St. Phi... Academy
St. 640 B... ...n Rd.
East Fallow... PA 19320
East (610) 486-1060 19320

COGNITIVE PSYCHOLOGY

Cognitive Psychology

A Student's Handbook

Michael W. Eysenck

Royal Holloway, University of London, UK

Mark T. Keane

University of Dublin, Trinity College, Ireland

 LAWRENCE ERLBAUM ASSOCIATES, PUBLISHERS
Hove (UK) Hillsdale (USA)

Lawrence Erlbaum Associates Ltd., Publishers
27 Church Road
Hove
East Sussex, BN3 2FA
UK

British Library Cataloguing in Publication Data
A catalogue record for this title is available from the British Library

ISBN 0-86377- 374-5 (Hbk)
ISBN 0-86377- 375-3 (Pbk)

Subject Index by Jackie McDermott
Printed and bound by BPC Wheatons Ltd., Exeter

To Christine with love
(M.W.E)

To a small person with a big name:
Alicia Paula Karla Byrne-Keane
(M.T.K.)

Discovery consists of seeing what everybody has seen and thinking what nobody has thought.

Albert Szent-Gyorgyi

Contents

Preface

As we indicated in the preface to the previous edition, it is a real challenge to write about the mushrooming area of cognitive psychology. In grappling with this challenge, we have followed the approach taken before. That is to say, we have focused on three major approaches within cognitive psychology: mainstream cognitive psychology; cognitive science, with its emphasis on computational modelling; and cognitive neuropsychology, which points up the effects of brain damage on cognition. By so doing, we hope that we have been able to impose some order on what might otherwise appear somewhat chaotic. You (the readers of this book) will sit in judgement on our efforts. However, it must be admitted that our busy professional lives have forced us to work hard to avoid chaos. For example, the first author wrote several parts of the book in India, and other parts were written in such far-flung places as Hong Kong, China, Egypt, Tenerife, Kuwait, and Turkey.

When I (Mark Keane) finished my PhD in 1987, it became clear to me that cognitive modelling was here to stay, and that I had better learn how to do it. The 1990 edition of this *Handbook* introduced this view to a whole generation of undergraduates. The idea of including cognitive neuropsychology was also important and has, I think, put the *Handbook* ahead of other texts. It is really only since 1990 that cognitive texts have started to include this sort of research, and few do it in the thoroughgoing manner we have adopted. However, the three views are not yet fully integrated: there are still research topics that reside wholly within experimental psychology. Much cognitive neuropsychological research is done without any computational modelling. There are few *integrated topics* where we have a computational model that captures both normal cognition and cognition under the influence of brain damage. If cognitive psychology follows the line of development suggested by this textbook, then these integrated topics should become commonplace rather than rare. It is my hope that this textbook will support that development.

I (Michael Eysenck) would like to express my profound gratitude to my wife Christine, to whom this book is appropriately dedicated. I am also very grateful to our three children (Fleur, Willie, and Juliet), with the whole family having shown great tolerance and understanding when I have been busy word-processing at home. Sadly, the children no longer interrupt me as they used to; instead they respond to my emergence into family life by beating me at everything from table tennis to *Countdown*, and from tennis to *Balderdash*.

We are very grateful to several people for reading an entire draft of this book, and for offering valuable advice on how it might be improved. They include Vicki Bruce, Trevor Harley, Al Parkin, and Philip Seymour. We would also like to thank those who commented on various chapters: Ruth Byrne, Gillian Cohen, Barry Smyth, John Towse, and John Richardson, and others who wish to remain anonymous.

Michael Eysenck and Mark Keane

1

Introduction

COGNITIVE PSYCHOLOGY AS A SCIENCE

In the last decades of the 20th century, as our understanding of the world and outer space has advanced, we have turned towards attempting to understand each other and our inner, mental spaces. This concern with our mental life has been marked by a tidal wave of research in cognitive psychology, and by the emergence of cognitive science as a unified programme for studying the mind.

In the popular media, there are numerous books, films, and television programmes on the more accessible aspects of cognitive research. In scientific circles, cognitive psychology is currently a thriving area. It deals with a bewildering diversity of phenomena constituting the nuts and bolts of an individual's cognition; thus, it is concerned with topics like perception, learning, memory, language, emotion, concept formation, and thinking.

In spite of its diversity, cognitive psychology is unified by a common approach based on an analogy between the mind and the digital computer; this is the information-processing approach. In the terminology of the philosophy of science, the information-processing approach is the dominant *paradigm* (theoretical orientation) in cognitive psychology (Kuhn, 1970).

Historical roots of cognitive psychology

It is notoriously difficult to pin-point the precise moment at which any major academic discipline started, but 1956 was a critical year in the development of cognitive psychology. At one meeting at the Massachusetts Institute of Technology, Chomsky gave a preliminary paper on his theory of language, George Miller presented a paper on the magic number seven in short-term memory (Miller, 1956), and Newell and Simon discussed their very influential computational model called the General Problem Solver (discussed in Newell, Shaw, & Simon, 1958; 1960; see also Chapter 15). In addition, the first systematic attempt to consider concept formation from a cognitive psychological perspective was reported (Bruner, Goodnow, & Austin, 1956).

Artificial intelligence was also founded in 1956 at the famous Dartmouth Conference, which was attended by Chomsky, McCarthy, Minsky, Newell, Simon, and Miller (see Gardner, 1985). With the benefit of hindsight, we can see that 1956 witnessed the birth of both cognitive psychology and cognitive science as major disciplines. Books devoted to certain aspects of cognitive psychology began to appear (e.g. Broadbent, 1958; Bruner et al., 1956). However, it took several years before the entire information-processing viewpoint reached undergraduate courses.

Information processing: Consensus

During the 1960s and most of the 1970s, it was the fashion to follow Broadbent (1958) in regarding much of cognition as consisting of a sequential series of processing stages. When a stimulus is presented (so the reasoning went), basic perceptual processes occur, followed by attentional processes that transfer some of the products of the initial perceptual processing to a short-term memory store. Thereafter, rehearsal serves to maintain information in the short-term memory store, and some of that information is transferred to a long-term memory store. One of the most sophisticated theories of this type was put forward by Atkinson and Shiffrin (1968; see also Chapter 6).

This kind of theoretical orientation provided a simple and coherent framework for textbook writers. It was possible to follow the stimulus input from the sense organs to its ultimate storage in long-term memory by means of successive chapters on perception, attention, short-term memory, and long-term memory. However, the sequential stage model makes the erroneous assumption that stimuli impinge on an inactive and unprepared organism. In fact, although processing is substantially affected by the nature of presented stimuli, it is also affected crucially by the individual's past experience, expectations, and so on.

Matters can be clarified by reference to a distinction that is often made between bottom-up or stimulus-driven processing and top-down or conceptually driven processing. Bottom-up processing refers to processing directly affected by stimulus input, whereas top-down processing refers to processing affected by what an individual brings to a stimulus situation (e.g. expectations determined by context and past experience). As an example of top-down processing, it is easier to read the word "well" when poorly written if it is presented in the context of the sentence "I hope you are quite _ _ _ _" than when it is presented on its own. Most cognitive activity involves these two kinds of processing in combination. The sequential stage model deals almost exclusively with bottom-up or stimulus-driven processing, and its failure to consider top-down processing adequately is its single greatest inadequacy.

Towards the end of the 1970s, theorists (e.g. Neisser, 1976) argued that virtually all cognitive activity consists of interactive bottom-up and top-down processes occurring at the same time (see Chapter 4). Perception and remembering might seem to be exceptions, because perception obviously depends heavily on the precise stimuli presented (and thus on bottom-up processing), and remembering depends crucially on stored information (and thus on top-down processing). However, perception is also much affected by the perceiver's expectations about to-be-presented stimuli (see Chapters 2, 3, and 4), and remembering depends far more on the exact nature of the environmental cues provided to facilitate recollection than was thought at one time (see Chapter 6).

By the end of the 1970s, most cognitive psychologists agreed that the information-processing paradigm was the appropriate way to study human cognition (see Lachman, Lachman, & Butterfield, 1979). It has several basic characteristics:

- People are viewed as autonomous, intentional beings who interact with the external world.
- The mind through which they interact with the world is a general-purpose, symbol-processing system (as used here, "symbols" are patterns stored in long-term memory which "designate or 'point to' structures outside themselves"; Simon & Kaplan, 1989, p.13).
- Symbols are acted on by various processes that manipulate and transform them into other symbols that ultimately relate to things in the external world.
- The aim of psychological research is to specify the symbolic processes and representations that underlie performance on all cognitive tasks.
- Cognitive processes take time, so that predictions about reaction times can often be made.
- The mind is a limited-capacity processor having both structural and resource limitations.
- This symbol system depends on a neurological substrate, but is not wholly constrained by it.

Many of these ideas stemmed from the view that human cognition can be understood by comparison with the functioning of computers. As Herb Simon (1980, p.45) expressed it:

It might have been necessary a decade ago to argue for the commonality of the information processes that are employed by such disparate systems as computers and human nervous systems. The evidence for that commonality is now overwhelming.

Most of the theories we examine in this book either assume these basic tenets of the information-processing framework or else attempt to clarify more precisely what they involve (e.g. the exact nature of the resource limitations or the processes involved in a given task). However, there are theorists who have explicitly rejected some of the ideas underlying the information-processing approach (e.g. see the later section on connectionist modelling methods).

It is difficult to identify the core ideas in the information-processing framework because of the open-ended nature of the computational metaphor. When scientists construct theories on the basis of metaphors or analogies to other mechanisms, the comparisons are usually clear and bounded. For example, in characterising light in terms of waves, the nature of waves is clear-cut, and their relevant aspects can be used directly to understand light. In the case of the computational metaphor, however, new extensions of it become possible as computer technology develops. In the 1950s and 1960s, researchers mainly used the general properties of the computer to understand the mind (e.g. that it had a central processor and memory registers). Many different programming languages had been developed by the 1970s, and this led to various aspects of computer software and languages being used (e.g. Johnson-Laird, 1977, on analogies to language understanding). More recently, as massively parallel machines have been developed, theorists have returned to the notion that cognitive theories should be based more closely on the parallel processing capabilities manifested by the brain.

Information processing: Diversity

In its most general sense, cognitive science is a broad, trans-disciplinary grouping of cognitive psychology, artificial intelligence, linguistics, philosophy, neuroscience, and cognitive anthropology. The common aim of these disciplines is the understanding of the mind. Figure 1.1 shows schematically the relative amount of overlapping interest that exists between cognitive psychology and each of the other cognitive sciences (note that it does not show how these other disciplines overlap with one another). To simplify matters, we will narrow the definition of cognitive science primarily to the important dependency between cognitive psychology and artificial intelligence, although the real richness of the interactions should be kept in mind.

This diversity is reflected in the different kinds of cognitive psychologists who have emerged. At the risk of over simplification, it is possible to identify at least three major groupings of cognitive psychologists:

• Experimental cognitive psychologists, who follow the experimental tradition of cognitive psychology, but do no computational modelling.
• Cognitive scientists, who construct computational models and who differ among themselves as to the value of rigorous experimentation.
• Cognitive neuropsychologists, who argue that investigation of the patterns of cognitive impairment shown by brain-damaged patients can provide valuable information concerning normal human cognition.

It is important to note that many researchers vacillate among the various categories, and so the distinctions are by no means absolute. Nevertheless, the proposed three categories possess some validity. It is a matter of current debate in cognitive psychology whether experimental cognitive psychologists are an endangered species, with the new, emergent species being cognitive scientists (see Gardner, 1985). This tension owes something to philosophical perspectives on the best route to the truth; these can be divided into empiricist and rationalist perspectives. Empiricists (e.g.

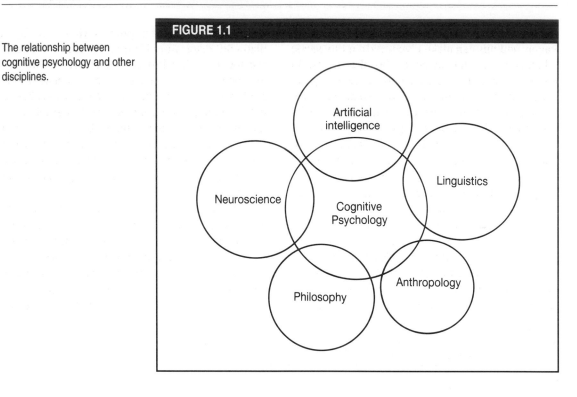

FIGURE 1.1

The relationship between cognitive psychology and other disciplines.

experimental cognitive psychologists) assume that the truth about the world is to be gained through observation and experimentation. In contrast, rationalists (e.g. hard-nosed cognitive scientists) assume that truth is to be found through the construction of formal systems such as those in mathematics and logic.

Our view is that empiricism and rationalism are both dangerous if taken to extremes. Empiricism can lead to unproductive and atheoretical experimentation, and rationalism can lead to elegant formal systems bearing little relationship to any external reality. We will focus on providing a synthesis of the insights that have emerged from the different approaches adopted by experimental cognitive psychologists, cognitive scientists, and cognitive neuropsychologists.

The activities of experimental cognitive psychologists should be familiar to you, but those of cognitive scientists and cognitive neuro-psychologists are probably rather less familiar. Therefore, in the following sections we will consider how they tackle the task of understanding human cognition.

COGNITIVE SCIENCE

Cognitive scientists are fond of constructing computational models to enhance their knowledge of human cognition. Computational models provide important information about whether the concepts used in a theory can be specified in detail, and they allow us to predict behaviour in new situations. Mathematical models are particularly useful for determining the variables that underlie a phenomenon and the relative importance of these variables to the phenomenon. We will concentrate on computational models in this section, because they are the hallmark of the cognitive science approach.

Computational modelling: From flowcharts to simulations

In the past many experimental cognitive psychologists cast their theories in a fairly informal mould. That is, a theory would only be stated verbally.

Such verbal statements tend to be extremely vague, and this can make it very difficult to decide whether or not the evidence fits the theory. In contrast, cognitive scientists produce computer programs that are meant to represent cognitive theories with all of the details made explicit. In the 1960s and 1970s, cognitive psychologists tended to use flowcharts rather than programs to characterise their theories. Computer scientists use flowcharts as a sort of plan or blueprint for a program, before they write the detailed code for it. Flowcharts are more specific than verbal descriptions, but they can still be under-specified, if not accompanied by a coded program. An example of a very inadequate flowchart is shown in Fig. 1.2. This is a flowchart of a bad theory about how we understand sentences. It assumes that a sentence is encoded in some form and then stored.

After that, a decision process (indicated by a diamond) determines if the sentence is too long. If it is too long, then it is broken up and we return to the encode stage to re-encode the sentence. If it is not too long, then another decision process decides if the sentence is ambiguous. If it is ambiguous, then its two senses are distinguished and we return to the encode stage. If it is not ambiguous, then it is stored in long-term memory. After one sentence is stored, we return to the encode stage to consider the next sentence.

In the days when cognitive psychologists only used flowcharts to describe their theories, sarcastic questions abounded, such as "What happens in the boxes?" or "What goes down the arrows?" Such comments do point to genuine criticisms. We really need to know what is meant by "encode sentence", how long is "too long", and how sentence

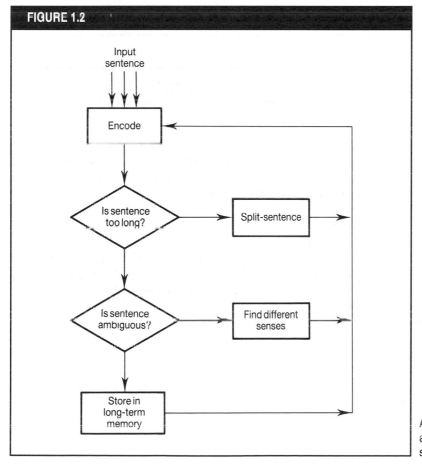

FIGURE 1.2

A flowchart of a bad theory about how we understand sentences.

ambiguity is tested. For example, after deciding that only a certain length of sentence is acceptable, it may turn out that it is impossible to decide whether the sentence portions are ambiguous without considering the entire sentence. Thus, the boxes may look all right at a superficial glance, but real contradictions may appear when their contents are specified.

In similar fashion, exactly what goes down the arrows is critical. If one examines all the arrows converging on the "encode sentence" box, it is clear that more needs to be specified. There are four different kinds of thing entering this box: an encoded sentence from the environment; a sentence that has been broken up into bits by the

"split-sentence" box; a sentence that has been broken up into several senses; and a command to consider the next sentence. This means that the "encode" box has to perform several different specific operations. In addition, it may have to record the fact that an item is either a sentence or a possible meaning of a sentence, or that an item may be part of another sentence. Thus, several other complex processes have to be specified within the "encode" box to handle these tasks, but the flowchart sadly fails to address these issues. The gaps in the flowchart show some similarities with those in the formula shown in Fig. 1.3.

Of course, not all theories expressed as flowcharts possess the deficiencies of the one we

FIGURE 1.3

"I THINK YOU SHOULD BE MORE EXPLICIT HERE IN STEP TWO."

The problem of being specific © 1977 by Sidney Harris in American Scientist Magazine. Reproduced with permission of the author.

have just considered. However, implementing a theory as a program is a good method for checking that it contains no hidden assumptions or vague terms. In the previous example, this would involve specifying the form of the input sentences, the nature of the storage mechanisms, and the various decision processes (e.g. those about sentence length and ambiguity). These computer programs are written in artificial intelligence programming languages, usually LISP (Norvig, 1992) or PROLOG (Shoham, 1993).

There are many issues surrounding the use of computer simulations and the ways in which they do and do not simulate cognitive processes. Palmer and Kimchi (1986) argued that it should be possible to decompose a theory successively through a number of levels (e.g. from descriptive statement to flowchart to specific functions in a program) until one reaches a written program. In addition, they argued that it should be possible to draw a line at some level of decomposition, and say that everything above that line is psychologically plausible or meaningful, whereas everything below it is not. This issue of separating psychological aspects of the program from other aspects arises because there will always be parts of the program that have little to do with the psychological theory, but which are there simply because of the particular programming language being used and the machine on which the program is running. For example, in order to see what the program is doing it is necessary to have print commands in the program which show the outputs of various stages on the computer's screen. However, no one would argue that such print commands form part of the psychological model.

Other issues arise about the relationship between the performance of the program and the performance of human subjects. For example, it is seldom meaningful to relate the speed of the program doing a simulated task to the reaction time taken by human subjects, because the processing times of programs are affected by psychologically irrelevant features. Programs run faster on more powerful computers, or if the program's code is interpreted rather than compiled. However, the various materials that are presented to the program should result in differences in program operation

time that correlate closely with differences in subjects' reaction times in processing the same materials. At the very least, the program should be able to reproduce the same outputs as subjects when given the same inputs.

In sum, computer programs or models are very useful tools for theorists because they both force and allow them to conceive of cognitive processes and representations in a concrete fashion. In addition, models can be used to run different materials in order to predict future behaviour.

Computational modelling techniques

The general characteristics of computational models of cognition have been discussed at some length. It is now time to deal with some of the main types of computational model that have been used in recent years. Three main types are outlined briefly here: semantic networks; production systems; and connectionist networks.

Semantic networks

Consider the problem of modelling what we know about the world (see Chapter 9 for further details). There is a long tradition from Aristotle and the British empiricist school of philosophers (Locke, Hume, Mill, Hartley, Bain) which proposes that all knowledge is in the form of associations. Three main principles of association have been proposed:

- Contiguity: two things become associated because they occurred together in time.
- Similarity: two things become associated because they are alike.
- Contrast: two things become associated because they are opposites.

There is a whole class of cognitive models that owe their origins to these ideas; they are called associative or semantic or declarative networks.

Semantic networks have the following general characteristics:

- Concepts are represented by linked nodes that form a network.
- These links can be of various kinds; they can represent very general relations (e.g. *is-associated-with* or *is-similar-to*), or specific,

simple relations like *is-a* (e.g. John is-a policeman), or more complex relations like *play*, *hit*, *kick*.

- The nodes themselves and the links among nodes can have various activation strengths which represent the similarity of one concept to another; thus, for example, a dog and a cat node may be connected by a link with an activation of 0.5, whereas a dog and a pencil may be connected by a link with a strength of 0.1.
- Learning can take the form of adding new links and nodes to the network or changing the activation values on the links between nodes; for example, in learning that two concepts are similar, the activation of a link between them may be increased.
- Various effects (e.g. memory effects) can be modelled by allowing activation to spread throughout the network from a given node or set of nodes.

- The way in which activation spreads through a network can be determined by a variety of factors; for example, it can be affected by the number of links between a given node and the point of activation, or by the amount of time that has passed since the onset of activation.

Part of a very simple network model is shown in Fig. 1.4. It corresponds closely to the semantic network model proposed by Collins and Loftus (1975). Such models have been successful in accounting for a variety of findings. For example, the word "dog" is recognised more readily if it is preceded by the word "cat", and this semantic priming effect (Meyer & Schvaneveldt, 1971) is easily modelled using such networks. At their best, semantic networks are both flexible and elegant modelling schemes.

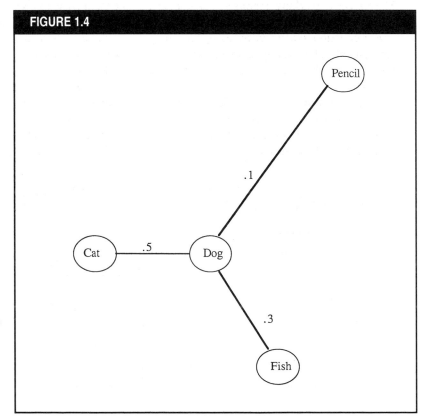

FIGURE 1.4

A schematic diagram of a simple semantic network with nodes for various concepts (i.e. dog, cat) and links between these nodes indicating the differential similarity of these concepts to each other.

Production systems

Another popular approach to modelling cognition involves production systems. Production systems are made up of productions, where a production is an "IF ... THEN" rule. These rules can take many forms, but an example we might want children to have is, "If someone smiles at you, then smile back." In a typical production system model there is a long-term memory that contains a large set of these IF ... THEN rules. There is also a working memory (i.e. a system holding information that is currently being processed). If information from the environment that "someone is smiling at you" reaches working memory, it will match the IF-part of the rule in long-term memory, and trigger the THEN-part of the rule (i.e. smile back). As a consequence, the world will be full of smiling children!

Production systems have the following general characteristics:

- They have a large number of IF ... THEN rules.
- They have a working memory that contains information.
- The production system operates by matching the contents of working memory against the IF-parts of the rules and executing the THEN-parts.
- If some information in working memory matches the IF-part of many rules, there may be a *conflict-resolution strategy* that selects one of these rules as the best rule to be executed.

Consider a very simple production system which operates on lists of letters involving As and Bs (see Fig. 1.5). The system has two rules:

1. IF a list in working memory has an A at the end THEN replace the A with AB.
2. IF a list in working memory has a B at the end THEN replace the B with an A.

If we give this system different inputs in the form of different lists of letters, then different things happen. If we give it CCC, this will be stored in working memory but will remain unchanged because it does not match either of the IF-parts of the two rules. If we give it A, then it will be modified by the rules after the A is stored in working memory. This A is a list of one item and as such it matches rule 1. Rule 1 has the effect of replacing the A with AB, so that when the THEN-part is executed, working memory will contain an AB. On the next cycle, AB does not match rule 1 but it does match rule 2. As a consequence, the B is replaced by an A, leaving an AA in working memory. The system will then continue in the same fashion, producing AAB, then AAA, then AAAB, and so on.

Many aspects of cognition can be specified as sets of IF ... THEN rules. For example, chess knowledge can readily be represented as a set of productions based on rules such as "If the Queen is threatened, then move the Queen to a safe square." In this way, people's basic knowledge of chess can

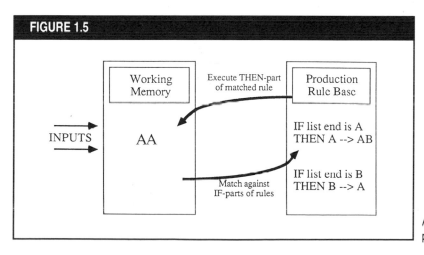

FIGURE 1.5

A schematic diagram of a simple production system.

be modelled as a collection of productions and gaps in this knowledge as the absence of some productions. Newell and Simon (1972) were the first psychologists to establish the usefulness of production system models in characterising cognitive processes like problem solving and reasoning (see Chapters 15 and 16). However, these models have a wider applicability. Anderson (1993) has modelled human learning using production systems (see Chapter 16), and Holland, Holyoak, Nisbett, and Thagard (1986) have shown that more elaborate versions of such systems can model many diverse aspects of cognition, from reinforcement behaviour in rats to memory phenomena and learning.

Connectionist networks

Connectionist networks, neural networks, or parallel distributed processing models as they are variously called are relative newcomers to the computational modelling scene. All previous techniques were marked by the need to program explicitly all aspects of the model, and by their use of explicit symbols to represent concepts. Connectionist networks, on the other hand, can to some extent program themselves, in that they can "learn" to produce specific outputs when certain inputs are given to them. Furthermore, connectionist modellers often reject the use of explicit rules and symbols and use distributed representations, in which concepts are characterised as patterns of activation in the network (see Chapter 9).

Early theoretical proposals about the feasibility of learning in neural-like networks were made by McCulloch and Pitts (1943) and by Hebb (1949). However, the first neural network models, called Perceptrons, were shown to have several limitations (Rosenblatt, 1959; Minsky & Papert, 1969, 1988). By the late 1970s, hardware and software developments in computing offered the possibility of constructing more complex networks that overcame many of these original limitations (e.g. Ballard, 1986; Feldman & Ballard, 1982; Hinton & Anderson, 1981; Rumelhart, McClelland, & The PDP Research Group, 1986; Rumelhart, McClelland, & The PDP Research Group, 1986a).

Connectionist networks typically have the following characteristics (see Fig. 1.6):

- The network consists of elementary or neurone-like *units* or *nodes*, which are connected together so that a single unit has many links to other units.
- Units affect other units by exciting or inhibiting them.
- The unit usually takes the weighted sum of all of the input links, and produces a single output to another unit if the weighted sum exceeds some threshold value.
- The network as a whole is characterised by the properties of the units that make it up, by the way they are connected together, and by the rules used to change the strength of connections among units.
- Networks can have different structures or layers; they can have a layer of input links, intermediate layers (of so-called "hidden units"), and a layer of output units.
- A representation of a concept can be stored in a distributed manner by a pattern of activation throughout the network.
- The same network can store many different patterns in this way without them necessarily interfering with each other if they are sufficiently distinct.
- An important learning rule used in networks is called *backward propagation of errors (BackProp)*.

In order to understand connectionist networks more fully, let us consider how individual units act when activation impinges on them. Any given unit can be connected to several other units (see Fig. 1.7). Each of these other units can send an excitatory or an inhibitory signal to the first unit. This unit generally takes a weighted sum of all these inputs. If this sum exceeds some threshold it produces an output. This output may feed into another unit which does the same. Figure 1.7 shows a simple diagram of just such a unit which takes the inputs from a number of other units and sums them to produce an output if a certain threshold is exceeded.

These networks can model cognitive behaviour without recourse to the kinds of explicit rules found in production systems. They do this by storing

FIGURE 1.6

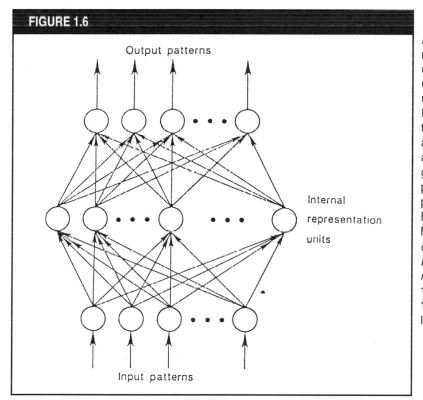

Output patterns

Internal
representation
units

Input patterns

A multi-layered connectionist network with a layer of input units, a layer of internal representation units or hidden units, and a layer of output units. Input patterns can be encoded, if there are enough hidden units, in a form that allows the appropriate output pattern to be generated from a given input pattern (reproduced with the permission of David E. Rumelhart & James L. McClelland from *Parallel distributed processing: Explorations in the microstructure of cognition* (Vol. 1), published by the MIT Press, 1986, the Massachusetts Institute of Technology)

FIGURE 1.7

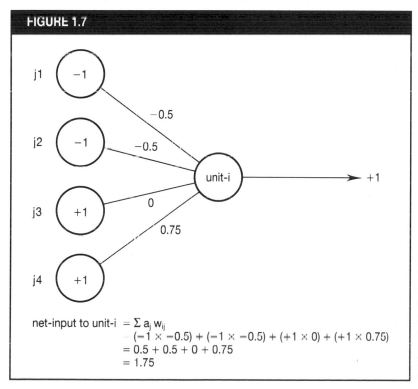

j1 -1

j2 -1 -0.5

j3 $+1$ 0

j4 $+1$ 0.75

-0.5

unit-i   → $+1$

$$net\text{-}input\ to\ unit\text{-}i = \Sigma\ a_j\ w_{ij}$$
$$= (-1 \times -0.5) + (-1 \times -0.5) + (+1 \times 0) + (+1 \times 0.75)$$
$$= 0.5 + 0.5 + 0 + 0.75$$
$$= 1.75$$

Diagram showing how the inputs from a number of units are combined to determine the overall input to unit-i. Unit-i has a threshold of 1; so if its net input exceeds 1 then it will respond with +1, but if the net input is less than 1 then it will respond with −1.

patterns of activation in the network that associate various inputs with certain outputs. The models typically make use of several layers to deal with complex behaviour. One layer consists of input units that encode a stimulus as a pattern of activation in those units. Another layer is an output layer, which produces some response as a pattern of activation. When the network has learned to produce a particular response at the output layer following the presentation of a particular stimulus at the input layer, it can exhibit behaviour that looks "as if" it had learned a rule of the form "IF such-and-such is the case THEN do so-and-so." However, no such rule exists explicitly in the model.

Networks learn the association between different inputs and outputs by modifying the weights on the links between units in the net. In Fig. 1.7 we see that the weight on the links to a unit, as well as the activation of other units, plays a crucial role in computing the response of that unit. A variety of learning rules are used to modify these weights in systematic ways. When we apply such learning rules to a network, the weights on the links are modified until the net produces the required output patterns given certain input patterns.

One such learning rule is called "backward propagation of errors" or BackProp. BackProp allows a network to learn to associate a particular input pattern with a particular output pattern. At the beginning of the learning period, the network is set up with random weights on the links among the units. During the early stages of learning, after the input pattern has been presented, the output units often produce a response that is not the required output pattern. What BackProp does is to compare this imperfect pattern with the known required response, noting the errors that occur. It then back-propagates activation through the network so that the weights between the units are adjusted in such a way that they will tend to produce the required pattern. This process is repeated with a particular stimulus pattern until the network produces the required response pattern. Thus, the model can be made to learn the behaviour with which the cognitive scientist is concerned, rather than being explicitly programmed to produce it.

Networks have been used to produce very interesting results. Several examples will be discussed throughout the text (see, for example, Chapters 10 and 16), but one concrete example may be mentioned here. Sejnowski and Rosenberg (1987) produced a connectionist network called NETtalk which takes an English text as its input and produces reasonable English speech as its output. Even though the network is trained on a limited set of words, it can pronounce the words from new text with approximately 90% accuracy. Thus, the network appears to have learned the "rules of English pronunciation", but it has done so without having explicit rules that combine and encode sounds in various ways.

Connectionist models such as NETtalk have great "gee whiz" value, and are the subject of considerable research interest. Some of these researchers might object to our classification of connectionist networks as merely one among a number of modelling techniques. Smolensky (1988) and others have argued that connectionism represents an alternative to the information-processing paradigm. Indeed, if one examines the fundamental tenets of the information-processing framework, then connectionist schemes seem to violate one or two of them. For example, symbol manipulation of the sort found in production systems does not seem to occur in connectionist networks. We will return to the complex issues raised by connectionist theories later in the book.

COGNITIVE NEUROPSYCHOLOGY

Cognitive neuropsychology is concerned with the patterns of cognitive performance in brain-damaged patients. Those aspects of cognition that are intact or impaired are identified, and this information is of value for two main reasons. First, the cognitive performance of brain-damaged patients can often be explained by theories within cognitive psychology. Such theories specify the processes or mechanisms involved in normal cognitive functioning, and it should in principle be possible to account for many of the cognitive impairments of brain-damaged patients in terms of selective damage to some of those mechanisms.

Second, it may be possible to use information from brain-damaged patients to *reject* theories proposed by cognitive psychologists, and to propose new theories of normal cognitive functioning. According to Ellis and Young (1988, p.4), a major aim of cognitive neuropsychology:

is to draw conclusions about normal, intact cognitive processes from the patterns of impaired and intact capabilities seen in brain-injured patients ... the cognitive neuropsychologist wishes to be in a position to assert that observed patterns of symptoms could not occur if the normal, intact cognitive system were not organised in a certain way.

Thus, the intention is that there should be bi-directional influences of cognitive psychology on cognitive neuropsychology, and of cognitive neuropsychology on cognitive psychology. Historically, the former influence was the greater one, but the latter has become progressively more important.

Before beginning to discuss the cognitive neuropsychological approach in more detail, it is useful to discuss a concrete example of cognitive neuropsychology in operation. Atkinson and Shiffrin (1968) argued there is an important distinction between a short-term memory store (containing information that is currently being processed) and a long-term memory store (containing information that has left consciousness), and that information enters into the long-term store as a result of rehearsal and other processing activities in the short-term store. Relevant evidence from the cognitive neuropsychological perspective was obtained by Shallice and Warrington (1970). They investigated a patient, KF, who had suffered damage to a part of the brain specialised for speech perception and production. KF appeared to have severely impaired short-term memory, but essentially intact long-term memory.

The investigation of this patient served two important purposes. First, it provided a new kind of evidence to support the theoretical distinction

between two memory systems. Second, it pointed to a real deficiency in the theoretical model of Atkinson and Shiffrin (1968). If, as this model suggests, long-term learning and memory depend on the short-term memory system, then it is very surprising that someone with a grossly deficient short-term memory system also has normal long-term memory. The appropriate interpretation of the findings from KF is discussed further in Chapter 6.

The case of KF illustrates very clearly the potential power of cognitive neuropsychology. The study of this one patient provided strong evidence that the dominant theory of memory at the end of the 1960s was seriously inadequate. This is no mean achievement for a study based on one subject!

Cognitive neuropsychological evidence

How do cognitive neuropsychologists set about the task of understanding how the cognitive system functions? A crucial goal is the discovery of *dissociations*, which occur when a patient performs normally on one task but is impaired on a second task. In the case of KF, a dissociation was found between performance on short-term memory tasks and on long-term memory tasks. As we have seen, such evidence can be used to argue that normal individuals possess at least two separate memory systems.

There is a potential problem in drawing sweeping conclusions from single dissociations, however. A patient may perform poorly on one task and reasonably well on a second task because the first task is more complicated and difficult than the second. In other words, the brain damage suffered by the patient may not have impaired specific aspects of cognitive functioning, but may instead have had the general effect of reducing the ability to cope with difficult tasks of all kinds. The solution to this problem is to look for *double dissociations*. A double dissociation between two tasks (1 and 2) is shown when one patient performs normally on task 1 and at an impaired level on task 2, and another patient performs normally on task 2 and at an impaired level on task 1. If a double dissociation can be demonstrated, then the results cannot be explained in terms of one task being intrinsically more difficult than the other.

In the case of short-term and long-term memory, such a double dissociation has been demonstrated. Whereas KF had impaired short-term memory but intact long-term memory, so-called amnesic patients have severely deficient long-term memory but intact short-term memory (see Chapter 7 for a review). These findings suggest that there are two distinct memory systems which can suffer damage separately from each other.

An alternative approach is based on *associations*, which is the tendency of different patients to exhibit impaired performance on the same set of tasks. If such an association across tasks is shown, it is tempting to assume there is a common cognitive process or mechanism underlying performance on all of the tasks showing impairment. However, damage often extends over a number of brain areas. Tasks may require different cognitive processes, but these processes may be very close together anatomically, so that damage to one cognitive process is usually accompanied by damage to all of the others. In general terms, the clearest indication that an association has occurred simply because of the accident of anatomical closeness in cognitive processes is finding some patients who do not show impaired performance across all of the tasks on which most patients are impaired.

If brain damage were usually very limited in scope and affected only a single cognitive process or mechanism, then cognitive neuropsychology would be a relatively simple enterprise. In fact, brain damage is often rather extensive, so that several different cognitive systems are all impaired to a greater or lesser extent. This means that considerable ingenuity is needed to make sense of the tantalising glimpses of human cognition provided by brain-damaged patients.

Theoretical assumptions

Most cognitive neuropsychologists subscribe to the following assumptions (with the exception of the last one):

• The cognitive system exhibits *modularity*, i.e. there are several relatively independent cognitive processors or modules, each of which can function to some extent in isolation from the rest of the processing system; brain damage will typically impair only some of these modules.
• There is a meaningful relationship between the organisation of the physical brain and that of the mind; this assumption is known as *isomorphism*.
• Investigation of cognition in brain-damaged patients can tell us much about cognitive processes in normal individuals; this important assumption is closely bound up with the other assumptions.
• Most patients can be categorised in terms of *syndromes*, which are based on co-occurring sets of symptoms.

Syndromes
The traditional approach within neuropsychology made considerable use of *syndromes*. It was claimed that certain sets of symptoms or impairments are usually found together, and each set of co-occurring symptoms was used to define a separate syndrome. Thus, for example, patients with intact short-term memory but severely impaired long-term memory were said to be suffering from the "amnesic syndrome".

This syndrome-based approach allows one to impose some order on the numerous cases of brain-damaged patients who have been studied, by assigning them to a relatively modest number of categories. It is also of use in identifying those areas of the brain primarily responsible for cognitive functions such as language, because one can look for those parts of the brain that are damaged in all those patients having a particular syndrome. However, a syndrome-based approach tends to exaggerate the similarities among different patients allegedly suffering from the same syndrome. In addition, those symptoms or impairments said to form a syndrome may be found in the same patients solely because the underlying cognitive processes are anatomically adjacent.

In recent years, there have been attempts to propose more specific syndromes or categories based on our theoretical understanding of cognition. One of the problems here is that the discovery of new patients with unusual patterns of deficits and the occurrence of theoretical advances mean that the categorisation system is in a constant state of flux. As Ellis (1987) pointed out, "a syndrome thought at time *t* to be due to damage to a single unitary module is bound to have fractionated by time *t* + 2 years into a host of awkward subtypes".

Ellis (1987) argued that cognitive neuropsychology should proceed on the basis of intensive single-case studies in which individual patients are studied on a wide variety of tasks. According to the logic of this approach, an adequate theory of cognition should be as applicable to the individual case as to groups of individuals, and so single-case studies provide a perfectly satisfactory test of cognitive theories. The great advantage of this approach is that there is no need to make simplifying assumptions about which patients do and do not belong to the same diagnostic categories.

Another argument for single-case studies is that for many purposes it is not possible to find a group of patients exhibiting very similar cognitive deficits. As Shallice (1991, p.432) pointed out, "as finer and finer aspects of the cognitive architecture are investigated in attempts to infer normal function, neuropsychology will be forced to resort more and more to single-case studies".

Ellis (1987) may have somewhat over-stated the value of single-case studies. If our theoretical understanding of an area (e.g. memory) is rather limited, it may make sense to adopt the syndrome-based approach until the major theoretical issues have been clarified. Furthermore, many experimental cognitive psychologists disapprove of attaching great theoretical significance to findings from individuals who may not be representative even of brain-damaged patients. As Shallice (1991, p.433) argued:

A selective impairment found in a particular task in some patient could just reflect: the patient's idiosyncratic strategy, the greater difficulty of that task compared with the others, a premorbid lacuna [gap] in that patient, or the way a reorganised system but not the original normal system operates.

We have seen that there are real problems with both group and single-case studies. A reasonable compromise is to carry out a number of single-case studies. If a theoretically crucial dissociation is found in a single patient, then there are various ways of interpreting the data. However, if the same dissociation in obtained in a number of individual patients, it is less likely that all of the patients had atypical cognitive systems prior to brain damage, or that they have all made use of similar compensatory strategies.

Modularity

The whole enterprise of cognitive neuropsychology is based on the assumption that there are numerous *modules* or cognitive processors in the brain. These modules function relatively independently, so that damage to one module does not directly affect other modules. Modules are anatomically distinct, so that brain damage will often affect some modules while leaving others intact. Cognitive neuropsychology may facilitate the discovery of these major building blocks of cognition. A double dissociation indicates that two tasks make use of different modules or cognitive processors, and so a series of double dissociations can be used to provide a sketch-map of our modular cognitive system.

The notion of modularity is closely associated with Fodor (1983), who published a book entitled *The modularity of mind*. He tried to identify the main distinguishing features of modules, and came up with the following suggestions:

- Informational encapsulation: each module functions independently from the functioning of other modules.
- Domain specificity: each module can process only one kind of input (e.g. words; faces).
- Mandatory (compulsory) operation: the functioning of a module is not under any form of voluntary control.
- Innateness: inborn.

Fodor's (1983) ideas have been influential. However, many psychologists have criticised mandatory operation and innateness as criteria for modularity. Some modules may operate in a rather automatic fashion, but there is little evidence to suggest that they all do. It is implausible to suppose that the modules underlying language skills, such as reading and writing are innate, as these are skills that the human race has possessed only in comparatively recent times.

From the perspective of cognitive neuropsychology, these criticisms do not pose any special problems. If the assumptions of informational encapsulation and domain specificity remain tenable, then data from brain-damaged patients can continue to be used in the hunt for cognitive modules. This would still be true even if it turned out that several modules or cognitive processors were neither mandatory nor innate.

It should be noted that it is not only cognitive neuropsychologists who subscribe to the notion of modularity. The great majority of experimental cognitive psychologists and cognitive scientists also believe in modularity. The three groups differ primarily in terms of the preferred methods for demonstrating modularity.

Isomorphism

Cognitive neuropsychologists assume there is a meaningful relationship between the way in which the brain is organised at a physical level and the way in which the mind and its cognitive modules are organised. This assumption has sometimes been called *isomorphism*, meaning that two things (e.g. brain and mind) have the same shape or form. Thus, it is expected that each module will have a somewhat different physical location within the brain. If this expectation is disconfirmed, then cognitive neuropsychology will become a more complicated enterprise.

An assumption that is related to isomorphism is that there is localisation of function, meaning that any specific function or process occurs in a particular location within the brain. The notion of localisation of function appears to be in conflict with the connectionist account, according to which a process (e.g. activation of a concept) can be distributed over a wide area of the brain. There is as yet no definitive evidence to support one view over the other.

Evaluation of cognitive neuropsychology

Are the various theoretical assumptions underlying cognitive neuropsychology correct? It is difficult to tell. In some sense, modules do not actually "exist"; rather, they are convenient theoretical devices used to clarify our understanding. Therefore, the issue of whether the theoretical assumptions are valuable or not is probably best resolved by considering the extent to which cognitive neuropsychology is successful in increasing our knowledge of cognition. In other words, the proof of the pudding is in the eating. As we will see in this book, the omens are basically favourable.

Although the reader may have formed the impression that cognitive neuropsychology is the best thing since sliced bread, it should be pointed out that it has several problematical aspects. Perhaps the most serious one stems from the difficulty in carrying out group studies. This has led to the increasing use of single-case studies; they are sometimes very revealing, but can provide misleading evidence if the patient had specific cognitive deficits prior to brain damage, or if he or she has developed unusual compensatory strategies to cope with the consequences of brain damage.

ORGANISING AND STRATIFYING COGNITIVE PSYCHOLOGY

There are two general theoretical issues that are worth considering at this point. The first issue concerns terms such as "framework", "theory", and "model". The second issue concerns the relationship between the various disciplines that have an impact on cognitive psychology. For example, how are we to integrate computational models, cognitive neuropsychology and neurophysiology, and evidence from psychological experiments?

The second issue resembles that confronted much earlier by physicists, chemists, and biologists. Whereas biology deals with the gross functioning of bodily organs, chemistry can deal with the same subject matter at a finer level in terms of molecular changes. At the most detailed level, quantum physics can characterise the activity of the sub-atomic particles that form atoms, which in turn make up the molecules. In some cases, different levels of description are appropriate for different levels of analysis. For instance, most of molecular chemistry could be characterised in terms of quantum physics, but the resultant theory would be too detailed and complicated to be of much use. As the disciplines relevant to cognitive psychology are still being developed, there is no consensus on how they might relate to each other. However, one possible view of how it might be done was proposed by David Marr (1982), and will be discussed shortly.

Frameworks, theories, models, and architectures

It is important to distinguish between a number of terms differing in their specificity: framework, theory, model, and architecture (see Fig. 1.8). A framework is a general set of ideas drawn on by theorists within a particular discipline (see Anderson, 1983). Other terms that are essentially synonymous with "framework" are approach, paradigm, and meta-theory (see Kuhn, 1970; Lachman, Lachman, & Butterfield, 1979). The general framework that is most commonly used by cognitive psychologists is the information-processing framework discussed earlier. Frame-

works should be regarded as useful or useless rather than correct or incorrect, because they consist of high-level assumptions that cannot be tested directly at an experimental level.

In contrast, theories should be stated in terms that permit researchers to determine whether they are correct or incorrect. Theories are more constrained than frameworks, and often provide precise accounts of the underlying mechanisms and influences giving rise to a set of phenomena. Theories differ considerably in their scope, i.e. the range of phenomena with which they are concerned.

Theories are typically too general to make predictions about specific situations. However, a model is a particular instantiation of a theory which relates that theory to a specific situation. This then makes it possible to make relatively detailed predictions. For example, suppose we have a theory stating that all problem solving simply involves trial and error. If we wanted to apply this theory to problem solving in chess, then we would have to construct a model of how we would expect trial and error to manifest itself in the chess situation.

There has been a proliferation of theories in cognitive psychology, but it is not clear how these

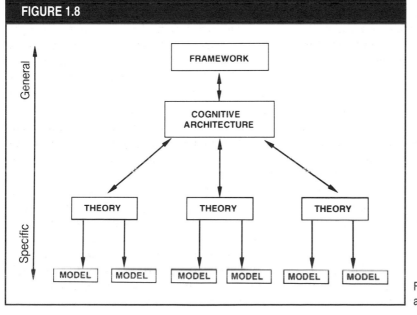

Frameworks, theories, models, and architectures.

theories relate to each other. A cognitive architecture is intended to provide the missing theoretical integration, and is thus far broader in scope than most theories. According to Anderson (1983, p.ix), cognitive architectures are designed to "capture the basic principles of operation built into the cognitive system". There are only a few theoretical formulations that lay claim to be cognitive architectures. These include Anderson's (1983, 1993) ACT models (for Adaptive Control of Thought) and Newell's SOAR system (standing for State, Operator, And Result; Newell, 1990).

A framework for theories in cognitive psychology

A very important issue for cognitive psychology concerns the marriage of psychological theory with computational modelling and with the neuro-sciences. One of the hopes behind connectionism was that it could relate psychological functioning to brain functioning rather directly because of the neurone-like properties of connectionist networks. However, connectionist networks actually differ substantially from brain neurones and synapses (Crick, 1989), and some have argued (e.g. Smolensky, 1988) that connectionist models should be thought of as operating above the neuronal level.

Marr (1982) proposed a very interesting framework for organising theories of mental processes. Although the general applicability of his framework has been questioned (Anderson, 1987a, 1989), it does nevertheless present a tantalising glimpse of how one might co-ordinate the different levels of theory within cognitive psychology.

Marr's research was mainly concerned with visual processes, and a more detailed treatment of his framework as applied to vision is to be found in Chapters 2 and 3.

Marr (1982) outlined three levels at which an information-processing theory should be characterised (see Table 1.1). The top level, which he called the computational level, contains a specification of what needs to be computed for a particular task to be carried out. This level constitutes a formal statement of the various outputs resulting from different inputs. Some people find the term "computational level" unhelpful, preferring the term "functional level", because, as Arbib (1987, p.478) states:

> it is far from indicating the steps—serial or parallel—whereby computation is to be undertaken; rather, it corresponds to what in computer program synthesis would be a specification of the program in input/output terms, plus perhaps a top-down sketch of program design.

The computational level is also concerned with specifying why the stated strategy and computations are appropriate. In other words, it is concerned with the purpose of the computation. In the case of visual perception, for example, the purpose is to transform input in the form of the pattern of light produced by the external environment into output in the form of information about environmental objects which can then be used to plan action.

At the intermediate, or algorithmic level, the exact nature of the computation is specified. At this

TABLE 1.1	
Marr's (1982) Framework for Theories	
Computational Level	The goal of the computation, why it is appropriate, what the logic of the strategy carried out might be.
Algorithmic Level	How can the computational theory be implemented, the representation for the input, and the algorithm for the transformation.
Hardware Level	How can the representation and the algorithm be realised physically.

level, the representations one is using and the algorithms or rules operating on those representations should be indicated. This level should capture the detailed processing steps that intervene between the inputs and outputs, and it should take account of the mechanisms people actually use.

The final level, the hardware level, is the brain. The brain imposes limitations on the kinds of representations and algorithms that can actually be used. We usually know so little of brain functioning that such knowledge hardly constrains theorising at the algorithmic level, but there are exceptions. As we will see later in this chapter, the discovery of cells within the brain's visual system that are especially sensitive to certain kinds of stimulus has influenced theories of vision.

It is important to note that these three levels are quite distinct from each other. Although there are some interdependencies among them, the different levels do not simply decompose into each other. Thus, there will be concepts at one level which have no corresponding entities at another level. It is also worth bearing in mind that Marr (1982) was proposing a framework. As such, it is neither right nor wrong, but stands or falls on the basis of its usefulness in research (for similar frameworks, see Newell, 1990, and Palmer, 1989).

EMPIRICAL METHODS FOR ASSESSING COGNITION

In most of the research discussed in this book, cognitive processes and structures were inferred from subjects' behaviour (e.g. speed of performance; accuracy of performance). This approach has proved to be extremely useful, and the data thus obtained have been used in the development and subsequent testing of most theories in cognitive psychology. However, there at least two major potential problems with the use of such data:

1. Measures of the speed and accuracy of performance provide rather *indirect* information about the internal processes and structures that are of central interest to cognitive psychologists.

2. Behavioural data are usually gathered in the artificial surroundings of the laboratory; the ways in which people behave in the laboratory may differ substantially from the ways in which they behave in everyday life (see Chapter 19).

Cognitive psychologists do not rely solely on behavioural data to obtain useful information from their subjects. Two major alternative approaches to data collection will be discussed here. First, there is the use of verbal reports or introspection (defined by the *Oxford English Dictionary* as "examination or observation of one's own mental processes"). The advantages and disadvantages of introspective evidence are discussed shortly.

Second, instead of attempting to explore cognitive processes indirectly by observing the behaviour to which they lead, it is possible to adopt the more direct approach of measuring actual brain functioning during performance of a cognitive task. Technological advances have enabled cognitive psychologists to measure brain activity much more precisely than before, and to compare the levels of activity in different areas of the brain. These advances offer real prospects of enhancing our understanding of human cognition.

Introspection

One way of studying cognitive processes is by making use of introspection. However, introspection depends on conscious experience, and each individual's conscious experience is by its nature personal and private. In spite of this, it is often assumed that introspection can provide useful evidence about some mental processes. However, Nisbett and Wilson (1977) disagreed, arguing that introspection is practically worthless. They illustrated their argument with various examples. In one study, subjects were presented with five essentially identical pairs of stockings and were asked to decide which pair was the best. After they had made their choice, they were asked to indicate why they had chosen that particular pair. Most subjects chose the right-most pair, and so their decisions were actually affected by relative spatial position. However, the subjects did not suggest spatial position as a reason for making their choice. Indeed, they vehemently denied that it had played any part in their decision, referring instead to slight differences in colour, texture, and so on among the pairs of stockings as having been important.

Nisbett and Wilson (1977) claimed that people are generally unaware of the processes influencing their behaviour. According to them (Nisbett & Wilson, 1977, p.248), accurate introspective reports can be explained in terms of a priori theories:

> When people are asked to report how a particular stimulus influenced a particular response, they do so not by consulting a memory of the mediating process, but by applying or generating causal theories about the effects of that type of stimulus on that type of response.

This view was supported by discovering that an individual's introspections about what is determining his or her behaviour are often no more accurate than the guesses about those determinants made by other people.

Striking evidence of the limitations of introspective evidence has emerged in much recent research on normal and on brain-damaged individuals. For example, there is the phenomenon of *implicit learning*, which was defined by Seger (1994, p.163) as "learning complex information without complete verbalisable knowledge of what is learned". One task that has been used to study implicit learning is artificial grammar learning, in which the subjects learn to decide whether strings of letters conform to the rules of an artificial grammar. There is a progressive improvement in performance, but subjects cannot explain the rules they are using (Reber, 1989).

Berry and Broadbent (1984) studied implicit learning by using a complex task in which a sugar-production factory had to be managed to maintain a specified level of sugar output. Subjects learned to perform this task effectively, but most of them could not explain the principles underlying their performance. Those subjects whose reports revealed good knowledge of the principles under-lying task performance tended to perform the task less well than those with poor knowledge. This

suggests that the task information available to conscious awareness was of no value to the learners.

In similar fashion, there has been a considerable amount of research on *implicit memory* (memory in the absence of conscious recollection). The relevant research is discussed in detail in Chapters 6 and 7, and demonstrates that normal and brain-damaged individuals can exhibit excellent memory performance even when there is no relevant introspective evidence. It is not entirely clear whether implicit learning and implicit memory are closely related, but Seger (1994, p.165) concluded that "there is probably no firm dividing line between implicit memory and implicit learning". However, it is noteworthy that implicit learning typically involves memory for relatively complex patterns, whereas implicit memory generally involves memory for specific stimuli.

Ericsson and Simon (1980, 1984) argued that Nisbett and Wilson (1977) had overstated the case against introspection. They proposed various criteria for distinguishing between valid and invalid uses of introspection:

- It is preferable to obtain introspective reports during the performance of a task rather than retrospectively, because of the fallibility of memory.
- Subjects are more likely to produce accurate introspections when asked to describe what they are attending to, or thinking about, than when required to interpret a situation or their own thought processes.
- People cannot usefully introspect about several kinds of processes (e.g. neuronal processes; recognition processes).

Careful consideration of the studies that Nisbett and Wilson (1977) regarded as striking evidence of the worthlessness of introspection reveals that subjects generally provided retrospective inter-pretations about information that had probably never been attended to fully. Thus, their findings are consistent with the approach of Ericsson and Simon (1980, 1984).

In sum, introspection is sometimes useful, but there is no conscious awareness of many cognitive processes or their products. This point is illustrated by the phenomena of implicit learning and implicit memory, but numerous other examples of the limitations of introspection will be presented throughout this book.

Technological advances

According to a popular view, scientific progress occurs as a result of a brilliant scientist suddenly having a flash of inspiration. A famous example of this might appear to be the discovery of the structure of deoxyribonucleic acid (DNA) by James Watson, Francis Crick, and Maurice Wilkins. According to Watson's (1968) account, the crucial insight that the DNA molecule has a double-helical structure was based on an intuitive leap from the inadequate evidence then available. However, there was more to it than that. In the early 1950s, Rosalind Franklin worked on the X-ray crystallographic study of the structure of DNA using new technology, and the diffraction images of DNA she produced were of major importance in producing the double-helix model of DNA structure.

The discovery of the structure of DNA illustrates the impact that technological advances have on scientific progress. Developments in technology have already exerted a major influence on cognitive psychology, but much of this influence has been somewhat indirect (e.g. the use of the computer metaphor by cognitive scientists). However, there are strong signs that the techniques for studying the brain which have been developed in recent years will prove tremendously important in increasing our knowledge of human cognition.

Some cognitive psychologists argue that we can understand cognition by relying on observations of subjects' performance on cognitive tasks. However, there are powerful arguments in favour of studying the brain. As Churchland & Sejnowski (1991, pp.17–18) have suggested:

> It would be convenient if we could understand the nature of cognition without understanding the nature of the brain itself. Unfortunately, it is difficult, if not impossible, to theorise effectively on these

matters in the absence of neurobiological constraints. The primary reason is that computational space is consummately vast, and there are many conceivable solutions to the problem of how a cognitive operation could be accomplished. Neurobiological data provide essential constraints on computational theories, and they consequently provide an efficient means for narrowing the search space. Equally important, the data are also richly suggestive in hints concerning what might really be going on.

As Churchland and Sejnowski (1991) pointed out, the various techniques for studying brain functioning differ in terms of their spatial and temporal resolution. Some techniques provide information about the neuronal level whereas others tell us about activity over the entire brain. In similar fashion, some techniques provide information about brain activity on a millisecond-by-millisecond basis, whereas others indicate brain activity only over much longer time periods such as minutes or hours.

A few of the main techniques will be discussed in order to give the reader some idea of the weapons available to cognitive psychologists. To provide a frame of reference, the spatial and temporal resolutions of some of these techniques are shown in Fig. 1.9. It may be unwise to assume that the spatial and temporal resolutions of some techniques are intrinsically superior to others: high spatial and temporal resolutions are advantageous if a very detailed account of brain functioning is sought, whereas low spatial and temporal resolutions are more useful if a more general view of brain activity is required. The use of optical dyes is included as a technique because it covers combinations of spatial and temporal resolutions not covered by other techniques. Blasdel and Salama (1986) applied a voltage-sensitive dye to the striate cortex of monkeys, after which one eye was closed and a visual stimulus was presented to the other eye. This provided evidence that there are columns in the striate cortex that are primarily affected by stimulation of either the left or the right eye.

The spatial and temporal ranges of some physiological techniques used to study human cognition. Adapted from Churchland and Sejnowski (1991).

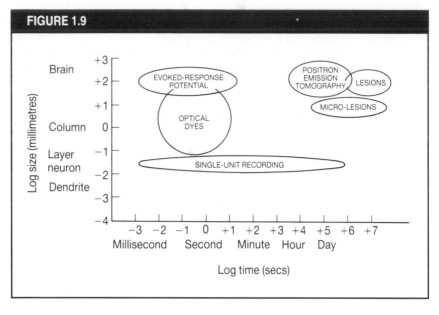

FIGURE 1.9

Single-unit recording

Single-unit recording is a fine-grain technique which was developed over 30 years ago to permit study of single neurones. A microelectrode is inserted into the brain to provide a record of extracellular potentials. Hubel and Wiesel (1962) used the single-unit recording technique with cats to study the neurophysiology of vision. They discovered three different kinds of cells (simple, complex, and hyper-complex) within the visual system. Recordings obtained when different visual stimuli were presented indicated that simple cells differ from each other in the kind of stimulus to which they are maximally responsive, leading them to be divided into edge detectors, slit detectors, and line detectors. Complex cells resemble simple cells, except that the exact location of the stimulus within the cell's receptive field is much less important in determining their responsiveness. Hyper-complex cells resemble complex cells, but their responsiveness is much affected by the length of the visual stimulus.

Such findings provided solid evidence that many brain cells respond to very specific aspects of visual stimuli, and this evidence has influenced most subsequent theories of visual perception. For example, Marr's (1982) very influential theory of

perception is based in part on the findings of Hubel and Wiesel (1962); see Chapters 2 and 3.

Averaged evoked response potentials

The electroencephalogram (EEG), which is based on electrical recordings taken from the scalp, was first used by Hans Berger over 65 years ago. It has proved useful in many ways (e.g. establishing the different stages of sleep), but it is a rather blunt instrument. Indeed, the EEG has been compared to trying to hear what people are saying in the next room by putting your ear to the wall. The EEG also has the disadvantage that it typically tells us little about cognitive processes, because spontaneous EEG potentials are not directly related to external events. Much more has been learned about cognition from averaged evoked response potentials (ERPs) extracted from EEG recordings. In essence, a stimulus is presented several times, and the EEG recordings obtained from each presentation are then averaged. There tends to be so much spontaneous EEG activity that it obscures the impact of stimulus processing on the EEG recording. As a consequence, several trials are needed to distinguish genuine effects of stimulation from background brain activity. Averaged evoked response potentials provide fairly detailed information about brain activity over time, but do not indicate precisely which regions of the brain are most involved in processing.

Averaged evoked response potentials have been used to investigate selective attention. One of the issues in research on selective attention has been whether unattended stimuli are processed as thoroughly as attended ones. It has been established that there are differences in averaged evoked response potentials between attended and unattended stimuli within approximately 60 milliseconds of stimulus presentation (Loveless, 1983). This finding suggests there are major differences in processing of the two kinds of stimuli at nearly all stages of processing, which is in line with the findings from several purely behavioural studies (see Chapter 5).

Positron emission tomography

Position emission tomography (PET scanning) is one of the most important techniques for assessing brain function. The way in which PET scanning works was described by Davison and Neale (1990, p.85):

> A substance used by the brain is labelled with a short-lived radioactive isotope and injected into the bloodstream ... The radioactive molecules of the substance emit a particle called a positron, which quickly collides with an electron. A pair of high-energy light particles shoot out from the skull in opposite directions and are detected by the scanner. The computer analyses millions of such recordings and converts them into a motion picture of the functioning brain in horizontal cross section, projected onto a television screen.

PET scans were used by Petersen et al. (1988) to investigate the parts of the brain involved in word processing. They discovered that there were highly localised areas of the brain most associated with visual and auditory word presentation, speech production, and the processing of meaning. An exciting implication of this research is that it may become possible to identify with some precision where in the brain different cognitive processes occur. As yet, however, the newness of the technology (and its great expense) mean that progress has been relatively slow.

Regional cerebral blood flow

A related method of investigating brain activity is based on the measurement of regional cerebral blood flow, using a small radioactive substance injected into the bloodstream. A scanner relays information about levels of radioactivity to a computer, which displays the information in the form of a coloured map revealing radioactivity levels in the different parts of the brain. There is greater blood flow to more active areas of the brain, and thus higher levels of radioactivity.

Regional cerebral blood flow was assessed by Tulving (1989). He compared two kinds of long-term memory: episodic or autobiographical memory and semantic memory (organised knowledge of the world). There has been some controversy as to whether there are relatively separate episodic and semantic memory systems (see Chapter 7), and Tulving was interested in discovering whether different parts of the brain are active in episodic and semantic memory. He found that the front part of the brain was more active when personal or episodic events were being thought about, whereas the back part of the brain was more active when knowledge in semantic memory was being considered. This evidence is clearly consistent with the view that there are important differences between episodic and semantic memory.

Squid magnetometry

PET scans and regional cerebral blood flow both provide reasonably precise information about those locations within the brain that are most active during the performance of a task. However, they only indicate the total amount of activity in each region of the brain over a period of several seconds or a few minutes, and do not reveal second-by-second changes in patterns of brain activity. Improved technology in the form of Squid magnetometry is set to allow such changes to be monitored. Squid stands for superconducting quantum interference device, and it measures the magnetic flux or field very accurately when a group of neurones in the brain is triggered. An important reason for this accuracy is that the skull is completely transparent to magnetic fields, which contrasts with the low electrical conductivity of bone (see Kutas & Van Petten 1994).

Although Squid magnetometry offers the prospect of observing the brain in action, there are problems associated with its use. The magnetic field generated by the brain when thinking is about 100 million times weaker than the Earth's magnetic field and a million times weaker than the magnetic fields around overhead power cables. As a consequence, it is very difficult to prevent irrelevant sources of magnetism from interfering with the measurement of brain activity. Another problem is that superconductivity requires temperatures close to absolute zero, which means that the Squid has to be immersed in liquid helium at four degrees above the absolute zero of $-273°C$. However, it is possible that these problems can be overcome, and that Squid magnetometry will become an important tool of cognitive psychologists.

Section summary

Valuable information about cognition can be obtained from human subjects in various ways, including the collection of behavioural data, reliance on introspective evidence, and the use of new technology to obtain relatively direct measurements of brain activity. Each type of measure possesses its own strengths and limitations, and so it is often desirable to use a number of different kinds of measures to study human cognition. If similar findings are obtained from two different types of measures, this is known as *converging evidence*; such evidence is valuable because it suggests that the measures are not providing distorted information.

What if two kinds of measures apparently produce very different findings? One possibility is simply that one (or both) of the measures provides inadequate or distorted information about the underlying cognitive processes. Another, more interesting possibility is that such discrepant findings are of theoretical importance. Consider,

for example, a patient, DB, who suffered from "blindsight": he was able to demonstrate some visual processing ability via his behaviour (e.g. reaching out to visual stimuli) in spite of having no introspective awareness of being able to see (Weiskrantz, 1986). These findings suggest that there can be much visual processing without accompanying conscious awareness.

OUTLINE OF THE BOOK

One of the problems with writing a textbook of cognitive psychology is that virtually all of the processes and structures of the cognitive system are interdependent. Consider, for example, the case of a student *reading* a book to prepare for a forthcoming examination. Hopefully, the student is *learning* something, but there are several other processes going on as well. *Visual perception* is involved in the intake of information from the printed page, and presumably there is *attention* to the content of the book (although attention may be captured by extraneous stimuli). In order for the student to profit from the book, he or she must possess considerable *language skills*, and must also have rich *knowledge representations* that are relevant to the material in the book. There may be an element of *problem solving* in the student's attempts to relate what is in the book to the possibly somewhat conflicting information he or she has learned elsewhere. Furthermore, what the student learns will depend on his or her *emotional state* at the time of learning. Finally, the acid test of whether the learning has been effective comes during the examination itself, when the material contained in the book must be *remembered*.

The words italicised in the previous paragraph indicate some of the major ingredients of human cognition, and they form the basis of our coverage of cognitive psychology. In view of the interdependent functioning of all aspects of the cognitive system, there is great emphasis in this book on the ways in which each process (e.g. perception) depends on other processes and on structures (e.g. attention; long-term memory; stored representations). This should facilitate the task of making sense of the complexities of the human cognitive system.

CHAPTER SUMMARY

There are reasons for arguing that 1956 marked the true beginnings of cognitive psychology. A major factor in the emergence of cognitive psychology was the development of computers. Initially, it was argued that there are some interesting similarities between human and computer functioning. More recently, however, there have been serious efforts to exploit the computer metaphor much more fully, using the so-called information-processing framework.

There are at least three major kinds of cognitive psychologists. First, there are experimental cognitive psychologists, who are primarily involved in empirical research on normal subjects. Second, there are cognitive scientists, who combine experimentation and the computational modelling of human cognition. Third, there are cognitive neuropsychologists, who investigate the patterns of cognitive impairment shown by brain-damaged patients, and relate them to normal functioning.

Theorising within cognitive psychology occurs at several different levels. A framework is very broad and consists of assumptions that cannot be submitted to experimental test. A theory is more precise; it makes various predictions that can be tested. A model is still more precise; it typically consists of a theory applied to a particular situation.

A cognitive architecture consists of an ambitious attempt to identify the crucial processes and mechanisms involved in all cognition.

Cognitive psychologists have made use of numerous different behavioural measures in order to understand cognition. They have also made use of introspection, which appears to be particularly useful when people are asked to describe the contents of focal attention rather than to interpret experience. Technological advances (e.g. PET scanners) mean that it is possible to measure activity in different parts of the brain more directly than was possible in the past; these advances promise to transform our knowledge of human cognition in the next few years.

FURTHER READING

Churchland, P. S., & Sejnowski, T. J. (1992). *The computational brain*. Cambridge, MA: MIT Press. This book provides a good description of many of the techniques available for studying human cognition, as well as much of the background to a neuroscience approach.

Johnson-Laird, P. N. (1993). *The computer and the mind* (2nd Edn.). London: Fontana. This book provides a very readable review of the cognitive science perspective in cognitive psychology from one of its main exponents.

Shallice, T. (1991). From neuropsychology to mental structure. *Behavioral and Brain Sciences, 14*, 429–439. Many of the key issues relating to cognitive neuropsychology are discussed in this article and in the commentaries that follow it.

2

Visual Perception: Basic Processes

INTRODUCTION

This chapter and the following two deal with visual perception. We can perhaps most appropriately begin with a consideration of the concept of "perception". Its definition has changed over the years as the study of perception has become increasingly dominated by the computational and cognitive perspectives. Roth (1986, p.81) provided a representative definition: "The term *perception* refers to the means by which information acquired from the environment via the sense organs is transformed into experiences of objects, events, sounds, tastes, etc."

Visual perception appears to be such a simple and effortless process that we tend to take it for granted. In fact, it is very complex, and several processes are involved in transforming and interpreting sensory information. Some of the complexities of visual perception only became clear when workers in artificial intelligence attempted to program computers to "perceive" the environment. Even when the environment is artificially simplified (e.g. consisting only of white solids) and the task is apparently relatively straight-

forward (e.g. deciding how many objects there are), computers require very complicated programming in order to succeed. It is still the case that there are no computers capable of matching more than a small fraction of the skills of visual perception possessed by nearly every adult human being.

As we will see later, the experimental, the computational, and the neuropsychological approaches have all been influential in increasing our understanding of visual perception. In addition, physiological studies have probably played a larger role in vision research than in other areas of cognitive psychology. At least 60% of the monkey cortex is devoted to visual processing (see Humphreys & Riddoch, 1994), and so this emphasis on physiological evidence is probably justified.

The primary emphasis in this chapter is on some of the basic processes involved in visual perception. Higher-level processes are considered in Chapter 3, with major theoretical orientations and motion perception being dealt with in Chapter 4. Much contemporary thinking has been strongly influenced by Marr's (1982) computational theory, which provides an account of both basic and higher-level processes. Accordingly, we will begin by discussing his theoretical approach.

MARR'S COMPUTATIONAL THEORY

The starting point for Marr's (1982) computational theory was that there are a number of different levels of explanation, which need to be distinguished. Consider, for example, the kinds of explanation that could be proposed for a car and its functioning. At one level, a car consists of an engine, four wheels, a chassis, gears, and numerous other bits and pieces. At another level, we could describe the role of the battery in supplying electricity, the engine-cooling characteristics of the radiator, the operations of the carburettor, and so on. Finally, we could explain a car in terms of its function, which is to transport people and their belongings from one place to another along the road system.

As we saw in Chapter 1, Marr (1982) identified three levels of explanation for visual perception. The top level is the computational level, which relates to the purpose of perception, and the bottom level is the hardware level (i.e. the brain). At an intermediate point, there is the algorithmic level, which is concerned with the detailed processes involved in perception.

Although all these levels of explanation are important in their own right, the computational theory level may well be of particular significance. An indication of why this is so can be obtained by referring back to the car example. It would be possible to have a thorough understanding of how each of the various components of a car works, but without knowing what a car is for there would be little grasp of *why* a car has those particular components interconnected as they are. Once we realise that a car is essentially a means of transport, it then follows that it needs a source of energy, aerodynamically sound shape, ways in which its movements can be controlled, and so on. It then becomes clear why cars are designed as they are.

The development of a computational theory is undoubtedly more complex in the case of visual perception than in that of the motor car. One reason for this is that visual perception fulfils a number of functions (Harris & Humphreys, 1994, p.179): "Vision is like a service industry which contributes to a broad range of behaviours including, among others, navigation, balance, object recognition, and the guidance of social interaction." As a consequence, it may prove necessary to develop somewhat separate computational theories for each of these functions.

We have dealt with some of the general characteristics of Marr's (1982) theoretical approach, and it is now time to consider in more detail his theory of visual perception. He proposed that the processes involved in vision produce a series of *representations* (i.e. descriptions) providing increasingly detailed information about the visual environment. Marr identified three major kinds of representation:

- *Primal sketch :* this provides a two-dimensional description of the main light-intensity changes in the visual input, including information about edges, contours, and blobs.
- $2\frac{1}{2}$-*D sketch :* this incorporates a description of the depth and orientation of visible surfaces, making use of information provided by shading, texture, motion, binocular disparity, and so on; like the primal sketch, it is observer-centred.
- *3-D model representation*: this describes three-dimensionally the shapes of objects and their relative positions in a way that is independent of the observer's viewpoint.

Primal sketch

According to Marr (1982), it is possible to identify two versions of the primal sketch: the *raw primal sketch* and the *full primal sketch*. The raw primal sketch contains information about light-intensity changes in the visual scene, and the full primal sketch is formed as a result of making use of this information to identify the number and outline shapes of visual objects.

A theoretical problem which arises is that light-intensity changes often provide ambiguous information about the appropriate way of organising the visual field. Marr (1976) devised a computational model to address this problem. In essence, various grouping rules are used to produce perceptual organisations which correspond well to those present in the visual environment. The details of how this was achieved are discussed later in the chapter.

$2\frac{1}{2}$-D sketch

According to Marr (1982), various stages are involved in the transformation of the primal sketch into the $2\frac{1}{2}$-D sketch. The first stage involves the construction of a *range map* ("local point-by-point depth information about surfaces in the scene", Frisby, 1986, p.164). After this, higher-level descriptions (e.g. of convex and concave junctions between two or more surfaces) are produced by combining information from related parts of the range map. More is known of the processes involved in constructing a range map than in proceeding from that to the $2\frac{1}{2}$-D sketch itself.

What kinds of information are used in changing the primal sketch into the $2\frac{1}{2}$-D sketch? Those used include shading, motion, texture, shape, and binocular disparity. Most of these factors are discussed later in the chapter.

Cognitive neuropsychological evidence is relevant to evaluating Marr's notion of the $2\frac{1}{2}$ D sketch. If a patient found it difficult to form $2\frac{1}{2}$-D sketches, but could form primal sketches and had access to semantic knowledge about objects, what would one expect of his or her perceptual performance? On the positive side, some basic processes of visual perception would be intact, including those involved in the initial analysis of light-intensity changes. In addition, objects would be identifiable from information provided by sense modalities other than the visual. On the negative side, such a patient would have severe shape-processing impairments, and would be unable to copy presented objects. He or she would also be unable to identify objects solely on the basis of visual information.

There are some brain-damaged patients whose perceptual abilities and deficits resemble those just described. S, who was studied by Benson and Greenberg (1969), retained some perceptual skills in the visual modality. He could distinguish between relatively small differences in brightness, he could detect the movements of small objects, and he was able to find his way safely around the hospital in which he was living. He could also identify objects provided that appropriate non-visual (e.g. auditory or tactile) cues were available. However, S was extremely poor at identifying objects on the basis of vision alone. His problems with shape and object perception were so great that he could not copy simple figures. He was even unable to decide which out of an array of four figures was the same as a sample figure.

S's perceptual performance apparently indicated that he could no longer make use of the form- and shape-processing abilities underlying the formation of $2\frac{1}{2}$-D sketches, but his residual visual abilities suggested he might well be able to form at least an approximation to the primal sketch representation. However, not everyone subscribes to the notion that patients such as S have relatively intact basic perceptual abilities. Campion and Latto (1985) investigated a patient, RC, who resembled S in a number of ways. Both patients had suffered from accidental carbon monoxide poisoning, showed poor object recognition only in the visual modality, and demonstrated some basic visual abilities. In the case of RC, however, it was discovered that he had numerous small areas of blindness within his field of vision, and these blind areas may well have contributed to his impaired object perception.

In sum, there are two schools of thought concerning the appropriate explanation of the perceptual deficits shown by patients such as S and RC. One possibility is that their perceptual problems are mainly at the level of form- and shape-processing, and a second possibility is that difficulties in forming $2\frac{1}{2}$-D sketches stem from perceptual impairments at a more basic level. It is likely that basic perceptual impairments (e.g. RC's blind areas) sometimes disrupt object perception. However, the fact that the extent of such impairments does not correlate highly with problems of object perception indicates that impaired object perception cannot be accounted for entirely in terms of sensory deficits.

3-D model representation

The $2\frac{1}{2}$-D sketch suffers from a number of limitations. It does not contain information about those surfaces of objects in the visual field that are hidden from view. It is observer-centred, which means the representation of an object will vary considerably depending on the angle from which it is observed. This enormous variety of representations obviously provides a poor basis for identifying the object by matching it up with stored object information in long-term memory. These are some of the reasons why it is important for perceivers to go on to compute the 3-D model representation, which does not have these limitations.

Most of the coverage of 3-D model representations and higher-level processes in object recognition is to be found in Chapter 3, which also contains an overall evaluation of Marr's theoretical position. The earlier stages of visual processing (relating to the primal sketch and the $2\frac{1}{2}$-D sketch) are considered in the remainder of this chapter.

Raw primal sketch

Some of the earliest stages of visual processing involve the formation of a raw primal sketch incorporating information about light-intensity changes, and a full primal sketch incorporating information about edges and object shapes. As there are usually light-intensity changes at the edges of an object, it may be wondered why two separate primal sketches need to be created. Part of the answer is that light-intensity changes can occur for several different reasons. The intensity of light reflected from a surface depends on the angle at which light strikes it, and is reduced by shadows falling on the surface. In addition, there can be substantial differences in light intensity reflected from an object due to variations in its texture. Thus, light-intensity changes provide a fallible guide to object shapes and edges.

The raw primal sketch is formed from what is known as a *grey-level representation* of the retinal image. This representation is based on the light intensities in each very small area of the image; these areas are called *pixels* (picture elements). Unfortunately, the construction of a useful grey-level representation is more complicated than one might imagine. One problem is that the intensity of light reflecting from any given pixel fluctuates constantly, and so there is a danger that the grey-level representation will be distorted by these momentary fluctuations. One approach is to average the light-intensity values of neighbouring pixels. This smoothing process can be effective in eliminating "noise", but it can produce a blurring

effect in which valuable information is lost along with the noise. The usual answer to this problem is to assume that several representations of the image are formed which vary in their degree of blurring. Information from these image representations is then combined to form the raw primal sketch.

Marr and Hildreth (1980) proposed an algorithm (specified procedure) for constructing the raw primal sketch. They used as their starting point the assumption that several different smoothed representations varying in their blurredness are formed from the grey-level representation. In more technical terms, the grey-level representation of an image is passed through a number of Gaussian filters differing in width, with the output of wide filters being more blurred than that of narrow filters. In essence, in a Gaussian filter, intensity information is pooled within a circular region of the image, with intensities from the central region being weighted most strongly; the precise weighting is based on a Gaussian or normal distribution with its peak in the centre of the circular region.

According to the Marr-Hildreth algorithm, the information contained in the various more- and less-blurred representations is then used to uncover what are known as *zero-crossings*. These zero-crossings are difficult to calculate, but some idea of what is involved can be grasped with reference to Fig. 2.1. We start with (a), which simply represents a rapid change in intensity at one location in the image. In (b), there is what is known as the first derivative of the intensity change, which provides an indication of the rate of change of intensity in (a). The rate of change is zero between d and e, rapid between e and f, and is once again zero between f and g. Finally, in (c), we have the second derivative of the intensity change; it is derived from (b). The curve in (b) is at zero between d and e, rises and falls rapidly between e and f, and then returns to zero. During the change from rapid increase to rapid decrease, the line crosses the horizontal mid-point; this is a zero-crossing. After that, *zero-crossing segments* (zero-crossings having the same orientation) are located.

What do these complex calculations of zero-crossings and zero-crossing segments give us (apart from a headache)? According to Marr and

FIGURE 2.1

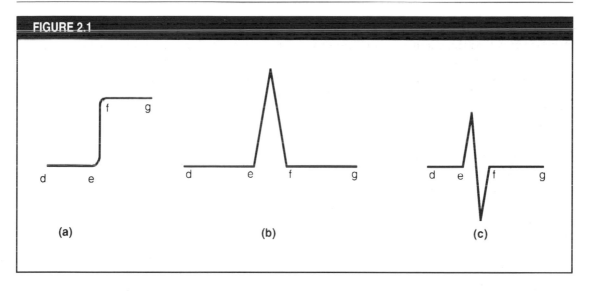

(a)   **(b)**   **(c)**

The Marr-Hildreth algorithm: (a) shows an intensity change, (b) is the first derivative, and (c) is the second derivative (zero-crossings occur when the line crosses the horizontal mid-point). Adapted from Marr (1982).

Hildreth (1980), they provide a reliable and valid way of identifying edges in the raw primal sketch.

It is important at this point in the story to note that it would be unwise to rely totally on the zero-crossing segments identified within any single blurred representation. The output of narrow filters includes a mixture of meaningful and meaningless zero-crossing segments, whereas the output of wide filters produces a highly blurred representation, which contains meaningful zero-crossing segments that cannot be localised with any precision. Common sense indicates that the next step should be to combine information about zero-crossing segments from the different filters, and that is precisely what Marr and Hildreth (1980) proposed. Their key assumption was as follows: zero-crossing segments or rapid intensity changes that are present in the outputs of two filters of adjacent width correspond to significant aspects of the visual environment, and so are represented in the raw primal sketch. In contrast, zero-crossing segments that are present in only one blurred representation are discarded.

According to Marr and Hildreth (1980), the raw primal sketch consists of four different tokens: edge-segments; bars; terminations; and blobs. Each of these tokens is based on a different pattern of light-intensity change in the blurred representations.

What evidence do we have that the complicated procedures incorporated into the Marr-Hildreth algorithm are on the right lines? Marr and Hildreth (1980) adopted the approach of computer simulation. Photographs of everyday scenes were converted into grey-level representations, and then a computer program applied the Marr-Hildreth algorithm to those representations. The results were encouraging, but it should be borne in mind that demonstrating that the raw primal sketch can be constructed in the way proposed by Marr and Hildreth (1980) does not prove that this is how the human visual system actually operates.

Evaluation
Watt (1988) pointed out some problems with the approach of Marr and Hildreth (1980). For example, although the intensity changes found at edges are revealed by zero-crossings, those associated with discontinuities of gradient are not (see Fig. 2.2). Watt and Morgan (1984) proposed their MIRAGE algorithm, which is more sensitive than the Marr-Hildreth algorithm to a wide range of intensity changes in the image. The MIRAGE

FIGURE 2.2

Discontinuities in gradient (1 and 2) do not lead to zero-crossings, whereas discontinuities in intensity (3 and 4) do lead to zero-crossings in Marr and Hildreth's (1980) algorithm. Adapted from Watt (1988).

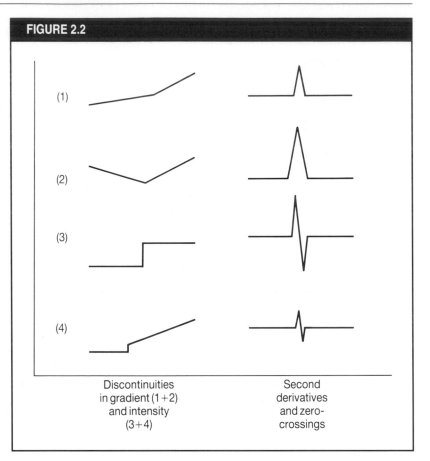

Discontinuities in gradient (1+2) and intensity (3+4)

Second derivatives and zero-crossings

system starts with a range of filters (as in the Marr-Hildreth algorithm). After that, however, differences appear between the two theoretical approaches. According to Marr and Hildreth (1980), edge information in the form of zero-crossings is obtained from each filter. In contrast, it is assumed with the MIRAGE system that information from all the filters is amalgamated. In this process of amalgamation, positive and negative outputs are dealt with separately to produce the S+ and S- signals, respectively. Sections of each signal deviating from zero are called "zero-bounded masses", and the locations of the boundaries of these zero-bounded masses in the S+ and S- signals are then used to identify lines, edges, and so on in the image.

The MIRAGE algorithm is often more in line with the evidence than the Marr-Hildreth algorithm. For example, Watt and Morgan (1984) considered the errors that were made when subjects decided whether two edges were aligned, with the contrast of the edges being varied. Comparison of the actual findings with those predicted by the MIRAGE and Marr-Hildreth approaches (see Fig. 2.3) indicates that the MIRAGE algorithm (centroids) predicted the data much better than did the Marr-Hildreth algorithm (zero-crossings).

In sum, the Marr-Hildreth algorithm, with its emphasis on zero-crossings, is lacking in sensitivity, in that it does not make full use of the intensity-change information contained in the grey-level representation. More specifically, important intensity changes such as those produced by gradients do not produce zero-crossings. Theoretical developments (such as that of Watt and Morgan) have had some success in eliminating these limitations of the Marr-Hildreth algorithm.

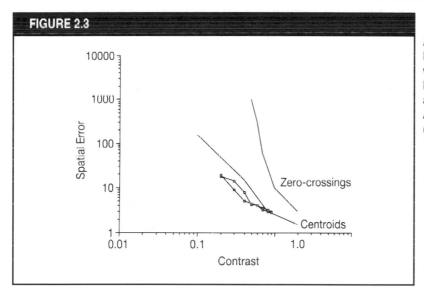

FIGURE 2.3

Accuracy of judgements of edge location (thick dots) compared with predictions from Marr and Hildreth (1980) (zero-crossings) and from MIRAGE (centroids). Adapted from Watt and Morgan (1984).

PERCEPTUAL ORGANISATION

We have seen that the basic visual information available to us consists of simple elements such as edges, lines, and blobs. Of course, that is not how we perceive the world. What we actually see is an organised world consisting of people and objects. A major issue in visual perception is to account for *perceptual segregation*, i.e. our ability to work out which parts of the visual information presented to us belong together and thus form separate objects.

Gestaltist approach

Historically, the first systematic attempt to study perceptual segregation and the perceptual organisation to which it gives rise was made by the Gestaltists. They were a group of German psychologists (including Koffka, Kohler, and Wertheimer) who emigrated to the United States between the two World Wars. Their fundamental principle of perceptual organisation was the law of Prägnanz, which Koffka (1935, p.138) expressed as follows: "Of several geometrically possible organisations that one will actually occur which possesses the best, simplest and most stable shape."

Although the law of Prägnanz was their key organisational principle, the Gestaltists also

proposed several other laws. Most of these laws (see Fig. 2.4) can be subsumed under the law of Prägnanz. The fact that three horizontal arrays of dots rather than vertical groups are perceived in Fig. 2.4 (a) indicates that visual elements tend to be grouped together if they are close to each other (the law of proximity). Figure 2.4 (b) illustrates the law of similarity, which states that elements will be grouped together perceptually if they are similar to each other. Vertical columns rather than horizontal rows are seen because the elements in the vertical columns are the same, whereas those in the horizontal rows are not. We see two crossing lines in Fig. 2.4 (c), because according to the law of good continuation we group together those elements requiring the fewest changes or interruptions in straight or smoothly curving lines. Figure 2.4 (d) illustrates the law of closure, according to which missing parts of a figure are filled in to complete the figure. Thus, a circle is seen in spite of the fact that it is incomplete.

Most of the Gestalt laws were derived from the study of static two-dimensional figures such as those presented in Fig. 2.4. However, they also proposed the law of common fate, according to which visual elements that appear to move together are grouped together. This was shown in an interesting experiment by Johansson (1973). He attached lights to each of the joints of an actor who

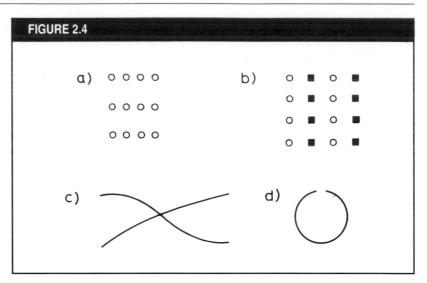

FIGURE 2.4

Examples of some of the Gestalt laws of perceptual organisation: (a) the law of proximity; (b) the law of similarity; (c) the law of good continuation; and (d) the law of closure.

wore dark clothes and then filmed him as he moved around in a dark room. Observers saw only a meaningless display of lights when the actor was at rest, but they perceived a moving human figure when he walked around. This was in spite of the fact that they could not actually see anything other than the lights.

The Gestalt laws of perceptual organisation make reasonable intuitive sense. However, they are descriptive statements possessing little or no explanatory power. The Gestaltists attempted to provide an explanation by means of their doctrine of *isomorphism*, according to which the experience of visual organisation is mirrored by a precisely corresponding organised process in the brain. It was assumed that there are electrical "field forces" in the brain which are of importance in producing the experience of a stable perceptual organisation when we look at our visual environment.

Unfortunately, the Gestaltists knew very little about the workings of the brain, and their pseudo-physiological ideas have not survived. Much damage was done to the theory by Lashley, Chow, and Semmes (1951) in a study on two chimpanzees. They placed four gold foil "conductors" in the visual area of one of the chimpanzees, and 23 gold pins vertically through the cortex of the other chimpanzee. Lashley et al. (1951) argued persuasively that the rather horrifying things they had done to these chimpanzees would have severely disrupted any electrical field forces. In fact, the perceptual abilities of the chimpanzees were hardly affected by their treatment, suggesting that electrical field forces are of much less significance than the Gestaltists claimed.

Section summary

The great strength of the Gestalt approach was that the Gestaltists identified several important phenomena, which have not been seriously challenged or undermined over the years. However, their approach also possessed important weaknesses. They were unduly concerned to demonstrate the correctness of their theory, and so failed to carry out experiments to reveal its limitations and inadequacies. In addition, with the failure of their doctrine of isomorphism they were left without any real explanation of the organisational phenomena they had discovered.

Subsequent theories

The Gestaltists emphasised the importance of the law of Prägnanz, according to which the perceptual world is organised into the simplest and best shape. However, they lacked any effective means of assessing what shape is the simplest and best, and so had to rely on subjective impression. Restle (1979) proposed an interesting way of clarifying the notion of simplicity. He studied how dots moving across a display are perceived. The most complicated approach would be to treat each dot as completely separate from all of the others, and to calculate its starting position, speed, and direction of movement, and so on. In contrast, it is possible to treat the moving dots as belonging to groups, especially if they move together in the same direction and at the same speed. The amount of processing or computation involved is much greater when the dots are treated separately rather than as members of groups, and Restle (1979) was able to calculate precisely how much processing would be involved. His main finding was that whatever grouping of moving dots in a display would involve the least calculation generally corresponds to what is actually perceived.

Julesz (1975) pointed out that most of the stimuli used by the Gestaltists and their followers were very limited in that they were based mainly on lines and shapes. He extended the Gestaltists' work by studying the effects of brightness and colour on perceptual organisation. He discovered that a visual display will be perceived as consisting of two regions if the average brightness in each region differs considerably. However, a display was not perceived as dividing into two regions if

the detailed pattern of brightnesses in each region was different but there was only a modest difference in the average brightness. In similar fashion, a visual display consisting of coloured squares is perceived as forming two regions if the average wavelength of light in each region is clearly different. Two regions are less likely to be perceived if there are different patterns of colours in each region, but the average wavelength differs only slightly (e.g. mostly red and green squares in one region, and mostly yellow and blue squares in the other region).

Julesz (1975) discovered that there are some exceptions to the notion that average brightness or wavelength is crucial in determining whether a display is perceived as consisting of two regions. Another important factor is granularity, which refers to the way in which the elements in a region are distributed. At one extreme, all of the elements could be evenly distributed within the field; at the other extreme, they could all be clumped together. Julesz (1975) found that a display in which the overall brightness is the same throughout the display but the granularity is greater in one half than the other will be perceived as consisting of two regions. This can be seen in Fig. 2.5, in which the

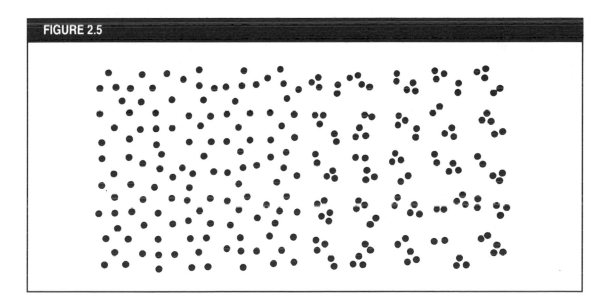

FIGURE 2.5

Even though the average brightness in the left and right areas is the same, there is a distinct boundary between the left and right halves of the figure because of a change in granularity. Adapted from Julesz (1975).

dots are clumped together to a much greater extent towards the right of the figure than to the left.

The grouping processes identified by Julesz are based on basic stimulus properties such as brightness, wavelength, and granularity. This suggests that the processes involved in perceptual organisation occur very early in visual perception. These considerations led Julesz (1981) to propose a theory based on *textons*, which are the basic elements of early vision. Textons consist of elongated blobs or line segments and their terminations; they correspond directly to the representations found in the raw primal sketch. As the raw primal sketch only contains basic information about a visual display, the initial perceptual organisation does not take account of subtle variations in texture. For example, as Julesz (1981) pointed out, it is very difficult to discriminate between two regions if one region consists of S-shaped elements looking like:

whereas the other region consists of 10-shaped elements looking like:

Full primal sketch

One of the limitations of the approach adopted by Julesz (1981) and by others is that relatively little is said about the detailed processes involved in perceptual organisation. However, workers in artificial intelligence have made some progress in this direction, and the work of Marr (1976, 1982) is an example. His starting point was the notion that basic perceptual organisation is achieved relatively early in perceptual processing, namely at the level of the two-dimensional primal sketch.

It will be remembered that the raw primal sketch contains information about light-intensity changes in the form of edges, blobs, bars, and terminations. Various processes need to be applied to this raw primal sketch to identify its underlying structure or organisation. Of particular importance is the fact that the information contained in the raw primal sketch is typically ambiguous, in the sense that it is compatible with several different underlying structures.

Marr (1976) discovered that it was valuable to make use of two rather general principles when designing a program to achieve perceptual organisation: the *principle of explicit naming*, and the *principle of least commitment*. According to the former principle, it is useful to give a name or symbol to a set of grouped elements. The reason is that the name or symbol can be used over and over again to describe other sets of grouped elements, all of which can then form a much larger grouping. According to the principle of least commitment, ambiguities are resolved only when there is convincing evidence as to the appropriate solution. This principle is useful because mistakes at an early stage of processing can lead on to several other mistakes.

With respect to the principle of explicit naming, Marr's program assigned *place tokens* to small regions of the raw primal sketch, such as the position of a blob or edge, or the termination of a longer blob or edge. Various edge points in the raw primal sketch are incorporated into a single place token on the basis of Gestalt-like notions such as proximity, figural continuity, and closure. Place tokens are then grouped together in various ways, in part on the basis of the grouping principles advocated by the Gestaltists. Some examples of the ways in which place tokens are combined are as follows:

- Clustering: place tokens that are close together can be combined to form higher-order place tokens.
- Curvilinear aggregation: place tokens that are aligned in the same direction will be joined to produce a contour.

Section summary

Marr's (1976, 1982) visual processing program was reasonably successful. One reason why the grouping principles applied to place tokens work is because they reflect what is generally the case in the real world. For example, visual elements that are close together are likely to belong to the same object, as are elements that are similar. It is particularly impressive that the program works well in spite of the fact that it typically does not rely on object knowledge or expectations when deciding what goes with what. However, there were cases of ambiguity when the program could not specify the contour or perceptual organisation until supplied with additional information.

Perhaps the greatest limitation of Marr's approach to grouping was that he assumed that grouping is based on two-dimensional representations. Although this may generally be the case, there is evidence that grouping can also be based on three-dimensional representations. For example, Enns and Rensick (1990) discovered that their subjects immediately perceived which in a display of block figures was the "odd-man out". The subjects were able to do this even though the figures differed only in their three-dimensional orientation, but not in their two dimensional orientation. This suggests that three-dimensional information can be used to group stimuli.

DEPTH PERCEPTION

One of the major accomplishments of visual perception is the way in which the two-dimensional retinal image is transformed into perception of a three-dimensional world. It is important to note that the term "depth perception" is used in two rather different senses (Sekuler & Blake, 1994). First, there is *absolute distance*, which refers to the distance away from the observer that an object is located. Second, there is *relative distance*. This refers to the distance between two objects, and is used, for example, when fitting a slice of bread into a toaster. Judgements of relative distance are generally more accurate than judgements of absolute distance.

In real life, cues to depth are often provided by movement either of the observer or of objects in the visual environment. However, the major focus here will be on cues to depth that are available even if the observer and the objects in the environment are static. These cues can conveniently be divided into monocular and binocular cues. *Monocular cues* are those that only require the use of one eye, although they can also be used readily when someone has both eyes open. Such cues clearly exist, because the world still retains a sense of depth with one eye closed. *Binocular cues* are those that involve both eyes being used together.

Monocular cues

There are various monocular cues to depth. They are sometimes called *pictorial cues*, because they have been used by artists attempting to create the impression of three-dimensional scenes while painting on two-dimensional canvases. One such cue is *linear perspective*. Parallel lines pointing directly away from us appear progressively closer together as they recede into the distance (e.g. railway tracks or the edges of a motorway). This convergence of lines can create a powerful impression of depth in a two-dimensional drawing.

Another aspect of perspective is known as *aerial perspective*. Light is scattered as it travels through the atmosphere, particularly if the atmosphere is dusty. As a consequence, more distant objects lose contrast and appear somewhat hazy. There is evidence (e.g. Fry, Bridgman, & Ellerbrock, 1949) that reducing the contrast of objects makes them appear to be more distant.

Another cue related to perspective is *texture*. Most objects (e.g. cobble-stoned roads; carpets) possess texture, and textured objects slanting away from us have what Gibson (e.g. 1979) described as a texture gradient. This can be defined an increased gradient (rate of change) of texture density as you look from the front to the back of a slanting object. If you were unwise enough to stand between the rails of a railway track and look along the track, the details would become less clear as you looked into the distance. In addition, the distance between the connections would appear to reduce. The resultant texture gradient is shown in Fig. 2.6. Evidence that texture gradient can be a useful cue to depth in the absence of other depth cues was provided by Todd and Akerstrom (1987).

A further cue is *interposition*, in which a nearer object hides part of a more distant object from view. Some evidence of how powerful interposition can be is provided by Kanizsa's (1976) illusory square. As can be seen in Fig. 2.7, there is a strong impression of a white square in front of four black circles, in spite of the fact that most of the contours

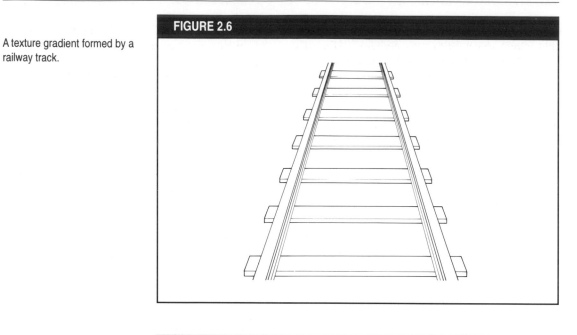

FIGURE 2.6

A texture gradient formed by a railway track.

FIGURE 2.7

Kanizsa's (1976) illusory square.

of the white square are missing. In other words, the visual system makes sense of the four sectored black discs by perceiving an illusory interpolated white square.

Another cue to depth is provided by *shading*. Flat, two-dimensional surfaces do not cast shadows, and so the presence of shading generally provides good evidence for the presence of a three-dimensional object. Ramachandran (1988) presented observers with a visual display consisting of numerous very similar circular dents, some of which were illuminated by one light source and the remainder of which were illuminated by a different light source. The observers incorrectly assumed that the visual display was lit by a single light source above the display, and this led them to assign different depths to different parts of the display (i.e. some dents were perceived as bumps).

The sun was easily the major source of light until comparatively recently in our evolutionary history, and this might explain why people assume that visual scenes are generally illuminated from above. Howard, Bergstrom, and Masao (1990) pointed out that the notion of "above" is ambiguous, in that it could be above with reference to gravity (as is assumed in the explanation just given), or it could be above with reference to the position of the head. Accordingly, they persuaded their subjects to view displays like those of Ramachandran (1988) with their heads upside down! The perceived source of light was determined with reference to head position rather than gravity, indicating that the location of the sun is not relevant to decisions about the direction of illumination.

Another cue to depth is provided by *familiar size*. It is possible to use the retinal image size of an object to provide an accurate estimate of its distance, but only when you know the object's actual size. Ittelson (1951) had subjects look at playing cards through a peep hole that restricted subjects to monocular vision and largely eliminated cues to depth other than familiar size. There were three playing cards (normal size, half-size, and double-size), and they were presented one at a time at a distance of 7.5ft from the observer. On the basis of familiar size, the judged distance of the normal card should have been 7.5ft, that of the half-size card 15.0ft, and that of the double-size card 3.8ft. The actual judged distances were 7.5ft, 15.0ft, and 4.6ft, indicating that familiar size can be a powerful determinant of distance judgements.

The final monocular cue we will discuss is *motion parallax*, which refers to the movement of an object's image over the retina. Consider, for example, two objects moving left to right across the line of vision at the same speed, but one object is much further away from the observer than is the other. In that case, the image cast by the nearer object would move much further across the retina than would the image cast by the more distant object.

Motion parallax is also involved if there are two stationary objects at different distances from the observer, and it is the observer's eyes that move. It would again be the case that the image of the nearer object would travel a greater distance across the retina. Some of the interesting properties of motion parallax can be observed through the window of a moving train. Objects that are closer to you than the fixation point appear to be moving in the opposite direction to the train, whereas objects that are beyond the fixation point appear to be moving in the same direction as the train.

Convincing evidence that motion parallax can generate depth information in the absence of all other cues was obtained by Rogers and Graham (1979). Their subjects looked at a display containing approximately 2000 random dots with only one eye. When there was relative movement of a section of the display (motion parallax) to simulate the movement produced by a three-dimensional surface, the subjects reported a three-dimensional surface standing out in depth from its surroundings. As Rogers and Graham (1979, p.134) concluded, "it has been clearly demonstrated that parallax information can be a subtle and powerful cue to the shape and relative depth of three-dimensional surfaces".

Binocular cues

The pictorial cues we have discussed could all be used as well by one-eyed people as by those with normal vision. However, there are various other cues that are available only to those possessing binocular vision. One such cue is *convergence*, which refers to the fact that the eyes turn inwards to focus on an object to a greater extent with a very close object than with one that is somewhat further away. Another cue is *accommodation*, which refers to the variation in optical power produced by a thickening of the lens of the eye when focusing on a close object. Finally, and most importantly, there is *stereopsis*, which is stereoscopic vision depending on the disparity in the images projected on the retinas of the two eyes. However, it must be noted that convergence, accommodation, and stereopsis are only effective in facilitating depth perception over relatively short distances.

There has been some controversy about the usefulness of convergence as a cue to distance. The findings have tended to be negative when real objects are used, but more promising findings have been obtained with use of the "wallpaper illusion" (Logvinenko & Belopolskii, 1994). In the wallpaper illusion, there is under-estimation of the apparent distance of a repetitive pattern when the fixation point is shifted towards the observer, and over-estimation when the fixation point moves away from the observer. It has generally been assumed that convergence of the eyes explains the wallpaper illusion, but Logvinenko and Belopolskii (1994) discussed evidence casting doubt on that assumption. It is possible to perceive two illusory patterns at two different apparent distances at once, which would be impossible if the phenomenon depended entirely on convergence. In addition, subjects can move their gaze around (and so change convergence) without any loss of the illusion. Such findings led Logvinenko and Belopolskii (1994, p.216) to conclude as follows:

> In view of the fact that the wallpaper illusion is commonly assumed to be the main evidence for convergence as a cue to distance, we conclude that convergence does not supply sufficient information for the perception of distance.

There is evidence that accommodation is also of very limited use. Its potential value as a depth cue is limited to the region of space immediately in front of you. However, distance judgements based on accommodation are rather inaccurate even when the object is at close range (e.g. Kunnapas, 1968).

The importance of stereopsis was demonstrated clearly by Wheatstone (1838), who is generally regarded as the inventor of the *stereoscope*. What happens in a stereoscope is that separate pictures or drawings are presented to an observer in such a way that the each eye receives essentially the information it would receive if the object or objects depicted were actually presented. This simulation of the disparity in the images presented to the two eyes produces a strong depth effect.

One might think that steropsis is a reasonably straightforward phenomenon. In fact, nothing could be further from the truth. It has proved surprisingly difficult to work out in detail how it is that two separate images turn into a single percept. In general terms, we must somehow establish *correspondences* between the information presented to one eye and that presented to the other eye. At one time, it was believed that the forms or objects presented to each eye were recognised independently, and that they were then fused into a single percept. However, this no longer seems likely. Crucial evidence was obtained by Julesz (1971), who made use of random-dot stereograms. Each member of such a stereogram appears to consist of a random mixture of black and white dots, i.e. neither member appears to contain a recognisable form. However, when the stereogram is viewed in a stereoscope, an object (e.g. a square) can be clearly seen.

If stereopsis does not result from a matching of the forms from each image, how does it happen? Part of the answer was obtained by Frisby and Mayhew (1976). They made use of a process known as filtering to remove certain spatial frequencies (these are determined by the closeness together of alternating dark and light bars). Stereopsis remained when only high spatial frequencies were removed from both halves of a stereogram, or when only low spatial frequencies were removed from both. However, when high spatial frequencies were removed from one half and low spatial frequencies from the other, stereopsis was lost and only one half of the stereogram could be seen at any one time. These findings indicate that some overlap of spatial frequencies between the two halves of a stereogram are necessary for stereopsis.

Marr and Poggio (1976) proposed three rules that might be useful in matching up information from the two eyes:

- *Compatibility constraint:* elements from the input to each eye are matched with each other only if they are compatible (e.g. having the same colour; edges having the same orientation).

- *Uniqueness constraint:* each element in one image is allowed to match with only one element in the other image.
- *Continuity constraint:* matches between two points or elements are preferred where the disparities between the two images are similar to the disparities between nearby matches on the same surface.

These three constraints were incorporated into a theory that was able to produce appropriate solutions to random dot stereograms (Marr & Poggio, 1976). However, Frisby (1986) pointed out that the continuity constraint is the least adequate. For example, if an object slants steeply away from the observer, then nearby matching points will not have very similar disparities. As a consequence, there may be a failure to match corresponding points with each other.

There are several other theories of stereopsis. For example, Mayhew and Frisby (1981) argued that stereopsis is very much bound up with the elaboration of descriptions in the raw primal sketch. This contrasts with the view of Marr and Poggio (1976), which is that stereopsis is rather separate from other aspects of visual processing. Mayhew and Frisby (1981) proposed a *figural continuity constraint:* most erroneous possible matches can be eliminated by considering the pattern of light-intensity changes in the area close to that of the potential match.

The emphasis in most theories of stereopsis has been on the basic visual processes involved. However, there is reasonably convincing evidence that cognitive factors can be important. A case in point is Gregory's (1973) "hollow face" illusion. In this illusion, observers looking at a hollow mask of a face from a distance of a few feet report seeing a normal face. What is happening is that stereoscopic information is ignored in favour of expectations about human faces based on previous experience.

Integrating cue information

The visual environment is typically rich in information, so that we generally have access to several different depth cues. In order to have a complete understanding of depth perception, we need to know how information from the various cues we have discussed is combined and integrated. For example, what do we do if two depth cues provide conflicting evidence about depth? One possibility is that we make use of information from both cues to reach some compromise solution, but another possibility is that we accept the evidence from one and ignore the other.

Some of the major issues of cue combination were investigated by Bruno and Cutting (1988). They identified three possible strategies that might be used by observers who had information available from two or more depth cues:

- *Additivity:* all of the information from different cues is simply added together.
- *Selection:* information from a single cue is used, with information from the other cue or cues being ignored.
- *Multiplication:* information from different cues interacts in a multiplicative fashion.

Bruno and Cutting (1988) tested these possibilities in a series of studies on relative distance in which three untextured parallel flat surfaces were arranged in depth. The observers viewed the displays monocularly, and there were four sources of information about depth: relative size; height in the projection plane; interposition; and motion parallax. The findings provided consistent support for the additivity notion (Bruno & Cutting, 1988, p.161): "Information is gathered by separate visual subsystems ... and it is added together in the simplest manner." There is growing evidence that many of the processes involved in visual perception operate in parallel (see the next section of this chapter), and the notion of additivity is entirely consistent with such evidence.

It is advantageous to have a visual system that combines information from different depth cues in an additive fashion. Any depth cue provides inaccurate information under some circumstances, and so relying exclusively on one cue would often lead to error. In contrast, hedging one's bets by taking equal account of all the available information about depth is generally the best way of ensuring that depth perception is accurate. Another advantage of having additive, independent mechanisms involved in depth perception can be seen in infants, because each mechanism can develop in its own time without having to wait for other mechanisms to develop before it can be used. As Bruno and Cutting (1988) pointed out, infants can use motion parallax before the age of three months, even though many of the other mechanisms involved in depth perception have not developed at that stage.

Bruno and Cutting (1988) did not investigate what happens when two cues provide conflicting information about depth. However, it would seem to follow from their general theoretical orientation that observers would attempt to combine the information from both cues in their depth perception. Support for this position was obtained by Rogers and Collett (1989, p.716). They set up a complex display in which binocular disparity and motion parallax cues provided conflicting information about depth, and discovered that the conflict was resolved by taking both cues into account: "Given apparently contradictory disparity and parallax information about the structure of 3-D objects, it would appear that the visual system attempts to find a solution that is maximally consistent with *all* the available information."

The evidence indicates that observers typically use information from all the available depth cues when attempting to judge relative or absolute distance. However, there are some exceptions. Woodworth and Schlosberg (1954) described a situation in which two normal playing cards of the same size are attached vertically to stands, with one card being closer to the observer than the other. The observer views the two cards monocularly, and the further card looks more distant. In the next phase of the experiment, a corner is clipped from the nearer card, and the two cards are arranged so that in the observer's retinal image the edges of the more distant card exactly fit the cutout edges of the nearer card. With monocular vision, the more distant card now appears to be in front of, and partially obscuring, the nearer card. In this case, the cue of interposition (which normally provides very powerful evidence about relative depth) completely overwhelms the cue of familiar size.

More research is needed to enhance our understanding of how information from different depth cues is combined. All the available information is generally taken into account in assessing depth, but there are some cases in which one or more cues are virtually ignored. The factors determining whether or not all of the available depth cues are used have not been clearly established.

BRAIN SYSTEMS

In recent years, considerable knowledge about basic processes and systems of vision has been obtained through direct study of the brain by neurobiologists and others. Much of this research has been summarised by Zeki (1992, 1993). His major assumption is that different parts of the cortex are specialised for different visual functions, and that in order to understand visual perception, we need to recognise that the visual system consists of a number of modules or relative independent processing units (see Chapter 1). This contrasts with the traditional view, according to which there was a reasonably unitary visual processing system.

Some of the main areas of the visual cortex in the macaque monkey are shown in Fig. 2.8. The retina connects primarily to what is known as the primary visual cortex or area V1; the links between the retina and area V1 are through a sub-cortical structure called the lateral geniculate nucleus. The importance of area V1 is demonstrated by the fact that lesions at any point along the pathway to it from the retina lead to total blindness within the affected part of area V1. However, the prestriate cortex (areas V2 to V5) is also of major significance in visual perception. In summary form, here are the main functions that Zeki (1992, 1993) ascribes to these areas:

- *V1 and V2:* these areas are involved at an early stage of visual perception; they contain different groups of cells responsive to colour and form, and may be said to "contain pigeonholes into which the different signals are assembled before being relayed to the specialised visual areas" (Zeki, 1992, p.47).

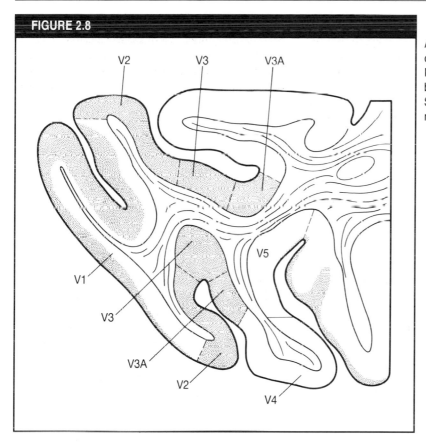

FIGURE 2.8

A cross-section of the visual cortex of the macaque monkey. From Zeki (1992). Reproduced by permission. © 1992 by Scientific American, Inc. All rights reserved.

- *V3 and V3A:* cells in these areas are responsive to form (especially the shapes of objects in motion) but not to colour.
- *V4:* the overwhelming majority of cells in this area are responsive to colour; many are also responsive to line orientation.
- *V5:* this area is specialised for visual motion (Zeki found in studies with macaque monkeys that all the cells in this area are responsive to motion, but they are not responsive to colour).

Experimental evidence

A central assumption made by Zeki (1992, 1993) is that colour, form, and motion are processed in anatomically separate parts of the visual cortex. The evidence that the visual cortex is organised in the way proposed by Zeki (1992, 1993) initially came from studies of monkeys. However, there is increasing evidence from positron emission tomography (PET; see Chapter 1) and from brain-damaged patients that the functional specialisation of the visual cortex in humans closely resembles that in monkeys.

Zeki (1992) discussed some of his research with PET scans. Normal human subjects viewing an abstract colour painting showed greatest brain activity in the fusiform gyrus, an area that is known as human V4. In contrast, viewing a pattern of moving black-and-white squares led to greatest activity in a different area known as human V5. These findings demonstrate that motion and colour are processed in different parts of the visual cortex in humans as well as in monkeys. In addition, the fact that there was considerable activity in area V1 (and also probably in area V2) with both stimuli suggests that these regions are involved in distributing signals to the relevant specialised areas of the prestriate cortex.

It would be expected from the notion of anatomically separate brain systems in visual perception that at least some patients with damage to the visual cortex should exhibit highly selective visual impairments. There are various conditions conforming to this expectation:

• *Achromatopsia:* this is a condition in which patients with damage to area V4 have no colour perception, and cannot even remember colours from the period before the brain damage; in spite of this, their form and motion perception are generally normal.
• *Akinetopsia:* this is a condition produced by damage to area V5 in which stationary objects can generally be perceived fairly normally, but objects in motion simply become invisible.
• *Chromatopsia:* this is a term devised by Zeki (1992) to refer to patients with widespread cortical damage caused by carbon monoxide poisoning who have good colour vision even though all other aspects of visual perception are very severely impaired.

It might be expected that some brain-damaged patients would suffer from severely impaired form vision, but Zeki (1992, p.47) claimed that "no one has ever reported a complete and specific loss of form vision". He argued that the reason for this might be that a lesion that was large enough to destroy areas V3 and V4 (the areas specialised for form perception) would probably destroy area V1 as well, and thus the patient would suffer from total blindness rather than simply loss of form perception.

There are other brain-damaged patients with extensive damage to area V1, in whom signals from the lateral geniculate nucleus appear to go directly to the specialised areas of the prestriate cortex without going via area V1. These patients are said to suffer from "blindsight" (Weiskrantz, 1986, 1990). They are blind in part of the visual field, in the sense that they have no conscious awareness of stimuli presented to it. In spite of this, they are able to make some accurate judgements and discriminations about visual stimuli presented to this blind area. For example, blindsight patients can indicate some knowledge of the location of objects in space by reaching towards them or by

appropriate eye movements. Patients have also been able to show above chance performance in deciding whether two stimuli (one presented to the blind area and the other to another part of the visual field) match or mismatch (Weiskrantz, 1990). Although it is generally assumed that blindsight patients have no conscious awareness of stimuli in the "blind" area, it should be noted that some patients find themselves in an intermediate state of awareness in which they have a "gut feeling" that there is something in the blind region (Weiskrantz, 1990).

Integration of information

As we have seen, there is convincing evidence that there are "four parallel systems concerned with different attributes of vision — one for motion, one for colour, and two for form" (Zeki, 1992, p. 47). This functional specialisation poses problems of integration, in that information about an object's motion, colour, and form needs to be brought together at some point. According to Zeki (1992, 1993), this is probably achieved at the end of the following sequence of processing stages:

• Initially, signals proceed from the retina to area V1 via the lateral geniculate nucleus.
• Signals go from area V1 to the various areas of the prestriate cortex specialised for form, motion, and colour processing.
• Signals from the specialised areas of the prestriate cortex are sent back to areas V1 and V2, because these are the areas that have the most precise maps of the visual field.

The complexities of integrating information about objects in the visual field also produce the "binding" problem: cells responding to any given object in the visual field may be distributed throughout area V1, and so a kind of binding is needed to combine these distributed sources of information. As yet, little is known of how the brain solves the binding problem. However, it appears likely that cells relating to a particular object fire in synchrony, and that this plays some part in producing the necessary integration of information for accurate perception of the visual world.

CHAPTER SUMMARY

A theoretical framework for understanding some of the basic processes in visual perception was provided by Marr (1982). He argued that the initial stages of processing involve the construction of two primal sketches: (1) the raw primal sketch, which incorporates information about light-intensity changes in the visual display; and (2) the full primal sketch, which utilises information from the raw primal sketch to identify the number and outline shapes of visual objects.

One of the most obvious characteristics of visual perception is that it is generally very organised. The Gestalt psychologists identified many of the factors (e.g. similarity; proximity) determining which elements of a visual display will be grouped together. They argued that we perceive the simplest or best organisation of a visual scene, but they failed to provide adequate measures of either of these organisational aspects. Marr incorporated many of the Gestalt principles into that part of his model concerned with explaining how the organised full primal sketch is obtained from the incoherent raw primal sketch.

One of the main achievements of visual perception is to permit us to perceive the world accurately in depth. We possess numerous cues to depth, some of which are monocular (requiring only one eye) and others of which are binocular (requiring both eyes). The monocular cues include linear perspective, aerial perspective, texture, interposition, shading, familiar size, and motion parallax. The binocular cues are convergence, accommodation, and stereopsis, but convergence and accommodation both seem to be of very limited usefulness. Stereopsis, which is based on the disparity of the retinal images from the two eyes, is much more important. However, it has proved rather difficult to produce an adequate theory of the processes involved in stereopsis. Information from the various depth cues is usually simply combined in an additive fashion, which is an efficient strategy for minimising errors in depth perception.

There is a growing consensus that there are a number of anatomically distinct systems in the visual cortex which are specialised for processing different kinds of information (form; motion; colour). Evidence to support this view comes from studies on monkeys, from PET scans, and from brain-damaged human patients. There is as yet only partial understanding of the complex processes required to integrate these disparate kinds of information into a unified image.

FURTHER READING

Harris, M.G., & Humphreys, G.W. (1994). Computational theories of vision. In A. M. Colman (Ed.), *Companion encyclopaedia of psychology,* (Vol. 1). London: Routledge. One of the more accessible accounts of Marr's theoretical views on basic visual processes is to be found in Chapter 3.2.

Sekuler, R., & Blake, R. (1994). *Perception* (3rd. Edn.). New York: Mcgraw-Hill. Chapter 7 in this book contains good coverage of the various cues used in depth perception.

Zeki, S. (1993). *A vision of the brain.* Oxford: Blackwell. This book provides a comprehensive account of knowledge about the major brain systems involved in visual perception.

3

Object Recognition

INTRODUCTION

Throughout the waking day we are bombarded with information from the visual environment. Most of the time we are able to make sense of that information, which usually involves identifying or recognising the objects that surround us. Object recognition generally occurs in such an effortless fashion that it is difficult to believe that it is actually a rather complex achievement.

The complexities of object recogniton can be grasped by discussing some of the processes that are involved. First, there are usually numerous different overlapping objects in the visual environment, and we must somehow decide where one object ends and the next starts. This requires a substantial amount of processing, as can be seen if we consider the visual environment of the first author as he is word-processing these words. There are well over 100 objects visible in the room in front of him and in the garden outside. Over 90% of these objects overlap, and are overlapped by, other objects.

Second, objects can be recognised accurately over a wide range of viewing distances and orientations. For example, there is a small table directly in front of the first author. He is confident that the table is round, although its retinal image is elliptical. The term "constancy" is used to refer to the fact that the apparent size and shape of an object do not change in spite of large variations in the size and shape of the retinal image.

Third, we recognise that an object is, say, a chair without any apparent difficulty. Chairs vary enormously in their visual properties (e.g. colour, size, shape), and it is not immediately obvious how we manage to allocate such heterogeneous visual stimuli to the same category. The discussion of the representation of concepts (e.g. Rosch et al., 1976) in Chapter 10 is relevant here.

In spite of the complexities of object recognition, we can generally go beyond simply identifying objects in the visual environment. For example, we can normally describe what an object would look like if viewed from a different angle, and we know its uses and functions.

All in all, there is more to object recognition than might initially be supposed. This chapter is devoted to the task of unravelling some of the mysteries of object recognition in normal and brain-damaged individuals.

PATTERN RECOGNITION

Given the complexities in recognising three-dimensional objects, it is sensible to start by considering the processes involved in the recognition of two-dimensional patterns. Much of this research has addressed the question of how alphanumeric patterns (alphabetical and numerical symbols) are recognised. A key issue here is the flexibility of the human perceptual system. For example, we can recognise the letter "A" rapidly and accurately across considerable variations in orientation, in typeface, in size, and in writing style. Why is pattern recognition so successful? Advocates of template theories, feature theories, and structural description theories have proposed different answers to this question. However, they agree that at a very general level pattern recognition involves matching information from the visual stimulus with information stored in memory.

Template theories

The basic idea behind template theories is that there is a miniature copy or template stored in long-term memory corresponding to each of the visual patterns we know. A pattern is recognised on the basis of which template provides the closest match to the stimulus input. This kind of theory is beguilingly simple, but it is not very realistic in view of the enormous variations in visual stimuli allegedly matching the same template.

One modest improvement to the basic template theory is to assume that the visual stimulus undergoes a normalisation process (i.e. producing an internal representation in a standard position, size, and so on) before the search for a matching template begins. Normalisation would facilitate pattern recognition for letters and digits, but it is improbable that it would consistently produce matching with the appropriate template.

Another way of attempting to improve template theory would be to assume that there is more than one template for each letter and numeral. This would permit accurate matching of stimulus and template across a wider range of stimuli, but only at the cost of making the theory much more unwieldy.

In general terms, template theories are ill-equipped to account for the adaptability shown by people when recognising alphanumeric stimuli. The limitations of template theories are especially obvious when the stimulus belongs to an ill-defined category for which no single template could possibly suffice (e.g. buildings).

Feature theories

According to feature theories, a pattern consists of a set of specific features or attributes. For example, a face could be said to possess various features: a nose, two eyes, a mouth, a chin, and so on. The process of pattern recognition is assumed to begin with the extraction of the features from the presented visual stimulus. This set of features is then combined, and compared against information stored in memory.

In the case of an alphanumeric pattern such as "A", feature theorists might argue that its crucial features are two straight lines and a connecting cross-bar. This kind of theoretical approach possesses the advantage that visual stimuli varying greatly in size, orientation, and minor details may nevertheless be identifiable as instances of the same pattern.

The feature-theory approach has received support in studies of visual search, in which a target letter has to be identified as rapidly as possible in a block of letters (see Fig. 3.1, for example). Neisser (1964) compared the time taken to detect the letter "Z" when the distractor letters consisted of straight lines (e.g. W, V) or contained rounded features (e.g. O, G). Performance was faster in the latter condition, presumably because the distractors shared fewer features with the target letter Z.

Although Neisser's classic research suggested that feature analysis plays an important role in letter perception, other evidence indicates it is not only the specific features that are important. Harvey, Roberts, and Gervais (1983) investigated spatial frequency (which is low when alternating light and darks bars are in close proximity). Individual letters were presented very rapidly, and subjects had to name them. Some letters (e.g. "K" and "N") having several features in common were not confused, whereas letters with similar spatial

FIGURE 3.1

LIST 1	LIST 2
IMVXEW	ODUGQR
WVMEIX	GRODUQ
VXWIEM	DUROQG
MIEWVX	RGOUDQ
WEIMXV	RQGOUD
IWVXEM	UGQDRO
IXEZVW	GUQZOR
VWEMXI	ODGRUQ
MIVEWX	DRUQGO
WXEIMV	UQGORD

Illustrative lists to study letter search; the distractors in List 2 share fewer features with the target letter Z than do the distractors in List 1.

frequencies but few common features tended to be confused.

It seems reasonable to assume that stimulus features play some role in pattern recognition. However, feature theories leave much that is of importance out of account. First, in common with template and structural description theories, they de-emphasise the effects of context and of expectations on pattern recognition. Consider a study by Weisstein and Harris (1974), in which the subjects' task was to detect a line that was embedded either in a briefly flashed three-dimensional form or in a less coherent form. According to feature theorists, the target line should always activate the same feature detectors, and so the coherence of the form in which it is embedded should not affect detection. In fact, target detection was best when the target line was part of a three-dimensional form. Weisstein and Harris (1974) called this the "object-superiority effect", and this effect is inconsistent with many feature theories.

Second, pattern recognition does not depend solely on listing the features of a stimulus. For example, the letter "A" consists of two oblique uprights and a dash, but these three features can be presented in such a way that they are not perceived as an A: \ / –. In order to understand pattern recognition, we need to consider the relationships among features as well as simply the features themselves.

Third, the limitations of feature theories are clearer with three-dimensional than with two-dimensional stimuli. The fact that observers can generally recognise three-dimensional objects even when one or more of the major features are hidden from view is difficult to account for on a theory that emphasises the role of features in recognition.

Structural descriptions

An approach to pattern recognition representing an advance on the theories considered so far is one based on structural descriptions. Structural descriptions consist of propositions, which are the smallest units of meanings to which we can assign a meaning. According to Bruce and Green (1990, p.186), "such propositions describe the nature of the components of a configuration and make explicit the structural arrangement of these parts". For example, a structural description of a capital letter T might include the following five propositions: there are two parts; one part is a horizontal line; one part is a vertical line; the vertical line supports the horizontal line; the vertical line bisects the horizontal line.

A structural description offers a more complete account of a visual stimulus than is usually provided by a feature analysis. Structural descriptions, and the models formed from them, focus on key aspects of stimuli rather than on less important ones. For example, the structural description of the letter T does not include propositions referring to the lengths of the vertical and horizontal lines. The reason is that the letter T can be recognised in spite of wide variations in the lengths of its constitutent lines.

So far we have considered structural descriptions only at the two-dimensional level. Not surprisingly, matters become more complicated when it comes to three-dimensional structural descriptions. In Fig. 3.2, we recognise both forms as representing the letter T. However, their equivalence is not captured by two-dimensional structural descriptions. It emerges only when three-dimensional structural descriptions are constructed.

Structural descriptions provide a more adequate basis for understanding pattern recognition than do templates or feature lists. However, more needs to be done at a theoretical level. In particular, it remains unclear how the information extracted from a visual stimulus is matched with the relevant stored structural description. In addition, structural descriptions do not take contextual information into account.

OBJECT RECOGNITION

When considering object recognition, it is important to note that the recognition of three-dimensional objects is not a unitary activity. When we recognise an object, we typically have access to several different kinds of information. Consider our experience when we recognise an object as a cat. We know what the cat would look like if viewed from different angles, we know what its functions are (e.g. a household pet), and we know that it is a member of the category of "cats".

These considerations led Humphreys and Bruce (1989) to propose a simple framework within which to understand object recognition (see Fig. 3.3). *Perceptual classification* involves matching the visual information extracted from an object with its stored structural description; *semantic classification* involves the retrieval of information about the functions and associates of the object; and *naming* involves the retrieval of the object's name. According to the framework presented in Fig. 3.3, perceptual classification precedes semantic classification, which in turn precedes name retrieval. However, this may be an over-simplification, as later processes may start before earlier ones have been completed.

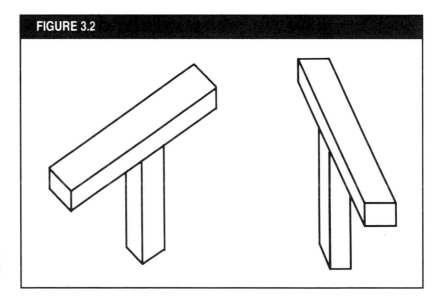

FIGURE 3.2

An example of forms that are equivalent at the three-dimensional level but not at the two-dimensional level. Adapted from Bruce and Green (1990).

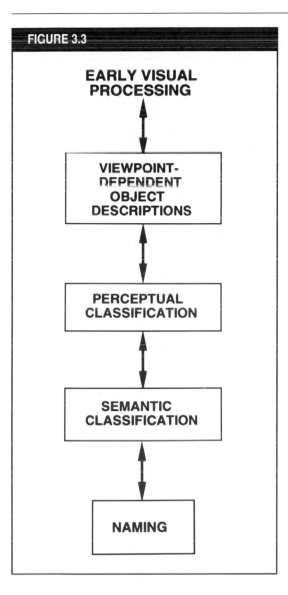

FIGURE 3.3

EARLY VISUAL
PROCESSING

VIEWPOINT-
DEPENDENT
OBJECT
DESCRIPTIONS

PERCEPTUAL
CLASSIFICATION

SEMANTIC
CLASSIFICATION

NAMING

Stages of processing in object recognition. Adapted from
Humphreys and Bruce (1989).

It follows from this approach that brain-damaged patients whose object recognition abilities are impaired should differ in terms of the precise nature of their impairment depending on which part or parts of the object-recognition system are damaged. As we will see, the available evidence from cognitive neuropsychology provides general support for this implication.

An interesting case of a patient having a particular problem with perceptual classification

was reported by Humphreys and Riddoch (1987). The patient, HJA, could not recognise most objects after suffering a stroke. Even when he was able to identify an object, it typically took him 20–30 seconds to do so. He was unable to distinguish between line drawings of real objects and of non-objects formed by interchanging parts of real objects. However, he was able to copy drawings of objects, and his semantic knowledge of objects appeared to be intact. He could provide good definitions of objects (even those he could not recognise), and he could draw objects accurately from memory.

Most of the findings from HJA suggest that he has problems with the *integration* of visual information. For example, he finds it easier to distinguish between real objects and non-objects when they are presented as silhouettes rather than as line drawings, presumably because the additional visual information presented in line drawings is more difficult for him to integrate or combine into a coherent representation.

Problems with perceptual representation might also occur because visual knowledge about objects is lost or inaccessible. This appears to be the case with some patients suffering from herpes simplex encephalitis. Warrington and Shallice (1984) discovered that such patients performed poorly on a number of tasks dependent on visual knowledge about objects. They found it difficult to identify objects presented visually. They were also poor at producing adequate definitions of objects, presumably because perceptual properties are important when defining most objects (the "yellowness" of bananas or the "roundness" of oranges, for example).

More direct evidence that patients with herpes simplex encephalitis have a particular problem with accessing visual information about objects was obtained by Silveri and Gainotti (1988). They asked their patients to name objects when provided with definitions emphasising either their visual (e.g. colour; size) or their functional properties (i.e. main uses). The patient performed better when provided with the functional information than with the visual information, indicating that it was specifically visual knowledge about objects that was unavailable or lost.

There are other patients who seem to possess intact visual knowledge, but who find it difficult to access their intact semantic knowledge following perceptual classification. Some of these patients suffer from *optic aphasia*, a condition with the following characteristics:

- Difficulties in naming objects from sight alone.
- Good ability to name objects that are touched.
- Use of some visually presented objects can be mimed.

Riddoch and Humphreys (1987) investigated a patient, JB, who suffered from optic aphasia. He performed at about the normal level when asked to decide whether line drawings represented real or meaningless objects, suggesting that his perceptual classification skills were reasonably good. In addition, the fact that he could name objects that he had touched or for which a definition had been provided means that he did not have a general problem with naming objects.

The clearest evidence that JB found it difficult to link semantic knowledge with visual knowledge came on an associative task, when he had to decide which two out of three visually presented objects were used together. This is an easy task for most people, but JB's performance was only slightly above chance level. His poor performance was not due to impaired semantic knowledge, because he performed virtually perfectly on the task when he was given the names of the objects. JB was also very poor at drawing objects from memory, even when he could remember relevant semantic information about the objects concerned. This suggests that he could not readily access visual knowledge from semantic knowledge.

There was one aspect of JB's performance that does not fit very well with the account given so far. He was able to mime the use of some visually presented objects (e.g. making a cutting gesture to indicate a knife). This suggests that some semantic knowledge can be accessed from visual informa-tion. According to Riddoch and Humphreys (1987), there may be direct associations between visual information and motor actions, so that appropriate gestures can be made without accessing the semantic system.

Whereas JB and other optic aphasics have intact semantic knowledge but often cannot access it, there are other patients who seem to have lost most of their associative and functional knowledge of objects. An example is a woman suffering from pre-senile dementia (Marin, 1987). She could access some visual knowledge, as was shown by her ability to arrange pictures in the correct orientation. However, she performed extremely poorly on all tasks requiring associative or functional knowledge about objects (e.g. deciding which objects belonged to the same category), and it made little difference whether the stimuli were presented visually or named out loud. This across-the-board impairment probably reflects substantial loss of associative and functional knowledge.

According to Fig. 3.3, the last stage in object recognition is naming. An implication is that successful object naming depends on having previously accessed relevant visual and semantic knowledge. This appears to be the case on the basis of the available evidence. In contrast, several patients suffering from *anomia* (characterised by problems in finding the names of objects) have been studied. Howard and Orchard-Lisle (1984) studied a patient, JCU, who was very poor at naming the objects shown in pictures unless she was given the first phoneme or sound of the name as a cue. If the cue was the first phoneme of a word closely related to the object shown in the picture, then she would often be misled into producing the wrong answer. She accepted this wrong answer as correct 76% of the time, indicating that she had only partial access to semantic knowledge about objects.

Section summary

There is compelling evidence that different kinds of information are involved in visual object recognition. It is reasonable to distinguish among visual knowledge, semantic (associative and functional) knowledge, and object naming, and studies on brain-damaged patients indicate the value of these distinctions. However, it is important to consider the detailed processes involved in perceptual and semantic classification. In the following sections we discuss theoretical approaches in which such processes are considered, especially those relating to perceptual classification.

Whole versus part processing

Several theorists (e.g. Watt, 1988) have argued (in similar fashion to the Gestaltists, whose views were discussed in Chapter 2) that visual processing typically proceeds from a rather global or general analysis of the whole pattern or object to a more detailed analysis of its component parts. One advantage of focusing initially on the overall structure is that this is less likely to vary from one instance to another than are the component parts. For example, two dogs will resemble each other at the global level (e.g. possessing a head at the front, a tail at the back, and four legs underneath), even though they may differ considerably at a more detailed level (e.g. in their markings, fur colour, size, and facial expressions).

Some evidence suggesting that global processing often precedes more specific processing was obtained by Navon (1977). He presented his subjects with stimuli such as the one shown in Fig. 3.4. In one of his experiments, subjects had to decide as rapidly as possible on

FIGURE 3.4

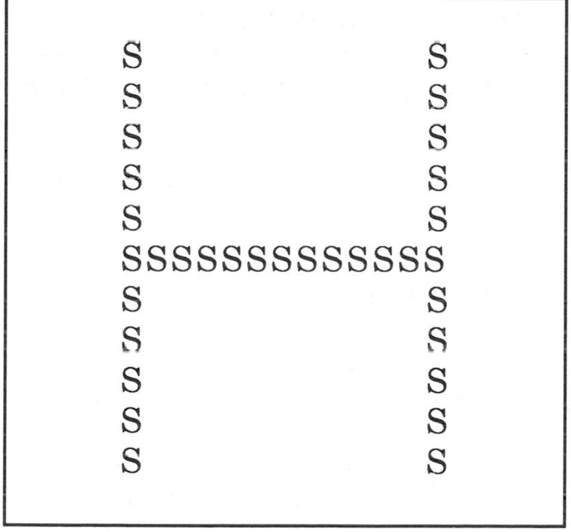

The kind of stimulus used by Navon (1977) to demonstrate the importance of global features in perception.

some trials whether the large letter was an "H" or an "S"; on other trials, they had to decide whether the small letters were Hs or Ss. Performance speed with the small letters was greatly slowed when the large letter was different to the small letters. In contrast, decision speed with the large letter was unaffected by the nature of the small letters. According to Navon (1977, p.354), these findings indicate that "perceptual processes are temporally organised so that they proceed from global structuring towards more and more fine-grained analysis. In other words, a scene is decomposed rather than built up".

Some of the available evidence is inconsistent with Navon's conclusion. For example, Kinchla and Wolfe (1979) used stimuli of a similar nature to those of Navon (1977), but of variable size. When the large letter was very large, they found that processing of the small letters preceded processing of the large letter. They argued that global processing occurs prior to more detailed processing only when the global structure of a pattern or object can be ascertained by a single eye fixation.

The main problem with research stemming from Navon's (1977) study is that it has not proved possible to identify precisely where in the visual processing system the global advantage occurs. In the words of Kimchi (1992, p.36):

> There seems to be evidence, though not entirely conclusive, that global advantage occurs at early perceptual processing. Certain findings suggest that the mechanisms underlying the effect may be sensory, but other findings are suggestive of attentional mechanisms.

Marr's computational theory

Marr's (1982) primal sketch and $2\frac{1}{2}$-D sketch were discussed in Chapter 2, and it is now time to focus on his 3-D model representation. The $2\frac{1}{2}$-D sketch provides a poor basis for identifying an object, primarily because it is viewpoint-centred; this means that the representation of an object will vary considerably depending on the angle from which it is viewed, and this variability greatly complicates object recognition. As a consequence, the 3-D model representation, which contains observer-independent information, is produced.

Marr and Nishihara (1978) identified three desirable criteria for a 3-D representation:

- Accessibility: the representation can be constructed easily.
- Scope and uniqueness: "scope" refers to the extent to which the representation is applicable to all the shapes in a given category, and "uniqueness" means that all the different views of an object produce the same standard representation.
- Stability and sensitivity: "stability" indicates that a representation incorporates the similarities among objects, and "sensitivity" means that it incorporates salient differences.

Marr and Nishihara (1978) proposed that the primitive units for describing objects should be cylinders possessing a major axis. These primitive units are hierarchically organised, with high-level units providing information about object shape and low-level units providing more detailed information. Why did Marr and Nishihara adopt this axis-based approach? In essence, they argued that the main axis or axes of an object are usually easy to establish regardless of the viewing position, but this is not true of other characteristics of objects (e.g. precise shape).

The flavour of Marr and Nishihara's (1978) theoretical approach can be seen in their description of the human form:

First the overall form of the 'body' is given an axis. This yields an object-centred coordinate system which can then be used to specify the arrangement of the 'arms', 'legs', 'torso', and 'head'. The position of each of these is specified by an axis of its own, which in turn serves to define a coordinate system for specifying the arrangement of further subsidiary parts. This gives us a hierarchy of 3D models ... The shapes ... are drawn as if they were cylindrical, but that is purely for ... convenience: it is the axes alone that stand for the volumetric qualities of the shape, much as pipecleaner models can serve to describe various animals.

This account of the hierarchical organisation of the human form is illustrated in Fig. 3.5, which shows how the human form can be decomposed into a series of cylinders with axes at different levels of generality. It was assumed that this overall 3-D description is stored in memory. The information contained in this description enables us to recognise appropriate visual stimuli as humans regardless of the angle of viewing.

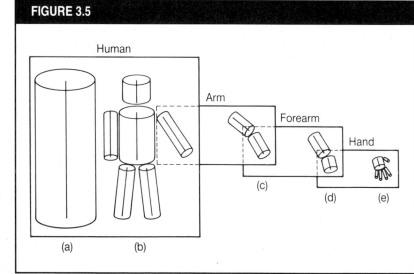

FIGURE 3.5

Human

Arm

Forearm

Hand

(a)   (b)   (c)   (d)   (e)

The hierarchical organisation of the human figure (Marr & Nishihara, 1978, reprinted by permission of the Royal Society) at various levels: (a) axis of the whole body; (b) axes at the level of arms, legs, and head; (c) arm divided into upper and lower arm; (d) a lower arm with separate hand; and (e) the palm and fingers of a hand.

According to Marr and Nishihara (1978), object recognition involves matching the 3-D model representation constructed from a visual stimulus against a catalogue of 3-D model representations stored in memory. In order for this to happen, it is necessary to identify the major axes of the visual stimulus. Marr and Nishihara (1978) proposed that concavities (areas where the contour points into the object) are identified first of all. With the human form, for example, there is a concave area in each armpit. These concavities are used to divide the visual image into segments (e.g. arms; legs; torso; head). Finally, the main axis of each segment is found.

There are some advantages associated with Marr and Nishihara's emphasis on concavities and axis-based representations. First, there is good evidence that the identification of concavities plays an important role in object recognition. Consider, for example, the faces–goblet ambiguous figure (Fig. 3.6), which was studied by Hoffman and Richards (1984). When one of the faces is seen, the concavities facilitate the identification of the forehead, nose, lips, and chin. In contrast, when the goblet is seen, the concavities serve to define its base, stem, and bowl.

Second, it is possible to calculate the lengths and arrangement of axes of most visual objects regardless of the angle of viewing. Third, information about axes can facilitate object recognition. As Humphreys and Bruce (1989) pointed out, humans can be readily distinguished from gorillas on the basis of the relative lengths of the axes of the segments or cones corresponding to arms and legs: in general, our legs are longer than our arms, whereas the opposite is true of gorillas.

FIGURE 3.6

An ambiguous drawing which can be seen either as two faces or as a goblet.

Cognitive neuropsychology

According to Marr's (1982) computational theory, it is theoretically possible for brain-damaged patients to have problems with object recognition because they cannot readily turn 2½-D sketches into 3-D model representations. What pattern of perceptual performance might one expect to find in such patients? They might be able to draw visually presented objects reasonably accurately, as this ability requires only an adequate 2½-D sketch. However, they would experience great difficulty in recognising objects presented in unusual angles, because they lack the ability to transform the viewpoint-centred 2½-D sketch into the object-centred 3-D model representation. If their semantic knowledge about objects were intact, then such patients might be able to recognise objects that were viewed from the most typical angle. In those circumstances, the 2½-D sketch would closely resemble the 3-D model representation, and so the problems of transforming one representation into the other would be minimised.

Warrington and Taylor (1978) studied patients with posterior injuries of the right cerebral hemisphere who approximated to the description given here. The stimuli presented to the patients consisted of pairs of photographs of objects, one member of each pair being a usual or conventional view and the other member being an unusual view. For example, the usual view of a flat-iron was photographed from above, whereas the unusual view showed only the base of the iron and part of the handle. When the photographs were shown one at a time, the patients were reasonably good at identifying the objects when they were shown in the usual or conventional view, but were extremely poor at identifying the same objects shown from an unusual angle.

Warrington and Taylor (1978) obtained more dramatic evidence of the perceptual problems of these patients when they presented pairs of photographs together, and asked the patients to decide whether the same object was depicted in both photographs. The patients performed poorly on this task, indicating that they found it difficult to identify an object shown from an unusual angle even when they knew what it might be on the basis of their identification of the accompanying usual view.

The findings obtained by Warrington and Taylor (1978) are plausibly explained by assuming that the patients found it difficult to transform unusual views of objects into appropriate 3-D model representations. However, Humphreys and Riddoch (1984, 1985) pointed out that the view of an object can be unusual in at least two different ways. It can be unusual because the object is foreshortened, thus making it difficult to determine its principal axis of elongation, or because a distinctive feature of the object is hidden from view. In order to investigate these two possibilities, Humphreys and Riddoch used photographs in which some of the unusual views were based on obscuring a distinctive feature, whereas others were based on foreshortening. Subjects either had to name the object in a photograph, or they had to decide which two out of three photographs were of the same object.

In four patients having right posterior cerebral lesions Humphreys and Riddoch (1984, 1985) found that they performed poorly with the foreshortened photographs but not with those lacking a distinctive feature. Marr and Nishihara (1978) argued that foreshortening makes it especially difficult to attain a 3-D model representation, and so the data are consistent with their theoretical position.

Biederman's recognition-by-components theory

Biederman (1987) proposed a theory of object recognition that resembles (but goes beyond) that of Marr and Nishihara (1978). The central assumption of his recognition-by-components theory is that objects can be regarded as consisting of basic shapes or components known as "geons" (geometric ions). Examples of geons are blocks, cylinders, spheres, arcs, and wedges. According to Biederman (1987), there are approximately 36 different geons. This may sound like a suspiciously small number to provide descriptions of all the objects we can identify. However, we can identify enormous numbers of spoken English words even though there are only approximately 44 phonemes in the English language. The reason is that these phonemes can be arranged in almost endless different orders, and the same is true of geons. Part of the reason for the richness of the object descriptions provided by geons stems from the different possible spatial relationships among them. For example, a cup can be described by an arc connected to the side of a cylinder, and a pail can be described by the same two geons, but with the arc connected to the top of the cylinder.

In order to understand recognition-by-components theory more fully, it will be useful to refer to Fig. 3.7. The stage which we have discussed so far is that of the determination of the components or geons of a visual object and their relationships. When this information is available, it is matched with stored object representations or structural models containing information about the

nature of the relevant geons, their orientations, sizes, and so on. In general terms, the identification of any given visual object is determined by whichever stored object representation provides the best fit with the component- or geon-based information obtained from the visual object.

As can be seen in Fig. 3.7, only part of Biederman's theory has been presented so far. What has been omitted has been any analysis of how an object's components or geons are determined. One major element is to decide how a visual object should be segmented to establish the number of parts or components of which it consists. Biederman (1987) agreed with Marr and Nishihara (1978) that the concave parts of an object's contour are of particular value in accomplishing the task of segmenting the visual image into parts.

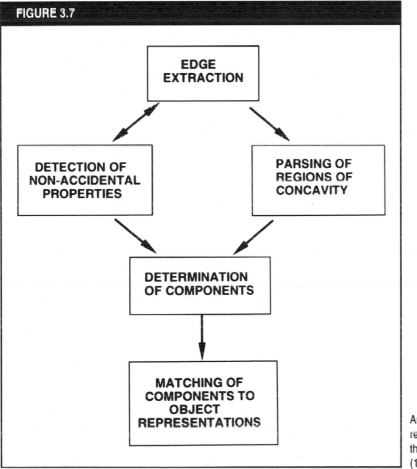

FIGURE 3.7

EDGE EXTRACTION

DETECTION OF NON-ACCIDENTAL PROPERTIES

PARSING OF REGIONS OF CONCAVITY

DETERMINATION OF COMPONENTS

MATCHING OF COMPONENTS TO OBJECT REPRESENTATIONS

An outline of Biederman's recognition-by-components theory. Adapted from Biederman (1987).

The other major element is to decide which edge information from an object possesses the important characteristic of remaining invariant across different viewing angles. According to Biederman (1987), there are five such invariant properties of edges:

- Curvature: points on a curve.
- Parallel: sets of points in parallel.
- Cotermination: edges terminating at a common point.
- Symmetry: versus asymmetry.
- Co-linearity: points in a straight line.

According to the theory, the components or geons of a visual object are constructed from these invariant properties. Thus, for example, a cylinder possesses curved edges and two parallel edges connecting the curved edges, whereas a brick possesses three parallel edges and no curved edges. According to Biederman (1987, p.116), the five properties:

have the desirable properties that they are invariant over changes in orientation and can be determined from just a few points on each edge. Consequently, they allow a primitive [component or geon] to be extracted with great tolerance for variations of viewpoint, occlusion [obstruction], and noise.

An important part of Biederman's theory with respect to the invariant properties is what he called the "non-accidental" principle. According to this principle, regularities in the visual image reflect actual (or non-accidental) regularities in the world rather than depending on accidental characteristics of a given viewpoint. Thus, for example, it is assumed that a two-dimensional symmetry in the visual image indicates symmetry in the three-dimensional object. Use of the non-accidental principle facilitates object recognition, but occasionally leads to error. For example, a straight line in a visual image usually reflects a straight edge in the world, but it might not (e.g. a bicycle viewed end-on).

Some visual illusions can be explained by assuming that we use the non-accidental principle.

For example, consider the Ames distorted room: It is actually of a most peculiar shape, but when viewed from a particular point it gives rise to the same retinal image as a conventional rectangular room. Of particular relevance here, misleading properties such as symmetry and parallellism can be derived from the visual image of the Ames room, and may underlie the illusion.

Biederman's (1987) theory makes it clear how objects can be recognised in normal viewing conditions. However, we are generally very good at recognising objects when the conditions are sub-optimal (e.g. the lighting is poor; an intervening object obscures part of the target object). According to Biederman (1987), there are various reasons why we are able to achieve object recognition in such conditions:

- The invariant properties (e.g. curvature; parallel lines) can still be detected even when only parts of edges can be seen.
- Provided that the concavities of a contour are visible, there are mechanisms allowing the missing parts of a contour to be restored.
- There is normally a considerable amount of redundant information available for recognising complex objects, and so they can still be identified when some of the geons or components are missing (e.g. a giraffe could be identified from its neck even if its legs were hidden from view).

Experimental evidence

A study by Biederman, Ju, and Clapper (1985) was designed to test the notion that complex objects can be detected even when some of the components or geons are missing. Line drawings of complex objects having six or nine components were presented briefly. Even when only three or four of their components were present, subjects displayed approximately 90% accuracy in identifying the objects.

Biederman (1987) discussed one of his studies in which subjects were presented with degraded line drawings of objects resembling those shown in Fig. 3.8. Object recognition was much harder to achieve when parts of the contour providing information about concavities were omitted than when other parts of the contour were deleted. This

FIGURE 3.8

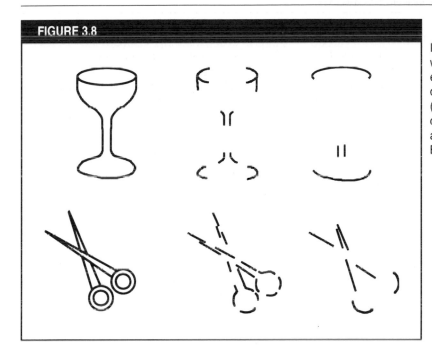

Intact figures (left-hand side), with degraded line drawings either preserving (middle column), or not preserving (far-right column), parts of the contour providing information about concavities. Adapted from Biederman (1987).

confirms the notion that information about concavities is important for object recognition.

According to Biederman's theory, object recognition depends on edge information rather than on other kinds of information (e.g. colour). To test this, subjects were presented with line drawings or full-colour photographs of common objects for between 50 and 100msec. Performance was comparable with the two types of stimuli: mean identification times were 11msec faster with the coloured objects, but the error rate was slightly higher. Even objects for which colour would appear to be important (e.g. bananas) showed no benefit from being presented in colour.

Biederman (1987) argued that the input image is initially organised into its constituent parts or geons, with geons forming the building blocks of object recognition. However, as we saw earlier in the chapter, global processing of an entire object often precedes more specific processing of its parts (see Kimchi, 1992). Additional evidence against Biederman's (1987) theory was reported by Cave and Kosslyn (1993). They argued that, on Biederman's (1987) theory, object recognition should be impaired if line drawings of objects were divided into parts in such a way that the geons were difficult to detect. However, they found that dividing objects into parts had very little effect on object recognition.

In sum, there is reasonable experimental support for the kind of theory proposed by Biederman (1987). However, the central theoretical assumptions have not been tested directly. For example, there is no convincing evidence that the 36 components or geons postulated by Biederman do actually form the building blocks of object recognition.

Evaluation

As Humphreys and Riddoch (1994) pointed out, many theories of object recognition (e.g. those of Marr and Nishihara, and of Biederman) propose that object recognition depends on a series of processes as follows:

- Coding of edges.
- Grouping or encoding into higher-order features.
- Matching to stored structural knowledge.
- Access to semantic knowledge.

These theories have the great advantage over earlier theories of being more realistic about the complexities of recognising three-dimensional objects. However, they are still rather limited in various ways. First, these theories are reasonably effective when applied to objects having readily identifiable constituent parts, but they are much less so when applied to objects that do not (e.g. clouds).

Second, Marr and Nishihara (1978), Biederman (1987), and others have emphasised the notion that object recognition involves matching an object-centred representation that is independent of the observer's viewpoint with object information stored in long-term memory. This theoretical view was explored by Biederman and Gerhardstein (1993). They argued that object naming would be primed as well by two different views of an object as by two identical views, provided that the same object-centred structural description could be constructed from both views. Their findings supported the prediction. However, in a related study, Lawson, Humphreys, and Watson (1994) discovered that object recognition was most efficient when the same viewpoint-specific object representation was activated by two successive pictures. This suggests that object-centred representations may be less important to object recognition than has generally been thought to be the case.

More evidence was reported by Perrett, Oram, Hietanen, and Benson (1994), who studied face-sensitive cells in the superior temporal sulcus of the monkey. They found that many cells were much more responsive to front views of the face than to profile views, whereas others were much more responsive to profile views. Although it appeared that these cells were basically responding in a viewpoint-specific fashion, there were also a few cells that responded to a range of different facial views in a more object-centred fashion. This neurophysiological evidence suggests that a complete theory may need to assume that object-centred and viewpoint-specific representations both play a substantial role in object recognition.

Third, the theories proposed by Marr and Nishihara (1978), Biederman (1987), and others were basically designed to account for relatively unsubtle perceptual discriminations, such as deciding whether the animal in front of us is a dog or a cat. These theories have little to say about subtle perceptual discriminations within classes of objects. For example, the same geons are used to describe almost any cup, but we can readily identify which one out of a varied collection of cups is the one we normally use.

Fourth, the theories we have considered have de-emphasised the important role played by context in object recognition. For example, Palmer (1975) presented a picture of a scene (e.g. a kitchen), followed by the very brief presentation of the picture of an object. This object was sometimes appropriate to the context (e.g. a loaf), or it was inappropriate (e.g. mailbox or drum). There was also a further condition in which no contextual scene was presented. The context had a systematic effect on the probability of identifying the object correctly, with the probability being greatest when the object was appropriate to the context, intermediate when there was no context, and lowest when the object was inappropriate to the context.

COGNITIVE NEUROSCIENCE APPROACH

The theories of object recognition that we have discussed so far in this chapter are mostly far removed from the biological realities of brain functioning. However, since about 1985 more and more theorists have been concerned to develop theories that take account of our knowledge of brain functioning. According to Van Kleeck and Kosslyn (1993), this is the era of *cognitive neuroscience*, in which theorists start with the assumption that "the mind is what the brain does".

Theorists within the cognitive neuroscience approach differ in terms of their primary focus. Some theorists (often known as "connectionists") are much influenced by the fact that there are enormous number of neurones in the brain; these neurones are either active or inactive at any given moment depending on whether they have received inputs from other neurones. We consider two connectionist models: WISARD, discussed by Stonham (1986); and the parallel distributed processing model of McClelland and Rumelhart (1985).

Other cognitive neuroscientists have also taken account of our increased knowledge of the brain, but have focused on producing theories at a much less detailed level than connectionist modellers. An example of a general theory in cognitive neuroscience, that of Kosslyn, Flynn, Amsterdam, and Wang (1990), is discussed later in the chapter.

WISARD

WISARD (Wilkie, Aleksander, and Stonham's Recognition Device) is an example of a connectionist model designed to recognise patterns (see Stonham, 1986). The stimulus display is regarded as consisting of a very large number of small regions called pixels (picture elements), each of which is either black or white. The entire display is then sampled by selecting successive groups of pixels of a given size ("n-tuples"); for example, each group might consist of four pixels, and these pixels would not necessarily be adjacent. The WISARD system stores away information about the pattern of black and white pixels obtained. As a consequence, the WISARD system learns to recognise patterns. For example, if WISARD is exposed repeatedly to five faces, they will each produce a rather different pixel pattern. When a new face is presented, WISARD will categorise it on the basis of the overall similarity of its pixel pattern to those of the five face patterns on which it has been trained.

WISARD is good at learning to recognise patterns in suitable conditions. When WISARD was presented with various views of 15 faces, it was subsequently able to identify accurately each of the 15 faces (Stonham, 1986). In spite of its success, however, the WISARD system is very limited. First, it performs well only when the conditions during testing are very similar to those during training. An alteration in the lighting conditions (e.g. having an indirect source of lighting that casts a shadow over the visual display) can produce a substantial change in the numbers and pattern of black and white pixels and thus disrupt pattern recognition. Second, the way in which WISARD performs pattern recognition is very different from that of humans. WISARD carries out simple processing operations on visual stimuli, and succeeds at pattern recognition because of its excellent memory. In contrast, humans show good pattern recognition because of the complex processing of visual stimuli rather than because of the power of their memory systems.

Connectionist approach

There has been increasing interest in another connectionist approach to object recognition based on the notion of parallel distributed processing (see Chapter 1). It is assumed that any given object category (e.g. "cat") is represented by a pattern of activity across different processing units spread out in space. This contrasts with the more usual assumption that information about each object category is stored in a specific location.

Most connectionist models are rather complex, but some of the main assumptions of a model proposed by McClelland and Rumelhart (1985) will be discussed here. They assumed that there is a network of processing units, in which all of the units are interconnected. Each unit can receive an external input from a visual stimulus and an internal input from other processing units. Connections between units can be either excitatory or inhibitory. Learning occurs as a consequence of an altered pattern of activity in the network, although this is reduced to some extent by the decay of activity in the system. After learning has occurred, the network activity corresponding to an entire stimulus pattern can be produced even when only part of the stimulus pattern is presented. This is done by calculating the difference ("delta") between the external and the internal input to each unit, and making adjustments so that the total internal input is the same as the total external input; this is known as the "delta rule".

McClelland and Rumelhart (1985) illustrated the learning powers of networks operating according to these rules. They considered a very small network of only 24 processing units; this network was exposed to two simple patterns called "Rover" and "Lassie"; these patterns were so limited that no real pattern processing was possible. Eight of the processing units were dedicated to the task of learning to associate the names correctly with their respective patterns, while the remaining 16 units were devoted to learning the general characteristics of the category "dog". There was a prototype pattern representing the common characteristics of dogs, but this pattern was always presented in a somewhat distorted fashion. The network succeeded in distinguishing between "Lassie" and "Rover" patterns, and at the same time it also learned the characteristics of the "dog" category. Its learning of the latter was so good that it was able to complete the prototype pattern when presented with only a part of it.

McClelland and Rumelhart (1985) also used a 24-unit network to perform a more complex pattern recognition task. It was presented during training with a number of very simple patterns designed to represent individual dogs, cats, and bagels, all of which consisted of distortions of their respective prototype patterns. When the network was tested after the training phase, it was able to produce the pattern of activation of the respective prototype when presented with an instance of the category (e.g. a specific dog). The network is also sensitive to details of presented instances, in that it produces greater activation in response to an instance that was presented recently than to one that was not.

These findings correspond well to those that have been obtained with human subjects. For example, consider a priming effect in which object recognition is facilitated by having presented the object previously. With faces, the greatest priming effect is obtained when the same photograph is presented twice, but a smaller priming effect is found when two different photographs of the same face are presented (see Bruce, 1988, for a review). In other words, our perceptual systems resemble McClelland and Rumelhart's (1985) network in being responsive to general, categorical information and to the specific information provided by instances of a category.

Evaluation

There are various limitations with connectionist models of pattern recognition. First, such models often use arbitrary sets of features as the input to the network (e.g. McClelland & Rumelhart, 1985). This does not resemble human object recognition, which appears to make extensive use of information about edges in the initial processing stages (Marr, 1982). Second, at a more technical level, two patterns that are represented by activity in the same processing units (e.g. "Rover" and "Lassie") cannot both be recognised at the same time, whereas this limitation is not present in human perception. Third, most of the proposed networks (such as the 24-unit network of McClelland & Rumelhart, 1985) are enormously oversimplified when compared to the complexities of the processes involved in human object perception.

General evaluation of connectionist approaches

It has only been possible to give a sketch of connectionist approaches to visual perception. Some of the more complex models have been omitted because they cannot be described briefly. For example, McClelland and Rumelhart (1985) proposed a relatively simple "single-layer" network, but "multi-layer" networks (with an additional intermediate layer of so-called "hidden units"), such as the one put forward by Rumelhart, Hinton, and Williams (1986b), are potentially much more powerful and flexible (see Chapter 1). As a consequence, some of the main achievements of connectionist modellers have not been presented.

Gordon (1989) discussed some of the valuable features of the connectionist or parallel distributed processing approach. He argued (p.220) that this approach was characterised by one major insight: "Systems using simple components can do very complicated things, provided these components are allowed to compete and interact."

One of the key issues (and one which is difficult to address satisfactorily) concerns the relationship between the distributed representations of connectionists and the symbolic representations of the visual world proposed by Marr (1982) and other theorists (see Chapter 9). In broad terms, connectionist models have been regarded either as fundamentally opposed to more traditional theories or as complementary to such theories. According to those who favour the latter alternative, connectionist models are at a more detailed or specific level than traditional theories; as such, they may offer insights into the processes involved in the formation of symbolic representations.

There are grounds for arguing that most connectionist models complement rather than challenge previous theories of pattern and object recognition. A number of connectionist models are based on symbol-processing theories. For example, Hummel and Biederman (1992) proposed a connectionist model of Biederman's (1987) geon theory. This model (known as JIM because the first names of the two theorists who proposed it are John and Irv) is a seven-layer connectionist network that takes as its input a representation of a line drawing of an object and produces as its output a unit representing its identity. The first three layers of the network produce the constituent geons of the object, and these geons are then used to identify the object. The success of this model provides concrete evidence that at least some connectionist and symbol-processing theories can be reconciled.

One of the major attractions of connectionist networks with their interconnected processing units is that they appear to resemble the network of neurons and synapses found in the human brain. This similarity may be only superficial, but there are some indications that it may not be. In one study (Lekhy & Sejnowski, 1988), a multi-layered network learned to recognise the curvatures of geometrical shapes. Hidden units within the network responded to edge and bar patterns, and the activity in these hidden units was affected by the orientation of the patterns. The properties of these hidden units correspond closely to those of the simple and complex cells identified by Hubel and Wiesel (1962) within the brain's visual system. Other potentially important similarities between connectionist networks and the detailed physiological functioning of the brain's visual system are discussed by Bruce and Green (1990).

General theory of high-level vision

Kosslyn et al. (1990) proposed an ambitious theory of high-level vision (visual processing involving the use of previously stored information). Evidence about brain functioning was used in its construction, and a computer simulation model was constructed to consider what components are necessary for high-level visual processing. This computer simulation model was also used to consider the consequences of different kinds of damage to the visual system.

The outline of the theory is shown in Fig. 3.9. There are various sub-systems within the overall visual perceptual system, and each of these sub systems consists of a parallel distributed network. In terms of the flow of information, the starting point is information approximating to that in Marr's (1982) $2\frac{1}{2}$-D sketch (i.e. edge, depth, and orientation information) being delivered to the *visual buffer*. There is more information available in the visual buffer than can be passed on to the later stages of visual processing, and so there needs to be an *attention window* to handle this problem.

One of the central assumptions of the theory is that the encoding of object information (i.e. "what" information) and of spatial information (i.e. "where" information) occurs in separate sub-systems (see the discussion of Zeki's theory in Chapter 2). There is a considerable amount of support for this assumption. For example, Mishkin and Ungerleider (1982) used a situation in which there were two food wells, each of which was covered by a lid. There was food in one of the wells, and monkeys were allowed to lift one lid in order to find it. Food was either associated with a specific lid pattern (object information) or with whichever food well was closer to a small model tower (spatial information). Monkeys whose inferior temporal lobes were removed had problems in using object information but not spatial information, whereas monkeys whose parietal lobes were removed experienced difficulty in using spatial information but not object information. These (and other) findings suggest that spatial properties are processed in a "dorsal" system running from the occipital lobe to the parietal lobe, whereas object properties are processed in a "ventral" system running from the occipital lobe to the inferior temporal lobe.

According to Kosslyn et al. (1990), the spatial information supplied to the *spatial properties sub-system* from the visual buffer is retinotopic (location is specified relative to the retina). One of the main characteristics of this sub-system is to transform this retinotopic representation into a

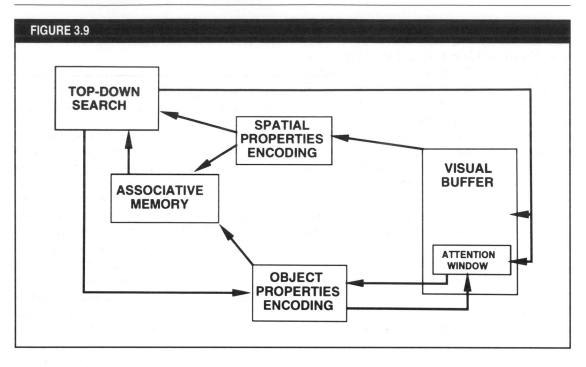

FIGURE 3.9

Kosslyn et al.'s theory of high-level vision. Adapted from Kosslyn et al. (1990).

spatiotopic representation, in which location is represented relative to objects in space. The *object properties sub-system* identifies the non-accidental properties of the input on the basis of edge, texture, colour, and intensity information in ways similar to those proposed by Biederman (1987). Kosslyn et al. (1990) left it open as to whether this sub-system produces viewpoint-centred or object-centred object representations.

The *associative memory sub-system* is responsible for integrating spatial and object information supplied by the spatial properties and object properties sub-systems. This information is compared against appropriate stored information in order to produce object recognition. This is an ongoing process: as spatial and object information accumulates in associative memory, a hypothesis of the object's identity is generated. Finally, *top-down search* tests the hypothesis. It can be used to look up in associative memory the properties the hypothesised object should have, or it can produce a shift in attention if this is needed for object recognition.

Computer simulation

The implications of damage to parts of the visual processing system were assessed by Kosslyn et al. (1990) using computer simulation. Two-dimensional stimulus arrays representing either a face or a fox were placed in the visual buffer, and limited arrays consisting of one-ninth of the original array were passed on via the attention window to the other sub-systems. Four different tasks were then given to the computer simulation program: (1) What is this?; (2) Who is this? (for faces only); (3) Are they the same? (for two pictures presented in succession); and (4) What is here? (for two pictures presented together).

The most striking finding of the computer simulation was that many perceptual problems can be caused by several different kinds of damage. One example is *visual agnosia* (involving deficient ability to recognise visual objects in spite of intact naming and attentional abilities), which was defined by poor performance on the first task listed earlier combined with intact performance on the third task. There were 34 different types of damage that produced this particular deficit. In similar fashion, there is *prosopagnosia* (difficulties in face recognition), which was defined by being able to identify a face as a face (first task) but being unable to identify correctly which face it was (second task). This pattern of performance was produced by 16 different types of damage.

Why can some disorders of visual perception be produced in numerous different ways? The main reason is because of the interconnected nature of the visual processing system shown in Fig. 3.9. For example, damage within the object properties sub-system means there is an impoverished output from that sub-system to the associative memory sub-system. As a consequence, the associative memory sub-system cannot function effectively, even though it may be intact.

Kosslyn et al. (1990) also discussed a condition known as *simultanagnosia*, in which only one object at a time can be perceived (see also Chapter 5). The computer simulation revealed that this condition arose only through partial damage to that part of the spatial properties sub-system responsible for producing a spatiotopic representation. It could thus be predicted that simultanagnosia should be rarer than most other forms of perceptual deficit, and that is indeed the case.

Evaluation

The theory proposed by Kosslyn et al. (1990) possesses at least three major strengths. First, it is the first theory to propose a collection of computational processing sub-systems underlying high-level vision that are in line with available knowledge of brain systems. Second, it provides a useful framework for cognitive neuropsychologists in their efforts to make theoretical sense of the data from brain-damaged patients. Third, the theory is one of the few in which attentional and perceptual phenomena are integrated.

On the negative side, it could be argued that the theory is at too great a level of generality. As a consequence, there is little clarification of the detailed processes operating within each of the sub-systems. This lack of specificity is perhaps especially noticeable so far as associative memory and top-down search are concerned. In both cases, it is much clearer *what* is accomplished by the particular sub-system than *how* it is accomplished.

FACE RECOGNITION

There are various reasons for devoting a separate section of this chapter to face recognition. First, as face recognition is the most common way of identifying people we know, the ability to recognise faces is of great signficance in our everyday lives. Second, as we will see, face recognition differs in a number of ways from other forms of object recognition. Third, there has been a substantial amount of impressive research and theorising on face recognition in recent years. As a consequence, we know more about the processes involved in face recognition than about those involved in most other forms of object recognition.

Some of the most interesting evidence that face processing differs in major ways from the processing of other objects has emerged from the study of a face-processing disorder known as *prosopagnosia*. Prosopagnosic patients are unable to recognise familiar faces, and this can even extend to their own faces seen in a mirror. However, they generally have few problems in recognising familiar objects. This inability to recognise faces does not occur as a result of having forgotten the people concerned, because they can still recognise familiar people from their voices and from their names.

There have been different opinions as to how to interpret the findings from prosopagnosic patients. It has been suggested that these patients have problems in recognising faces simply because more precise discriminations are required to distinguish between one face and another than to distinguish between different objects (e.g. a chair and a table). An alternative position is that there are specific processing mechanisms that are only used for face recognition, and which are not involved in object recognition. Evidence supporting the notion of face-specific processes was obtained by DeRenzi (1986). The prosopagnostic patient studied by DeRenzi was very good at making fine discriminations (e.g. between Italian coins and others; between his own handwriting and that of others), but he was unable to recognise friends and relatives by sight.

Some interesting evidence that different regions of the brain may be involved in face recognition and in object recognition was reported by Sergent, Ohta, and MacDonald (1992). Normal subjects categorised objects as living or natural versus non-living or man-made, or they categorised well-known faces as belonging to actors or non-actors. They found that the brain areas specifically active in face identification tended to be forward to those active in object identification. They also discovered that several regions in the right hemisphere were more active in face identification than in object identification. This latter finding is of particular interest in view of the fact that prosopagnosic patients typically have damage to the right hemisphere.

Configural information

When we recognise a face shown in a photograph, there are two major kinds of information presented in the photograph which we might use: (1) information about the individual features (e.g. eye colour); or (2) information about the configuration or overall arrangement of the features. Many approaches to face recognition are based on a feature approach. For example, police forces often make use of Identikit to facilitate face recognition in eyewitnesses. Identikit involves constructing a face resembling that of the criminal on a feature-by-feature basis.

Evidence that the configuration of facial features also needs to be considered was obtained by Young, Hellawell, and Hay (1987). They constructed faces from photographs by combining the top halves and bottom halves of different famous faces. When the two halves were closely aligned, subjects experienced great difficulty in naming the top halves. However, their performance was much better when the two halves were not closely aligned. Presumably close alignment produced a new configuration which interfered with face recognition.

There is considerable evidence that people have particular problems with inverted faces, with recognition memory for such faces being rather poor (e.g. Valentine, 1988). Young et al. (1987) discovered that the halves of closely aligned different famous faces were recognised faster when the faces were inverted than when they were the right way up. This finding may sound surprising, but presumably happened because the configural processing that disrupted face recognition with the upright faces had much less effect with the inverted faces.

The fact that face recognition depends to a large extent on the overall configuration of the face is relevant to the understanding of our ability to recognise faces even when considerably transformed. For example, Rhodes, Brennan, and Carey (1987) found that grossly distorted caricatures were often more recognisable than accurate line drawings of the same faces. Caricatures seem to emphasise any discrepancies between an individual face and the average face whether in terms of individual features or the relationships among features. Rhodes et al. (1987) discovered that an artificial caricature-generator operating on that basis produced very effective caricatures.

Of course, face recognition does not depend solely on configural information. There is much evidence that some facial features tend to be more important than others in facilitating recognition. Recognition of unfamiliar faces seems to depend more on external features such as face outline and hair style than on internal features, whereas the opposite is the case for familiar faces (Ellis, Shepherd, & Davies, 1979). Studies focusing specifically on internal features have indicated that the area around the eyes is of most importance for recognition and the area around the nose is of least importance (Roberts & Bruce, 1988).

Most of the research on face recognition has used photographs or other two-dimensional stimuli. There are at least two potential limitations of such research. First, viewing an actual three-dimensional face provides more information for the observer than does viewing a two-dimensional representation. Second, people's faces normally exhibit considerable motion, registering emotional states, agreement or disagreement with what is being said, and so on. None of these dynamic changes over time are available in a photograph. The importance of these changes was demonstrated by Bruce and Valentine (1988). Small illuminated lights were spread over a face which was then filmed in the dark so that only the lights could be seen. Subjects showed some ability to determine the sex and the identity of each face on the basis of the movements of the lights, and were very good at identifying expressive movements (such as smiling or frowning).

Bruce and Young's model

Bruce and Young (1986) proposed an influential model of face recognition. They argued that there

are several different types of information that can be obtained from faces, and which correspond to the eight components of their model (see Fig. 3.10). It is worth noting here and now that not all of these components are involved in recognising every face. According to Bruce and Young (1986), there are major differences in the processing of familiar and unfamiliar faces. The recognition of familiar faces depends primarily on structural encoding, face recognition units, person identity nodes, and name generation, whereas the processing of unfamiliar faces involves structural encoding, expression analysis, facial speech analysis, and directed visual processing.

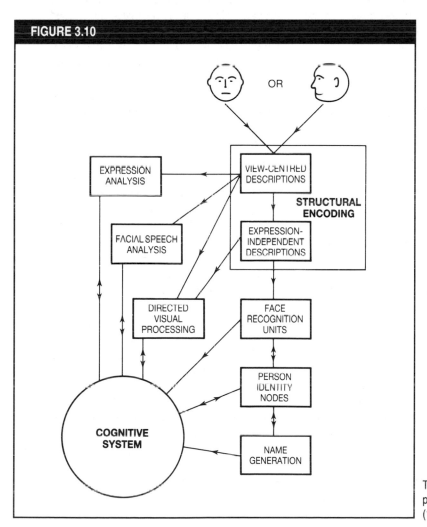

FIGURE 3.10

The model of face recognition proposed by Bruce and Young (1986).

The eight components of the model are as follows:

- *Structural encoding:* this produces various representations or descriptions corresponding approximately to those identified within Marr's (1982) model.
- *Expression analysis:* an individual's emotional state can be inferred from an analysis of information about his or her facial features.
- *Facial speech analysis:* speech perception can be facilitated by detailed observation of a speaker's lip movements (McGurk & MacDonald, 1976).
- *Directed visual processing:* for certain purposes (e.g. to decide whether most psychologists have beards), specific facial information may be processed selectively.
- *Face recognition units:* each face recognition unit contains structural information about one of the faces known to the viewer.
- *Person identity nodes:* these provide information about the person concerned (e.g. his or her occupation, interests, friends, contexts in which encountered).
- *Name generation:* a person's name is stored separately from other information about them.
- *Cognitive system:* the cognitive system contains additional information (e.g. that actors and actresses tend to have attractive faces) that is sometimes of use in face recognition; it also plays a part in determining which component or components of the system receive attention.

Experimental evidence

One of the major theoretical assumptions made by Bruce and Young (1986) is that familiar and unfamiliar faces are processed in different ways. Some components of the model (e.g. expression analysis; facial speech analysis; directed visual processing) can be used with familiar and unfamiliar faces, but others (e.g. face recognition units; person identity nodes; name generation) cannot be used with unfamiliar faces. If it were possible to find patients who showed good recognition of familiar faces but poor recognition of unfamiliar faces, and other patients who showed the opposite pattern, then this would provide strong evidence that the processes involved in the recognition of familiar and unfamiliar faces are different.

Malone, Morris, Kay, and Levin (1982) obtained findings in line with these theoretical predictions. They tested one patient who showed reasonable ability to recognise photographs of famous statesmen (14 out of 17 correct), but who was severely impaired in a task involving matching unfamiliar faces. A second patient was quite different, performing at a normal level on matching unfamiliar faces, but having great difficulties in recognising photographs of famous people (only 5 out of 22 correct).

Let us return to the model shown in Fig. 3.10. It indicates that the name generation component can be accessed only via the appropriate person identity node. In other words, the model makes the strong prediction that we should never be able to put a name to a face without at the same time having available other information about that person (e.g. his or her occupation; the contexts in which he or she has been encountered in the past). At a purely anecdotal level, the model has the advantage of explaining why it is that so many people complain about their frequent embarrassment at forgetting other people's names.

More convincing evidence was obtained by Young, Hay, and Ellis (1985). They asked their subjects to keep a diary record of the specific problems they experienced in face recognition day by day. There were 1008 incidents altogether, but not once did a subject report putting a name to a face while knowing nothing else about that person. In contrast, there were 190 occasions on which a subject could remember a fair amount of information about the person, but was quite unable to think of his or her name.

Cognitive neuropsychological evidence also supports this prediction of the model. There are no convincing cases in which a brain-damaged patient has been able to put names to faces without knowing anything else about the person, but there are several patients who show the opposite pattern. For example, Flude, Ellis, and Kay (1989) studied a patient, EST, who was able to retrieve the occupations for 85% of very familiar people when presented with their faces, but could recall only 15% of their names.

According to the model, another kind of problem should be fairly common. If the appropriate face recognition unit is activated, but the person identity node is not, then there should be a feeling of familiarity coupled with the inability to think of any relevant information about the person (e.g. where he or she has been seen before; what he or she does for a living; his or her name). In the set of incidents collected by Young et al. (1985), this was reported on 233 occasions.

Reference back to Fig. 3.10 suggests further predictions about familiar faces. When we look at a familiar face, familiarity information from the face recognition unit should be accessed first, followed by information about that person (e.g. occupation) from the person identity node, followed by that person's name from the name generation component. It follows that familiarity decisions about a face should be made faster than decisions based on person identity nodes. As predicted, Young, McWeeny, Hay, and Ellis (1986b) discovered that the decision as to whether a face was familiar was made faster than the decision as to whether it was the face of a politician.

It also follows from the model that decisions based on person identity nodes should be made faster than those based on the word generation component. Young, McWeeny, Hay, and Ellis (1986a) found that subjects were much faster to decide whether a face belonged to a politician than they were to produce the person's name.

Evaluation and theoretical advances

Although the model proposed by Bruce and Young (1986) has been deservedly influential, it was clear from the outset that some of the components and processes involved in face recognition were insufficiently specified. For example, as Bruce and Young (1986, p.324) admitted, the cognitive system "serves to catch all those aspects of processing not reflected in other components of our model". In addition, the account given of the processing of unfamiliar faces is much less detailed than the one offered of familiar faces.

One of the features of the Bruce and Young (1986) model is that there is a separate store for names which can be accessed only via relevant autobiographical information stored at the person identity nodes. Evidence contradicting that assumption was provided by de Haan, Young, and Newcombe (1991), who investigated an amnesic patient, ME. She was able to match the faces and names of 88% of famous people for whom she was unable to recall any autobiographical information. The fact that her person identity nodes were damaged (revealed by the inability to retrieve autobiographical information) should have prevented her from matching faces and names.

Burton, Bruce, and Johnston (1990) and Burton and Bruce (1992) revised and developed the Bruce and Young (1986) model in various ways. As can be seen in Fig. 3.11, they assumed that there are three pools of information:

- *Face-recognition units:* view-independent units which are activated by the presentation of any familiar face.
- *Person identity nodes:* domain- and modality-free gateways into semantic information.
- *Semantic information units:* name information and other information about an individual (e.g. occupation; interests).

There are bi-directional excitatory links between the pools, but within pools each unit is linked to the others by means of inhibitory connections. A face is recognised as familiar when the level of activity in the appropriate person identity node reaches a threshold level of activation, and the same mechanism is involved in recognition on the basis of name, voice, or other information. Some of the main differences between this version of the model and the original one are:

- There is now no separate store for names; information about names is stored in the same way as other information about an individual; name information is difficult to access because it tends to be unique (how many people with your first and last names do you know?) and is thus poorly integrated with other semantic information.
- Familiarity decisions are made at the person-identity nodes rather than at the face recognition units; in a sense, it is now the person rather than the face that is recognised.

FIGURE 3.11

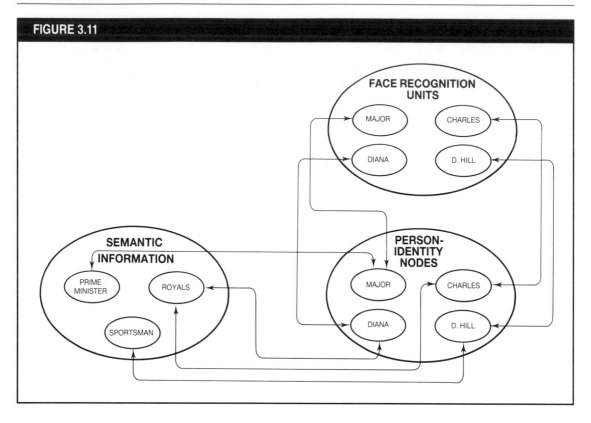

Modified version of the Bruce and Young (1986) model. Adapted from Burton et al. (1990).

• The model is now more precise, in that Burton et al. (1990) provided a reasonably detailed interactive activation model in place of the generalities of the Bruce and Young (1986) model.

What are the advantages of the revised model over the original one? First, it is now possible to account for the findings of de Haan et al. (1991). Their patient ME was able to match the names and faces of famous people about whom she could not remember any relevant information because name and face information can be linked without requiring access to autobiographical information (see Fig. 3.11).

Second, it is argued within the revised model that the name is generally harder to access than other information about a person because it is poorly integrated with other information. According to this account, names might be easier to retrieve than other person-relevant information if they were more semantically integrated. In contrast, this could not happen on the original model. Cohen (1990) found that faces produced better recall of names than occupations when the names were meaningful and the occupations were meaningless.

Third, the greater precision of the revised model means that it can be evaluated in ways not feasible with the original model. For example, Burton et al. (1990) provided a computer simulation of the revised model. This simulation led to improvements in the model, and also suggested some additional predictions that could be tested empirically (see Burton et al., 1990, for details).

CHAPTER SUMMARY

Various attempts have been made to identify the processes involved in the recognition of two-dimensional patterns. Template theorists argue that stimuli are matched against miniature copies or templates of previously presented patterns. Unless the implausible assumption is made that there is an almost infinite number of templates to handle all eventualities, template theories are generally inadequate to account for the versatility of perceptual processing. Feature theorists emphasise that any stimulus can be regarded as consisting of a number of specific features, and that feature analysis plays a crucial role in pattern recognition. The effects of context and of expectations are de-emphasised in most feature theories, as are the inter-relationships among features. A more adequate way of accounting for pattern recognition is provided by theories based on structural descriptions, which specify the structural arrangement of the constituent parts of a pattern.

The recognition of three-dimensional objects involves a number of sequential stages, including perceptual classification, semantic classification, and naming. Supporting evidence for the existence of these stages has been obtained by studying brain-damaged patients. A more specific theory was proposed by Marr and Nishihara (1978). They argued that many objects can be described as consisting of a hierarchical set of generalised cones. The segments of an object corresponding to the generalised cones are identified by making use of concavities in its contour. A related but more general theory was proposed by Biederman (1987). He argued that objects can be regarded as consisting of basic shapes called "geons" (geometric ions). He also argued that perceivers assume that regularities in the visual image reflect regularities in the world (the "non-accidental" principle). The theories proposed by Marr and Nishihara, and by Biederman, are not well designed to account for the perception of objects lacking readily identifiable constituent parts. In addition, these theories cannot explain perceptual discriminations among stimuli that possess considerable overall similarity (e.g. different faces).

Connectionist models generally incorporate a network of processing units resembling the network of neurons found in the brain's visual system. In many cases, connectionist models seem to complement symbol-processing theories, such as those of Marr and Nishihara, and Biederman, in that they provide a detailed account of some of the processes involved in the formation of symbolic representations.

One of the most important and complex of visual objects is the human face. Several different processing components need to be postulated in order to account for face recognition, as is illustrated by the eight-component model proposed by Bruce and Young (1986). Their model provides a convincing account of many of the phenomena of face recognition, but some of the components involved (e.g. the cognitive system) are clearly under-specified. In addition, their description of the processing of familiar faces is more convincing than that of the processing of unfamiliar faces. Some of the limitations of the Bruce-Young theory have been overcome in revised versions of the theory proposed by Burton et al. (1990) and by Burton and Bruce (1992).

FURTHER READING

Bruce, V., & Green, P. R. (1990). *Visual perception: Physiology, psychology, and ecology* (2nd Edn.). Hove, UK: Lawrence Erlbaum Associates Ltd. Some of the main approaches to object recognition are discussed, and there is good coverage of connectionism. Chapters 8 and 9 are of most relevance to object recognition.

Humphreys, G. W., & Bruce, V. (1989). *Visual cognition: Computational, experimental and neuro-psychological perspectives.* Hove, UK: Lawrence Erlbaum Associates Ltd. There is a good account of object recognition in Chapter 3 of this book.

Van Kleeck, M. H., & Kosslyn, S. M. (1993). Visual information processing: A perspective. In D. E. Meyer & S. Kornblum (Eds.), *Attention and performance (*Vol. XIV). London: MIT Press. This chapter provides an instructive account of the main developments in research on visual perception over the past 30 years.

4

Theories of Perception, Movement, and Action

INTRODUCTION

Some of the main contemporary cognitive and computational theories of perception were discussed in the previous two chapters. Most of these theories are based on the assumption that perception is a complex achievement. Most theorists assume that several different kinds of information processing are required in order to transform the mosaic of light intensities on the retina into accurate and detailed perception of the visual environment. In other words, perception is *indirect* in the sense that it depends on numerous internal processes. Those (e.g. Bruner, 1957; Gregory, 1970) who have emphasised internal processes not stemming directly from the stimulus input are sometimes known as *constructivist theorists*.

Gibson (1950, 1966, 1979) developed an approach to visual perception that is in conflict with most cognitive and computational theories. His is a theory of *direct* perception: the information provided by the visual environment is allegedly sufficient to permit the individual to move around and to interact directly with that environment without the involvement of internal processes and representations.

Those theorists who argue that perception is indirect tend to suggest that top-down or conceptually driven processes are of importance in perception. In contrast, Gibson and other direct theorists typically emphasise the role of bottom-up or data-driven processes in perception. It is important to consider these two viewpoints. Not only do they represent important approaches within perception theory, but also they serve to illuminate some major issues relating to the nature of perception.

Gibson's direct theory of visual perception is generally regarded as an ecological approach, because of his insistence that we should study perception as it operates in the real world. In addition, he argued that perception and action are closely intertwined. Perception provides valuable information in the organisation of action, and action and movement by the organism facilitate accurate perception. Some of these issues will be addressed later in the chapter.

CONSTRUCTIVIST THEORIES

Helmholtz (1821–1894) discovered that a piece of grey paper appeared slightly green when placed on a red surface, and he wondered why there was this discrepancy between the information presented to the eyes and the final perception. Helmholtz knew that green is the complementary colour to red (i.e. when mixed together they produce white), and he assumed that observers made use of their knowledge that placing a grey stimulus next to a red one should produce the complementary colour.

This account is inaccurate, because the effect actually depends on basic physiological mechanisms. However, it illustrates a major theoretical approach to perception which was introduced by Helmholtz. He argued that the inadequate information provided by the senses is augmented by *unconscious inferences*, which add meaning to sensory information. He assumed that these inferences were unconscious, because we typically have little or no awareness that we are making inferences while perceiving.

The approach advocated by Helmholtz, which we will call the constructivist approach, remains influential to this day. Theorists such as Bruner (1957), Neisser (1967), and Gregory (1972, 1980) all subscribe to a number of assumptions resembling those originally proposed by Helmholtz:

• Perception is an active and constructive process; it is "something more than the direct registration of sensations ... other events intervene between stimulation and experience" (Gordon, 1989, p.124).
• Perception is not directly given by the stimulus input, but occurs as the end-product of the interactive influences of the presented stimulus and internal hypotheses, expectations, and knowledge, as well as motivational and emotional factors; in other words, sensory information is used as the basis for making informed guesses or inferences about the presented stimulus and its meaning.
• Because it is influenced by hypotheses and expectations that will sometimes be incorrect, perception is prone to error.

The flavour of this theoretical approach was captured by Gregory (1972), who claimed that perceptions are constructions "from floating fragmentary scraps of data signalled by the senses and drawn from the brain memory banks, themselves constructions from the snippets of the past." Thus, the frequently inadequate information supplied to the sense organs is used as the basis for making inferences or forming hypotheses about the nature of the external environment.

We can illustrate this approach by considering the role of contextual information in making inferences about the nature of a visual stimulus. Palmer (1975) presented a scene (e.g. a kitchen) in pictorial form, followed by the very brief presentation of the picture of an object (this study was mentioned in Chapter 3). This object could be appropriate to the context (e.g. loaf), or it could be inappropriate (e.g. mailbox or drum). There was also a further condition in which no contextual scene was presented. The context had a systematic effect on the probability of identifying the object correctly: that probability was greatest when the object was appropriate to the context, intermediate when there was no context, and lowest when the object was inappropriate to the context.

According to constructivist theorists, perception involves using inferential processes (e.g. hypotheses; expectations) to make sense of the information presented to the sense organs. It follows that the formation of incorrect hypotheses or expectations will lead to errors of perception. An interesting demonstration of how perceptual errors can occur was provided by Ittelson (1952), who argued that the perceptual hypotheses formed may be very inaccurate if a visual display appears familiar but is actually novel. An example of this is the well-known Ames distorted room. The room is actually of a peculiar shape, but when viewed from a particular point it gives rise to the same retinal image as a conventional rectangular room.

It is perhaps not surprising that observers decide that the room is like a normal one. However, what is somewhat puzzling is that they maintain this belief even when someone inside the room walks backwards and forwards along the rear wall, apparently growing and shrinking as he or she proceeds! The reason for the apparent size changes is that the rear wall is not perpendicular to the viewing point: one corner is actually much further away from the observer than the other corner. As might be expected by constructivist theorists, there is a greater likelihood of the room being perceived as having an odd shape and the person walking inside it remaining the same size when that person is the spouse or close relative of the observer.

Another illustration of the possible pitfalls involved in relying too heavily on expectations or hypotheses comes in a classic study by Bruner, Postman, and Rodrigues (1951). Their subjects expected to see conventional playing cards, but some of the cards used were incongruous (e.g. black hearts). When these incongruous cards were presented briefly, subjects sometimes reported seeing brown or purple hearts. Here we have an almost literal blending of stimulus information (bottom-up processing) and stored information (top-down processing).

Motivation and emotion

One of the central assumptions of the constructivist approach is that perception is not determined entirely by external stimuli. As a consequence, it is assumed that current motivational and emotional states may influence people's perceptual hypotheses and thus their visual perception. Consider, for example, a study by Schafer and Murphy (1943). They prepared drawings consisting of an irregular line drawn vertically through a circle so that either half of the circle could be seen as the profile of a face. During initial training, each face was presented separately. One face in each pair was associated with financial reward, whereas the other face was associated with financial punishment. When the original drawings were then presented briefly, subjects were much more likely to report perceiving the previously rewarded face than the previously punished one. In subsequent research, Smith and Hochberg (1954) found that administering a shock when one of the two profile faces was presented decreased its tendency to be perceived subsequently.

An interesting study on motivation was carried out by Bruner and Goodman (1947). They asked rich and poor children to estimate the sizes of coins. The poor children over-estimated the size of every coin more than did the rich children. Although this finding might reflect the greater value of money to poor children, a simpler explanation is that rich children had more familiarity with coins and so were more accurate in their size estimates. Ashley, Harper, and Runyon (1951) introduced an ingenious modification to the experimental design used by Bruner and Goodman (1947). They hypnotised adult subjects into believing that they were rich or poor, and found that the size estimates of coins were consistently larger when the subjects were in the "poor" state.

There are several other studies that allegedly demonstrate effects of motivation and emotion on perception. However, it is important to distinguish between effects on perception and on response. For example, it is well established from work on operant conditioning by Skinner and others that reward and punishment both influence the likelihood of making any given response. Thus, it is possible that reward and punishment in the study by Schafer and Murphy (1943) affected subjects' responses without necessarily affecting actual visual perception.

Visual illusions

According to Gregory (1970, 1980), many of the classic visual illusions can be explained by assuming that previous knowledge derived from the perception of three-dimensional objects is applied inappropriately to the perception of two-dimensional figures. For example, people typically see a given object as having a constant size despite variations in the retinal image by taking account of its apparent distance. Size constancy means that an object is perceived as having the same size whether it is looked at from a short or a long distance away. This constancy contrasts with the size of the retinal image, which becomes progressively smaller as an object recedes into the distance. Gregory's (1970, 1980) misapplied size-constancy theory argues that this kind of perceptual processing is applied wrongly to produce several visual illusions.

In the Muller-Lyer illusion (see Fig. 4.1), the vertical line in the figure on the left appears longer than the vertical line in the figure on the right, although they are actually the same length. The

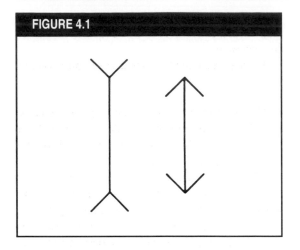

FIGURE 4.1

The Muller-Lyer illusion.

Muller-Lyer figures can be regarded as simple perspective drawings of aspects of three-dimensional objects. Thus, the figure on the left can be thought of as the inside corner of a room, and the figure on the right as the outside corner of a building. In other words, the outgoing fins represent lines approaching us, whereas the ingoing fins stand for lines receding into the distance. Thus, the vertical line on the left is in some sense further away from us than the vertical line on the right. Because the retinal images of the two vertical lines are the same size, the implication of size-constancy scaling is that a more distant line of the same retinal size as a less distant line must actually be longer, and that is the Muller-Lyer illusion.

The misapplied size-constancy theory claims that the internal processes that use apparent distance to gauge apparent size are misapplied to illusion figures, such as those of the Muller-Lyer. But, you may well argue, why is it that the figures appear flat and two-dimensional if they are treated in many ways as three-dimensional objects? According to Gregory (1970, 1980), cues to depth are used in a relatively automatic way to trigger constancy scaling whether or not the figures are seen to be lying on a flat surface. The fact that the Muller-Lyer figures take on a three-dimensional appearance when they are presented in the dark as luminous two-dimensional outlines supports this point of view.

This theory is ingenious, but has not gained univeral acceptance. Gregory's claim that luminous Muller-Lyer figures are seen three-dimensionally by everyone is incorrect. It is puzzling that the illusion can still be obtained when the fins on the two figures are replaced by other attachments such as circles or squares. This suggests that the vertical line may appear longer or shorter than its actual length simply because it is part of a large or a small object. In all probability, more than one factor contributes to the Muller-Lyer illusion.

Evaluation

As we have seen, the constructivist approach has led to the discovery of a wide range of interesting perceptual phenomena. It is almost indisputable that processes resembling those postulated by constructivist theorists underlie most of these phenomena. However, many theorists disagree strongly with the constructivist viewpoint. They are unconvinced of the central constructivist assumption that perceivers resemble the great detective Sherlock Holmes as they struggle to make sense of the limited "fragmentary scraps of data" available to them. Some of the major problems for the constructivist approach will now be discussed.

First, the constructivist approach appears to predict that perception will often be in error, whereas in fact perception is typically accurate. If we are constantly using hypotheses and expectations to interpret sensory data, why is it that these hypotheses and expectations are correct nearly all of the time? Presumably the answer is that the environment provides considerably more information than the "fragmentary scraps" assumed by constructivist theorists.

Second, many of the experiments and demonstrations carried out by constructivist theorists involve artificial or unnatural stimuli. As Gordon (1989, p.144) indicated, such studies involve:

the perception of patterns under conditions of brief exposure, drawings which could represent the corners of buildings, glowing objects in darkened corridors … none of these existed in the African grasslands where human perceptual systems reached their present state of evolutionary development.

Of particular importance, many of the studies supporting the constructivist approach (e.g. Bruner et al., 1951; Palmer, 1975) involved presenting visual stimuli very briefly. Brief presentation reduces the impact of bottom-up processes, allowing more scope for top-down processes (e.g. hypotheses; inferences) to operate.

Third, it is not always clear what hypotheses observers would form. Let us return to the study (Ittelson, 1952) in which someone walks backwards and forwards along the rear wall of the Ames room. Subjects could interpret what they are seeing by hypothesing that the room is distorted and the person remains the same size, or by assuming that the room is normal but the person grows and shrinks. The former hypothesis strikes the authors as more plausible, but subjects seem to favour the latter hypothesis.

Fourth, constructivist theorists assume that the hypotheses formed by perceivers represent the "best guess" in the light of the available information. However, it often proves extremely difficult to persuade perceivers to change their hypotheses. For example, there is the hollow face illusion (Gregory, 1973), which was discussed in Chapter 2. Even when observers know that it is a hollow face, they still report that it looks like a normal face.

DIRECT PERCEPTION

As we have seen, Gibson's theoretical approach to perception can be regarded as a bottom-up theory, in that he claimed that there is much more information potentially available in sensory stimulation than is generally realised. However, he emphasised the role played in perception by movement of the individual within his or her environment, so his is not a bottom-up theory in the sense of an observer passively receiving sensory stimulation. Indeed, Gibson (1979) called his theory an *ecological approach* to emphasise that

the primary function of perception is to facilitate interactions between the individual and his or her environment.

Some of his main theoretical assumptions are as follows:

- The pattern of light reaching the eye can be thought of as an *optic array* ; this structured light contains all of the visual information from the environment striking the eye.
- This optic array provides unambiguous or invariant information about the layout of objects in space. This information comes in many forms, including texture gradients, optic flow patterns, and affordances (all of which are described later).
- Perception involves "picking up" the rich information provided by the optic array in a direct fashion via resonance with little or no information processing involved.

In order to understand Gibson's theoretical position, it is useful to consider how his interest in perceptual phenomena developed. He was given the task in the Second World War of preparing training films describing the problems experienced by pilots when taking off and landing. This led him to wonder exactly what information pilots have available to them while performing these manoeuvres. He discovered what he termed *optic flow patterns* (Gibson, 1950), which can be illustrated by considering a pilot approaching the landing strip. The point towards which the pilot is moving (called the "pole") appears motionless, with the rest of the visual environment apparently moving away from that point. The further away any part of the landing strip is from that point, the greater is its apparent speed of movement. Over time, aspects of the environment at some distance from the pole pass out of the visual field and are replaced by new aspects emerging at the pole. A shift in the centre of the outflow indicates that there has been a change in the direction of the plane.

According to Gibson (1950), optic flow patterns can provide pilots with unambiguous information about their direction, speed, and altitude. Gibson was so impressed by the wealth of sensory information available to pilots in optic flow patterns that he subsequently devoted himself to an analysis of the kinds of information available in sensory data under other conditions. For example, he argued that *texture gradients* provide very useful information. As we saw in Chapter 2, objects slanting away from you have an increased gradient (rate of change) of texture density as you look from the near edge to the far edge. Gibson (1966, 1979) claimed that observers "picked up" this information about the gradient of texture density from the optic array. As a consequence, at least some aspects of depth are perceived directly.

The optic flow pattern and texture density illustrate some of the information inherent in the optic array which can be used to provide an observer with an unambiguous spatial layout of the environment. In more general terms, Gibson (1966, 1979) argued that certain higher-order characteristics of the visual array change (transpositions) whereas others remain unaltered (invariants) when observers move around their environment.

The fact that they remain the same over different viewing angles makes invariants of particular importance. The lack of apparent movement of the point towards which we are moving forms one of the invariant features of the optic array. Another invariant is useful in terms of maintaining size constancy: the ratio of an object's height to the distance between its base and the horizon is invariant regardless of its distance from the viewer. This invariant is known as the horizon ratio relation (Sedgwick, 1973).

Meaning: Affordances

How can the Gibsonian approach handle the problem of meaning? Gibson (1979) rejected the conventional view that we perceive a meaningful environment because of the involvement of the relevant knowledge stored in long-term memory. Instead, he claimed that all of the potential uses of objects (or what he referred to as their *affordances*) are directly perceivable. For example, a ladder "affords" ascent or descent, and a chair "affords" sitting. The notion of affordances was even applied to postboxes (Gibson, 1979, p.139): "The postbox … affords letter-mailing to a letter-writing human in a community with a postal system. This fact is perceived when the postbox is identified as such, and it is apprehended whether the postbox is in

sight or out of sight." Most objects give rise to more than one affordance, with the particular affordance that influences behaviour depending on the perceiver's species and on his or her current psychological state. Thus, a hungry person will perceive the affordance of edibility when presented with an orange and eat it, whereas a person who is angry may detect the affordance of a projectile and throw the orange at someone.

Gibson assumed that most perceptual learning has occurred during the history of mankind, and so does not need to occur during the individual's lifetime. However, we do have to learn which affordances will satisfy particular goals we may have, and we need to learn to attend to the appropriate aspects of the visual environment. According to Gibson's theory (Gordon, 1989, p.161), "The most important contribution of learning to perception is to educate attention".

The notion of affordances is very important to Gibson's theoretical position. It forms part of his attempt to demonstrate that all the information needed to make sense of the visual environment is directly present in the visual input, and it conforms to the notion that there is a close relationship between perception and action. If he had not proposed the notion of affordances, or something very similar, then he would have been forced to admit that the meaning of objects is stored in long-term memory rather than being directly perceivable.

Resonance

How exactly do human perceivers manage to "pick up" the invariant information that is supplied by the visual world? According to Gibson, there is a process of *resonance*, which he explained by analogy to the workings of a radio. In most houses throughout the Western world, there is almost non-stop electromagnetic radiation from various radio transmitters. When a radio set if turned on, there may be only a hissing sound. However, if it is turned properly, speech or music will be clearly audible. In Gibson's terms, the radio is now resonating with the information contained in the electromagnetic radiation.

This analogy suggests that perceivers can pick up information from the environment in a relatively automatic and effortless way provided that they are attuned to that information. The radio operates in a holistic fashion, in the sense that damage to any part of its circuitry would prevent it working. In a similar fashion, Gibson assumed that the nervous system works in a holistic way when perceiving.

Evaluation

The ecological approach to perception advocated by Gibson has proved very successful in a number of ways. First, his views have had a major impact at the philosophical level. One of his main concerns was to overturn the conventional view that perceptual experience is clearly distinct from the objective world. According to Gibson (1979, p.8), "The words 'animal' and 'environment' make an inseparable pair. Each term implies the other. No animal could exist without an environment surrounding it. Equally, though not so obvious, an environment implies an animal (or at least an organism) to be surrounded". As Gordon (1989, p.176) expressed it, "Direct perceptionists can be said to have restored the environment to its central place in the study of perception … organisms did not evolve in a world of simple isolated stimuli".

Second, Gibson was right to claim that visual stimuli provide considerably more information than had previously been thought to be the case. Traditional laboratory research had generally involved static observers looking at impoverished visual displays, often with chin rests or other restraints being used to prevent movement of the eyes relative to the display. Not surprisingly, such research had failed to reveal the richness of the information available in the everyday environment. In contrast, Gibson correctly emphasised that we spend much of our time in motion, and that the consequent moment-by-moment changes in the optic array provide a considerable amount of useful information (discussed more fully later in the chapter).

Third, Gibson was correct in arguing that inaccurate perception often depends on the use of very artificial situations. However, the notion that visual illusions are merely unusual trick figures dreamed up by psychologists to baffle ordinary decent folk does not apply to all of them. There are at least some visual illusions that produce effects

similar to those to be found in normal perception. Consider, for example, the vertical–horizontal illusion shown in Fig. 4.2. The two lines are actually the same length, but the vertical line appears to be longer than the horizontal one. This tendency to over-estimate vertical extents relative to horizontal ones can readily be shown with real objects by taking a teacup, saucer, and two similar spoons. Place one spoon horizontally in the saucer and the other spoon vertically in the cup, and you should find that the vertical spoon looks much longer than the horizontal spoon.

Fourth, in part for reasons already given, it should not be assumed that the numerous laboratory studies apparently providing support for constructivist theories necessarily cast doubts on Gibson's direct theory. As Cutting (1986, p.238) pointed out, "Given that most visual stimuli in experiments are pictures (virtual rather than real objects) and that Gibson stated that picture perception is indirect, most psychological experiments have never been relevant to the direct/indirect distinction as he construed it".

Fifth, some contemporary theorists are attempting to develop the ideas originally proposed by Gibson. For example, Greeno (1994, p.337) has argued in favour of situation theory, according to which the primary focus should be on "interactive processes in which agents participate, cooperatively, with other agents and with the

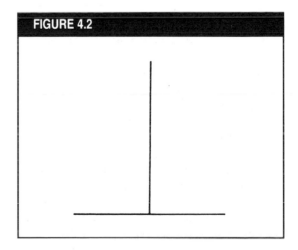

FIGURE 4.2

The vertical–horizontal illusion.

physical systems that they interact with". Greeno has not as yet developed situation theory in detail, but he believes that the Gibsonian notion of "affordance" is of central importance in understanding these interactive processes.

On the negative side, Gibson's direct theory of perception has attracted a considerable amount of criticism, and some of the main criticisms will be considered here. First, the processes involved in identifying invariants in the environment, in discovering affordances, in "resonance", and so on, are considerably more complicated than was implied by Gibson. In the words of Marr (1982, p.30), the major shortcoming of Gibson's analysis:

> results from a failure to realise two things. First, the detection of physical invariants, like image surfaces, is exactly and precisely an information-processing problem, in modern terminology. And second, he vastly under-rated the sheer difficulty of such detection.

Second, Gibson's theoretical approach applies much more effectively to some aspects of perception than to others. The distinction between "seeing" and "seeing as" is useful in addressing this issue (Bruce & Green, 1990). According to Fodor and Pylyshyn (1981, p.189), "What you see when you see a thing depends upon what the thing you see is. But what you see the thing as depends upon what you know about what you are seeing". This may sound incomprehensible, but Fodor and Pylyshyn (1981) illustrated the point by considering someone called Smith who is lost at sea. Smith sees the Pole Star, but what matters in terms of his survival is whether he sees it as the Pole Star or as simply another star. If it is the former, then this will be useful for navigational purposes; if it is the latter, then he remains as lost as ever. Gibson's approach is reasonably informative about *seeing*, but has little to say about *seeing as*.

Third, Gibson's argument that there is no need to postulate internal representations (e.g. memories; $2\frac{1}{2}$-D sketches) in order to understand perception seems flawed. Bruce and Green (1990) cite the work of Menzel (1978) as an example of the problems flowing from Gibson's argument.

Chimpanzees were carried around a field, and shown the locations of 20 pieces of food. When each chimpanzee was released, it moved around the field picking up the pieces of food in a rather efficient fashion. As there was no information in the light reaching the chimpanzees to guide their search, they must have made use of memorial representations of the locations of the pieces of food. This is quite contrary to the assumptions made by Gibson.

THEORETICAL SYNTHESIS

In general terms, the constructivist theorists have emphasised the importance of top-down processes in perception, whereas Gibson argued that bottom-up processes are of paramount importance. The relative importance of top-down and bottom-up processes undoubtedly depends on various factors. Visual perception may be largely determined by bottom-up processes when the viewing conditions are good, but may increasingly involve top-down processes as the viewing conditions deteriorate because of very brief presentation times or lack of stimulus clarity. In line with this analysis, Gibson concentrated on visual perception occurring under optimal viewing conditions, whereas constructivist theorists have tended to use sub-optimal viewing conditions (e.g. brief tachistoscopic presentation).

In many circumstances, perception undoubtedly involves the combined influence of bottom-up and top-down processes. Total reliance on bottom-up processes would be unwise because of the ambiguous and imprecise nature of much visual stimulation, and exclusive reliance on top-down processing would lead to hallucinations. The contribution of both kinds of processing to word perception was shown by Tulving, Mandler, and Baumal (1964). The role of bottom-up processing was manipulated by altering the exposure duration, and the involvement of top-down processing was varied by changing the amount of relevant sentence context provided before the word was presented. Correct word identification increased directly as a function of both exposure duration and the amount of context. In addition, the impact of context was progressively reduced as the target words were presented for longer durations, suggesting that the clearer the stimulus input, the less necessary it is to make use of other sources of information.

Neisser (1976) provided a synthesis of the different theoretical positions we have been considering. The basic outline of his theoretical position is shown in Fig. 4.3. He assumed that there is a perceptual cycle involving schemata, perceptual exploration, and the stimulus environment. Schemata contain collections of knowledge derived from past experience which serve the function of directing perceptual exploration towards relevant environmental stimuli. Such exploration often leads the perceiver to sample some of the available stimulus information. If the information obtained from the environment fails to match information in the relevant schema, then the information in the schema is modified appropiately.

The perceptual cycle described by Neisser incorporates elements of bottom-up and top-down processing. Bottom-up processing is represented by the sampling of available environmental information which can modify the current schema. Top-down processing is represented by the notion that schemata influence the course of the information processing involved in perception.

Evaluation

Neisser's cyclic theory of perception illustrates one way in which bottom-up and top-down processes may interact and combine in the course of perception. The theory suffers from the severe limitation that it is very sketchy, and that it fails to specify in any detail the processes involved in perception. However, it may well be that the theory is on the right lines. More specific theories based on the assumption that bottom-up and top-down processes interact with each other are discussed at various points in the book (e.g. the theory of spoken language comprehension proposed by Marslen-Wilson and Tyler, 1980, discussed in Chapter 12).

MOTION, PERCEPTION, AND ACTION

As was mentioned earlier in the chapter, most research on visual perception used to involve a motionless observer viewing one or more static objects. Such research lacked ecological validity or

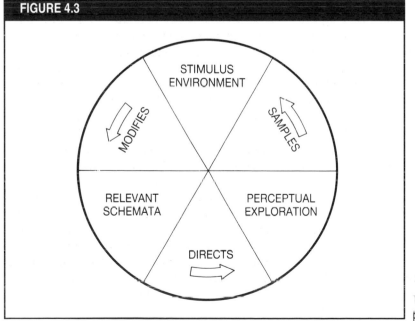

FIGURE 4.3

The perceptual cycle as proposed by Neisser (1976).

relevance to our everyday experiences in a number of ways. We reach out for objects, and we walk, run, or drive through the environment; at other times, we are stationary but other living creatures or objects in the environment are in movement relative to us. Gibson was instrumental in producing an increased interest in issues such as visually guided action and the perception of movement; in the words of Greeno (1994, p.341), Gibson believed that "perception is a system that picks up information that supports coordination of the agent's actions with the systems that the environment provides".

We will start with the role of eye movements in visual perception. The retinal image of the environment changes a number of times each second, even when we are stationary and observing a stationary environment. We are generally very efficient at deciding whether changes in the retinal image reflect actual movements made by ourselves or objects in the environment, or whether they simply reflect eye movements. After that, we consider the visual processes involved in facilitating human movement or action. Finally, we consider how we perceive object motion. Related issues sometimes arise in these last two areas. For example, the processes involved in perceiving how long it will be before we collide with an object in front of us may be rather similar whether we are moving at 30mph (48 kilometres an hour) towards it, or it is moving at the same speed towards us.

There is one central issue running through much of the research. That issue is whether Gibson (1979) was correct in assuming that we interact with the environment in a direct fashion making use of invariant information. As we will see, there is evidence that directly available information (e.g. about optic flow patterns) is used in some of our interactions with the environment, but it remains controversial whether this is generally the case.

Eye movements

Our eyes move approximately three or four times a second, and these eye movements generally produce substantial effects on the retinal image. In spite of that, we normally perceive the environment as stable and unmoving. There are several ways in which our visual systems could achieve this

stability. One possibility is that the visual system monitors actual changes in the extra-ocular muscles controlling eye movements, and then uses that information to interpret changes in the retinal image. However, it would be important for information about eye-muscle movements to be used *before* the retinal image changed, because otherwise the altered retinal image might be misinterpreted. The second possibility was originally put forward by Helmholtz (1866). He proposed an outflow theory, in which image movement is interpreted by making use of information about intended movement sent to the eye muscles. The fact that the visual world appears to move when the side of the eyeball is pressed supports this theory: there is movement within the retinal image unaccompanied by commands to the eye muscles, and so it is perceived as genuine.

One way of testing outflow theory is to study the effects of immobilising the eyes by means of a paralysing drug. According to the theory, the visual world should appear to move when subjects given such a drug try unsuccessfully to produce eye movements. This prediction has been supported (e.g. Brindley & Merton, 1960). However, Stevens et al. (1976) obtained a slightly different effect. Their subject reported that attempted eye movements following muscle paralysis produced a kind of relocation of the visual world but without movement.

Convincing evidence for Helmholtz's theory was reported by Duhamel, Colby, and Goldberg (1992). They carried out physiological research on the brains of monkeys, and found that the parietal cortex (the upper, rear portion of the side of the cortex) is of major importance to an understanding of how the visual system handles eye movements. On the basis of their findings, Duhamel et al. (1992, p.91) arrived at the following conclusion: "At the time a saccade [rapid, jerky eye movement] is planned, the parietal representation of the visual world undergoes a shift analogous to the shift of the image on the retina." In other words, visual processing in the parietal cortex anticipates the next eye movement in the period between its planning and execution.

In spite of the successes of outflow theory, it cannot be the whole story. As Tresilian

(1994, p.336) pertinently remarked, outflow theory "predicts that if the eyes are stationary in the head as the head rotates, the resulting image motion will be interpreted as motion of the environment, yet everyone knows that this does not happen". What probably happens is that we do not rely exclusively on information about intended eye movements to perceive a stable environment. It is likely that movement of the entire retinal image is attributed to movement of the head or eye, whereas movement of part of the retinal image is interpreted as movement of an external object.

VISUALLY GUIDED ACTION

From an ecological perspective, it is of central interest to focus on how we move around the environment. If we are to avoid premature death, we have to ensure that we are not hit by cars when crossing the road; we must avoiding falling over the edges of cliffs; and when driving we must avoid hitting cars coming the other way. Visual perception plays a major role in facilitating human locomotion and ensuring our safety.

Reaching and grasping
One of the major functions of visually guided action is to allow us to interact effectively with our immediate environment. If we want to pick up a knife and fork, to kick a football, or to shake someone's hand, our actions need to be visually guided if they are to be effective. Although it is obvious that the visual system plays a crucial role in guiding action, it is more difficult to specify its role in detail. However, the evidence of Mishkin and Ungerleider (1982; see Chapter 3) provides a useful starting point. They discovered that separate brain systems process information about object location ("where is it?") and about object identification ("what is it?"). The parietal lobes are involved in processing information about object location, whereas the inferior temporal lobes process information about object identification. It is probable that both kinds of information are very useful in visually guided reaching and grasping, but it could reasonably be argued that knowledge of an object's location is even more important than knowledge of what it is.

Common sense may suggest that an observer needs to have conscious awareness of an object's location before being able to make appropriate movements in its direction. However, there is increasing evidence that some of the basic processes in reaching and grasping may not require such conscious awareness. For example, some patients with blindsight (see Weiskrantz, 1990, and Chapter 2) are able to point to, or reach towards, the locations of stimuli of which they have no conscious awareness.

Evidence from normal subjects also indicates that appropriate reaching movements towards an object do not necessarily depend on prior conscious awareness of its location. In a study by Castiello, Paulignan, and Jeannerod (1991), subjects were presented with an object which moved suddenly as they began a grasping movement. Subjects averaged 107 milliseconds to adjust their motor movements to the new location of the object, but it took them 420 milliseconds on average to indicate their awareness that the object had moved by saying "Tah!". The fact that corrective action was taken almost one-third of a second before subjects indicated their awareness that such action was needed suggests that action does not need to await awareness of an object's current location. This was borne out by the subjects' reports: they said that they only saw the object moving its location as they were in the process of completing their corrective movement.

It was mentioned earlier that object location and object identification are dealt with by different processing systems. According to Milner, Carey, and Harvey (1994), the parietal system which locates objects is used to guide reaching for objects and also guides the grasping of those objects; this system makes use of viewer-centred information such as would be available in the $2\frac{1}{2}$-D sketch representation identified by Marr (1982; see Chapter 2). In contrast, the temporal system for object recognition makes use of Marr's (1982) 3-D model representation (see Chapter 2).

What would we expect to find in a brain-damaged patient whose visual systems for object location and object identification are intact, but in whom the two systems can no longer communicate effectively with each other? So far as visually guided reaching and grasping are concerned, such a patient should be able to grasp objects efficiently simply by using the parietal system. However, as information about the nature of the object being grasped would not be available to that system, the patient should often grasp the object inappropriately, not knowing precisely what to do with it. A patient exhibiting just those characteristics was discussed by Milner et al. (1994).

It follows from the theoretical position of Milner et al. (1994) that a patient with substantial damage to the temporal system involved in object recognition would still be able to reach for (and to grasp) objects reasonably effectively. In fact, they arrived at their theoretical position partly on the basis of previous research on such a patient (Milner et al. 1991). The patient (DF) had a severe deficit in visual recognition, indicating that there was substantial damage to the temporal system. In spite of this, as Milner et al. (1991, p.418) pointed out, she "had little difficulty in everyday activity such as opening doors, shaking hands, walking around furniture, and eating meals ... she could accurately reach out and grasp a pencil orientated at different angles". The pattern of intact and impaired visual abilities shown by DF is generally known as "visual form agnosia".

In sum, visually guided reaching and grasping towards an object can be reasonably efficient when detailed information about the nature of the object is not available, and even when there is a lack of conscious awareness of the present location of the object. An implication of the available evidence is that reaching and grasping require primarily basic spatial information provided by the parietal visual system. More evidence, and a theoretical position somewhat different to that of Milner et al. (1994), are discussed by Jeannerod (1994).

Time to contact

There are numerous situations in everyday life in which we want to know when we are going to reach some object (e.g. the car immediately in front of us). It would be possible to make these calculations by estimating the initial distance away of the object

(e.g. car; ball), estimating our speed, and then combining these two estimates into an estimate of the time to contact by dividing distance by speed. However, there are two problems with that approach: (1) two possible sources of error are present in the calculation (i.e. perceived distance and perceived velocity); and (2) it is relatively complex to combine the two kinds of information.

Lee (1976) argued that it is not necessary to perceive either the distance or speed of an object we are approaching in order to work out the time to contact, provided that we are approaching it with constant velocity. He claimed that time to contact could be calculated using only a single variable, namely, the rate of expansion of the object's retinal image: the faster the image is expanding, the less time there is to contact. Lee (1976) used this notion to propose a measure of time to contact which he called T or tau, and which is defined as the inverse of the rate of expansion of the retinal image of the object: $T = 1/$ (rate of expansion of object's retinal image). This theory is in general agreement with Gibson's approach, because it is assumed that information about time to contact is directly available.

According to Lee, information about tau is used when an object is approaching us as well as when we are approaching an object. It is also used in various sports when we need to be prepared to catch or hit an approaching ball, when long jumpers approach the take-off board, and so on. For the present, we are concerned with time to contact when a person is moving towards an object; later in the chapter, we will turn to the issue of time to contact when it is the object rather than the person that is in movement.

Cavallo and Laurent (1988) tested Lee's (1976) theory in a study in which experienced drivers and beginners indicated when they expected a collision with a stationary obstacle to occur. They manipulated how easy it was to assess speed by comparing normal and restricted visual fields, and they manipulated ease of distance assessment by comparing binocular and monocular vision. Their findings did not indicate that the rate of expansion of the obstacle's retinal image was the major determinant of time-to-contact judgements. Accuracy of time-to-contact estimation was greater when speed and distance were relatively easy to assess, and there was evidence that the beginners were making use of both speed and distance information in their estimates. In contrast, experienced drivers seemed to make more use of distance than of speed information.

Stewart, Cudworth, and Lishman (1993) argued that tau may be difficult to assess accurately when an object is some distance away, and that as a consequence most drivers may rely more on judgements of speed and distance. More specifically, they claimed that familiar size may be used as an indication of distance; for example, if the retinal image of a pedestrian is small, it is assumed that he or she is relatively far away. These ideas led them to a novel explanation of the high percentage of road accidents involving children (Stewart et al., 1993, p.1241): "If a child is misperceived as a larger person at a greater distance, time-to-collision will be over-estimated." This over-estimation means that drivers will brake later when approaching children than adults.

Stewart et al. (1993) tested their theory by examining accident data. They argued that this over-estimation would be less likely to occur at zebra crossings, because the road markings at such crossings provide valuable information about distance. As a consequence, children should be relatively less vulnerable on zebra crossings than elsewhere. This was supported by the evidence. The percentage of casualties who were children was 36% away from zebra crossings, but was only 24% on zebra crossings. This, and other findings, led Stewart et al. (1993, p.1241) to conclude that over-estimation of the time-to-collision with children "causes over half of Britain's daily toll of about 60 child pedestrian casualties".

Some interesting research on US Air Force pilots by Kruk and Regan (1983) may be relevant to Lee's (1976) theory. They assessed the pilots' sensitivity to change in the size of a square which changed size in an unpredictable fashion. As calculation of tau involves making use of information about size expansion, sensitivity to size changes is an indirect measure of sensitivity to tau. Kruk and Regan (1983) also assessed the pilots' ability to land a plane smoothly using a cockpit simulator. There was a strong tendency for the pilots who produced the smoothest landings to have the greatest sensitivity to size changes. It is thus possible that individual differences in pilots' landing abilities reflect their sensitivity to tau.

Walking and running

Walking and running may seem like extremely simple and automatic activities requiring only very limited visual information (e.g. about large objects that we must avoid bumping into). In fact, a considerable amount of visual monitoring of the environment is often needed. Anyone who has walked over rough ground at night under poor lighting conditions will probably remember that it can be a difficult and uncomfortable experience.

Some of the processes involved in running were investigated by Lee, Lishman, and Thomson (1982). They took films of female long jumpers during their run-up. Jumps are disqualified if the long jumper oversteps the take-off board, so precise positioning of the feet is important. Most coaches and athletes used to assume that expert long jumpers develop a stereotyped stride pattern that is repeated on each run-up, and which relies very little on visual information. In contrast, Lee et al. (1982, p.456) argued that there are two major processes involved: (1) control consists "in regulating just one kinetic parameter, the vertical impulse of the step—keeping it constant during the approach phase and then adjusting it to regulate flight time in order to strike the board"; and (2) tau is used late in the run-up, because time-to-arrival at the board is "specified directly by a single optical parameter, the inverse of the rate of dilation of the image of the board".

Lee et al. (1982) obtained evidence in favour of their theoretical position. The athletes showed a gradual increase in inconsistency in their stride patterns during most of the run-up, which is in conflict with the view that there is a stereotyped stride pattern. This was followed by a marked increase in the variability of stride lengths over the last three strides, which seemed to be due to alterations in the leap or flight time of each stride. This had the effect of allowing the athletes' last stride to land in an appropriate position with respect to the take-off board. According to Lee et al. (1982), these adjustments are visually guided by tau. Lee et al. (1982) concluded that most of a long jumper's run-up is determined by internal processes, with visual processes assuming great importance only in the last few strides.

Berg, Wade, and Greer (1994) pointed out that Lee et al. (1982) had used only three jumpers, and had tested them under non-competitive conditions. Accordingly, they set out to replicate and extend the earlier findings under competitive conditions. Their findings with expert long jumpers were comparable to those of Lee et al. (1982), and they also found that novice long jumpers had similar run-up patterns. This suggests that using tau to regulate stride pattern comes naturally, and does not require extensive experience.

Section summary

Lee's (1976) theory that decisions about time to contact are based primarily on tau or the inverse of the rate of expansion of an object's retinal image has received mixed support from studies in which the individual moves towards the object. There is more support from studies of long jumpers than from studies of drivers. There are at least two plausible reasons why the findings from these two groups of subjects might differ. First, tau may be hard to calculate accurately when the time-to-contact is short, which would reduce its value to drivers. For example, the stopping time for a driver at 31 miles per hour (50 kilometres an hour) is three seconds. Second, there may be more information about speed and distance available to drivers than to long jumpers, because of speedometers, road markings, changing position on the road relative to other drivers, and so on. As a consequence, there may be less need for drivers to rely on tau.

Heading: Optic flow

One of the most important notions put forward by Gibson (1950) was that of the optic flow pattern. When someone is moving forwards, the point towards which he or she is heading appears motionless, whereas the visual field around that point appears to be moving away (this is known as the "outflow"). As optic flow provides relatively precise information about the direction in which someone is heading, it follows from Gibson's (1950) theoretical position that heading judgements should generally be fairly accurate. In fact, however, heading errors of between 5° and 10° were reported in most of the early research (e.g. Warren, 1976). With that low level of accuracy, it is doubtful whether optic flow could provide adequate information for the control of locomotion.

Warren, Morris, and Kalish (1988) argued that there were some limitations with previous research. Heading judgements were generally obtained by requiring the subjects to point, and this may provide an insensitive measure. Accordingly, Warren et al. (1988) used a rather different task. They produced films consisting of moving dots, with each film simulating the optic flow that would be produced if someone were moving in a given direction. The subjects' task was to decide whether they seemed to be heading to the left or to the right of a stationary target positioned at some point along the horizon of the display. The mean error with this measure of heading accuracy varied with dot density, but averaged out at about 1.2°. As Warren et al. (1988, p.659) concluded, "optical flow can provide an adequate basis for the control of locomotion and other visually guided behaviour".

At a theoretical level, there are various aspects of optic flow that might be of crucial importance to the perception of heading. Gibson (1950) proposed a global radial outflow hypothesis, according to which it is the overall or global outflow pattern that specifies the direction of heading. Other hypotheses are discussed by Warren et al. (1988). For example, there is the local focus of outflow hypothesis, according to which the direction of heading is determined by locating the one element in the flow field that is stationary. This hypothesis appears incorrect, as Warren et al. (1988) found that heading judgements were very accurate even when there was no stationary element. Their finding that heading judgements were very good with as few as 10 moving dots disproved several hypotheses in which it is assumed that valuable information cannot be extracted from optic flow with such an impoverished flow field. However, as Warren et al. (1988, p.646) concluded, their findings "are consistent with Gibson's (1950) original global radial hypothesis for perception of heading".

Section summary

Various aspects of visually guided action have been considered in this section of the chapter, including reaching and grasping, time to contact, and the use of optic flow information to decide the direction in which we are heading. It appears that relatively basic visual information is often (but not always) sufficient to allow us to perform these actions efficiently:

- Reaching and grasping seem to depend mainly on information about spatial location.
- Time-to-contact decisions can be based on the rate of expansion of the retinal image, especially when the time to contact is relatively short.
- Judgements about the direction of heading can be based on the outflow pattern of the optic flow.

Gibson argued that visually guided action is determined mainly by invariant information obtained from optic flow patterns. His theoretical position is thus very much in line with the evidence that rate of expansion of the retinal image and outflow patterns are used in the guidance of action. However, other evidence is perhaps less consistent with the Gibsonian position. Decisions about time to contact sometimes depend on speed, distance, or familiar size information rather than on the rate of expansion of the retinal image. In addition, appropriate grasping movements often require the combining of information about spatial location with information about object identification in complex ways.

PERCEPTION OF OBJECT MOTION

Perception of object motion is important for a number of reasons. It allows us to avoid colliding with moving objects, but it also facilitates detection of small or camouflaged objects, and it can also permit us to identify an object's three-dimensional shape (known as the kinetic depth effect). A simple example of the kinetic depth effect was provided by Sekuler and Blake (1994). A wire hanger is twisted into a random three dimensional shape, and a light shining on it produces a shadow on a piece of paper. If the wire hanger is motionless, it is impossible to work out the three-dimensional shape of the wire hanger from the shadow. However, if the hanger rotates, its three-dimensional shape is readily perceived.

Several studies of the kinetic depth effect have used random-dot surfaces taken from three-dimensional objects. It has been found in several studies that three-dimensional structures can be perceived accurately even when only two different random-dot surfaces taken from the same object are presented alternately (see Todd & Norman, 1991). This is an impressive achievement, especially as computational analyses have suggested that a minimum of three distinct views should be required in order to identify an object's three-dimensional structure (e.g. Huang & Lee, 1989).

Evidence of the vital importance of the ability to perceive object motion is provided by the case of a female patient, LM, who had suffered brain damage in both hemispheres. She was good at locating stationary objects by sight, she had good colour discrimination, and her binocular visual functions (e.g. stereoscopic depth perception) were normal, but her movement perception was grossly deficient. According to Zihl, von Cramon, and Mai (1983, p.315):

> She had difficulty ... in pouring tea or coffee into a cup because the fluid appeared to be frozen, like a glacier. In addition, she could not stop pouring at the right time since she was unable to perceive the movement in the cup (or a pot) when the fluid rose ... In a room where more than two other people were walking she felt very insecure ... because 'people were suddenly here or there but I have not seen them moving'.

The focus in the first part of this section is on the perception of objects that are genuinely in motion. Two issues will be addressed. The first one is how we decide when an object moving in our direction will reach us. The second issue is how we are able to perceive biological movement even when we are only provided with rather impoverished information.

In the second part of this section, we consider two illusory phenomena related to object motion. The first phenonemon is known as *apparent movement*, and occurs when movement is perceived even though the observer is presented with a series of static images. Apparent movement is seen every time you see a film or watch television. The second phenomenon is known as *perceived causality*. If objects move around in certain specified ways, it is difficult to avoid attributing intentionality to their movements, even though we know that objects do not really possess intentions.

Time to contact

We saw earlier that people moving through an environment (e.g. long jumpers) seem to make use of information about the rate of expansion of an object's retinal image to predict the time to contact; the measure generally used is tau, which is the inverse of the rate of object expansion (Lee, 1976). There has been much research interest in attempting to see whether the same is true when an object moves towards a motionless observer.

Schiff and Detwiler (1979) obtained evidence that tau, rather than perceived distance or perceived velocity, is used to calculate time to contact. They found that adults were reasonably accurate at predicting when an object on a film would have hit them. Their accuracy was little affected by whether the object was filmed against a blank or a textured background, suggesting that information about the rate of expansion of the retinal image is sufficient to decide when an object will arrive.

Lee, Young, Reddish, Lough, and Clayton (1983) investigated the relevance of tau to performance in a situation in which subjects had to jump up and punch balls that were dropped from various heights above them. The speed of a dropping ball increases over time, but the calculation of tau ignores such changes in velocity. It follows that the actual time to contact will be less than tau. The key finding was that the subjects' leg and arm movements were determined more closely by tau than by the actual time to contact.

Lee's (1976) main theoretical assumption is that the rate of expansion of an object's retinal image is the crucial factor influencing judgements of time to contact. It would thus be valuable in tests of this theory to manipulate the rate of expansion as directly as possible. Savelsberg, Whiting, and Bootsma (1991) had the ingenious idea of achieving this by requiring subjects to catch a deflating ball that was approaching them, with the subjects being unaware that the ball was deflating. The rate of expansion of the retinal image is less for a deflating than for a non-deflating ball, and so on Lee's theory subjects should assume that the deflating ball will take longer to reach them. As predicted, the grasping movements involved in catching occurred later for a deflating than for a non-deflating ball.

Savelsberg et al. (1991) wondered whether factors other than the rate of expansion of the retinal image played a part in judgements about time of arrival of the ball. They compared performance under binocular and monocular vision to see whether the ability to see the various binocular cues (accommodation; convergence; stereopsis; see Chapter 2) improved catching performance with the deflating ball. Performance was not improved when the ball was viewed by both eyes, strengthening the argument that rate of expansion of the retinal image was the most important information used by the subjects.

Biological movement

Most people are very good at interpreting the movements of other people, and can decide very rapidly whether someone is walking, running, limping, or whatever. How successful would we be at interpreting biological movement if the visual information available to us were substantially reduced? In research mentioned in Chapter 2, Johansson (1975) addressed this issue by attaching lights to actors' joints (e.g. wrists; knees; ankles). The actors were dressed entirely in black so that only the lights were visible, and were then filmed at they moved around. Reasonably accurate perception of a moving person could be achieved even with only six lights and a short segment of film. Most observers were able to describe accurately the posture and movements of the actors, and it almost appeared as if their arms and legs could be seen.

Subsequent research using the same basic paradigm has indicated that observers can make very precise discriminations when viewing point-light displays. Cutting and Kozlowski (1977) found that observers were reasonably good at identifying themselves and others known to them from point-light displays, and Kozlowski and Cutting (1978) discovered that observers were correct approximately 65% of the time when guessing the sex of someone walking. Judgements were better when joints in both the upper and lower body were illuminated than when only the upper body or only the lower body was illuminated, presumably because good judgements depend on some overall bodily feature or features.

Cutting, Proffitt, and Kozlowski (1978) pointed out that men tend to show relatively greater side to side motion (or swing) of the shoulders than of the hips, whereas women show the opposite. The reason for this is that men typically have broad shoulders and narrow hips compared to women. The shoulders and hips move in opposition to each other, that is, when the right shoulder is forward, the left hip is forward. One can identify the *centre of moment* in the upper body, which is the neutral reference point around which the shoulders and hips swing. The position of the centre of moment is determined by the relative swings of the shoulders and hips, and is typically lower in men than in women. Cutting et al. (1978) found that the centre of moment correlated well with the sex judgements made by observers.

Cutting (1978) extended the findings of Cutting et al. (1978) by using artificial moving dot displays in which only the centre of moment was varied. Judgements of the sex of "male" and "female" walkers were correct over 80% of the time, confirming the importance of centre of moment. Above-chance performance was still obtained when the lights conveying information about the centre of moment were not illuminated, indicating that observers can make use of other, more indirect, sources of information.

Some of the most interesting findings with point-light displays were reported by Runeson and Frykholm (1983). In one experiment, they asked the actors to lift a box weighing four kilograms and to carry it to a table, while trying to give the impression that the box weighed 6.5, 11.5, or 19 kilograms. Observers detected the actors' intentions from the pattern of lights, and thus were not deceived about the weight of the box.

In another experiment, Runeson and Frykholm (1983) asked the actors to carry out a sequence of movements naturally or as if they were a member of the opposite sex. Observers guessed the gender of the actor correctly 85.5% of the time when he or she acted naturally, and there was only a modest reduction to 75.5% correct in the deception condition.

Theoretical account

A key theoretical issue is whether our good ability to perceive biological motion accurately involves complex cognitive processes. Most of the available evidence suggests it does not. For example, Fox and McDaniel (1982) presented two different motion displays side by side to infants. One display consisted of dots representing someone running on the spot, and the other showed the same activity but presented upside down. Infants four months of age spent most of their time looking at the display that was the right way up, suggesting that they were able to detect biological motion.

More evidence suggesting that the detection of biological motion occurs in a rather straightforward fashion was reported by Johansson, von Hofsten, and Jansson (1980). They discovered that observers who saw the moving lights for only one-fifth of a second perceived biological movement with no apparent difficulty.

These findings are consistent with Johansson's (1975) view that the ability to perceive biological motion is innate. However, it is clearly possible that four-month-old infants have learned from experience how to perceive biological motion. Runeson and Frykholm (1983) argued for a Gibsonian position, according to which aspects of biological motion provide invariant information. These invariants can be perceived with the impoverished information available from point-light displays, and can be identified even when there are deliberate attempts to deceive observers. The main problem with their theoretical approach is that the alleged invariants of biological motion remain to be identified.

Apparent motion

As was mentioned earlier, anyone who has ever watched television or seen a film has experienced *apparent motion*: what is presented to the viewer is a rapid series of still images, but what is perceived is the illusion of continuous motion. Apparent motion was demonstrated under laboratory conditions by Wertheimer (1912). He used a display in which two vertical lines in different spatial locations were presented alternately. When the delay between successive presentations was approximately one-twentieth of a second, observers often reported that there was one line that moved smoothly from place to place.

Probably the main issue that needs to be resolved by the visual system in apparent motion is that of *correspondence*. This involves deciding which parts of successive still images belong to the same object in motion. Correspondence could be achieved by comparing each small part of successive images, but this would be very cumbersome with complex displays. For example, apparent motion can be created by using two large random-dot patterns which are identical except that dots in a square central position in one pattern are shifted to the left in the other pattern (discussed by Ramachandran & Anstis, 1986). When these two patterns are superimposed and presented in rapid alternation, a central square appears to move from side to side. As there are thousands of dots in each display, it seems improbable that the visual system meticulously compares each and every dot.

According to Ramachandran and Anstis (1986), the visual system focuses on certain features of a display when attempting to detect correspondence. For example, the visual system seems good at detecting correspondences between areas of brightness and darkness (technically known as areas of low spatial frequency). A white square on a black background was presented for one-tenth of a second, and was replaced by a display with an outline square of the same size but coloured black on the left and a white circle on the left. The white square appeared to move towards the circle rather than towards the black square, suggesting that "the visual system tends to match areas of similar brightness in preference to matching sharp outlines" (Ramachandran & Anstis, 1986, p. 82).

Another characteristic of the visual system is that it prefers to perceive apparent motion in ways that would make sense in the real world. For example, we take account of the fact that objects in motion typically proceed along a straight path. This was demonstrated in a two-stage experiment (Ramachandran & Anstis, 1986). In the first stage, two dots were presented rapidly at diagonal corners of an imaginary square, and were then replaced by identical dots in the opposite diagonal corners. Approximately half of the observers perceived two dots moving horizontally, with the other observers seeing the dots moving vertically. In the second stage, all the observers perceived two dots moving horizontally. The reason was that the display was embedded in the centre of a larger display in which two rows of dots moved horizontally in opposite directions. Perceiving the two central dots moving horizontally created an impression of linear movement in the larger display.

Ramachandran and Anstis (1986) argued that the visual system makes use of two other rules which affect decisions about correspondences or matches between successive images: the rule of rigidity and the rule of occlusion. According to the rule of rigidity, it is assumed that objects are rigid; thus, if part of an object moves, all the rest of it moves as well. According to the rule of occlusion, an object continues to exist when it is hidden (or occluded) behind an intervening object. The relevance of these rules to apparent motion was demonstrated using displays like those shown in Fig. 4.4. The two displays were superimposed and then presented alternately. As you can see from Fig. 4.4, four pie-shaped wedges are added and four are taken away, but what is seen is a white square moving right and left, occluding and uncovering discs in the background. This effect illustrates use of the rule of rigidity, because the dots within the square appear to move with it, even though in fact they remain stationary. The rule of occlusion is involved, because observers assume that the four circles remain intact, but that parts of them are occluded or partially obscured some of the time.

Theoretical account

It appears that the rules used by observers to detect correspondence and perceive apparent motion are

FIGURE 4.4

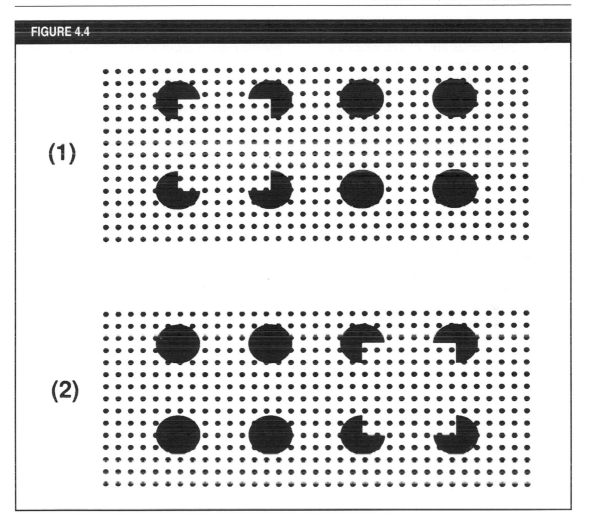

The stimuli shown in (1) are superimposed on, and alternated with, those shown in (2), creating the impression that a white square is moving forwards and backwards. Adapted from Ramachandran and Anstis (1986).

largely based on their knowledge of regularities in the world and of the properties of objects. Ramachandran and Anstis (1986) argued that only relatively low-level processes are needed to produce the various effects they obtained. The experiments they described all involved rapid rates of stimulus presentation, and they claimed that it is unlikely that higher-level cognitive processes could have operated at those speeds. They also refer to neurobiological research (see Chapter 2), which has indicated that some nerve cells are sensitive to the motion of images with low spatial frequencies; these nerve cells may play a part in detecting correspondence at an early stage of visual processing.

Other theorists have argued that there is more than one kind of apparent motion. For example, Braddick (1980) proposed that apparent motion sometimes, but not always, depends on the stimulation of low-level direction-selective cells. There is substantial evidence (Regan, Beverley, & Cynader, 1979) for direction-selective cells in the visual cortex, which respond mainly to a particular direction of movement. Particularly impressive evidence for their existence was obtained by Salzman, Murasugi, Britten, and Newsome (1992). They studied the perceived direction of movement in random-dot displays in their monkey subjects. Electrical stimulation of direction-selective cells biased the monkeys' perception of motion; when, for example, cells responding to rightward movement were stimulated, this increased the probability of the display appearing to move in a rightward direction.

According to Braddick (1980), apparent motion of the central square when two large random-dot patterns are superimposed and alternated (see earlier description) involves low-level, direction-selective cells. However, he assumed that apparent motion of line stimuli (e.g. Wertheimer, 1912, discussed earlier) may involve higher-level, more cognitive processes.

Braddick (1980) discussed some of the evidence indicating important differences between apparent motion with random-dot and line displays. Apparent motion with random-dot displays requires the stimuli to be much closer together than is the case in order to perceive apparent motion with line displays, and there need to be much shorter intervals of time between stimuli (under 100 milliseconds versus 300 milliseconds, respectively). In addition, apparent motion with random-dot displays is not observed when the two stimuli are presented to different eyes, but is still perceived with line displays. At the very least, then, it would appear that rather different processes underlie different phenomena of apparent motion.

Further evidence that apparent motion can be produced in more than one way was reported by Shiffrar and Freyd (1990). In part of their experiment, observers were presented in rapid succession with two photographs of a man with his hand held out and his palm facing forward. In one photograph, his hand was twisted as far left as possible, and in the other photograph it was twisted as far right as possible; there was a rotation of the wrist of about 270° between the two photographs. Apparent motion could either be seen in the longer (270°) but biologically possible direction, or in the shorter (90°) but biologically impossible direction. When there was rapid alternation of the

photographs, the shorter rotation was perceived; however, the longer and more plausible rotation was perceived when the rate of alternation was slower. Thus, knowledge of what is physically possible influenced apparent motion when there was enough time for that information to be accessed.

Perception of causality

Heider and Simmel (1944) discovered an interesting phenomenon. They presented their subjects with two triangles of different sizes and a disc, all of which moved around in an enclosure with a movable flap in one side. When the subjects were asked to describe what they saw, nearly all of them described the motions of these objects in terms normally used to refer to human social interactions. For example, they described objects fighting or one chasing another, and they often attributed motives or intentions to the objects.

Michotte (1963) extended our knowledge of perceived causality in a series of studies. For example, observers might watch as one square moved towards a second square, with the first square stopping and the second square moving off at a slower rate than the first one as they came into contact. According to Michotte, observers perceived that the first square had caused the motion of the second square, and the term "launching effect" was used to describe it. The perception of causality disappeared when there was a time interval between the contact and the second square moving off, or if the second square moved off in a different direction to that of the first square. The first square seemed to "trigger" rather than "launch" the second square if the second square moved faster than the first one had done. Although the existence of the launching effect depended on factors such as timing, direction of motion, and speed of motion, it did not seem to be affected by the nature of the objects. The launching effect could be observed even if the two objects were very different from each other.

Michotte (1963) claimed that nearly everyone perceived causality in his displays under the appropriate conditions, and he also argued that causality is perceived in a rather direct fashion which does not rely on inference or other processes. Both of these claims have been disputed. Beasley (1968) found that only 65% of subjects reported the impression of causality with the launching display, and even fewer did so with other displays allegedly giving rise to causal impressions. In strong contrast to Michotte's (1963) findings, he found that 45% reported causal impressions when the second object moved off at a 90° angle to the direction of motion of the first object.

Evidence more supportive of Michotte (1963) was reported by Dittrich and Lea (1994). They identified three separate factors, all of which contributed to the perception of intentional motion in an object:

- The object moved in a direct fashion.
- The object moved faster than other objects.
- The goal towards which the object was moving was visible.

The fact that intentional motion depended on three separate factors suggests that intentionality is a rather complex concept. In spite of its complexity, however, Dittrich and Lea (1994, p.265) concluded that "the perception of intentionality can be a relatively immediate, bottom-up process, probably occurring quite early in the visual processing".

Section summary

Various aspects of the perception of object motion have been considered, including decisions about time to contact, detection of biological motion, apparent movement, and perceived causality or intentionality. It has been claimed for each of these phenomena that they occur in a relatively direct fashion not dependent on elaborate visual processing. It has proved difficult to establish precisely what processes are involved. However, there is good evidence that basic information about rate of expansion of the retinal image determines time-to-contact decisions, and fairly basic processes may often underlie the detection of biological motion and perceived causality. In contrast, apparent motion seems to be more complex. It sometimes depends on low level processes, but in other situations it involves higher-level cognitive processes.

CHAPTER SUMMARY

The constructivist approach to perception has been a popular one for a very long time. According to constructivist theorists, perception is an active and constructive process depending on hypotheses and expectations. This approach has been applied with reasonable success to many of the errors found in perception (e.g. those found in visual illusions). Constructivist theories are most applicable to the perception of degraded or briefly presented stimuli, but they predict far more errors in normal perception than are actually found.

Gibson proposed an ecological approach to visual perception. He argued that perception is direct, in the sense that the stimulus input provides us with all the information needed for accurate perception. More specifically, the optic array is said to contain invariant or unambiguous information about the layout of objects in the visual environment. We pick up this invariant information by means of a process of resonance. Within Gibson's theory, meaning is dealt with by assuming that affordances (the potential uses of an object) are directly perceivable. Gibson was correct in assuming that the visual input provides a much richer source of information than is acknowledged by most constructivist theorists. However, he substantially under-estimated the complexity of the processes involved in visual perception, and his notion of affordances is inadequate as a way of understanding the role of meaning in perception. His theory is informative about some of the processes involved in "seeing", but is considerably less so with respect to "seeing as".

It is of importance to us to distinguish between movements in the retinal image that are due to the movements of objects in the environment and those that are due to eye movements. Most of the evidence supports outflow theory, according to which movement of the retinal image is interpreted by making use of information about intended movement sent to the eye muscles. However, it cannot account for the fact that the environment appears stable when we move our heads without moving our eyes.

Vision is very important in the guidance of action. One issue is to explain how vision guides reaching and grasping behaviour. The evidence suggests that the parietal visual system, which processes information about spatial location, is of primary importance. Reaching and grasping towards an object can both be reasonably efficient in the absence of detailed information about the nature of the object.

Another issue that is raised by visually guided action is how we are able to judge when we will hit some object if we fail to take avoiding action. This time-to-contact could be calculated by working out perceived distance and perceived velocity. However, Lee has argued persuasively that we often take account of tau, which is based on the rate of expansion of an object's retinal image. A further issue is how we adjust our style of walking or running to take account of difficulties (e.g. uneven terrain). There is evidence that tau is often relevant here as well.

For many purposes (e.g. a pilot coming in to land), it is essential to know the direction in which we are heading. Gibson (1950) argued that there is an optic flow, with the point towards which we are heading remaining stationary whereas the visual field around it appears to be moving away. The available evidence indicates that information about the overall or global outflow away from the point towards which we are heading is utilised.

Several issues have been considered in connection with the perception of object motion. It appears that we decide how long it will before a moving object reaches us on the basis of its rate of expansion in the retinal image. Biological movement, and its significance, can be perceived surprisingly well even with the impoverished information provided by point-light displays. The fact that biological movement is perceived very rapidly and can also be perceived by infants suggests that relatively low-level processes are involved.

Apparent motion is involved every time we watch television or a film. Correspondence or matching between objects in successive still images generally involves making use of our knowledge of the properties of objects and of regularities in the world. It is likely that apparent motion sometimes depends mainly on low-level, direction-selective cells, whereas in other circumstances it depends more on higher-level cognitive processes.

Michotte argued that perceived causality of movement occurs in a rather direct fashion that does not depend on learning. More recent research, however, indicates that relevant experience is more important than Michotte thought.

FURTHER READING

Banks, W. P., & Krajicek, D. (1991). Perception. In M. R. Rosenzweig & L. W. Porter (Eds.), *Annual review of psychology* (Vol. 42). Palo Alto, CA: Annual Reviews Inc. Some of the major theoretical approaches to perception, including that of Gibson, are discussed in detail.

Bruce, V., & Green, P.R. (1990). *Visual perception: Physiology, psychology, and ecology.* Hove, UK: Lawrence Erlbaum Associates Ltd. This good (but difficult) book contains substantial coverage of the work of Gibson and the ecological approach to perception.

Sekuler, R., & Blake, R. (1994). *Perception* (3rd Edn.). New York: McGraw-Hill. The major processes involved in the perception of motion are discussed in detail in Chapter 8 of this textbook.

Wertheim, A.H. (1994). Motion perception during self-motion: The direct versus inferential controversy revisited. *Behavioral and Brain Sciences, 17,* 293–311. This article provides a detailed consideration of various theories about how it is that we perceive a stable world in spite of constantly varying retinal images.

5

Attention and Performance Limitations

INTRODUCTION

The concept of "attention" was considered to be important by many philosphers and psychologists in the late 19th century, but fell into disrepute because the behaviourists regarded all internal processes with the utmost suspicion. Attention became fashionable again following the publication of Broadbent's book *Perception and communication* in 1958, but more recently many have argued that it is too vague to be of value. Moray (1969) pointed out that attention is sometimes used to refer to the ability to select part of the incoming stimulation for further processing, but it has also been regarded as synonymous with concentration or mental set. It has been applied to search processes in which a specified target is looked for, and it has also been suggested that attention co-varies with arousal (e.g. the drowsy individual is in a state of low arousal and attends little to his or her environment).

There is an obvious danger that a concept that is used to explain everything will turn out to explain nothing. However, attention is most commonly used to refer to selectivity of processing. This was the sense emphasised by William James (1890, pp.403–404):

> Everyone knows what attention is. It is the taking possession of the mind, in clear and vivid form, of one out of what seem several simultaneously possible objects or trains of thought. Focalisation, concentration, of consciousness are of its essence. It implies withdrawal from some things in order to deal effectively with others.

An issue of some importance concerns the relationship between attention and consciousness. In order to discuss this, we need first to define "consciousness". According to Baars (1988, p.15): "We will consider people to be conscious of an event if (1) they can say immediately afterwards that they were conscious of it *and* (2) we can independently verify the accuracy of their report." In the context of that definition, attention is "that which controls access to conscious experience" (Baars, 1988, p.302). More specifically, by attending to certain visual or auditory stimuli rather than others, we can determine in part the contents of consciousness.

If we ask what makes us attend to some things rather than others, then the usual answer is that we choose to attend to sources of information that are relevant in the context of our present activities and goals. That is true as far as it goes, but attention is sometimes "captured" involuntarily by certain stimuli. For example, Muller and Rabbitt (1989) instructed their subjects to allocate visual attention on the basis of an arrow and to ignore briefly brightened squares presented in the periphery of vision. In spite of these instructions, subjects' attention was drawn to the brightened squares.

There is an important distinction between focused and divided attention (see Fig. 5.1). Focused attention is studied by presenting people with two or more stimulus inputs at the same time, and instructing them to process and respond to only one. Work on focused attention can tell us how effectively people can select certain inputs rather than others, and it enables us to investigate the nature of the selection process and the fate of unattended stimuli. Divided attention is also studied by presenting at least two stimulus inputs at the same time, but with instructions that all stimulus inputs must be attended to and responded to. Studies of divided attention provide useful information about an individual's processing limitations, and may tell us something about attentional mechanisms and their capacity.

There are two important limitations in most research on attention. First, although we can attend to either the external environment or the internal environment (i.e. our own thoughts and information in long-term memory), most of the work on attention has been concerned only with attention to the external environment. Why should this be so? Experimenters can identify and control the stimuli presented in the external environment in a way that is simply not possible with internal determinants of attention.

Second, as Tipper, Lortie, and Baylis (1992) pointed out, most studies of attention are very artificial. In the real world, we generally attend to three-dimensional people and objects, and decide

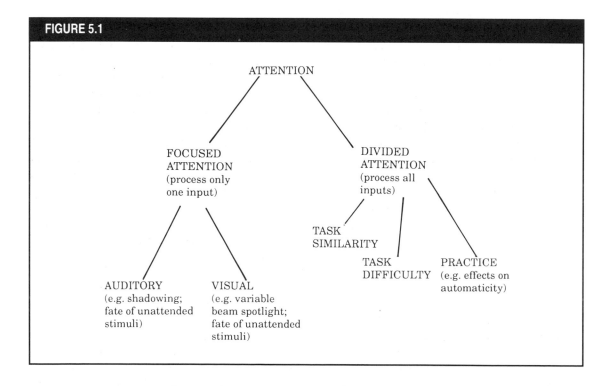

FIGURE 5.1

The ways in which different topics in attention are related to each other.

what actions might be appropriate with respect to them. In the laboratory, in contrast, the emphasis, according to Tipper et al. (1992, p.902), is on "experiments that briefly present static 2D displays and require arbitrary responses. It is clear that such experimental situations are rarely encountered in our usual interactions with the environment". Tipper et al. (1992) carried out a series of experiments under fairly naturalistic conditions. As their findings resembled those obtained in traditional laboratory studies, the artificiality of most laboratory research may not always undermine its validity.

FOCUSED AUDITORY ATTENTION

Systematic research on focused attention was initiated by the British scientist Colin Cherry (1953). He was working in an electronics research laboratory at the Massachusetts Institute of Technology, but somehow managed to find himself involved in psychological research. What fascinated Cherry was the "cocktail party" problem, i.e. how are we able to follow just one conversation when several different people are talking at once? Cherry discovered that this ability involves making use of physical differences to select among the auditory messages. These physical differences include differences in the sex of the speaker, in voice intensity, and in the location of the speaker. When Cherry presented two messages in the same voice to both ears at once (thereby eliminating these physical differences), listeners found it remarkably difficult to separate out the two messages on the basis of meaning alone.

Cherry also carried out experiments in which one auditory message had to be shadowed (i.e. repeated back, out loud) at the same time as a second auditory message was played to the other ear. Very little information seemed to be extracted from the second or non-attended message. Listeners seldom noticed when that message was spoken in a foreign language or in reversed speech. In contrast, physical changes such as the insertion of a pure tone were almost always detected. The

conclusion that unattended auditory information receives practically no processing was supported by other evidence. For example, there is practically no memory for words on the unattended message even when they are presented 35 times each (Moray, 1959).

Broadbent's theory

Broadbent (1958) felt that the findings from the shadowing task were important. He was also impressed by data from a memory task in which three pairs of digits were presented to a subject dichotically, i.e. three digits were heard one after the other by one ear, at the same time as three different digits were presented to the other ear. Subjects demonstrated a clear preference for recalling the digits ear by ear rather than pair by pair. In other words, if 496 were presented to one ear and 852 to the other ear, recall would be 496852 rather than 489562.

Broadbent (1958) accounted for the various findings by making the following assumptions (see Fig. 5.2):

• Two stimuli or messages presented at the same time gain access in parallel (i.e. at the same time) to a sensory buffer.
• One of the inputs is then allowed through a filter on the basis of its physical characteristics, with the other input remaining in the buffer for later processing.
• This filter is necessary in order to prevent overloading of the limited-capacity mechanism beyond the filter; this mechanism processes the input thoroughly.

This theory handles Cherry's basic findings, with unattended messages being rejected by the filter and thus receiving minimal processing. It also accounts for performance on Broadbent's dichotic task because the filter selects one input on the basis of the most prominent physical characteristic distinguishing the two inputs (i.e. the ear of arrival). However, it fails to explain other findings. It assumes that the unattended message is always rejected at an early stage of processing, but this is not correct. The original shadowing experiments made use of subjects who had little or no previous

FIGURE 5.2

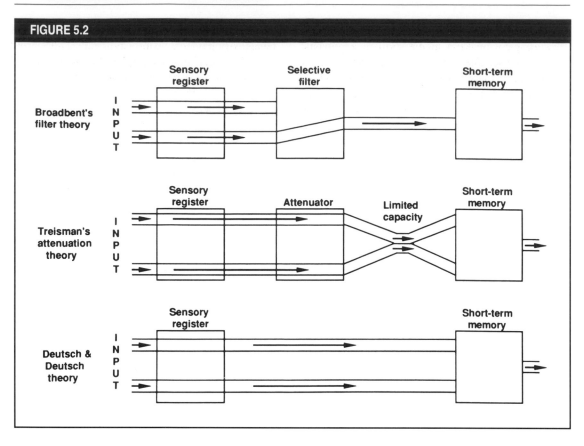

A comparison of Broadbent's theory (top): Treisman's theory (middle); and Deutsch and Deutsch's theory (bottom).

experience of shadowing messages, so that nearly all of their available processing resources had to be allocated to the shadowing task. Underwood (1974) asked subjects to detect digits presented on either the shadowed or the non-shadowed message. Naive subjects detected only 8% of the digits on the non-shadowed message, but an experienced researcher in the area detected 67% of the non-shadowed digits.

In most of the early work on the shadowing task, the two messages were usually rather similar (i.e. they were both auditorily presented verbal messages). Allport, Antonis, and Reynolds (1972) discovered that the degree of similarity between the two messages had a major impact on memory for the non-shadowed message. When shadowing of auditorily presented passages was combined with auditory presentation of words, memory for the

words was very poor. However, when the same shadowing task was combined with picture presentation, memory for the pictures was very good (90% correct). Thus, if two inputs are dissimilar from each other, they can both be processed more thoroughly than was allowed for on Broadbent's filter theory.

In the early studies, it was concluded that there was no processing of the meaning of unattended messages because the subjects had no conscious awareness of their meaning. This left open the possibility that meaning might be processed without awareness. Von Wright, Anderson, and Stenman (1975) gave their subjects two auditorily presented lists of words, with instructions to shadow one list and to ignore the other. When a word that had previously been associated with electric shock was presented on the non-attended list, there was sometimes a noticeable physiological reaction in the form of a galvanic skin response. The same effect was produced by presenting a word very similiar in sound or meaning to the shocked word. These findings suggest that information on the unattended message was processed in terms of both sound and meaning, even though the subjects were not consciously aware that the previously shocked word had been presented. However, as galvanic skin responses were detected on only a fraction of the trials, it is likely that thorough processing of unattended information occurred only some of the time.

In sum, there can be far more thorough processing of the non-shadowed message than would have been expected on Broadbent's (1958) theory. He proposed a relatively inflexible system of selective attention that cannot account for the great variability in the amount of analysis of the non-shadowed message. The same inflexibility of the filter theory is also shown in its assumption that the filter selects information on the basis of physical features. This assumption is supported by the tendency of subjects to recall dichotically presented digits ear by ear, but a small change in the basic experiment can alter the order of recall considerably. Gray and Wedderburn (1960) made use of a version of the dichotic task in which "Who 6 there" might be presented to one ear at the same time as "4 goes 1" was presented to the other ear. The preferred order of report was not ear by ear; instead, it was determined by meaning (e.g. "who goes there" followed by "4 6 1"). The implication is that selection can occur either before the processing of information from both inputs or afterwards. The fact that selection can be based on the meaning of presented information is inconsistent with filter theory.

Alternative theories

Treisman (1964) proposed a theory in which the analysis of unattended information is attenuated or reduced (see Fig. 5.2). Whereas Broadbent had suggested that there was a bottleneck early in processing, Treisman claimed that the location of the bottleneck was more flexible. She proposed that stimulus analysis proceeds in a systematic fashion through a hierarchy starting with analyses based on physical cues, syllabic pattern, and specific words, and moving on to analyses based on individual words, grammatical structure, and meaning. If there is insufficient processing capacity to permit full stimulus analysis, then tests towards the top of the hierarchy are omitted.

Treisman's theory accounts for the extensive processing of unattended sources of information that proved embarrassing for Broadbent, but the same facts were also explained by Deutsch and Deutsch (1963). They argued that all stimuli are fully analysed, with the most important or relevant stimulus determining the response (see Fig. 5.2). This theory resembles those of Broadbent and of Treisman in assuming the existence of a bottleneck in processing, but it places the bottleneck much nearer the response end of the processing system.

Treisman and Geffen (1967) provided support for Treisman's theory. Subjects shadowed one of two auditory messages, and at the same time tapped when they detected a target word in either message. According to Treisman's theory, there should be attenuated analysis of the non-shadowed message, and so fewer targets should be detected on that message than on the shadowed one. According to Deutsch and Deutsch, there is complete perceptual analysis of all stimuli, and so it might be predicted that there would be no difference in detection rates between the two messages. In fact, the shadowed or attended message showed a very large advantage in detection rates over the non-shadowed message (87% vs. 8%).

According to Deutsch and Deutsch (1967), their theory assumes that only important inputs lead to responses. As the task used by Treisman and Geffen (1967) required their subjects to make two responses (i.e. shadow and tap) to target words in the shadowed message, but only one response (i.e. tap) to targets in the non-shadowed message, the shadowed targets were more important than the non-shadowed ones.

Treisman and Riley (1969) handled this argument by carrying out a study in which exactly the same response was made to targets occurring in either message. They told their subjects to stop shadowing and to tap as soon as they detected a target in either message. Many more target words were still detected on the shadowed message than on the non-shadowed message.

Johnston and Heinz's theory

Deutsch and Deutsch (1963) assumed that selection always occurs after full analysis of all inputs has taken place, which suggests that the processing system is rather rigid. In contrast, Johnston and Heinz (1978) proposed a more flexible model in which selection is possible at several different stages of processing. They made the following two main assumptions:

- The more stages of processing that take place prior to selection, the greater are the demands on processing capacity.
- Selection occurs as early in processing as possible given the task demands (in order to minimise demands on capacity).

Johnston and Wilson (1980) tested these theoretical ideas. Pairs of words were presented together dichotically (i.e. one word to each ear), and the task was to identify target items consisting of members of a designated category. The targets were ambiguous words having at least two distinct meanings. For example, if the category were "articles of clothing", then "socks" would be a

possible target word. Each target word was accompanied by a non-target word biasing the appropriate meaning of the target (e.g. "smelly"), or a non-target word biasing the inappropriate meaning (e.g. "punches"), or by a neutral non-target word (e.g. "Tuesday").

When subjects did not know which ear targets would arrive at (divided attention), appropriate non-targets facilitated the detection of targets and inappropriate non-targets impaired performance (see Fig. 5.3). Thus, when attention needed to be divided between the two ears, there was clear evidence that the non-target words were processed for meaning. On the other hand, when subjects knew that all the targets would be presented to the left ear, the type of non-target word presented at the same time had no effect on target detection. This suggests that non-targets were not processed for meaning in this focused attention condition, and that the amount of processing received by non-target stimuli is only as much as is necessary to perform the experimental task.

Section summary

The analysis of unattended auditory inputs can be greater than was originally thought. However, the full analysis theory of Deutsch and Deutsch (1963) seems rather dubious in view of the findings

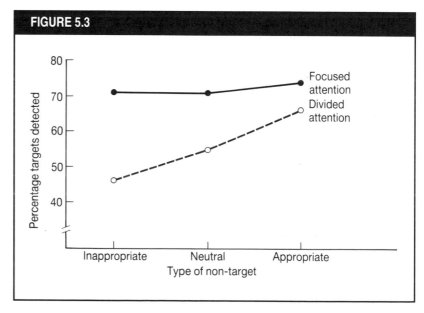

FIGURE 5.3

Effects of attention condition (divided vs. focused) and of type of non-target on target detection. Data from Johnston and Wilson (1980).

obtained by Treisman and Geffen (1967) and Treisman and Riley (1969). The most reasonable account of focused attention may be along the lines suggested by Treisman (1964), with reduced or attenuated processing of sources of information outside focal attention. The extent of such processing is probably flexible, being determined in part by task demands (Johnston & Heinz, 1978).

FOCUSED VISUAL ATTENTION

Zoom-lens model

It has often been argued that focused visual attention is rather like a spotlight: everything within a relatively small area can be seen clearly, but it is much more difficult to see anything not falling within the beam of the spotlight. According to the zoom-lens model proposed by Eriksen (1990), there is an attentional spotlight, but this spotlight has an adjustable beam so that the area covered by the beam can be increased or decreased.

Relevant evidence was obtained by LaBerge (1983). In his study, five-letter words were presented. A probe requiring a rapid response was occasionally presented instead of, or immediately after, the word. The probe could appear in the spatial position of any of the five letters of the word. In one condition, an attempt was made to focus the subjects' attention on the middle letter of the five-letter word by asking them to categorise that letter. In another condition, the subjects were required to categorise the entire word. It was expected that this would lead the subjects to adopt a broader attentional beam.

The findings on speed of detection of the probe are shown in Fig. 5.4. In order to interpret them, we need to make the reasonable assumption that the probe was responded to faster when it fell within the central attentional beam than when it did not. On this assumption, the results indicate that the attentional spotlight can have either a very narrow (letter task) or rather broad beam (word task).

It is attractively simple to regard focused visual attention in terms of a zoom lens or variable-beam spotlight, but there is increasing evidence that the analogy is over-simplified. For example, consider a study by Juola, Bowhuis, Cooper, and Warner (1991). A target letter (L or R) which had to be identified was presented in one of three rings having the same centre: an inner, a middle, and an outer ring (see Fig. 5.5). The subjects fixated the centre of the display, and were given a cue which mostly provided accurate information as to the ring in which the target would be presented. If visual

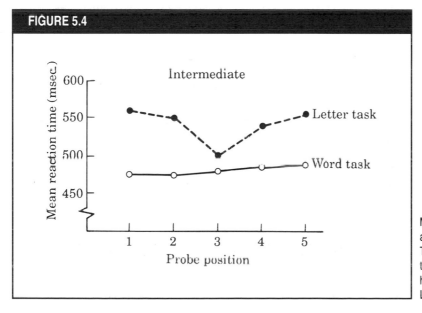

FIGURE 5.4

Mean reaction time to the probe as a function of probe position. The probe was presented at the time that a letter string would have been presented. Data from LaBerge (1983).

An indication of the stimulus display used by Juola et al. (1991).

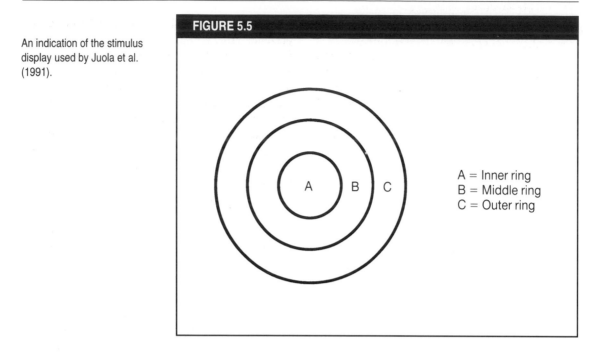

FIGURE 5.5

A = Inner ring
B = Middle ring
C = Outer ring

attention is like a spotlight, then it would be expected that speed and accuracy of performance would be greatest for targets presented in the inner ring. In fact, performance was best when the target appeared in the ring that had been cued. This suggests that visual attention could be allocated in an O-shaped pattern to include only the outer or the middle ring.

Evidence that is even more difficult to reconcile with the zoom-lens model was reported by Neisser and Becklen (1975). They superimposed two moving scenes on top of each other, and found that their subjects could readily attend to one scene while ignoring the other. The zoom-lens model proposes that the focus of attention is a given area in visual space, but these findings suggest that this is sometimes incorrect. It appears that objects within the visual environment can be the major focus of visual attention.

Section summary

There is some mileage in the zoom-lens model: attention is typically focused on only part of the visual environment, and the area covered by focal attention is variable. However, the evidence suggests that focused visual attention operates in a more flexible fashion than is envisaged within the zoom-lens model. Attention does not have to be focused on an entire area in visual space, but can be directed to certain objects within that area or to certain significant parts of that area.

Unattended visual stimuli

We saw earlier in the chapter that there is generally rather limited processing of unattended auditory stimuli. What happens to unattended visual stimuli? Johnston and Dark (1986, p.56) reviewed the relevant evidence, and came to the following conclusion: "Stimuli outside the spatial focus of attention undergo little or no semantic processing." In contrast, Allport (1989) argued that the meaning of unattended visual stimuli is generally processed. In order to understand how these different conclusions were arrived at, it is worth considering some of the evidence.

Francolini and Egeth (1980) reported findings that are consistent with the conclusions of Johnston and Dark (1986). Subjects were presented with a circular array of red and black letters or numerals. Their task was to count the number of red items and to ignore the black items. Performance speed was reduced when the red items consisted of numerals conflicting with the answer, but there was no distraction effect from the black items. These findings suggest that there was little or no processing of the to-be-ignored black items.

Subsequent research by Driver (1989) contradicted this conclusion. He used the same task as Francolini and Egeth (1980), but focused on whether or not conflicting numerical values had been presented on the previous trial. He found that there was an interference effect, and that this interference effect was of comparable size from red and black items. The fact that performance on trial *n* was affected by the numerical values of distracting items presented on trial *n* − 1 means that those items must have been processed.

Driver's (1989) findings demonstrate the phenomenon of *negative priming*. In this phenomenon, the processing of a target stimulus is inhibited if that stimulus or one very similar to it was an unattended or distracting stimulus on the previous trial. For example, Tipper and Driver (1988) found that having a picture as the unattended stimulus on one trial slowed the processing of the corresponding word on the next trial. The details of the processes producing this negative priming effect are not known, but it is clear that the meaning of the unattended picture must have been processed.

Section summary

The fact that processing and responding to attended visual stimuli are often unaffected by the nature of distracting or unattended stimuli has suggested to many theorists that there is very little processing of unattended stimuli. However, the phenomenon of negative priming indicates that this conclusion is unwarranted. It is probable that there is generally at least some processing of the meaning of unattended visual stimuli, but that this processing often does not disrupt responding to attended stimuli.

Visual search

So far we have considered some of the general characteristics of focused visual attention. In so doing, we have not discussed in detail the various underlying processes involved in focused attention. Some progress in identifying these processes has been obtained from the use of visual search tasks. In such tasks, subjects are presented with a visual display containing a variable number of stimuli. A target stimulus (e.g. red letter G) is present on half of the trials and absent on the other half, and the subjects' task is to decide as rapidly as possible whether the target is present in the display. The effects of variations in the nature of the target and the nature of the non-targets on the speed of response are observed.

Perhaps the most influential theory based on visual search is the *feature integration theory* proposed by Treisman (1988, 1992). This theory has been criticised by various theorists including Duncan and Humphreys (1989). Duncan and Humphreys (1992) proposed an alternative explanation of the visual search findings known as *attentional engagement theory*. Both of these theories will now be discussed.

Feature integration theory

Treisman (1988) drew a distinction between the features of objects (e.g. colour, size, lines of particular orientation) and the objects themselves. Her theory based on this distinction includes the following assumptions:

• There is a rapid initial parallel process in which the visual features of objects in the environment are processed together; this is not dependent on attention.
• There is a second, serial process in which features are combined to form objects (e.g. a large, red chair).
• The second serial process is slower than the initial parallel process, especially when several stimuli need to be processed.
• Features can be combined by focused attending to the location of the object, in which case focused attention provides the "glue" that constructs unitary objects from the available features.
• Feature combination can also be influenced by stored knowledge (e.g. bananas are usually yellow).
• In the absence of focused attention or relevant stored knowledge, features will be combined from different objects in a random fashion, producing what are known as "illusory conjunctions".

Treisman and Gelade (1980) had previously obtained apparently good support for this feature integration theory using a visual search task. In one of their experiments, subjects searched for a target in a visual display containing between 1 and 30 items. The target was either an object (a green letter T), or it consisted of a single feature (either a blue letter or an S). When the target was a green letter T, all of the non-targets shared one feature with the target (i.e. they were either the brown letter T or the green letter X). It was predicted that focused attention would be needed to detect the former target (because it is defined by a combination of features), but that the latter target could be detected in the absence of focal attention because it is defined by a single feature.

The findings were as predicted (see Fig. 5.6). The number of items in the visual display had a substantial effect on detection speed when the target was defined by a combination or conjunction of features (i.e. a green letter T), presumably because focused attention was required. However, there was practically no effect of display size when the target was defined by a single feature (i.e. a blue letter or an S).

According to the feature integration theory, lack of focused attention produces a state of affairs in which the features of different objects are processed but remain "unglued". This should lead to the random combination of features and illusory conjunctions referred to earlier. This prediction was confirmed by Treisman and Schmidt (1982). They obtained numerous illusory conjunctions when attention was widely distributed, but not when the stimuli were presented to focal attention.

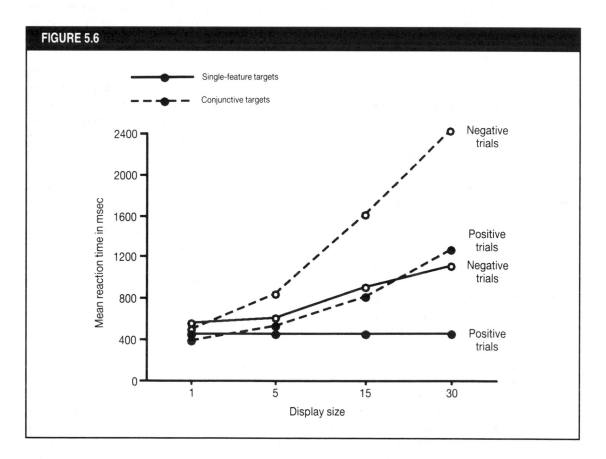

FIGURE 5.6

Performance speed on a detection task as a function of target definition (conjunctive vs. single feature) and display size. Adapted from Treisman and Gelade (1980).

Treisman has modified her feature integration theory in recent years. For example, Treisman and Sato (1990) argued that the degree of similarity between the target and the distractors is a factor influencing visual search time. They claimed (with supporting evidence) that visual search for an object target defined by more than one feature is typically limited to those distractors possessing at least one of the features of the target. For example, if you were looking for a blue circle in a display containing blue triangles, red circles, and red triangles, then you would ignore red triangles. This contrasts with the views of Treisman and Gelade (1980), who argued that none of the stimuli would be ignored in such circumstances.

Attentional engagement theory

Duncan and Humphreys (1989, 1992) have proposed an attentional engagement theory of visual attention. They assumed that the time taken to detect a target in a visual display depends on two major factors:

1. Search times will be slower when the similarity between the target and the non-targets is increased.
2. Search times will be slower when there is reduced similarity among non-targets. Thus, the slowest search times are obtained when non-targets are dissimilar to each other, but similar to the target.

Some evidence that visual search can be very rapid when the non targets are all the same was obtained by Humphreys, Riddoch, and Quinlan (1985). Subjects were asked to detect a target of an inverted T against a background of Ts the right way up. The time taken to detect the target was scarcely affected by the number of non-targets, presumably because they were all the same. According to feature integration theory, the fact that the target was defined by a combination or conjunction of features (i.e. a vertical line and a horizontal line) means that visual search should have been slow and much affected by the number of non-targets.

At a more explanatory level, the following assumptions are incorporated into the attentional engagement theory:

- There is an initial parallel stage of perceptual segmentation and analysis involving all of the visual items together.
- There is a subsequent stage of processing in which selected information is entered into visual short-term memory; this corresponds to selective attention.
- The speed of visual search depends on how easily the target item enters visual short-term memory.
- Visual items that are well matched to the description of the target item are most likely to be selected for visual short-term memory; thus, non-targets that are similar to the target slow the search process.
- Visual items that are perceptually grouped (e.g. because they are very similar) will tend to be selected (or rejected) together for visual short-term memory; thus, dissimilar non-targets cannot be rejected together and this slows the search process.

Some of the differences between this theory and Treisman's feature integration theory can be seen if we reconsider the study by Treisman and Gelade (1980). It will be remembered that there were long search times to detect a green letter T in a display containing an approximately equal number of brown Ts and green Xs (see Fig. 5.6), and Treisman and Gelade (1980) argued that this occurred because of the need for focal attention to produce the necessary conjunction of features. In contrast, Duncan and Humphreys (1989, 1992) claimed that the slow performance resulted from the high similarity between the target and non-target stimuli (all of the latter possessed one of the features of the target stimulus) and the dissimilarity among the non-target stimuli (the two different non-targets did not share any features).

Section summary

The speed of visual search appears to depend on a number of factors. It is likely that the similarity between target and non-targets (accepted by Duncan and Humphreys, and by Treisman), the degree of similarity among non-targets (emphasised by Duncan and Humphreys), and conjunction of features (emphasised by Treisman) all affect visual search. There are indications that the differences between feature integration theory and attentional engagement theory are becoming less as the theories are modified. As Treisman (1992, p.589) concluded: "There is substantial convergence between the respective theories, but it still appears that conjoining features poses a special problem that cannot be explained solely by the grouping and matching mechanisms of Duncan and Humphreys."

Disorders of visual attention: Cognitive neuropsychology

Michael Posner (e.g. Posner & Petersen, 1990) proposed a theoretical framework within which various disorders of visual attention in brain-damaged patients can be understood. In essence, he argued that at least three separate abilities are involved in visual attention:

- The ability to *disengage* attention from a given visual stimulus.
- The ability to *shift* attention from one target stimulus to another.
- The ability to *engage* attention on a new visual stimulus.

Disengagment of attention

Problems with the disengagement of attention have been studied in patients suffering from what is known as *unilateral visual neglect.* The most common form of unilateral visual neglect is when patients with damage to the right hemisphere neglect or ignore visual stimuli in the left side of space. The problem is not simply one of being unable to see what is presented to the affected side because such patients can also show neglect on tasks involving images rather than visual perception (Bisiach & Luzzati, 1978).

Posner, Walker, Friedrich, and Rafal (1984) carried out a study on patients with unilateral visual neglect in which cues to the locations of forthcoming targets were presented. The patients generally coped reasonably well with this task, even when the cue and the target were both presented to the impaired visual field. However, there was one major exception: when the cue was presented to the unimpaired visual field and the target was presented to the impaired visual field,

the patients' performance was extremely poor. These findings suggest that the patients found it particularly difficult to disengage their attention from visual stimuli presented to the unimpaired side of visual space.

Patients with unilateral visual neglect have suffered damage to the parietal region of the brain (Posner et al., 1984). A different kind of evidence that the parietal area is important in attention was obtained by Petersen, Corbetta, Miezin, and Shulman (1994), who made use of PET scans (see Chapter 1). They used a variety of tasks, and discovered that there was generally considerable activation within the parietal area when attention shifted from one spatial location to another.

Problems with disengaging attention are also found in patients suffering from *simultanagnosia*. In this condition, only one object (out of two or more) can be seen at any one time, even when the objects are close together in the visual field. As most of these patients have full visual fields, it seems that the attended visual object exerts a "hold" on attention that makes disengagement difficult. However, there is evidence that neglected stimuli are processed to some extent. For example, Coslett and Saffran (1991) observed strong effects of semantic relatedness between two briefly presented words in a patient with simultanagnosia.

Shifting of attention

Posner, Rafal, Choate, and Vaughan (1985) investigated problems of shifting attention by studying patients suffering from *progressive supranuclear palsy*. Such patients have damage to the midbrain. As a consequence of this brain damage, they find it very difficult to make voluntary eye movements, especially in the vertical direction. These patients were given the task of responding to visual targets, and there were sometimes cues to the locations of forthcoming targets. There was a short, intermediate, or long interval between the cue and the target. At all intervals, valid cues (i.e. cues providing accurate information about target location) speeded up responding to the targets when the targets were presented to the left or the right of the cue. However, only cues at the long interval facilitated responding when the targets were presented above or below the cues. These findings suggest that the patients had difficulty in shifting their attention in the vertical direction.

Attentional deficits apparently associated with shifting of attention have been studied in patients with *Balint's syndrome*. These patients, who have damage to the occipital-parietal area, have difficulty in reaching for stimuli using visual guidance. Humphreys and Riddoch (1993) presented two Balint's patients with 32 circles in a display; the circles were either all the same colour, or half were one colour and the other half a different colour. The circles were either close together or spaced, and the subjects' task was to decide whether they were all the same colour. On trials where there were circles of two colours, one of the patients (SA) performed much better when the circles were close together than when they were spaced (79% vs. 62%, respectively), whereas the other patient (SP) performed equivalently in the close together and spaced conditions (62% vs. 59%). Apparently some patients with Balint's syndrome (e.g. SA) find it difficult to shift attention appropriately within the visual field.

Engaging attention
Rafal and Posner (1987) investigated problems of engaging attention in patients with damage to the pulvinar nucleus of the thalamus. These patients were given the task of responding to visual targets that were preceded by cues. The patients responded faster when the cues were valid than when the cues were invalid, regardless of whether the target stimulus was presented to the same side as the brain damage or to the opposite side. However, they responded rather slowly following both kinds of cues when the target stimulus was presented to the side of the visual field opposite to that of the brain damage. According to Rafal and Posner (1987), these findings reflect a particular problem the patients have in engaging attention to such stimuli.

Additional evidence that the pulvinar nucleus of the thalamus is involved in controlling focused attention was obtained by LaBerge and Buchsbaum (1990). They took positron emission tomography (PET) measurements (see Chapter 1) during an attention task, and discovered that there was increased blood flow in the pulvinar nucleus when

subjects were instructed to ignore a given stimulus. Thus, the pulvinar nucleus appears to be involved in preventing attention from being focused on an unwanted stimulus as well as in directing attention to significant stimuli.

Section summary
As Posner and Petersen (1990, p.28) pointed out, the findings indicate that "the parietal lobe first disengages attention from its present focus, then the midbrain area acts to move the index of attention to the area of the target, and the pulvinar nucleus is involved in reading out data from the indexed locations". At a more theoretical level, the major implication is that the attentional system is considerably more complex than has been assumed by most theorists. As Allport (1989, p.644) expressed it, "spatial attention is a distributed function in which many functionally differentiated structures participate, rather than a function controlled uniquely by a single centre".

DIVIDED ATTENTION

What happens when people try to do two things at once? The answer obviously depends on the nature of the two "things". Sometimes the attempt is successful, as when an experienced motorist drives a car and holds a conversation at the same time, or a tennis player notes the position of his or her opponent while running at speed and preparing to make a stroke. At other times, as when someone tries to rub their stomach with one hand while patting their head with the other, there can be a complete disruption of performance. In this section of the chapter, we will be concerned with some of the factors determining how well two tasks can be performed concurrently (i.e. at the same time).

Hampson (1989) made the important point that focused and divided attention are more similar in some ways than one might have imagined. Factors such as use of different modalities which facilitate focused or selective attention generally also make divided attention easier. According to Hampson (1989, p.267), the reason for this is that "anything which minimises interference between processes, or keeps them 'further apart' will allow them to be dealt with more readily either selectively or together".

At a more theoretical level, the breakdowns of performance often found when two tasks are combined shed light on the limitations of the human information-processing system. It has been assumed by many theorists that such breakdowns reflect the limited capacity of a single multi-purpose central processor or executive that is sometimes simply referred to as "attention". Other theorists are more impressed by our apparent ability to perform two relatively complex tasks at the same time without disruption or interference. Such theorists tend to favour the notion of several specific processing resources, arguing that there will be no interference between two tasks provided that they make use of different processing resources.

More progress has been made at the empirical level than at the theoretical level. It is possible to predict reasonably accurately whether or not two tasks can be combined successfully, but the accounts offered by different theorists are very diverse. Accordingly, we will make a start by discussing some of the factual evidence before moving on to the murkier issue of how the data are to be explained.

Factors determining dual-task performance

Task similarity

When we think of pairs of activities that are performed well together in everyday life, the examples that come to mind usually involve two rather dissimilar activities (e.g. driving and talking; reading and listening to music). There is much evidence that the degree of similarity between two tasks is of great importance. As we saw earlier in the chapter, when people attempt to shadow or repeat back prose passages while learning auditorily presented words, their subsequent recognition-memory performance for the words is at chance level (Allport et al., 1972). However, the same authors found that memory was excellent when the to-be-remembered material consisted of pictures.

There are various kinds of similarity that need to be distinguished. Wickens (1984) reviewed the evidence and concluded that two tasks interfere to the extent that they have the same stimulus modality (e.g. visual or auditory), make use of the same stages of processing (input, internal processing, and output), and rely on related memory codes (e.g. verbal or visual). Response similarity is also important. McLeod (1977) required subjects to perform a continuous tracking task with manual responding at the same time as a tone-identification task. Some of the subjects responded vocally to the tones, whereas others responded with the hand not involved in the tracking task. Performance on the tracking task was worse with high response similarity (manual responses on both tasks) than with low response similarity (manual responses on one task and vocal ones on the other).

Similarity of stimulus modality has probably been investigated most thoroughly. For example, Treisman and Davies (1973) found that two monitoring tasks interfered with each other much more when the stimuli on both tasks were presented in the same sense modality (visual or auditory) than when they were presented in different modalities.

Although it is clear that the extent to which two tasks interfere with each other is a function of their similarity, it is often very difficult to measure similarity. How similar are piano playing and poetry writing, or driving a car and watching a football match? Only when there is a better understanding of the processes involved in the performance of such tasks will sensible answers be forthcoming.

Practice

Common sense suggests that the old saying, "Practice makes perfect", is especially applicable to dual-task performance. For example, learner drivers find it almost impossible to drive and to hold a conversation at the same time, whereas expert drivers find it relatively easy. Support for this commonsensical position was obtained by Spelke, Hirst, and Neisser (1976) in a study on two students called Diane and John. These students received five hours' training a week for four months on a variety of tasks. Their first task was to read short stories for comprehension at the same time as they wrote down words to dictation. They found this very difficult initially, and their reading speed and handwriting both suffered considerably. After six weeks of training, however, they were able to read as rapidly and with as much comprehension when taking dictation as when only reading, and the quality of their handwriting had also improved.

In spite of this impressive dual-task perform-ance, Spelke et al. were still not satisfied. They discovered that Diane and John could recall only 35 out of the thousands of words they had written down at dictation. Even when 20 successive dictated words formed a sentence or came from a single semantic category, the two subjects were unaware of the fact. With further training, however, they learned to write down the names of the categories to which the dictated words belonged while maintaining normal reading speed and comprehension.

Spelke et al. (1976) wondered whether the popular notion that we have limited processing capacity is accurate, basing themselves on the dramatic findings with John and Diane. They observed (1976, p.229): "People's ability to develop skills in specialised situations is so great that it may never be possible to define general limits on cognitive capacity." However, there are alternative ways of interpreting their findings. Perhaps the dictation task was performed rather automatically, and so placed few demands on cognitive capacity, or there might have been a rapid alternation of attention between reading and writing. Hirst et al. (1980) claimed that writing to dictation was not done automatically because the subjects understood what they were writing. They also claimed that reading and dictation could only be performed together with success by the strategy of alternation of attention if the reading material were simple and highly redundant. However, they discovered that most subjects were still able to read and take dictation effectively when less redundant reading matter was used.

It is sometimes claimed that the studies by Spelke et al. (1976) and by Hirst et al. (1980) demonstrate that two complex tasks can be performed together without disruption, but this is

not so. One of the subjects used by Hirst et al. was tested at dictation without reading, and made fewer than half the number of errors that occurred when reading at the same time. Furthermore, the reading task gave the subjects much flexibility in terms of when they attended to the reading matter, and such flexibility means that there may well have some alternation of attention between tasks.

There are other cases of apparently successful performance of two complex tasks, but the requisite skills were always highly practised. Expert pianists can play from seen music while repeating back or shadowing heard speech (Allport et al., 1972), and an expert typist can type and shadow at the same time (Shaffer, 1975). These studies are often regarded as providing evidence of completely successful task combination, but there are signs of interference when the data are inspected closely (Broadbent, 1982).

There are several reasons why practice might facilitate dual-task performance. First, subjects may develop new strategies for performing each of the tasks so as to minimise task interference. Second, the demands that a task makes on attentional or other central resources may be reduced as a function of practice. Third, although a task initially requires the use of several specific processing resources, practice may permit a more economical mode of functioning relying on fewer resources. These possibilities are considered in more detail a little later in the chapter.

Task difficulty

The ability to perform two tasks together undoubtedly depends on their difficulty, but there are several ways in which one task can be more difficult than another one. However, there are several studies showing the expected pattern of results. For example, Sullivan (1976) gave her subjects the two tasks of shadowing an auditory message and detecting target words on a non-shadowed message. When the shadowing task was made more difficult by using a less redundant message, fewer targets were detected on the non-shadowed message.

It has sometimes been assumed that the demands for resources of two tasks when performed together equal the sum of the demands of the two tasks when performed separately. However, the necessity to perform two tasks together often introduces fresh demands of co-ordination and avoidance of interference. Duncan (1979) asked his subjects to respond to closely successive stimuli, one requiring a left-hand response and the other a right-hand response. The relationship between each stimulus and response was either corresponding (i.e. rightmost stimulus calling for response of the rightmost finger) or crossed (e.g. leftmost stimulus calling for response of the rightmost finger). Performance was rather poor when the relationship between stimulus and response was corresponding for one stimulus but crossed for the other. In these circumstances, the subjects were sometimes confused, as indicated by the fact that the errors were largely those expected if the inappropriate stimulus–response relationship had been selected. Thus, the uncertainty caused by mixing two different stimulus–response relationships added a complexity to performance that did not exist when only one of the tasks was performed.

Theoretical accounts of dual-task performance

Several theories of dual-task performance have been proposed over the years, and some of the main theoretical approaches are discussed here. As we will see, there have been theoretical disagreements about the relative importance of general and specific processes in this area. However, we will first of all consider the work of Welford (1952), who provided one of the first systematic attempts to account for dual-task performance.

Bottleneck theories

Welford (1952) argued that there is a bottleneck in the processing system which makes it difficult (or impossible) for two decisions about the appropriate responses for two different stimuli to be made at the same time. Much of the supporting evidence for this theory came from studies of the *psychological refractory period*. In the standard task, there are two stimuli (e.g. two lights) and two responses (e.g. button presses), and the subject's task is to respond to each stimulus as rapidly as possible. When the second stimulus is presented very shortly after the

first stimulus, there is generally a marked slowing of the response to the second stimulus: this is known as the psychological refractory period effect (see Welford, 1952).

Although the existence of this psychological refractory period effect is consistent with the notion of a bottleneck in processing, it could be argued that it occurs because people are not used to having to respond to two immediately successive stimuli. However, Pashler (1993) discussed one of his experiments in which the effect was still observable after more than 10,000 trials of practice. Another objection to the notion that the delay in responding to the second stimulus reflects a bottleneck in processing is that the effect may instead be due to similarity of stimuli and/or similarity of responses.

Pashler (1990) carried out a study to decide between the bottleneck and similarity-based accounts of the psychological refractory period effect. According to the bottleneck theory, the effect should be present even when the two stimuli and the two responses differ considerably. In contrast, the effect should disappear if similarity is crucial to its existence. In one of Pashler's (1990) experiments, the stimuli were a tone requiring a vocal response and a visual letter requiring a button-push response. Some of the subjects were told the order in which the stimuli would be presented, whereas others were not. The findings are shown in Fig. 5.7. In spite of a lack of either stimulus or response similarity, there was a psychological refractory period effect, and it was somewhat greater when the order of the stimuli was known than when it was not. Thus, the findings provided strong support for the bottleneck position.

Earlier in the chapter we considered various studies (e.g. Hirst et al., 1980; Spelke et al., 1976) in which two complex tasks were performed remarkably well together. Such findings make it difficult to argue for the existence of a bottleneck in processing. However, as Pashler (1993) pointed out, studies of the psychological refractory period effect have the considerable advantage that there is very precise assessment of the time taken to respond to any given stimulus. The coarse-grained measures obtained in studies such as those of

FIGURE 5.7

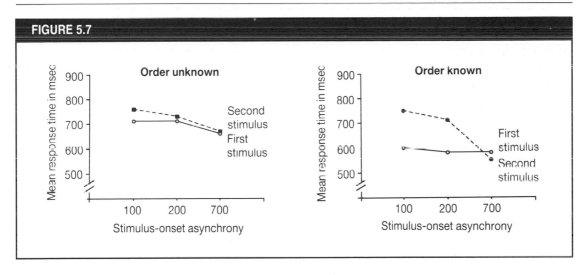

Response times to the first and second stimuli as a function of time between the onset of the stimuli (stimulus–onset asynchrony) and whether or not the order of the stimuli was known beforehand. Adapted from Pashler (1990).

Spelke et al. (1976) and Hirst et al. (1980) may simply be too insensitive to permit detection of bottlenecks.

Even if there is a bottleneck that disrupts dual-task performance, it is clearly not the only relevant factor. Accordingly, we now turn to theoretical accounts that consider other factors such as the effects of practice and similarity.

Central capacity theories

An apparently straightforward way of accounting for many of the dual-task findings is to assume there is some central capacity which can be used flexibly across a wide range of activities (e.g. Johnston & Heinz, 1978). This central processor possesses strictly limited resources, and is sometimes known as attention or effort. The extent to which two tasks can be performed together depends on the demands that each task makes on those resources. If the combined demands of the two tasks do not exceed the total resources of the central capacity, then the two tasks will not interfere with each other. However, if the resources are insufficient to meet the demands placed on them by the two tasks, then performance disruption is inevitable.

According to central capacity theories, the crucial determinant of dual-task performance is the difficulty level of the two tasks, with difficulty being defined in terms of the demands placed on the resources of the central capacity. However, the effects of task difficulty are often swamped by those of similarity between the tasks. For example, Segal and Fusella (1970) combined image construction (visual or auditory) with signal detection (visual or auditory). As can be seen in Fig. 5.8, the auditory image task impaired detection of auditory signals more than the visual task did, suggesting to central capacity theorists that the auditory image task is more demanding than the visual image task. However, the auditory image task was less disruptive than the visual image task when each task was combined with a task requiring detection of visual signals, which suggests exactly the opposite conclusion. In this study, task similarity was clearly a much more important factor than task difficulty.

Many theorists have become so disenchanted with the notion of a central capacity or attentional system that they deny the existence of any such capacity or system. For example, Allport (1989, p.647) argued that the findings "point to a multiplicity of attentional functions, dependent on a multiplicity of specialised subsystems. No one of these subsystems appears uniquely 'central'". According to Allport, it is possible to "explain"

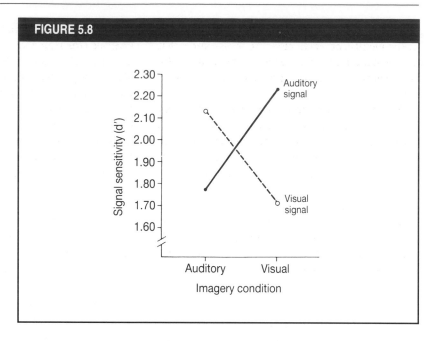

FIGURE 5.8

Sensitivity (d') to auditory and visual signals as a function of concurrent imagery modality (auditory vs. visual). Adapted from Segal and Fusella (1970).

dual-task interference by assuming that the resources of some central capacity have been exceeded, and to account for a lack of interference by assuming that the two tasks did not exceed those resources. However, in the absence of any independent assessment of central processing capacity, this is more like a re-description of the findings rather than a proper explanation.

Modular theories

The views of central capacity theorists can be compared with those of cognitive neuro-psychologists. It was pointed out in Chapter 1 that cognitive neuropsychologists assume that the processing system is modular (i.e. it consists of numerous relatively independent processors or modules). Some of the most convincing evidence for modularity comes from the study of language in brain-damaged patients (see Chapters 12 and 14). This has revealed, for example, that reading is a complex skill involving several rather separate processing mechanisms. If the processing system consists of a large number of specific processing mechanisms, then it is clear why the degree of similarity between two tasks is so important: similar tasks compete for the same specific processing mechanisms or modules, and thus

produce interference, whereas dissimilar tasks involve different modules, and so do not interfere with each other.

Allport (1989) and others have argued that dual-task performance can be accounted for in terms of modules or specific processing resources, but there are significant problems with this theoretical approach. First, there is no consensus regarding the nature or number of these processing modules. Second, and following on from the first point, modular theories cannot at present be falsified. Whatever the findings of any given experiment, it is always possible to account for them after the event by postulating the existence of appropriate specific modules. Third, if there were a substantial number of modules operating in parallel, then there would be substantial problems in terms of co-ordinating their outputs in order to produce coherent behaviour.

Synthesis theories

Other theorists (e.g. Baddeley, 1986; Eysenck, 1982) have opted for a compromise position based on a hierarchical structure. The central processor, central executive, or attention is at the top of the hierarchy, and is involved in the co-ordination and control of behaviour. Below this level are specific processing mechanisms operating relatively independently of each other. It is assumed that control of these specific processing mechanisms by the central processor prevents chaos from developing.

Perhaps the major problem with the notion that there are several specific processing mechanisms and one general processing mechanism is that there does not appear to be a unitary attentional system. As we saw in the earlier discussion of cognitive neuropsychological findings, it appears that somewhat separate mechanisms are involved in disengaging, shifting, and engaging attention. If there is no general processing mechanism, then it may be unrealistic to assume that the processing system possesses a hierarchical structure.

AUTOMATIC PROCESSING

As we saw earlier in the chapter, one of the key phenomena in studies of divided attention is the dramatic improvement that practice often has on performance. The commonest explanation for this phenomenon is that some processing activities become automatic as a result of prolonged practice. Numerous definitions of "automaticity" have been been proposed, but there is reasonable agreement on some criteria:

- Automatic processes are fast.
- Automatic processes do not reduce the capacity for performing other tasks (i.e. they demand zero attention).
- Automatic processes are unavailable to consciousness.
- Automatic processes are unavoidable (i.e. they always occur when an appropriate stimulus is presented, even if that stimulus is outside the field of attention).

As Hampson (1989, p.264) pointed out, "Criteria for automatic processes are easy to find, but hard to satisfy empirically". For example, the requirement that automatic processes should not need attention means that they should have no influence on the concurrent performance of an attention-demanding task. This is rarely the case in practice (see Hampson, 1989, for a review). There are also problems with the unavoidability criterion. The Stroop effect, in which the naming of the colours in which words are printed is slowed down by using colour words (e.g. the word YELLOW printed in red), has often been regarded as involving unavoidable and automatic processing of the colour words. However, Kahneman and Henik (1979) discovered that the Stroop effect was much larger when the distracting information (i.e. the colour name) was in the same location as the to-be-named colour rather than in an adjacent location. This means that the processes producing the Stroop effect are not entirely unavoidable, and thus are not completely automatic in the strict sense of the term.

Relatively few processes are fully automatic in the sense of conforming to the criteria described earlier, with a much larger number of processes being only partially automatic. Later in this section we consider a theoretical approach (that of Norman & Shallice, 1986) which distinguishes between fully automatic and partially automatic processes.

Shiffrin and Schneider's theory

Shiffrin and Schneider (1977) and Schneider and Shiffrin (1977) argued for a theoretical distinction between controlled and automatic processes. According to them:

- Controlled processes are of limited capacity, require attention, and can be used flexibly in changing circumstances.
- Automatic processes suffer no capacity limitations, do not require attention, and are very difficult to modify once they have been learned.

Schneider and Shiffrin tested these ideas in a series of experiments. They made use of a task in which subjects memorised one, two, three, or four letters (the memory set), were then shown a visual display containing one, two, three, or four letters, and finally decided as rapidly as possible whether any one of the items in the visual display was the same as any one of the items in the memory set. In many of their experiments, the crucial manipulation was the kind of mapping used. With consistent mapping, only consonants were used as members of the memory set, and only numbers were used as distractors in the visual display (or vice versa). In other words, if a subject were given only consonants to memorise, then he or she would know that any consonant detected in the visual display must be an item from the memory set. With varied mapping, a mixture of numbers and consonants was used to form the memory set and to provide distractors in the visual display.

There were striking effects of the mapping manipulation (see Fig. 5.9). The numbers of items in the memory set and visual display both greatly affected decision speed in the varied mapping conditions, whereas decision speed was almost unaffected by the sizes of the memory set and visual display in the consistent mapping conditions. According to Schneider and Shiffrin (1977), a controlled search process was used with varied mapping; this involves serial comparisons between each item in the memory set and each item in the visual display until a match is achieved or until all the possible comparisons have been made. In contrast, performance with consistent mapping

reflects the use of automatic processes operating independently and in parallel. According to Schneider and Shiffrin (1977), these automatic processes evolve as a result of years of practice in distinguishing between letters and numbers.

The notion that automatic processes develop through practice was tested by Shiffrin and Schneider (1977). They used consistent mapping with the consonants B to L forming one set and the consonants Q to Z forming the other set. As before, items from only one set were always used in the construction of the memory set, and the distractors in the visual display were all selected from the other set. There was a substantial improvement in performance over a total of 2100 trials, and it appeared to reflect the growth of automatic processes.

The most obvious problem with automatic processes is their lack of flexibility, which is likely to disrupt performance when there is a change in the prevailing circumstances. This was confirmed in the second part of the study just described. The initial 2100 trials with one consistent mapping were followed by a further 2400 trials with the reverse consistent mapping. This reversal of the

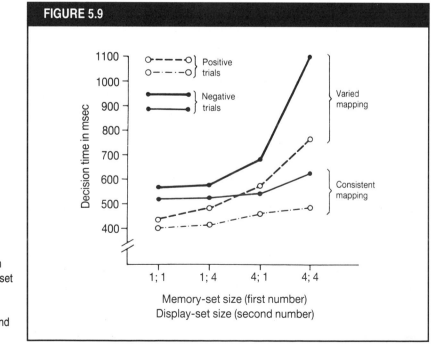

FIGURE 5.9

Response times on a decision task as a function of memory-set size, display-set size, and consistent versus varied mapping. Data from Shiffrin and Schneider (1977).

mapping conditions had a markedly adverse effect on performance; indeed, it took nearly 1000 trials under the new conditions before performance recovered to its level at the very start of the experiment!

Shiffrin and Schneider (1977) conducted further experiments in which subjects initially attempted to locate target letters anywhere in a visual display, but were then instructed to detect targets in one part of the display and to ignore targets elsewhere in the display. Subjects were less able to ignore part of the visual display when they had developed automatic processes than when they had made use of controlled search processes. In general terms, as Eysenck (1982, p.22) pointed out: "Automatic processes function rapidly and in parallel but suffer from inflexibility; controlled processes are flexible and versatile but operate relatively slowly and in a serial fashion."

Evaluation

Shiffrin and Schneider's (1977) theoretical approach is important, but it is open to various criticisms. For example, there is a puzzling discrepancy between theory and data with respect to the identification of automaticity. The theoretical assumption that automatic processes operate in parallel and place no demands on capacity means that there should be a slope of zero (i.e. a horizontal line) in the function relating decision speed to the number of items in the memory set and/or in the visual display when automatic processes are used. In fact, as can be seen in Fig. 5.8, decision speed was slower when the memory set and the visual display both contained several items.

The greatest weakness of Shiffrin and Schneider's approach is that it is descriptive rather than explanatory. The claim that some processes become automatic with practice is uninformative about what is actually happening. Practice may simply lead to a speeding up of the processes involved in performing a task, or it may lead to a dramatic change in the nature of the processes themselves. Cheng (1985) used the term "restructuring" to refer to the latter state of affairs. For example, if you are asked to add ten twos, you could do this in a rather laborious way by adding two and two, and then two to four, and so on.

Alternatively, you could short-circuit the whole process by simply multiplying ten by two. The crucial point is that simply discovering that practice leads to automaticity does not make it clear whether the same processes are being performed more efficiently or whether entirely new processes are being used.

Cheng (1985) argued that most of Shiffrin and Schneider's findings on automaticity were actually based on restructuring. More specifically, she claimed that subjects in the consistent mapping conditions did not really search systematically through the memory set and the visual display looking for a match. If, for example, they knew that any consonant in the visual display had to be an item from the memory set, then they could simply scan the visual display looking for a consonant without any regard to which consonants were actually in the memory set.

Schneider and Shiffrin (1985) admitted that some of their earlier findings could be accounted for if by assuming that subjects in consistent mapping conditions made use of knowledge about the categories being used. However, they pointed that other findings could not be explained in terms of restructuring. For example, the finding that subjects could not ignore part of the visual display after automatic processes had been acquired does not lend itself to a restructuring explanation.

Norman and Shallice's theory

Norman and Shallice (1986) discussed a theory taking account of the distinction between fully automatic and partially automatic processes. Instead of the usual distinction between automatic and attentional or controlled processes, they identified three different levels of functioning:

- Fully automatic processing controlled by schemas (organised plans).
- Partially automatic processing involving contention scheduling without deliberate direction or conscious control; contention scheduling is used to resolve conflicts among schemas.
- Deliberate control by a supervisory attentional system.

According to Norman and Shallice (1986), fully automatic processes occur with very little conscious awareness of the processes involved. Such automatic processes would frequently disrupt behaviour if left entirely to their own devices. As a consequence, there is an automatic conflict resolution process known as contention scheduling, which selects one of the available schemas on the basis of environmental information and current priorities. There is generally more conscious awareness of the partially automatic processes involving contention scheduling than of fully automatic processes. Finally, there is a higher level control mechanism known as the supervisory attentional system. This system is involved in decision making and trouble-shooting, and it permits flexible responding in novel situations. As is discussed in Chapter 6, the supervisory attentional system may well be located in the frontal lobes.

Section summary

The theoretical approach of Norman and Shallice (1986) incorporates the interesting notion that there are two separate control systems: contention scheduling and the supervisory attentional system. This contrasts with the views of many previous theorists that there is a single control system. The approach of Norman and Shallice is preferable, because it provides a more natural explanation for the fact that some processes are fully automatic whereas others are only partially automatic.

Automaticity as memory retrieval

Logan (1988) pointed out that most theories of automaticity do not indicate clearly how automaticity develops through prolonged practice. He tried to fill this gap by making these assumptions:

• Separate memory traces are stored away each time a stimulus is encountered and processed.
• Practice with the same stimulus leads to the storage of increased information about the stimulus, and about what to do with it.
• This increase in the knowledge base with practice permits rapid retrieval of relevant information when the appropriate stimulus is presented.

• "Automaticity is memory retrieval: performance is automatic when it is based on a single-step direct-access retrieval of past solutions from memory" (Logan, 1988, p.493).
• In the absence of practice, responding to a stimulus requires thought and the application of rules; after prolonged practice, the appropriate response is stored in memory and can be accessed very rapidly.

These theoretical views make coherent sense of many of the characteristics of automaticity. Automatic processes are fast because they require only the retrieval of "past solutions" from long-term memory. Automatic processes have little or no effect on the processing capacity available to perform other tasks because the retrieval of heavily over-learned information is relatively effortless. Finally, there is no conscious awareness of automatic processes because no significant processes intervene between the presentation of a stimulus and the retrieval of the appropriate response.

In sum, Logan (1988, p.519) encapsulated his theoretical position in the following way: "Novice performance is limited by a lack of knowledge rather than by a lack of resources … Only the knowledge base changes with practice." Logan is probably right in his basic assumption that an understanding of automatic, expert performance will require detailed consideration of the knowledge acquired with practice, rather than simply the changes in processing which occur.

ACTION SLIPS

Some of the theoretical notions considered so far in this chapter are relevant to an understanding of action slips (the performance of actions that were not intended). At the most general level, it seems clear that attentional failures usually underlie action slips, and this is recognised at a commonsensical level in the notion of "absent-mindedness". However, there are several different kinds of action slips, and each one may require its own detailed explanation.

Diary studies

One of the main ways of studying action slips is to collect numerous examples via diary studies. Sellen and Norman (1992, p.317) gave the following examples of action slips from a diary study: "I planned to call my sister Angela but instead called Agnes (they are twins). What I heard myself say did not match what I was thinking," and "I wanted to turn on the radio but walked past it and put my hand on the telephone receiver instead. I went to pick up the phone and I couldn't figure out why."

In one diary study, Reason (1979) asked 35 people to keep diaries of their action slips over a two-week period. Over 400 action slips were reported, most of which belonged to five major categories. Forty percent of the slips involved *storage failures*, in which intentions and actions were either forgotten or recalled incorrectly. Reason (1979, p.74) quoted the following example of a storage failure: "I started to pour a second kettle of boiling water into a teapot of freshly made tea. I had no recollection of having just made it."

A further 20% of the errors were *test failures* in which the progress of a planned sequence was not monitored sufficiently at crucial junctures. An illustrative test failure from one person's diary went as follows (Reason, 1979, p.73): "I meant to get my car out, but as I passed through the back porch on my way to the garage I stopped to put on my wellington boots and gardening jacket as if to work in the garden." *Subroutine failures* accounted for a further 18% of the errors; these involved insertions, omissions, or re-orderings of the component stages in an action sequence. Reason (1979, p.73) gave the following example of this type of error: "I sat down to do some work and before starting to write I put my hand up to my face to take my glasses off, but my fingers snapped together rather abruptly because I hadn't been wearing them in the first place."

There were relatively few examples of action slips belonging to the two remaining categories of *discrimination failures* (11%) and *programme assembly failures* (5%). The former category consisted of failures to discriminate between objects (e.g. mistaking shaving cream for toothpaste), and the latter category consisted of inappropriate combinations of actions (e.g. Reason, 1979, p.72): "I unwrapped a sweet, put the paper in my mouth, and threw the sweet into the waste bucket."

Evaluation

It would be unwise to attach much significance to the percentages of the various kinds of action slips for a number of reasons. First, the figures are based on those action slips that were detected, and we simply do not know how many cases of each kind of slips went undetected. Second, the number of occurrences of any particular kind of action slip is meaningful only when we know the number of occasions on which that kind of slip might have occurred but did not. Thus, the small number of discrimination failures may reflect either good discrimination or a relative lack of situations requiring anything approaching a fine discrimination.

Another issue is that two action slips may appear to be superficially similar, and so be categorised together, even though the underlying mechanisms are different. For example, Grudin (1983) conducted videotape analyses of substitution errors in typing involving striking the key adjacent to the intended key. Some of these substitution errors involved the correct finger moving in the wrong direction, whereas others involved an incorrect key being pressed by the finger that normally strikes it. According to Grudin (1983), the former kind of error is due to faulty execution of an action, whereas the latter is due to faulty assignment of the finger. We would need more information than is generally available in most diary studies to identify such subtle differences in underlying processes.

Laboratory studies of action slips

Several techniques have been used to produce action slips in laboratory conditions. What is often done is to provide a misleading context which increases the activation of an incorrect response at the expense of the correct response. Reason (1992) discussed a study of the "oak–yolk" effect illustrating this approach. Some subjects were asked to respond as rapidly as possible to a series of questions (the most frequent answers are given):

Q: What do we call the tree that grows from acorns?
A: Oak.
Q: What do we call a funny story?
A: Joke.
Q: What sound does a frog make?
A: Croak.
Q: What is Pepsi's major competitor?
A: Coke.
Q: What is another word for cape?
A: Cloak.
Q: What do you call the white of an egg?
A: Yolk.

The correct answer to the last question is "albumen". However, 85% of these subjects gave the wrong answer because it rhymed with the answers to the previous questions. In contrast, of those subjects only asked the last question, a mere 5% responded "yolk".

Although it is possible to produce large numbers of action slips under laboratory conditions, it is not clear that such slips resemble those typically found under naturalistic conditions. As Sellen and Norman (1992, p.334) pointed out, many naturally occurring action slips occur:

> ... when a person is internally preoccupied or distracted, when both the intended actions and the wrong actions are automatic, and when one is doing familiar tasks in familiar surroundings. Laboratory situations offer completely the opposite conditions. Typically, subjects are given an unfamiliar, highly contrived task to accomplish in a strange environment. Most subjects arrive motivated to perform well and ... are not given to internal preoccupation ... In short, the typical laboratory environment is possibly the least likely place where we are likely to see truly spontaneous, absent-minded errors.

Theories of action slips

At a general level, most theorists (e.g. Reason, 1992; Sellen & Norman, 1992) have assumed that action slips occur in part because there are two modes of control:

- An automatic mode, in which motor performance is controlled by schemas or organised plans; the schema that determines performance is the strongest available one.
- A conscious control mode based on some central processor or attentional system; it can oversee and override the automatic control mode.

Each mode of control has its own advantages and disadvantages. Automatic control is fast and it permits valuable attentional resources to be devoted to other processing activities. However, automatic control is relatively inflexible, and action slips occur when there is undue reliance on this mode of control. Conscious control has the advantages that it is less prone to error than automatic control and it responds flexibly to environmental changes. However, it operates relatively slowly, and is an effortful process.

It follows from this theoretical analysis that action slips occur when an individual is in the automatic mode of control and the strongest available schema or motor programme is not appropriate. The involvement of the automatic mode of control can be seen in many of Reason's (1979) action slips. One common type of action slip involves repeating an action unnecessarily because the first action has been forgotten (e.g. attempting to start a car that has already started, or brushing one's teeth twice in quick succession). We know from studies in which listeners attend to one message and repeat it back while ignoring a second message presented at the same time, that unattended information is held very briefly and then forgotten. When the initial starting of a car or brushing one's teeth occurs in the automatic mode of control, it would be predicted that subsequent memory for what has been done should be extremely poor, and so the action would often be repeated.

Sub-routine failures occur when a number of distinct motor programmes need to be run off in turn. Although each motor programme can be carried out without use of the conscious mode of control, a switch to that mode is essential at certain points in the sequence of actions, especially when a given situation is common to two or more motor programmes, and the strongest available motor programme is inappropriate. The person who put on his gardening clothes instead of getting the car out exemplifies the way in which strong but unplanned actions can occur in the absence of attentional control.

Schema theory

A more detailed theory was proposed by Norman (1981) and by Sellen and Norman (1992). According to them, actions are determined by hierarchically organised schemas or organised plans. The highest-level schema represents the overall intention or goal (e.g. buying a present), and the lower-level schemas correspond to the actions involved in accomplishing that intention (e.g. taking money out of the bank; taking the train to the nearest shopping centre). A schema determines action when its level of activation is sufficiently high and when the appropriate triggering conditions exist (e.g. getting into the train when it stops at the station). The activation level of schemas is determined by current intentions and by the immediate environmental situation.

According to this schema model, action slips occur for various reasons:

- Errors in the formation of an intention.
- Faulty activation of a schema, leading to activation of the wrong schema or to loss of activation in the correct schema.
- Faulty triggering of active schemas, leading to action being determined by the wrong schema.

Many of the action slips recorded by Reason (1979) can be related to this theoretical framework. For example, discrimination failures can lead to errors in the formation of an intention, and storage failures for intentions can produce faulty triggering of active schemas.

Evaluation

One of the positive characteristics of recent theories is the notion that errors or action slips should not be regarded as special events produced by their own mechanisms; rather, they emerge from the interplay of conscious and automatic control, and are thus "the normal by-products of the design of the human action system" (Sellen & Norman,

1992, p. 318). On the negative side, the notion that behaviour is determined by the automatic or conscious mode of control is rather simplistic. As we saw earlier in the chapter, there are considerable doubts about the notion of automatic processing, and it is improbable that there is a unitary attentional system. More needs to be discovered about the factors determining which mode of control will dominate. It is correctly predicted by contemporary theory that action slips should occur most frequently with highly practised activities, because it is under such circumstances that the automatic mode of control has the greatest probability of being used. However, the incidence of action slips is undoubtedly much greater with actions that are perceived to be of minor importance than those regarded as very important. For example, many circus performers carry out well-practised actions, but the danger element ensures that they make minimal use of the automatic mode of control. It is not clear that recent theories are equipped to explain such phenomena.

Behavioural efficiency

It might be argued that people would function more efficiently if they placed less reliance on relatively automatic processes and more on the central processor. However, such an argument is suspect because automated activities can sometimes be disrupted if too much attention is paid to them. For example, it can become more difficult to walk down a steep spiral staircase if attention is paid to the leg movements involved. Moreover, Reason's diarists produced an average of only one action slip per day, which does not indicate that their usual processing strategies were ineffective. Indeed, most people seem to alternate between the automatic and attention-based modes of control very efficiently. The optimal strategy involves very frequent shifts from one mode of control to the other, and it is noteworthy that these shifts are performed with great success for the most part.

Action slips are the consequences of a failure to shift from automatic to attention-based control at the right time. Although they are theoretically important, action slips usually have a minimally disruptive effect on everyday life. However, there may be some exceptions, such as absent-minded professors who focus on their own profound inner thoughts rather than on the world around them!

Section summary

Action slips (i.e. the performance of actions that were not intended) have been investigated by means of diary studies in which subjects keep daily records of any slips they make. Various categories of action slip have been identified, but they all typically involve highly practised activities. Highly practised skills mostly do not require detailed attentional monitoring except at critical decision points. Failures of attention at such decision points cause many action slips. Failure to remember what was done a few seconds previously is responsible for many other action slips.

EVALUATION OF THEORIES OF ATTENTION

Attention: Unitary or multiple systems?

Most research has been based on the notion that there is a single, limited-capacity, attentional system. So far as focused attention tasks are concerned, the limitations of this system allegedly produce bottlenecks in processing. So far as divided attention tasks are concerned, attentional limitations often prevent successful performance of two tasks together, and lead to the development of automatic processes that are not reliant on attentional capacity.

One of the reasons for the long-lasting popularity of the view that attention is unitary (i.e. there is a single system) is that it fits well with introspective evidence. It seems as if we have a single attentional system which can (in the visual modality) be directed like a variable-beam spotlight to some part of the environment. However, this view is wrong. As was discussed earlier in the chapter, Posner and Petersen (1990) have identified three separate attentional processes: disengagement of attention from a stimulus; shifting of attention from one stimulus to another; and engagement of attention on a new stimulus.

The fact that attention is not unitary has grave implications for most theory and research on attention. The notion that any given process either requires attention or does not (i.e. is automatic) is clearly a drastic over-simplification if there are a number of different attentional processes. In similar fashion, it may not be sensible to ask whether attentional selection occurs early or late in processing if there is no unitary attentional system. In the words of Allport (1993, pp.203–204):

There is no one uniform function, or mental operation (in general, no one causal mechanism), to which all so-called attentional phenomena can be attributed ... It seems no more plausible that there should be one unique mechanism, or computational resource, as the causal basis of all attentional phenomena than that there should be a unitary causal basis of thought, or perception, or of any other traditional category of folk psychology ... Reference to attention (or to the central executive, or even to the anterior attention system) as an unspecified causal mechanism explains nothing.

Functions of attention

A major limitation of most theories of attention, and the research to which they have give rise, is that the functions of attention receive little consideration. In most research, what subjects attend to is determined by the experimental instructions. In the real world, however, what we attend to is determined in large measure by our motivational states and by the goal we are currently pursuing. This point is emphasised by Allport (1989, p.664): "What is important to recognise ... is not the location of some imaginary boundary between the provinces of attention and motivation but, to the contrary, their essential inter-dependence."

Concern with the functions of attention suggests that attention theorists may need to change the focus of their research. For example, Allport (1989,

1993) identified the following (relatively un-investigated) issues as being of major importance:

- Segmentation of different parallel processing streams.
- Priority assignment among multiple goals.
- Co-ordination between sensory input and action: selection for action.

CHAPTER SUMMARY

The concept of "attention" is generally used in connection with either selective processing or mental effort and concentration. Selective attention has been investigated in studies of focused attention, in which the subject's task is to respond to one stimulus (the attended stimulus) and to ignore the other stimulus (the unattended stimulus). The issue of what happens to the unattended stimulus has been investigated in the auditory and visual modalities. Studies in the auditory modality suggest there is typically some processing of unattended stimuli, with the amount of such processing varying as a function of how easy it is to discriminate between the attended and unattended stimuli. Similar findings have been obtained when focused attention has been investigated in the visual modality.

Visual attention has been compared to a spotlight with an adjustable beam and to a zoom lens. However, although such analogies are intuitively appealing, there appears to be more processing of unattended visual stimuli outside the attentional beam than would be expected. It is also the case that visual attention operates in a more flexible fashion than is implied by the zoom-lens model.

Research by cognitive neuropsychologists has indicated that the attentional system is not unitary. Attention appears to involve at least three different processes (i.e. disengagement of attention from one stimulus; shifting of attention; engagement of attention on to a new stimulus), and brain damage sometimes selectively affects one or other of these processes.

Studies of divided attention involve presenting subjects with two tasks at the same time, with instructions to perform both tasks as well as possible. At an empirical level, the main issue is to identify those factors determining whether two tasks can be performed successfully at the same time. Three of the main factors are task similarity, task difficulty, and practice. Two tasks are performed well together when they are dissimilar, when they are relatively easy, and when they are well practised. In contrast, the worst levels of performance occur when two tasks are highly similar, rather difficult, and have been practised very little.

Several theorists have argued that practice leads to automatic processing. It is generally assumed that automatic processes are fast, that they do not reduce the capacity available for other tasks, and that there is no conscious awareness of them. Logan (1988) proposed that increased knowledge about what to do with different stimuli is stored away with practice, and that automaticity occurs when this information can be retrieved very rapidly.

Absent-mindedness or action slips occur as a result of attentional failure. What often happens is that an individual runs off a sequence of highly practised and over-learned motor programmes. Attentional control is not required during the time each programme is running, but is needed when there is a switch from one programme to another. Failure to attend at these choice points can lead to the wrong motor programme being activated, especially if it is stronger than the appropriate programme. As optimal performance requires very frequent shifts between the presence and absence of attentional control, it is perhaps surprising that action slips are not more prevalent.

Most theory and research on attention are limited in various ways. Many of the major issues studied in attention research become relatively meaningless when it is accepted that attention is not unitary but rather involves multiple systems. Attention is closely bound up with motivation in the real world, but this interdepence of attention and motivation is not reflected in most theories of attention.

FURTHER READING

Allport, A. (1993). Attention and control: Have we been asking the wrong questions? A critical review of twenty-five years. In D. E. Meyer & S. Kornblum (Eds.), *Attention and performance* (Vol. XIV). London: MIT Press. Most of the traditional assumptions of attention theorists are examined and rejected in this thought-provoking chapter.

Kinchla, R. A. (1992). Attention. In M. R. Rosenzweig & L.W. Porter (Eds.), *Annual review of psychology* (Vol. 43). Palo Alto, CA: Annual Reviews Inc. This chapter gives a clear and up-to-date account of research on visual attention.

Walsh, V., & O'Mara, S.M. (1994). A selection on attention: Special issue on attention. *Cognitive Neuropsychology*, *11*, 97–98. This short article introduces an interesting collection of papers on the cognitive neuropsychology of attention (pp.97–263).

6

Memory: Structure and Processes

This chapter and the two chapters that follow it are all concerned with human memory. This chapter and Chapter 8 deal with normal human memory, whereas Chapter 7 deals with the memory problems of brain-damaged patients suffering from amnesia. The main difference between this chapter and Chapter 8 is that laboratory research is the focus of this chapter, with more naturalistic research being the focus of Chapter 8. As we will see, many theoretical issues are relevant to brain-damaged and normal individuals (whether tested in the laboratory or the field).

INTRODUCTION

Theories of memory generally consider both the *structure* of the memory system and the *processes* operating within that structure. Structure refers to the way in which the memory system is organised, and process refers to the activities occurring within the memory system. Nearly all memory theorists agree that structure and process are both important,

but some of them emphasise one or the other in their theoretical formulations.

Learning and memory involve a series of stages. Those processes occurring during the presentation of the learning material are referred to as "encoding". This is the first stage. As a result of encoding, some information is stored within the memory system. Thus, *storage* is the second stage. The third, and final, stage is *retrieval*, which involves recovering or extracting stored information from the memory system.

We have emphasised the importance of the distinctions between structure and process and among encoding, storage, and retrieval. However, it is worth noting that one cannot have structure without process, or retrieval without previous encoding and storage. It is only when processes operate on the essentially passive structures of the memory system that the system becomes active and of use. As far as storage and retrieval are concerned, Tulving and Thomson (1973, p.359) pointed out that: "Only that can be retrieved that has been stored, and ... how it can be retrieved depends on how it was stored."

THE STRUCTURE OF MEMORY

Spatial metaphor

When people think about the mind, they often liken it to a physical space, with memories and ideas as objects contained within that space. Thus, we speak of ideas being in the dark corners or dim recesses of our minds, and of holding ideas in mind. With respect to the processes involved in memory, we talk about storing memories, searching or looking for lost memories, and sometimes of finding them. There appears to be general adherence to what might be called the spatial metaphor. According to advocates of the spatial metaphor:

- Memories are treated as objects stored in specific locations within the mind.
- The retrieval process involves a search through the mind to find specific memories.

The ancient Greek philosopher Plato compared the mind to an aviary, in which the specific memories were represented by birds. Information was remembered when the appropriate bird was caught, whereas an error in recall occurred when the wrong bird was seized. Plato's bird–brain analogy anticipates some recent theories of memory. However, technological advances have led to changes in the precise form of analogy used (Roediger, 1980), with aviaries being replaced by switchboards, gramophones, tape recorders, libraries, conveyor belts, and underground maps. More recently, the workings of human memory have been compared to computer functioning (e.g. Atkinson & Shiffrin, 1968), and it has been proposed that the various memory stores found in computers have their counterparts in the human memory system.

The spatial metaphor suffers from various limitations. For example, it does not explain how it is that we can often decide very rapidly that we do not know something (e.g. that "mantiness" is not an English word; that we have never visited a given city). The most obvious assumptions based on the spatial metaphor are that there would be a thorough memory search in order to ascertain that

the relevant piece of information was not present, and that this search would be relatively time-consuming.

The spatial metaphor implies that the storage system is rather inflexible. If everything we know is stored within a three-dimensional space, then some kinds of information must be stored closer together than others. Perhaps the organisation of information within the memory system resembles a library, with items of similar content being stored together. However, the cataloguing system in most libraries would break down completely if a novel category of books were requested (e.g. books with red covers or with more than 700 pages). In contrast, retrieval from memory demonstrates much greater flexibility than this. In essence, reliance on the spatial metaphor leads to an over-emphasis on the ways in which information is represented in the memory system, and to an under-emphasis on the processes operating on those memorial representations.

There are various alternatives to the spatial metaphor. According to parallel distributed processing theorists, information about an individual or an event is stored in the form of numerous connections among units and is not stored in a single place. Some of the advantages of this approach to human memory will be considered later in this chapter.

Memory stores

Several memory theorists (e.g. Atkinson & Shiffrin, 1968) attempted to describe the basic architecture of the memory system in terms of a number of stores. The various theories overlapped considerably, so that it is possible to discuss the multi-store approach on the basis of the common features of the various theories. Three types of memory store were proposed:

- Sensory stores, each of which holds information very briefly and is modality-specific (limited to one sensory modality).
- A short-term store of very limited capacity.
- A long-term store of essentially unlimited capacity which can hold information over extremely long periods of time.

The basic ingredients of the multi-store model are shown in Fig. 6.1. Information from the environment is initially received by the sensory stores. These stores are modality-specific, with a separate sensory store corresponding to each of the sensory modalities (e.g. vision; hearing). Information is held very briefly in the sensory stores, with some of it being attended to and processed further by the short-term store. In turn, some of the information processed in the short-term store is transferred to the long-term store. Long-term storage of information often depends on rehearsal, with a direct relationship between the amount of rehearsal in the short-term store and the strength of the stored memory trace.

There is clearly a considerable overlap between the areas of attention and memory. Broadbent's (1958) theory of attention (discussed in Chapter 5) was the main precursor of the multi-store approach to memory, and there is a definite resemblance between the notion of a sensory store and his "buffer" store.

The multi-store approach incorporated a number of structural and processing assumptions. The memory stores themselves form the basic structure, and processes such as attention and rehearsal control the flow of information between the memory stores. However, the main emphasis within this approach to memory was on structure.

Sensory stores

Our senses are constantly bombarded with an enormous amount of information, most of which does not receive any attention. If you are sitting down in a chair as you read this, then tactile information from that part of your body in contact with the chair is probably available. However, if you are focusing on what you are reading, then you have probably been unaware of that tactile information until now. Information in all of the sense modalities persists for some time after the end of stimulation, facilitating the task of extracting its most important aspects for further analysis.

Iconic store

Most research has concentrated on the visual and auditory modalities, which are the most important ones in our everyday lives. The classic work on the *visual* or *iconic store* was carried out by Sperling (1960). When he presented a visual array containing three rows of four letters each for 50 milliseconds, he discovered that his subjects could usually report only four or five of the letters. However, they claimed to have seen many more letters than they had been able to report. Sperling (1960) wondered whether this happened because visual information was available for only a brief period of time after the stimulus had been turned off, and so had faded before most of it could be

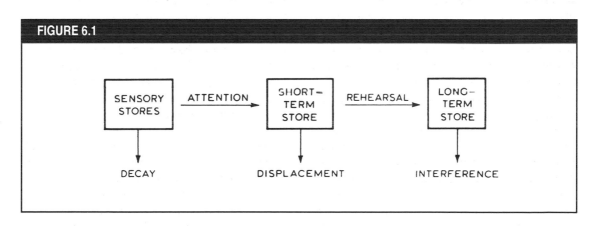

FIGURE 6.1

The multi-store model of memory.

reported. He tested this by using a tone to cue the subjects to report the letters from only one row. Because the three rows were tested at random, it was possible to estimate the total amount of information available immediately after stimulation by multiplying the number of letters recalled by three. When the tone was presented immediately before or after the onset of the visual display, approximately nine letters appeared to be available. However, performance dropped to six letters when the tone was heard 0.3 seconds after the presentation of the display, and it fell to 4.5 letters with an interval of 1 second. These findings suggest that information in visual or iconic storage decays within approximately 0.5 seconds.

How useful is iconic storage? Haber (1983) claimed that the iconic store is irrelevant to normal perception, except possibly when attempting to read in a lightning storm! He argued that "frozen iconic storage of information" may be valuable in the laboratory when you are confronted with very brief presentations of single stimuli, but that similar conditions practically never occur normally. In the real world, the icon formed from one visual fixation would be rapidly masked by the next fixation, and so could not assist perception. In fact, Haber is quite mistaken. He assumed that the icon is created at the offset of a visual stimulus, whereas it is actually created at its onset (Coltheart, 1983a). Thus, even with a continuously changing visual world, there is plenty of opportunity for iconic information to be used. Indeed, the mechanisms responsible for visual perception invariably operate on the icon rather than directly on the visual environment. Thus, the iconic store is an integral part of visual perception, not a laboratory curiosity.

Echoic store
There is considerable evidence for a transient store in the auditory modality known as the *echoic store* consisting of relatively unprocessed auditory input. For example, suppose that someone who is reading a newspaper or book is asked a question. The person addressed will sometimes ask, "What did you say?", and at the same time realise that he or she does know what has been said. This "playback" facility depends on the workings of echoic memory.

A related phenomenon was explored by Treisman (1964), who asked people to shadow (repeat back aloud) the message presented to one ear while ignoring a second message presented to the other ear. When the second or non-shadowed message preceded the shadowed message, the two messages were only recognised as being the same when they were within 2 seconds of each other. This suggests that the temporal duration of unattended auditory information in echoic storage is approximately 2 seconds, although other estimates are somewhat longer (e.g. Darwin, Turvey, & Crowder, 1972).

Short- and long-term stores
The distinction between a short-term and a long-term store is like the one proposed by William James (1890) between primary memory and secondary memory. Primary memory relates to information that remains in consciousness after it has been perceived and forms part of the psychological present. Secondary memory contains information about events that have left consciousness, and are therefore part of the psychological past.

Attempting to remember a telephone number for a few seconds is an everyday example of the use of the *short-term store* or *primary memory*. It illustrates two key characteristics that are usually attributed to this store:

- Extremely limited capacity (only about seven digits can be remembered).
- Fragility of storage, as any distraction usually causes forgetting of the number.

It is difficult to provide an accurate estimate of the capacity of short-term memory, in part because the assumption that there is a single short-term storage capacity is incorrect. As we will see later in the chapter, there are actually various different components of short-term memory, each of which has its own capacity. Historically, there were two major ways in which the capacity of short-term memory was assessed: span measures, and the recency effect in free recall. An example of a span measure is digit span, in which subjects have to repeat back a list of random digits in the correct order as soon as they have been spoken. The span of immediate memory is generally "seven, plus or minus two" whether the units are numbers, letters, or words (Miller, 1956). More specifically, Miller claimed that approximately seven chunks (integrated pieces or units of information) could be held in short-term memory at any one time; for example, "IBM" is one chunk for those familiar with the company name International Business Machines but three chunks for everyone else. However, Simon (1974) discovered that the number of chunks in the span was less with larger chunks (e.g. eight-word phrases) than with smaller chunks (e.g. one-syllable words).

A problem with span measures of short-term storage capacity is that long-term memory may play a part in determining the span. For example, when digit strings are presented for immediate serial recall, and one digit string is surreptitiously repeated several times, performance on the repeated string becomes progressively superior to that on the non-repeated strings (Bower & Winzenz, 1969). This suggests that some information about the repeated digit string is stored in long-term memory.

The recency effect in free recall (recalling the to-be-remembered items in any order) refers to the finding that the last few items in a list are usually much better remembered in immediate recall than are the items from the middle of the list. Counting backwards for only 10 seconds between the end of list presentation and the start of recall virtually eliminates the recency effect but has no effect on recall of the other list words (Glanzer & Cunitz, 1966; see Fig. 6.2). The two or three words susceptible to the recency effect may be in the short-term store at the end of the list presentation, and thus are vulnerable to the interpolated task of counting backwards. However, a complication is that recency effects have also been demonstrated in long-term memory (e.g. Tzeng, 1973).

Span measures indicate a larger short-term memory capacity than do recency effect measures. Probably an important reason for this relates to different patterns of rehearsal. Subjects performing a span task generally attempt to rehearse as many different items as possible, whereas subjects asked to learn a list for free recall concentrate their rehearsal on only a few items at a time. Span and recency effect measures both indicate that the

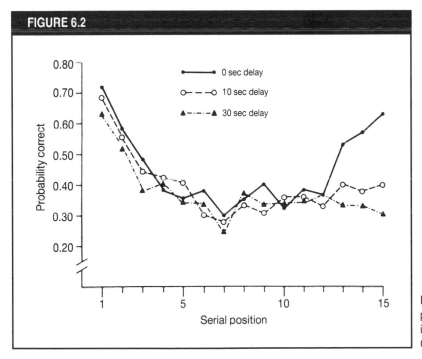

FIGURE 6.2

0 sec delay
10 sec delay
30 sec delay

Probability correct

Serial position

Free recall as a function of serial position and duration of the interpolated task. Adapted from Glanzer and Cunitz (1966).

capacity of short-term memory is strictly limited. In contrast, no effective limits on the capacity of long-term memory have been discovered.

Some of the strongest evidence for the distinction between short-term and long-term memory stores comes from the study of brain-damaged patients. As was discussed in Chapter 1, rather convincing evidence that two tasks involve different processing mechanisms can be obtained if there is a double dissociation, i.e. some patients perform normally on task A but very poorly on task B, whereas other patients perform normally on task B but very poorly on task A. A double dissociation involving short-term and long-term memory has been demonstrated using amnesic patients.

Korsakoff patients, who suffer from memory problems as a result of alcoholism, have extremely poor long-term memory for many kinds of information (see Chapter 7). However, they have virtually normal short-term memory as assessed by digit span and by the recency effect in free recall (Baddeley & Warrington, 1970; Butters & Cermak, 1980). The reverse problem of very poor short-term memory combined with normal long-term memory is relatively rare, but a few such cases have been reported. These cases include KF, a patient who suffered damage in the left parieto-occipital region of the brain following a motorcycle accident. KF had no difficulty with long-term learning and recall, but his digit span was grossly impaired (a ceiling of two items) and he had a recency effect in free recall of only one item under some circumstances (Shallice & Warrington, 1970). It is rather difficult to explain these various patterns of memory impairment without assuming that there are separate short-term and long-term memory systems. However, it should be noted that KF did not perform badly on all short-term memory tasks (see next section of the chapter).

A major distinction between the short-term and long-term stores concerns the ways in which forgetting occurs. We saw in the study by Glanzer and Cunitz (1966) that counting backwards caused forgetting from the short-term store. This may have happened either because counting backwards is a source of interference, or because it diverts attention away from the information in short-term memory. The available evidence suggests that interference and diversion of attention both play a part (e.g. Reitman, 1974). Forgetting from the long-term store, which is discussed more fully later in the chapter, appears to involve rather different mechanisms. As Tulving (1974) pointed out, we must distinguish between trace-dependent forgetting (i.e. the relevant memory traces are lost from the memory system) and cue-dependent forgetting (i.e. the memory traces are still in the memory system, but are inaccessible to most retrieval cues). There is much evidence of the importance of cue-dependent forgetting. For example, many people report that they cannot remember much about their early childhood experiences. However, if they revisit the area they were brought up in, the streets and houses often serve as powerful retrieval cues that enable them to reconstruct many childhood events.

Evaluation

The multi-store model served an important function historically. It provided a systematic account of the structures and processes involved in memory. The conceptual distinction between three different kinds of memory stores (sensory stores, short-term store, and long-term store) still makes sense. In order to justify the notion that there are three qualitatively different types of memory store, it is necessary to demonstrate that there are important differences among them. Precisely this has been done. The memory stores differ from each other in at least the following ways:

- temporal duration;
- storage capacity;
- forgetting mechanism;
- effects of brain damage.

Many contemporary memory theorists have used the multi-store model as the starting point of their theories. For example, much theoretical effort has gone into the attempt to provide a more detailed account of the long-term store than that offered by Atkinson and Shiffrin (1968, 1971). Such attempts constitute a refinement rather than an outright rejection of the multi-store approach.

The multi-store model is very oversimplified. It was assumed that both the short-term and long-term stores are unitary, i.e. that each store always operates in a single, uniform fashion. Evidence that the short-term store is not unitary was obtained by Warrington and Shallice (1972). They carried out further investigations on KF, who was initially found to have an apparently impaired short-term store but an intact long-term store. Warrington and Shallice discovered that KF's short-term forgetting of auditory letters and digits was considerably greater than his forgetting of visual stimuli. Shallice and Warrington (1974) then found that KF's short-term memory deficit was limited to verbal materials such as letters, words, and digits, and did not extend to meaningful sounds such as cats mewing or telephones ringing. Thus, we cannot simply argue that KF had impaired short-term memory. According to Shallice and Warrington (1974), his problems centred on the "auditory–verbal short-term store". In other words, their evidence compelled them to abandon the simple-minded view of the short-term memory store put forward by the multi-store theorists.

The multi-store model is similarly over-simplified when it comes to long-term memory. There is an amazing wealth of information stored in our long-term memory, including knowledge that Kevin Costner is a film star, that $2 + 2 = 4$, that we had eggs and bacon for breakfast, and perhaps information about how to ride a bicycle and to play the piano. It seems improbable that all of this knowledge is stored in precisely the same form within a single long-term memory store (see Chapter 7).

Multi-store theorists assume that the major way in which information is stored in long-term memory is via rehearsal in the short-term store. In fact, the role played by rehearsal in our everyday lives is considerably less than was assumed by multi-store theorists. At a more general level, multi-store theorists can be criticised for focusing on structural aspects of memory at the expense of an adequate view of the processes involved in learning and memory.

WORKING MEMORY

We have seen that the multi-store model fell into disfavour because its accounts of short-term and long-term memory were over-simplified. Contemporary views on short-term memory will be discussed here, leaving detailed consideration of modern views on long-term memory for later in this chapter and for Chapter 7.

Baddeley and Hitch (1974) argued that the concept of the short-term store should be replaced with that of working memory. According to them, the working memory system consists of three components:

- A modality-free central executive resembling attention.
- An articulatory or phonological loop which holds information in a phonological (i.e. speech-based) form
- A visuo-spatial scratch pad (now known as sketch pad) which is specialised for spatial and/or visual coding.

The most important component of working memory is the central executive. It has limited capacity, and is used when dealing with most cognitively demanding tasks. The articulatory loop and the visuo-spatial sketch pad are slave systems that can be used by the central executive for specific purposes. The articulatory loop preserves information (e.g. word order).

Articulatory loop

Information about the articulatory loop was obtained in a word-span study by Baddeley, Thomson, and Buchanan (1975). They discovered that subjects' ability to reproduce a sequence of words was better with short words than with long words. Further investigation of this *word-length effect* indicated that subjects could provide immediate serial recall of approximately as many words as they could read out loud in 2 seconds. This suggested that the capacity of the articulatory loop is determined by temporal duration in the same way as a tape loop.

Strong evidence that the word-length effect depends on the articulatory loop was obtained by Baddeley et al. (1975). The number of visually presented words (out of five) that could be recalled was assessed. In order to study the role of the articulatory loop, some subjects were given the articulatory suppression task of repeating the digits 1 to 8 over and over again while performing the main task. The argument was that this task would pre-empt the use of the articulatory loop and prevent it being used on the word-span task. As can be seen in Fig. 6.3, articulatory suppression eliminated the word-length effect, indicating that the effect depends critically on the articulatory loop.

An important implication of the study by Baddeley et al. (1975) is that memory span depends on the rate of rehearsal. This contrasts with the views of Miller (1956) and Simon (1974) discussed earlier, both of whom argued that memory span depends on the number of chunks or integrated units of information. Zhang and Simon (1985) compared these rival accounts. They investigated memory span for three different kinds of Chinese material: radicals (which do not have common names); two-syllable words; and one-syllable characters. Because radicals, words, and characters are all familiar units to Chinese people, it follows from the chunking hypothesis that memory span should be the same for all three kinds of material. In contrast, it follows from the articulatory loop hypothesis that memory span should be greater for characters than for words, because characters take less time to rehearse; span should be worst for radicals, because they cannot be pronounced. The results were much more consistent with the articulatory loop hypothesis: the span for characters was 6.4, against 3.8 for words, and 2.7 for radicals.

The articulatory loop now appears to be more complex than was originally envisaged by Baddeley and Hitch (1974). For example, although

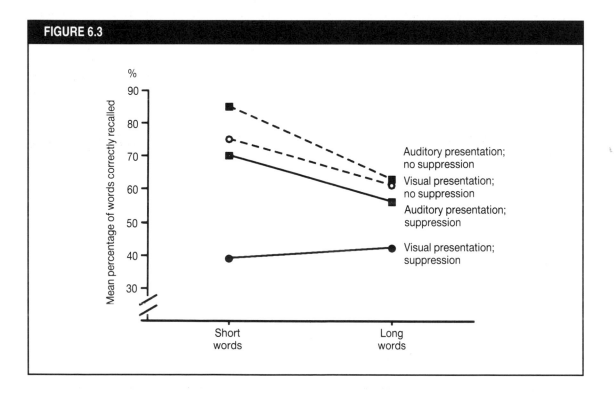

FIGURE 6.3

Immediate word recall as a function of modality of presentation (visual vs. auditory), presence versus absence of articulatory suppression, and word length. Adapted from Baddeley et al. (1975).

Baddeley et al. (1975) found that articulatory suppression eliminated the word-length effect with visual presentation of the words, it did not do so with auditory presentation (see Fig. 6.3). Basso, Spinnler, Vallar, and Zanobio (1982) studied a patient, PV, who did not seem to use the articulatory loop when tested on memory span. Her memory span for visually presented letters remained the same whether or not articulation was prevented by an articulatory suppression task, and there was also evidence that she did not use articulation with spoken letters. In spite of this, her memory span for spoken letters was worse when the letters were phonologically similar (i.e. they sounded alike) than when they were phonologically dissimilar. Thus, PV seemed to be processing phonologically (in a speech based manner), but without making use of articulation.

Baddeley (1986, 1990) put forward a revised account of the articulatory loop, which is now more appropriately known as the phonological loop. He drew a distinction between a phonological (speech-based) store and an articulatory control process (see Fig. 6.4). According to Baddeley, the phonological loop consists of:

• A passive phonological store which is directly concerned with speech perception.

• An articulatory process that is linked to speech production and gives access to the phonological store.

According to this revised account, words that are presented auditorily are processed differently from words that are presented visually. Auditory presentation of words permits *direct* access to the phonological store regardless of whether the articulatory control process is being used. In contrast, visual presentation of words only permits *indirect* access to the phonological store through subvocal articulation. Some of these issues are dealt with further in the discussion of inner speech (see Chapter 13).

This revised account helps us to make sense of some of the findings. Suppose that the word length effect observed by Baddeley et al. (1975) depends on the rate of articulatory rehearsal (see Fig. 6.3). Articulatory suppression eliminates the word-length effect with visual presentation because access to the phonological store is prevented. Articulatory suppression does not affect the word-length effect with auditory presentation because information about the words enters the phonological store directly.

Why was PV's letter memory span with auditory presentation affected by phonological

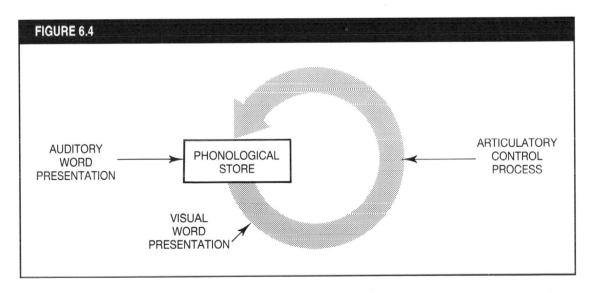

FIGURE 6.4

AUDITORY WORD PRESENTATION → PHONOLOGICAL STORE ← ARTICULATORY CONTROL PROCESS

VISUAL WORD PRESENTATION

Phonological loop system as envisaged by Baddeley (1990).

similarity even though she did not use subvocal articulation? The effects of phonological similarity occurred because the auditorily presented letters entered directly into the phonological store even in the absence of subvocal articulation.

Does subvocal articulatory activity within the phonological loop require use of the speech musculature? Suggestive evidence was obtained by Baddeley and Wilson (1985). They studied an Oxford University student, GB (who was unable to speak apart from a single meaningless sound), and five further similar cases. These patients all suffered from *anarthria*, in which general language ability is intact even though damage to the system controlling the speech musculature prevents speech. In spite of having essentially no use of their speech musculature, the patients seemed able to engage in subvocal rehearsal or articulation. Baddeley (1986, p.107) concluded: "The loop and its rehearsal processes are operating at a much deeper level than might at first seem likely, apparently relying on central speech control codes which appear to be able to function in the absence of peripheral feedback."

What is the value of the phonological loop? The phonological loop is used to increase memory span, but this is far removed from most of the activities of everyday life. A major function of the phonological loop is to facilitate the reading of difficult material, making it easier for readers to retain information about the order of words in text during the process of comprehension (see Chapter 13). It is also possible that the phonological loop aids comprehension by providing information about stress patterns and rhythm within a sentence.

Visuo-spatial sketch pad

The characteristics of the visuo-spatial sketch pad are less clear than those of the articulatory loop. Baddeley (1986, p.109) defined it as "a system especially well adapted to the storage of spatial information, much as a pad of paper might be used by someone trying for example to work out a geometric puzzle". Baddeley, Grant, Wight, and Thomson (1975) studied the visuo-spatial sketch pad. Subjects heard the locations of digits within a matrix described by means of an auditory message that was either easily visualised or was rather

difficult to visualise, and were then asked to reproduce the matrix. When this task was combined with pursuit rotor (i.e. tracking a light moving along a circular track), performance on the easily visualised message was greatly impaired, but there was no adverse effect on the non-visualisable message.

The most obvious interpretation of these findings is that the pursuit rotor involves visual perception, and it is for this reason that it interferes with performance on the visualisable message. However, Baddeley and Lieberman (1980; see also Chapter 9) found that a specifically visual concurrent task (making brightness judgements) actually disrupted performance more on the non-visualisable message than the visualisable one. The results were very different when a spatial task with no visual input was performed while the message was being presented; this involved subjects attempting to point at a moving pendulum while blindfolded, with auditory feedback being provided. This spatial tracking task produced a substantial reduction in recall of the visualisable messages, but had little effect on the non-visualisable messages. It thus appears that recall of visualisable messages of the kind used by Baddeley et al. (1975) and by Baddeley and Lieberman (1980) is interfered with by spatial rather than by visual tasks, implying that processing of visualisable messages within the visuo-spatial sketch pad relies on spatial rather than visual coding.

More recent evidence suggests that visual coding can also be of importance within the visuo-spatial sketch pad. Logie (1986) asked subjects to learn word lists using either visual imagery or rote rehearsal, with irrelevant line drawings or irrelevant speech being presented at the same time. The use of imagery was disrupted more by the line drawings than by the speech, whereas the opposite was the case with rote rehearsal (see Fig. 6.5). Presumably the disruptive effects of line drawings in the imagery condition occurred because the processing of the drawings and forming images of the list words both competed for the visual processing capacity of the visuo-spatial sketch pad. However, there is evidence (Smyth & Scholey, 1994) that the

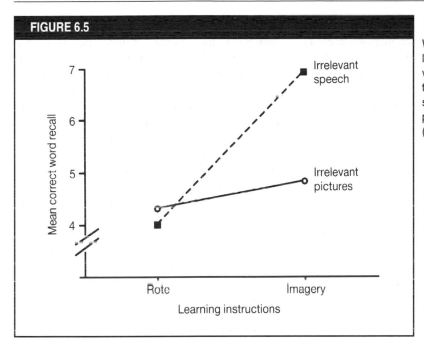

FIGURE 6.5

Word recall as a function of learning instructions (rote vs. imagery) and the nature of the distractors (irrelevant speech vs. irrelevant pictures). Adapted from Logie (1986).

requirement to attend to different spatial locations also disrupts visuo-spatial memory, which tends to go against the notion that maintenance of information in the visuo-spatial sketch pad is analogous to verbal rehearsal.

How useful is the visuo-spatial sketch pad in everyday life? Some suggestions about its uses were put forward by Baddeley (1990, p.113–114):

It seems likely that the spatial system is important for geographical orientation, and for planning spatial tasks. Indeed, tasks involving visuo-spatial manipulation have long formed an important component of intelligence test batteries, and have tended to be used as selection tools for professions where visuo-spatial planning and manipulation are thought to be important, such as engineering and architecture.

There may be important links between the visuo-spatial sketch pad and the spatial medium identified by Kosslyn (e.g. 1983). The spatial medium is used for manipulating visual images, and appears to share some characteristics with Baddeley's visuo-spatial sketch pad (Brandimonte, Hitch, & Bishop, 1992; see also Chapter 9).

Central executive

The central executive, which is rather like an attentional system, is the most important and versatile component of the working memory system. However, relatively little is known of its functioning. Baddeley (1986, 1990) suggested that the central executive may resemble the supervisory attentional system described by Norman and Shallice (1980) and by Shallice (1982) (see Chapter 5). According to Shallice (1982), the supervisory attentional system has limited capacity, and is used for a variety of purposes. These include trouble-shooting when lower processing systems seem inadequate; tasks requiring planning or decision making; and situations where poorly mastered response sequences are involved.

Baddeley (1986, 1990) argued that extensive damage to the frontal lobes may cause impairments to the central executive or supervisory attentional system. Patients with frontal lobe damage present a wide variety of symptoms, but Rylander (1939, p.20) described the classical frontal syndrome as involving "disturbed attention, increased distractibility, a difficulty in grasping the whole of a complicated state of affairs ... well able to work along old routine lines ... cannot learn to master new types of task, in new situations". In other words, patients with the frontal syndrome behave as if they lacked a control system that allowed them to direct, and to re-direct, their processing resources flexibly and appropriately. Most of their processing resources appear to be intact, but there is no overall direction of the kind that in most people is provided by the central executive or supervisory attentional system.

Evidence that may indicate the kinds of memory problem associated with damage to the central executive was discussed by Parkin (1993). Parkin and his colleagues studied a patient, CB, who had suffered a stroke which damaged part of his frontal lobes. CB performed extremely poorly on a recall test, but performed slightly better than control subjects on a standard recognition test. Strategic or problem-solving processes are used more frequently on recall than on recognition tests, and it may be these strategic processes that have been impaired by damage to the central executive (there is additional discussion of the effects of frontal lobe damage on memory in Chapter 7).

Evaluation

There are several advantages of the working memory model over the earlier formulation of Atkinson and Shiffrin (1968). First, the working memory system is concerned with both active processing and transient storage of information, and so is of relevance to activities such as mental arithmetic (Hitch, 1978), verbal reasoning (Hitch & Baddeley, 1976), and comprehension (Baddeley & Hitch, 1974), as well as to traditional memory tasks. Second, the working memory model is better placed to provide an explanation of the partial deficits of short-term memory that have been observed in brain-damaged patients. If brain damage affects only one of the three components of working memory, then selective deficits on short-term memory tasks would be expected. Third, the working memory model incorporates verbal rehearsal as an optional process that occurs within only one component (i.e. the articulatory loop). This is more realistic than the enormous significance given to verbal rehearsal within the multi-store model of Atkinson and Shiffrin (1968).

On the negative side, there has been relatively little clarification of the role played by the central executive. It is claimed that the central executive is of limited capacity, but it has proved difficult to measure that capacity. It is also claimed that the central executive is "modality-free" and used in numerous processing operations, but the precise constraints on its functioning are unclear.

Of particular importance, there is increasing evidence that the central executive is not unitary. Eslinger and Damasio (1985) investigated a former accountant, EVR, who had had a large cerebral tumour removed. He had a high IQ, and performed well on tests requiring reasoning, flexible hypothesis testing, and resistance to distraction and memory interference, suggesting that his central executive was essentially intact. However, he exhibited extremely poor decision making and judgement (e.g. he would often take hours to decide where to eat), and as a consequence he was dismissed from a number of jobs. The most reasonable interpretation of these findings is that EVR's central executive was partially intact and partially damaged, which implies that the central executive is not unitary, but rather consists of two or more component systems. Such evidence is entirely consistent with the growing body of evidence that the attentional system is not unitary (see Chapter 5).

MEMORY PROCESSES

Suppose you were interested in looking at the effects of learning processes on subsequent long-term memory. One method that has been used very frequently is to present several groups of subjects with the same list of nouns, and to ask each group to perform a different activity or orienting task with the list. The tasks used range from counting the number of letters in each word to thinking of an appropriate adjective for each word.

If subjects were told that their memory was going to be tested, they would presumably realise that a task such as simply counting the number of letters in each word would not enable them to remember very much. There would thus be a natural temptation for them to process the words more thoroughly. Therefore, in order to control the subjects' processing actvities as much as possible, the experimenter does not tell them there is going to be a memory test (this is known as incidental learning). Finally, all the subjects are unexpectedly asked to recall as many words as they can. As the various groups are presented with exactly the same words, any differences in recall must reflect the influence of the processing tasks.

Hyde and Jenkins (1973) carried out an experiment using the approach just described. Words were either associatively related or unrelated in meaning, and different groups of subjects performed each of the following five orienting tasks:

1. rating the words for pleasantness;
2. estimating the frequency with which each word is used in the english language;
3. detecting the occurrence of the letters "e" and "g" in the list words;
4. deciding the part of speech appropriate to each word;
5. deciding whether the list words fitted sentence frames.

Half of the subjects in each condition were told to try to learn the words (intentional learning), whereas the other half were not (incidental learning). There was a test of free recall shortly after the orienting task finished.

The main results are shown in Fig. 6.6. Rating pleasantness and rating frequency of usage presumably both involve semantic processing (processing of meaning), whereas the other three orienting tasks do not. If we make these assumptions, then retention was 51% higher after the semantic tasks than the non-semantic tasks on the list of associatively unrelated words; with the list of associatively related words, there was an 83% superiority for the semantic tasks. Somewhat surprisingly, incidental learners recalled the same number of words as intentional learners. This suggests that intent to learn is not of crucial importance; rather, it is the nature of the processing activity that determines how much is remembered subsequently.

Levels-of-processing theory
Craik and Lockhart (1972) proposed a broad framework within which memory phenomena

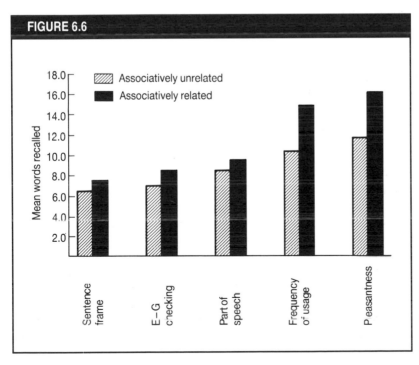

FIGURE 6.6

Mean words recalled as a function of list type (associatively related or unrelated) and orienting task. Data from Hyde and Jenkins (1973).

could be understood. They argued that it was too general to be regarded as a theory; however, because they made a number of specific predictions, it will be treated here as a theory. They assumed that the attentional and perceptual processes operating at the time of learning determine what information is stored in long-term memory. They argued that there are a number of different levels of processing, ranging from shallow or physical analysis of a stimulus (e.g. detecting specific letters in words) to deep or semantic analysis. The crucial notion of depth of processing was further explained by Craik (1973, p.48): " 'Depth' is defined in terms of the meaningfulness extracted from the stimulus rather than in terms of the number of analyses performed upon it."

The most important theoretical assumptions made by Craik and Lockhart (1972) were as follows:

- The level or depth of processing of a stimulus has a substantial effect on its memorability.
- Deeper levels of analysis produce more elaborate, longer lasting, and stronger memory traces than do shallow levels of analysis.

The findings of Hyde and Jenkins (1973), as well as those of numerous other researchers, are in line with the predictions of the levels-of-processing approach. However, it became apparent that the approach was over-simplified, and so various modifications and additions were proposed.

Elaboration

Craik and Tulving (1975) obtained evidence that the depth of processing is not the only factor determining long-term memory. They discovered that elaboration of processing (i.e. the amount of processing of a particular kind) is also important. In one of their experiments, subjects were presented on each trial with a word and a sentence containing a blank, and were asked to decide whether the word fitted appropriately into the blank space. Elaboration was manipulated by varying the complexity of the sentence frame between the simple (e.g. "She cooked the ____") and the complex (e.g. "The great bird swooped down and carried off the struggling ____"). Cued recall was twice as high for words accompanying complex sentences, suggesting that elaboration benefits long-term memory.

Subsequent research indicated that memory depends on the kind of elaboration as well as on the amount of elaboration. Bransford, Franks, Morris, and Stein (1979) presented either minimally elaborated similes (e.g. "A mosquito is like a doctor because they both draw blood") or multiply elaborated similes (e.g. "A mosquito is like a raccoon because they both have heads, legs, jaws"). Recall was much better for the minimally elaborated similes than for the multiply elaborated ones, indicating that the nature and degree of precision of semantic elaborations are relevant when predicting the effects of elaboration on retention.

Distinctiveness

Eysenck (1979) argued that long-term memory is affected by distinctiveness of processing as well as by the depth and elaboration of processing. In other words, memory traces that are distinctive or unique in some way will be more readily retrieved than memory traces that closely resemble a number of other memory traces. Eysenck and Eysenck (1980) tested this theory by using nouns having irregular grapheme–phoneme correspondence (i.e. words not pronounced in line with pronunciation rules, such as "comb" with its silent "b"). Subjects performed the shallow or non-semantic orienting task of pronouncing such nouns as if they had regular grapheme–phoneme correspondence, which presumably produced distinctive and unique memory traces (non-semantic, distinctive condition). Other nouns were simply pronounced in their normal fashion (non-semantic, non-distinctive condition), and still others were processed in terms of their meaning (semantic, distinctive and semantic, non-distinctive).

On a subsequent and unexpected recognition-memory test, words in the non-semantic, distinctive condition were much better remembered than those in the non-semantic, non-distinctive condition (see Fig. 6.7). Indeed, they were remembered almost as well as the words

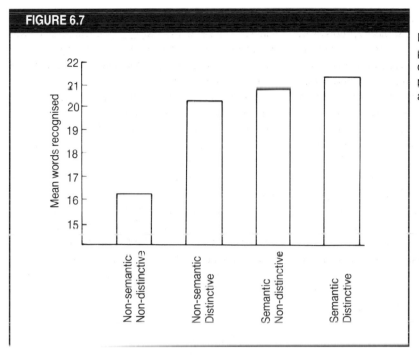

FIGURE 6.7

Recognition-memory performance as a function of the depth and distinctiveness of processing. Data from Eysenck and Eysenck (1980).

in the semantic conditions. These findings demonstrate the importance of distinctiveness to long-term memory.

Evaluation

The processes that occur at the time of learning have a major impact on subsequent long-term memory. That may sound obvious, but surprisingly little research pre-1972 involved an investigation of learning processes and their effects on memory. It is also valuable that elaboration and distinct-iveness of processing have been identified as factors that need to be considered when comparing the effectiveness of different learning processes.

On the negative side, it is difficult with many orienting tasks to know the level of processing involved. For example, Hyde and Jenkins (1973) argued that the task of deciding the part of speech to which a word belongs is a shallow processing task, but other researchers claimed that the task involves deep or semantic processing. It is difficult to be sure who is right. In essence, the problem is caused by the lack of any independent measure of processing depth. This can lead to the unfortunate state of affairs described by Eysenck (1978, p.159):

In view of the vagueness with which depth is defined, there is a danger of using retention-test performance to provide information about the depth of processing, and then using the putative depth of processing to 'explain' the retention-test performance, a self-defeating exercise in circularity.

However, it is sometimes possible to provide an independent measure of depth (see Parkin, 1979).

Craik and Lockhart (1972) argued that deep or semantic processing will always lead to superior long-term memory compared to shallow or non-semantic processing, but some of the evidence disconfirms this prediction. Morris, Bransford, and Franks (1977) argued that stored information is remembered only to the extent that it is of *relevance* to the memory test. Their subjects had to answer semantic or shallow (rhyme) questions for lists of words. Memory was tested by a standard recognition test, in which a mixture of list and non-list words was presented, or it was tested by a rhyming recognition test. On this latter test, subjects were told to select words that rhymed with list words; note that the list words themselves were not presented.

Some of the findings are shown in Fig. 6.8. If one considers only the results obtained with the standard recognition test, then the predicted superiority of deep processing over shallow processing was obtained. However, the opposite result was obtained with the rhyme test, and this represents an experimental disproof of the notion that deep processing always enhances long-term memory.

Morris et al. (1977) argued that their findings supported a *transfer-appropriate processing theory*. According to this theory, different kinds of processing lead learners to acquire different kinds of information about a stimulus. Whether the stored information leads to subsequent retention depends on the relevance of that information to the kind of memory test used. For example, storing semantic information is essentially irrelevant when the memory test requires the identification of

words rhyming with list words. What is required for this kind of test is shallow rhyme information.

A final problem with the levels-of-processing approach is that it describes rather than explains. Craik and Lockhart (1972) argued that deep processing leads to better long-term memory than does shallow processing, but they failed to provide a detailed account of exactly why it is that deep processing is so effective.

REMEMBERING AND FORGETTING

There have been several theoretical approaches to remembering and forgetting over the years, and some of the most important ones will be discussed shortly. Memory theorists have been especially concerned with the ways in which the probability of retrieval is affected by the precise form of retention test that is used. More specifically, it has been found repeatedly that recognition memory is

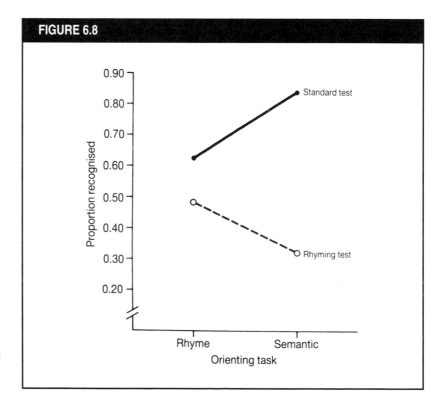

FIGURE 6.8

Mean proportion of words recognised as a function of orienting task (semantic or rhyme) and of the type of recognition test (standard or rhyming). Data are from Morris et al. (1977), and are from positive trials only.

usually much better than recall (see Parkin, 1993), and many theorists have tried to understand why this should be the case. However, before turning to their theories, we will consider a rather different approach focusing on the role of interference in forgetting.

Interference theory

The dominant approach to forgetting during much of this century was based on interference theory. It was assumed that our subsequent ability to remember what we are currently learning may be disrupted or interfered with by what we have previously learned or by what we learn in the future. When previous learning interferes with later learning, this is known as *proactive interference*, and when later learning disrupts earlier learning there is *retroactive inteference*. Methods of testing for proactive and retroactive inteference are shown in Fig. 6.9.

Interference theory can be traced back to Hugo Munsterberg in the 19th century. He had for many years kept his pocket-watch in one particular pocket. When he started keeping it in a different pocket, he often fumbled about in confusion when asked for the time. In essence, he had learned an association between the stimulus "What time is it?" and the response of removing the watch from his pocket. Later on, the stimulus remained the same, but a different response was now associated with it. Subsequent research using methods such as those shown in Fig. 6.9 revealed that both proactive and retroactive interference tend to be maximal when two different responses have been associated with the same stimulus; intermediate when two similar stimuli are involved; and minimal when two different stimuli are involved (Underwood & Postman, 1960).

As proactive and retroactive interference have both been demonstrated numerous times, why is it

---

FIGURE 6.9

Proactive interference

Group	Learn	Learn	Test
Experimental	A–B	A–C	A–C
	(e.g. Cat–Tree)	(e.g. Cat–Dirt)	(e.g. Cat–Dirt)
Control	—	A–C	A–C
		(e.g. Cat–Dirt)	(e.g. Cat–Dirt)

Retroactive interference

Group	Learn	Learn	Test
Experimental	A–B	A–C	A–B
	(e.g. Cat–Tree)	(e.g. Cat–Dirt)	(e.g. Cat–Tree)
Control	A–B	—	A–B
	(e.g. Cat–Tree)		(e.g. Cat–Tree)

Note: for both proactive and retroactive interference, the experimental group exhibits interference. On the test, only the first word is supplied, and the subjects must provide the second word.

Methods of testing for proactive and retroactive interference.

that inteference theory no longer enjoys the popularity that it once did? There are two major reasons. First, interference theory is uninformative about the internal processes involved in learning and memory. Second, it requires special circumstances for substantial interference effects to occur (i.e. the same stimulus paired with two different responses), and these circumstances seem relatively rare in everyday life.

Two-process theory

One of the most influential attempts to account for the superiority of recognition memory to recall is the two-stage or two-process theory (see Watkins & Gardiner, 1979, for a review). Several slightly different versions of this theory have been proposed, but what they have in common are the following assumptions:

- Recall involves a search or retrieval process, which is followed by a decision or recognition process based on the apparent appropriateness of the retrieved information.
- Recognition involves only the second of these processes.

Two-process theory therefore claims that recall involves two fallible stages, whereas recognition involves only a single fallible stage. It is for this reason that recognition is superior to recall. According to this theory, recall requires an item to be retrieved and then recognised. The notion that the probability of recall is determined by the probability of retrieval multiplied by the probability of recognition was tested by Bahrick (1970) using cued recall (words were presented as cues for to-be-remembered list words). He used the probability of the cue producing the to-be-remembered word in free association as an estimate of the retrievability of the to-be-remembered word, and he ascertained the probability of recognition by means of a standard recognition test. The level of cued recall was predicted reasonably well by multiplying together those two probabilities.

Further evidence that people can recall information by making extensive use of the retrieval process and then deciding which of the items produced are appropriate was obtained by Rabinowitz, Mandler, and Patterson (1977). They compared recall of a categorised word list (a list containing words belonging to several different categories) under standard instructions and under instructions to generate as many words as possible from the categories represented in the list, saying aloud only those that subjects thought had actually been presented. Subjects given the latter generation-recognition instructions recalled 23% more words than those given standard recall instructions. Thus, the generate-recognise strategy described by the two-process theory can be useful in increasing recall.

Evaluation

Despite the success of two-process theory, it has attracted much criticism. Recall is sometimes better than recognition, which simply should not happen according to two-process theory. In a study by Muter (1978), subjects were presented with names of people (e.g. DOYLE, FERGUSON, THOMAS) and asked to circle those they "recognised as a person who was famous before 1950". They were then given recall cues in the form of brief descriptions plus first names of the famous people whose surnames had appeared on the recognition test (e.g. author of the Sherlock Holmes stories: Sir Arthur Conan _____ ; Welsh poet: Dylan _____). Subjects recognised only 29% of the names but recalled 42%.

A related phenomenon that also poses considerable problems for two-process theory is known as recognition failure of recallable words, or simply recognition failure. This occurs when learning is followed by a recognition memory test and then a test of recall, and some of the items that are not recognised are nevertheless subsequently recalled (e.g. Tulving & Thomson, 1973). According to two-process theory, recognition failure should practically never happen. This is because recall allegedly requires both retrieval and recognition of the to-be-remembered item.

Another problem with two-process theory is that its account of recognition memory is threadbare. As we will see later in the chapter, recognition memory can involve at least two different kinds of processes (see Gardiner & Java,

1993), and the theory simply cannot handle such complexities.

Encoding specificity

Tulving (1982, 1983) assumed there are basic similarities between recall and recognition. He also assumed that contextual factors are important, and that what is stored in memory represents a combination of information about the to-be-remembered material and about the context.

Tulving embodied these ideas into his encoding specificity principle (Wiseman & Tulving, 1976, p.349): "A to-be-remembered (TBR) item is encoded with respect to the context in which it is studied, producing a unique trace which incorporates information from both target and context. For the TBR item to be retrieved, the cue information must appropriately match the trace of the item-in-context." Subsequently, Tulving (1979, p.408) proposed a more precise formulation of the encoding specificity principle: "The probability of successful retrieval of the target item is a mono-tonically increasing function of informational overlap between the information present at retrieval and the information stored in memory." For the benefit of any reader wondering what on earth "monotonically increasing function" means, it refers to a generally rising function that does not decrease at any point. In other words, memory performance depends directly on the similarity between the information in memory and the information available at retrieval.

Note that the encoding specificity principle does not refer explicitly to either recall or recognition. The reason is that it is intended to apply equally to both forms of retention test. Attempts to test the encoding specificity principle typically involve two learning conditions and two retrieval conditions. This allows the experimenter to demonstrate (as is claimed in the encoding specificity principle) that memory depends on both the information in the memory trace stemming from the learning experience and the information available in the retrieval environment.

A concrete example of this research strategy is a study by Thomson and Tulving (1970). They presented pairs of words in which the first word was the cue and the second word was the to-be-remembered word. The cues were either weakly associated with the list words (e.g. "Train-BLACK") or were strongly associated (e.g. "White-BLACK"). Some of the to-be-remembered items were tested by weak cues (e.g. "Train-?") and others were tested by strong cues (e.g. "White-?"). The results are shown in Fig. 6.10. As would be expected on the encoding specificity principle, recall performance was best when the cues provided at recall were the same as those provided at input. Any change in the cues lowered recall, even when the shift was from weak cues at input to strong cues at recall.

What does Tulving have to say about the relationship between recall and recognition? The general superiority of recognition over recall is accounted for in two ways. First, the overlap between the information contained in the memory test and that contained in the memory trace will typically be greater on a recognition test (when the entire item is presented) than on a recall test. Second, Tulving (1983) argued that a greater amount of informational overlap is required for successful recall than for successful recognition. The reason is that recall involves naming a previous event, whereas recognition involves only a judgement of familiarity.

In spite of these considerations, the encoding specificity principle predicts there should be cases in which items that cannot be recognised can nevertheless be recalled (this is the phenomenon of recognition failure mentioned earlier). Tulving and Thomson (1973) obtained evidence of recognition failure using a rather complex four-stage design. In the first stage, subjects were presented with weakly associated word pairs (e.g. "black-ENGINE") and instructed to learn the second word. In the second stage, they were told to produce associations to a strong associate of each to-be-remembered word (e.g. "steam"). In the third stage, they were asked whether they recognised any of the words generated as corresponding to list words (e.g. "engine" would normally have been generated). In the fourth stage, they were given the context words presented in the first stage (e.g. "black") and told to recall the to-be-remembered words. In many cases, the to-be-remembered words that were not recognised in stage three were recalled in stage

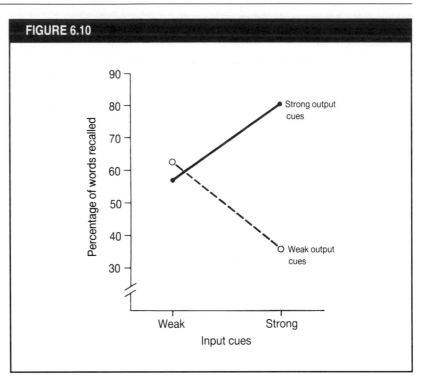

FIGURE 6.10

Mean word recall as a function of input cues (strong or weak) and output cues (strong or weak). Data from Thomson and Tulving (1970).

four. Information about the context word (e.g. "black") was stored in the memory trace, and so the presentation of this word on the recall test but not the recognition test increased the overlap between test information and trace information for recall relative to recognition.

When the findings from the various recognition-failure studies are considered together (Tulving & Flexser, 1992), it appears that recall performance depends much less on recognition performance than would be predicted from two-process theory. The relationship between recall and recognition is shown in Fig. 6.11. The broken line indicates what would be the case if there were no relationship between recall and recognition. The solid line showing the actual weak relationship has been called the "Tulving-Wiseman function".

Flexser and Tulving (1978) provided an explanation of this function based on the encoding specificity principle. According to them, there is some relationship between recall and recognition because both tests are directed at the same memory trace. However, the relationship is weak because the information contained in the recognition test is unrelated to that contained in the recall test.

As we have seen, there are some studies (e.g. Muter, 1978) in which recall was actually superior to recognition. In general terms, it is assumed within the encoding specificity principle that this happens when the information in the recall cue overlaps more than the information in the recognition cue with the information stored in the memory trace. This could explain why, for example, the recall cue "Welsh poet: Dylan ____" produced better memory performance than the recognition cue "Thomas" in the study by Muter.

Evaluation

One of the valuable aspects of Tulving's approach is the notion that memory depends jointly on the nature of the memory trace and on the information available in the retrieval environment. Another valuable aspect is the emphasis on the role played by contextual information in retrieval. Contextual influences had usually been ignored or de-emphasised prior to Tulving's encoding specificity principle, but there is now compelling

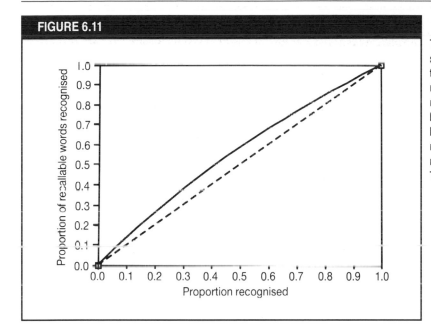

FIGURE 6.11

The Tulving-Wiseman function, showing in the solid line that there is only a limited relationship between recall and recognition performance (the broken line indicates what would happen if there were no relationship between recall and recognition). Adapted from Tulving and Flexser (1992).

evidence that recall and recognition are both affected greatly by the similarity of context at learning and at test.

On the negative side, there is a danger of circularity in applying the encoding specificity principle. Memory is said to depend on "informational overlap", but there is seldom any direct measure of that overlap. It is tempting to infer the amount of informational overlap from the level of memory performance, which produces completely circular reasoning.

Another serious problem associated with Tulving's theoretical position is his view that the information available at the time of retrieval is compared in a very simple and direct fashion with the information stored in memory to ascertain the amount of informational overlap. This is implausible if one considers what happens if memory is tested by asking the question, "What did you do six days ago?" Most people answer a question like that by engaging in a rather complex problem-solving strategy which takes some time to reconstruct the relevant events. Tulving's approach has very little to say about how retrieval operates under such circumstances.

A final limitation of Tulving's approach concerns context effects in memory. Tulving assumed that context affects recall and recognition in the same ways, but that is not entirely true. Baddeley (1982) proposed a distinction between *intrinsic context* and *extrinsic context*. Intrinsic context has a direct impact on the meaning or significance of a to-be-remembered item (e.g. strawberry versus traffic as intrinsic context for the word "jam"), whereas extrinsic context (e.g. the room in which learning takes place) does not. According to Baddeley, recall is affected by both intrinsic and extrinsic context, whereas recognition memory is affected only by intrinsic context.

Convincing evidence that extrinsic context has quite different effects on recall and recognition was obtained by Godden and Baddeley (1975, 1980). In the study by Godden and Baddeley (1975), subjects learned a list of words either on land or 20 feet underwater, and were then given a test of free recall on land or underwater. Those who had learned on land recalled more on land than underwater, and those who learned underwater did better when tested underwater. Retention was approximately 50% higher when learning and recall took place in the same extrinsic context (see Fig. 6.12). Godden and Baddeley (1980) carried out a very similar study, but using recognition instead of recall. Recognition memory

FIGURE 6.12

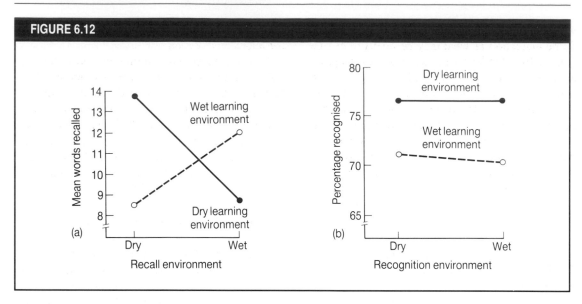

(a) Recall in the same versus different contexts, data from Godden and Baddeley (1975); (b) Recognition in the same versus different contexts. Data from Godden and Baddeley (1980).

was not affected by extrinsic context (see Fig. 6.12).

Multiple-route approaches

Most approaches to recall and recognition (including the two-process and encoding specificity theories) are very over-simplified. It has often been assumed that there is only one way in which recall occurs and only one way in which recognition occurs. This is implausible, because it implies that memory operates in a rather fixed and inflexible fashion. In fact, there are various strategies that can be used in order to recall or recognise stored information. Some of the flavour of these multiple-route approaches will be given here.

Recall
Jones (e.g. 1982) argued that there are two different routes to recall:

- The direct route, in which the cue permits direct accessing of the to-be-remembered information.
- The indirect route, in which the cue leads to recall via the making of inferences and the generation of possible responses.

Jones (1982) reported some interesting findings supporting this theoretical position. Subjects were shown a list of apparently unrelated cue-target word pairs (e.g. "regal-BEER"), followed by a test of cued recall (e.g. "regal-?"). Some of the subjects were told after learning but before recall that reversing the letters of each cue word would produce a new word that was related to the target word (e.g. "regal" turns into "lager", which in turn suggests "BEER"). Subjects who were told about reversing the letters of the cue word recalled more than twice as many words as uninformed subjects. According to Jones (1982), uninformed subjects made use only of the direct route, whereas informed subjects were able to use the direct and indirect routes, and so recalled many more words.

It is possible to relate Jones' two recall routes to two of the theories discussed earlier in the chapter. In approximate terms, recall is assumed to occur via the direct route according to the encoding specificity principle. In contrast, the indirect route closely resembles the recall process as described by the two-process theorists.

Recognition
It has been proposed by several theorists (e.g. Gardiner & Java, 1993) that there are two different

ways in which recognition memory can occur. Some indication of what may be involved can be gleaned from the following anecdote. Several years ago, the first author walked past a man in Wimbledon, and felt immediately that he recognised him. However, he was somewhat puzzled because it was difficult to think of the situation in which he had seen the man previously. After a fair amount of thought about it (this is the kind of thing academic psychologists do think about!), he realised that the man was a ticket-office clerk at Wimbledon railway station, and this greatly strengthened his conviction that the initial feeling of recognition was correct. This anecdote suggests that recognition can be based either on familiarity or on remembering relevant contextual information.

Gardiner and Java (1993) discussed several studies in which an attempt was made to distinguish between these two forms of recognition memory. Subjects were presented with a list of words followed by a recognition memory test. For each word recognised, subjects had to make either a "know" or a "remember" response: know responses were to be made if there were feelings of familiarity only, whereas remember responses

were to be made if retrieval were accompanied by conscious recollection.

In order to provide strong evidence for the reality of the know/remember distinction, it is necessary to find some experimental manipulations that affect remember responses but not know responses, and vice versa. This has been done. Gardiner and Parkin (1990) used two learning conditions: (1) attention was devoted only to the list of words to be remembered (undivided attention); (2) attention had to be divided between the list and another task (divided attention). As can be seen in Fig. 6.13, the attentional manipulation affected only the remember responses.

Rajaram (1993) presented a word below the conscious threshold to subjects immediately prior to each test word that was presented for recognition memory. This word was either the same as the test word or different. As can be seen in Fig. 6.14, the relationship between the subliminal word (masked prime) and the test word made a difference to know responses but not to remember responses.

In sum, there are important differences in recognition memory between "know" and "remember" responses. Remember decisions appear to depend more than know decisions on the

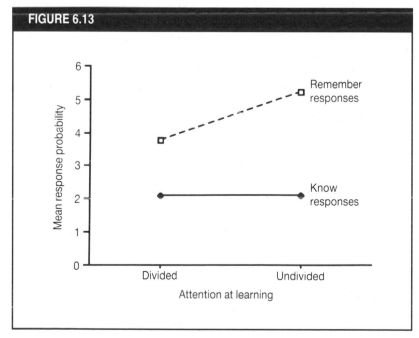

FIGURE 6.13

Mean probabilities of remember and know responses on a recognition test as a function of whether attention at learning was divided or undivided. Adapted from Gardiner and Parkin (1990).

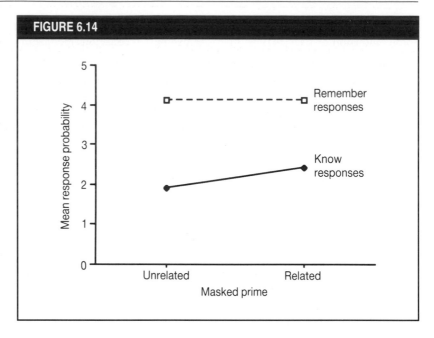

FIGURE 6.14

Mean probabilities of remember and know responses on a recognition test as a function of whether masked primes were related or unrelated. Adapted from Rajaram (1993).

involvement of conscious attention, but the detailed processes involved remain unclear.

Section summary

One of the implications of the various multi-route approaches is that there is no simple answer to the question of the similarity between the processes involved in recall and recognition. If there are at least two recall processes and two recognition processes, then the degree of similarity clearly depends on which recall process is being compared with which recognition process. One of the issues for the future is to identify more precisely the circumstances in which each particular process is used.

IMPLICIT MEMORY

Definitions

Traditional measures of memory, such as free recall, cued recall, and recognition, all involve use of direct instructions to retrieve information about specific experiences. As a consequence, they can all be regarded as measures of explicit memory (Graf & Schacter, 1985, p.501): "Explicit memory

is revealed when performance on a task requires conscious recollection of previous experiences." In recent years, researchers have become increasingly interested in understanding implicit memory (Graf & Schacter, 1985, p.501): "Implicit memory is revealed when performance on a task is facilitated in the absence of conscious recollection." Indeed, implicit memory has become the "hot" topic within memory research.

It should be noted at the outset that the terms "explicit memory" and "implicit memory" tell us nothing about memory structures, and relatively little about the processes involved. As Schacter (1987, p.501) pointed out, explicit and implicit memory "are *descriptive* concepts that are primarily concerned with a person's psychological experience at the time of retrieval".

Evidence

In order to understand what is involved in implicit memory, we will consider a study by Tulving, Schacter, and Stark (1982). Initially, they asked their subjects to learn a list of multi-syllabled and relatively rare words (e.g. "toboggan"). One hour or one week later, they were simply asked to fill in the blanks in word fragments to make a word (e.g. _ O _ O _ GA_). The solutions to half of the fragments were words from the list that had been learned, but the subjects were not told this. As conscious recollection was not required on the word-fragment completion test, it can be regarded as a test of implicit memory.

There was evidence for implicit memory, with the subjects completing more of the fragments correctly when the solutions matched list words. This effect is known as *repetition priming*. A sceptical reader might argue that repetition priming occurred because the subjects deliberately searched through the previously learned list, and thus the test actually reflects explicit memory. However, Tulving et al. (1982) reported an additional finding which goes against that possibility: repetition priming was no greater for target words that were recognised than for those that were not. In other words, the repetition priming effect was unrelated to explicit memory performance as assessed by recognition memory.

This finding suggests that repetition priming and recognition memory involve different forms of memory. Further support for that view came when Tulving et al. (1982) discovered that the length of

the retention interval had different effects on recognition memory and fragment completion. As can be seen in Fig. 6.15, recognition memory was considerably worse after one week than after one hour, whereas fragment-completion performance did not change significantly over time.

In terms of the definition of implicit memory, it is important to ensure that effects on memory performance are demonstrated in the absence of conscious recollection. This is easier said than done. The usual method is to ask the subjects at the end of the experiment about their awareness of any conscious recollection, but subjects may forget or the questioning may be insufficiently probing. Jacoby, Toth, and Yonelinas (1993) came up with an ingenious way of measuring the respective contributions of explicit and implicit memory processes to performance on a test of cued recall. A list of words was presented (e.g. "mercy"), and there were two different conditions at the time of the test:

• Inclusion test: subjects were instructed to complete the cues or word stems (e.g. "mer__")

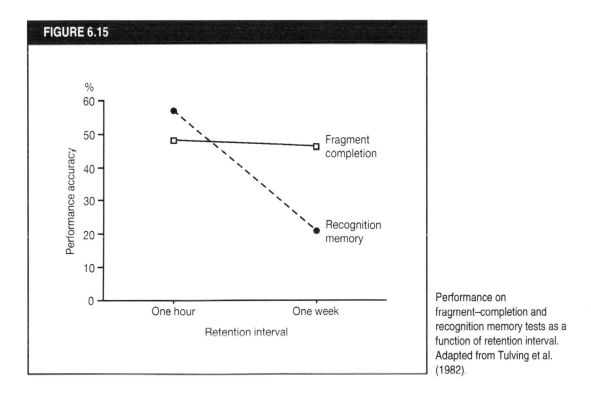

FIGURE 6.15

Performance on fragment–completion and recognition memory tests as a function of retention interval. Adapted from Tulving et al. (1982).

with list words they recollected or failing that with the first word that came to mind.

• Exclusion test: subjects were instructed to complete the word stems (e.g. "mer__") with words that were not presented on the list.

If conscious recollection (explicit memory) were perfect, then 100% of the completions on the inclusion test would be list words compared to 0% on the exclusion test. In contrast, a complete lack of conscious recollection would produce a situation in which subjects were as likely to produce list words on the exclusion test as on the inclusion test. This would indicate that the subjects could not tell the difference between list and non-list words. Jacoby et al. (1993) assessed the impact of attention on explicit and implicit memory by using full-attention and divided-attention conditions. In the full-attention condition, subjects were instructed to remember the list words for a subsequent memory test; in the divided-attention condition, they had to perform a complex listening task while reading the list words and they were not told there would be a memory test.

The findings are shown in Fig. 6.16. Most studies of cued recall only use a condition resembling the inclusion test, and inspection of

those findings suggests that there was reasonable explicit memory performance in both attention conditions. However, the picture looks very different when the exclusion test data are also considered. Subjects in the divided-attention condition produced the same level of performance on the inclusion and exclusion tests, indicating that they were not making any use of conscious recollection or explicit memory. However, subjects in the full-attention condition did much better on the inclusion test than on the exclusion test, indicating considerable reliance on explicit memory. It also appeared that implicit memory processes were used equally in the divided-attention and full-attention conditions. An important implication of these findings is that attention at the time of learning is of crucial importance to subsequent conscious recollection, but is irrelevant to implicit memory.

In sum, these findings confirm that the crucial distinction between explicit and implicit memory is in terms of the involvement of conscious recollection. This poses problems for researchers, because it is generally difficult to decide whether conscious recollection influences any given memory performance. In spite of this, there is now convincing evidence that the distinction between

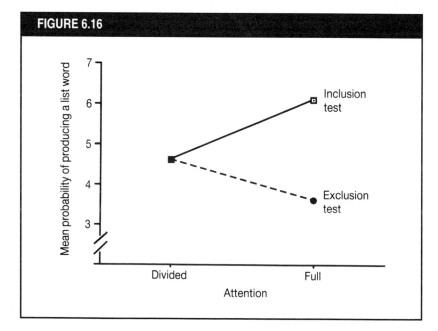

Performance on inclusion and exclusion memory tests as a function of whether attention at learning was divided or full. Adapted from Jacoby et al. (1993).

explicit and implicit memory is both valid and important. Many memory tests (e.g. cued recall; Jacoby et al., 1993) involve a mixture of explicit memory and implicit memory.

Theoretical considerations

Several theoretical accounts of the differences between explicit and implicit memory have been offered in recent years. Some theorists (e.g. Squire, Knowlton, & Musen, 1993) have focused on the underlying brain structures and their associated memory systems. Because such theorists typically rely heavily on evidence from amnesic patients, we will consider their theories in Chapter 7. In contrast, Roediger (1990) has proposed an influential theory in which the focus is on the processes underlying explicit and implicit memory in normal individuals, and this theory will be discussed here. The broader issue of the relative usefulness of structural and processing theories in this area is discussed in Chapter 7.

Roediger's theory
Roediger (1990) based his theoretical approach on the following assumptions:

• There is an important distinction between data-driven processes (those triggered off directly by external stimuli) and conceptually driven processes (those initiated by the subject).

• Data-driven processes often underlie performance on tests of implicit memory, whereas conceptually driven processes frequently sustain performance on tests of explicit memory.

• Memory performance will generally be best when the processing required on the memory test *matches* that used at the time of learning; this assumption closely resembles those incorporated into the transfer-appropriate processing theory of Morris et al. (1977), discussed earlier in the chapter.

The potential usefulness of these theoretical assumptions can be seen if we consider a study by Jacoby (1983). Subjects were initially given words to learn in three different conditions: no context (e.g. XXX - COLD); context (e.g. hot -COLD); and generate (hot - ?). In the last condition, subjects were instructed to generate the opposite of the word presented. An explicit memory test (recognition memory) and an implicit memory test (perceptual identification: recognising rapidly presented words) followed. As can be seen in Fig. 6.17, the learning conditions had very different effects on the two memory tests. Explicit memory was best in the generate condition and worst in the no context

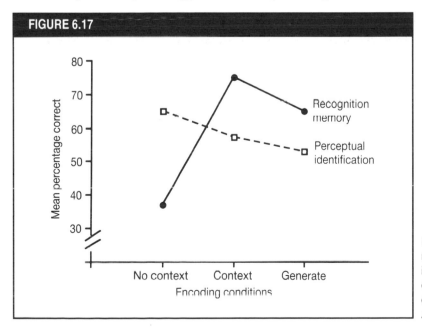

FIGURE 6.17

Mean percentage correct (y-axis: 30, 40, 50, 60, 70, 80)

Recognition memory

Perceptual identification

Encoding conditions: No context, Context, Generate

Performance on recognition memory and perceptual identification tests as a function of conditions at learning (no context; context; or generate). Adapted from Jacoby (1983).

condition, whereas precisely the opposite was the case for implicit memory.

According to Roediger (1990), the perceptual identification task used by Jacoby (1983) involved data-driven processing, and so should have been performed best when learning involved similar data-driven processes (i.e. perceptual processing of the target word in the context and no context conditions) than when it did not (i.e. the generation condition). In contrast, recognition memory depends to a large extent on conceptually driven processes, and so should be performed better when acquisition involved similar conceptually driven processes (i.e. generation condition) than when it did not (i.e. context and no context conditions). The various findings were in line with these expectations.

It follows from the views of Roediger (1990) that manipulations of conceptually driven processes at the time of learning should affect performance mainly on conceptually driven memory tests but should not affect performance on data-driven memory tests. There is relevant evidence in studies that have considered the effects of the levels-of-processing manipulation on memory performance. Deep or semantic proces-sing involves more conceptually driven processing than shallow or non-semantic processing, but deep and shallow processing probably involve comparable amounts of data-driven processing. As expected, deep processing typically produces superior memory performance to shallow processing on a conceptually driven memory test such as free recall (e.g. Hyde & Jenkins, 1973). The position is different if we consider implicit memory tests involving data-driven processes (e.g. word-fragment completion; perceptual identification). With such tests, the levels-of-processing manipulation generally has a non-significant effect (e.g. Jacoby & Dallas, 1981).

It also follows from Roediger's (1990) theoretical position that manipulations of data-driven processes should primarily affect data-driven memory tests. One popular way of manipulating data-driven processes is by varying the modality of presentation (i.e. visual vs. auditory). In general terms, memory on visual data-driven memory tests is better when there is visual presentation at learning than when there is auditory presentation (e.g. Roediger & Blaxton, 1987), but there are only modest effects of modality on more conceptually driven memory tests such as recognition (e.g. Blaxton, 1989).

Evaluation
Roediger's theoretical approach is evaluated at some length in Chapter 7, so only a few comments will be made here. On the positive side, there is a substantial amount of evidence supporting the view that memory performance is better when the processing at encoding (data-driven or conceptually driven) matches the processing at retrieval than when it does not. In addition, it is reasonable to assume that the distinction between data-driven and conceptually driven processing is important.

On the negative side, it has been assumed too often that most tasks (encoding or memory) involve only data-driven or only conceptually driven processes. It is far more likely that most involve a mixture of data-driven and conceptually driven processes (see Challis & Brodbeck, 1992). This then poses the (largely unsolved) problem of how we determine the relative importance of these two types of processing on any given encoding or memory task. As we will see in Chapter 7, there is much evidence indicating that rather different memory structures are involved in explicit and implicit memory, but Roediger (1990) did not include any assumptions about structure.

Varieties of implicit memory
Many researchers have discussed implicit memory as if it refers to a single memory system. However, the fact that there are numerous different kinds of implicit memory tasks ranging from motor skills to word completion suggests there are probably a number of different memory systems involved. Relevant research was reported by Witherspoon and Moscovitch (1989), who compared priming performance on perceptual-identification and fragment-completion tasks. They obtained statistical independence (lack of correlation) between the two implicit tasks: subjects who had a large priming effect on one task showed no particular tendency to have a large priming effect

on the other task. The lack of relationship between performance on the two tasks suggests they involve different processes. In the words of Witherspoon and Moscovitch (1989, p.22): "The results are not consistent with current multiple memory system interpretations that assign all implicit, priming tests to one system and explicit tests to another."

It remains unclear how many varieties of implicit memory need to be identified. It has been suggested by several researchers (e.g. Tulving & Schacter, 1990) that there are important differences between *perceptual* and *conceptual implicit tests*. On most perceptual implicit tests, the stimulus presented at study is presented at test in a degraded form (e.g. word-fragment completion; word-stem completion; perceptual identification). On conceptual implicit tests, on the other hand, the test provides information that is conceptually related to the studied information, but there is no perceptual similarity between the study and test stimuli (e.g. general knowledge questions such as "What is the largest animal on earth?"; generation of category exemplars from a category such as "four-footed animals").

Some evidence supporting the distinction between perceptual and conceptual implicit memory tests was reported by Srinivas and Roediger (1990). They discovered that manipulation of the level of processing (i.e. semantic vs. non-semantic) at the time of learning affected priming on a conceptual test but did not affect priming on a perceptual test. There are several other studies reporting that the level of processing had no effect on perceptual priming, but a note of caution is in order. Challis and Brodbeck (1992) reviewed the literature, and concluded that the level of processing has some effect on implicit perceptual tests, albeit smaller than the effect on implicit conceptual tests.

In Chapter 7, evidence is reported from brain-damaged patients suggesting that different systems are involved in priming on the word-completion task and in motor skills learning (Butters, Heindel, & Salmon, 1990). Much current research is investigating these issues, and it is likely that the number and nature of memory systems involved in implicit memory will soon be much better established.

Section summary

Some understanding of the differences between explicit and implicit memory can be achieved by considering the role of data-driven and conceptually driven processes. However, it is often difficult to establish the relative contributions of these two types of processing to task performance, and it is probable that memory structures should be taken into account. It is likely that there are various forms of implicit memory. This is not surprising when one considers that implicit memory is defined only by the absence of conscious recollection. There could be numerous quite different forms of memory which do not involve conscious recollection. As the distinction between explicit and implicit memory has been used extensively in research on amnesic patients, a fuller theoretical discussion of the issues will be delayed until after the amnesia research has been considered in Chapter 7.

MEMORY FROM A CONNECTIONIST PERSPECTIVE

Parallel distributed processing (PDP) models or connectionist networks provide an alternative way of considering human learning and memory (parallel = more than one process occurring at a time; distributed processing = processing occurring in a number of different locations). The basic characteristics of this approach were considered in Chapter 1, and should perhaps be re-read by any reader who has forgotten what was said there. Although several different connectionist or PDP models have been proposed, the focus here will be on those assumptions that are common to most of them.

It is assumed in most of the theories discussed earlier in this chapter that there are huge numbers of memory traces stored in long-term memory, and that retrieval involves gaining access to the information in a particular memory trace. The assumptions incorporated into connectionist models are very different. It is assumed within such models that the information about a person, object, or event is stored in several interconnected units rather than in a single place. Thus, for example, you may have a friend called Rebecca, who is a post-graduate student, 26 years old, married, with no children. According to the connectionist model put forward by McClelland (1981), each of these pieces of information about Rebecca is stored in a separate unit. Learning involves gaining access to one or more of these units, which then activate the other units and re-create your knowledge of Rebecca. It is also assumed that each unit is involved in the representation of several different individuals or objects.

What are the advantages of the connectionist approach? The notion that knowledge about a person or object is distributed across several units rather than being concentrated in a single memory trace means that the system can often function reasonably well even if a unit is damaged or imperfect information is supplied to it. Consider, for example, the task of deciding which prime minister this century was male, very domineering, and won three consecutive general elections. You may well have thought of the answer almost immediately in spite of being misled by the first piece of information or cue (i.e. maleness). This is readily explained by connectionist models. All three cues activate their respective units, and these units then activate other units associated with them. As a consequence, there is more activation of the name "Thatcher" than any other.

In contrast, consider a theory according to which retrieval works in a serial fashion in which only one cue at a time is considered. The cue "male" restricts the search to the names of male prime ministers, and then an attempt is made to think of domineering male prime ministers. From that smaller list, there is no one who also won three elections running, and so retrieval fails.

Another virtue of the PDP approach to learning and memory is that it permits what McClelland, Rumelhart, and Hinton (1986) refer to as "spontaneous generalisations" (see also Chapter 10). These involve "remembering" general information that was not learned in the first place. For example, if someone asks you whether right-wing people tend to be older or younger than left-wing people, you might happen to know the answer because it is part of your stock of knowledge. According to PDP theorists, however, you might be able to come up with the right answer simply on the basis of specific information about individuals. The cue "right-wing" would activate information about all of the right-wing people you know, including information about their ages, and the same thing would happen for the cue "left-wing". In other words, novel and spontaneous generalisations can be produced readily even though the sought-for information is not directly stored in memory.

McClelland et al. (1986) pointed out that PDP models allow for what they term "default assignment", in which missing information about an individual or an object is filled in on the basis of information about similar individuals or objects (see also Chapter 11). Suppose, for example, that you forget how old your friend Rebecca is. When Rebecca's characteristics (e.g. a friend; post-graduate student; married; no children) are activated, they will activate units containing information about other individuals resembling Rebecca. If most of the married post-graduate students you know who have no children are in their twenties, then that information will be activated. In other words, Rebecca's age becomes "mid-twenties" through default assignment, and you may not be aware that your assessment of her age was not based on direct knowledge.

There is plenty of experimental evidence for default assignment (see Chapter 13 for a fuller account). For example, Bower, Black, and Turner (1979) presented stories involving everyday events such as going to a restaurant. On a subsequent recognition memory test, subjects claimed that information which would naturally form part of such an event (but which had not been stated explicitly) had actually been presented. The reason for this is presumably because subjects filled in the missing information by means of default assignments.

More potential advantages of the PDP approach to memory are discussed by McClelland and Rumelhart (1986 a,b), but there is space here to discuss only two more. People typically behave as if they had both general and specific information stored in long-term memory, and an issue that has to be faced by memory theorists is how to account for the relationship between these two kinds of information. For example, we have stored information about specific dogs we have encountered, but we also have more general and abstract information about what a "dog" is. The PDP approach provides a reasonably convincing account of how general information can emerge from specific information (see McClelland & Rumelhart, 1986a,b, for details). In essence, presentation of the word "dog" leads to the activation of numerous units relating to specific dogs we know. This leads via an averaging process to a set of attributes (e.g. size, colour) corresponding in some sense to a "typical" dog.

The PDP approach to memory also has advantages in its account of amnesia. Amnesic patients tend to be better at learning and remembering the *common* features of situations than the *idiosyncratic* features found in only one situation. Some understanding of this pattern of impairment can be gained if we make the simple assumption that learning experiences produce a smaller increase in the connection strengths among the relevant units for amnesic patients than for other people. This slower rate of learning means that amnesics should show very poor memory for the non-repeated, idiosyncratic features of situations, because connection strengths remain low. This prediction is certainly in accord with the evidence. On the other hand, amnesic patients should eventually show learning for repeated information as the relevant connection strengths slowly increase, and this is also supported by the evidence. The fact that amnesic patients can learn some things (e.g. many motor skills) as rapidly as normal people is accounted for by arguing that the kinds of learning involved are those that are not facilitated by large increases in the strengths of connections among units.

Evaluation

It is difficult to evaluate the PDP or connectionist approach to learning and memory, because it is still being developed. However, the main reason for the great interest in it is that it appears to offer a strong conceptual framework within which to consider the functioning of human memory. In particular, a memory system in which processing is parallel is potentially more powerful and flexible than one in which processing does not occur in parallel. Psychophysiological assessment of brain activity indicates that processing typically occurs in a parallel rather than a serial fashion, and that gives the connectionist approach a certain plausibility. There is current controversy about the similarity between connectionist networks and brain functioning. Johnson-Laird (1988, p.193) argued that: "Whatever sort of computations brain cells carry out—and little is known of their nature—they are not satisfactorily idealised by network units. The brain is not wired up in a way that resembles any of the current connectionist proposals." However, it may well be that that is an unduly negative view.

As we grow older, so our brains lose substantial numbers of brain cells each day. It might be expected that this would have dramatic effects on our ability to learn and remember, but what generally happens is a modest reduction in the efficiency of the brain. This effect is known as *graceful degradation*, and is exactly what would be predicted if memories are widely distributed in the brain. If, on the other hand, memories are stored in specific places, then the normal ageing process might have devastating effects on parts of our memory systems. Thus, evidence for graceful degradation supports the connectionist approach over rival theories.

One of the characteristics of PDP theories that makes evaluation difficult is that the issues addressed by PDP theorists overlap only partially with those of the other theorists considered in this chapter. However, there must be some doubts as to whether the complexities of memory processes and structures identified by cognitive psychologists can be captured adequately by the PDP emphasis on strengths of connections among units. Baddeley (1990) argued that connectionist models may prove successful when accounting for low-level systems or modules such as the phonological store in the working memory system; however, they may not be able to account for a more complex system such as the central executive, which co-ordinates information from a number of different modules. Future prospects for the PDP and connectionist approaches are discussed in Chapter 19.

CHAPTER SUMMARY

This chapter has been concerned with major theories of learning and memory. These theories differ in terms of whether they are concerned mainly with the structures or processes involved in memory. They also differ in terms of whether they focus on the storage of information or its subsequent retrieval.

According to the multi-store theory, there are separate sensory, short-term, and long-term stores. There is strong evidence to support the notion of various qualitatively different memory stores, but this approach provides a very over-simplified view. For example, multi-store theorists assumed there are unitary short-term and long-term stores, whereas the reality is much more complex.

Baddeley (e.g. 1986) proposed replacing the unitary short-term store with a working memory system consisting of three components: an attention-like central executive; an articulatory loop holding speech-based information; and a visuo-spatial sketch pad specialised for spatial and/or visual coding. This working memory system is concerned with both active processing and transient storage of information, and so is of relevance to non-memory activities such as comprehension and verbal reasoning.

One of the main criticisms of the multi-store approach was that it focused too much on the structure of memory and not enough on the processes involved. Craik and Lockhart (1972) attempted to remedy this situation in their levels-of-processing theory. They (and their followers) identified depth of processing (i.e. extent to which meaning is processed), elaboration of processing, and distinctiveness of processing as key determinants of long-term memory. The emphasis is too much on what happens at the time of learning, with insufficient attention being paid to the relationship between the processes at

learning and those at the time of test. Other problems are that the theory is insufficiently explanatory and that it is generally difficult to assess the depth of processing.

Several theories of retrieval have considered recall and recognition. There has been much controversy as to whether the processes involved in recall and recognition are basically similar. Two-process theorists focused on differences between these two kinds of memory tests, whereas Tulving with his encoding specificity principle argued that the informational overlap between retrieval environment and memory trace is crucial for both recall and recognition. There is a growing awareness that recall sometimes occurs in a relatively fast and direct fashion, whereas at other times it occurs in an indirect fashion which can resemble problem solving. In similar fashion, recognition sometimes occurs mainly on the basis of familiarity, and sometimes it involves conscious recollection. An implication is that there is no single or simple relationship between recall and recognition.

Recall and recognition depend mainly on explicit memory, in that they involve conscious recollection. In contrast, memory tests such as word-fragment completion or word-stem completion mainly depend on implicit memory, because conscious recollection is generally not involved. However, these differences are relative rather than absolute. Roediger (1990) has proposed that explicit memory usually depends on conceptually driven processes, whereas implicit memory depends on data-driven processes; however, this approach ignores the memory structures involved.

The traditional notion of specific memory traces containing all of the information we possess about objects and people has been challenged by parallel distributed processing theorists. They claim that information is distributed across numerous interconnected units. The fact that connectionist networks learn from experience, function reasonably well when partially damaged, and exhibit phenomena, such as spontaneous generalisation and default assignment, suggests that they may represent a valuable way of conceptualising human memory.

FURTHER READING

Baddeley, A. D. (1990). *Human memory: Theory and practice*. Hove, UK: Lawrence Erlbaum Associates Ltd. This book has two major strengths: it is very well written, and it is unusually comprehensive in its coverage.

Parkin, A. J. (1993). *Memory: Phenomena, experiment and theory*. Oxford: Blackwell. This is a very good textbook which provides coverage of most of the topics discussed in this chapter. It also provides interesting discussion of developmental issues.

Squire, L. R., Knowlton, B., & Musen, G. (1993). The structure and organisation of memory. *Annual Review of Psychology*, *44*, 453–495. Although this article covers several topics, it is especially interesting on the distinction between explicit and implicit memory. This is due in part to Squire's knowledge of the brain structures involved in long-term memory.

7

Memory and Amnesia

INTRODUCTION

One way of increasing our knowledge about human memory is by studying brain-damaged patients suffering from amnesia. Such patients generally have extensive memory problems, which are sometimes so great that they cannot remember that they read the newspaper or ate a meal within the previous hour. There has been considerable interest during this century in identifying the precise nature of their problems, and in attempting to help overcome those problems. Over the past 20 years or so, however, there has been a dramatic increase in the amount of research that cognitive psychologists and cognitive neuropsychologists have carried out on amnesic patients.

Why exactly are amnesic patients of interest to cognitive psychologists and cognitive neuro-psychologists? One major reason is that the study of amnesia provides a good *test-bed* for existing theories of normal memory. Data from amnesic patients can strengthen or weaken the experimental support for memory theories. For example, the notion that there is a valid distinction between short-term and long-term memory stores has been tested with amnesic patients. The discovery that some patients have severely impaired long-term memory but intact short-term memory, whereas a few patients show the opposite pattern, is rather strong evidence that there are separate short-term and long-term stores.

The second major reason is that amnesia research has led to new theoretical developments. Studies of amnesia have suggested theoretical distinctions which then prove to be of relevance to an understanding of memory in normal individuals. Relevant examples are discussed during the course of this chapter.

Although much valuable information about the workings of human memory has been obtained from amnesic patients, it is rather difficult to make rapid progress. There are many reasons for this, but some of the main ones were neatly encapsulated by Hintzman (1990, p.130):

> The ideal data base on amnesia would consist of data from thousands of patients having no other disorders, and having precisely dated lesions [injuries] of known location and extent, and would include many reliable measures spanning all types of knowledge and skills, acquired at known times ranging from the recent to the distant past. Reality falls near the opposite pole of each dimension of this description.

One of the main difficulties in amnesia research stems from the fact that amnesic patients often have relatively widespread brain damage. This makes it difficult to interpret the findings obtained from them. It is especially difficult to know which brain area is primarily responsible for a particular memory deficit if, say, three different brain areas are all damaged.

A major concern of this chapter is with theories of memory, and with the theoretical implications of amnesia research. However, in order to make sense of the findings from amnesic patients, it is clearly necessary to have some background understanding of the amnesic condition. The first point that needs to be emphasised is that the reasons why patients have become amnesic are very varied. Bilateral stroke is one factor causing amnesia, but closed head injury is the most common cause of amnesia. However, patients with closed head injury often have a range of cognitive impairments, and this makes it rather difficult to interpret their memory deficit. As a consequence, most experimental work has focused on patients who have become amnesic because of chronic alcohol abuse (Korsakoff's syndrome). It is a matter of some controversy whether there are sufficient similarities in the nature of the memory impairment among these various groups to justify considering them together.

Those who believe that most amnesic patients form a similar or homogeneous group often refer to the "amnesic syndrome". The main character-istics of this syndrome are as follows:

• There is a very marked impairment of the ability to remember new information which was learned after the onset of the amnesia; this is known as anterograde amnesia.
• There is often great difficulty in remembering events that occurred prior to amnesia; this is known as retrograde amnesia, and is especially pro-nounced in patients with Korsakoff's syndrome.
• Patients suffering from the amnesic syndrome generally have only slightly impaired immediate or short-term memory as indexed by measures such as digit span (i.e. the ability to repeat back a random string of digits immediately after presentation): this is shown at an informal level by the fact that it

is possible to have a normal conversation with an amnesic patient.
• It has been known for a long time that patients with the amnesic syndrome usually have some remaining learning ability after the onset of the amnesia, in spite of their generally poor long-term memory for new information.

It has been established that many amnesic patients conform reasonably well to the characteristics of the "amnesic syndrome". However, some theorists (e.g. Parkin, 1990) have argued that there are actually a number of somewhat distinct syndromes. Some of the major issues here are discussed in the next section.

THE AMNESIC SYNDROME OR SYNDROMES?

The amnesic syndrome can be produced by damage to a number of different brain structures (Parkin & Leng, 1993). These structures are to be found in two separate areas of the brain: a sub-cortical region called the diencephalon, and a cortical region known as the medial temporal lobe. It can be difficult to locate the precise location of damage in any given patient, in part because attempts to do so often occur only on post-mortem examination.

Some of the brain areas that can produce the amnesic syndrome when damaged are shown in Fig. 7.1. Chronic alcoholics who develop Korsakoff's syndrome have brain damage in the diencephalon (especially the mamillary bodies and dorsothalamic nucleus), but typically the frontal cortex is also damaged (Wilkinson & Carlen, 1982). In contrast, herpes simplex encephalitis (which involves inflammation of the brain) has been found to cause widespread damage to the lateral and medial temporal cortex, often extending to the orbito-frontal cortex and the parietal lobe. There are also a number of cases in which some of the temporal lobe was removed from epileptic patients in an attempt to reduce the incidence of epileptic seizures. As a consequence, many of these patients (including the much-studied HM) became severely amnesic (Scoville & Milner, 1957).

FIGURE 7.1

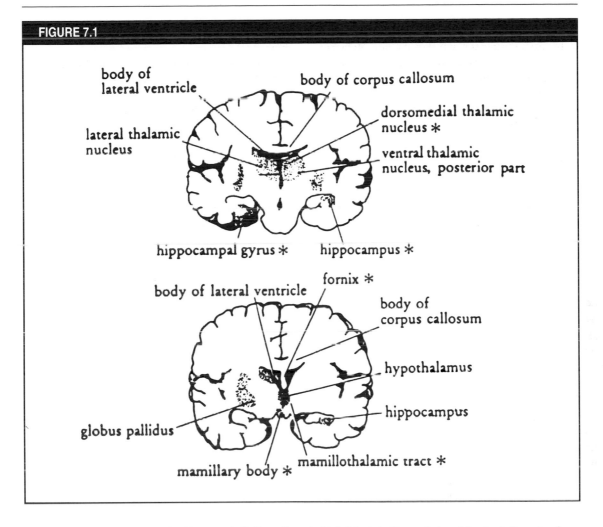

Some of the brain structures involved in amnesia (indicated by asterisks). Adapted with permission of Academic Press Inc. from Butters and Cermak (1980).

Some theorists (e.g. Parkin, 1990) have argued that there are important differences between the effects of damage to the diencephalon and to the temporal lobes, with damage to the temporal lobes being associated with faster forgetting than damage to the diencephalon. Other theorists (e.g. Squire, Knowlton, & Musen, 1993) have argued that the diencephalon and the temporal lobes (which are close together anatomically) both form part of a single system. The precise involvement of these, and other, brain structures in producing impaired memory performance will be discussed towards the end of the chapter.

Korsakoff patients

Most investigations of amnesia have made use almost exclusively of Korsakoff patients. This means that the majority of statements about the characteristics of the amnesic syndrome are actually based on findings obtained from Korsakoff patients. As that is the case, it is worth considering in more detail how suitable such patients are from the point of view of understanding the processes underlying amnesia. Unfortunately, there are two major difficulties posed by Korsakoff patients. The first is that the amnesia usually has a gradual onset, although this is by no means always the case. It is caused by an increasing deficiency of the vitamin thiamine, which is associated with chronic alcoholism. This means that it is often difficult to know whether past events occurred before or after the onset of amnesia, so poor memory for such events may reflect either retrograde or anterograde amnesia.

The second difficulty, as we have seen, is that brain damage in many Korsakoff patients is rather widespread. Structures within the diencephalon, such as the hippocampus and the amygdala, are usually damaged, and these structures appear to be of vital significance to memory. In addition, there is very often damage to the frontal lobes. This may produce a range of cognitive deficits which are not specific to the memory system, but which have indirect effects on memory performance. Cognitive neuropsychologists would find it easier to make coherent sense of findings from Korsakoff patients if brain damage were limited to the diencephalon, but this is rarely the case.

RESIDUAL LEARNING CAPACITY

If we are to understand amnesia, it is extremely important to consider which aspects of learning and memory remain relatively intact in amnesic patients. These aspects are commonly referred to as "residual learning ability". It would be useful to draw up lists of those memory abilities impaired and not impaired in amnesia. By comparing the two lists, it might be possible to identify those processes and/or memory structures that are primarily affected in amnesic patients. Theoretical accounts could then proceed based on a solid foundation of knowledge. The available evidence is less extensive than would be desirable, but we will consider it in some detail. In this section of the chapter we consider residual learning capability, and in the next section there is a discussion of theoretical distinctions involving categorisation of intact and impaired memory skills.

Short-term memory
We saw in the last chapter that amnesic patients have a reasonably intact short-term memory

system but a severely deficient long-term memory system. However, a few brain-damaged patients show the opposite pattern. It has been found (e.g. Butters & Cermak, 1980) that Korsakoff patients perform almost as well as normals on the digit-span task, in which random digits must be repeated back immediately in the correct order. It is especially noteworthy that similar results have also been reported in non-Korsakoff patients, details of two of which will now be given.

NA became amnesic as a result of having a fencing foil forced up his nostril and into his brain. This caused widespread diencephalic and medial temporal damage. Teuber, Milner, and Vaughan (1968) discovered that he performed at the normal level on span measures.

HM had an operation that damaged the temporal lobes, together with partial removal of the hippocampus and amygdala. He also turned out to have a normal level of short-term memory performance as indexed by immediate span (Wickelgren, 1968).

It should be noted that span measures are by no means the only way in which short-term memory can be assessed. However, Baddeley and Warrington (1970) observed normal performance by amnesic patients on a number of other tasks allegedly measuring short-term memory. Although amnesic patients have reasonably intact short-term memory, the few brain-damaged patients who have been found to have memory problems mainly involving short-term memory are of great theoretical interest. As we saw in Chapter 6, the development of theories of short-term memory has been much influenced by evidence obtained from brain-damaged patients with partial deficits in short-term memory.

Skills
Most evidence of residual learning capability in amnesics has been obtained from tasks involving motor or other skills. The tasks on which amnesics have been shown to acquire skills are very varied (see Parkin & Leng, 1993, for a review). These tasks include the following: dressmaking; billiards; finger mazes; tracking a moving target on a pursuit rotor (involving a rotating turntable); jigsaw completions; reading mirror-reversed script; and

mirror drawing. In addition, there is good evidence that skills acquired before the onset of amnesia tend to be retained. For example, Schacter (1983) described an amnesic patient whose golfing skills remained intact.

There are two issues that are important in considering the learning of skills by amnesics. One is whether these skills all reflect the same underlying mechanisms, and the other is whether amnesics' ability to acquire these skills is as good as that of normals. On the first issue, it is still not clear whether the range of preserved skills identified so far makes any psychological sense, but there is a suspicion that it may not. On the second issue, there are some cases in which amnesics learn skills as rapidly as normals, and other skills where their rate of learning is significantly slower. It is to some of these apparent inconsistencies in the literature that we now turn.

Speed of skills acquisition

Corkin (1968) reported that the amnesic patient HM was able to learn the pursuit rotor, which involves manual tracking of a moving target, and mirror drawing. His rate of learning was slower than that of normals on the pursuit rotor, but was approximately normal on the mirror-drawing task. In contrast, Cermak, Lewis, Butters, and Goodglass (1973) found that Korsakoff patients learned the pursuit rotor as fast as normals. However, the amnesic patients were slower than the normals at learning a finger maze.

There have been a number of studies of reading mirror-reversed script. In these studies it is possible to distinguish between general improvement in speed of reading produced by practice and more specific improvement produced by re-reading the same groups of words or sentences. Cohen and Squire (1980) reported that amnesics demonstrated general and specific improvement in reading mirror-reversed script, and there was still evidence of improvement after a delay of three months. Martone et al. (1984) also obtained evidence of general and specific improvement in amnesics. However, although the general practice effect was as great in amnesics as in normals, the specific practice effect was not. It may be that normals (but not amnesics) are able to use speed-reading

strategies to facilitate reading of repeated groups of words.

What skills are preserved?

Amnesic patients show good, or even normal, rates of learning for several tasks involving different skills. What is much more difficult to do is to describe what (if anything) these tasks have in common. However, a start has been made by Moscovitch (1984), who argued that amnesics typically perform well on tasks possessing three characteristics:

*   it is obvious to the patient what is required;
*   the necessary responses are already in the patient's repertoire;
*   there is no need to refer to any specific past event in order to solve the task.

Moscovitch has provided a useful description of some of the main features of those tasks on which amnesics show good skill learning. However, it is rather difficult to move from the descriptive to the explanatory level. Possible explanations will be considered later in the chapter.

Priming effects

Suppose that someone is presented with the same stimulus on two separate occasions, and asked to perform the same task on it each time. For example, a word might be presented briefly, and people could be asked to identify it (i.e. say what word it is). Performance is generally better the second time that the stimulus is presented, presumably because useful information is stored in memory as a result of the first encounter with the stimulus. This improved performance is known as the repetition-priming effect (see Chapter 6). As we will see, amnesics generally demonstrate normal or nearly normal priming effects on most tasks.

Cermak, Talbot, Chandler, and Wolbarst (1985) compared the performance of Korsakoff patients and non-amnesic alcoholics. The patients were presented with a list of words followed by a priming task. This task was perceptual identification, and involved presenting the words at the minimal exposure time needed to identify them correctly. As can be seen in Fig. 7.2, the

FIGURE 7.2

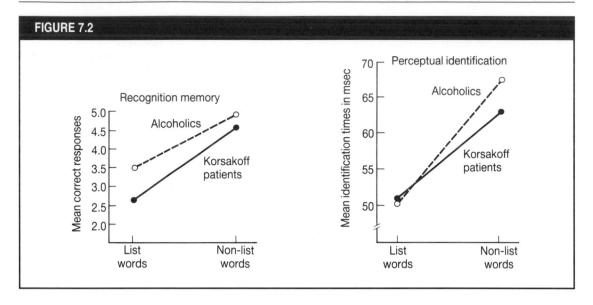

Recognition memory and perceptual identification of Korsakoff patients and non-amnesic alcoholics; delayed conditions only. Data from Cermak et al. (1985).

performance of the Korsakoff patients resembled that of the control subjects, with identification times being faster for the primed list words than for the unprimed non-list words. In other words, the amnesic patients showed as great a perceptual priming effect as the controls. Cermak et al. (1985) also used a conventional test of recognition memory for the list words. In line with much previous research, the Korsakoff patients did significantly worse than the controls on this task (see Fig. 7.2).

A somewhat different task was used by Crovitz, Harvey, and McClanahan (1981). On two successive days they presented "picture puzzles" that were difficult to identify. The time taken by amnesic patients to identify these pictures was much less on the second day than it had been on the first one, indicating that a considerable amount of perceptual learning had occurred. However, the amnesics were very poor in terms of recogniton memory for the repeated pictures.

An especially interesting and important repetition-priming effect was investigated by Graf, Squire, and Mandler (1984). Word lists were presented, with the subjects deciding how much they liked each word. The lists were followed by one of four memory tests. Three of the tests were conventional memory tests (free recall; recognition memory; cued recall), but the fourth test (word completion; see Chapter 6) measured a priming effect. On this last test, subjects were given three-letter word fragments (e.g. STR__) and simply had to write down the first word they thought of which started with those letters (e.g. STRAP; STRIP). Priming was assessed by the extent to which the word completions corresponded to words the list previously presented. Amnesic patients did much worse than controls on all of the conventional memory tests, but there was no difference between the two groups in the size of their priming effect on the word-completion task (see Fig. 7.3).

Section summary

Amnesic patients exhibit a variety of repetition-priming effects. Their performance is greatly improved by the prior presentation of stimuli even when there is an absence of conscious awareness that these stimuli have previously been presented (as indicated by poor recognition memory performance). There has been some controversy as to whether this disparity between

FIGURE 7.3

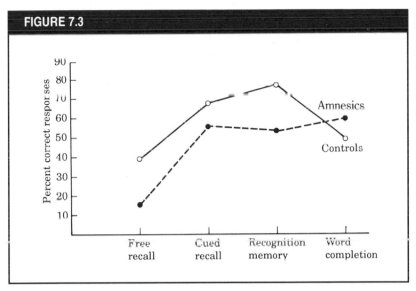

Free recall, cued recall, recognition memory, and word completion in amnesic patients and controls. Data from different experiments reported by Graf et al. (1984).

performance and conscious awareness on priming tasks is unique to amnesic patients. Some evidence that it is not was obtained by Meudell and Mayes (1981). They used a task in which cartoons had to be searched for specified objects. When amnesics repeated the task seven weeks later, they found the objects faster than the first time in spite of very poor recognition memory for the cartoons. When normals were tested at the much longer interval of 17 months, they showed exactly the same pattern. This indicates that repetition-priming effects in the absence of conscious awareness of having seen the stimuli before can be found in normal individuals as well as in amnesic patients.

It used to be thought that amnesic patients were at a severe disadvantage to other people with respect to all forms of learning and the long-term retention of information. However, it has become increasingly clear that many amnesic patients are actually surprisingly good at acquiring a variety of skills and knowledge. The most obvious reason why the learning abilities of amnesic patients used to be under-estimated is because amnesics often have very limited or non-existent conscious awareness of what they have learned. It is only when learning is assessed in ways that place no reliance on introspective evidence that the true extent of amnesics' residual learning capability becomes clear.

One of the major requirements of a good theory of amnesia is that it should permit us to understand why some skills and abilities are more or less intact in amnesic patients, whereas other skills and abilities are severely impaired. It cannot be claimed that any current theory has achieved that goal, but there are several theories that represent useful first steps to understanding. Ideally, theories of amnesia should also help to explain memory functioning in normal individuals. It is to such theories that we now turn.

THEORIES OF MEMORY AND AMNESIA

As was mentioned earlier in the chapter, there has been an interesting change in theories of amnesia. Until recently, most theorists attempted to apply pre-existing theories of normal memory functioning to amnesics. Thus, for example, the evidence of Baddeley and Warrington (1970) and others seemed at one time to provide strong support for the multi-store approach which was discussed in Chapter 6. A few years later, Cermak (1979) attempted to apply the levels-of-processing approach to amnesia. He argued that amnesics typically fail to process the meaning of to-be-remembered information, and that this lack of semantic processing causes the severely impaired long-term memory found in amnesic patients. This theory has been abandoned, because there is strong evidence that most amnesic patients are well able to process meaning.

More recent theorists have shown less of a tendency to adopt the approach of attempting to make previously existing theories fit the facts of amnesia. Instead, they have started by considering the pattern of deficits exhibited by amnesic patients, and have then constructed new theories designed to accommodate that pattern. More recently still, some of these theories have been modified in the light of additional testing on normal individuals. In other words, theorists are increasingly inclined to take account of data from both amnesic patients and normal individuals in the construction and development of their theories of human memory.

The assumption that there is a single, unified long-term memory system has been rejected by all of the theorists we will be considering. Most theorists have argued that there are at least two major types of processing associated with long-term memory; however, other theorists have focused on memory systems, and have attempted to identify the underlying brain systems involved. Some of the general issues relating to the processes–systems distinction will be discussed later in the chapter after the various theories have been considered.

An important point that is worth emphasising is that many of the theories to be discussed overlap with each other. This fact, coupled with the imprecision of many of the theoretical constructs used, means that it is very difficult to decide which theoretical approaches are more promising than others.

Episodic versus semantic memory

As was discussed in Chapter 6, our long-term memories contain an amazing variety of different kinds of information. As a consequence, there is a natural temptation to assume that there are a number of different long-term memory systems, each of which is specialised for certain types of information. Tulving (1972) argued for a distinction between *episodic memory* and *semantic*

memory. This distinction, and some of the available evidence from normal individuals, will be discussed before its potential relevance to amnesia is considered.

Episodic memory has an autobiographical flavour about it, referring to the storage of specific events or episodes which occurred in a particular place at a particular time. Thus, memory for what you had for breakfast this morning or what happened last Christmas Day are examples of episodic memory. In contrast, semantic memory contains information about our stock of knowledge about the world. Tulving (1972, p.386) defined semantic memory in the following way:

It is a mental thesaurus, organized knowledge a person possesses about words and other verbal symbols, their meanings and referents, about relations among them, and about rules, formulas, and algorithms for the manipulation of these symbols, concepts, and relations. Semantic memory does not register perceptible properties of inputs, but rather cognitive referents of input signals.

There has been some controversy about the usefulness of the distinction between episodic and semantic memory. There is a clear difference in *content* between the information in episodic and semantic memory, but it is less obvious that there is a difference in the *processes* involved. One of the reasons for doubting that there are two separate memory systems is the fact that episodic and semantic memory are strongly interdependent in their functioning. Consider, for example, memory concerning what you had for breakfast this morning. Although this is basically stored in episodic memory, semantic memory is also involved, in that your knowledge of the world allowed you to identify what was on your plate as bacon, eggs, sausages, toast, or whatever. Thus, episodic and semantic memory typically work in tandem.

Tulving (1989) reported some evidence that appears to go against the thrust of the previous paragraph. A small dose of radioactive gold was injected into the bloodstream of volunteers, who were asked to think about personal events or

reason is that implicit memory consists of a large and apparently unrelated collection of skills and processes. This is unsurprising, given that the term covers all forms of memory performance occurring in the absence of conscious recollection. One reasonable sub-division within implicit memory is between priming and motor skills, and some evidence for this was discussed earlier (Butters et al., 1990).

There have been various attempts to identify the major categories of procedural or implicit learning. According to Tulving and Schacter (1990), the various implicit priming effects that have been demonstrated depend on three different neural systems:

- A perceptual representation system underlying priming for words.
- A structural description representation system underlying priming for pictures and objects.
- A semantic memory system underlying priming on conceptual implicit memory tasks (e.g. producing instances to category names).

A more inclusive list was provided by Squire (1987). He identified five major types of procedural or implicit learning:

- cognitive skill learning;
- perceptual learning;
- motor skill learning;
- repetition learning;
- classical conditioning.

At present, it is clear that there are various systems involved in implicit memory, but there is no consensus on the number and nature of these systems.

Why are humans equipped with rather separate brain systems underlying declarative or explicit memory and procedural or implicit memory? Squire et al. (1993, pp.485–486) argued that each major brain system has its own particular value:

One system involves limbic/diencephalic structures, which in concert with neocortex provides the basis for conscious recollections. This system is fast, phylo-genetically recent, and specialised for one-trial learning ... The system is fallible in the sense that it is sensitive to interference and prone to retrieval failure. It is also precious, giving rise to the capacity for personal autobiography and the possibility of cultural evolution.

Other kinds of memory have also been identified ... Such memories can be acquired, stored, and retrieved without the participation of the limbic/diencephalon brain system. These forms of memory are phylogenetically early, they are reliable and consistent, and they provide for myriad, nonconscious ways of responding to the world ... they create much of the mystery of human experience.

Theories: Processes versus systems

It can be argued that each of the main theories of explicit and implicit memory emphasises either processes or memory systems. Roediger (1990) is a prominent processing theorist, and Cohen (e.g. 1984) and Squire (e.g. Squire et al., 1993) are leading systems theorists. Processing theorists tend to be cognitive psychologists whose main focus is on normal memory functioning, whereas those who advocate memory systems tend to be neuroscientists whose main focus is on brain-damaged patients.

Which approach is more useful? This issue is the subject of much controversy at present, but we believe that the memory systems approach possesses certain advantages. First, it seems more convincing and in line with the evidence to account for amnesia in terms of damage to a brain system involving structures within the limbic system than in terms of impaired conceptually driven processing.

Second, there are many findings that can only be understood by taking account of brain processes and systems. For example, Marsolek, Kosslyn, and Squire (1992) found that changing the visual appearance of stimuli between study and test had an effect when the test items were presented to the right hemisphere, but not when they were presented to the left hemisphere. It is not clear how Roediger (1990) would account for these findings, given that the stimuli and the processing requirements remained the same whichever hemisphere received the target items. From a memory or brain systems perspective, the findings are consistent with other evidence that the brain systems in the right hemisphere are more sensitive to the specific characteristics of visual stimuli (Schacter, 1992).

Third, and most important, memory systems theorists make use of a much greater range of information than processing theorists. Many systems theorists adopt a thoroughgoing multi-disciplinary approach based on the findings of cognitive psychologists, neurophysiologists, and neuroanatomists. Constructing theories from multi-disciplinary evidence is more difficult, but ultimately more valuable, than constructing them from a more limited data base.

The reader may be wondering whether it is really necessary for theorists to focus on processes at the expense of memory systems, or on memory systems at the expense of processes. It is likely that theorists in future will follow systems theorists in taking account of our knowledge of brain functioning, and will follow processing theorists in focusing on the precise processes involved in performing different encoding and retrieval tasks.

MEMORY IN ALZHEIMER'S DISEASE

As was mentioned earlier, Alzheimer's disease is a form of dementia or loss of mental abilities. There is extensive brain damage, including numerous senile plaques (patches or lesions) and neuro-fibrillary tangles in the frontal, parietal, and temporal lobes of the cortex. It is progressive in the sense that there is a steady deterioration, with memory impairment in the early stages being followed by more general cognitive impairments. The progressive nature of Alzheimer's disease poses problems for research, because the impairments shown by a patient at one time may be only a small fraction of the impairments shown by that patient on re-testing.

Scientists are currently working on drugs that might reduce the extent of the brain damage. In order for such drugs to be of most use, it will clearly be necessary to diagnose Alzheimer's disease as early as possible before the brain damage becomes widespread. Because memory problems are among the first symptoms of the disease, this gives research into the memory deficit in Alzheimer's disease major practical significance.

Most research on memory in Alzheimer patients has focused on patients in the early stages of the disease. If Alzheimer patients in the later stages of the disease were to be tested, there would be massive impairments on virtually all memory tasks. It should also be noted that many of the studies used patients who should strictly be described as suffering from dementia of the Alzheimer's Type. The complexities of diagnosis mean that it is often not certain whether or not a given patient is actually suffering from Alzheimer's disease. However, for convenience we will use the term Alzheimer's disease in preference to the wordier "dementia of the Alzheimer's Type".

Basic findings

As with Korsakoff patients, there is a marked impairment of long-term memory in Alzheimer patients as assessed by tests of explicit memory. As Morris (1991) pointed out in his review, Alzheimer patients show severely impaired recall and recognition memory for numerous types of stimuli including word lists, faces, and stories. This appears to happen, at least in part, because of deficient semantic processing. For example, the recognition memory of Alzheimer patients is no better following instructions to process the meanings of words than following instructions to perform a non-semantic task such as deciding whether list words rhyme with other words (Corkin, 1982).

Alzheimer patients differ from Korsakoff patients in that their short-term memory is significantly impaired on various tests such as memory span. The articulatory loop component of the working memory system (Baddeley, 1986; see Chapter 6) is used on memory span tasks, but appears to be unimpaired in Alzheimer patients. Relevant evidence was obtained by Morris (1987). Subjects were prevented from using the articulatory loop on a memory span task by being required to perform an articulatory suppression task (involving saying something simple repeatedly) at the same time. Articulatory suppression reduced performance on the memory span task as much for Alzheimer's patients as for normal controls, suggesting that Alzheimer patients normally make as much use as normals of the articulatory loop.

If the short-term memory deficit in Alzheimer patients is not due to an impairment in the articulatory loop, to what is it due? According to Baddeley et al. (1986), the problem lies in the central executive component of working memory (Chapter 6). More specifically, they argued that it is the ability of the central executive to co-ordinate activities which is impaired in Alzheimer patients. In order to test this notion, Baddeley et al. (1986) gave Alzheimer's patients easy versions of a pursuit tracking task and a digit span task to perform separately. The tasks were made sufficiently easy that performance in terms of time on target and numbers of errors, respectively, was comparable for Alzheimer patients, the normal elderly, and young control subjects. When the two tasks had to be performed together, however, the performance of the Alzheimer patients was considerably more disrupted than that of the other two groups. This finding suggests that Alzheimer patients have difficulty in co-ordinating two tasks, but it may also reflect reduced processing capacity.

Alzheimer patients are only slightly impaired on tests of vocabulary, which might suggest that their semantic memory is essentially intact. However, they do show significant impairment on some measures of semantic memory. Flicker, Ferris, and Crook (1987) used two tasks. The first task involved presenting a picture of an object or a name (e.g. chair), followed by a question about category membership (e.g. "Is this an article of furniture?"). The performance of Alzheimer patients was unimpaired on this task. The second task involved presenting a picture, followed by either the correct name or a false one from the same category. Alzheimer patients were much worse than normal controls in deciding accurately whether the name described the picture. These findings suggest that Alzheimer patients retain some knowledge about semantic categories, but often have insufficient knowledge available to make fine discriminations between members of the same category.

We have now discussed various memorial limitations of Alzheimer patients. However, there are some memory tasks on which their performance is either normal or nearly so. As we saw earlier, Alzheimer patients show reasonably good learning on the pursuit rotor (Butters et al., 1990), a finding that has been reported by other researchers (see Morris, 1991, for a review). Alzheimer patients also show good memory performance on priming tasks. For example, Nebes, Brady, and Huff (1989) used a lexical decision task, in which subjects have to decide whether a string of letters forms a word. There is a semantic priming effect on this task, in which a previously presented semantically related word can speed up lexical decision (e.g. subjects can decide more rapidly that BUTTER is a word if it has been preceded by the word BREAD). Nebes et al. (1989) discovered that the semantic priming effect was actually greater for Alzheimer patients than for controls.

Theoretical implications

There are a number of similarities in memory performance between Korsakoff patients and Alzheimer patients. Both groups of patients have poor long-term explicit memory as assessed by tests such as recall and recognition. In addition, both groups have reasonably intact priming effects and learning of motor skills. However, there are also some differences. Alzheimer patients have impaired short-term memory and semantic memory for knowledge acquired before the onset of disease, whereas Korsakoff patients do not. Baddeley (1990, p.429) summarised the overall findings in the following way: "Alzheimer patients ... show a combination of the amnesic syndrome together with the disturbance in central executive functioning." In addition, Alzheimer patients suffer from a much more pronounced problem with semantic memory than do Korsakoff patients.

At a theoretical level, it is true in approximate terms that Alzheimer patients have reasonably good implicit memory but a severe impairment of explicit memory. However, that statement needs to be qualified. Although implicit memory tasks are usually well performed by Alzheimer patients, Butters et al. (1990) discussed findings which showed that they do relatively better on some implicit memory tasks (e.g. pursuit rotor) than on others (e.g. word completion).

Section summary

Alzheimer patients typically exhibit a wider range of memory impairments than do Korsakoff patients and other brain-damaged patients suffering from the amnesic syndrome. The findings from Alzheimer patients have so far proved of less theoretical interest than those from amnesic patients. This may be due in part to the difficulty associated with accounting for the multiple memory deficits found in Alzheimer patients. It may also reflect the fact that there has been considerably more research on amnesic patients than on Alzheimer patients.

CHAPTER SUMMARY

Many of the most important theoretical advances in recent years arose out of the substantially increased amount of research on amnesia. Although that research has proved fruitful, it has also proved complex. Many theorists have identified an "amnesic syndrome", but the pattern of memory impairment depends at least in part on the area of the brain that is damaged.

The study of amnesic patients has provided a new way of evaluating theories of normal memory. For example, the multi-store model is based on the view that there is a single short-term store and a single long-term memory store. This view appears woefully limited when one considers those amnesic patients who have a complex pattern of intact and impaired aspects of long-term memory functioning. In similar fashion, advocates of the levels-of-processing approach were disconcerted by the discovery that most amnesic patients can process information in terms of its meaning, but that this deep processing has practically no beneficial effect on long-term memory. Finally, the distinction between episodic and semantic memory has been influential, but its theoretical significance

has been reduced because the memory deficits in amnesia cannot be accounted for in terms of the distinction.

The most exciting result of amnesia research has been the introduction and development of new theoretical distinctions. The distinction between procedural (knowing how) and declarative (knowing that) knowledge was put forward many years ago, but only became important when it was found that it could help to account for the memory deficits of amnesics. In similar fashion, the distinction between implicit and explicit memory is one that has received its strongest support from the study of amnesic patients, and it is now generally felt to be of major significance. The evidence from amnesic patients indicates that much information that cannot be accessed on direct tests of explicit memory is available on indirect tests of implicit memory. The implication that memory can be demonstrated by performance (implicit memory) in the absence of any conscious awareness of recollection (explicit memory) means that conscious awareness is of much less importance to memory than had been previously thought.

Accounts of explicit and implicit memory can be divided into processing theories (e.g. Roediger, 1990) and memory systems theories (e.g. Squire et al., 1993). Those favouring memory systems attempt to identify the brain systems underlying different aspects of memory by making use of data from amnesic patients. In future, it is likely that theorists will attempt to integrate processing and memory systems notions in their formulations.

The investigation of Alzheimer patients has revealed some interesting similarities and differences between their memory performance and that of Korsakoff patients. Both groups of patients have poor long-term explicit memory but relatively intact implicit memory (e.g. motor skills; priming effects). However, the memory impairment in Alzheimer patients is more severe than in Korsakoff patients, as it also includes short-term memory and semantic memories formed before brain damage. The variety of memory impairments found in Alzheimer patients presumably reflects the widespread brain damage associated with Alzheimer's disease.

FURTHER READING

Graf, P., & Masson, M. E. J. (1993). *Implicit memory: New directions in cognition, development, and neuropsychology*. Hove, UK: Lawrence Erlbaum Associates Ltd. As the title suggests, this is a valuable source book for anyone interested in making a detailed study of implicit memory.

Morris, R. G. (1991). The nature of memory impairment in Alzheimer-type dementia. In J. Weinman & J. Hunter (Eds.), *Memory: Neurochemical and abnormal perspectives*. London: Harwood. This chapter is very accessible, and gives a good overall account of our current knowledge about memory in Alzheimer patients.

Parkin, A. J., & Leng, N. R. C. (1993). *Neuropsychology of the amnesic syndrome*. Hove, UK: Lawrence Erlbaum Associates Ltd. The effects of different kinds of brain damage on memory are discussed at length. This book is especially useful for those interested in the details of brain structure and its relationship to memory functioning.

Squire, L. R., Knowlton, B., & Musen, G. (1993). The structure and organisation of memory. *Annual Review of Psychology, 44*, 453–495. This chapter is complex, but it is very valuable for its coverage of the brain or memory systems approach to amnesia.

8

Everyday Memory

INTRODUCTION

When most people think about memory, they consider it in the context of their own everyday experience. They wonder why their own memory is so fallible, or why some people's memories seem much better than others. Perhaps they ask themselves what they could do in order to improve their own memories. Although these are the issues of general concern, we saw in Chapters 6 and 7 that psychologists have carried out a considerable amount of research on human memory which seems of only marginal relevance to these issues. Neisser (1978, pp.4–5) drew attention to this unfortunate state of affairs:

> The results of a hundred years of the psychological study of memory are somewhat discouraging. We have established firm empirical generalisations, but most of them are so obvious that every ten-year-old knows them anyway ... If X is an interesting or socially significant aspect of memory, then psychologists have hardly ever studied X.

Neisser's (1978) arguments seem persuasive, and many psychologists responded to them by conducting research on everyday memory. However, some psychologists are concerned about the lack of experimental and scientific rigour that characterise research in the field. According to Banaji and Crowder (1989, p.1185):

> The other sciences would have been hopelessly paralyzed if they had been deprived of the methods of science. Imagine astronomy being conducted with only the naked eye, biology without tissue cultures, physics without vacuums, or chemistry without test tubes! The everyday world is full of principles from these sciences in action, but do we really think their data bases should have been those of everyday applications? Of course not. Should the psychology of memory be any different? We think not."

Some of the key issues about the ultimate value of everyday memory research will be discussed at the end of this chapter. For the moment, however, three points should be borne in mind:

1. The distinction between laboratory-based and everyday memory research is by no means absolute. For example, everyday memory has often been studied in the laboratory, e.g. much of the research on eyewitness testimony discussed later in the chapter.

2. It is probably most accurate to regard laboratory and real-world memory research as *complementary*. Laboratory research is well controlled but may lack applicability to everyday life, whereas real-world research possesses that applicability but is often poorly controlled.

3. With luck, there will be cross-fertilisation between the two approaches to research. Everyday memory provides interesting and important phenomena which can be studied in the laboratory under controlled conditions, whereas laboratory research provides theories and principles which may be of use in understanding real-world memory.

AUTOBIOGRAPHICAL MEMORY

The distinction between episodic or auto-biographical memory and semantic memory (knowledge of the world, language, and so on) was discussed at some length in Chapter 7. The focus of that discussion was on the issue of whether there are two separate memory systems underlying episodic and semantic memory. Irrespective of the outcome of that theoretical controversy, however, there are other important issues about episodic or autobiographical memory that need to be addressed. For example, how are our personal memories organised? What kinds of personal information do we remember best?

One of the reasons why it is of value to understand autobiographical memory is because it relates to our major life goals, our most powerful emotions, and our personal meanings. As Cohen (1989) pointed out, our sense of identity or self-concept depends on being able to recollect our personal history. The importance of auto-biographical memory can be seen if we consider the case of individuals (e.g. stroke victims) who are unable to recall the events of their lives. To the distress of their relatives and friends, such individuals have in an almost literal sense lost their identity.

Structure of autobiographical memory

We have an enormous amount of information stored away in autobiographical memory, ranging from the highly specific to the very general, and from the trivial to the very important. In the attempt to identify the underlying organisation or structure of autobiographical memory, it is possible to make inferences from observations of the patterns of retrieval of personal information.

Conway and Bekerian (1987), who made an ambitious attempt to establish the major structural levels within autobiographical memory, identified three different levels:

- *Lifetime periods:* substantial periods of time defined by major ongoing situations (e.g. living with someone; working for a particular firm).
- *General events:* repeated and/or extended events (e.g. a holiday in Italy) covering a period of days to months.
- *Event-specific knowledge:* images, feelings, and details relating to general events and spanning time periods from seconds to hours.

Each of these levels has its own special value. Lifetime periods are much more effective cues to many kinds of memory retrieval than are most other cues (Conway & Bekerian, 1987). Each lifetime period contains its own set of themes, goals, and emotions, and indexes a particular subset of the autobiographical knowledge base. This applies even to lifetime periods that overlapped in time.

There is considerable overlap between autobiographical memory and episodic memory, in that the recollection of personal events and episodes occurs with both types of memory. However, there can be episodic memory without autobiographical memory (Nelson, 1993, p.357): "What I ate for lunch yesterday is today part of my episodic memory, but being unremarkable in any way it will not, I am sure, become part of my autobiographical memory—it has no significance to my life story." It is also likely that there can be autobiographical memory without episodic memory. Autobiographical memories for lifetime periods seem to lack the specific reference to episodes or events that characterises episodic memory. In essence, autobiographical memories typically possess a personal significance that is often lacking from episodic memories, and episodic memories have a specificity of reference that is not necessary for autobiographical memories.

When people are asked to produce auto-biographical memories in a relatively uncon-strained fashion, then most of the memories produced consist of general events. Why should this be so? The information in general events is neither too general (as with lifetime periods) nor too specific (as with event-specific knowledge). Anderson and Conway (1994) investigated the relevance of temporal information and distinctive knowledge to the organisation of general events. When subjects were simply asked to provide information about a general event, they typically started with the most distinctive details and then worked through the event in approximately the correct chronological order. The importance of distinctive knowledge was also shown in another experiment by Anderson and Conway (1994). The knowledge in general events was accessed more rapidly via distinctive-detail cues than by other kinds of cue. As Conway and Rubin (1993, p.106) concluded:

> general events are organised in terms of contextualising distinctive details that distinguish one general event from another, and which also represent the theme or themes of a general event ... this thematic organisa-tion is also supplemented by temporal organisation, and the order in which action sequences occurred is, at least partly, preserved in general events.

Brewer (1988) carried out a study of event-specific knowledge. Subjects received randomly timed signals indicating that they should record the event happening at that time. Subsequently, they were tested for their recall of these events. A key finding was that recall of sensory details was highly predictive of accurate recall of other aspects of the event. When recall of an event was very good, subjects generally reported that the sensory re-experience closely resembled the actual experience.

Barsalou (1988), Conway and Rubin (1993), and others have suggested that autobiographical memories possess a hierarchical structure. Barsalou (1988) made the more specific suggestion that there are hierarchical *partonomies*, with event-specific knowledge forming part of a general event, and each general event forming part of a lifetime period. Evidence from brain damaged patients appears to support this hierarchical viewpoint. According to Conway and Rubin (1993), there are no reports of amnesic patients who can retrieve episode-specific knowledge but who are unable to retrieve knowledge about general events and lifetime periods, and there are no patients who can retrieve general event knowledge but not lifetime period knowledge. Thus, information at the top of the hierarchy (i.e. lifetime period knowledge) is the least vulnerable to loss and that at the bottom of the hierarchy (i.e. episode-specific knowledge) is the most vulnerable. Presumably the fact that we possess enormous amounts of information about lifetime periods helps to ensure that most forms of brain damage do not prevent access to such know-ledge.

Memories across the lifetime

Suppose that we ask people approximately 70 years old to think of personal memories suggested by cue words (e.g. nouns referring to common objects). From which parts of their lives would most of the memories come? Would they tend to think of recent experiences or the events of childhood or young adulthood? Answers to these questions were provided by Rubin, Wetzler, and Nebes (1986), who re-analysed the data from a number of studies. As can be seen in Fig. 8.1, there are various interesting features about the findings:

- A *retention function* for memories up to 20 years old, with the older memories being less likely to be recalled than more recent ones.
- A *reminiscence bump*, consisting of a surprisingly large number of memories coming

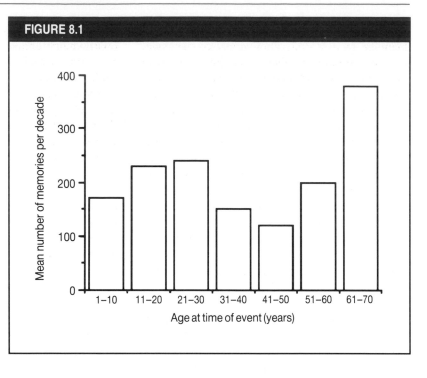

FIGURE 8.1

Memory for past events in the elderly as a function of the decade in which the events occurred. Based on Rubin et al. (1986).

from the years between 10 and 30 and especially between 15 and 25.

- *Childhood amnesia*, demonstrated by the almost total lack of memories coming from the first five years of life.

The reminiscence bump has not generally been found in people younger than 30 years of age, and has not often been observed in 40-year-olds (see Jansari and Parkin, submitted). However, Jansari and Parkin (submitted) discovered that an important reason for this is that younger people tend to retrieve mostly rather recent memories. When they were instructed to avoid recent memories, subjects in their thirties demonstrated the reminiscence bump.

Before attempting to account for the various findings, the work of Schuman and Rieger (1992) should be mentioned. They asked 1410 Americans to list one or two important public events from the past 50 years, and found that public events which had occurred when the respondents were in their late teens or early twenties were most likely to be reported. Thus, there is a reminiscence bump for

public events resembling the one found for personal events.

The retention function presumably reflects the normal time course of forgetting over time, and is thus relatively easy to explain. The reminiscence bump is more mysterious and more interesting, and exactly what produces it is not known. However, some factors that may well be relevant can be identified. First, many new or first-time experiences are likely to be associated with a time of rapid change such as adolescence and early adulthood, and it appears that such experiences are especially memorable. Cohen and Faulkner (1988) found that 93% of vivid life memories were either of unique one-off events or of first times. Impressive evidence that first-time experiences are particularly memorable was obtained by Pillemer, Goldsmith, Panter, and White (1988). They asked their subjects to recall four memories from their first year at college more than 20 years previously. No fewer than 41% of the memories came from September (the starting month of the college year).

Second, adolescence and early adulthood are associated with the development of a stable adult self-concept for most people. As a consequence, there are greater similarities in self-concept (and probably in dominant themes and goals) between old age and early adulthood than between old age and childhood, and these similarities may facilitate the retrieval of memories. Thus, pre-adolescent events are not well remembered because at that time the adult self-concept had not developed, whereas post-adolescent events are not well remembered because most events are not being experienced for the first time.

It is not clear why there is a reminiscence bump for public events (Schuman & Rieger, 1992). However, part of the explanation may be that it is not until adolescence and early adulthood that most public events are perceived as having any real relevance to an individual's life.

Childhood amnesia has been explained in many ways. Freud argued that the few memories of early childhood that can be recalled are "screen" memories which have been made up to hide the emotionally disturbing events of those early years. From a more cognitive perspective, young children have limited or no ability to store information in a verbal form, and they tend to lack a detailed and well-organised framework of knowledge to which they can relate their experiences. In addition, it is probable that the ways in which young children organise their memories differ markedly from those of adults. For example, an adult might remember a family holiday in terms of where and when it was, whereas a young child might remember only the friend that he or she made at the camp site or vomiting after a foreign meal. The available evidence does not permit a choice among the various possible explanations, and it is likely that there is some merit in most of them.

Diary studies

One of the major problems with investigating autobiographical memory is that it is often difficult, or even impossible, to assess the accuracy of an individual's recollections of the events of his or her own life. A rather drastic solution to this problem was adopted by Linton (1975) and by Wagenaar (1986). Both of them carried out diary studies in which they made a daily note of events

that happened to them, and both of them tested their own memory for these events at numerous different retention intervals. We will consider these diary studies in turn.

Linton (1975) wrote down brief descriptions of at least two events each day over a six-year period. Every month she selected two of these descriptions at random, and endeavoured to recall as much as possible about the events in question. She discovered that forgetting depended substantially on whether or not a particular event had been tested before. For example, over 60% of events that had happened 4.5 years ago were completely forgotten if they had not previously been tested, compared to under 40% of events of the same age that had been tested once before. This indicates the crucial importance of rehearsal in the prevention of forgetting.

One of the main reasons why events were forgotten was because many events were similar to each other. For example, Linton occasionally attended meetings of a distinguished committee which met in a distant city. Although the first such meeting was clearly remembered, most of the subsequent meetings blended into one another in her mind. As Linton (1975) expressed it, her semantic memory (or general knowledge) about the meetings increased over time, whereas her episodic memory (or memory for specific events) decreased.

One might have assumed that those events which were regarded at the time to be important and high in emotionality would be much better remembered than those which were thought to be lacking importance and emotionality. In fact, the impact of importance and emotionality of events on their subsequent recallability was relatively modest, perhaps because many events that seemed at the time to be important and high in emotionality no longer appeared so with the benefit of hindsight.

What strategies do we use to remember events from our past? Linton (1975) addressed this issue by considering how she set about the task of recalling as many events as possible from a particular month in the past. When the month in question was under two years ago, the main strategy was based on working through events in the order in which they occurred. In contrast, there was more use of recall by category (e.g. sporting events attended; dinner parties given) at longer retention intervals.

Wagenaar (1986) recorded over 2000 events over a six-year period. For each event, he noted down information about who, what, where, and when, together with the rated pleasantness, saliency or rarity, and emotionality of each event. He then tested his memory by using the who, what, where, and when information cues either one at a time or in combination. He discovered that "what" information provided the most useful retrieval cue, perhaps because our autobiographical memories are organised in categories. "What" information was followed in order of declining usefulness by "where", "who", and "when" information. "When" information on its own was almost totally

ineffective. Not surprisingly, the more cues that were presented, the higher was the resultant probability of recall (see Fig. 8.2). However, even with three cues almost half of the events were forgotten over a five-year retention interval. When these forgotten events involved another person, that person was asked to provide further information about the event. In nearly every case, this proved sufficient for Wagenaar to remember the event and to supply additional information about it, suggesting that the great majority of the events of our lives may be stored away in long-term memory.

High levels of salience, emotional involvement, and pleasantness were all found to be associated with high levels of recall, especially high salience or rarity. The effects of salience and emotional involvement remained strong over retention intervals ranging from one to five years, whereas

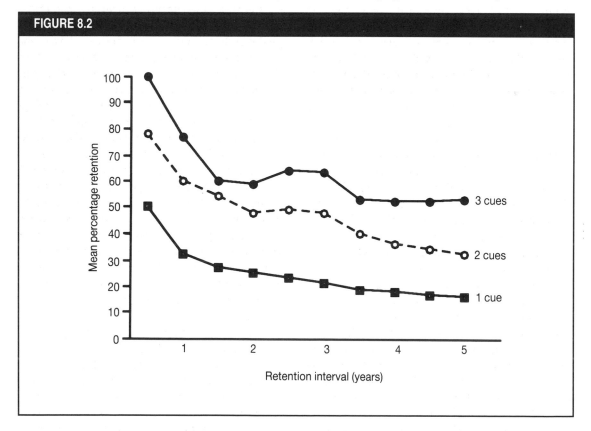

FIGURE 8.2

Memory for personal events as a function of the number of cues available and the length of the retention interval. Adapted from Wagenaar (1986).

the effects of pleasantness were substantial after one year but rather small after five years. It is not known why the impact of pleasantness on recall declines in this fashion.

The case studies of Linton (1975) and of Wagenaar (1986) are of considerable interest, but we need to be cautious about assuming that everyone's autobiographical memory systems function in the same way. For example, as we will see in Chapter 18, anxious and depressed individuals tend to recall a disproportionate number of negative events, and this recall bias may colour the way in which they remember their own past. It may well be that what we remember of our own lives is to some extent a reflection of our personalities.

Dating autobiographical memories

Linton (1975) and Wagenaar (1986) both discovered that they were reasonably good at dating the events of their lives. How do we remember when past events happened? As we saw earlier in the chapter, people often relate the events of their lives to major lifetime periods (Conway & Bekerian, 1987). In addition, we sometimes draw inferences about when an event happened on the basis of how much information about it we can remember. For example, if we can remember very little about an event, we may assume that this is because it happened a long time ago. This notion was investigated by Brown, Rips, and Shevell (1985). People were asked to date several news events over a five-year period (1977 to 1982). On average, those events about which much was known (e.g. the shooting of President Reagan) were dated as too recent by over three months, whereas low-knowledge events were dated as too remote by approximately two months.

In a follow-up study, Brown, Shevell, and Rips (1986) asked their subjects to date public events that were either political (e.g. the signing of an important treaty) or non-political (e.g. the eruption of Mount St. Helens). The subjects made considerable use of landmarks, i.e. events whose date they knew reasonably well. For example, someone might be able to date the eruption of Mount St. Helens by relating it to the landmark of becoming engaged shortly beforehand (the start

and end of lifetime periods are effective landmarks). Brown et al. (1986) discovered that landmarks were used approximately 70% of the time to facilitate the dating of public events, with the landmarks being either public or personal events. There was an interesting difference in the strategies used to date political and non-political events. Over 60% of political events were dated with reference to other political events, compared to only 31% which were related to personal events; in contrast, two thirds of the landmarks used to date non-political events were personal events.

Accuracy of autobiographical memories

How accurate are our memories of our past experiences? It is rather difficult to answer this question, because we do not generally have access to objective information about what actually happened at the time. An interesting and dramatic exception to this occurred with respect to the Watergate scandal in the early 1970s, in which it gradually became clear that President Nixon and his associates had engaged in a "cover-up" of the White House involvement in the Watergate burglary. What makes the case of interest to memory researchers is the fact that tape recordings had been made of all of the conversations that had taken place in the Oval Office of the White House.

Neisser (1981) took the opportunity provided to compare the tape recordings of conversations with the testimony to the Watergate Committee of John Dean, who had been counsel to the President. Of particular interest was Dean's recollection approximately nine months later of a conversation involving President Nixon, Bob Haldeman (Nixon's chief of staff), and John Dean on 15 September 1972 to discuss the Watergate situation. According to Neisser (1981, p.12):

It is clear that Dean's account of the opening of the September 15 conversation is wrong both as to the words used and their gist ... His testimony had much truth in it, but not at the level of "gist". It was true at a deeper level. Nixon was the kind of man Dean described, he had the knowledge Dean attributed to him, there was a cover-up. Dean remembered all of that; he just didn't recall the actual conversation he was testifying about.

It may be unwise to attach too much weight to John Dean's testimony, as he did not know at the time that tape recordings had been made. In order to defend himself effectively, he needed to claim that he remembered the details of conversations held several months previously. Nevertheless, the key notion that our recollections are more likely to be "true" in a broad sense than to be strictly accurate is supported by other evidence. Barclay (1988) used tests of recognition memory to assess the accuracy of people's memories for personal events that they had recorded in diaries. The recognition-memory tests were made difficult by using as distractors events that had not actually happened to a given individual, but which possessed many of the characteristics of the events that had happened. The subjects made many errors, thus appearing inaccurate, but their auto-biographical memory was truthful in the sense that it corresponded to the gist or flavour of their actual experiences.

It is likely that our autobiographical memories are sometimes rather less truthful than has been suggested so far. For example, Dean's memory for the conversations with the President fairly consistently gave Dean a more active and significant role than that indicated by the tape recordings. It is as if Dean remembered the conversations as he wished them to have been rather than the way they actually were. The findings can perhaps be explained by assuming that individuals have a self-schema (organised knowledge about themselves) which influences how they perceive and remember personal information. Someone who was as ambitious and egotistical as Dean might have focused particularly on those aspects of the conversations in which he played a dominant role, and this selective attention may then have affected what he recalled subsequently.

Evaluation

There has been reasonably good progress in understanding autobiographical memory in recent years. It appears that autobiographical memories are stored in categories, and that these memories are organised in a hierarchical fashion. It has also been found that new or first-time experiences tend to be especially memorable, thus giving rise to the reminiscence bump.

Future research should focus more on the relationship between the self-concept or personality and autobiographical memory. It is likely that people's personalities help to determine what they can readily recall of their lives and the errors and distortions in their personal recollections. After all, one of the reasons why people read autobiographies is because they believe that what the author remembers, and how he or she remembers it, sheds light on the author's character.

MEMORABLE MEMORIES

There are many reasons why we remember some events much better than others. For example, as we saw earlier in the chapter, personal memories with an emotional involvement or possessing rarity value (Wagenaar, 1986) are much better remembered than personal memories lacking those characteristics. Attempts to identify other factors associated with especially memorable or long-lasting memories have led to the discovery of two interesting phenomena: the self-reference effect and flashbulb memories.

It is intuitively reasonable that information about oneself should be better remembered than information of a more impersonal kind, because we are particularly interested in such information. This intuition defines the self-reference effect, which has been studied in detail in recent years.

Flashbulb memories are produced by very important, dramatic, and surprising public or personal events, such as the assassination of President Kennedy or the explosion of the space shuttle *Challenger*. Brown and Kulik (1977) coined the term "flashbulb memories", arguing that such memories are generally very accurate and essentially immune from forgetting.

These two phenomena (the self-reference effect and flashbulb memories) will now be discussed at length. The crucial issue (but one that is difficult to resolve) is whether the processes underlying these phenomena are quite different from those underlying ordinary memories.

Self-reference effect

One of the first investigations of the self-reference effect was reported by Rogers, Kuiper, and Kirker (1977). They presented a series of adjectives, and asked some of their subjects to make self-reference judgements (i.e. describes you?). Other subjects had to make semantic judgements (i.e. means the same as —?), phonemic judgements (i.e. rhymes with—?), or structural judgements (i.e. capital letters?). As would be anticipated on the basis of Craik and Lockhart's (1972) levels-of-processing theory (see Chapter 6), subsequent recall of the adjectives was much higher following semantic judgements than either phonemic or structural judgements (see Fig. 8.3). However, the most important finding was that recall was approximately twice as high following self-reference than semantic judgements, and this self-reference effect has been replicated several times since then (see Eysenck, 1992).

Why is self-reference so effective in increasing memory? According to Rogers et al. (1977), each individual possesses an extensive self-schema (an organised long-term memory structure incorporating our self-knowledge). This self-schema is activated when self-referent judgements are made, especially when those judgements are affirmative. At the time of recall, the self-schema may lead to the activation of a network of associations which assist the retrieval process. In other words, the stored self-schema serves as an effective retrieval cue.

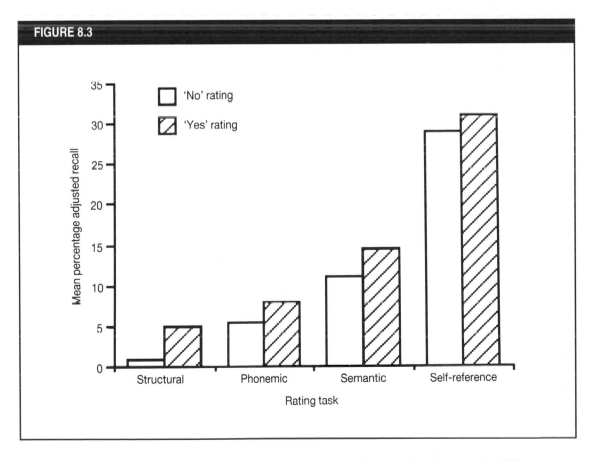

FIGURE 8.3

Recall performance as a function of orienting task, and yes versus no ratings. Based on data in Rogers et al. (1977).

From a theoretical perspective, the most important issue is whether there is something so special about self-knowledge that memory will always be superior following self-reference judgements than following any other kinds of judgements. The evidence increasingly suggests that self-knowledge probably does not possess special characteristics. For example, Bower and Gilligan (1979) compared recall following the self-reference task with recall following other-person reference tasks. Although other-person reference tasks generally produced rather poor levels of recall, good memory performance approaching that found with self-reference was obtained when a very well-known other person (e.g. one's own mother) was used as a referent.

Klein and Kihlstrom (1986) carried out a study in which they compared the importance of self-reference and organisation as factors determining memory. Subjects were presented with a list of occupations, and had to perform one of the following four tasks on each word:

1. Semantic, organised: Does this job require a college education?
2. Semantic, unorganised: Different questions for each word (e.g. Does this person perform operations?).
3. Self-reference, organised: Have you ever wanted to be a ——?
4. Self-reference, unorganised: Different questions for each word (e.g. I place complete trust in my ——-).

Klein and Kihlstrom (1986) discovered that organisation made a substantial difference to memory. However, self-reference was no more effective than ordinary semantic processing when the extent to which the information is organised was controlled. In fact, self-reference was associated with poorer recall than normal semantic processing if it failed to encourage organisation (i.e. conditions one and four). On this line of reasoning, the self-reference effect reported by Rogers et al. (1977) and by others is found when the self-reference task encourages organisation to a greater extent than does the rival semantic task.

In sum, relating information to oneself typically leads to good long-term memory for that information. This is probably due in a general way to the fact that we possess a rich network of knowledge about ourselves which can facilitate the storage and subsequent retrieval of self-relevant information. However, the details of the processes involved in the self-reference effect remain unclear, although it is likely that self-knowledge can be used as a basis for organising information in long-term memory.

Flashbulb memories

Brown and Kulik (1977) were impressed by the fact that we seem to retain very vivid and detailed memories of certain dramatic world events (e.g. the assassination of President Kennedy; the resignation of Mrs. Thatcher) even though we did not witness the events themselves. They suggested that there may be a special neural mechanism that is activated by such events, provided that they are perceived by the individual as surprising and are regarded as having real consequences for that person's life. This mechanism serves the purpose of "printing" the details of such events permanently in the memory system. According to Brown and Kulik (1977), flashbulb memories are not only accurate and very long-lasting, but also often include the following categories of information: informant (person who supplied the information); place where the news was heard; ongoing event; own emotional state; the emotional state of others; and aftermath or consequences of the event for the individual.

The central point that Brown and Kulik (1977) made is that flashbulb memories are quite different from most other memories in terms of their longevity, accuracy, and reliance on a special neural mechanism. However, this view has proved rather controversial. One of the problems is that flashbulb memories may be remembered clearly because they have been rehearsed on numerous occasions subsequently, rather than because of the processing occurring at the time of learning about the dramatic event. Another problem is checking up on the accuracy of reported flashbulb memories. At one time, Neisser (1982) was convinced that he was listening to a baseball game on the radio when he heard the news that the Japanese had bombed Pearl Harbor. However, the bombing of Pearl Harbor took place in December, which is not in the baseball season. It turned out that he was almost certainly listening to an American football game, but the location of the match and the names of the teams involved were suggestive of a baseball game.

Some of the strongest evidence against the views of Brown and Kulik (1977) was obtained by McCloskey, Wible, and Cohen (1988). They tested their subjects' memory of the explosion of the space shuttle *Challenger* a few days after the event and then again approximately nine months later. There was clear evidence for forgetting between the two testing conditions, and there were several inaccuracies (i.e. the information that was recalled differed between memory tests for some of the subjects). These findings suggest that flashbulb memories are like other memories rather than being inherently much more memorable. In addition, what could be recalled was often rather fragmentary, and encompassed only a few of the six categories of information (listed earlier) which were identified by Brown and Kulik (1977). Even in their original study, Brown and Kulik found that

subjects on average recalled information from fewer than three of the six categories.

Bohannon (1988) tested people's memory for the explosion of *Challenger* either two weeks or eight months afterwards. They were asked seven questions about the incident, and recall fell from 77% at the short retention interval to 58% at the long retention interval. This again suggests that flashbulb memories are subject to forgetting in the same way as ordinary memories. However, he did find that long term memory was best when the news had caused a strong emotional reaction and the event had been rehearsed or recounted several times subsequently (see Fig. 8.4). It is thus possible that a proportion of flashbulb memories are relatively immune to forgetting.

Conway et al. (1994) refused to accept that flashbulb memories are simply stronger versions of ordinary memories. As they pointed out, it is not clear that the subjects in studies such as those of Bohannon (1988) and McCloskey et al. (1988) regarded the explosion of *Challenger* as having consequences for their lives. If they did not, then one of the central criteria for flashbulb memories proposed by Brown and Kulik (1977) was not fulfilled.

FIGURE 8.4

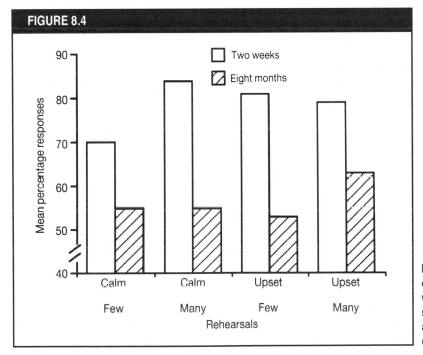

Memory for the *Challenger* explosion as a function of whether the event upset the subjects, the extent of rehearsal, and the retention interval. Based on data in Bohannon (1988).

Conway et al. (1994) studied flashbulb memories for the resignation of Mrs. Thatcher in 1990. This event was certainly perceived as surprising and consequential by most people in the United Kingdom, and so should theoretically have produced flashbulb memories. Their subjects were tested within a few days of the event, and again after 11 months, with some being re-tested 26 months after the event. They discovered that 86% of their United Kingdom subjects still had flashbulb memories after 11 months, compared with 29% in other countries. As they concluded (1994, pp.337–338): "The striking finding of the present study was the high incidence of very detailed memory reports provided by the U.K. subjects, which remained consistent over an 11-month retention interval and, for a smaller group, over a 26-month retention interval."

Section summary

It remains unclear whether flashbulb memories are substantially different from other memories. In common with most memories, they appear to be prone to inaccuracy, forgetting, and often contain fragmentary details rather than complete information. However, the findings of Conway et al. (1994) suggest that very consequential events may produce flashbulb memories that are relatively immune to forgetting. This would not necessarily indicate that flashbulb memories are very different from more ordinary memories. Factors associated with good long-term memory (e.g. deep or semantic processing, elaborative processing, and distinctive processing) were considered in Chapter 6, and may be of relevance to an understanding of flashbulb memories. More specifically, events such as the downfall of Mrs. Thatcher or the assassination of President Kennedy are clearly distinctive, and this distinctiveness probably contributes to their memorability.

EYEWITNESS TESTIMONY

A disturbing feature of the criminal justice system in most countries is the fact that many innocent individuals have been put in prison purely on the basis of eyewitness testimony. As Fruzzetti, Toland, Teller, and Loftus (1992) pointed out, even a very low rate of mistaken identifications could lead to several hundreds or thousands of people a year being convicted of crimes they did not commit. Eyewitness testimony, and the factors that increase or decrease its reliability, have been the focus of much interest in recent years.

One way in which eyewitness memory can be distorted is via what is known as *confirmation bias*. In essence, confirmation bias occurs when what is remembered of an event corresponds to the observer's expectations rather than to what actually happened. For example, students from two universities in the United States (Princeton and Dartmouth) were shown a film of a football game involving both universities. The students showed a strong tendency to report that their opponents had committed many more fouls than had their own team.

Does it make any difference to the memory of an eyewitness whether the crime observed by him or her is violent or not? A study by Loftus and Burns (1982) suggests that the answer is "yes". They showed their subjects two filmed versions of a crime. In the violent version, a young boy was shot in the face near the end of the film as the robbers were making their getaway. The main finding was that inclusion of the violent incident caused impaired memory for details presented up to two minutes earlier. Presumably the memory-impairing effects of violence would be even greater in the case of a real-life crime, because the presence of violent criminals might endanger the life of any eyewitness.

Post-event information

Of particular importance in research on eyewitness testimony has been the research of Elizabeth Loftus. She has demonstrated very clearly that the memory an eyewitness has of an incident can be systematically distorted by the questioning that occurs subsequently. To illustrate this point, we will consider a study by Loftus and Palmer (1974).

In that study, subjects were shown a film of a multiple car accident. After viewing the film, the subjects described in their own words what had happened, and then answered a number of specific questions. Some of the subjects were asked, "About how fast were the cars going when they smashed into each other?", whereas for other subjects the verb "hit" was substituted for "smashed into". Control subjects were not asked a question about car speed. The estimated speed was affected by the verb used in the question, averaging 10.5mph when the verb "smashed" was used versus 8.0mph when "hit" was used. This suggests that the information implicit in the question affected the way in which the multiple car accident was remembered.

One week later, all of the subjects were asked the following question: "Did you see any broken glass?" In spite of the fact that there was actually no broken glass in the accident, 32% of the subjects who had been asked previously about speed using the verb "smashed" said they saw broken glass. In contrast, only 14% of the subjects asked using the verb "hit" said they saw broken glass, and the figure was 12% for the control subjects who had not been asked a question about speed. Thus, our memory for events is relatively fragile and susceptible to distortion.

Loftus showed subsequently that even apparently trivial differences in the way in which a question is asked of an eyewitness can have a marked effect on the answers elicited. For example, Loftus and Zanni (1975) showed people a short film of a car accident, and then asked them various questions about the accident. Some of the eyewitnesses were asked, "Did you see a broken headlight?", whereas others were asked, "Did you see the broken headlight?" In fact, there was no broken headlight in the film, but the latter question implies that there was. Only 7% of those asked about a broken headlight said that they had seen it, against 17% of those asked about the broken headlight.

How does misleading post-event information distort what eyewitnesses report? According to Loftus (1979), information from the misleading questions permanently alters the memory representation of the incident: the previously formed memory is "overwritten" and destroyed. In support of this position, she has demonstrated that it can be extremely difficult to retrieve the original memory. In one study involving misleading

questions, Loftus (1979) offered her subjects $25 if their recall of an incident was accurate. This incentive completely failed to prevent their recollections being distorted by the misleading information they had heard.

McCloskey and Zaragoza (1985) and Zaragoza and McCloskey (1989) disagreed with Loftus (1979). They argued that misleading information provided after an incident affects eyewitness reports because subjects are trying to do what they think is expected of them rather than because the memory traces have been altered. Suppose, for example, that subjects see slides of an incident involving a man using a hammer, but then read an account of the incident in which the instrument is called a screwdriver. They are then asked to decide whether the instrument used by the man in the slides was a hammer or a screwdriver. Subjects who cannot recollect the instrument shown in the slides may remember that it was described in the subsequent account as a screwdriver. They may feel that they will best please the experimenter and demonstrate that they were paying attention to the slides by selecting the screwdriver. In other words, the subjects are simply playing along with what they think is expected of them; this is known as responding to the *demand characteristics* of the experimental situation.

Evidence suggesting that there is more to it than demand characteristics was reported by Lindsay (1990). He presented misleading information in a narrative account after showing slides in which a maintenance man stole money and a calculator from an office. After that, the eyewitnesses were told truthfully that any information in the narrative account which was relevant to the subsequent memory test was wrong. Presumably these instructions should have prevented distorted memory performance. In fact, memory for the incident by the misled subjects were considerably distorted by the post-event information, suggesting that this information had genuinely affected memory.

Much of the research in this area can be interpreted within the framework of a theory of memory proposed by Bartlett (1932; see Chapter 11). According to Bartlett, retrieval involves a process of *reconstruction*, in which all of the available information about an event is used to reconstruct the details of that event on the basis of "what must have been true". One of the major implications of Bartlett's reconstructive hypothesis is that new information that is relevant to a previously experienced event can affect recollection of that event by providing a different basis for reconstruction. Perhaps such re-constructive processes are involved in eyewitness studies on post-event information.

In sum, the distorting effects of misleading post-event information on eyewitnesses' recollections may sometimes be due to the demand characteristics of the situation. However, most such distortions probably reflect real effects on memory. These effects could take the form of altering the memory traces of the original incident as Loftus (1979) has suggested, or they might involve difficulties of gaining access to the original memory traces (e.g. because of interference). It is likely that most of the distortions occur as a consequence of the reconstructive processes emphasised by Bartlett (1932).

One limitation of this entire line of research is that much of the research has focused on memory for peripheral details of events (e.g. presence or absence of broken glass). As Fruzzetti et al. (1992) pointed out, it is generally more difficult to distort witnesses' memory by misleading post-event information for key details (e.g. the murder weapon) than for minor details.

Eyewitness identification

There has been a considerable amount of research in recent years on eyewitness identification, much of it based on identification parades or line-ups (see Wells, 1993, for a review). The central finding is that eyewitness identification is often extremely fallible. Shapiro and Penrod (1986) discussed the evidence, and concluded that eyewitness identification experiments typically produce inferior memory performance to more traditional face recognition experiments. An important part of the reason for this discrepancy is that the same stimuli (e.g. photographs) are often used at acquisition and at test in traditional studies of face recognition, whereas the facial appearance of someone may differ substantially between a staged incident and the subsequent identification parade or line-up.

One of the factors determining the likelihood of an incorrect identification is the *functional size* of the line-up, which can be defined as the number of people in the line-up who match the eyewitness' description of the culprit. If, for example, the eyewitness recalled only that the culprit was a man, then the functional size of a line-up consisting of three men and two women would be three. When the actual culprit is not present, low functional size of line-up is associated with a greater probability of mistaken identification (Lindsay & Wells, 1980).

Another factor that can affect the probability of a mistaken identification is whether or not the eyewitness is warned that the culprit might not be in the line-up (Wells, 1993). This is probably especially important with real-life line-ups, where the eyewitness may feel that the police would not have gone to the trouble of setting up an identification parade unless they were reasonably certain that the actual culprit was present.

According to Wells (1993, p.560), small functional size of the line-up and a failure to warn of the possible absence of the culprit in the line-up are problematical mainly because of the eyewitness' tendency to use *relative judgements*: "The eyewitness chooses the line-up member who most resembles the culprit *relative to the other members of the line-up*." How can we reduce eyewitnesses' reliance on the relative judgement strategy? One reasonable method is to use *sequential line-ups*, in which members of the line-up or identification parade are presented one at a time. Lindsay et al. (1991) discovered that the use of sequential line-ups reduced the effects on mistaken identification of functional size and failure to warn of possible culprit absence, presumably because the eywitnesses were less likely to use the relative judgement strategy.

Other factors in eyewitness testimony

Researchers have investigated several other factors of relevance to the use of eyewitness testimony in criminal cases. There is not the space to discuss all of this research here. Instead, we will focus on those findings that possess two important qualities:

1. They are regarded by eyewitness experts as generally reliable and valid.
2. They do not correspond to common sense.

Kassin, Ellsworth, and Smith (1989) have collected the relevant information. Here are the findings that were judged by most experts to be reliable, but not to be in accord with common sense (with percentages of experts believing each statement to be commonsensical in brackets):

• An eyewitness's confidence is not a good predictor of his or her identification accuracy (3%).
• Eyewitnesses tend to over-estimate the duration of events (5%)
• Eyewitness testimony about an event often reflects not only what the eyewitness actually saw but information they obtained later on (7.5%).
• There is a conventional forgetting curve for eyewitness memories (24%).
• An eyewitness's testimony about an event can be affected by how the questions put to that witness are worded (27%).
• The use of a one-person line up increases the risk of misidentification (29%).

The position of Kassin et al. (1989) contrasts strongly with that of McCloskey and Egeth (1983). They argued that there was rather little eyewitness research that was both reliable and non-obvious. According to them, psychologists should not put themselves forward in court cases as experts in eyewitness testimony, because there is so little research that is both reliable and non-obvious. According to the "Frye test" which applies in the United States, scientific evidence "must be sufficiently established to have gained general acceptance in the particular field in which it belongs" in order to warrant its use in criminal cases. McCloskey and Egeth (1983) argued that the evidence on eyewitness testimony fails to meet the Frye test.

As we have seen, Kassin et al. (1989) have convincingly refuted the arguments of McCloskey and Egeth (1983). It is now generally accepted that psychologists can make a very valuable contribution to ensuring that justice is done in criminal cases. For example, there is the case of John Demjanjuk. He was convicted of being Ivan the Terrible, the person who operated the gas chambers at Treblinka concentration camp, on the basis of the eyewitness testimony given by survivors of the camp some 40 years after the end of the war. Psychologists involved in the case warned about the fallibility of eyewitness testimony over such long periods, and their warnings appear to have been justified by the subsequent overturning of the conviction.

Interviewing eyewitnesses: Improvements

The research of Loftus and others has obvious implications for the interviewing of eyewitnesses. In essence, there is a great danger that the questions asked during a police interview may unwittingly distort an eyewitness's memory and thus reduce its reliability. Investigation of actual police procedures indicates that what typically happened until comparatively recently was that an eyewitness's account of what had happened was repeatedly interrupted, and that the question answer format was used excessively. The interruptions obviously made it difficult for the eyewitness to concentrate fully on the process of retrieval, and may thus have reduced the amount that could be recalled. As a result of psychological research, the Home Office has recently issued guidelines recommending that police interviews should proceed from free recall to general open-ended questions, concluding with more specific questions.

Apart from correcting these deficiencies in the interviewing techniques of the police, are there any other changes that have been (or should be) introduced in order to improve eyewitness testimony? According to Fisher and Geiselman (e.g. Geiselman, Fisher, MacKinnon, & Holland, 1985), interview techniques should take account of some basic characteristics of human memory:

• Memory traces are usually complex and contain a number of different features or kinds of information.
• The effectiveness of a retrieval cue depends on the extent to which the information it contains

overlaps with information stored in the memory trace; this is the encoding specificity principle (e.g. Tulving, 1979), which was discussed in detail in Chapter 6.

• If one combines the first two points, it follows that there are various different retrieval cues which may permit access to any given memory trace; if you could not immediately remember the name of an acquaintance, it might be worth using any information you have about that person as retrieval cues (e.g. form an image of the person; think of the names of the person's friends; try to think of the first letter of the person's name; think of the situations in which you have met the person).

Geiselman et al. (1985) used these considerations to develop what they called the *basic cognitive interview*. This incorporates the following basic retrieval strategies:

• The eyewitness attempts to recreate mentally the context that existed at the time of the crime, including environmental and internal (e.g. mood state) information.
• The eyewitness simply reports everything he or she can think of relating to the incident, even if the information is fragmented.
• The eyewitness reports the details of the incident in a number of different orders.
• The eyewitness reports the events from various perspectives, an approach based on the Anderson and Pichert (1978) study (see Chapter 11).

Geiselman et al. (1985) compared the effectiveness of the basic cognitive interview with that of the standard police interview. The average number of correct statements produced by eyewitnesses was 41.1 using the basic cognitive interview against only 29.4 using the standard police interview. They also investigated the effectiveness of interviewing under hypnosis. This produced an average of 38.0 correct statements, making it somewhat less useful than the basic cognitive interview in improving eyewitness recollection.

Fisher et al. (1987) devised an *enhanced cognitive interview*. This incorporates the key aspects of the basic cognitive interview, but also makes use of the following recommendations (Roy, 1991, p.399):

Investigators should minimise distractions, induce the eyewitness to speak slowly, allow a pause between the response and next question, tailor language to suit the individual eyewitness, follow up with interpretive comment, try to reduce eyewitness anxiety, avoid judgmental and personal comments, and always review the eyewitness's description of events or people under investigation.

According to the evidence obtained by Fisher et al. (1987), this enhanced cognitive interview is even more useful than the basic cognitive interview: eyewitnesses produced an average of 57.5 correct statements when given the enhanced interview compared to 39.6 with the basic interview. However, the number of incorrect statements was approximately 28% greater with the enhanced interview.

The main limitation of the study by Fisher et al. (1987) is that it was carried out under artificial conditions. Fisher, Geiselman, and Amador (1990) have examined the use of the enhanced interview in field conditions. Detectives working for the Robbery Division of Metro-Dade Police Department in Miami were trained in the techniques involved in the enhanced cognitive interview. Police interviews with eyewitnesses and the victims of crime were tape recorded and then scored for the number of statements obtained and the extent to which these statements were corroborated or confirmed by a second eyewitness. Training produced an increase of 46% in the number of statements produced. Where corroboration was possible, over 90% of the statements were accurate.

Section summary

Research on eyewitness testimony has proved very successful at the theoretical and practical levels. Theoretically, the ways in which human memory can be distorted and its fragility are more clearly understood. At the practical level, the findings of psychologists are slowly but surely influencing various aspects of the legal process (e.g. interviewing techniques; advice given to jurors). It would appear that the interventions of psychologists have had an almost entirely beneficial effect in terms of ensuring that criminals are arrested and convicted, and that innocent people are not.

SUPERIOR MEMORY ABILITY

Most research on human memory has focused on its limitations (e.g. omissions; distortions). However, it is also useful to study individuals possessing unusually good memories if we want to understand the principles involved in efficient human learning. Probably the best-known mnemonist or memory expert is S, whose amazing powers were investigated by the Russian neuropsychologist Luria (1975). After only three minutes' study, S learned a matrix of 50 digits perfectly, and was then able to recall them effortlessly in any direction. More strikingly, he showed almost perfect retention for much of what he had learned for several years thereafter.

In our search for an explanation of S's exceptional memory, we should take into account his frequent use of synaesthesia (the tendency for one sense modality to evoke another). His usual strategy was to encode all kinds of material in vivid visual terms. For example, S once said to the psychologist Vygotsky, "What a crumbly yellow voice you have" (Luria, 1975, p.24). Unfortunately, we do not know why S possessed such strong synaesthesia and such exceptional memory. However, the fact that he did not appear to dedicate much time to improving his memory suggested to Luria (1975) that his abilities were innate. Wilding and Valentine (1991) developed this line of argument, suggesting that S may have had more brain tissue devoted to processing sensory information than most people.

S was rather unusual among those with superior memory ability in two ways. First, his memory powers were much greater than those of most other people with superior memory ability. Second, his superiority apparently owed little to the use of highly practised memory techniques. More typical is the case of the young man studied by Ericsson and Chase (1982). He was paid to practise the digit-span task for one hour a day for two years. The digit span (the number of random digits that can be repeated back in the correct order) is typically about seven items, but this subject eventually attained a span of 80 items. He accomplished this by making use of his extensive knowledge of running times. For example, if the first few digits presented were "3594", he would probably note that this was Bannister's time when he broke the four-minute barrier for the mile, and that would be the information he would store away. In other words, he made use of long-term memory to reduce 80 digits to a much smaller number of running times.

Ericsson (1988) has proposed that there are three requirements to achieve very high memory skills of the kind just described:

- *Meaningful encoding:* the information should be processed meaningfully, relating it to pre-existing knowledge (this is reminiscent of the levels-of-processing theory already discussed in Chapter 6).
- *Retrieval structure:* cues should be stored with the information to facilitate subsequent retrieval (this is reminiscent of the encoding specificity principle discussed in Chapter 6).
- *Speed-up:* there is extensive practice so that the processes involved in encoding and retrieval function progressively faster (these resemble the automatic processes discussed in Chapter 5).

Ericsson (1988) went on to argue more dubiously that nearly everyone who exhibits superior memory does so because of their extensive reliance on highly practised memory strategies. However, Wilding and Valentine (1994) discovered that matters are more complicated than that. They took advantage of the fact that the World Memory Championships were being held in London to assess the memory performance of some of the contestants as well as a few members of the audience who showed outstanding memory abilities.

First of all, Wilding and Valentine (1994) classified their subjects into two groups: (1) strategists, who reported frequent use of memory strategies; and (2) naturals, who claimed naturally superior memory ability from early childhood, and who possessed a close relative exhibiting a comparable level of memory ability. Second, they used two kinds of memory tasks: (1) strategic tasks (e.g. recalling names to faces) that seemed to be susceptible to the use of memory strategies; and (2) non-strategic tasks (e.g. recognition of snow crystals).

The main findings (shown in Fig. 8.5) revealed important differences between the strategists and the naturals. The strategists performed much better on strategic tasks than on non-strategic tasks. In contrast, the naturals did well on both kinds of memory tasks. The data are plotted in percentiles, so we can see how the two groups compared against a normal control sample (50th percentile = average person's score). The findings suggest that superior ability can depend on either natural ability or on the use of highly practised strategies. However, there was partial support for Ericsson's view of the importance of the memory strategies:

easily the most impressive memory performance (surpassing that of more than 90% of the population) was obtained by strategists on strategic tasks.

Mnemonic techniques

A basic notion in attempts to improve memory is that relevant previous knowledge is very useful in permitting the efficient organisation and retention of new information. It has been found that expert chess players can remember the positions of approximately 24 chess pieces provided that the arrangement of the pieces forms a feasible game position (De Groot, 1966; see also Chapter 16). Unskilled amateur players can remember the positions of only about 10 pieces. These findings reflect differences in knowledge of the game rather than in memory ability, because experts do no better than amateurs when remembering the positions of randomly placed pieces.

Several mnemonic techniques to increase long-term memory have been devised. Most of them involve some or all of the requirements for superior memory skills identified by Ericsson (1988): meaningful encoding; retrieval structure;

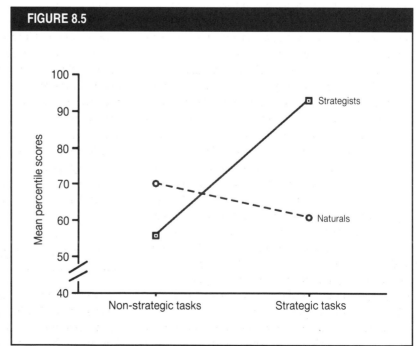

FIGURE 8.5

Memory performance of strategists and naturals on strategic and non-strategic tasks. Based on data in Wilding and Valentine (1994).

and speed-up. For example, there are the various peg systems, in which to-be-remembered items are attached to easily memorised items or pegs. The most popular of the peg systems is the "one-is-a-bun" mnemonic, which is based on the rhyme, "one is a bun, two is a shoe, three is a tree, four is a door, five is a hive, six is sticks, seven is heaven …" One mental image is formed associating the first to-be-remembered item with a bun, a second mental image links a shoe with the second item, and so on. The seventh item can be retrieved by thinking of the image based on heaven. This mnemonic makes use of all Ericsson's requirements, and doubles recall (Morris & Reid, 1970).

The "one-is-a-bun" mnemonic is successful because it provides an organisational framework for unorganised learning material; because it provides effective and specific retrieval cues; and because it involves interactive imagery. However, from a scientific rather than a practical perspective, it is unfortunate that it is not known which of these factors is of greatest importance.

The key word method is a mnemonic technique that has been applied extensively to the task of acquiring foreign vocabulary. First, an association is formed between each spoken foreign word and an English word or phrase sounding like it (the keyword). Second, a mental image is created in which the keyword acts as a link between the foreign word and its English equivalent. For example, the Russian word "zvonok" is pronounced "zvah-oak" and means bell. This can be learned by using "oak" as the keyword, and forming an image of an oak tree festooned with bells.

The keyword technique is more effective when the keywords are provided than when learners must provide their own. In one study (Atkinson & Raugh, 1975), 120 Russian words and their English equivalents were presented. The beneficial effects of the keyword method at short and long (six-week) retention intervals are shown in Fig. 8.6. Pressley and McDaniel (1988) confirmed the effectiveness of the keyword method in producing good recall. In addition, they found that it was associated with a high level of comprehension.

There is a very different technique known as SQ3R (Survey, Question, Read, Recite, Review) which can be used for learning complex, integrated material. The initial Survey stage involves skimming through the material while attempting to construct a framework to facilitate comprehension. In the Question stage, the learner asks himself or herself questions based on the various headings in the material; the idea here is to make reading purposeful. The material is read thoroughly at the Read stage, with the questions from the previous stage being borne in mind. The material is re-read at the Recite stage, with the learner describing the essence of each section to himself or herself after it has been read. Finally, the learner reviews what has been learned. Part of the rationale for this study method is that the Survey stage activates previous knowledge, with the subsequent stages involving active, goal-directed processes designed to integrate that knowledge with the stimulus material.

Evaluation

Although memory researchers have traditionally focused on failures of memory, it is also important to consider situations in which there is very high memory performance. Ericsson (1988) has made a contribution towards understanding the requirements of successful memory strategies, but theoretical progress has been slow. Most of the mnemonic techniques are very effective, but we generally do not know why in detail.

At the practical level, some of the techniques require time-consuming training, and they are often of little applicability. For example, few of us need to learn the order of a list of unrelated words, which is what the "one-is-a-bun" mnemonic permits us to do. General memory aids (e.g. the SQ3R method of study) tend to be less effective than very specific memory aids, but unfortunately it is the general memory aids that typically have the greatest applicability to everyday life.

PROSPECTIVE MEMORY

The overwhelming proportion of studies of human memory (whether laboratory-based or naturalistic) have been concerned with retrospective memory. The focus has been on the past, particularly on

FIGURE 8.6

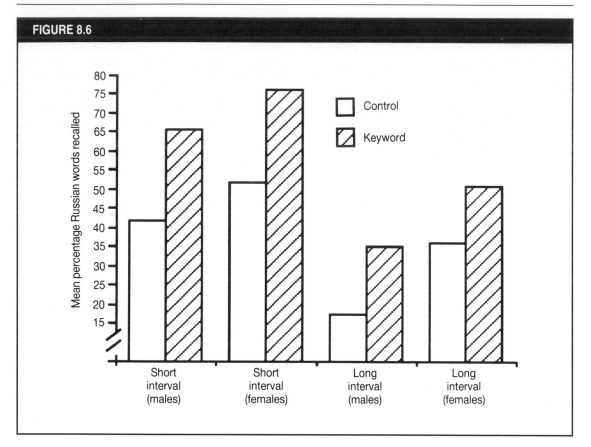

Effects of the keyword method on recall at short and long delays in males and females. Based on data in Atkinson and Raugh (1975).

people's ability to remember events that they have experienced or knowledge that they acquired previously. In contrast, much of everyday life is concerned with prospective memory, which involves remembering to do things at the appropriate time (e.g. meet a friend at eleven o'clock; attend a lecture at three o'clock). Forgetting to carry out some habitual action (e.g. feeding the cat before going off to work) fits this definition of prospective memory, but most theorists would prefer to categorise such lapses as action slips rather than failures of prospective memory (see Chapter 5).

As Baddeley (1990) pointed out, retrospective and prospective memory do not differ only with respect to their past versus future time orientation. Retrospective memory tends to involve

remembering *what* we know about something and can be high in information content, whereas prospective memory typically focuses on *when* to do something and has a fairly low informational content. Another difference is that prospective memory is obviously of relevance to the plans or goals that we form for our daily activities in a way that is not true of retrospective memory. Evidence that these goals are of importance to memory was obtained by Brewer and Dupree (1983). They discovered that subjects tended to remember the goals underlying the actions of other people even when the steps leading to those goals had been forgotten.

Another difference between prospective and retrospective memory is that there are generally more external cues available in the case of retrospective memory. If external cues are often lacking, why is prospective memory generally successful? Morris (1992) referred to a study at Lancaster University in which there was evidence that cues only marginally related to the to-be-remembered action could sometimes suffice to trigger a prospective memory. For example, a subject who had been told to phone the experimenter as part of an experiment was reminded by seeing a poster for another psychology experiment.

Some evidence that prospective and retrospective memory are very different from each other was obtained by Kvavilashvili (1987). Subjects were instructed to remind the experimenter to pass on a message. Those subjects who remembered to remind the experimenter (i.e. those showing good prospective memory) were no better than those who did not remind the experimenter (i.e. those showing poor prospective memory) at remembering the content of the message. These findings suggest that prospective memory ability may be unrelated to retrospective memory ability.

In spite of the findings of Kvavilashvili (1987), it seems likely that there are some similarities between prospective memory and retrospective memory. For example, prospective memory involves remembering the intention to perform an action over a period of time, and at least in this regard would appear to resemble retrospective memory. Hitch and Ferguson (1991) studied memory for intentions by asking members of a film society to list films they intended to see as well as those they had seen during that season. Memory for films that had been seen showed a recency effect, with films that had been seen most recently being most likely to be remembered; in similar fashion, memory for the intention to see films in the future was best for films that were due to be seen soonest. Ability to recall specific films that had been seen was inversely related to the number of such films, and ability to remember the intention to see specific films in the future was also inversely related to the number of such films. Hitch and Ferguson (1991) also reported a correlation of +0.27 between retrospective memory for films already seen and prospective memory for films yet to be seen. An

important difference between their study and that of Kvavilashvili (1987) was that they did not assess whether subjects actually carried out their intentions to see various films, leading them to the following speculation (Hitch & Ferguson, 1991, p.292): "It is translating intentions into actions that contributes particularly to differences between prospective and retrospective memory."

Meacham (1988) suggested an interesting way of considering prospective memory. According to him, the distinctive feature of prospective remembering is that it has its basis in interpersonal relations. More specifically, prospective remembering is concerned primarily with having a memory of one's public commitments or promises to perform some action. Meacham (1988) discussed some of his own research in which prospective memories that involved other people were more likely to be remembered than prospective memories that did not involve anyone else.

There are probably several different kinds of prospective memory. Ellis (1988) distinguished between pulses and steps. If one has to remember to do something at a specific time (e.g. be at a bridge session at 7.30 p.m.), then a pulse is involved. If one has to remember to do something that can be done within a broader period of time (e.g. book seats for a forthcoming football match), then a step is involved. Ellis (1988) carried out a diary study, and found that there were a number of differences between pulses and steps. Pulses are usually regarded as more important than steps, and they are more likely to be remembered by resorting to a diary, because they necessitate a restructuring of the day's activities. Pulses are either remembered only at the specific time when the event in question is supposed to occur or they are thought about throughout the day. In contrast, steps tend to be thought about sporadically throughout the day, and they are more likely to be recorded in memos than in a diary.

Harris and Wilkins (1982) made an interesting attempt to study prospective memory under laboratory conditions. Their subjects watched a film, having been instructed to hold up cards at pre-specified times. Their watches were removed, but there was a clock behind them which they were free to consult. It was thus possible for the experimenters to assess how frequently the subjects checked the time, and how accurate they were in performing the task of holding up the cards.

In general, the number of observations of the clock described a J-shaped pattern, in which there were frequent observations at the beginning and end of the time period but very few in the middle period. The high number of observations near the time when the card was to be held up presumably occurred because the subjects wanted to be as accurate as possible. It is less clear why there were so many clock observations early on, but this may have happened because the subjects wanted to establish the relationship between the subjective and objective passage of time (Ceci, Baker, & Bronfenbrenner, 1988).

Common sense indicates that motivation plays a part in determining whether or not we remember to do things. For example, it seems probable that we are more likely to remember to do something enjoyable (e.g. visit the theatre) than to do something we dislike (e.g. visit the dentist). Freud (1901, p.157) certainly subscribed to that point of view, going so far as to argue that the motive behind many of our failures of prospective memory "is an unusually large amount of unavowed contempt for other people". Freud's views (as usual) may have been somewhat over the top, but there is evidence that motivation makes a difference to prospective memory. Meacham and Singer (1977) instructed their subjects to post postcards at one weekly intervals. Performance on this prospective memory task was higher when a financial incentive was offered than when it was not.

As Cohen (1989) has pointed out, prospective memory should be considered with respect to the action plans that we form. Action plans can be routine (e.g. have lunch) or novel (e.g. buy a new car), they can be general (e.g. organise a dinner party) or specific (e.g. buy a bottle of gin), they may form part of a network of plans (e.g. organise the arrangements for a business trip) or they may be isolated (e.g. buy a collar for the cat), and they may be high or low in priority. Direct evidence is lacking, but it seems probable that memory is likely to be good for plans that are routine, high in priority, and relate to a network of plans (see Cohen, 1989). Networking may be of particular importance: we rarely forget to carry out actions (e.g. having lunch; catching the 7.35a.m. train) that are well embedded in our daily plans.

EVALUATION OF EVERYDAY MEMORY RESEARCH

As was pointed out at the beginning of this chapter, there is considerable controversy concerning the value of research on everyday memory. Now that we have considered some of this research, it is easier to evaluate. Strong views against everyday memory were expressed by Banaji and Crowder (1989, p.1190). According to them: "We have not been able to see any new principles of memory emerging from the everyday memory studies. Again and again, what seem at first like new, dramatic, emergent principles turn out to be everyday manifestations of laboratory wisdom." They supported this argument with reference to two phenomena: the self-reference effect and flashbulb memories. As they pointed out, it was initially argued that information that was processed in relation to the self was especially memorable because of the involvement of the self-schema. However, subsequent research indicated that information not processed in relation to the self could be as well remembered provided that the information was well organised or related to some rich network of knowledge.

So far as flashbulb memories are concerned, it was claimed by Brown and Kulik (1977) that there is a special "print now" neural mechanism which ensures that dramatic and surprising events are accurately remembered over extremely long periods of time. Some so-called flashbulb memories are forgotten in the same way as other memories, but others seem more immune to forgetting. It is still not clear whether there is anything very special about flashbulb memories to distinguish them from other memories.

Even if research on everyday memory has not been very productive of theoretical insights, it has certainly been valuable in identifying interesting new phenomena. A particularly clear example is prospective memory. Memory researchers have traditionally attempted to study memory in isolation from normal functioning, but research on prospective memory has indicated that memory in real life is typically embedded in a rich social and motivational context. Instead of assessing the capacities of different memory systems, researchers might be better advised to follow the lead of those who study prospective memory and address the key issue of the functions that memory serves in our lives.

Banaji and Crowder (1989) also criticised research into everyday memory on the grounds that much of it focuses on specific situations or phenomena, with the consequence that the findings cannot be generalised to other situations or phenomena. They have a point when they argue that the generalisability of research findings is important. However, much traditional laboratory-based memory research also suffers from a lack of generalisability, and it is not clear that practical memory research is inferior in that regard.

Everyday memory research has been of value in testing theories that have been developed on the basis of laboratory research. Consider, for example, the interview techniques that are used with eyewitnesses. Tulving's encoding specificity principle and the notion that memory traces are complex integrations of information have been applied with great success to the task of obtaining additional information from eyewitnesses.

On the negative side, there are some methodological problems with much research on everyday memory. Although the experimenter may have good control over the conditions at the time of retrieval, he or she typically is not able to control what happens at the time of learning. Furthermore, because the experimenter was usually not present at the time of learning, it is difficult to establish the accuracy or otherwise of an individual's recollections of some past experience. This problem can often be handled by investigating the phenomena of everyday memory under controlled laboratory conditions, as has happened in the case of research on eyewitness testimony and the self-referent effect. Even when this is not possible, everyday memory research can still be of considerable value. As Gruneberg and Morris

(1992b, p.7) pointed out: "Practical application of memory research is of value in its own right, and ... it is preferable to carry out research with technical limitations in terms of laboratory control, than to abandon application because control is less than perfect."

We can draw up a balance sheet which indicates the advantages and the limitations of everyday memory. The following are some of the major advantages of such research:

* Important, non-obvious phenomena have been discovered.
* There is direct applicability to everyday life.
* The functions served by memory in our lives are considered.
* It provides a test-bed for theories of memory developed from laboratory research.

The following are some of the major limitations of everyday memory research:

* There is often poor experimental control, especially of the learning stage.
* The accuracy of everyday memories often cannot be assessed.
* Relatively few new theoretical insights have emerged.

CHAPTER SUMMARY

Autobiographical memory, the memory we have of our own past, appears to be organised in a hierarchical fashion. It tends to be good for relatively recent events and for the years of adolescence and early adulthood, but it is rather poor for the middle years of adulthood and for early childhood (childhood amnesia). Autobiographical memories that are high in rarity or salience are generally very well remembered. Autobiographical memories tend to blur into each other, so that recall of a given event is often true in a general sense but inaccurate in a specific sense.

The self-reference effect and flashbulb memories are two phenomena that have attracted much interest. The evidence suggests that enhanced recall for self-relevant information occurs because we possess a rich network of information about ourselves, and because that information is organised. Flashbulb memories often seem to be very vivid and immune from forgetting, but research has indicated that they are subject to forgetting and can be inaccurate in the same way as ordinary memories.

Research on eyewitness testimony has uncovered several phenomena that are reliable and counter-intuitive. Of particular importance, it has been discovered that an eyewitness's memory for an incident is rather fragile, and can easily be distorted by inaccurate information about that incident which is provided subsequently. Some of the obtained findings may reflect the demand characteristics of the situation, but it is probable that memory itself is usually changed. Psychologists have devised techniques for increasing the amount of information that can be obtained from eyewitnesses. Many of these techniques are based on the assumption that there are various access routes to a memory trace, and thus it is useful to employ several different retrieval cues in order to maximise recall.

One way of attempting to improve people's memory is to study individuals who have superior memories. Most individuals with superior memory have devoted substantial amounts of time to practising specific memory techniques, but there are others who are blessed with a "naturally good" memory. Techniques for improving memory usually involve relating the to-be-learned information in a meaningful way to existing knowledge, storing cues for retrieval, and then devoting considerable practice in order to speed up the processes involved. There are several mnemonic techniques that have been developed for specific purposes (e.g. putting names to faces; remembering long lists of words). These techniques are generally very effective but of

limited practical usefulness. However, some techniques (e.g. the keyword method for vocabulary acquisition; the SQ3R method of study) are of more general relevance.

Prospective memory refers to memory for future actions. Prospective memories are usually rooted in interpersonal relations for two reasons: there is a public commitment to perform the future action, and the action itself involves other people. Future actions that we are highly motivated to remember are more likely to be performed than those where motivation is lower. Prospective memories should be considered in relation to the action plans we form. Those prospective memories that form part of a large integrated action plan are more likely to be remembered than those that are isolated. It is important to distinguish between remembering a future action and actually performing it: for example, one may remember a dentist's appointment but decide not to fulfil it because of the potential pain involved.

FURTHER READING

Banaji, M. R., & Crowder, R. G. (1989). The bankruptcy of everyday memory. *American Psychologist*, *44*, 1185–1193. As the title suggests, this article focuses on the alleged deficiencies and limitations of everyday memory research.

Conway, M. A., & Rubin, D. C. (1993). The structure of autobiographical memory. In A. F. Collins, S. E. Gathercole, M. A. Conway, & P. E. Morris (Eds.), *Theories of memory*. Hove, UK: Lawrence Erlbaum Associates Ltd. Contemporary views of the rapidly growing area of autobiographical memory are discussed in a clear and interesting fashion.

Gruneberg, M., & Morris, P. (Eds.) (1992a). *Aspects of memory: Vol. 1. The practical aspects*. London: Routledge. This book contains substantial chapters dealing in an up-to-date way with most of the topics discussed in this chapter.

9

Mental Representation:
Propositions and Images

INTRODUCTION

As in Adams' (1979) *Hitch-hiker's guide to the galaxy*, any chapter titled "Mental representation" should be prefaced with the comforting words "Don't panic!" For centuries philosophers, linguists, and psychologists have puzzled over how we come to represent the world "inside our heads". Paivio (1986) has proposed that the problem of mental representation might be the most difficult one to solve in all of the sciences. Of course, topics that experts find difficult become waking nightmares for students. You should, therefore, read this chapter carefully and thoughtfully.

This chapter is a foundation for many subsequent chapters. Here we talk about the different types of representations that exist, whereas in Chapters 10 and 11 we deal with how these representations are organised as knowledge in memory. In subsequent chapters, we consider how this knowledge is used in other mental activities, like reading, speaking, problem solving, and reasoning.

Several distinctions can be made among types of representation (see Fig. 9.1). A broad distinction can be made between the external representations

of everyday life (e.g. writing, pictures, and diagrams) and our "internal", mental representations. The two types of representations should not be confused. In the next section, we discuss different classes of external representations (e.g. pictures and words) because this is a good introduction to the distinctions that are made among mental representations. Mental representations can be viewed from two main perspectives. Traditionally, they are characterised as symbolic representations; where a symbol is a pattern stored in long-term memory which denotes or refers to something outside itself (Vera & Simon, 1994). However, with the emergence of connectionism, theorists have proposed the notion of sub-symbolic, mental representations; these are "distributed representations" stored as patterns of activation in connectionist networks (see Chapter 1). We use the term "perspective" rather than "distinction" for this division as several theorists have argued that distributed representations are merely symbolic representations at a more detailed level. Most of this chapter presents the traditional symbolic view, but later we review the alternative connectionist position.

Symbolic, mental representations divide into analogical and propositional representations. The

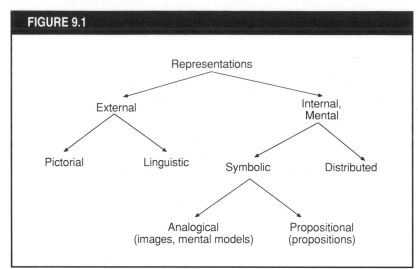

FIGURE 9.1

Outline of the different types of representations discussed in this chapter and the distinctions that can be made among them.

classic analogical representation is the visual image, although it is important to remember that we can form images based on other modalities: auditory images from hearing, and olfactory images from our sense of smell. Propositional representations are more abstract, language-like representations; they are meant to capture the conceptual content of situations and things. For example, when you think about a book being on a table, the conceptual content of those thoughts is supposed to be mentally represented by propositions [which might be written as ON(BOOK, TABLE)]. You should always remember that propositional representations are only *language-like*; they are *not* words but rather capture abstract, ideational content. The analogical–propositional distinction is controversial, as some theorists have argued that images are not really a separate type of representation but can be reduced to propositional representations. This debate, which we outline later in the chapter, has been termed the imagery–propositional debate.

WHAT IS A REPRESENTATION ?

A representation is any notation or sign or set of symbols that "re-presents" something to us. That is, it stands for some thing in the absence of that thing; typically, that thing is an aspect of the external world or an object of our imagination (i.e. our own internal world). External representations come in many different forms: maps, menus, oil paintings, blueprints, written language, and so on. However, broadly speaking, external representations are either written notations (typically words) or graphical notations (pictures and diagrams). Consider a practical example of how these two types of external representation can be used to achieve the same end.

External representations: Written versus graphical representations

Imagine you have to work out office allocations for several people. You might draw a diagram of the floor of the building with its corridor, the rooms along it, and the occupants of each room (see Fig. 9.2a for one possibility). Essentially the same information can be captured in the description shown in Fig. 9.2b. Both of these representations have a critical characteristic that is common to all representations; namely, they only represent some aspects of the world. Neither representation shows us the colour of the carpet in the corridor, or the thickness of the walls, or the position of fire exits because these things are not relevant to our purpose.

However, the words and diagrams also differ in one important respect; the diagram has a "closer" relationship to the world than the linguistic description. The diagram tells us about the relative

FIGURE 9.2

(a)

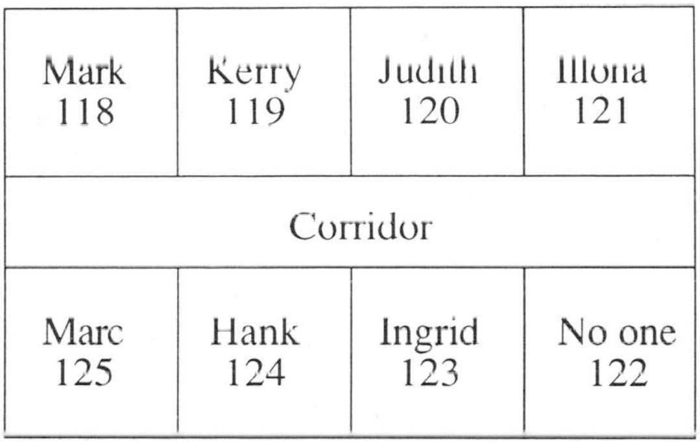

Mark 118	Kerry 119	Judith 120	Illona 121
Corridor			
Marc 125	Hank 124	Ingrid 123	No one 122

(b) Mark is in Room 118   No one is in Room 122
Kerry is in Room 119   Ingrid is in Room 123
Judith is in Room 120   Hank is in Room 124
Illona is in Room 121   Marc is in Room 125

An example of the two main types of external representations: (a) a pictorial representation of the occupants of several rooms along a corridor, and (b) a linguistic description of the same information.

spatial position of the rooms. For example, we know that Hank's room faces Kerry's room and that Illona's room is at the opposite end of the corridor to Marc's room. Were the linguistic description to include this information, we would have to include several further sentences.

Pictures and diagrams are "closer" to the world because their structure resembles the structure of the world. In this case, the spatial configuration of the rooms in the diagram is the same as that of the actual rooms in the world. This structural resemblance is often termed *analogical*. Typically, linguistic descriptions do not have this analogical property because the relationship between a linguistic symbol and that which it represents is arbitrary (de Saussure, 1960). There is no inherent reason why small, furry, household pets should be labelled by the word "cats". If the English language had developed along other lines, cats might well have been designated by the word "sprogdorfs". Even onomatopoeic words (like "miaow") that seem to resemble the sound they represent are really arbitrary; as evidenced by their failure to be used in every language. In Irish, for example, the word for "miaow" is "meamhlach" (pronounced "me-all-och").

Differences between external representations

The critical difference between written and graphical representations explained earlier has several specific implications. Consider another example involving two alternative representations of a book on a desk (see Fig. 9.3). There are several ways in which these two representations differ (see Kosslyn, 1980, 1983).

First, the linguistic representation is made up of discrete symbols. The words can be broken down into letters but these are the smallest units that can be used. A quarter of the letter "B" is not a symbol that can be used in the language. However, a pictorial representation has no obvious smallest unit. It can be broken up in arbitrary ways and these parts can still be used as symbols (e.g. the corner of the table, half the spine of the book, or even just a single dot from the picture).

Second, a linguistic representation has explicit symbols to stand for the things it represents (e.g. words for the "book" and the "desk" and the relation between them, "on"). The picture does not have distinct symbols for everything it represents. In particular, there is no explicit symbol for the relation between the book and the desk. "On-ness" is shown implicitly by the way the book and the

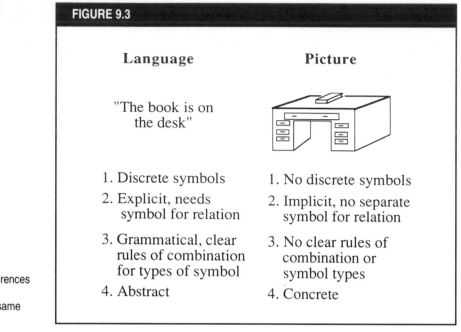

FIGURE 9.3

Language

Picture

"The book is on
the desk"

1. Discrete symbols

2. Explicit, needs
   symbol for relation

3. Grammatical, clear
   rules of combination
   for types of symbol

4. Abstract

1. No discrete symbols

2. Implicit, no separate
   symbol for relation

3. No clear rules of
   combination or
   symbol types

4. Concrete

Some of the major differences between two external representations of the same situation.

desk are placed; that is, "on" cannot be represented by itself but only in a given context.

Third, in the linguistic representation the symbols are organised according to a set of rules (i.e. a grammar). One cannot say "on is table the book" and have a meaningful combination. These rules of combination exploit the fact that there are different classes of symbols (e.g. nouns and verbs). Pictures do not seem to have grammars of the same sort in that (i) they have less distinct classes of symbol, (ii) if there are rules of combination they are less constrained than in a linguistic representation.

Fourth, the linguistic representation is *abstract* in that the information it characterises could have been acquired from any form of perception (e.g. by touch, by vision) and bears no direct relationship to a given modality. In contrast, the picture is more *concrete* in the sense that, although the information it represents could have been acquired from a variety of perceptual sources, it is strongly associated with the visual modality.

Differences between internal, mental representations

Many of the points we have made about external representations have parallels in our internal, mental representations. First, mental representa-

tions only represent some aspects of the environment (whether that environment be the external world or our own imagined world). Second, the difference between written and graphical representations is paralleled in mental representations, by the difference between analogical and propositional representations (see Table 9.1). *Analogical representations* tend to be images that may be either visual, auditory, olfactory, tactile, or kinetic. *Propositional representations* are language-like representations that capture the ideational content of the mind, irrespective of the original modality in which that information was encountered.

Analogical and propositional representations also reflect the detailed differences between types of external representations. Analogical representations are non-discrete, can represent things implicitly, have loose rules of combination, and are concrete in the sense that they are tied to a particular sense modality. Propositional representations are discrete, explicit, are combined according to rules, and are abstract. They are abstract in the sense that they can represent information from any modality; but it should also be stressed that, unlike the words of a language, they usually refer to distinct and unambiguous

TABLE 9.1

Summary of the Major Differences Between Analogical and Propositional Representations

Analogical	Propositional
Non-discrete	Discrete
Implicit	Explicit
Loose combination rules	Strong combination rules
Modality-specific	Amodal (abstract)

entities. That is, the propositions for the example in Fig. 9.3 [represented as ON(BOOK, DESK) to distinguish it from the linguistic representation] refer to a specific book and a specific desk and to a specific relationship of ON between them. These differences between analogical and propositional representations are now widely accepted in psychological theory. However, as a counterpoint, you should be aware of some commentators' view that it is next to impossible to really distinguish between the two forms of representation (for good discussions see Boden, 1988, and Hayes, 1985).

In conclusion, several aspects of external representations have parallels in mental representations. In later sections, we consider the differences between mental representations in some detail, as well as the debate that has arisen over these differences. Most of this chapter and of the literature on analogical representations concentrates on visual images.

PROPOSITIONS AS MENTAL REPRESENTATIONS

As we saw earlier, propositional representations are considered to be explicit, discrete, abstract entities that represent the ideational content of the mind. They represent conceptual objects and relations in a form that is not specific to any language (whether it be it Russian, Serbo-Croat, or Urdu) or to any modality (whether it be vision, audition, olfaction, or touch). Thus, they constitute a universal, amodal, mentalese; the basic code in which all cognitive activities are proposed to be carried out. However, this leaves us with a puzzle. If propositional representations are abstract, language-non-specific, and amodal how do we characterise them? Well, when theorists want to be explicit about the use of propositional representations they use aspects of a logical system called the *predicate calculus*.

One can imagine that the contents of the mind might be object-like entities that are related together in various ways by conceptual relations. The predicate calculus provides a convenient notation for realising these intuitions; the links on relations are represented as *predicates* and the object-entities as *arguments* of these predicates. By definition, a predicate here is anything that takes an argument or a number of arguments. The terminology sounds daunting but the idea is relatively simple. If you want to express the idea that "the book is on the table", then the link or relationship between the book and the table is represented by the predicate ON (where the capitals represent the notion that we are dealing with the mental content of ON and not the word "on"). The arguments that the ON-predicate links are the conceptual entities, the BOOK and the TABLE. In order to indicate that ON takes these two arguments, the objects are usually bracketed in the following manner:

ON(BOOK, TABLE)

Predicates can take any number of arguments; so, the sentence "Mary hit John with the stick and the stick was hard" can be notated as follows:

HIT(MARY, JOHN, STICK) and
HARD(STICK)

The predicates HIT and HARD are first-order predicates; that is, they take object constants as their arguments. Whenever one has a predicate and a number of arguments combined in this fashion the whole form is called a *proposition*, as can the combination of a number of such forms (i.e. the whole of the expression is also a proposition).

There are also second-order predicates that take propositions as their arguments. So, in characterising the sentence "Mary hit John with the stick and he was hurt" we can use the second-order predicate CAUSE to link the two other propositions:

CAUSE[HIT(MARY, JOHN, STICK),
        HURT(MARY, JOHN)   ]

Cognitive psychologists have used these notations to express *mental, propositional representations*. However, psychologists do not use all the strictures employed by logicians when they use the predicate calculus. In logic, a proposition can be either true or false and this has important consequences for logical systems. Most psychologists are not overly concerned with the formal properties of propositions (one important exception is the work on deductive reasoning in Chapter 17). In short, typically, theorists merely use the notion that ideational content can be stated in terms of predicates taking one or more arguments.

In an empirical context, the basic properties of propositions are rarely tested directly but are simply assumed. Their characteristics are, however, tested at a more gross level when they are combined to represent knowledge. Chapters 10 and 11 review several areas where propositional representations have been used heavily to represent semantic networks and schemata (see e.g. Collins & Quillian, 1969; Rumelhart & Ortony, 1977). Finally, in practical terms propositional representations are very useful for computational modelling. The predicate calculus can be implemented very easily in artificial intelligence computing languages like LISP (Norvig, 1992; Steele, 1990) or PROLOG (Clocksin & Mellish, 1984; Shoham, 1993). This has allowed researchers to be very precise about theories based on propositional representations and to construct and run computer models of cognitive processes.

EMPIRICAL DISTINCTIONS BETWEEN IMAGES AND PROPOSITIONS

Historically, visual imagery has been studied for a long time. Over 2000 years ago, Aristotle regarded imagery as the main medium of thought. Furthermore, orators in ancient Greece used imagery-based, mnemonic techniques to memorise speeches (see Yates, 1966); a technique that is still used today as an aid to improving one's memory. This interest in imagery can be traced in a continuous line through philosophers like Bishop Berkeley at Trinity College Dublin to the 19th-century research of Galton (see Mandler & Mandler, 1964). Galton (1883) distributed a questionnaire among his eminent scientific colleagues, asking them to, for example, imagine their breakfast table that morning. Surprisingly enough, several reported no conscious mental imagery at all.

As in Galton's studies, much of this early research relied on the use of introspective evidence. During the behaviourist era, when introspection fell into disrepute and mental representations were in a sense "banned", research on imagery lay fallow for a number of years. However, with the emergence of cognitive science, the study of mental representations once again became respectable. The main motivation behind this was the perceived necessity to be representationally precise about possible cognitive mechanisms. However, no sooner had researchers returned to examining imagery using new and more rigorous experimental methods, than further controversy arose.

The debate on imagery boils down to two basic questions. First, are images really different from propositional representations? Some researchers argued that images were distinct picture-like representations that operate in their own special medium. Others maintained that ultimately images are not really a different form of representation, they are merely propositional representations in a different guise. In this section, we review empirical evidence for the first view. Later, we consider some of the theoretical points that emerged in this debate.

The second question is related to the first but is subtly different. It is concerned with whether imagery has any *functional significance*. It is possible to accept that images are distinct and yet argue that they are merely epiphenomenal. An epiphenomenon is something that has no causal significance to some event. For example, the lights blinking on the outside of a computer indicate something about its internal operations but are not causally necessary for this activity to occur. If some of the bulbs were broken, the machine's internal computations would go on regardless. Thus, the bulbs are epiphenomenal to the system's processing. In a similar way, one can argue that imagery may occur in the mind but that it has no causal significance to cognition; if these images were suppressed then cognition would go on operating as normal.

Paivio's dual-coding theory

Allan Paivio's dual-coding theory (see Paivio, 1971, 1979, 1983, 1986, 1991) is devoted to determining the minimal basic differences between imagistic and propositional representations, grounded in empirical data from a large corpus of experiments. The basic proposals of the theory are shown in Panel 9.1.

Stated simply, the essence of dual-coding theory is that there are two distinct systems for the representation and processing of information. A verbal system deals with linguistic information and stores it in an appropriate verbal form. A separate non-verbal system carries out image-based processing and representation (see Fig. 9.4). Each of these systems is further divided into sub-systems that process either verbal or non-verbal information in the different modalities (i.e. vision, audition, haptic, taste, smell; see Table 9.2). However, it should be noted that there are no corresponding representations for taste and smell in the verbal system.

Within a particular sub-system when, for example, a spoken word is processed it is identified by a logogen for the auditory sound of the word. The concept of a *logogen* comes from Morton's (1969, 1979) theories of word recognition. Paivio (1986, p.66) characterises a logogen as a modality-specific unit that "can function as an

---

(Panel 9.1) Pavio's Dual-coding Theory

- Two basic independent but interconnected coding or symbolic systems underlie human cognition: a non-verbal system and a verbal system.

- Both systems are specialised for encoding, organising, storing, and retrieving distinct types of information.

- The non-verbal (or imagery) system is specialised for processing non-verbal objects and events (i.e. processing spatial and synchronous information) and thus enters into tasks like the analysis of scenes and the generation of mental images.

- The verbal system is specialised for dealing with linguistic information and is largely implicated in the processing of language; because of the serial nature of language it is specialised for sequential processing.

- Both systems are further sub-divided into several sensorimotor sub-systems (visual, auditory, and haptic) (Table 9.2).

- Both systems have basic representational units: *logogens* for the verbal system and *imagens* for the non-verbal system that come in modality-specific versions in each of the sensorimotor sub-systems.

- The two symbolic systems are interconnected by referential links between logogens and imagens.

FIGURE 9.4.

A schematic outline of the major components of dual-coding theory. The two main symbolic systems—the verbal and non-verbal systems—are connected to distinct input and output systems. Within the two systems are associative structures (involving logogens and imagens) that are linked to one another by referential connections. Adapted with permission from *Mental representations: A dual coding approach*, by Allan Paivio, 1986, published by Oxford University Press.

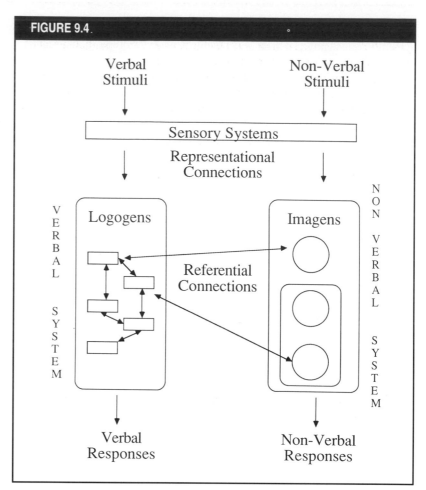

TABLE 9.2

The Relationship Between Symbolic and Sensorimotor Systems and Examples of the Types of Information Represented in Each Sub-system in Paivio's Dual-coding Theory

	Symbolic systems	
Sensorimotor	*Verbal*	*Non-verbal*
Visual	Visual words	Visual objects
Auditory	Auditory words	Environmental sounds
Haptic	Writing patterns	"Feel" of objects
Taste	—	Taste memories
Smell	—	Olfactory memories

integrated, informational structure or as a response generator": for example, there may be logogens for the word "snow". Logogens are modality-specific, in the sense that there are separate logogens for identifying the spoken sound "snow" and its visual form (i.e. the letters "s-n-o-w"). The corollary of logogens in the non-verbal system are imagens. Imagens are basic units that identify and represent images, in the different sensorimotor modalities. The important point to note about logogens and imagens is that they allow the theorist to posit a processing unit that identifies or represents a particular item (i.e. an image of a dog or a particular word) without having to specify the internal workings of this processing unit or the detailed representation of the item being processed. This lack of specification is one criticism of Paivio's work, although it is a deficit that is compensated for by later computational theories (like Kosslyn's, 1980).

The verbal and non-verbal systems communicate in a functional fashion via relations between imagens and logogens. The simplest case of such a relation is the referential link between an object and its name. That is, if you see a visual object (e.g. a dog runs by) it would be recognised by an imagen and a link between this imagen and an auditory logogen for the word "dog" may bring the word "dog" to mind. Thus, the links between these basic units constitute the fundamental ways in which the sub-parts of the two symbolic systems are interconnected.

Evidence for dual-coding theory

Evidence for dual coding theory has been provided in a number of distinct task areas: for instance, in memory tasks, in neuropsychological studies, and in problem solving. These studies tend to show that either the two symbolic systems operate in an independent fashion or that they produce joint effects, depending on specific circumstances. For example, an experiment might show that memory for words is quite distinct from memory for pictures, or that memory is enhanced when something is encoded in *both* pictures *and* words. Consider three classic cases from memory experiments designed to test the theory: the differences between recalling pictures and words,

the effects of word imaging and concreteness, and repetition effects.

Effects of dual codes on free recall

Consider an experiment in which subjects are given either a set of pictures or a list of words to memorise. If the pictures are of common objects then subjects are likely to name them spontaneously while memorising them (see Paivio, 1971). So, people should encode them using both verbal and non-verbal systems. In contrast, the words are more likely to be memorised using the verbal system alone (assuming that subjects do not spontaneously image the objects referred to by the words). Memory for pictures should, therefore, be better than that for words because of the joint influence of both systems in the former case. Paivio (1971) found that pictures were remembered, in both free-recall and recognition tasks, more readily than words. In fact, pictures are recalled so much more easily than words that Paivio has proposed that the image code is mnemonically superior to the verbal code, although exactly why this should be so is not clear.

These joint effects are not only found for pictures and words. Initial results indicated that they could also be found between different classes of words. Some words are concrete and evoke images more readily than other words. If words are concrete, in the sense of denoting things that can be perceived by one of the sense modalities, rather than abstract, they appear to be retrieved more easily (see Paivio, Yuille, & Madigan, 1968, for evidence of this). As in the case of the picture–word differences, words that are rated as being high in their image-evoking value or concreteness (or both) are likely to be encoded using two codes rather than just one (for reviews of the results of item-memory tasks see Cornoldi & Paivio, 1982; Richardson, 1980). So, again there seems to be a joint contribution to performance when both systems are involved in the task.

However, there is some controversy on the dual-code explanation of recall differences for concrete and abstract words. Part of the problem is that the results are of a correlational nature, they merely show that the imagibility/concreteness of words *correlates* with good recall performance.

They do not show a causal connection between concreteness and recall. We can test for such a causal connection by varying the instructions given to subjects when they are memorising the words. If you employ interactive-imagery instructions (e.g. "Form images depicting objects interacting in some way"), then it is typically found that performance is improved for concrete material but not for abstract materials (see Richardson, 1980). This is perfectly consistent with dual-code theory because the imagery instructions should involve both coding systems for the concrete words but not for the abstract words.

Unfortunately, similar instructions that do not involve imaging have similar effects; verbal mediation instructions (e.g. "Form short phrases including the list of items") result in concrete materials being recalled more readily than abstract materials. On the basis of these results, Bower (1970, 1972) proposed that interactive imagery and verbal mediation instructions were both effective in that they increased the organisation and cohesion of the to-be-remembered information. To test this hypothesis, Bower presented subjects with pairs of concrete words using three different types of instructions for different subject groups: interactive-imagery instructions, separation-imagery instructions (i.e. "Construct an image of two objects separated in space"), or instructions to memorise by rote. On a subsequent cued-recall task, the interactive-imagery subjects performed much better than the separation-imagery subjects, who in turn performed no better than subjects instructed to use rote memorisation. In other words, interactive imagery instructions are effective because they enhance relational organisation. So, recall differences between concrete and abstract words create some difficulties for Paivio's theory.

However, we should point out that Paivio has gone some way towards accounting for these results by including organisational assumptions within each of his symbolic systems that account for differences between interactive-imagery and separation-imagery instructions (see Paivio, 1986, Chapters 4 and 8). Having said this, the issue has not been fully resolved. Recent research has shown that concreteness effects are not due solely to the effects of imagery but may also involve factors like distinctiveness and relational information (see Marschark & Cornoldi, 1990; Marschark & Hunt, 1989; Marschark & Surian, 1992; Plaut & Shallice, 1993). Furthermore, in a review of the literature, Marschark, Richman, Yuille, and Hunt (1987) have rejected the proposal that imaginal codes are stored in long-term memory, arguing instead that verbal and imaginal processing systems operate on a more generic, conceptual memory.

Studies of free recall also support the additivity and functional independence of the two systems (Paivio, 1975; Paivio & Csapo, 1973). In these experiments, subjects were shown a series of concrete nouns and asked either to image to the presented noun or to pronounce it. During the five-second intervals between items they were asked to rate the difficulty of imaging or pronouncing the word. In one manipulation, subjects were presented with a given word repeatedly. In some cases, the repetition encouraged dual coding, in that subjects had to image it on one occurrence and pronounce it on the next. In other cases, the repetition merely promoted encoding in a single code when subjects either imaged or pronounced the word again. After doing this task, without prior warning, subjects were asked to recall the presented words.

Several interesting results were found to support dual-coding theory. First, the probability of imaged words being recalled was twice as high as that for pronounced words, indicating the superiority of non-verbal codes in recall. Second, the imagery-instructions raised the level of recall to the same high level that is normally seen for the encoding of pictures under comparable conditions. Third, in the conditions that predicted dual coding, there was a statistically additive effect on recall relative to recall levels calculated for once-presented items that had been imaged or pronounced. Fourth, in contrast to these results, when a repeated word was encoded in the same way on each presentation, the massed repetitions did not produce similar additive effects (see Fig. 9.5).

Interference within a single system
Paivio's theory sees the routes taken by perception and imagery as basically the same. For example, in

FIGURE 9.5

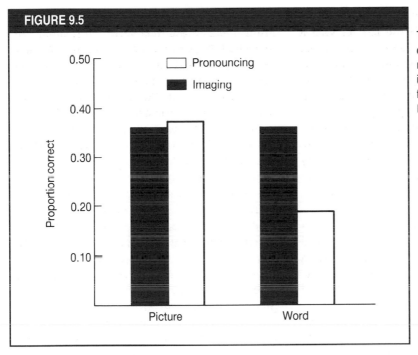

The relative proportions of correct responses when subjects repeatedly pronounced or imaged pictures or words in a free recall task. Adapted from Paivio and Csapo (1973).

talking about the non-verbal system he says that it is responsible both for the cognitive task of forming visual images and the perceptual task of scene-analysis. Therefore, any findings that demonstrate interference between perceptual and imagery tasks are a further source of evidence for the theory. That is, if performance on a perceptual task is disrupted by carrying out an imagery task, and vice versa, it is likely that both tasks are using related processing components. Such interference has been found on a regular basis. For example, Segal and Fusella (1970) asked subjects to form both visual and auditory images and then asked them to perform a visual or auditory detection task. They found that auditory images interfered more with the detection of auditory signals and visual images interfered more with visual detection. As there was some interference in all conditions it seems reasonable to conclude that there is a generalised effect of mental imagery on perceptual sensitivity in addition to a large modality-specific effect.

However, it is not enough to simply demonstrate interference. One needs to pin-point the specific processes that are responsible for the interference and also, if possible, to show how perceptual and image-based processing differ. More detailed evidence of this sort has been found in a task used by Baddeley, Grant, Wight, and Thomson (1975). In this experiment, subjects listened to a description of locations of digits within a matrix and were then asked to reproduce the matrix. The description was either hard or easy to visualise. The interfering task involved a pursuit rotor (i.e. visually tracking a light moving along a circular track). This task results in a distinct type of interference—performance on easily visualised messages is retarded, whereas the non-visualisable message is unaffected—but the interference is not due specifically to the perceptual processes involved in vision. Baddeley and Lieberman (1980) have shown that if the concurrent task is specifically visual (e.g. the judgement of brightness), rather than visual and spatial (as the pursuit rotor seems to be) then the interference effects disappear. Similarly, when the concurrent task is purely spatial (i.e. when blindfolded subjects were asked to point at a moving pendulum on the basis of auditory feedback) the pattern of interference found reproduces the effects found in the original Baddeley et al. experiment. In summary, it appears that the recall of visualisable (or easily imagined) messages of the kind used in these experiments is interfered with by spatial processing rather than by visual processing, indicating that these spatial processes are somehow shared by perceptual and image-based processing within the non-verbal system (see Logie & Baddeley, 1989, for a review).

These experiments show that Paivio's interference predictions really rest on the assumption that visual imagery involves visual rather than spatial representations. However, Farah, Hammond, Levine, and Calvanio (1988) have suggested that it is a mistake to argue that imagery is either visual *or* spatial. Rather they have shown, using neuropsychological evidence, that imagery is both visual and spatial, and taps into distinct visual and spatial representations.

Neuropsychological evidence for dual coding

A natural question that arises about Paivio's theory is whether there is neuropsychological evidence for the localisation of the two symbolic systems within the brain. For instance, for most people the left hemisphere is implicated in tasks that involve the processing of verbal material. In contrast, the right hemisphere tends to be used in tasks that are of a non-verbal nature (e.g. face identification, memory for faces, and recognising non-verbal sounds). Furthermore, within each hemisphere there seems to be some localisation for the sensorimotor sub-systems: visual, auditory, and tactile (see Cohen, 1983). Although dual-coding theory posits distinct symbolic systems, Paivio does not maintain that these distinct systems reside in distinct hemispheres, although the systems are localised to some extent (for evidence against this see e.g. Zaidel, 1976).

There is some evidence for localisation differences on concrete and abstract words that disrupt a simple left–right division. Word recognition studies, using tachistoscopes, have shown that there are hemispheric differences in the processing of concrete and abstract words (see Paivio, 1986, Chapter 12). Typically, abstract words that are presented to the right visual field, and hence are processed by the left hemisphere, are recognised more often than those presented to the

left visual field (i.e. processed by the right hemisphere). However, concrete words are recognised equally well irrespective of the visual field (and hence the hemisphere) to which they are presented. It should be pointed out that these findings have not been consistent although there is a tendency for the performance asymmetries to be less consistent for concrete than for abstract words (Boles, 1983). Converging evidence also comes from so-called deep-dyslexic patients, who have widespread lesions in the left hemisphere. Generally, they have greater difficulty reading abstract, low-imagery words than concrete high-imagery words (see Coltheart, Patterson, & Marshall, 1980; Paivio & te Linde, 1982). Plaut and Shallice (1993) have modelled these concrete–abstract effects by lesioning a connectionist net (see also Hinton & Shallice, 1991). However, the effects were modelled by representing concrete concepts with more features than abstract concepts, rather than using imagery representations. We shall see later, in the presentation of Kosslyn's theory, that some more recent evidence presents a clearer picture of what might be happening in both hemispheres (see Farah, 1984; Kosslyn, 1987).

Section summary

In conclusion, several sources of evidence support Paivio's proposals that there are two separate but interdependent symbolic systems. First, the theory accounts for the pictorial–word and concrete–abstract word differences in free-recall studies, although it is not the only possible explanation of some of the latter results. The interference that dual-coding theory predicts between perceptual and image-based processes within the non-verbal system has been found, although its locus in the visual modality seems to lie in spatial processing. Finally, there is some evidence for the localisation of different symbolic systems within different parts of the cerebral hemispheres. So, on the issue of the broad distinctions between verbal and non-verbal processing in the brain, dual-coding theory is moderately successful. However, in later sections we will see that this picture of imagery behaviour can be construed in a more complicated fashion.

THE STRUCTURE OF VISUAL IMAGES: SOME EMPIRICAL EVIDENCE

Paivio's theory addresses the distinction between imagery and propositional codes, but it says little about the structure of imagery. It tells us little about how images appear to us (in our mind's eye), and about the sort of things that images allow us to do. Happily, other researchers have concentrated on the structure of imagery *per se*. Two sets of studies illustrate several important properties of mental images. First, studies on *mental rotation* show how people can rotate visual images. Second, studies on *image scanning* give us some idea of how people can "mentally scan" a visual image.

Mental rotation

In a series of experiments the mental rotation of a variety of imaged objects has been examined (e.g. Cooper, 1975; Cooper & Podgorny, 1976; Cooper & Shepard, 1973; Shepard, 1978 for a review; Shepard & Metzler, 1971). For example, Cooper and Shepard (1973) presented subjects with alphanumeric items in either their normal form or

in reversed, mirror-image form (see Fig. 9.6). In the experiment subjects were asked to judge whether a test figure was the normal or reversed version of the standard figure. The test figures were presented in a number of different orientations (see Fig. 9.6). The main result was that the further the test figure was rotated from the upright standard figure, the more time subjects took to make their decisions (see Fig. 9.7). These experiments have been carried out on a variety of different objects, indicating that there was some generality to the findings; for instance, digits, letters, or block-like forms have been used. (For recent research on mental rotation see Cohen & Kubovy, 1993; Takano, 1989; Tarr & Pinker, 1989.)

The impression we get from these experiments is that visual images have all the attributes of actual objects in the world—that is, they take up some form of mental space in the same way that physical objects take up physical space in the world, and that these objects are mentally moved or rotated in the same way that objects in the world are manipulated. In short, the image seems to be some "quasi-spatial simulacrum of the 3-D object" (see Boden, 1988). This view, however, is not wholly justified as there

FIGURE 9.6

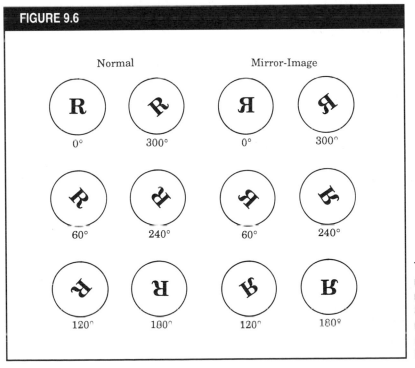

Normal   Mirror-Image

The different degrees of rotations performed on the materials in Cooper and Shepard (1973) for mirror-imaged letters (on the right) and normal letters (on the left).

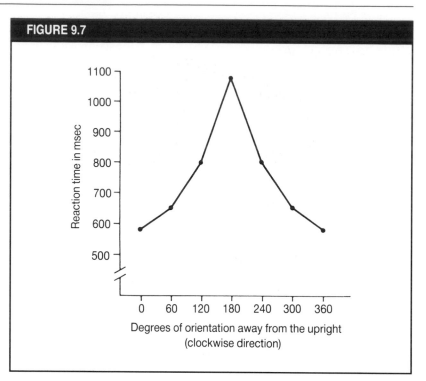

FIGURE 9.7

The mean time to decide whether a visual stimulus was in the normal or mirror-image version as a function of orientation. Data from Cooper and Shepard (1973).

are conditions under which mental rotation effects differ from physical rotation. If the imagined object becomes more complex, subjects are less able to make correct judgements about its appearance when rotated (Rock, 1973). Such a problem would not arise in the physical rotation of a physical object.

Similarly, people's capacity to imagine rotated objects (even simple cubes) depends crucially on the description of the object they implicitly adopt (Boden, 1988; Hinton, 1979; and later section on re-interpreting images). Hinton (1979) provides a practical demonstration of this proposal when you are asked to imagine a cube placed squarely on a shelf with its base level with your eyes. Imagine taking hold of the bottom corner that is nearest your left hand with your left hand, and the top corner that is farthest away from your left hand with your right hand, taking the cube from the shelf and holding it so that your right hand is vertically above your left. What will be the location of the remaining corners? Most subjects tend to reply that they will form a square along the "equator" of the cube. In fact, the middle edge of the cube is not horizontal but forms a zigzag. This occurs because one does not take the image of the cube (as it is in reality) and rotate it, rather one is working off some less elaborate, structural description. Inconsistencies like this have fuelled the imagery–propositional debate we consider later.

Image scanning

Image scanning studies give us another insight into the nature of mental images. In these studies, subjects usually have to scan mentally an imaged map (e.g. Kosslyn, Ball, & Reiser, 1978). Typically, in these experiments subjects are given a fictitious map of an island with landmarks indicated by Xs (see Fig. 9.8 for an example). Initially, subjects spend some time memorising the map, until they can reproduce it accurately as a drawing. They are then given the name of an object, and are asked to image the map and focus on that object. Five seconds later, a second object is named and subjects are instructed to scan from the first object to the second object by imaging a flying black dot. Because the objects on the map have been placed at different distances from one another,

FIGURE 9.8

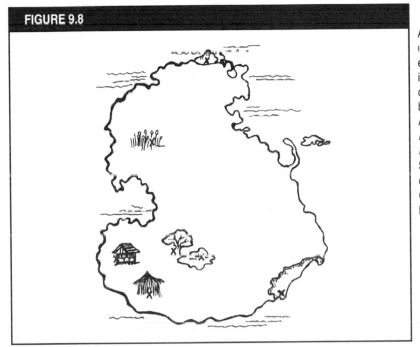

An example of the materials used in mental scanning experiments. Subjects had to image a black dot moving from one point on the map (indicated by the x-ed features) to another. Adapted from *Ghosts in the mind's machine: Creating and using images in the brain* by Stephen Kosslyn, by permission of the publisher, W.W. Norton & Company Inc. Copyright © 1983 by Stephen M. Kosslyn.

it is possible to determine whether the time taken to scan from one object on the map to another is related to the actual distance on the map between these two points. Using experimental procedures of this type, it has repeatedly been found that the scanning time is related linearly to the actual distance between points on the map; that is, the scanning time increases proportionately with the actual distance between two points. This result lends support to the view that images have special, spatial properties that are analogous to those of objects and activities in the world.

However, there is a worry about these results, which we will elaborate in detail later. It is expressed succinctly by Baddeley (1986, p.130) when he says:

I have a nagging concern that implicitly, much of the experimental work in this field consists of instructing the subject to behave as if he were seeing something in the outside world ... Whether such results tell us how the system works, or indeed tell us much about the phenomenology, I am as yet uncertain.

THEORETICAL DISTINCTIONS: THE IMAGERY-PROPOSITIONAL DEBATE

Mental representation is a central topic in modern cognitive psychology. For this reason, the resurgence of research in the area was accompanied by a heated debate about the status of imagery. In the 1970s and 1980s several commentators became embroiled in this debate (notably Pylyshyn, 1973, 1979). Initially, the thrust of Pylyshyn's arguments was that imagery was too vague a construct, but later he argued that images were epiphenomenal.

Are images a distinct type of representation?

Several arguments have been mounted against imagery theories as a separate representational construct. First, Pylyshyn (1973) argued that images could not be picture-like entities, as many imagery theories assumed, because when we forget parts of an image, we forget meaningful parts not random parts as would be the case if an image was like a picture (e.g. a corner of a picture that does not represent a meaningful part can be torn off). Second, he argued that you had to postulate some form of propositional code to mediate between verbal and non-verbal codes. As these two codes were in different formats there had to be an interlingua (i.e. a language or code that can translate between two other codes) to relate one to the other. Third, others pointed out that it is impossible to determine unequivocally the format of a representation used in any cognitive task; because any theory that proposes a certain representation in combination with a certain set of processes can be mimicked by another theory using a different representation and a different set of processes (see Anderson, 1978, p.263). So, any theory that proposed an imagery representation along with some process to explain, say, mental rotation could be mimicked and replaced by a theory positing a propositional representation and some other process.

Consider how this might be done for mental rotation studies. We could use a propositional code to represent an object in its different orientations. For example, a letter in its upright orientation could be represented propositionally by predicates that specify the features of the letter that are at the top, bottom, left, and right; for the letter "A" one could have the proposition top(35°-vertex, letter-a) to indicate that the pointed feature is the top of the letter A. So when one has to rotate the object by 180° a set of processes switch the top to be the bottom and the bottom to be the top. Now, an opponent of this account might argue that this would not predict differences in rotation times; because the processes that change the orientation predicates (i.e. top, bottom, 5° tilt) will carry out any rotation (whether it be of 180° or 30°) in the same number of steps. However, an extra assumption can be added to handle this objection. A propositional theorist could argue that although rotation could be done in one step by a propositional system, it is often important to simulate how the object would actually rotate in space; e.g. one might simulate, step by step, the arc of a bouncing ball to see if it will clear an object in its path. Similarly, the propositional operators might change the orientation predicates in a step-by-step fashion (e.g. from top to 30° tilt, from 30° tilt to 60° tilt, and so on until 150° is changed to bottom) thus leading to the same predictions as the imagery account.

These objections to imagery theories appear to be quite serious, although they have been countered in the literature. First, Kosslyn (1980, 1981) pointed out that few theorists held to the images-as-pictures view, but rather maintained the view that images are quasi-spatial entities generated from some store of perceptual experience in long-term memory. Second, Pylyshyn's requirement for an interlingua is flawed, because if it is true it leads to an infinite regress: if you need a propositional code to intervene between a verbal and non-verbal code then surely one also needs another code to come between the verbal code and the propositional code, and so on (see Anderson, 1978).

Third, the mimicry argument can be answered by considering what a theory should do. Theories can be evaluated in two main ways: you can assess how much evidence they explain or you can evaluate their *suggestiveness* or *generativity* (i.e. the extent to which they "naturally" suggest a set of novel, untested phenomena). The propositional explanation of mental rotation works, but it is tortuous and *ad hoc*. The propositional theory, unlike the imagery theory, does not *suggest* that people might carry out mental rotation but it can explain it after the fact. So, it should be noted that even poorly developed imagery theories can be more *generative* than propositional theories.

Does it matter if images are cognitively penetrable?

Further arguments against imagery have been proposed, which are really directed towards the mental scanning studies (see Pylyshyn, 1981, 1984). Stated simply the suggestion is that subjects in mental scanning experiments are simply doing what they are told to do, they are simulating what it would be like to look at something and scan across it, rather than reflecting special properties of imagery (see Baddeley's, 1986, comment quoted earlier). More generally, this criticism hinges on the cognitive penetrability of imagery.

Cognitive penetrability is best understood by analogy to the computer. Every computer has hardware (silicon chips and wiring) and software (the programs that run on the hardware). The hardware is unchanging, unless we physically open the machine and add new components. The software, on the other hand, can be changed in a number of different ways; programs can generate new programs or create data that can be stored in memory. However, software cannot modify the hardware of the computer directly. Pylyshyn argues that the mind has a *functional architecture*. This consists of unchanging constraints on the mind that, like the hardware of the computer, cannot be modified by the higher-level, software-like processes of the mind (i.e. our beliefs, goals, and wishes). If images operate in a special medium, he argues, then they must be part of the functional architecture of the mind. Because your beliefs and goals cannot modify or penetrate the functional architecture of the mind, your beliefs should not be able to penetrate images. In short, images should be *cognitively impenetrable*. As beliefs and goals are inherently propositional entities, if you can show that images *are* cognitively penetrable then they must be fundamentally the same sort of stuff as propositional representations; and hence be reducible to propositional representations.

Pylyshyn has used these proposals to reinterpret the mental scanning experiments. Recall that in these experiments subjects were instructed to image moving a black dot from one point on an imaged map to another. In a series of experiments, Pylyshyn (1984; Bannon, 1981) found, as Kosslyn had done, that if subjects were asked to image a real spot moving or really walking from one point to another, the times taken by subjects to "scan" corresponded to the relative distance between points on the map. However, he also found that if subjects were asked to image shifting their gaze as quickly as possible from one point to another, the effects disappeared. Similarly, if subjects were asked to imagine running (instead of walking) the time taken to complete the task between points was quicker than in the original (walking) experiments. This shows two things: (i) that people did not seem

to be scanning an image in a uniform fashion, because these instructions should not have increased the scan rate; and (ii) that imagery was clearly under the control of the kind of transformations one expected or believed to occur. In short, it was cognitively penetrable. "To imagine" something means to represent something *as if* it were real. Thus imagining traversing a space entails imagining being successively at intermediate points — otherwise it would not be traversing that was being imagined. So, subjects are rather better at following the instructions than you might expect, and a special representational format is not required to explain the results. The mental rotation studies can be accounted for in the same way. Research that is consistent with this view has been done by Rock (1973) who has shown that it is harder to judge rotation effects in more complex 3-D shapes (see also Hinton's earlier comments).

Several theorists have tried to answer Pylyshyn's cognitive penetrability arguments. Boden (1988) has proposed that representations be categorised into propositions, analogue-as-special-medium representations, and simply analogical representations (in a sense that lacks any special medium claims). This means that even though images may be cognitively penetrable (and therefore based on propositions) it does not follow that imagery *has* to be explained in terms of propositional representations; they could be explained in terms of analogue representations that do not operate in a special medium. Johnson-Laird (1983) has pointed out that Pylyshyn's penetrability argument can be turned against its creator. He points out that a thoroughgoing materialist (e.g. Churchland, 1981) might maintain that Pylyshyn's constructs of beliefs and goals are epiphenomenal because they can be "imagistically penetrated"; that is, the way in which they govern behaviour can be influenced in a rationally explicable way by images. Johnson-Laird concludes (1983, p. 152): "The moral is plain: images and beliefs are both high-level constructs, and it is a mistake to argue that they are epiphenomenal just because they 'penetrate' each other."

KOSSLYN'S COMPUTATIONAL MODEL OF IMAGERY

Throughout the late 1970s and 1980s Stephen Kosslyn and his associates tested and developed a theory that can be viewed as a response to the early criticisms of imagery theory. Kosslyn's position was that imagery is worth examining as a separate construct because it has its own privileged properties, even if it is partly based on propositional representations.

The theory and model

Kosslyn's theory has been specified in a computational model and is roughly summarised in Panel 9.2 (see also Fig. 9.9; Kosslyn, 1980, 1981, 1987, 1994; Kosslyn & Shwartz, 1977).

Consider the basic task of generating an image of a duck. The theory maintains that several structures and processes are involved: the spatial medium in which the duck is to be represented, the propositional and image files that store the knowledge about the duck, and the processes that generate the image in the medium from these files.

The spatial medium

The spatial medium in which the duck is to be represented is modelled as a television screen in Kosslyn's computational model (see Kosslyn & Shwartz, 1977). That is, the medium has a surface that can be divided up into dots or pixels, each of which can be characterised by co-ordinates indicating where a dot is on the screen. The theory mentions four properties of this spatial medium. First, that it functions as a space, in the sense that it preserves the spatial relations of the objects it represents. So, if an object is represented in the extreme top left of this space, and another object in the extreme bottom left, then the relative position of the two objects will be preserved (i.e. the second object will be beneath the first object). The spatial medium is also like a physical space in that it has a limited extent and is bounded. If images move too far in any direction they will overflow the medium, like a slide projected on a screen. Finally, the space has a definite shape; although the central area of highest resolution is roughly circular, the medium becomes more oblong at the periphery.

The second main attribute of this spatial medium is that it does not necessarily represent images at a uniform resolution. Rather, at the centre of the medium, an image is represented at its highest resolution. From there outwards it begins to get fuzzier. This is akin to the visual field, which also has its highest resolution at the centre of the scene being viewed.

Third, the medium has a grain. The grain of a photograph or a VDU refers to the size of the basic dots of colour that make it up. If these dots are very large then the detail one can represent is limited, whereas if the dots are very small more detailed

---

(Panel 9.2) Kosslyn's Theory of Imagery

- Visual images are represented in a special, spatial medium.

- The spatial medium has four essential properties: (i) it functions as a space, with limited extent, it has a specified shape and a capacity to depict spatial relations; (ii) its area of highest resolution is at its centre; (iii) the medium has a grain that obscures details on "small" images; (iv) once the image is generated in the medium it begins to fade.

- Long-term memory contains two forms of data structures: image files and propositional files. Image files contain stored information about how images are represented in the spatial medium and have an analogical format. Propositional files contain information about the parts of objects, how these parts are related to one another and are in a propositional format. Propositional files and image files are often linked together.

- A variety of processes use image files, propositional files, and the spatial medium in order to generate, interpret, and transform images.

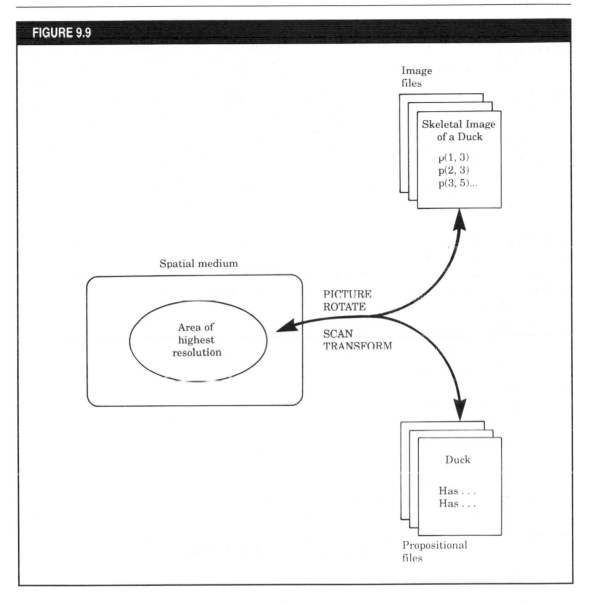

FIGURE 9.9

Image files

Skeletal Image of a Duck

p(1, 3)
p(2, 3)
p(3, 5)...

Spatial medium

Area of highest resolution

PICTURE
ROTATE

SCAN
TRANSFORM

Duck

Has . . .
Has . . .

Propositional files

A schematic diagram of Kosslyn's computational model of imagery. Images are constructed and manipulated (using the PICTURE, ROTATE, SCAN, and TRANSFORM processes) in the highest area of resolution in the spatial medium using the information stored in image files and propositional files in long-term memory.

images can be represented. A good example of this is the comparison between a conventional Teletype computer screen and the Apple Macintosh screen. The latter has the grain to depict different letter fonts and pictures in a manner that is impossible on the Teletype screen. Thus, the grain of the spatial medium determines what can and cannot be represented clearly. It also means that when an image is reduced in size then parts of it may disappear, because the grain may not be detailed enough to represent these parts. Specifically, a part of the larger image that was represented by a configuration of dots may, when the image is reduced, be represented by a single dot.

Finally, as soon as an image is generated in the medium it begins to fade and so, if the image is to be maintained in the medium, it needs to be regenerated or refreshed. A similar type of fading occurs with after-images in the visual system. When we look at bright lights and then close our eyes, we see after-images caused by the over-stimulation of our retinal cells. Although these after-images are not the same as visual images, they have this same quality of rapidly fading after they first appear.

Image and propositional files

Returning to our duck, we have a fair idea of where she is represented but not how we come to represent her. In Kosslyn's computational model it is assumed that there are image files that represent the co-ordinates of dot-like points in the spatial medium. These image files can represent a whole object or various parts of an object. Specifically, some image files characterise a *skeletal image* that depicts the basic shape of the object, but lacks many of the object's details. These detailed parts of images may be represented in other image files, for reasons that will become apparent later. In terms of our example, the image in Fig. 9.10a is a rough, skeletal image of the duck, whereas Fig. 9.10b shows the addition of one of her parts (i.e. the wings).

The propositional files list the properties of ducks (e.g. HAS_WINGS, HAS_FEET), and the relationships between these properties and a "foundation part" of the duck (i.e. its body). The foundation part is the part that is central to the representation of the object and will be linked to the skeletal image file for the object. The propositional file for the duck might, thus, contain entries that relate the wing parts of the duck to the foundation part: for example, WINGS LOCATION ON_EITHER_SIDE BODY indicating that the wings are on either side of the body. Each of these parts would have a corresponding image file that contains the basic material for constructing the image of a given part in the spatial medium. Propositional files also contain more information about the rough size category of the object (e.g. very small, small, large, enormous) and information about superordinate categories of the objects (e.g. in the duck case, that BIRD would be the most likely superordinate; see Kosslyn, 1980, 1983, for details; and Chapter 10).

The information in the propositional files is connected to the image files. So, for example, the foundation part in the propositional file has a link or pointer to the image file that contains the skeletal image of the object. Similarly, the detailed parts of the object have links to image files containing images of these parts. For example, the wings part is linked to an image file containing co-ordinate information for the construction of an image of a wing.

FIGURE 9.10

(a)

(b)

According to Kosslyn's theory, images are constructed in parts, so one might first form (a) a skeletal image of a duck, and then (b) add a wing part to this initial skeletal image.

Imaging processes

Finally, when someone is asked to image a duck several processes use the propositional and image files to generate an image of the duck in the spatial medium. In the model, the main IMAGE process involves three sub-processes: PICTURE, FIND, and PUT. When asked to image, the IMAGE process first checks to see whether the object (i.e. the duck) mentioned in the instructions has, in its propositional-file definition, a reference to a skeletal-image file. If such a file is present then the PICTURE process takes the information about the co-ordinates of the image and represents it in the spatial medium (see Fig. 9.10). Unless the location or size of the image is specified (e.g. image a giant duck), the image is generated in the part of the spatial medium with the highest resolution and at a size that fills this region. The PUT process directs the PICTURE process to place the remaining image-parts at the appropriate locations on the skeletal image. For example, PUT might use the propositional information about the location of the wings to add them to the side of the skeletal image of the body. PUT, however, must use FIND to locate the objects or parts already in the image to which the new, to-be-imaged parts can be related. When the appropriate size and location of the wings are known they are added to the image (see Fig. 9.10b).

In cases where more specific instructions are given, like "Does the duck have a rounded beak?" or "Image a fly on the tip of the duck's wing, up close" or "Rotate the duck 180 degrees", further processes called SCAN, LOOKFOR, PAN, ZOOM, and ROTATE operate on the image (see Kosslyn, 1983, Chapter 7; and Kosslyn, 1980, for more details). The names of these processes are self-explanatory and each one has been modelled as a set of specified procedures in the model that, for instance, SCAN and ROTATE images. These processes are used to explain the results of mental scanning and mental rotation studies.

Empirical evidence for Kosslyn's theory

Kosslyn's work has several important and welcome features. First, by specifying computationally the processes and representations involved in imagery, he avoids the vagueness criticism. Second, the claims he makes for the properties of imagery are clear. Third, many of these detailed proposals are supported by empirical evidence. Consider some of the evidence for his proposals on limited extent and granularity, the fading of images, and the area of high resolution in the spatial medium.

The image tracing task

Kosslyn (1975, 1976, 1980) has used an "image tracing task" to test his proposals on the limited extent of the spatial medium and on granularity. As in the duck example, in these experiments subjects were asked to image an object and then to try to "see" some property of the imaged object (e.g. "Can you 'see' the duck's beak?"). The critical manipulation in the experiment was the context in which the animal was imaged. The "target" animal (e.g. a rabbit) was imaged along with another animal that was either much larger or much smaller (i.e. an elephant and a fly, respectively). The rationale here was that in the case where the elephant and the rabbit were imaged together, the elephant would take up most of the space and as a result the rabbit would be represented as being much smaller relative to the elephant. In contrast, in the case where the fly and the rabbit were imaged together, the rabbit would take up most of the space relative to the fly (see Fig. 9.11a and b). Given the hypothesis that the spatial medium has granularity, the two different images of the animal pairs should result in differences in the "visible" properties of the rabbit. In the rabbit–elephant pair many of the rabbit's properties should be hard to "see" whereas in the rabbit–fly pair most of its properties should be easy to "see". This difficulty in "seeing" properties should translate itself into differential response times in deciding on the presence of a property (e.g. whether the rabbit has a pointed nose).

This is exactly what Kosslyn found in his studies. Subjects take longer to see parts of the rabbit in the rabbit–elephant pair relative to seeing the same parts in the rabbit–fly pair. Furthermore, Kosslyn noted that subjects' introspective reports suggested that they were "zooming in" to see the parts of the subjectively smaller images.

FIGURE 9.11

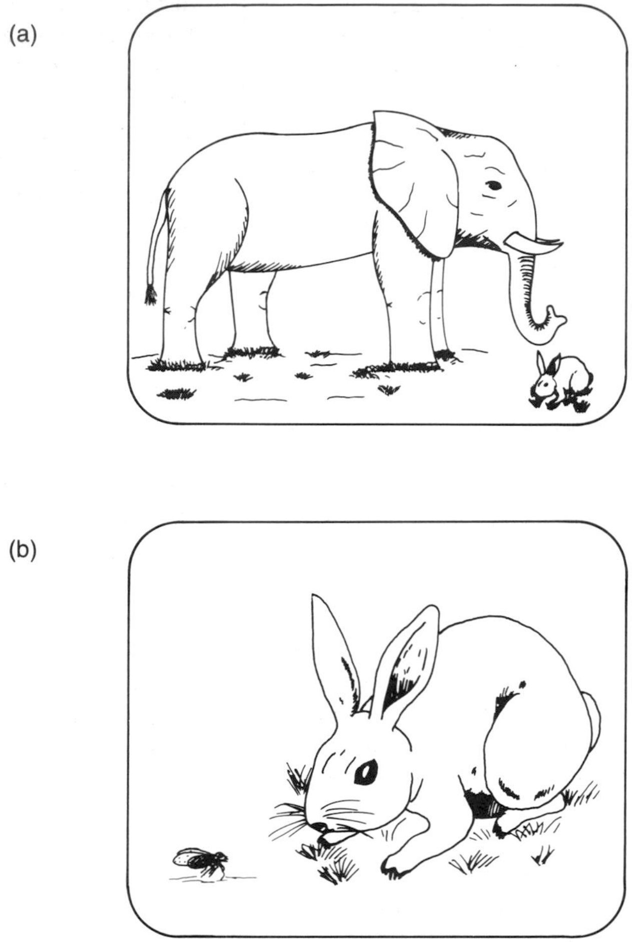

A schematic diagram of how the image of (a) an elephant and a rabbit, and (b) a fly and a rabbit might result in the rabbit being imaged at different levels of detail. Adapted from *Ghosts in the mind's machine: Creating and using images in the brain* by Stephen Kosslyn, by permission of the publisher, W.W. Norton & Company Inc. Copyright © 1983 by Stephen M. Kosslyn.

(a)

(b)

Reinterpreting images of ambiguous figures

Recently, there has been considerable interest in how people reinterpret visual images of ambiguous figures (see Fig. 9.12). This research was not designed to support Kosslyn's theory, but it ties in nicely with several aspects of it and refines some of its proposals. Chambers and Reisberg (1985) presented subjects with ambiguous figures like the duck/rabbit, which can be interpreted in different ways; for example, as a rabbit facing to the right or a duck facing to the left. Subjects viewed a figure for five seconds and were asked to image it before it was taken away. Then, still imaging it, they were asked to give a second interpretation of the figure.

In spite of several different interventions to aid subjects, 100% of them could not produce another interpretation of the figure. However, the same subjects could draw their image of the figure and having drawn it, could produce a reinterpretation of it.

This finding suggests several theoretical conclusions. First, it shows how the propositional code influences the construction of the image, to such an extent that details needed for the reinterpretation are omitted. As Chambers and Reisberg (1992) put it: "What an image depicts depends on what it means." Second, this finding also suggests that the definition of images in the

FIGURE 9.12

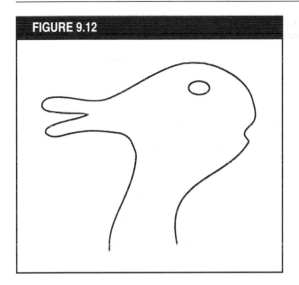

An example of an ambiguous figure from Chambers and Reisberg's (1985) study. It can be seen as either a duck or a rabbit.

spatial medium may not be as clear as Kosslyn suggests. Recent research has shown that the definition of the image towards the "face" of the figure is better than at the "back" of the figure (see Brandimonte & Gerbino, 1993; Chambers & Reisberg, 1992; Peterson, Kihlstrom, Rose, & Glinsky, 1992).

Experiments in the spatial medium

A further set of experiments by Kosslyn (1978) examined the idea of the limited spatial extent of the medium. Assume our visual field consists of a 100 degree visual arc in front of us. If we are looking at something in this visual field, then at a given distance the object will take up a portion of this arc. If we move closer to the object and it is a large object — like a double-decker bus — then eventually it will completely fill the visual arc and may even overflow it. That is, it may stretch beyond our field of view. Kosslyn employed the same idea to test the limited extent of the spatial medium. If one assumes that the spatial medium has a limited extent and has a similar visual-image arc, then one way of measuring the size of an imaged object is in terms of the arc it subtends. At some point an object of a certain size should overflow the medium (see Fig. 9.13). To test this prediction, subjects

were asked to close their eyes and to image an object (usually an animal again) far away in the distance. They were then asked to "mentally walk" towards the image until they reached a point where they could see all the object at once (i.e. the point just prior to overflow). Finally, they were asked to estimate how far away the animal would be if they were seeing it at that subjective size. If the spatial medium has a limited extent of a constant size then the larger the object, the further away it would seem at the point of overflow. This was the result found by Kosslyn. In general, the estimated distance of the point of overflow increases linearly with the size of the imaged object.

As we have seen throughout this book, one strong test of a theory is to see whether it is consistent with neuropsychological evidence from the study of individuals with brain injuries. As we shall see in the next section, Kosslyn's theory has also been applied to understanding the patterns of behaviour manifested by brain-damaged patients.

THE NEUROPSYCHOLOGY OF VISUAL IMAGERY

Farah (1984) carried out a review of imagery deficits following brain injuries using Kosslyn's theory to understand these deficits. She abstracted the general component processes and structures of the theory and analysed various test tasks in terms of them. She then showed that different deficiencies in brain-damaged patients could be traced to problems with particular components. For instance, Kosslyn's theory posits a process that generates images from long-term memory representations, so if this process is damaged then the patient should not be able to describe the appearance of objects from memory or draw objects from memory. However, the same patient should be able to recognise and draw visually presented objects because these involve component processes other than those used in image generation. Several studies have reported patients with this pattern of behaviour (e.g. Lyman, Kwan, & Chao, 1938; Nielsen, 1946).

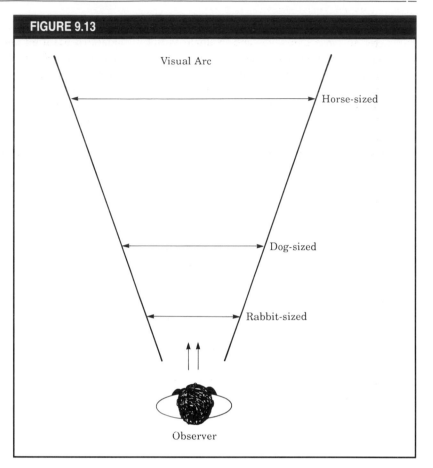

FIGURE 9.13

Diagram of the relative amounts of the visual arc that are taken up by different-sized animals. Adapted from *Ghosts in the mind's machine: Creating and using images in the brain* by Stephen Kosslyn, by permission of the publisher, W.W. Norton & Company Inc. Copyright © 1983 by Stephen M. Kosslyn.

Traditionally, imagery has been viewed as being a right hemisphere function (see Ehrlichman & Barrett, 1983, for a review). Farah challenged this view in arguing that at least one component — the imagery generation component — appears to be a left hemisphere function (see Farah, 1984; Farah, Peronnet, Gonon, & Giard, 1988; Kosslyn, 1987; Kosslyn, Holtzmann, Farah, & Gazzaniga, 1985). In a study involving split-brain patients, Farah, Gazzaniga, Holtzmann, and Kosslyn (1985) have shown that the disconnected left hemisphere could perform a task requiring image generation when the right hemisphere could not; and that the right hemisphere could be shown to have all the components of the imagery task except for image generation (see also Kosslyn et al., 1985). This work has also dealt with the link between the imagery system and visual system (Farah, 1988; Farah, Weisberg, Monheit, & Peronnet, 1990).

There has been considerable debate about the lateralisation of imagery processes (see Corballis, 1989; Farah, 1988; Goldberg, 1989; Kosslyn, 1987; Sargent, 1990). Some of this work has questioned the original evidence used by Farah (see Sargent, 1990), whereas other theorists have tried to argue that there are distinct types of imagery information involved in image generation that may arise in both hemispheres (see Kosslyn, 1987). Having said this, the emerging consensus in this debate appears to be that the left hemisphere has a direct role in the generation of visual images, although the left may not be its sole preserve. Both hemispheres are likely to contribute to image generation but in different ways (see Tippett, 1992, for a review).

Recently, Kosslyn, Alpert, Thompson, and Maljkovic (1993) have used PET techniques to investigate the localisation of imagery processing in the brain. They found that when subjects were instructed to close their eyes and evaluate visual mental images of uppercase letters that were either small or large, the small mental images engendered more activation in the posterior portion of the visual cortex whereas the large mental images engendered more activation in anterior portions of the visual cortex (see also Kosslyn, 1994).

All of this research represents an important step from psychology into neuropsychology. Apart from showing how psychological theories can include neuropsychological evidence, it also has important implications for the imagery–propositional debate. Farah (1984) has pointed out that in propositionalist terms there should be no difference between the recall and manipulation of information about the appearances of objects and information about other memory contents (e.g. historical facts or philosophical arguments). Hence, the occurrence of selective impairments to these types of information should be as likely as a selective impairment of imagery. However, specific impairments of historical ability do not occur, but selective impairments of imagery do; moreover we can identify separate brain areas dedicated to this imagery ability.

REPRESENTATION IN CONNECTIONISM: A NEW PARADIGM?

In most of this chapter we have concentrated on the traditional symbolic approach to mental representation (see also Chapter 1). The basic view of this approach is that human cognition is centrally dependent on the manipulation of symbolic representations by various rule-like processes. Kosslyn's imagery theory is a prime example of theorising from this viewpoint, in which rule-based processes — like IMAGE and PUT — manipulate various symbols. Even though the symbolic approach has been the dominant one within information-processing psychology, some have questioned whether it is ultimately the best way to understand human cognition. These critics have highlighted some of the difficulties in the symbolic approach.

First, as we have seen in this chapter, within a symbolic tradition one has to state explicitly how mental contents are represented (whether they be images or propositions). Moreover, one has to specify how these representations are manipulated by various rules. So, even for relatively simple tasks, symbolic theories can be very complicated. When one moves away from laboratory tasks and looks at everyday tasks (like driving a car) it is sometimes difficult to envisage how such a complicated scheme could work. People can operate quite efficiently by taking multiple sources of information into account at once. Although a symbolic account might be able to account for driving, many feel that this account would be too inelegant and cumbersome. A second worry about the symbolic approach is that it has tended to avoid the question of how cognitive processes are realised in the brain. Granted, it provides evidence for the gross localisation of cognitive processes in the brain, but we are left with no idea of how these symbols are represented and manipulated at the neural level.

In response to these and other issues, in the 1980s a parallel processing approach re-emerged called *connectionism* (see Chapter 1; Ballard, 1986; Feldman & Ballard, 1982; Hinton & Anderson, 1981; McClelland, Rumelhart, & the PDP Research Group, 1986; Rumelhart, McClelland, & The PDP Research Group, 1986a). As we saw in Chapter 1, connectionists use computational models consisting of networks of neurone-like units that have several advantages over their symbolic competitors.

As we shall see, connectionist schemes can represent information without recourse to symbolic entities like propositions; they are said to represent information sub-symbolically in *distributed representations* (see Smolensky, 1988). Second, they have the potential to model complex behaviours without recourse to large sets of explicit, propositional rules (see e.g. Holyoak & Thagard, 1989; Rumelhart, McClelland, & The PDP Research Group, 1986a). Third, in their use of neurone-like processing units they suggest a more direct link to the brain (but see Smolensky, 1988). Connectionism clearly provides significant answers to many questions about human cognition.

However, it is unclear how much of human cognition can be characterised in this way.

Distributed representation: The sight and scent of a rose

The concept of a distributed representation can be illustrated by an example involving a simple network called a *pattern associator*. Within the symbolic tradition, the sight and the scent of a rose might be represented as some set of co-ordinates (for the image of the rose) or as a proposition, i.e. ROSE(x). A distributed representation does not have symbols that explicitly represent the rose but rather *stores the connection strengths between units that will allow either the scent or vision of the rose to be re-created* (see Hinton, McClelland, & Rumelhart, 1986). Consider how this is done in the simple network in Fig. 9.14a.

The sight and scent of the rose can be viewed as being coded in terms of simple signals in certain

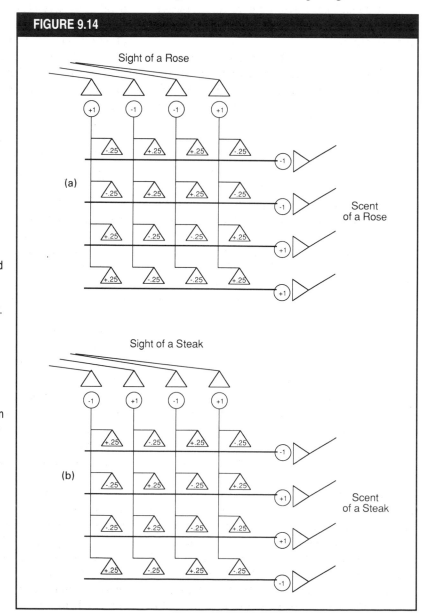

FIGURE 9.14

Two simple pattern associators representing different information. The example assumes that the patterns of activation in the vision units, encoding the sight of (a) a rose or (b) a steak, can be associated with the patterns of activation in olfaction units, encoding the smell of (a) a rose or (b) a steak. The synaptic connections allow the outputs of the vision units to influence the activations of the olfaction units. The synaptic weights shown in the two networks are selected to allow the pattern of activation shown in the vision units to reproduce the pattern of activation in the olfaction units without the need for any olfactory input. Adapted with the permission of David E. Rumelhart and James L. McClelland from *Parallel distributed processing: Explorations in the microstructure of cognition*, Volume 1. The MIT Press, © 1986 by The Massachusetts Institute of Technology.

input cells (i.e. as pluses and minuses, see Fig. 9.14a). The input cells that take signals from vision are called vision units and those that take signals from the smell senses are called olfaction units. Essentially, the network is capable of associating the pattern of activation that arrives at the vision units with that arriving at the olfaction units. The distributed representation of the sight and scent of the rose is thus represented by the "matrix" of activation in the network; without recourse to any explicit symbol for representing the rose. Consider how this coding of the representation is achieved in more detail.

Figure 9.14a shows the vision and olfaction units. The sight of the rose is represented by a particular pattern of activation on the vision units (characterised by $+1, -1, -1, +1$), while the pattern of olfactory excitation is shown on the olfaction units (from top to bottom $-1, -1, +1, +1$). The effect of a single vision unit on an olfaction unit is determined by multiplying the activation of the vision unit by the strength of its link to the olfaction unit. So, all the vision units produce the output of the first olfaction unit in the following fashion:

1st	Vision unit $+1$ x -0.25 (1st link)	$= -0.25$
2nd	Vision unit -1 x -0.25 (2nd link)	$= 0.25$
3rd	Vision unit -1 x $+0.25$ (3rd link)	$= -0.25$
4th	Vision unit $+1$ x -0.25 (4th link)	$= -0.25$

| 1st | Olfaction unit | -1 |
| | | (by summation) |

In cases where the pattern associator does not learn the association, the links between the vision and olfaction units can be set so that given the vision input of $+1, -1, -1, +1$ the olfaction output $-1, -1, +1, +1$ is produced and vice versa (according to the method of combining activation just described). In this way, the pattern associator has represented the association between the sight and scent of the rose in a distributed fashion. We could also represent the sight and smell of another object by a different pattern of activation in the *same network*. For example, the sight and smell of a steak could be characterised by the vision pattern $(-1, +1, -1, +1)$ and the olfactory pattern $(-1, +1, +1, -1)$. The different pattern of activation for this is shown in Fig. 9.14b. Note the differences in the weights of the links in the network.

Distributed versus local representations

Not all connectionist models use distributed representations. They also use representations similar to those used in the symbolic approach, even though the models still use networks of units. Connectionists call the latter *local representations*. The crucial difference between distributed and local representations is sometimes subtle. According to Rumelhart, Hinton, and McClelland, (1986c, p.47) a *distributed representation* is one in which "the units represent small feature-like entities [and where] the pattern as a whole is the meaningful unit of analysis". The essential tenet of the distributed scheme is that different items correspond to alternative patterns of activity in the same set of units, whereas a local representation has a one-unit-one-concept representation in which single units represent entire concepts or other large meaningful units.

To be clear about this distinction, consider two networks that deal with the same task domain; one of which uses a local representation and the other a distributed representation. These networks represent the mappings between the visual form of a word (i.e. c-a-t) and its meaning (i.e. small, furry, four-legged; see Figs 9.15a and 9.15b). The network in this case has three layers. A layer for identifying letters of the word (consisting of grapheme units that indicate the letter and its position in the word); a middle layer; and a layer that encodes the semantic units that constitute the meaning of the word (see Chapter 10 for further details on such semantic primitives; here we call them sememe units).

In the localist version of the model, the middle layer of the network has units that represent one word. So, a particular grapheme string activates this word unit and this activates whatever meaning is associated with it. In short, there is a one-unit-one-concept representation in the middle layer (see Fig. 9.15a). In the distributed version of the network, the grapheme units feed into word-set units that in turn feed into the semantic units. A word-set unit is activated whenever the pattern of the grapheme units activate an item in that set. A

FIGURE 9.15

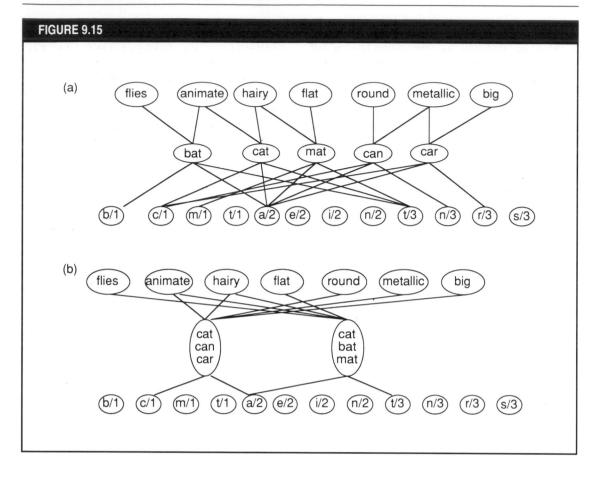

Two examples of a three-layered connectionist network. The bottom layer contains units that represent particular graphemes in particular positions within a word. The middle layer contains units that recognise complete words, and the top layer contains units that represent semantic features of the meaning of the word. Network (a) uses local representations of words in the middle layer, whereas network (b) has a middle layer that uses a more distributed representation. Each unit in the middle layer of network (b) can be activated by the graphemic representation of any one of a whole set of words. The unit then provides input to every semantic feature that occurs in the meaning of any of the words that activate it. Only those word sets containing the word "cat" are shown in network (b). Notice that the only semantic features that receive input from all these word sets are the semantic features of "cat". Adapted with the permission of David E. Rumelhart and James L. McClelland from *Parallel distributed processing: Explorations in the microstructure of cognition*, Volume 1. The MIT Press, © 1986 by The Massachusetts Institute of Technology.

set could be something like all the three-letter words beginning with CA or all the words ending in AT. So, in this distributed representation, activation goes from the grapheme units to many different word-set units and these in turn send activation to the sememe layer, to indicate uniquely which set of semantic features is associated with this particular configuration of graphemes. This representation is distributed because each word-set unit participates in the representation of many

words. Stated another way, different items correspond to alternative patterns of activity in the same set of units (see Fig. 9.15b).

Without wishing to be confusing, it should be noted that the local–distributed representation distinction can often be equivocal. For example, Hinton et al. (1986) admit that semantic networks that use spreading activation (see Chapters 1 and 10) are not very distinguishable from other distributed representations, even though they have units that correspond to single concepts. Similarly, it must be admitted that the word-sets in the distributed representation just described are not very feature-like entities but could be categorised as meaningful wholes. However, until more is known about the characteristics of these networks the distinction is heuristically useful.

Distributed representations and propositions/ images

The sixty-four million dollar question, which we have been ignoring until now, is "What is the relationship between distributed representations and symbolic representations?" Hinton et al. (1986) argue that these views do not contradict one another, but rather are complementary. By this they mean that the high-level representations, like propositions, may be represented by lower-level distributed representations. However, this complementarity depends on the properties of the lower-level distributed representation being recognised as fundamental aspects of the higher-level representations.

Distributed representations have several properties that make them very attractive relative to symbolic representations. First, distributed representations are *content-addressable*. This is an important general characteristic of human memory and refers to the fact that apparently any part of a past occurrence or scene can lead to its later retrieval from memory. For instance, you may remember your holiday on the Côte d'Azur on hearing a certain song, on smelling the aroma of ratatouille, or seeing the sun reflected in a certain way on a woman's hair. It seems that any part of the memory can reinstate all of the original memory. Similarly, in distributed representations, a partial representation of an entity is sufficient to reinstate the whole entity. For example, if we present a slight variant of the original scent of the rose (say, $-1, -1, +1, 0$ instead of $-1, -1, +1, +1$) to the network in Fig. 9.14a, it will still excite the vision units in roughly the same way. Second, distributed representations allow automatic generalisation. That is, in a manner related to the content-addressibility property, patterns that are similar will produce similar responses.

In conclusion, one can view the symbolic framework as characterising the macro-structure of cognitive representation (i.e. the broad outlines of symbols and their organisation), whereas the distributed representations characterise the micro-structure of cognitive representation (see McClelland et al., 1986; Rumelhart et al., 1986a). However, the full ramifications of the relationship between the two levels requires substantial elaboration.

CHAPTER SUMMARY

Most sciences are in a constant state of flux. At any point in time there are dominant themes that large groups of researchers are investigating. When a dead end is reached or the problems in the area seem to be solved sufficiently, many researchers turn to other issues. The pejorative name for this activity is "bandwagon research", and the imagery–propositional debate could be viewed as a prime example of it. For a time in the 1970s and early 1980s it was one of the most hotly researched issues. Now research continues on imagery, but the emphasis has shifted away from attempting to prove that images are a vacuous representational construct. The current consensus could be summarised in two points. First, the whole effort to prove that one format of representation is redundant was a waste of time; the terms of the argument were either misplaced or the issue is not empirically decideable, or both groups of proponents were attempting to answer radically different questions (Anderson, 1990; Baddeley, 1986; Marschark et al., 1987). Second, there is general agreement that different representational constructs are needed to characterise the richness of human cognition, and that imagery should be counted as one of these constructs (see e.g. Anderson, 1983; Johnson-Laird, 1983). However, even though the debate may have been ill-conceived in itself, it has provoked a clarification of the concept of imagery and led to some creative experimentation. These developments have then allowed researchers to tackle the more practical concerns of the effects of brain injury on imagery ability.

The emergence of connectionism has attracted similar if not more attention than the imagery debate, although this is not to say that it suffers from the same faults. As a concluding comment, it should be noted that we have taken the ecumenical position proposed by Hinton et al. (1986) on the relationship between symbolic and connectionist representations, in saying that the two are complementary. Not everyone shares this view. For example, Smolensky's (1988) "proper treatment of connectionism" argues against this position for some forms of cognition. One of the current interesting issues in cognitive psychology concerns the final resolution of this debate.

FURTHER READING

Churchland, P.S., & Sejnowski, T.J. (1992). *The computational brain*. Cambridge, MA: MIT Press. Chapter 4 of this book provides a fuller context to the issues of representation in connectionist systems.

Kosslyn, S.M. (1994). *Image and brain: The resolution of the imagery debate*. Cambridge, MA: MIT Press. This is a very readable summary of Kosslyn's research over the years.

Kosslyn, S., & Koenig, O. (1992). *Wet mind: The new cognitive neuroscience*. New York: Free Press. This gives some of the wider background to the cognitive neuropsychology approach to imagery.

Paivio, A. (1986) *Mental representations*. Oxford: Oxford University Press. This book provides a good treatment of dual-coding theory and the empirical evidence that supports it.

10

Objects, Concepts, and Categories

INTRODUCTION

In the previous chapter, we saw how knowledge can be represented. However, we have said little about what was represented; about the content of that knowledge. In this chapter and the next, we consider the content and organisation of human knowledge. Here, we deal with object concepts and categories before turning to more elaborate knowledge structures, like schemata, in the next chapter. Beyond these chapters, much of the remainder of the book is about how this knowledge is used in the important activities of problem solving, reasoning, and decision making. Before we plunge into this chapter, we should pause to consider why we need knowledge and why that knowledge needs to be organised.

Constraints on concepts: Economy, informativeness, and naturalness

Why do we need knowledge? We need to know about things to behave and act in the world. In its most general sense our knowledge is all the information that we have inherited genetically or learned through experience. Without this

knowledge we simply cannot do certain things. If you have not acquired the knowledge for bicycle riding, by spending hours falling off bicycles and grazing your knees, then you cannot carry out this behaviour. If you have not read the chapter on concepts in this book (or any other), then the likelihood is you will not do very well in an exam question on the topic. In short, knowledge informs and underlies all of our daily activitites and behaviour.

Why do we need to organise knowledge? It is not enough just to acquire experience and store it; we need to organise this knowledge in an economic and informative fashion. The South American writer Jorge-Luis Borges (1964, pp.93–94) describes a fictional character who had a perfect memory of every second of his life; a man called Funes, who had no need to organise or categorise his experience:

> … Funes remembered not only every leaf of every tree of every wood, but also every one of the times he had perceived or imagined it. … He was, let us not forget, almost incapable of ideas of a general, Platonic sort. Not only was it difficult for him to comprehend that

the generic symbol dog embraces so many unlike individuals of diverse size and form; it bothered him that the dog at three fourteen (seen from the side) should have the same name as the dog at three fifteen (seen from the front). His own face in the mirror, his own hands, surprised him every time he saw them.

No human being is like Funes, because we have to organise our knowledge. We identify categories of things, like dogs, in part to avoid having to remember every individual dog we have seen (or indeed every different angle from which we have seen a specific dog). Our memory systems clearly require a certain economy in the organisation of our experience. If we were like Funes, our minds would be cluttered with many irrelevant details. So, we seem to abstract away from our experience to develop general concepts (Borges suggests that Funes could not think and reason because he lacked abstract categories). *Cognitive economy* is achieved by dividing the world into classes of things to decrease the amount of information we must learn, perceive, remember, and recognise (Collins & Quillian, 1969). Once concepts have been formed they can, in turn, be organised into hierarchies; where *animal* is a superordinate concept (i.e. more general or encompassing) of *dog*, and where *living thing* is a superordinate of *animal* and *plant*. However, this sort of cognitive economy has to be balanced by informativeness.

If our minds went too far in applying the economy constraint then we would end up with too many general concepts and lose many important details. If we generalised all of our object concepts to be just three (animals, plants, and everything else) then we would have a very economic conceptual system, but we would not have a very informative conceptual system; for instance, we would not have abstractions to distinguish between, say, chairs and tables.

Finally, there is a sense in which some concepts are more "natural" than others. A category that included pints-of-Guinness and birds-that-flew-on-one-wing, does not seem likely or natural. Human concepts cohere in certain ways making certain groupings of entities more likely to occur than other groupings. One problem is to specify the basis for this naturalness or cohesiveness.

In short, for reasons of storage and effective use it seems to be necessary to organise and categorise experience. In human memory, this organisation appears to be guided by the principles of cognitive economy, informativeness, and natural coherence. One of the marvels of human memory is that it balances these principles in the acquisition of conceptual systems that allow us to get around and understand our world.

The study of human knowledge

Human knowledge consists of everything that we know. In any attempt to characterise this knowledge a starting point for research is hard to find. Traditionally, a distinction has been made between "objects" (*dog*, *cat*, *dishwasher*, *spigot*) and the "relations" between things (*above*, *below*, *kick*, *hit*). Research on concepts has been heavily influenced by philosophy; especially the British Empiricist philosophers (e.g. Locke, 1690) who viewed concepts as being atomic units that were combined in molecule-like ways into more complex structures. More recently, the psychological literature has concentrated on how different objects come to be grouped together in a common category (e.g. how we consider the mongrel next door and the winner of Crufts to be instances of the category *dog*) and how these concepts are related to one another hierarchically, for example, how the concepts *dog* and *cat* are subordinates (i.e. more specific versions) of the more general *animal* concept. This research on the organisation of *object concepts* (like *dog*, *bird*, *chair*, *furniture*) has been marked by several theoretical stances, which we review under the headings of the defining-attribute view; the defining- and characteristic-attribute views; and the prototype view. This research tradition has tended to ignore *relations* in favour of objects (see Chapter 11). All of these treatments of concepts are also said to be similarity-based, in that concept formation is based on the similarities between conceptual entities. In Chapter 11, we will encounter a different approach, the explanation-based view, which uses different mechanisms in forming concepts.

Of course, there is a lot more to be said about human knowledge beyond the organisation of object concepts. Most of our knowledge is structured in complex ways; we typically think in terms of events (e.g. the time I failed my first-year psychology exams). The structures that encode this knowledge, which are called schemata, involve many different entities (e.g. pens, exam scripts, student cards) connected by many diverse relations (e.g. concentrate, write, fail). Until recently, there was less research on these more complex knowledge formations (but see Chapter 11, and Chapter 8 on autobiographical memory). It is these structures that underlie the alternative explanation-based view of concepts that has emerged in recent years.

THE DEFINING-ATTRIBUTE VIEW

The basic intuition behind traditional theories of concepts is quite simple and plausible. It is that we generalise from instances of objects by noting their similarities and ruling out their differences. So, for example, we form the general concept, dog, by noting that many instances of dogs (Alsations, Irish Wolfhounds, Red Setters) have certain attributes in common (e.g. having four legs, barking, fur) and differing attributes that can be ignored (e.g. different sizes and colours). Similarity is, therefore, seen as the central process in concept formation (see later section). This basic intuition is specified more clearly in the defining-attribute or classical view of concepts (see Medin & Smith, 1984; Smith & Medin, 1981).

The defining-attribute view is based on ideas developed in philosophy and logic. This view, elaborated by the logician Gottlob Frege (1952), maintains that a concept can be characterised by a set of *defining attributes*. Frege clarified the distinction between a concept's intension and its extension. The *intension* of a concept consists of the set of attributes that define what it is to be a member of the concept, and the *extension* is the set of entities that are members of the concept. So, for example, the intension of the concept bachelor might be its set of defining attributes (*male, single,*

adult), whereas the extension of the concept is the complete set of all the bachelors in the world (from the Pope to Mr. Jones next door). Related ideas have appeared at various times in linguistics and psychology (see e.g. Glass & Holyoak, 1975; Katz & Fodor, 1963; Leech, 1974).

There are two important terminological points to be made at this stage. Throughout this chapter we will use the term "attribute" when discussing the intensions of concepts. However, many other terms are used in the literature, including "property", "semantic marker", and "feature". Some of these terms can have special connotations but, in general, they can be treated as being interchangeable with the term "attribute". Second, in talking about one of the set of objects in the world that make up a category, we will use the terms "instance" and "member" interchangeably.

The general characteristics of defining-attribute theories are summarised in Panel 10.1. It can be seen that the theory maintains that if defining attributes of the concept *bachelor* are *male, single, adult*, then for Mr. Jones to be a bachelor it is necessary for him to have each attribute (i.e. *male, single,* and *adult*) and it is enough for him to have all these three attributes together; that is, no other attributes enter into determining whether he is an instance of the concept. So, each of the properties is singly necessary, and all are jointly sufficient, for determining whether Mr. Jones is a member of the concept *bachelor*. This has the implication that what is and is not a *bachelor* is very clear. If Mr. O'Shea is an adult and male but is married then he cannot be considered to be a member of the category bachelor. So, the defining-attribute theory predicts that concepts should divide up individual objects in the world into distinct classes and that the boundaries between categories should be well-defined and rigid. Similarly, the theory predicts that all members of the category are equally representative of it. That is, Mr. Jones cannot be considered to be a better example of a bachelor than, say, Mr. Smith, who is also *male, adult,* and *single*. As we shall see, these two predictions have been disconfirmed by findings in the literature.

Finally, consider two other concepts to understand how defining-attribute hierarchies nest

---

(Panel 10.1) Defining-attribute Theories of Concepts

- The meaning of a concept can be captured by a conjunctive list of attributes (i.e. a list of attributes connected by ANDs).

- These attributes are atomic units or primitives which are the basic building blocks of concepts.

- Each of these attributes is necessary and all of them are jointly sufficient for something to be identified as an instance of the concept.

- What is and is not a member of the category is clearly defined; thus, there are clear-cut boundaries between members and non-members of the category.

- All members of the concept are equally representative.

- When concepts are organised in a hierarchy then the defining attributes of a more specific concept (e.g. sparrow) in relation to its more general relative (its superordinate; e.g. bird) includes all the defining attributes of the superordinate.

---

within one another. Assume that you have the specific concept *sparrow* (defined as *feathered, animate, two-legged, small, brown*) and its superordinate, *bird* (defined as *feathered, animate, two-legged*). The subordinate concept *sparrow* will contain all the attributes of the superordinate, although it will also have many other attributes (such as *brown*), to distinguish it from other subordinate concepts (e.g. *canary*, defined as *feathered, animate, two-legged, small, yellow*). This means that a specific concept will tend to have more attributes in common with its immediate superordinate than with a more distant superordinate. For example, *sparrow* should have more attributes in common with its immediate superordinate, *bird*, than with its more distant superordinate, *animal*.

There is evidence that people can treat concepts in ways that agree with the tenets of the defining-attribute view. Indeed, they expect concepts to adhere to the defining-attribute view (see e.g. Armstrong, Gleitman, & Gleitman, 1983). In particular, the influential work of Bruner, Goodnow, and Austin (1956) looked at how people acquire concepts of shapes involving different attributes. In Bruner et al.'s experiments, subjects were shown an array of stimuli (see Fig. 10.1) that had different attributes (e.g. shape, number of shapes, shading of shapes) with different values (e.g. cross/square, one/three, plain/shaded). From the experimenter's viewpoint, certain items in the array were instances of a rule; for example, the rule *three, square shapes* identifies items 20, 23, 26 as members of it and all other items as non-members. In one of their tasks, subjects were shown one example of the rule and had to discover the correct rule by asking the experimenter whether other items were instances of the rule.

Bruner et al. identified several different strategies used by subjects in these experiments that could be viewed as possible ways in which people might acquire concepts in everyday life, assuming that the defining-attribute view of concepts is true. However, Bruner et al.'s work was carried out in a domain of fairly artificial categories. Can we expect people to operate according to the defining-attribute view in more natural categories, involving the commonplace objects of everyday life? A means of testing this proposal arose when Allan Collins and Ross Quillian developed a theory and computational model that was a version of the defining-attribute view.

Collins and Quillian's network theory and model

The work of Collins and Quillian (1969, 1970) is one of the prime examples of the burgeoning of cognitive science research. Quillian (1966) had developed a computational model that represented

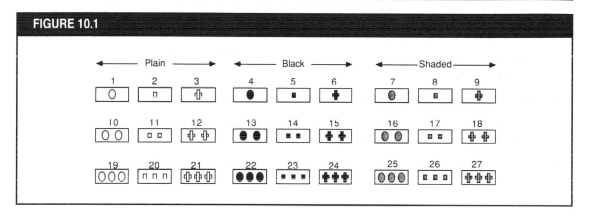

A sample of the sorts of materials used in Bruner et al.'s (1956) study of concept acquisition.

concepts as hierarchical networks (see also Chapter 1). This model was amended with some additional psychological assumptions to characterise the structure of semantic memory; a model of how concepts and their attributes were organised with respect to one another. The basic view of concepts taken in the theory was essentially the defining-attribute view. The details of the model are described in Panel 10.2 (see also Fig. 10.2).

In the sentence-verification tasks used by Collins and Quillian to test their theory, subjects were asked to say whether simple sentences of two forms were true or false. First, they were asked whether "an INSTANCE was a member of a SUPERORDINATE" (e.g. "Is a canary an animal?" or "Is a canary a fish?"). Second, subjects were asked whether "an INSTANCE had a certain ATTRIBUTE" (e.g. "Can a canary fly?", "Does a canary have skin?"). In both of these cases Collins and Quillian's predictions were confirmed. In the INSTANCE–SUPERORDINATE sentence it was found that the greater the distance between the subject and predicate of the sentence in the hierarchy, the longer it took to verify the sentence. And in the INSTANCE–ATTRIBUTE case the place of the attribute in the hierarchy relative to the instance, predicted the time taken to verify the sentence.

Evaluating defining-attribute theories

The defining-attribute view and various models that realise it can be challenged in two ways. First, and less seriously, it has been pointed out that the

theory fails to capture significant aspects of conceptual behaviour. The second, more serious criticism is that the central assumption of the view, that concepts depend the conjunction of necessary features, is wrong.

Prediction failures of defining-attribute theory

First, in the defining-attribute view all attributes are equally important or salient in determining the members of a concept. However, Conrad (1972) discovered that certain attributes of concepts were mentioned more often by subjects than other attributes and, hence, are considered to be more important or salient. For example, the attribute of a salmon *is-pink* is mentioned more often than the attribute *has-fins*. Not only does this suggest that attributes are not given equal weight by subjects, but Conrad showed that, in Collins and Quillian's experiments, the fast verifications of some sentences could be due to the attribute's salience.

Second, the defining-attribute prediction that all members of a category are equally important or representative was shown to be untrue. Certain members of natural categories are considered to be more typical or better examples of the concept. For example, Rosch (1973) asked people to rate the typicality of different members of a concept and consistently found that some members were rated as being much more typical than others (see also Rips, Shoben, & Smith, 1973). For example, a *robin* was considered to be a better example of a *bird* than a *canary*. This argument can even be

(Panel 10.2) Collins and Quillian's Network Model

• Concepts are represented as hierarchies of interconnected concept-nodes (e.g. *animal, bird, canary*).

• Any concept has a number of associated attributes at a given level of the hierarchy (e.g. an *animal* has the attributes *has-skin* and *eats,* while a *bird* has the attributes *has-wings* and *can-fly*).

• Some concept-nodes are superordinates of other nodes (e.g. *bird* is a superordinate of *canary,* and *animal* a superordinate of *bird*); by definition some nodes are therefore subordinates of others (e.g. *canary* is a subordinate of *bird*).

• For reasons of cognitive economy, subordinates *inherit* the attributes of their superordinate concepts; that is, as *animal* and *bird* are superordinates of *canary, canary* inherits their attributes (so a *canary* has the properties *eats, has-skin, has-wings, can-fly, is-yellow, can-sing*).

• Some instances of a concept are excepted from the defining attributes of its superordinates; for example, *ostrich* is excepted from the defining attribute of *can-fly,* for the bird category (see Fig. 10.2; this is one of the model's differences from the defining-attribute view).

• Various processes search these hierarchies for information about the concepts represented.

• So, in concept verification tasks (e.g. in determining whether one concept is an instance of another; "Is a canary a bird?") a search must be made from one node to another: this leads to the prediction that the greater the distance between nodes the longer it should take to verify the statement (e.g. "Is a canary a bird?" should be responded to more quickly than "Is a canary an animal?").

• Similarly, if someone is asked whether a concept has a particular property (e.g. "Can a canary sing?" as opposed to "Can a canary fly?") it should take longer to answer the latter because the attribute needs to be inferred from the superordinate *bird* node, rather than produced directly from the *canary* node.

FIGURE 10.2

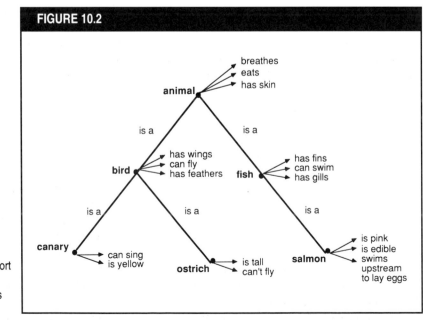

A schematic diagram of the sort of hierarchical, semantic networks proposed by Collins and Quillian (1969).

made about the hallowed concept of *bachelor*; clearly, Tarzan is not a good example of a bachelor because, alone with the apes of the jungle, he did not have the opportunity to marry (see Fillmore, 1982; Lakoff, 1982, 1987). The finding that members of a category differ in terms of their typicality is fairly serious, but it was also found that the typicality of members of a concept was a good predictor of the time subjects took to make verification judgements. That is, subjects took longer to verify statements involving less typical members (e.g. "A penguin is a bird") than statements involving more typical members (e.g. "A robin is a bird").

These results do not wholly finish the defining-attribute view. They are still consistent with the proposal that concept membership depends on a conjunction of necessary attributes. However, other lines of research have attacked this central assumption.

Fundamental problems with the conjunctive-attribute assumption

First, it has proved to be very difficult to determine the defining attributes of many concepts, despite attempts by several generations of linguists, philosophers, and psychologists (for examples of the latter see Hampton, 1979; McNamara & Sternberg, 1983). Some, therefore, argue that the whole enterprise of trying to break down concepts into their necessary and sufficient attributes is fundamentally ill-conceived (Fodor, Garrett, Walker, & Parkes, 1980; Wittgenstein, 1958). Some concepts simply do not seem to have defining attributes. Consider Wittgenstein's example of the concept of a *game*. There are clusters of attributes that characterise sets of games (that they involve pieces, involve balls, involve one or more players) but hardly any attribute holds for all the members of the concept. Members of the category *game*, like the faces of the members of a family, bear a *family resemblance* to one another but they do not share a distinct set of necessary and sufficient attributes. Empirical evidence supports this criticism. In terms of the defining-attribute view, people should list the same attributes for all the members of a category (i.e. the defining set). However, people do not do this, but tend to mention

non-necessary attributes (Conrad, 1972; Rosch & Mervis, 1975).

Second, the assumption that category membership is clear-cut, as determined by defining attributes, is undermined by evidence indicating that some categories are fuzzy. That is, even though some highly typical instances are considered by most people to be category members, and less typical instances are considered to be non-members of the category, between these two extremes people differ on whether an object is a member of the category and are also inconsistent in their judgements. That is, sometimes they think the object is a member of the category and other times they think it is not. McCloskey and Glucksberg (1977) found evidence for this view. Their subjects were sure about saying that a *chair* was a member of the category *furniture*, and that a *cucumber* was not a member of this category. But they disagreed with one another on whether *book-ends* were a member of the category *furniture*, and differed in their own category judgements from one session to the next (see also Barsalou, 1987, and the later sub-section on concept instability).

Third, the predictions made about nested concepts in hierarchies are not wholly confirmed. Contrary to Collins and Quillian's findings, Smith, Shoben, and Rips (1974) showed that more distant superordinates can be verified more quickly than immediate superordinates. So, when asked "Is a chicken a bird?" and "Is a chicken an animal?", contrary to Collins and Quillian's node-distance prediction, subjects responded faster to the latter than to the former. Hampton (1982) has shown that the defining-attribute prediction that hierarchies of concepts are transitive is not confirmed (i.e. as "An X is a Y" and "A Y is a Z" are true, " An X is a Z" is also true).

The evidence found in response to the Collins and Quillian work led to a reassessment of the defining-attribute approach to concepts. Several alternative formulations emerged to deal with this evidence. We will treat two general classes of these theories. The first class of theories make an attempt to save the defining-attribute view by adding the notion of characteristic attributes. The second class of theories take a more radical line in attempting to replace the defining-attribute view with one that lends a central role to the notion of prototypes.

Section summary

The traditional theory of concepts received from philosophy and linguistics defines concepts in terms of necessary and jointly sufficient attributes. This view thus asserts that (i) such attributes can be found, (ii) membership of a category is not a matter of degree but is an all-or-nothing affair, (iii) that there are clear boundaries between conceptual categories, and (iv) that a subordinate concept should contain all the attributes of its superordinate concept. Collins and Quillian produced a computational model which confirmed several of the central predictions of this view. However, all of these assumptions are either highly questionable or have been shown to be untrue of natural categories. Alternative theories have therefore been proposed to account for this evidence.

DEFINING-ATTRIBUTE AND CHARACTERISTIC-ATTRIBUTE THEORIES

When long-established theoretical views are challenged, researchers in a field tend to respond in one of several ways. One response involves a damage-limitation exercise which tries to shore up the traditional view by adding some new assumptions that account for troublesome evidence. So, in concept research, we find theories that retain the idea that there are defining attributes but add the extra assumption that concepts have characteristic attributes. Consider feature-comparison theory as one version of this class of theories (Rips et al., 1973; Smith et al., 1974).

Feature-comparison theory

Feature-comparison theory dispenses with the network proposals of Collins and Quillian and assumes that there are two types of attributes acted on by simple comparison processes. It may be noted that using a network model or attribute lists is not really a critical theoretical difference, as both can be used to generate the same empirical predictions (see Hollan, 1975). The main points of the theory are summarised in Panel 10.3.

Examples and evidence

Consider how this theory deals with two sentences: "A robin is a bird" and "An ostrich is a bird". If a subject is asked to determine the truth or falsity of these sentences, the former is answered more quickly than the latter. In the robin case, all the attributes of the concepts are compared in the first stage, and as many of the attributes of robin and bird match, a quick "yes" answer is given. However, in the ostrich case, the first stage returns a low number of overlapping attributes and, therefore, processing proceeds to the second stage, where only the defining attributes are compared. There are sufficient overlapping attributes in this second stage between the two concepts for a "yes" response to be returned. However, the response will be slower because two processing stages are involved. In contrast, sentences like "A cabbage is

---

(Panel 10.3) Feature-comparison Theory

- A concept is represented by a set of two types of attributes; defining and characteristic attributes.

- Defining attributes constitute the core definition of a concept and are shared by all members of it.

- Characteristic attributes determine how typical or representative a member of the category is likely to be judged.

- The process of verifying concepts (e.g. A canary is a bird) is carried out in two steps: first, all the attributes (both defining and characteristic) of the mentioned concepts are compared; second, only the defining attributes are compared.

- The second step is only applied if the first stage fails to produce a clear result.

a bird" can be quickly judged to be false because little or no attribute overlap is found between the two concepts in the initial stage of comparison. Other sentences, like "A bat is a bird", may proceed to the second comparison stage before being judged as false, because there is sufficient attribute overlap in the first stage. Subjects may even, when quick responses are demanded, make errors in the bat case and say that the sentence is true, because they do not proceed to the second stage of processing.

With respect to judgements about concepts within hierarchies, Smith et al. (1974) predicted that the speed of verification was a function of the similarity of the subordinate to a superordinate; hence they were able to account for "Is a chicken an animal?" being verified more quickly than "Is a chicken a bird?" (unlike Collins and Quillian).

This theory thus accounts for some of the objections raised to the defining-attribute view. First, it includes Conrad's (1972) finding that some attributes are more salient or characteristic of a concept than others. Second, it can account for some instances of a concept being viewed as being more typical than others. Third, verification times for positive and negative statements concur with people's judgements of subordinates and their relationship to near or distant superordinates.

Evaluating feature-comparison theory
Feature-comparison theory is clearly an improvement on the classical theory but it still has several theoretical and empirical limitations. Theoretically, it is limited in being bound to a specific sentence-verification task. It really only deals with "A something is a another-thing" type of sentences. If all of everyday categorisation could be reduced to this task then the theory would be fine, but as it cannot, its generality is questionable. Methodologically, it is limited by the failure to distinguish between defining and characteristic attributes in any objective fashion. So, it falls foul of a major criticism of the defining-attribute approach; namely, that it is impossible to define the defining attributes. Indeed, some have argued that there is little evidence that defining attributes exist at all (Rosch & Mervis, 1975; but see McNamara & Sternberg, 1983).

Empirically, some evidence does not compare favourably with the predictions made by the theory. First, the theory still predicts that members of a category should be clear-cut (as determined by the core of defining attributes) but as we saw earlier, people consider category membership to be fuzzy. Furthermore, some evidence for the theory has been shown to be the result of confounding semantic relatedness and the familiarity of the concepts (McCloskey, 1980). In their experiments, Smith et al. had manipulated the semantic relatedness of concepts in their verification tasks and found their predicted results on reaction times. However, McCloskey (1980) has shown that the effects found may reflect the familiarity of the stimuli used in the verification sentence rather than the proposed manipulation.

More seriously, Loftus (1973) has shown that if the nouns in the sentences are reversed, there are effects on verification speed not predicted by feature-comparison theory. She presented instances and asked subjects to list categories that the instances belonged to, and also presented categories and asked for a list of instances. This provided measures of instance-to-category production frequency and of category-to-instance production frequency, respectively. She then measured the reaction times in a verification task in which either the instance preceded the category ("Is a wren a bird?") or the category preceded the instance ("Is a bird a wren?"). According to the feature-comparison model, verification time should be unaffected by this manipulation of noun order. In fact, Loftus discovered that instance-to-category production frequency predicted the reaction time when the instance preceded the category, whereas the category-to-instance production frequency predicted the reaction time when the category preceded the instance (see Collins & Loftus, 1975, for a revised network model of these results).

Other models and evidence
Feature-comparison theory is only one of a number of defining- and characteristic-attribute theories. Another variant of this view, identified by Smith and Medin (1981) is based on Miller and Johnson-Laird's (1976) distinction between the

"core" of a concept and its "identification procedure". The *core* of the concept consists of defining attributes, and is important in revealing the relations between a given concept and other concepts. That is, the conceptual core of bachelor (male, single, adult) is important in revealing why a bachelor and a spinster (female, single, adult) are similar or why the terms "bachelor" and a "single male" are considered synonymous. The *identification procedure* plays a role in identifying objects in the real world and is responsive to their characteristic attributes. Thus, the core retains the defining-attribute theory while the identification procedure can account for typicality effects.

Armstrong et al. (1983) carried out a study that suggests evidence for this view. They examined concepts that clearly have defining attributes (e.g. even number, odd number, plane geometry figure) and found that members of these categories were judged to be more or less typical of the category. For instance, 22 was rated as being more typical of the concept even number than 18, and was also categorised more quickly. Thus, these concepts seemed to have a conceptual core and yet in categorisation tasks made use of characteristic attributes. Similarly, McNamara and Sternberg (1983) asked subjects to list the attributes of several different types of nouns (artefacts, natural kinds, and proper names) and to rate the necessity, sufficiency, and importance of each attribute to the word's definition. An inspection of subjects' ratings revealed that they considered some of the words to have defining attributes (i.e. necessary and sufficient attributes) and characteristic attributes. But only half could be defined by the defining attributes produced by subjects. McNamara and Sternberg also showed that these same distinctions were implicated in the real-time processing of the concepts, when read as words.

If we assume that concepts have a conceptual core and then other characteristic features, then one would expect there to be linguistic hedges in the language to take this distinction into account. Lakoff (1973, 1982) has argued that such hedges exist and are signalled by terms like "true" and "technically speaking" or "strictly speaking". These terms qualify assertions we might make

about category members. For example, if one says a "a duck is a true bird" the core definition of the concept bird is being explicitly marked, whereas the sentence "technically speaking, a penguin is a bird", marks the fact that you know a penguin is a non-representative example of the category but wish to include it within the category.

PROTOTYPE (OR CHARACTERISTIC-ATTRIBUTE) THEORIES

Although defining- and characteristic-attribute theories retain something of the traditional defining-attribute view, another family of theories has taken a very different line. Prototype theories were designed to rectify the deficits of the defining-attribute view. According to this view, categories are organised around central prototypes. However, different theories characterise prototypes in different ways.

In some theories, the prototype is a set of characteristic attributes; there are no defining attributes but rather only characteristic attributes of differential importance within the concept (see e.g. Hampton, 1979; Posner & Keele, 1968; Rosch, 1978). An object is a member of the concept if there is a good match between its attributes and those of the prototype. In other prototype theories, the prototype is literally the best example of the concept (e.g. Brooks, 1978; Estes, 1994; Hintzman & Ludlam, 1980; Medin & Shaffer, 1978). So, for example, if *robin* is the exemplar for the *bird* category, then it would be the prototype. Another object is a member of the bird category if it shares many attributes with the exemplar. As such, exemplar theories reject the idea that abstractions underlie our concepts, and argue that individual entities lie at the heart of our concepts. Recent research has shown that exemplar versions of prototype theory provide a better account of the evidence (see Barsalou & Medin, 1986; Nosofsky, 1988, 1991). For the purposes of this chapter, we combine these two variants of prototype theory in a single treatment that is summarised in Panel 10.4.

(Panel 10.4) Prototype Theory of Concepts

- Concepts have a prototype structure; the prototype is either a collection of characteristic attributes or the best example (or examples) of the concept.

- There is no delimiting set of necessary and sufficient attributes for determining category membership; there may be necessary attributes, but they are not jointly sufficient; indeed membership often depends on the object possessing some set of characteristic, non-necessary attributes that are considered more typical or representative of the category than others.

- Category boundaries are fuzzy or unclear; what is and is not a member of the category is ill-defined; so some members of the category may slip into other categories (e.g. tomatoes as fruit or vegetables).

- Instances of a concept can be ranged in terms of their typicality; that is, there is a typicality gradient which characterises the differential typicality of examples of the concept.

- Category membership is determined by the similarity of an object's attributes to the category's prototype.

Evidence for the prototype view

There is now a considerable body of empirical evidence that supports the prototype view, including research on colour, natural, and artificial categories. There is also work on the the nature of conceptual hierarchies in human categorisation, that has grown out of the protoype view.

Colour categories

One of the most striking pieces of evidence for the prototype view has come from cross-cultural studies on colour categories. There are many different colour terms used in the languages of the world. Some cultures have terms for a wide variety of colours (e.g. in Western Europe we have a huge diversity from magenta to sky-blue to red and so on), whereas other cultures have very few terms (e.g. the Dani of Papua New Guinea have only two colour terms for dark and bright). Berlin and Kay (1969) suggested that this diversity was only apparent if one distinguished between focal colours and non focal colours. In their studies they identified basic colour terms using four criteria: (i) the term must be expressed as one morpheme, so something like sky-blue would be ruled out; (ii) its meaning cannot include that of another term, ruling out scarlet because it includes red; (iii) it must not be restricted to a small class of objects, ruling out terms like blond which really only apply to hair and possibly furniture; and (iv) it must be a frequently

used term, like green, rather than turquoise. Berlin and Kay discovered that all languages draw their basic colour terms from a set of 11 colours. English has words for all of this set and they are: black, white, red, green, yellow, blue, brown, purple, pink, orange, and grey.

Using the basic colour terms derived from this analysis, they set about examining some 20 languages in detail, by performing experiments using a set of over 300 colour chips. In these studies, native speakers of the languages in question were asked two questions about the colour chips. First, they were asked what chips they would be willing to label using a particular, basic colour term. Second, they were asked what chips were the best or most typical examples of a colour term. What they found was that the speakers of different languages agreed in their identification of focal colours; people consistently agreed on the best example of, say, a red or a blue. This together with the finding that subjects were uncertain about category boundaries, suggested that category membership was judged on the basis of resemblance to focal colours. These results were also found for cultures with a very limited colour terminology like the Dani. Rosch (when her name was Heider, 1972; also Rosch, 1975a) showed that the Dani could remember focal colours better than non-focal colours and that, even though they only had two colour terms, they could learn names of focal colours more quickly than those for non-focal colours. It should be pointed out that Lucy and Schweder (1979, p.610) have shown that some of these memory results need to be questioned because "the colour array previously used to demonstrate the influence of focality on memory was discriminatively biased in favour of focal chips".

Thus, there seems to be a universality in people's categorisation of certain colours and in the structure of colour categories; in particular, it seems that these categories have a prototype structure. However, it is noteworthy that these categories have a strong physiological basis in the colour vision system (see Gordon, 1989). As such, some of these colour categories may be special cases. So, it is necessary to demonstrate similar effects for other categories.

Natural and artificial categories

Research on both natural categories (i.e. categories of things in the world, like birds and furniture) and artificial categories (e.g. numbers and dot patterns) has also supported detailed aspects of the prototype view. As we saw earlier, some members of categories are considered to be highly representative or highly typical. Subjects rate the typicality of instances of a concept differentially (Rips et al., 1973; Rosch, 1973). These typicality effects have considerable generality; for instance, they have also been found in psychiatric classifications (Cantor, Smith, French, & Mezzich, 1980), in linguistic categories (Lakoff, 1982, talks of degrees of noun-ness and verb-ness), and in various action concepts (e.g. to lie, and to hope; see Coleman & Kay, 1981, Vaughan, 1985). Furthermore, the most typical members of a concept play a special role in human categorisation.

First, the typicality gradient of members of a concept is a good predictor of categorisation times. In verification tasks (e.g. "A canary is a bird") typical members, like robin, are verified faster than atypical members like ostrich. This has proved to be a very robust finding (for reviews see Danks & Glucksberg, 1980; Kintsch, 1980; Smith, 1978; Smith & Medin, 1981). Second, typical members are likely to be mentioned first when subjects are asked to list all the members of a category (Battig & Montague, 1969; Mervis, Catlin, & Rosch, 1976). Similarly, Rosch, Simpson, and Miller (1976) found that when subjects were asked to sketch the exemplar of a particular category they were more likely to depict the most typical member. Third, the concept members that children learn first are the typical members, as measured by semantic categorisation tasks (Rosch, 1973). Fourth, Rosch (1975b) has found that typical members are more likely to serve as cognitive reference points than atypical members; for example, people are more likely to say "An ellipse is almost a circle" (where circle is the more typical form and occurs in the reference position of the sentence) than "A circle is almost an ellipse" (where ellipse, the less typical form, occurs in reference position).

A final important finding is the extent to which estimates of family resemblance correlate highly with typicality. Using Wittgenstein's term *family resemblance*, Rosch and Mervis (1975) have shown that one can derive a family-resemblance score for each member of a category by noting all the attributes that that member has in common with all the other members of the category. Rosch and Mervis found that typical members have high family-resemblance scores and share few (if any) attributes in common with related, contrast categories. This is rather direct evidence for the idea that the typicality gradient of a concept's instances is a function of the similarity of those members to the prototype of the category.

Conceptual hierarchies in prototype theory

Collins and Quillian's model had several levels of generality in its concept hierarchy. However, solid evidence for these levels was not found. As an adjunct to prototype theory, Rosch and her associates proposed that conceptual hierarchies had three levels of generality (see Panel 10.5; Rosch et al., 1976).

There is considerable evidence to support this conception of conceptual hierarchies. From the Roschian viewpoint, these levels reflect the optimal manner in which one can organise a set of categories. At the top level, the superordinate level, one has general designations for very general categories, like furniture. At the lowest level, there

---

(Panel 10.5) Prototype Theory of Concept Hierarchies

- People use hierarchies to represent relationships of class inclusion between categories; that is, to include one category within another (e.g. the category of chair within the category for furniture).

- Human conceptual hierarchies have three levels; a superordinate level (e.g. weapons, furniture), a basic level (e.g. guns, chair), and a subordinate level of specific concepts (e.g. hand-guns, rifles, kitchen chairs, armchairs).

- The basic level is the level at which concepts have the most "distinctive attributes" and it is the most cognitively economic; it is the level at which a concept's attributes are *not* shared with other concepts at that level.

- Categories at the basic level are critical to many cognitive activities; for example, they contain concepts that can be interacted with using similar motor movements, they have the same general shape, and they may be associated with a mental image that represents the whole category.

- The position of the basic level can change as a function of individual differences in expertise and cultural differences.

---

are specific types of objects (e.g. my favourite armchair, a kitchen chair). In between these two extremes is the basic level, which is critical to our everyday cognitive activities. Although we often talk about general categories (that furniture is expensive) and about specific concepts (my new Cadillac), typically, we deal with objects at the intermediate, basic level (whether there are enough chairs and desks in the office). It is at the basic level also that there is a maximal, within-category similarity relative to between-category similarity. That is, categories that are similar are grouped together in a way that sharpens their difference from other categories.

The idea of a basic level arose out of anthropological studies of biological and zoological categories (Berlin, 1972; Berlin, Breedlove, & Raven, 1973; Brown et al., 1976). Berlin (1972) noted that the classification of plants used by the Tzeltal Indians of Mexico corresponded to the categories at a particular level in the scientific taxonomy of plants. For instance, in the case of trees, the cultures studied by Berlin were more likely to have terms for a genus, such as beech, than for general, superordinate groupings (e.g. deciduous, coniferous) or for individual species (e.g. silver beech, copper beech). The reason Berlin gave for this basic level was that categories, such as "beech" and "birch", were

naturally distinctive and coherent groupings; that is, the species they include tend to have common patterns of attributes such as leaf shape, bark colour, and so on. The basic level was the best level at which to summarise categories.

Several aspects of the basic level were studied by Rosch et al. (1976). They asked people to list all the attributes of items at each of the three levels (e.g. furniture, chair, easy chair) and discovered that very few attributes were listed for the superordinate categories (like furniture) and many attributes were listed for the categories at the other two levels. However, at the lowest level very similar attributes were listed for different categories (e.g. easy chair, living-room chair). As such, the intermediate-level categories (like chair) are noted by a balance between informativeness (the number of attributes the concept conveys) and economy (a sort of summary of the important attributes that distinguish it from other categories). Informativeness is lacking at the highest level because few attributes are conveyed, and economy is missing at the lowest level because too many attributes are conveyed.

Rosch et al. (1976) also found evidence that basic-level categories have special properties not shared by categories at other levels. First, the basic level is the one at which adults spontaneously name objects and is also the one that is usually acquired first by young children. Furthermore, the basic level is the most general level at which people use similar motor movements for interacting with category members; for instance, all chairs can be sat on in roughly the same way, and this differs markedly to the way we interact with tables. Category members at the basic level also have fairly similar overall shapes and so a mental image can capture the whole category. Finally, objects at the basic level are recognised more quickly than objects at the higher and lower levels.

However, it is important to note that basic-level concepts do not always correspond to intermediate terms (e.g. "chair" in furniture-chair-armchair). In non-biological categories (like furniture) the intermediate term tends to correspond to the basic level. However, in biological categories the superordinate term tends to correspond to the basic level (e.g. "bird", in bird-sparrow-song sparrow). This difference is seen as being a function of the amount of experience people have with members of biological categories. That is, one's experience with the instances of a category will lead to differences in one's basic level. So, ornithologists would be more likely to consider *sparrow* to be the basic level for the bird category because, given their expertise, this is the most distinctive level. Similarly, Berlin's findings with the Tzeltal Indians probably reflects their expertise concerning the differences between trees (see also later section on neurological evidence).

Evaluation of the prototype view

Three main criticisms can be made of the prototype view. First, not all concepts have prototypic characteristics. Hampton (1981) has shown that only some abstract concepts (like "science", "crime", "a work of art", "rule", "belief") exhibit a prototype structure. This difference occurs because of the endless flexibility in membership of some abstract categories, in contrast to concrete categories. For instance, it seems impossible to specify the complete set of possible rules or beliefs. Thus, there are limits to the generality of prototype theory.

The prototype view is also incomplete as an account of the sort of knowledge people have about concepts. People seem to know about the relations between attributes, rather than just attributes alone, and this information can be used in categorisation (Malt & Smith, 1983; Walker, 1975). Consider the following case (see also Holland, Holyoak, Nisbett, & Thagard, 1986). Imagine going to a strange, Galapagos-like island for the first time, accompanied by a guide. On the journey, one sees a beautiful, blue bird fly out of a thicket and the guide indicates that it is called a "warrum". Later in the day, we meet a portly individual and are told that he is a member of the "klaatu" tribe. A day later, wandering without the guide one sees another blue bird, like the first, and considers it to be another warrum; however, on meeting another fat native one does not assume that he is a member of the klaatu tribe. The reason being that we know that colour is a particularly diagnostic and invariant attribute of the bird category, but physical weight is not a particularly diagnostic attribute of tribal affiliations and is known to be a highly variable attribute. Hence, we know that some attributes are more likely to vary than others. The fact that people can make reasonable guesses about the meaning of new terms on the basis of a single exposure to an instance is an important ability about which prototype theory is silent (see later sections and Chapter 11).

Finally, the prototype view does not provide a good account of what makes some categories natural and coherent; what makes us group certain objects together in one category rather than in another. The traditional answer given by the prototype and other views is that similarity is responsible for category cohesion. Stated simply, things form themselves into categories because they all have certain attributes in common. However, similarity cannot be the only mechanism, because we often form categories that are only tenuously based on shared attributes but which are nevertheless coherent (e.g. see Barsalou's work on *ad hoc* categories later). Murphy and Medin (1985) point to the biblical categories of clean and unclean animals; clean animals include most fish, grasshoppers, and some locusts, whereas unclean animals include camels, ostriches, crocodiles, mice, sharks, and eels (see also Douglas, 1966; Lakoff, 1987). Later, we will return to this issue of category cohesiveness.

These criticisms should cause us to pause for thought before accepting the prototype view. But if we do reject it, what can we put in its stead? In Chapter 11, we will see that there is an emerging view, called the explanation-based view, that is gaining ground as a candidate to fill this explanatory vacuum.

Section summary

The final view taken on concepts can be labelled the prototype view. This is a family of theories that views concepts as being organised around prototypes, expressed as clusters of attributes or some exemplar. This view can account for gradients of typicality, for fuzzy boundaries, and for levels of abstraction in both natural and artificial categories. Prototype theorists have proposed a three-level structure to conceptual hierarchies; a superordinate level, a basic level, and a subordinate level. The basic level is the level that is the most informative and economical. There are some queries about the generality of the prototype view, as some abstract concepts do not exhibit prototype structure. More seriously, the view is silent on the knowledge people have about the relations between properties, and it cannot adequately account for category cohesiveness.

HOW CONCEPTS ARE FORMED

Up to now, we have assumed that concepts come into being through noting the similarities between objects in the world, a similarity that uses the attributes of instances of that concept. We form the concept *dog* by noting the similarity between the different dogs we encounter. However, we have said little about exactly how this similarity works. In this section, we outline the dominant model of similarity and relate recent research that extends this model.

Tversky's contrast model of similarity

One of the longest-standing models in cognitive psychology is Tversky's contrast model (Tversky, 1977). This model accounts for the similarity judgements made by people involving concepts

described verbally or diagrammatically. It is also the model implicitly or explicitly assumed by most concept theorists (see Smith, 1988). Since 1977, the contrast model has been developed and tested extensively by Tversky and his colleagues (Tversky, 1977; Tversky & Gati, 1978).

The model maintains that the similarity of two concepts is based on some function of the attributes shared by the concepts, less the attributes that are distinctive to both:

$$s(a, b) = \theta f(A \cap B) - \alpha f(A - B) - \beta f(B - A)$$

where *a* and *b* are two concepts, *s* is the similarity of these two concepts, *A* is the set of attributes of concept *a*, and *B* is the set of attributes of concept *b*. In this formula, $A \cap B$ gives you the attributes that are common to the two objects, $A - B$ gives you the attributes that are distinctive to *a*, and $B - A$ the attributes that are distinctive to *b* (note that this is not an absolute distinctiveness, but just what is distinctive in one concept relative to the other). In general, this formula predicts that as the number of common features increases and the number of distinctive features decrease, the two objects *a* and *b* become more similar. The function *f* has a role in weighting certain attributes according to their salience and importance. The parameters θ, α, and β are used to reflect the relative importance of the common and distinctive attribute-sets. For instance, when people judge the similarity of two objects they tend to weight the common-features set as being more important than the distinctive-feature sets, whereas the distinctive-feature sets assume more importance in judgements of difference.

The effects of these θ, α, and β parameters also feature in the asymmetries that appear in similarity judgements; where it has been found that the similarity of *a* to *b* is not equal to the similarity of *b* to *a*: $s(a, b) \neq s(b, a)$. Tversky points out that in similarity statements there is a subject and a referent, we say that "a [subject] is like b [referent]". Furthermore, the choice of the referent and the subject is in part determined by the most important or salient concept; the more prominent concept being the referent. We say that "North Korea is like Red China", when Red China is the more prominent concept in the pair. When we reverse the roles of the concept the similarity of the two concepts changes; as in "Red China is like North Korea". In short, similarity statements are asymmetric.

Tversky and Gati (1978) found evidence for these proposals in a study involving similarity judgements for pairs of countries. They first confirmed that subjects preferred similarity statements in which the prominent country was in the referent rather than the subject position. The $s(q, p)$ column of figures in Table 10.1 shows the mean similarity judgements where the prominent country (p) was in the referent position (i.e. q is like p). The $s(p, q)$ column shows the mean similarity judgements when the prominent concept is in the subject position (i.e. p is like q). As you can see from Table 10.1, in almost every pair the similarity judgements are asymmetric; with $s(q, p)$ forms being judged consistently as being more similar than $s(p, q)$ forms.

Extending similarity models to include relations

The contrast model has stood the test of time well. However, recently, a number of studies have shown that it might have to be adjusted in a number of respects. All of the theories in this chapter and Tversky's model assume that concepts can be adequately characterised by attribute lists.

However, at the beginning of the chapter, we pointed out that relational concepts might also be important. Traditionally, relations (e.g. *flies, on-top-of, connected-to*) would be treated as attributes in a concept definition. Running against this treatment, some recent research has examined similarity judgements of stimuli where attributes and relations have been separated out (see Goldstone, Medin, & Gentner, 1991; Medin, Goldstone, & Gentner, 1990, 1993).

For instance, Medin et al. (1990) gave subjects the stimuli shown in Fig. 10.3. In these experiments, subjects had to choose whether the A or B stimulus was more similar to T. In each case, one of the choice stimuli always shared a unique attribute with the T stimulus (e.g. in Fig. 10.3, A and T share the unique attribute of having a chequered circle) and the other shared a unique relation with T (e.g. in Fig. 10.3, B and T share the unique relation of *same-shading*). They found that the stimulus with the relational similarity tended to be chosen as the more similar of the two, indicating that people were sensitive to relations in their judgements and that they also weighted relational matches as being more important. Further research along these lines has found support for what Goldstone et al. (1991) call the MAX hypothesis; that attributional and relational similarities are pooled separately, and shared similarities affect judged similarity more if the pool that they are in

TABLE 10.1

Some of the Mean Similarity Judgements for Countries from Tversky and Gati (1977) Showing the Asymmetries Between Judgements of the Form 'q is like p' and 'p is like q' (p is the Prominent Concept)

p	q	(q is like p) $s(q, p)$	(p is like q) $s(p, q)$
United States	Mexico	7.65	6.45
China	Albania	9.16	8.69
United States	Israel	3.69	3.41
Belgium	Luxembourg	16.14	15.54
France	Algeria	7.94	7.86
Germany	Austria	15.20	15.60

FIGURE 10.3

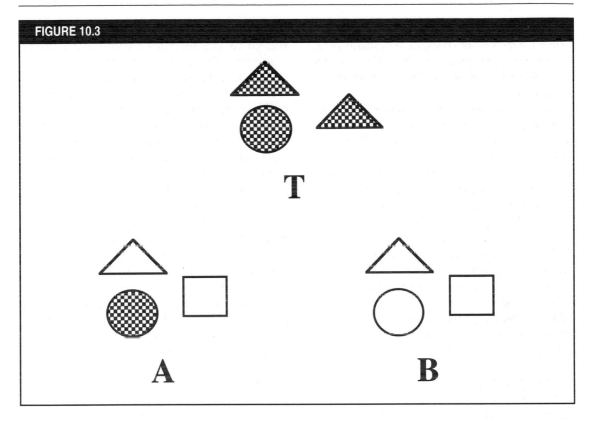

A sample of the materials used by Medin et al. (1990). The sample stimulus T is attributionally similar to A because they both have a chequered circle. B has not got this attributional similarity, but B does share a matching relation—same shading—with T.

is relatively large. Other research has also found support for the importance of relational information in similarity through the effects of structural alignment (see Markman & Gentner, 1993a,b).

A connectionist model of concept learning

Most of the computational models of concepts have been semantic networks in the Collins and Quillian style. More recently, several connectionist models have been used to model concepts. Indeed, there is a close relationship between semantic networks and some types of connectionist nets (see the section on localist representations in Chapter 9). Connectionist nets make good concept learners because they can learn from specific instances and implement similarity mechanisms. Their strengths lie in extracting the commonalities between a set of examples. In feedforward networks that use backpropagation of errors (see Chapter 1), the

network learns the central tendency of a set of target examples and encodes this as a pattern of activation in the network. Other forms of networks, called interactive activation nets (IAC), can find the commonalities between a set of concepts by the way activation is passed between the nodes of the network. McClelland (1981) provides a neat demonstration of how such networks can manifest many of the properties of human conceptual systems.

McClelland's IAC net was given an attribute description of the individuals in the Jets and Sharks gangs from *West Side Story* (see Table 10.2). In the network, each attribute is represented as a node; so there are nodes for gang names (Jets, Sharks), for education (junior high, college, high school), and jobs (pusher, burglar, bookie). Attributes that are related are grouped into "pools" (see Fig. 10.4); so, the pusher, burglar, and bookie nodes are grouped together in a pool because they are all occupations,

TABLE 10.2

The Attributes Used to Characterise the Individual Members of Two Gangs, the Jets and Sharks, from McClelland (1981)

Person	Name	Age	Education	Marital Status	Job	Gang
_Art	Art	40s	junior high	single	pusher	Jets
_Al	Al	30s	junior high	married	burglar	Jets
_Sam	Sam	20s	college	single	bookie	Jets
_Clyde	Clyde	40s	junior high	single	bookie	Jets
_Mike	Mike	30s	junior high	single	bookie	Jets
_Jim	Jim	20s	junior high	divorced	burglar	Jets
_Greg	Greg	20s	high school	married	pusher	Jets
_John	John	20s	junior high	married	burglar	Jets
_Doug	Doug	30s	high school	single	bookie	Jets
_Lance	Lance	20s	junior high	married	burglar	Jets
_George	George	20s	junior high	divorced	burglar	Jets
_Pete	Pete	20s	high school	single	bookie	Jets
_Fred	Fred	20s	high school	single	pusher	Jets
_Gene	Gene	20s	college	single	pusher	Jets
_Ralph	Ralph	30s	junior high	single	pusher	Jets
_Phil	Phil	30s	college	married	pusher	Sharks
_Ike	Ike	30s	junior high	single	bookie	Sharks
_Nick	Nick	30s	high school	single	pusher	Sharks
_Don	Don	30s	college	married	burglar	Sharks
_Ned	Ned	30s	college	married	bookie	Sharks
_Karl	Karl	40s	high school	married	bookie	Sharks
_Ken	Ken	20s	high school	single	burglar	Sharks
_Earl	Earl	40s	high school	married	burglar	Sharks
_Rick	Rick	30s	high school	divorced	burglar	Sharks
_Ol	Ol	30s	college	married	pusher	Sharks
_Neal	Neal	30s	high school	single	bookie	Sharks
_Dave	Dave	30s	high school	divorced	pusher	Sharks

FIGURE 10.4

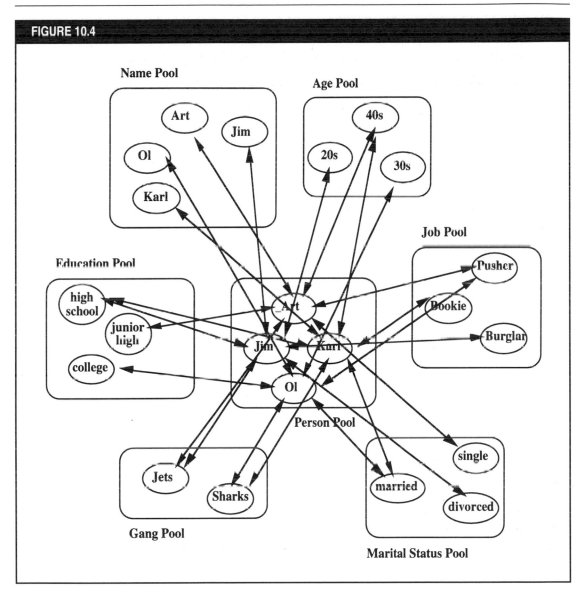

McClelland's (1981) Interactive Activation Constraint network for encoding the members of Jets and Sharks (with only some of the nodes and links shown). There are separate pools of nodes for the different properties (name, age, job, etc.). Within a pool all the nodes are interlinked in an inhibitory fashion (note that these links are not shown here). A particular individual is defined by establishing excitatory links between a given node in the person pool and the attribute nodes that define that individual.

and all the names of the people are in a "name pool". There is a special "person pool" for each individual in the list. This pool contains nodes that do not encode any specific attribute, and that stand for a particular individual. The links between nodes within a pool are all inhibitory or negative (these links are not explicitly shown in Fig. 10.4). This

means that the Jets node in the "gang pool" will pass negative activation to the Sharks node and vice versa. So, if one of these nodes has a high activation then it will force down the activation of the other node.

In this network, an individual is encoded by establishing excitatory links between the individual node and the nodes for the attributes of that individual. So, to encode Art, excitatory links are established between the _Art person node and the Art name node, the Jets node, the 40s age node, the junior high-school education node, the single marital-status node, and the pusher job node (see Fig. 10.4). This means that if activation is high at one of these nodes it will pass positive excitation to all of its connected nodes. Each of these nodes will then attempt to force down the activation of nodes within its respective pool, via the inhibitory links within the pool.

After the nodes and links have been built in this network it goes through a number of cycles where activation is passed between all the nodes in the network. In this way the activation in one node will interact with the activation in all the other nodes. Typically, after a number of cycles the network will settle into a state where the activation levels in the nodes are relatively unchanging. This network model can be used to demonstrate a number of properties of human conceptual systems. For example, if you want to determine the attributes of a given individual you can "clamp" a particular person-node (e.g. _Art); *clamping* is a term used to mean that you keep the activation in this node at a constant level on each cycle; you fix its activation at a given level so it does not change. When this is done, after a number of cycles all of Art's attributes will have high activations, indicating that these are his attributes. Furthermore, because activation passes out from some of these nodes to other instance nodes, all the individuals that share key attributes with Art will be activated to varying degrees. So, for example, the person nodes for _Clyde and _Ralph will also have high activations reflecting their similarity to _Art. More interestingly, the network can form a "generalisation" about the key attributes of different classes of individuals. If we clamp the Jets node, then when the network settles we have a weighted attribute description of the typical attributes of Jets gang-members; namely, that they tend to be single, are in their 20s, and have only been to junior high school. A generalisation for the Sharks gang can also be determined in this way.

The important point about this model is that you do not have to explicitly encode general knowledge, rather this knowledge emerges from a collection of instances over which certain computations are carried out. As such, one of the implications of this model is that it demonstrates the feasibility of an exemplar-based model of the prototype view of concepts. Other more advanced models exist in the literature that are specifically designed to model many aspects of the exemplar version of prototype theory (see e.g. Hintzman, 1986; Kruschke, 1992; Nosofsky, 1991).

CONCEPTUAL COMBINATION

The bulk of this chapter has been given over to examining the acquisition and organisation of single concepts. However, new concepts can also be created by combining existing concepts in novel ways. We develop concepts like *pet fish*, *fake gun*, and *blue-striped shirt*. These *conceptual combinations* or *complex concepts* should also be explained by concept theories (Osherson & Smith, 1981). Concept combinations come in a number of different forms: including adjective–noun combinations (e.g. red fruit, large bird), adverb–adjective–noun combinations (e.g. very red fruit, slightly large bird) and noun–verb combinations (e.g. birds eat insects). We will concentrate on the most commonly examined of these; namely, adjective–noun combinations (see Costello & Keane, 1992; Hampton, 1983, 1987, 1988; Jones, 1982b; Osherson & Smith, 1981, 1982; Smith, 1988; Smith & Osherson, 1984; Smith, Osherson, Rips, Albert, & Keane, 1988; Zadeh, 1982).

The phenomena surrounding adjective–noun combinations raise problems for both the defining-attribute and the prototype views. Defining-attribute theories predict that a combined concept should contain a set of entities that are a conjunction of the members that belong to the two constituent concepts. So, a red apple should refer to objects that are in both the categories *red-things* and *apples*. However, this is nowhere near a complete account. As Lakoff (1982) indicates, a *fake gun* is not a member of the category *gun*.

Osherson and Smith (1981, 1982) pointed out several serious problems for any prototype explanation of conceptual combination. They proved formally that the typicality of the member of the conjunction of two concepts could not be a simple function of the two constitutent typicalities. Intuitively, a *guppy fish* is a good example of a pet fish, but a guppy is not typical of the category of pets (who are generally warm and furry) nor is it typical of the category of fish (who are generally larger; see Hampton, 1988).

Several models have been proposed to account for conceptual combination and to predict the typicality of members of the combined concept (Cohen & Murphy, 1984; Hampton, 1983; Murphy & Medin, 1985; Smith & Osherson, 1984; Thagard, 1984). Hampton's (1983) model talks of the formation of a composite prototype, by combining various attributes of the constituent concepts in an interactive fashion. Hampton (1987, 1988) produced evidence in favour of this model which shows that the similarity of an object to the *composite prototype* of the combined concepts determines the typicality and class membership of that object. Murphy and Medin (1985) maintain that conceptual combination is another case where background conceptual knowledge or theories about the concepts in question play a role. They point out that *ocean drives* are not both *oceans* and *drives*, and *horse races* are not both *horses* and *races*. Some circumstantial evidence for this view has been found by Medin and Shoben (1988).

The work on conceptual combination is an interesting and important extension of the corpus of phenomena that any theory of concepts must explain. What is notable about research in this area is that although the defining-attribute view does not seem at all feasible, the two alternative formulations—the defining-attribute and characteristic-attribute, and prototype views— have had to work hard to be able to deal with the empirical evidence in this area. It is against this background that views about the role of knowledge or theories in conceptualisation have begun to emerge; these phenomena make a simple attribute-based, similarity-driven conceptual system harder to defend.

CONCEPT INSTABILITY

The research on concept combination suggests that purely similarity-based analysis of concepts using attribute-list representations is not sufficient. Another source of troublesome evidence comes from research on concept instability. Barsalou (1989, p.65) has pointed out that all concept theories share the assumption that:

> … knowledge structures are stable: knowledge structures are stored in long-term memory as discrete and relatively static sets of information; they are retrieved intact when relevant to current processing; different members of the population use the same basic structures; and a given individual uses the same structures across contexts.

In his research on concept instability, Barsalou (1987, 1989) argues convincingly that this assumption may be unwarranted. He points out that the way people represent a concept changes as a function of the context in which it appears. For example, Anderson and Ortony (1975) have shown that if people are given sentences to memorise like "The man lifted the piano" and "The man tuned the piano", that "something heavy" is a better cue to the former sentence than "something with a nice sound" and vice versa. One explanation of this result is that the representation of the concept's attributes in both sentences is different; the piano has attributes to do with weight in the lifting case and attributes to do with musicality in the tuning case. It seems that only a subset of the knowledge about a category becomes active in a given context; what Barsalou (1982) calls *context-dependent information*. So, for example, when people read "frog" in isolation, "eaten by humans" typically remains inactive in memory. However, "eaten by humans" becomes active when reading about frogs in a French restaurant. Thus, concepts are unstable to the extent that different information is incorporated into the representation of a concept in different situations.

Instability has also been found in the graded structure of category exemplars (see Barsalou,

1985, 1989). As we saw earlier, a category's graded structure is simply the ordering of its exemplars from most to least typical. For instance, in the bird category, American subjects order the following instances as decreasing in typicality from *robin* to *pigeon* to *parrot* to *ostrich*. Instability shows itself in the rearrangement of this ordering as a function of the population, the individual, or context (see Barsalou, 1989). For example, even though Americans consider a robin to be more typical than a swan, they treat a swan as being more typical than a robin when they are asked to take the viewpoint of the average Chinese citizen.

Furthermore, some categories are not well established in memory but seem to be formed on-the-fly (Barsalou, 1983). These so-called *ad hoc categories* are constructed by people to achieve certain goals. For example, if you wanted to sell off your unwanted possessions you might construct a category of "things to sell at a garage sale". Barsalou has shown that the associations between instances of these concepts and the concept itself are not well established in memory but can be constructed if required.

So, how can these views be squared with the research we have reviewed in this chapter. Barsalou's account is reminiscent of some of the defining- and characteristic-attribute theories we met earlier in this chapter. He posits that concepts have a conceptual core of *context-independent information* that gives rise to the more stable aspects of conceptualisation. As well as this core information, there is also context-dependent information activated by the current context, and recent context-dependent information activated in recent contexts. In Barsalou's (1989) view a person possesses a tremendous amount of loosely organised knowledge for a category in long-term memory. Even though much of this knowledge may be shared with other members of the population, because of the different subsets of knowledge that can become active in a given context (as a function of context dependence or recent experiences) more often than not conceptualisation will give the appearance of instability rather than stability. Barsalou's contribution is an important antidote to the view that everybody conceives of things in the same way. However, it remains to be seen whether a theory of the sort proposed by him can account for the extensive evidence on conceptualisation in the literature.

NEUROLOGICAL EVIDENCE ON CONCEPTS

Throughout this chapter we have concentrated on attempts to understand the nature of "normal" knowledge organisation. However, in the last 20 years a parallel research stream has examined impairments in knowledge that arise after neurological damage. This research has revealed a number of interesting and important findings.

First, people with a variety of neurological damage develop specific impairments of their semantic memory. When the cognitive systems involved in reading and speaking remain intact, there is evidence that the storage of knowledge or access to it, or both, can be disrupted. For example, Schwartz, Marin, and Saffran (1979; Schwartz, Saffran, & Marin, 1980) studied a patient, WLP, suffering from a severe dementing disease. WLP's ability to read was intact but her comprehension was poor. For example, when she was asked to indicate which one of a set of words a picture represented (using basic-level words, like "spoon", "apple", "cigarette"), she was poor at selecting the correct word for the picture. Furthermore, when she chose the wrong word, she tended to choose one that was related semantically to the correct choice. So, for example, for a picture of a fork she chose the word "spoon" and for a picture of a brush she chose "comb".

A second noteworthy finding is the way in which knowledge about superordinate concepts seems to be less susceptible to damage than more subordinate information (Warrington, 1975). Warrington (1975; see also Coughlan & Warrington, 1978) studied a patient, EM, also with a dementing illness, using a forced-choice decision task; that is, the patient was given a question like "Is cabbage an animal, a plant, or an inanimate object?" or "Is cabbage green, brown, or grey?" and had to choose one of the alternatives. It was discovered that EM was only wrong in 2% of cases on the former type of question but was wrong 28% of the time on the latter type of question. The point being that more subordinate attribute information about the *cabbage* concept was lost, even though the superordinate classification of a cabbage as a plant was retained (although see Rapp & Caramazza, 1989, for a recent challenge of this finding). Similar evidence has been found by Martin and Fedio (1983) in the naming errors made by Alzheimer's patients. These patients tend to give superordinates when they name objects wrongly. So, for example, asparagus is named as a vegetable and a pelican as a bird.

A third, and perhaps most surprising, finding from the neurological literature is evidence that patients have deficits in their knowledge of specific categories of objects. For example, Dennis (1976) has reported a patient who had difficulties only with the category "body parts". Warrington and Shallice (1984) have studied patients with similar deficits following damage to the medial temporal lobes, arising from herpes simplex encephalitis. These patients were very good at identifying inanimate objects by either verbal description or picture but were considerably poorer on objects that were living things or foods. More specifically, Hart, Berndt, and Caramazza (1985) have reported a patient, MD, with a deficit specific to the naming and categorisation of fruits and vegetables. Even though lesioned connectionist models manifest these sorts of deficits (see Plaut & Shallice, 1993), some researchers have argued that they may be artefactual (see Funnell & Sheridan, 1992; Parkin & Steward, 1993; Steward, Parkin, & Hunkin, 1992). Funnell and Sheridan (1992) proposed that studies showing category-specific effects did not control for important variables like the familiarity of the objects and their name frequency. In a patient they examined, they found that when they controlled for such factors there was no evidence of category-specific deficits.

Many of these effects can be found together in Alzheimer's disease where there is considerable degradation of patient's abilities in semantic memory tasks (see Nebes, 1989, for a review). How are we to understand these findings in the light of the previous theories of concepts? Shallice (1988) suggests that the salience of superordinate information indicates that the Roschian basic level is less important than previously thought. In terms of specific psychological models he suggests that these results favour later network models (e.g. Collins & Loftus, 1975) and distributed memory schemes (McClelland & Rumelhart, 1985). In distributed memory models, patterns of activation encoding superordinate information are less disrupted than patterns of activation representing exemplars (Shallice, 1988). As the status of category-specific deficits is questionable, it is unwise at this stage to draw definite conclusions about what they might mean for the normal conceptual system.

CHAPTER SUMMARY

The organisation of knowledge is one of the oldest and most researched areas in cognitive psychology. As such, it should act as a barometer of the state of the discipline. Has progress been made? Well, it is clear that research is not standing still. Researchers have used everything in the cognitive science cupboard (from empirical tests, to formal tests and computational models) to challenge each others' and often their own theories (e.g. Medin appears as the proposer of several different theories). It is clear that certain theoretical views have been modified by the evidence found, or in some cases wholly defeated. For instance, straight defining-attribute views have had their day, even though it has been the dominant view of conceptualisation for most of the intellectual history of Western Europe.

It is hard to draw clear lines between the other views and to say which one is dominant. As both the defining- and characteristic-attribute and the prototype approaches really consist of confederacies of many specific theories, arbitrating between both approaches is very difficult. What is clear, is that no single view can encompass all of the diverse evidence (see Komatsu, 1992). Furthermore, the area is not now hampered by unfruitful wrangles about basic philosophical positions.

We are, however, left with two big questions at the end of this chaper. First, how do we deal with more complex knowledge structures beyond object concepts, like relations and schemata? Second, how can these attribute-based theories be extended or modified to deal with evidence that suggests that theoretical and schematic knowledge has an important role to play in the nature and formation of object concepts and combined concepts? These are the issues we turn to in the next chapter on relations, events, and schemata.

FURTHER READING

Estes, W.K. (1994). *Classification and cognition.* Oxford: Oxford University Press. This book gives a very good account of exemplar-based approaches to categorisation which have not been covered in great detail here.

Komatsu, L.K. (1992). Recent views of conceptual structure. *Psychological Bulletin, 112,* 500–526. This article provides a recent review of the concept literature, with a comprehensive bibliography of references.

Smith, E.E., & Medin, D. (1981) *Categories and concepts.* Cambridge, MA: Harvard University Press. This is a classic and extensive review of the different concept approaches taken up to 1980. Although it is quite old now, it is still a very useful review.

Van Mechelen, I., Hampton, J., Michalski, R.S., & Theuns, P. (1993). *Concepts and categories.* London: Academic Press. This is a recent collection of articles on prominent areas in concept research.

11

Relations, Events, and Schemata

In the previous chapter, we proposed that our ideas about the world could be divided into objects, relations, and complex combinations of these things (e.g. events and scenes). However, as we have seen, most research on conceptualisation deals only with object concepts. In the previous chapter, we also hinted that a full characterisation of object concepts requires some notion of how they are embedded in more complex relational structures. In this chapter, we turn to the often-neglected study of relational concepts, and then to work on more complex conceptual structures, so-called schemata. Recently, one of the major developments in the area of object concepts has been to integrate them with schematic knowledge, to form a new perspective on concepts called the explanation-based view of concepts. So, at the end of this chapter, we return to the subject of object concepts and review this perspective.

RELATIONAL CONCEPTS

There is a lot more to knowledge than "object concepts" (e.g. *cats*, *dogs*, *tables*, *chairs*) even though most research has concentrated on them. A significant part of our knowledge is in the form of "relational concepts" (like *hit*, *bounce*, and *kiss*).

Quillian's (1966) semantic network model bucked this trend in emphasising relational as well as object concepts. In this and later network models, relational concepts, like *hit* and *kick*, were represented as labelled links between the nodes in the network (see Anderson, 1976, 1983; Collins & Loftus, 1975; Norman & Rumelhart, 1975). Psychological models of relational concepts were strongly influenced by previous work in linguistics and artificial intelligence.

Representing relational concepts

We saw earlier that object concepts could be characterised by attribute lists. Relational concepts may have received less attention because something different was required for their representation. Under influence of the linguist, Charles Fillmore (1968), relational concepts have been represented as a *case grammar*: as predicates taking a number of arguments (see e.g. Kintsch, 1974; Norman & Rumelhart, 1975). For example, the relational concepts for *hit* and *collide* are:

hit(Agent, Recipient, Instrument)
collide(Object1, Object2)

Here *hit* and *collide* are predicates and the bracketed terms are arguments (see Chapter 9). On understanding a sentence about hitting and colliding, people were supposed to construct a mental representation of this sort. So, the sentence:

Karl hit Mark with a champagne bottle.

would be represented as

hit(Karl, Mark, champagne bottle)

People must know which objects can fill the argument slots in the representation; that is, they should be able to determine that Karl is an agent, Mark is a recipient, and that the champagne bottle is an instrument and therefore assign them to their proper roles in the situation.

This method of representing relations has been used widely, even though it is not without its critics. Johnson-Laird, Herrmann, and Chaffin (1984) have argued, convincingly, that these propositional representations are not constrained enough to constitute an adequate theory of the meaning of relations; any theory of meaning can be represented by these network representations. In Johnson-Laird et al.'s terms they were "only connections". Johnson-Laird et al. (1984) also pointed out, using the intensional–extensional distinction, that these theories say little about extensional phenomena (see Chapter 10 for a discussion of the intensional–extensional distinction). For example, semantic networks ignore the gap there is between a linguistic description and a mental representation of that description. The statement "The cat is on the mat" could be mentally represented in many different ways; for instance, the cat in the middle of the mat, the cat on the left corner of the mat, the cat wearing a red-striped, top-hat standing with one foot on the mat. These are alternative mental models (or extensions) of the linguistic description that have semantic implications (see Johnson-Laird et al., 1984; Johnson-Laird, 1983, on mental models).

Semantic decomposition of relational concepts

One partial answer to Johnson-Laird et al.'s criticisms is to specify more about the *semantic primitives* that underlie a particular relation (see, for example, Gentner, 1975; Miller &

Johnson-Laird, 1976; Norman & Rumelhart, 1975). Roger Schank's *conceptual dependency theory* is one influential attempt to do this in artificial intelligence (see Schank, 1972).

Schank proposed that the core meaning of a whole set of action verbs could be captured by 12 to 15 primitive actions. These primitives were called *acts* and the main ones are listed in Table 11.1.

These primitive acts are used in a case-frame fashion to characterise the semantic basis of a whole range of verbs. For example, ATRANS can characterise any verb that involves the transfer of possession:

Actor:	person-2
Act:	ATRANS
Object:	physical object
Direction TO:	person-1
Direction FROM:	person-2

This structure is a type of *schema*; it is made up of a series of *variables* (the terms Actor, Act, Object, etc.) and in a specific case certain *values* are assigned to these variables. So, "John gave Mary a necklace" would be represented as:

Actor:	John
Act:	ATRANS
Object:	necklace
Direction TO:	Mary
Direction FROM:	John

A variable, as its name suggests, can take on any of a number of values. Computer scientists often use the terms *slot* for variable and *slot filler* for a value; this taps into a spatial metaphor which suggests that slots are like holes in the schema into which specific objects are put (like a necklace). ATRANS can be used to characterise many relations: like *receive*, *take*, *buy*, and *sell*. In a more complicated fashion, certain verbs can be characterised by a combination of primitives.

TABLE 11.1

The Meaning of the Main Primitive Acts in Schank's Conceptual Dependency Theory, with Instances of the Verbs They Are Used to Characterise

Primitive	Meaning	Sample Verbs
ATRANS	transfer of possession	give, lend, take
PTRANS	physical transfer from one location to another	move, walk, drive
MTRANS	transfer of mental information	order, advise
MBUILD	build memory structures	remember, understand
ATTEND	receive sensory input	see, hear
PROPEL	apply force to physical object	push, hit
MOVE	move a body part	wave, kick
INGEST	intake of food or air	breathe, eat
EXPEL	reverse of ingest	vomit, excrete

Other schemes have been used that are similar to this one, but they all share the characteristic of representing the relational term as a primitive or set of interconnected primitives. As such, in its simplest form, this approach has some aspects of the defining-attribute view of object concepts. As we shall see later, evidence suggests that the defining-attribute view is also inadequate in this area.

Evidence for semantic decomposition

In general, there has been more theoretical analysis of relations than empirical testing of these theories. Some research has examined whether relations are decomposed into their primitives in the course of comprehending a sentence. Some theorists have argued that this *semantic decomposition* does not occur (Fodor, Fodor, & Garrett, 1975; Kintsch, 1974), but others have taken the opposite view (Gentner, 1975, 1981). Several studies failed to find evidence for semantic decomposition; they showed that complex sentences as opposed to simple sentences (i.e. involving relations with more primitives) did not differ in memorability or take longer to process (see Carpenter & Just, 1977; Kintsch, 1974). However, Gentner (1975, 1981)

argued that these studies confounded two distinct types of complex or specific sentences. She maintained that "poorly connected" specific sentences should take less time to process than "well-connected" specific sentences, and that previous studies had confounded this difference (see Fig. 11.1)

Consider the three main types of materials Gentner (1981) used in her study. First, she distinguished between general and specific sentences: for instance, "Ida *gave* her tenants a clock" was considered to be more general than "Ida *mailed* her tenants a clock" or "Ida *sold* her tenants a clock". This was because *give* involves just a transfer of possession, whereas both *mail* and *sell* involve a transfer of possession and something else; in *mail* there are the associated actions of mailing something, and in *sell* there is a transfer of goods and of money. However, even though the mailed and sold sentences are both specific, they differ in the degree to which their elements are well connected. Mailing involves Ida as a principal agent who performs a mail routine that causes a transfer of possession to certain recipients (i.e. her tenants). Selling involves Ida as a principal agent who transfers possession of goods to the tenant

FIGURE 11.1

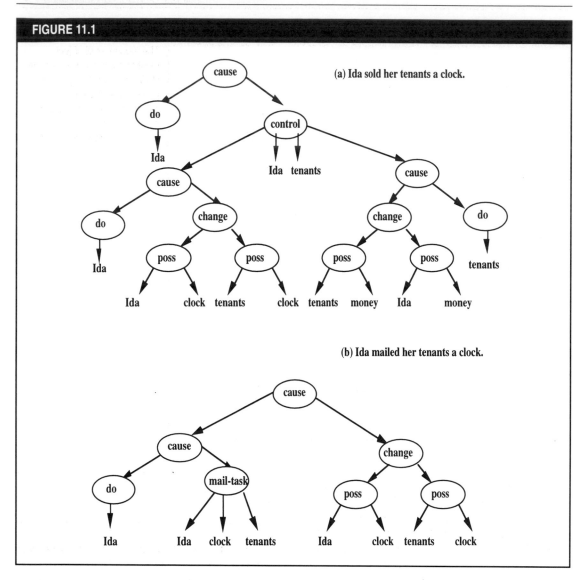

Representations from Gentner (1981) of two complex sentences that differ in terms of the degree to which their elements (e.g. Ida and her tenants) are integrated or connected: (a) the representation of the sentence "Ida sold her tenants a clock", and (b) the representation of the sentence "Ida mailed her tenants a clock".

recipients, but she is also a recipient for the transfer of money from the tenants acting as principal agents. Gentner, therefore, argued that more connections between Ida and the tenants are elaborated in the selling case than in the mailing case; that the former is better connected than the latter (see Fig. 11.1). If this hypothesis is true then objects from the well-connected, specific sentence should be better recalled than the poorly connected,

specific sentence when cued by other nouns from the sentence. These predictions were confirmed in her results (see Fig. 11.2).

Gentner's research suggests that there are defining primitives for relational concepts. However, Coleman and Kay (1981; also Vaughan, 1985) have shown that these primitives should be treated as characteristic attributes rather than defining attributes. Coleman and Kay posited that

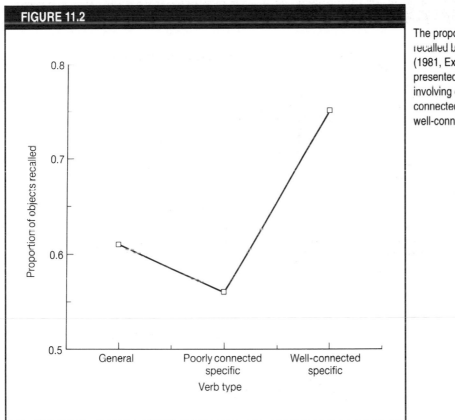

FIGURE 11.2

The proportion of objects recalled by subjects in Gentner (1981, Experiment 3), when presented with sentences involving either general, poorly connected-specific or well-connected-specific verbs.

the verb *to lie* (prevaricate) had three semantic components or attributes; in which (i) the statement made is false, (ii) the speaker believes the statement is false, and (iii) the speaker intends to deceive the hearer. They then made up stories in which they explicitly cancelled some or all of these attributes, and asked subjects to judge the degree to which the incident in the story could be regarded as a lie. For example, a story about a railway porter telling a traveller that the train to London leaves from Platform 5, when this was not true and the porter was not aware of its falsity, cancels the second two attributes. Using this method they found that different usages were considered to be better or worse examples of *lying*. Furthermore, the attributes that made up the representation of the verb were considered to be differentially important in characterising a good example of a lie. These results thus favour a prototype view of relational concepts.

SCHEMATA, FRAMES, AND SCRIPTS

As we said earlier, there is clearly more to human knowledge than attribute-like information about single concepts and hierarchies of these concepts (i.e. the subordinate, basic, and superordinate levels). It is more plausible to assume that there are more complex forms of conceptual organisation; that concepts are related to one another in ways that reflect the temporal and causal structure of the world. For instance, in order to represent the notion of an event (e.g. reading your exam results on the noticeboard) it is necessary to have a knowledge structure that relates the act of reading to the objects involved (e.g. you and the noticeboard). The knowledge structures that can represent this type of information have been variously called schemata, frames, and scripts.

Historical antecedents of schema theories

The most commonly used construct to account for complex knowledge organisation is the schema. A *schema* is a structured cluster of concepts; usually, it involves generic knowledge, and may be used to represent events, sequences of events, precepts, situations, relations, and even objects. The philosopher Kant (1787/1963) originally proposed the idea of schemata as innate structures used to help us perceive the world. Kant was strongly nativist in his view that innate, a priori structures of the mind allow us to conceive of time, three-dimensional space, and even geometry (even though many school children might disagree).

In the 1930s, the concept of a schema found its way, via Head's neurophysiology, into the research of Bartlett at Cambridge University. Bartlett (1932) was struck by how people's understanding and remembrance of events was shaped by their expectations. He suggested that these expectations were mentally represented in a schematic fashion, and carried out experiments illustrating their

effects on cognition. In one famous experiment, he gave English subjects a North American Indian folk tale to memorise and recall later at different time intervals. The folk tale had many strange attributions and a causal structure that was contrary to Western expectations. He found that subjects "reconstructed" the story rather than remembering it verbatim, and that this reconstruction was consistent with a Western world-view (see Table 11.2 and Chapter 13 for recent replications of this study). Finally, in a developmental context, Piaget (1967, 1970) had also used the schema idea to understand changes in children's cognition.

Schema theories re-emerged as a dominant interest in the 1970s. These theories came in several, superficially different forms: Schank's (1972) conceptual dependency theory essentially uses schemata to represent relational concepts; "story grammars" were proposed to underlie the comprehension of stories by Rumelhart and others (Rumelhart, 1975; Stein & Glenn, 1979; Thorndyke, 1977; and Chapter 13). Schemata

---

TABLE 11.2

Part of the Original *War of the Ghosts* Story and One Subject's Subsequent Recall of it (from Bartlett, 1932)

The War of the Ghosts

One night two young men from Edulac went down the river to hunt seals, and while they were there it became foggy and calm. Then they heard war-cries, and they thought: "Maybe this is a war-party". They escaped to the shore, and hid behind a log. Now canoes came up, and they heard the noise of paddles, and saw one canoe coming up to them. There were five men in the canoe, and they said: "What do you think? We wish to take you along. We are going up the river to make war on the people."

... one of the young men went but the other returned home ... [it turns out that the five men in the boat were ghosts and after accompanying them in a fight, the young man returned to his village to tell his tale] ... and said: "Behold I accompanied the ghosts, and we went to fight. Many of our fellows were killed, and many of those who attacked us were killed. They said I was hit, and I did not feel sick."

He told it all and then he became quiet. When the sun rose he fell down. Something black came out of his mouth. His face became contorted ... He was dead. (p.65)

A subject's recall of the story (two weeks later)
There were two ghosts. They were on a river. There was a canoe on the river with five men in it. There occurred a war of ghosts ... They started the war and several were wounded and some killed. One ghost was wounded but did not feel sick. He went back to the village in the canoe. The next morning he was sick and something black came out of his mouth, and they cried: "He is dead." (p.76)

containing organised sequences of stereotypical actions, called *scripts*, were proposed by Schank and Abelson (1977) to account for people's knowledge of everyday situations. Rumelhart and Ortony (1977; also Rumelhart, 1980) proposed a general theory of schemata; and, in artificial intelligence, Marvin Minsky (1975) suggested similar structures called "frames", which he mainly implicated in visual perception (see Alba & Hasher, 1983, Thorndyke & Yekovich, 1980, for reviews).

SCHEMATA: AN EXAMPLE AND EVIDENCE

The concept of a schema is a very loose one in many respects. Because it is an organising structure for knowledge, it tends to take on ostensibly different forms when representing different sorts of knowledge. However, schemata have certain common characteristics (see Panel 11.1).

We have illustrated the notion of a schema with respect to the very simple schemata that characterise relations. More elaborate examples occur in Schank and Abelson's (1977) script theory, which attempts to capture the knowledge we use to understand commonplace events like going to a restaurant.

Schank and Abelson's script theory

Schank and Abelson were interested in capturing the knowledge people use to comprehend extended texts, like the following one:

> Ruth and Mark had lunch at a restaurant today. They really enjoyed the meal but were worried about its cost. However, when the bill arrived after the ice-cream, they were pleasantly surprised to find that it was very reasonable.

In reading this passage, we use our knowledge to infer that the meal (mentioned in the second sentence) was at the restaurant where they had lunch (mentioned in the first sentence), that the meal involved ice-cream, and that the bill did not walk up to them but was probably brought by a waiter. Schank and Abelson argued that we must have predictive schemata to make these inferences and to fill in aspects of the event that are left implicit. The specific schemata they proposed were called scripts. *Scripts* are knowledge structures that encode the stereotypical sequence of actions in everyday happenings. For example, if you often eat in restaurants then you would have a script for "eating in restaurants". This "restaurant script" would encode the typical actions that occur in this scenario along with the sorts of objects and actors you would encounter in this context. The restaurant

---

(Panel 11.1) Definition of Schemata

- They consist of various relations and variables/slots, and values for these variables.

- The *relations* can take a variety of forms; they can be simple relations (e.g. *is-a, hit, kick*) or they can be more complex, "causal" relations (e.g. *enable, cause, prevent, desire*).

- Variables/slots contain concepts or other sub-schemata; any concept that fills a slot usually has to satisfy some test [e.g. the argument-slot "Agent" in the relation HIT (Agent, Object, Instrument) requires that the concept that fills it is an animate object].

- *Values* refers to the various specific concepts that fill or instantiate slots.

- Schemata, thus, encode general or *generic* knowledge that can be applied to many specific situations, if those situations are instances of the schema; for example, the HIT relation could characterise a domestic dispute (e.g. Harry hit the child) or a car crash (e.g. the van hit the lorry).

- Schemata can often leave slots "open" or have associated with them *default concepts* that are assumed if a slot is unfilled; for instance, we are not told what instrument Harry used (in "Harry hit the child"), but we tend to assume a default value (like a stick or a hand).

script proposed by Schank and Abelson had four main divisions: entering, ordering, eating, and leaving. Each of these general parts had sub-actions for what to do: for instance, entering breaks down into walking into the restaurant, looking for a table, deciding where to sit, going to a table, and sitting down (see Table 11.3).

Within this schema the relations are the various actions, like walking or sitting. The slots in the script are either roles (e.g. waiter) or headings for other sub-schemata (e.g. entering). *Role slots* capture the various "parts" in the script like the waiter, the customers, and the cook, and are filled by the specific people in the situation (e.g. the tall waiter with the receding hairline). Ordinarily, these roles can only be filled by an object that satisfies

the test of being human (e.g. a waiter who is a dog is unexpected and extraordinary). The general components of the script (e.g. entering, ordering) are different types of slots that contain sub-schemata (concerning the various detailed actions of walking, sitting, and so on). In this way, it is possible to create structures that characterise people's knowledge of many commonplace situations.

Evidence for script theory

Several studies have investigated the psychological plausibility of scriptal notions (see Abelson, 1981; Bower, Black, & Turner, 1979; Galambos, Abelson, & Black, 1986; Graesser, Gordon, & Sawyer, 1979; Sanford & Garrod, 1981; Walker & Yekovich, 1984). Bower, Black, and

---

TABLE 11.3

The Components and Actions of the Restaurant Script Proposed by Schank and Abelson (1977)

Script Name	Component	Specific Action
Eating at a restaurant	Entering	Walk into restaurant Look for table Decide where to sit Go to table Sit down
	Ordering	Get menu Look at menu Choose food Waiter arrives Give orders to waiter Waiter takes order to cook Wait, talk Cook prepares food
	Eating	Cook gives food to waiter Waiter delivers food to customer Customer eats Talk
	Leaving	Waiter writes bill Waiter delivers bill to customer Customer examines bill Calculate tip Leave tip Gather belongings Pay bill Leave restaurant

Turner (1979) asked people to list about 20 actions or events that usually occurred when eating at a restaurant. In spite of the varied restaurant experiences of their subjects, there was considerable agreement in the lists produced. At least 73% of subjects mentioned sitting down, looking at the menu, ordering, eating, paying the bill, and leaving. In addition, at least 48% included entering the restaurant, giving the reservation name, ordering drinks, discussing the menu, talking, eating a salad or soup, ordering dessert, eating dessert, and leaving a tip. So, there appear to be at least 15 key events involved in people's restaurant-visiting knowledge. Other evidence from Galambos and Rips (1982) has shown that when subjects have to make a rapid decision about whether or not an action is part of a script (e.g. determining that "getting to a restaurant" is part of a restaurant script), they answer rapidly when the action is part of the script but take longer when it is not a script action. Evidence for script theory has also been found in more applied contexts concerning eyewitness testimony for robberies (see Holst & Pezdek, 1992).

General evidence for schemata

There is considerable evidence in several different areas for the operation of schema like knowledge structures (see e.g. Alba & Hasher, 1983; Graesser, Woll, Kowalski, & Smith, 1980). After Bartlett, many studies have shown that when people have different expectations about a target event they interpret and recall it in different ways (see e.g. Anderson & Pichert, 1978; Bransford & Johnson, 1972; and Chapter 13).

Furthermore, schemata have also been implicated in perception, where they reduce the need to analyse all aspects of a visual scene. When we view everyday scenes, like our bedroom or a lecture theatre, we have clear expectations about what objects are likely to be present. Schemata reduce the amount of processing the perceptual system needs to carry out to identify expected objects (see Chapter 3), thus freeing resources for processing more novel and unexpected aspects of the scene (like the lecturer's dress-sense). Friedman (1979) has shown this by presenting subjects with detailed line drawings of six different scenes (from a city, a kitchen, a living room, an office, a kindergarten, and a farm). Each picture contained objects you would expect in the setting and a few unexpected objects. Friedman found that the duration of the first look was almost twice as long for unexpected as for expected objects, indicating the role of schemata in processing the latter. The differences between expected and unexpected objects were even more marked on a subsequent recognition-memory test. Subjects rarely noticed missing, or partially changed, expected objects even when only those expected objects that had been looked at were considered. In contrast, deletions or replacements of unexpected objects were nearly always detected. As Friedman concluded (1979, p.343): "The episodic information that is remembered about an event is the difference between that event and its prototypical, frame representation in memory."

These effects regarding the recollection of unexpected items have been found repeatedly in a number of different experiments, although they can be modified by conditions that interfere with subjects' attention to the processing of the unexpected objects (see Henderson, 1992; Mäntylä & Bäckman, 1992).

SCHEMA ACQUISITION

In general, little is known about the mechanisms of schema acquisition (see Anderson's ACT models, in Chapter 16, as one counter-example). Many theorists are either silent about how schemata are formed, or assume that some type of ill-specified, induction is used. The inductive account says that on first entering a particular restaurant you somehow learn what to do and muddle through (maybe on the basis of other related knowledge structures; e.g. going to a shop to buy food). When you have a second restaurant experience you note the similarities between the two episodes and form an abstraction which excludes the characteristics that differ between both situations. For example, you might notice that there were waiters in the first restaurant and waiters and waitresses in the second and, therefore, form the abstraction that servers can be both male and female. So, the schema is induced or abstracted from many specific experiences. However, this is a fairly loose account and many of its details need to be specified and proven; indeed, this type of induction has encountered several significant problems in artificial intelligence programs (see Hinton, 1989, for a review).

One of the most elaborated accounts on schema acquisition has been made by Rumelhart and Norman (1981; Rumelhart, 1980). They proposed that there are three basic ways in which learning can occur in a schema-based system: accretion, tuning, and restructuring. In learning by *accretion*, you simply record a new instance of an existing schema and add it to your repertoire of knowledge. *Tuning* refers to the elaboration and refinement of concepts in the schema through experience. So, for example, you may discover that a new type of object can fill a particular slot, and change the tests on possible filler-concepts for that slot. *Restructuring* involves the creation of new schemata either by analogy (see Gentner, 1983; Holyoak, 1985; Keane, 1988) or by schema induction (via the repetition of a spatio-temporal configuration of schemata). In the analogy case, some aspects of an existing schema are mapped onto a novel situation by changing some of its slot fillers (see Chapter 16 on analogy). Unfortunately, there have been few concerted attempts to test these proposals in a direct fashion.

More recently, some more specific theoretical accounts of schema acquisition have been proposed in the connectionist literature (see McClelland, Rumelhart, & The PDP Research Group, 1986; Rumelhart, McClelland, & The PDP Research Group, 1986a). Ironically, these accounts also argue against the idea that schemata are explicit knowledge structures. We will consider this approach in a later section on the problems that arise with schema theories.

SCHANK'S DYNAMIC MEMORY THEORY

Many schema theories have been described in a very abstract way (see e.g. Bobrow & Norman, 1975; Minsky, 1975; Rumelhart, 1980; Rumelhart

& Ortony, 1977). In contrast, Roger Schank and his associates have proposed a succession of specific schema theories grounded in particular problems (see Schank, 1972, 1982, 1986; Schank & Abelson, 1977). Most of this work has been purely computational, but it has attracted psychologists because of its specificity and scope. This influence has not all been one-way, from computational models to psychological testing, as Schank's (1982, 1986) later work has been inspired, in part, by psychological research indicating the limitations of script theory.

The main problem with script theory is the inflexibility of script structures. We know much about stereotypical situations but we can also deal with the unexpected. We are not thrown when we go to a restaurant that violates a previous script. For example, people do not grind to a halt on their first trip to MacDonald's, where you have to pay for the food before eating it. Furthermore, there are situations where we could not possibly have a script, but where we manage to act in a goal-directed way (e.g. your first time in a nightclub). Schank and Abelson's scripts were only formed from direct personal experience, so few of us should be able to understand bank robbery situations. However, we clearly can understand such situations. This means that we must have a more abstract set of structures that allow us to overcome the rigid structure of scripts and to understand the actions and goals of others in situations we have never experienced personally. Schank and Abelson had the concept of a plan to capture such abstract structures. *Plans* contained knowledge about abstract goals that any actor might have (like achieving the goal of satisfying a bodily need). However, the dividing line between scripts and plans was never clear (see Schank, 1982, Chapter 1).

Psychological evidence had also shown that the script idea was wrong in some respects. Bower et al. (1979) found that subjects confused events that, according to script theory, were stored separately and should not have interfered with one another. For example, recognition confusions were found between stories that called on distinct but related scripts; visits to the dentist and visits to the doctor. As scripts had been defined as structures that were specific experiences in specific situations, one clearly could not have a "visit to a health professional" script. In response to these problems, Schank revised script theory, in his dynamic memory theory.

MOPs, TOPs, and TAUs

In his reorganisation of script theory, Schank (1982) introduced the notion of Memory Organisation Packets (MOPs). MOPs are generalised clusters of events called *scenes*. Scenes are collections of the high-level components of scripts (i.e. you could have a set of entering scenes for different contexts; like entering the dentist's office or entering a restaurant). Rather than having a set of components organised together in a script, MOPs organised sets of scenes adding specific contextual information (see Fig. 11.3). Consequently, one could have a waiting room scene that contained a set of specific, waiting-room events (e.g. waiting at the doctor's, waiting at the dentist's, waiting at the solicitor's). At a higher level, MOPs co-ordinated these scenes together, pointing to the waiting room scene at the doctor's, the paying scene at the doctor's, and so on (see Fig. 11.3). The introduction of MOPs and scenes makes the system more flexible because the scenes can be combined and recombined in any desired organisation. This provides a way to deal with unexpected orderings of components in new-ish situations. Furthermore, MOPs make central use of the idea that different specific scenes (about doctor visits and dentist visits) are similar and are therefore stored in the same place. Abbot, Black, and Smith (1985) found support for this type of organisation by showing that various parts of what were formerly called scripts are hierarchically organised. At the top level is the general goal (e.g. eating at a restaurant), at the intermediate level are scenes that denote sets of actions (e.g. entering, leaving, ordering), and at the lowest level there are the actions themselves.

There are also higher levels of organisation above MOPS and scenes. Schank proposed Thematic Organisation Points (TOPs) that could generally apply to the theme of a whole sequence of episodes. For example, the theme of *Romeo and Juliet* can be characterised as "Mutual Goal Pursuit against Outside Opposition". Romeo and Juliet, in loving each other, have the "mutual goal" of being together. The "outside opposition" comes from their parents. This theme is identical to *West Side Story*, which is a modern equivalent of *Romeo and Juliet*. Schank argues that because we consider the play and the movie to be thematically similar, we must possess higher-order structures that capture

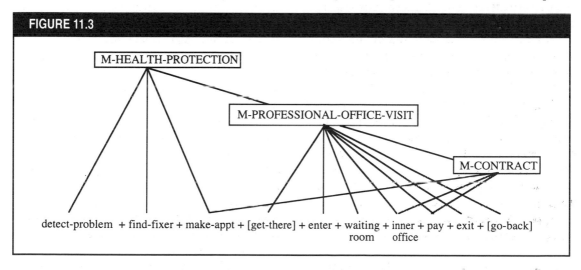

FIGURE 11.3

detect-problem + find-fixer + make-appt + [get-there] + enter + waiting + inner + pay + exit + [go-back]
room   office

According to Schank's (1982) dynamic memory theory there are three Memory-Organisation Packets (MOPs) active in a visit to a doctor: M-HEALTH-PROTECTION, M-CONTRACT, and M-PROFESSIONAL-OFFICE-VISIT. These organise specific scenes (e.g. get-there, enter) which are each coloured with the specifics of a visit to a doctor.

the general character of whole sequences of episodes. From a psychological perspective, Schank viewed TOPs as being implicated centrally in reminding. That is, he proposed that when one was reminded of something a TOP had been accessed in long-term memory (e.g. of *Romeo and Juliet* while watching *West Side Story*). Schank supposed that this sort of access occurred automatically, but as we shall see this is not supported by the evidence.

Dyer (1983) has proposed related knowledge structures called Thematic Abstraction Units (TAUs). TAUs capture plan–goal patterns reflected in common adages, like "A stitch in time saves nine". In plan–goal terms this suggests that "plans that satisfy a goal are best performed earlier than later, or else a lot more work may have to be done". TAUs raise the interesting idea that adages and proverbs summarise important high-level knowledge structures about the failure of plans and goals (see Kolodner, 1984; Kolodner & Simpson, 1986; Lehnert et al., 1983; Wilensky, 1983; for other developments of the work of Schank and Abelson's Yale Group of Researchers).

Evidence for dynamic memory theory
Some psychological research been directed at these proposals. Seifert and Black (1983) have shown, using Dyer's TAU structures, that if subjects are given stories that involve a common TAU and are asked to write similar stories, most produce stories that match the hypothesised TAU. They also found that subjects could sort stories reliably according to their TAU pattern. Seifert, McKoon, Abelson, and Ratcliff (1986) have examined the processing of story-episodes to see whether thematic structures are activated automatically when processing stories with a related episodic structure. They used a priming technique that looked at whether the verification time for a test sentence from one story was speeded by an immediately preceding test sentence from a thematically similar story. They concluded (1986, p.220) that:

> during the reading of an episode, thematic information may be encoded so as to lead to activation of similar episodes and formation of connections in memory between episodes,

but such encoding is not automatic and depends on subjects' strategies and task difficulty.

Finally, Keane (1987, 1988) showed that TOPs could be used to account for the differential frequencies with which subjects retrieved analogous problems, in a problem-solving situation (see also Chapter 16). However, the evidence suggests that reminding is not automatic but only occurs when subjects were specifically searching for an analogous problem (see also Gick & Holyoak, 1980). So, all of this research indicates that something like Schank's thematic structures may mediate retrieval from long-term memory, but contrary to his views on reminding these structures are not accessed automatically.

FUNDAMENTAL PROBLEMS WITH SCHEMA THEORIES

Schema theories are not without their problems. Although they remain the most overarching set of proposals on the structure and organisation of knowledge in long-term memory, they have a number of faults.

The unprincipled nature of schema theories

There is a broad consensus among many researchers that schema theories are unprincipled. This stems from the fact that it is often possible to create any particular content for the knowledge structures used, to account for the pattern of evidence found. Schank deals, in part, with this problem by attempting to delimit all the possible structures in long-term memory, but the theory is still underspecified. However, problems still remain; for example, what are the specific contents of all of these structures? In general, then, schema theories tend to be good at accounting for results in an *ad hoc* fashion but are not as predictive as one would like them to be.

There are two remedies to this situation. First, the theorist could specify the content of structures that *are* used; at least for a definable set of situations. That is, if you were using dynamic memory theory, you could specify all the possible scenes that people use, all the MOPS that organise these scenes, and all the TOPs that relate MOPs to one another. Unfortunately, this is probably impossible given the breadth of human knowledge and the possible variability in knowledge structures from one individual to the next. The other option is to be clearer about how these structures are acquired (see earlier section). If we knew more about this issue then we could begin to test how different selected experiences might be combined to form hypothetical structures in a more controlled fashion.

The problem of inflexibility and connectionist schemata

Although dynamic memory theory was developed to overcome many of the inflexibilities of script theory, some prominent theorists still consider that the intuitive flexibility of the schematic approach has not been realised in any of the present schemes (see Rumelhart, Smolensky, McClelland, & Hinton, 1986d). For example, Rumelhart and Ortony (1977) had proposed that the slots/variables in schemata should have two distinct characteristics. First, as stated earlier, they should test to see whether a certain object is an appropriate filler for the slot or provide a default value. Second, there should be interdependencies among the possible slot fillers. That is, if one slot is filled with a particular value then it should initiate changes in the default values for the other slots in the schema. For example, assume that you have a schema for rooms that includes slots for the furniture, the small objects found in it, and the usual size of the room. So, a kitchen schema would have the following structure and defaults:

Furniture:	kitchen table, chairs …
Small objects:	coffee pot, bread bin …
Size:	small

Other rooms would have different defaults; for example a bathroom would also be small but would have a toilet, bath, and sink as furniture, and toothbrushes as small objects. Rumelhart and Ortony's proposal was that, when the small-objects slot is filled with coffee pot, there should be an automatic change in the default value for the furniture slot to kitchen table and chairs. However, this second characteristic of schemata was never realised in the schema theories of the 1970s and 1980s.

Rumelhart et al. (1986d) proposed to remedy this state of affairs with a connectionist treatment of schemata. In this view, schemata emerge at the moment they are needed from the interaction of large numbers of parallel processing elements all working in concert with one another (for a treatment of connectionist ideas, see Chapters 1 and 9). In this scheme, there is no explicitly represented schema but only patterns of activation that produce the sorts of effects attributed to schemata in previous research. When inputs are received by a parallel network, certain coalitions of units in the network are activated and others are inhibited. In some cases where coalitions of units tend to work closely together, the more conventional notion of a schema is realised; but where the units are more loosely interconnected the structures are more fluid and less schema-like.

Rumelhart et al. (1986d) have illustrated the utility of such a scheme by encoding schema-type knowledge in a connectionist network. First, they chose 40 descriptors (e.g. door, small, sink, walls, medium) for five types of rooms (e.g. kitchen, bathroom, and bedroom). To get the basic data to construct the network they asked subjects to judge whether each descriptor characterised an example of a room type they were asked to imagine (e.g. a kitchen). When Rumelhart et al. built a network that reflected this information, they found that when activation was kept high in the ceiling unit and then some other unit (e.g. oven), the network settled into a state with high activation in units that corresponded to the typical features of a kitchen (e.g. coffee-pot, cupboard, refrigerator). Similarly, runs starting with other objects resulted in the emergence of descriptors for other prototypical rooms.

This connectionist work could solve the problem of the unprincipled nature of schema theories, in that it promises to specify a means by which schemata acquire their contents. Ironically, it does this without having to specify these schematic contents. However, a lot more needs to be done for it to replace the more explicit symbolic approach of Schank and others.

EXPLANATION-BASED VIEWS OF CONCEPTS

We saw in the previous chapter that traditional views of object concepts have been similarity-based, attribute-list views. These theories have been quite successful in accounting for the evidence of typicality judgements, sentence-verification tasks, and other results involving object concepts. However, we also saw that offshoots of this research on concept combination and concept instability have proved hard to explain; rather more complex formations of knowledge than attribute lists are required (see Putnam, 1975a and b, for arguments in philosophy on this point). Thus far, in this chapter, we have reviewed some of these more complex formations, so now is a good time to see how they might be introduced into theories of object concepts to improve them.

Initially, in Chapter 10, we introduced three guiding constraints for conceptual systems; informativeness, economy, and coherence. In attribute-based theories, concepts cohere because members of a category have similar attributes. However, there are concepts that have little similarity between their attributes. We have already seen how Barsalou's (1983) *ad hoc* categories upset this view of coherence (e.g. the category of things-to-sell-in-a-garage-sale). Murphy and Medin (1985) point out that in the Bible, the dietary rules associated with the abominations of Leviticus produce the categories of clean and unclean animals. What is it that makes camels, ostriches, crocodiles, mice, sharks, and eels *unclean*, and gazelles, frogs, most fish, grasshoppers, and some locusts *clean*?

Murphy and Medin argued that it was not the similarity of members of the concepts that determined the conceptual distinction but some theory or explanatory framework. The concept of clean and unclean animals rests on a theory of how the features of habitat, biological structure, and

form of locomotion should be correlated in various animals (see Douglas, 1966). Roughly speaking, creatures of the water should have fins and scales, and swim, and creatures of the land should have four legs. If a creature conforms with this theory, then it is considered clean. But any creature that is not equipped for the right kind of locomotion is considered unclean (e.g. ostriches). Murphy and Medin's notion of a *theory* refers to any of a number of mental "explanations" (rather than a complete scientific account): for example (Murphy & Medin, 1985, p.290):

> causal knowledge certainly embodies a theory of certain phenomena; scripts may contain an implicit theory of entailment between mundane events; knowledge of rules embodies a theory of the relations between rule constitutents; book-learned, scientific knowledge certainly contains theories.

They therefore argue that even though similarity notions are important they are not sufficient to determine which concepts will be coherent or meaningful. These arguments have informed a newly emergent view of concepts that has been termed the knowledge-based or explanation-based view.

The explanation-based view of object concepts

The explanation-based view of concepts sees concepts as involving more than attribute-lists; concepts also contain causal and other background knowledge that might be represented by schemata. For example, living things with wings, feathers, and light bones are seen as forming a natural category because they are, according to a certain theory, manifestations of a single, genetic code; the category coheres because we have a theory that explains the co-occurrence of these attributes.

Miller and Johnson-Laird (1976) were among the first to propose that concept representations involved schematic knowledge, although others have made similar proposals (Cohen & Murphy, 1984; Keil, 1989; Lakoff, 1987). For the most part, this view of concepts has been marked by several general statements of the view rather than many concrete realisations of it; see Lakoff (1987) on Idealised Cognitive Models, Johnson-Laird's (1983) mental models account, and Medin and Ortony's (1989) psychological essentialism. Some of the main proposals of the view are shown in Panel 11.2.

A thorough-going elaboration of this view with respect to the specific evidence of concept research remains to be carried out. However, it is clear at present that many theorists in the field are leaning towards theoretical proposals with these sorts of properties.

Evidence for explanation-based views

There are several sources of evidence for explanation-based views. Some studies have shown that there is a dissociation between similarity and categorisation judgements, thus demonstrating that similarity could not be the sole mechanism behind categorisation (see Rips, 1989a). Other studies have shown how background knowledge (either causal or specific knowledge) can influence the application and learning of categories (see Ahn, Brewer, & Mooney, 1992; Malt, 1994; Medin, Wattenmaker, & Hampson, 1987; Pazzani, 1991a; Wisniewski & Medin, 1994).

Rips (1989a) has shown a dissociation between similarity judgements and categorisation, in a study where one group of subjects was asked whether an object five inches in diameter was more likely to be a coin or a pizza, and a second group was given the same information and asked to judge the similarity of the object to either the coin or the pizza. Although the object's size was roughly midway between a large coin and a small pizza (as determined by prior norms), subjects in the categorisation group tended to categorise it as a pizza. However, the similarity group judged the object to more similar to the coin. If categorisation was based on similarity alone, subjects' judgements in both groups should have tallied. The fact that they did not indicates that some other variable was at work. Rips maintained that this variable was knowledge (or a theory) about the variability of the sizes of the objects in question. Coins have a size that is mandated by law, whereas pizzas can vary greatly in size.

Further evidence comes from Medin, Wattenmaker, and Hampson (1987) who have shown that conceptual knowledge seems to drive the application of a family-resemblance strategy in concept sorting. Recall that within the prototype view the typicality of a concept member is closely related to the family resemblance score for that instance; that is, the score that reflects the extent to which the instance's attributes are the same as those of other instances of the category. Medin et al. (1987) found that, in a sorting task, subjects persisted in sorting on the basis of a single dimension instead of using many dimensions, as a

---

(Panel 11.2) Explanation-based Approach to Concepts

- Concepts can have attributes:

- But they also have relations between these attributes, which form explanatory connections between the attributes (e.g. that wings, feathers, and light bones enable birds to fly).

- Concepts are not necessarily stored as static knowledge in memory, but may be dynamically constructed in working memory using attribute-definitions and other background knowledge (e.g. causal knowledge); hence, the phenomenon of *ad hoc* categories.

- Concept coherence and naturalness emerge from the underlying theoretical knowledge of concepts, not from similarity alone.

- Context effects on concept representations emerge from the way the concepts come to be constructed in working memory using background knowledge (e.g. a lifting or playing sentential-context for a piano, results in *weight*, and *musical* attributes becoming salient, respectively).

family-resemblance account would predict. Further exploration revealed that subjects abandoned this uni-dimensional sorting strategy in favour of a strategy that used several dimensions when the item had causally related, correlated properties. That is, when subjects were given conceptual knowledge that made inter-property relationships more salient, family-resemblance sorting became very common. The moral being that correlated-attribute dimensions are really only used in sorting when there is some background knowledge or theory that connects them together.

Finally, one of the earliest findings in concept formation was that conjunctive concepts were easier to learn than disjunctive concepts (see Bruner et al., 1956). So, for example, it is easier for people to learn a concept called DRAF consisting of the conjoined features —*black* and *round* and *furry* — than when its features are disjunctive — "black OR round OR furry". Pazzani (1991a) has demonstrated a reversal of this phenomenon when the disjunctive concept is consistent with background knowledge. In this study, groups of subjects were shown pictures of people (adults or children) carrying out actions (stretching or dipping in water) with balloons of different colours and sizes. One set of instructions required subjects to determine whether a given stimulus situation (e.g. a child dipping a large, yellow balloon in water) was an *alpha* situation. Another set of instructions required subjects to predict whether the balloon would *inflate* after the stimulus event. Groups receiving either of these instructions had to learn either a conjunctive concept (size-small and balloon-yellow) or a disjunctive concept (age-adult *or* action-stretching-balloon). Pazzani established that most people know that stretching a balloon makes it easier to inflate and that adults can inflate balloons more easily than children (but note that this knowledge does not correspond directly to the disjunctive definition subjects had to learn).

Pazzani found that the alpha groups found the conjunctive concept easier to acquire than the disjunctive concept (see Fig. 11.4). As in previous

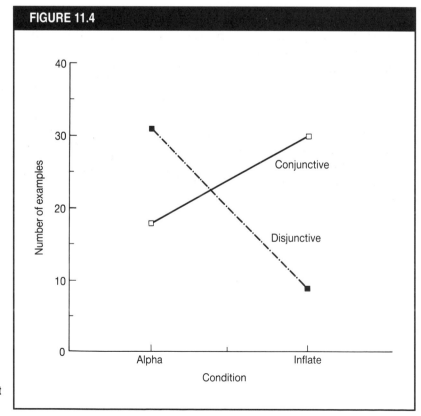

FIGURE 11.4

From Pazzani (1991a, Experiment 1), the ease of learning (as measured by number of examples taken to learn a concept) either a conjunctive or disjunctive concept as a function of the instructions given (to classify as alpha, or predict inflation). The disjunctive concept is consistent with background knowledge on the ease of inflating balloons, whereas the conjunctive concept violates this knowledge.

research, this result occurred because the background knowledge about inflating balloons was irrelevant to learning the alpha categorisation. However, in conditions receiving the instructions to predict inflation of the balloon the opposite was found; the group learning the disjunctive concept found it easier to learn than the conjunctive concept. This was due to the fact that subjects' background knowledge informed the formation of the disjunctive concept but did not support the learning of the conjunctive-inflate concept. Pazzani developed a computational model of these phenomena and confirmed several further simulations empirically. This work is a very important and concrete demonstration of the effects that background knowledge can have on concept formation and conceptualistation (see also Ahn, Brewer, & Mooney, 1992; Pazzani, 1990, 1993; Rips & Collins, 1993; for further more recent work).

CHAPTER SUMMARY

We concluded the previous chapter with two questions. First, how do we deal with more complex knowledge structures beyond object concepts, like relations and schemata? Second, how can attribute-based theories of object concepts be extended to included the theory-knowledge required to explain concept combination and other phenomena? Hopefully, we now have answers to both of these questions.

In this chapter, we have reviewed some of the theoretical proposals on the nature of relational concepts. We have seen that they are typically characterised as schematic structures and that these same structures can be used to handle more complex forms of knowledge (e.g. events, themes, and stereotypical sequences of events). We have also considered how object concepts can be modelled from this perspective in the explanation-based view.

Much still remains to be done in this research area. Essentially, the explanation-based view needs to be reconciled with the bulk of evidence amassed within the attribute-based tradition. This is a task that will require further theoretical development of this view and should entertain the research community for some time to come.

FURTHER READING

Pazzani, M. (1990). *Creating a memory of causal relationships.* Hillsdale, NJ: Lawrence Erlbaum Associates Inc. This book provides a full computational account of how concept learning can occur within a schematic framework.

Schank, R.C. (1982). *Dynamic memory.* Cambridge: Cambridge University Press. All of Schank's books are very readable and interesting. They constitute a good account of an attempt to push the explicit schema view to its limits.

Schank, R.C., & Abelson, R. (1977). *Scripts, plans, goals and understanding.* Hillsdale, NJ: Lawrence Erlbaum Associates Inc.

Van Mechelen, I., Hampton, J., Michalski, R.S., & Theuns, P. (1993). *Concepts and categories.* London: Academic Press. This is a recent collection of articles on prominent areas in concept research.

12

Speech Perception and Reading

INTRODUCTION

One of the fundamental ways in which humanity excels is in its use of language. Indeed, language is of such fundamental importance to human cognition that we will be devoting this chapter and the following two to an exploration of its many facets. In this chapter, we will focus on some of the basic processes involved in listening to speech and in reading. For many purposes, it may not make much difference whether a message is presented to our ears or to our eyes. For example, we would normally understand a sentence such as "You have done exceptionally well in your cognitive psychology examination" in much the same way regardless of whether we hear it or read it. Thus, many of the processes involved in comprehension are the same or highly similar whether we are reading a text or listening to someone talking.

In spite of the similarities, speech perception and reading differ in a number of significant ways. One important difference is that in reading, each word can be seen as a whole, whereas a spoken word is spread out in time. A more important difference between speech perception and reading is that speech generally provides a much more ambiguous and unclear signal than does printed text. When words were spliced out of spoken sentences and presented on their own, they were recognised only approximately half the time (Lieberman, 1963). Anyone who has studied a foreign language at school will remember the initial shock at being totally unable to understand the extremely rapid and apparently uninterrupted flow of speech produced by a native speaker of that language.

There are other significant differences. The demands on memory are greater when we are listening to speech than reading a text, because the words that have already been spoken are no longer accessible. So far, we have indicated ways in which listening to speech is more difficult than reading a text. However, there is at least one major way in which listening to speech is easier than reading. Speech usually contains numerous hints to sentence structure and the intended meaning, in the form of variations in the speaker's pitch, intonation, stress, and timing (e.g. a rising intonation on the last word in a sentence typically indicates that a question is being asked). These various hints are known collectively as *prosodic cues*. In contrast, the main cues to sentence structure in text are punctuation marks (e.g. commas, semi-colons), and these are often less informative than the prosodic cues contained in speech.

The fact that listening to speech and reading are quite different in some ways can be demonstrated most easily by considering children and brain-damaged patients. Young children often have good comprehension of spoken language, but struggle to read even simple stories. As we will see later in the chapter, there are some adult brain-damaged patients who can understand spoken language but cannot read properly, and there are others who can read perfectly well but cannot understand the spoken word.

Basic processes specific to listening to speech are dealt with first in the chapter, followed by a consideration of basic processes specific to reading. The subsequent language comprehension processes that are common to listening and to reading are discussed in the next chapter. However, the alert reader may spot the occasional deviation from this structure, which occurs in the interests of providing a coherent account.

LISTENING TO SPEECH

There has been some controversy about the size of the basic acoustic unit in speech perception, but it is generally thought that it corresponds approximately to the syllable. Some relevant evidence was obtained by Huggins (1964). Subjects listened to a stream of speech which switched backwards and forwards from one ear to the other. It was easy to follow the message when there were either 20 switches per second or only one, but it was very difficult to understand at intermediate rates of switching. Huggins assumed that maximal disruption would occur when each speech segment was somewhat smaller than the basic unit in speech perception. The most disruptive rate corresponded to 60% of the length of the average syllable, which supports the view that the syllable is of particular importance in speech perception.

Problems of speech perception

Accurate perception of speech is a more complex achievement than might be imagined, partly because language is spoken at a rate of up to 10 phonemes per second (Liberman, Cooper,

Shankweiler, & Studdert-Kennedy, 1967). As a consequence, phonemes (basic speech sounds) overlap and there is co-articulation, in which producing one speech segment affects the production of the following segment. This is sometimes referred to as the "linearity problem".

Another problem related to the linearity problem is the "non-invariance problem". This problem arises because the sound pattern for a particular speech component such as a phoneme (a sound unit conveying meaning) is not invariant; rather, it is affected by the sound or sounds preceding and following it. This is especially the case for consonants, because their sound patterns often depend on the following vowel.

A further problem is that speech typically consists of a continuously changing pattern of sound with relatively few periods of silence. This contrasts with our perception of speech as consisting of a series of separate sounds. The continuous nature of the speech signal produces the "segmentation problem" (i.e. deciding how the continuous stream of sound should be divided up into words).

The linearity, invariance, and segmentation problems experienced by listeners to speech were summarised in terms of an interesting analogy by Hockett (1955, p.210):

Imagine a row of Easter eggs carried along a moving belt; the eggs are of various sizes, and variously coloured, but not boiled. At a certain point, the belt carries the row of eggs between the two rollers of a wringer, which quite effectively smash them and rub them more or less into each other. The flow of eggs before the wringer represents the series of impulses from the phoneme source; the mess that emerges from the wringer represents the output of the speech transmitter. At a subsequent point, we have an inspector whose task it is to examine the passing mess and decide, on the basis of the broken and unbroken yolks, the variously spread-out albumen, and the variously coloured bits of shell, the nature of the flow of eggs which previously arrived at the wringer.

Spectrograms

Much valuable information about characteristics of the speech signal has been obtained from use of an instrument known as a *spectrograph*. In essence, sound enters through a microphone, and is then converted into an electrical signal. This signal is fed to a bank of filters selecting narrow-frequency bands. Finally, the spectrograph produces a visible record of the component frequencies of sound over time; this is known as a *spectrogram* (see Fig. 12.1). The spectrogram provides information about *formants*, which are frequency bands emphasised by the vocal apparatus when saying a phoneme. Vowels have three formants; these are numbered first, second, and third, beginning with the formant of lowest frequency. Even though vowels have three formants, they can usually be identified on the basis of the first two formants. The spectrogram reveals that most vowel sounds fall below 1200 Hertz (Hz), which is a measure of sound frequency; in contrast, many consonants have sounds falling in the region from 2400 Hz upwards.

Spectrograms may appear to provide an accurate picture of those aspects of the sound wave having the greatest influence on the human auditory system, but this is not necessarily the case.

For example, formants look important in a spectrogram, but this does not prove that they are of value in human speech perception. However, reasonably convincing evidence that the spectrogram is of value has been provided by making use of a *pattern playback* or *vocoder*, which allows the spectrograph to be played back. In other words, the pattern of frequencies in the spectrogram was produced by speech, and pattern playback permits the spectrogram to be re-converted into speech again. Liberman, Delattre, and Cooper (1952) constructed "artificial" vowels on the spectrogram based only on the first two formants of each vowel. They discovered that these vowels were easily identified when they were played through the vocoder, indicating that formant information is used to recognise vowels.

Spectrograms were also investigated by Cole, Rudnisky, Zue, and Reddy (1980). Victor Zue was successful in learning to interpret spectrograms with a high degree of accuracy, indicating that they contain a considerable amount of useful information. The richness of information in speech sounds presumably offsets the difficulties for listeners posed by the linearity, non-invariance, and segmentation problems.

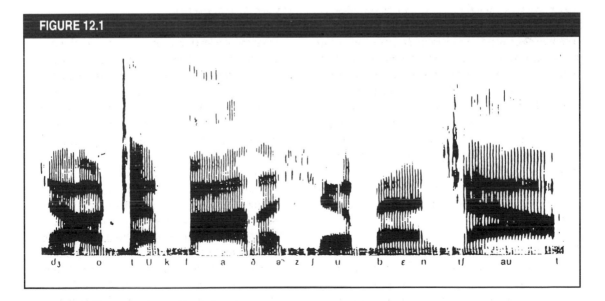

FIGURE 12.1

Spectrogram of the sentence "Joe took father's shoe bench out". From *Language Processes* by Vivien C. Tartter (1986, p.210).

Speech perception and auditory perception

Speech perception differs from other kinds of auditory perception in a number of ways. For example, there is a definite left-hemisphere advantage for perception of speech that does not extend to other auditory stimuli. Speech perception also appears to exhibit what is known as "categorical perception": listeners generally show superior ability to discriminate between a pair of sounds belonging to different phonetic categories (e.g. "ba" and "pa") compared to a pair of sounds belonging to the same category (Repp, 1984, provides a review). For example, the Japanese language does not distinguish between [l] and [r]; as these sounds belong to the same category for Japanese listeners, it is no surprise that they find it extremely difficult to discriminate between them. This is different from the case with ordinary sounds, where discrimination between pairs of sounds is superior to the ability to label them as belonging to separate categories.

The major differences between speech perception and auditory perception in general led Mattingly and Liberman (1990) to argue that speech perception involves a special module or cognitive processor functioning independently of other modules (the notion of a "module" is discussed in Chapter 1). This theory can be evaluated by considering some of the criteria for modularity proposed by Fodor (1983). According to him, modules are innate, and they exhibit informational encapsulation or independence of functioning from other modules. The innateness issue can be addressed by considering speech perception in infants. There is some evidence that infants notice changes between speech categories but not those within speech categories (Eimas, 1985), and this suggests that aspects of speech perception might be innate. Other evidence (e.g. Eimas, Miller, & Jusczyk, 1987) confirms that infants possess surprisingly good speech-perception skills.

The issue of whether speech perception demonstrates informational encapsulation, and is thus independent from other cognitive processes in its functioning, was addressed by Remez, Rubin, Pisoni, and Carrell (1981). According to them, utilisation of the speech perception module (if it exists) should not be influenced by some quite separate factor such as the listener's belief about the nature of the signal. They played a specially prepared series of tones to two groups of subjects. One group was told that they would be listening to synthetic or artificial speech, and their task was to write down what was said. These subjects had no difficulty in carrying out this task. The other group was simply told to describe what they heard; they reported hearing electronic sounds, tape-recorder problems, radio interference, and so on, but they did not perceive any speech. The dependence of speech processing on the manipulation of the listeners' expectations suggests that speech perception does not demonstrate informational encapsulation, and so does not involve a special module.

Section summary

It is probable that some of the mechanisms involved in speech perception are different from those required for other forms of auditory perception. It is also likely that infants possess many of the processes involved in speech perception. However, the available evidence (such as the study by Remez et al., 1981) does not justify the assumption that there is a specialised module for speech perception.

Word recognition

One of the key issues in research on speech perception is to identify the processes involved in spoken word recognition. There is now a considerable body of evidence on this topic (see Lively, Pisoni, & Goldinger, 1994, for a review). We will first consider some of the major processes involved, and will then turn to a discussion of influential theories of spoken word recognition.

Bottom-up and top-down processes

There is general agreement that spoken word recognition is generally achieved by a combination of bottom-up or data-driven processes triggered by the acoustic signal, and top-down or conceptually driven processes generated from the linguistic context. However, as we will see later, there have been disagreements about precisely how information from bottom-up and top-down processes is combined to produce word recognition.

Spoken language consists of a series of sounds or phonemes, each of which incorporates various features. Among the features for phonemes are the following: *manner of production* (oral vs. nasal vs. fricative, involving a partial blockage of the airstream); *place of articulation*; and *voicing* (the larynx vibrates for a voiced but not for a voiceless phoneme). The notion that bottom-up processes in word recognition make use of feature information was supported in a classic study by Miller and Nicely (1955). They gave their subjects the task of recognising consonants that were presented auditorily against a background of noise. The key finding was that the most frequently confused consonants were those that differed from each other on the basis of only one feature.

Convincing evidence that top-down processes based on context can be involved in speech perception was obtained by Warren and Warren (1970). They investigated what is known as the *phonemic restoration effect*. Twenty people were presented with a recording of the sentence: "The state governors met with their respective legi*latures convening in the capital city." The asterisk indicates a 0.12-second portion of the recorded sentence that had been removed and replaced with the sound of a cough. Warren and Warren found that all but one of their subjects claimed there was no missing sound, and the remaining subject identified the wrong sound as missing.

Warren and Warren (1970) then modified the basic experimental technique slightly to provide a more striking demonstration of the ways in which top-down processing based on stored knowledge can affect perception. Their subjects were presented with one of the following sentences (the asterisk indicates a deleted portion of the sentence):

- It was found that the *eel was on the axle.
- It was found that the *eel was on the shoe.
- It was found that the *eel was on the table.
- It was found that the *eel was on the orange.

The perception of the crucial element in the sentence (i.e. "*eel") was much affected by sentence context. Subjects listening to the first sentence tended to hear "wheel", those listening to the second sentence heard "heel", whereas those exposed to the third and fourth sentences heard "meal" and "peel", respectively. All the subjects heard the same speech sound (i.e. "*eel"), so what differed was the contextual information that was available.

Samuel (1981) pointed out that there are two possible explanations for the effects of context in the phonemic restoration effect. First, the context may interact directly with bottom-up processes; this would be a sensitivity effect. Second, the context may simply provide an additional source of information which is taken into account by the listener; this would be a response bias effect. In one of Samuel's (1981) experiments, subjects listened to sentences, and meaningless noise was presented briefly during each sentence. On some trials, this noise was superimposed on one of the phonemes of a word in the sentence; on other trials, that phoneme was deleted. The subject's task was to decide whether or not the crucial phoneme had been presented. A final aspect of the design was that the word containing this phoneme was either predictable or unpredictable from its sentence context.

Performance in Samuel's study was better when the word was predictable than when it was unpredictable, indicating the importance of context. If context improves sensitivity, then the ability to discriminate between phoneme plus noise and noise alone should be improved by predictable context. If context affects response bias, then subjects should simply be more likely to decide that the phoneme was present when the word was presented in a predictable context. The findings indicated that context affected response bias but not sensitivity, suggesting that contextual information did not have a direct effect on bottom-up processing.

Prosodic patterns

Most spoken speech contains prosodic cues in the form of stress, intonation, and so on. This information can be used by the listener to work out the syntactic or grammatical structure of each sentence. For example, in the ambiguous sentence,

"The old men and women sat on the bench", the women may or may not be old. If the women are not old, then the spoken duration of the word "men" will be relatively long, and the stressed syllable in "women" will have a steep rise in pitch contour. Neither of these prosodic features will be present if the sentence means that the women are old.

Most of the studies on listeners' ability to use prosody to interpret ambiguous sentences have only assessed this after an entire sentence has been presented. These studies have established that prosodic patterns are generally interpreted correctly, but they do not indicate whether prosodic information is used during presentation of the sentence or only after it has finished. This issue was addressed by Beach (1990). Subjects heard a sentence fragment, and then had to decide which of two sentences it had come from. For example, the fragment "Sherlock Holmes didn't suspect" could be from the sentence "Sherlock Holmes didn't suspect the beautiful young countess from Hungary" or the sentence "Sherlock Holmes didn't suspect the beautiful young countess could be a fraud". Subjects were reasonably accurate at predicting the overall structure of sentences on the basis of a small fragment, indicating that prosodic information can be used rapidly by listeners without needing to hear the entire sentence.

Lip-reading

Many people (especially those who are hard of hearing) are aware that they make some use of lip-reading to understand what someone is saying to them. However, this seems to happen to a far greater extent than is generally believed among those whose hearing is entirely normal. McGurk and MacDonald (1976) provided a striking demonstration of the importance of lip-reading. They prepared a videotape of someone repeating "ba" over and over again, but then changed the sound channel so there was a voice saying "ga" repeatedly in synchronisation with the lip movements. Subjects reported that they heard "da" rather than either "ga" or "ba", representing almost literally a blending of the visual and the auditory information.

The reason why visual information from lip movements is used to make sense of speech sounds is presumably because the information conveyed by the speech sounds is often inadequate (cf. Lieberman, 1963). Much is now known about the ways in which visual information provided by the speaker is used in speech perception (see Dodd & Campbell, 1986). Of course, there are circumstances (e.g. listening to the radio) in which no relevant visual information is available. We can usually follow what is said on the radio because broadcasters are trained to articulate clearly.

Theories of word recognition

There are several theories of spoken word recognition, three of which will be discussed here. The first theory (motor theory of speech perception) is of historical importance, and merits inclusion for that reason. The other two theories (cohort theory and the TRACE model) have been especially important and influential in recent years, and incorporate much contemporary wisdom.

Motor theory of speech perception

The key issue in speech perception is to explain how it is that listeners perceive words accurately even though the speech signal typically provides variable and inconsistent information. Liberman et al. (1967) gave an influential explanation in their motor theory of speech perception. In essence, they argued that listeners engage in a certain amount of mimicking of the articulatory movements of the speaker, but this need not involve measurable articulatory responses. The motor signal thus produced was claimed to provide much less variable and inconsistent information about what the speaker is saying than is given in the speech signal itself. In other words, the motor signal produced by articulation is more informative than the speech signal, and it is our reliance on the motor signal that allows spoken word recognition to be reasonably accurate.

Some evidence consistent with the motor theory was reported by Dorman, Raphael, and Liberman (1979). A tape was made of the sentence, "Please say shop," and a 50 millisecond period of silence was inserted between "say" and "shop." As a consequence, the sentence was misheard as "Please say chop". Our speech musculature forces us to pause between "say" and "chop", but not between "say" and "shop", and so the evidence from internal articulation would favour the wrong interpretation of the last word in the sentence.

Unfortunately for the motor theory, the major assumption that the motor signal provides invariant information about speech segments is incorrect. There are, for example, as many different motor manifestations of a given consonant as there are acoustic manifestations (MacNeilage, 1972). Such findings rather undermine the main reason for proposing the motor theory in the first place.

It follows from the motor theory that infants with limited expertise in articulation of speech should be very poor at speech perception. In fact, as we have seen, infants typically perform extremely well on a variety of tests of speech perception (e.g. Eimas et al., 1987). Thus, the ability to produce and make use of the motor signal does not appear to be necessary for good levels of speech perception. There are other findings that are difficult to reconcile with motor theory. For example, simultaneous translators can listen to speech in one language while producing fluent speech in another language at the same time, and it is difficult to see how this could happen on the motor theory.

In spite of experimental disconfirmations of aspects of the motor theory, it has influenced contemporary thinking. For example, one of the attractive features of motor theory was that it drew a clear distinction between the processing of speech and the processing of other auditory stimuli. A related position has been adopted by those contemporary theorists (e.g. Mattingly & Liberman, 1990) who argue that there is a separate module for speech perception.

Cohort theory

One of the most influential theories of spoken word recognition was proposed by Marslen-Wilson and Tyler (1980). This theory incorporated the following assumptions:

• Early in the auditory presentation of a word, those words known to the listener that conform to the sound sequence that has been heard so far become active; this collection of candidates for the presented word is the "word-initial cohort"

• words belonging to this cohort are then eliminated because they cease to match further information from the presented word, or because they are inconsistent with the semantic or other context.

• Processing of the presented word needs to continue only until contextual information and information from the word itself is sufficient to eliminate all but one of the words in the word-initial cohort; this is known as the "recognition point" of a word.

According to cohort theory, various knowledge sources (e.g. lexical, syntactic, semantic) interact and combine with each other in complex ways to produce an efficient analysis of spoken language. This approach can be contrasted with the notion (e.g. Forster, 1979) that processing proceeds in a serial fashion, with spoken language being analysed in a relatively fixed and invariant series of processing stages. As we will see, the evidence favours the interactive approach of cohort theory over the alternative serial processing approach

Marslen-Wilson and Tyler (1980) tested some of their theoretical notions in a word-monitoring task, in which subjects had to identify pre-specified target words presented within spoken sentences. There were normal sentences, syntactic sentences (grammatically correct but meaningless), and random sentences (unrelated words), and the target was a member of a given category, a word that rhymed with a given word, or a word that was identical to a given word. The measure of interest was the speed with which the target could be detected.

It is predicted by cohort theory that sensory information from the target word and contextual information from the rest of the sentence are both used at the same time in word recognition. In contrast, it is predicted by serial theories that sensory information is extracted prior to the use of contextual information. The results conformed more closely to the predictions of cohort theory than to those of a serial model. As can be seen in Fig. 12.2, complete sensory analysis of the longer words was not needed when there was adequate contextual information. It was only necessary to listen to the entire word when the sentence context

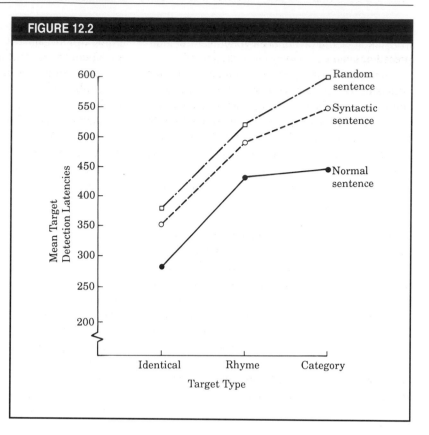

FIGURE 12.2

Detection times for word targets presented in sentences. Adapted from Marslen-Wilson and Tyler (1980).

contained no useful syntactic or semantic information (i.e. in the random word order condition)

Additional support for the interactive approach of cohort theory comes from a consideration of the great speed of word recognition in the normal sentence context. In that context, subjects initiated their responses approximately 200 milliseconds after the onset of the target word when it was identical to the given word. This figure should be compared against the mean spoken duration of target words, which was 369 milliseconds. The first 200 milliseconds of a word typically correspond to the first two phonemes of a word, and there are usually numerous English words consistent with those two phonemes. Therefore, contextual information must be used very early in processing. This is assumed by interactive models, such as cohort theory, but is rather inconsistent with serial models in which contextual information is used only after several processes have occurred.

Evaluation

The general approach to spoken word recognition adopted by Marslen-Wilson and Tyler (1980) is a valuable one. However, it is limited in a number of ways. For example, too much significance is given to the initial part of the word in cohort theory. It is assumed that a spoken word will generally not be recognised if its initial phoneme is unclear or ambiguous, but this is often not correct. Connine, Blasko, and Titone (1993) referred to a study in which a spoken word ending in "ent" had an ambiguous initial phoneme somewhere between "d" and "t". The theory predicts that neither of the words "dent" or "tent" would be activated, but in fact they both were.

The major problem with the initial version of cohort theory was its assumption that spoken word recognition proceeds in an extremely efficient fashion. In fact, processing is often less efficient than is assumed by the theory. For example, Bard, Shillcock, and Altmann (1988) found that under relatively unfavourable listening conditions subjects made use of *subsequent* (rather than preceding) context to identify spoken words.

Marslen-Wilson (1990) responded to the criticisms by producing a modified version of cohort theory which is better able to account for relatively inefficient spoken word recognition. In the original version of the theory, words were either in or out of the word cohort; in the revised version, candidate words vary in their level of activation, and so membership of the word cohort is now more a matter of degree. It is now assumed that the word-initial cohort contains words having phonetically similar initial phonemes, rather than being limited exclusively to words possessing the initial phoneme of the presented word. These, and other, changes to cohort theory allow it to account for findings such as those of Bard et al. (1988) and Connine et al. (1993). The major disadvantage with the revised version of cohort theory follows from the fact that many of the theoretical assumptions have been weakened. As a consequence, it is more difficult to derive testable predictions from the revised version than from the original theory.

TRACE model

McClelland and Elman (1986) and McClelland (1991) produced a network model of speech perception based on connectionist principles (see Chapter 1). Their TRACE model of speech perception resembles cohort theory in some ways. For example, it is argued within both cohort theory and the TRACE model that several sources of information combine interactively to achieve word recognition. It is also worth mentioning that the TRACE model is similar in some ways to the inter-active activation model of visual word recognition put forward by McClelland and Rumelhart (1981), which is discussed later in the chapter.

The TRACE model is based on the following theoretical assumptions:

- There are individual processing units or nodes at three different levels: features (e.g. voicing; manner of production), phonemes, and words.
- Feature nodes are connected to phoneme nodes, and phoneme nodes are connected to word nodes.

- Connections between levels operate in both directions, and are only facilitatory.
- There are connections among units or nodes at the same level; these connections are inhibitory.
- Nodes influence each other in proportion to their activation levels and the strengths of their interconnections.
- As excitation and inhibition spread among nodes, a pattern of activation or trace develops.
- The word that is recognised is determined by the activation level of the possible candidate words.

One of the key characteristics of the TRACE model is the assumption that bottom-up and top-down processing interact during speech perception. Bottom-up activation proceeds upwards from the feature level to the phoneme level and on to the word level, whereas top-down activation proceeds in the opposite direction from the word level to the phoneme level and on to the feature level. Strong evidence that top-down processes are involved in spoken word recognition was discussed earlier in the chapter (e.g. Marslen-Wilson & Tyler, 1980; Warren & Warren, 1970).

Much of the evidence discussed already in this chapter is consistent with the TRACE model. In addition, Elman and McClelland (1988) tested the assumption that activation of a phoneme node produced by top-down processes has the same effect as its activation by bottom-up processes. As was mentioned earlier, a speaker's articulation of one speech segment can be distorted by his or her articulation of the previous speech segment; this is termed "co-articulation". Evidence that listeners take co-articulation into account during speech perception was obtained by Elman and McClelland (1988). They produced a set of speech sounds ranging between "tapes" and "capes", and found that subjects were more likely to perceive "capes" following "Christmas" than following "foolish". Presumably this occurred because bottom-up processing caused the final phonemes of "Christmas" and "foolish" to be activated, and listeners then took co-articulation into account.

Elman and McClelland (1988) next decided to find out whether the phenomenon could be produced solely by top-down processing. To do this, an ambiguous sound midway between the final sounds of "Christmas" and of "foolish" replaced the original sounds. They still found that "capes" was more likely to be perceived after "Christmas" than after "foolish", even though the immediately preceding phoneme was the same in both conditions. This happened because the phoneme that normally comes at the end of each word was activated by top-down processes operating at the word level (i.e. the listeners expected the words "Christmas" and "foolish" to end on different phonemes). Thus, these findings substantiate the notion that top-down processes can affect phoneme activation in the same way as bottom-up processes.

Evaluation

Spoken word recognition is a temporally extended event, in the sense that the underlying processes take some time to reduce the number of candidate words to only one. This notion is fully incorporated into the TRACE model, because the excitatory and inhibitory processes that ultimately lead to word recognition change dynamically over time as additional information becomes available. Another strength of the TRACE model is its assumption that bottom-up and top-down processes interact and combine to achieve spoken word recognition. The processes involved are made explicit by assuming that there are bi-directional connections between the various levels of representation (i.e. feature; phoneme; word).

The major limitation of the TRACE model is that it appears to exaggerate the importance of top-down processes. There is reasonable evidence of top-down effects from the word level when stimuli are degraded, but much less when they are not. For example, Elman and McClelland (1988) used slightly degraded stimuli in their experimental demonstration of top-down effects, but these effects could not be replicated when the stimuli were not degraded (see Norris, 1994). In a study by Frauenfelder, Segui, and Dijkstra (1990) on non-degraded stimuli, subjects were given the task of detecting a given phoneme. The key condition was one in which a non-word closely resembling an actual word was presented (e.g.

"vocabutaire" instead of "vocabulaire"). Top-down effects from the word node corresponding to "vocabulaire" should have inhibited the task of identifying the "t" in "vocabutaire", but they did not. The implication is that top-down processes did not affect phoneme-level processes in this study.

Another significant limitation of the TRACE model is that its architecture is rather implausible. As Norris (1994) pointed out, the TRACE model requires there to be multiple copies of the basic lexical network. If an utterance consists of 40 phonemes, then there need to be 40 lexical networks to process it.

Finally, tests of the model have relied heavily on computer simulations involving a small number of one-syllable words. As a consequence, it is not entirely clear whether the model would perform satisfactorily if applied to the vastly larger vocabularies possessed by most people.

Section summary

The most important general point about theories of spoken word recognition is that they are becoming increasingly similar to each other. As Lively et al. (1994) pointed out, most theorists agree that activation of several candidate words occurs early in the process of word recognition. It is also generally assumed that the speed with which word recognition is usually achieved indicates that most of the processes involved proceed in parallel, or at the same time, rather than occurring serially. There is also general agreement that the activation levels of candidate words are graded rather than being either very high or very low. Finally, nearly all theorists agree that bottom-up and top-down processes combine in some fashion to produce word recognition. The revised version of cohort theory and the TRACE model are both in line with contemporary thinking in that they incorporate all of these assumptions.

There are two general issues that are in need of further research. First, there is still very little agreement on the size and number of the basic perceptual units in spoken word recognition, with theorists differing in the importance they attach to features, phonemes, syllables, and so on. Second, and more important, there is the issue of precisely how contextual and other forms of top down information are used in spoken word recognition. Most theorists (e.g. Marslen-Wilson, 1990; McClelland, 1990) assume that bottom-up and top-down processes interact directly with each other, but some research (e.g. Samuel, 1981) suggests that top-down processes may influence spoken word recognition in a rather different fashion (i.e. via response bias). It would be valuable to know in detail the factors determining whether or not top-down processes interact with bottom-up processes.

Cognitive neuropsychology of word processing

An apparently simple task is to repeat a spoken word immediately after hearing it. However, there are many brain-damaged patients who experience difficulties with this task even though audiometric testing reveals that they are not deaf. Detailed analysis of these patients suggests there are various processes that can be used to permit repetition of a spoken word.

Information from such patients was used by Ellis and Young (1988) to propose a model of the processing of spoken words (see Fig. 12.3). In essence, the model consists of five components:

- The *auditory analysis system* is used to extract phonemes or other sounds from the speech wave.
- The *auditory input lexicon* contains information about spoken words known to the listener, but does not contain information about their meaning; the purpose of the auditory input lexicon is to recognise familiar words via the activation of the appropriate word units.
- The meanings of words are stored within the *semantic system* (cf. semantic memory, which is discussed in Chapter 10).
- The speech output lexicon serves to provide the spoken forms of words.
- Speech sounds themselves are available at the phoneme level.
- These components can be used in various combinations, so that there are three different routes between hearing a spoken word and saying it.

It will be noticed in Fig. 12.3 that there is a bi directional arrow linking the auditory input lexicon and the semantic system. We saw earlier that Marslen-Wilson and Tyler (1980) found evidence that word recognition is affected by the semantic context in which a word is presented, and the arrow going from the semantic system to the auditory input lexicon acknowledges such evidence.

The most striking feature of the model is the notion that saying a spoken word can be achieved using three different routes. It is this feature of their model to which we will devote the most attention.

Route 1

This route makes use of the auditory input lexicon, the semantic system, and the speech output lexicon. It represents the normal way in which familiar words are identified and comprehended by those with no brain damage. If a brain-damaged patient could use only this route, then one would expect familiar words to be said correctly. However, there would be severe problems with saying unfamiliar words and non-words, because they do not have entries in the auditory input lexicon, and therefore require use of Route 3.

McCarthy and Warrington (1984) described a patient, ORF, who fits the bill reasonably well. ORF repeated words much more accurately than non-words (85% vs. 39%, respectively), indicating that Route 3 was severely impaired. However, the fact that he made a fair number of errors in repeating words suggests there was also some impairment to other parts of the system.

Route 2

If a patient could use Route 2 (and possibly Route 3), but Route 1 was severely impaired, one would expect that he or she would be able to repeat familiar words but would often find it difficult to understand their meaning. Patients suffering from a condition known as "word-meaning deafness" seem to fit this description. Ellis (1984) has reprinted the case of a young woman suffering from word-meaning deafness which was originally reported by Bramwell (1897). She could understand written sentences reasonably well, and she could say sentences that were spoken to her,

FIGURE 12.3

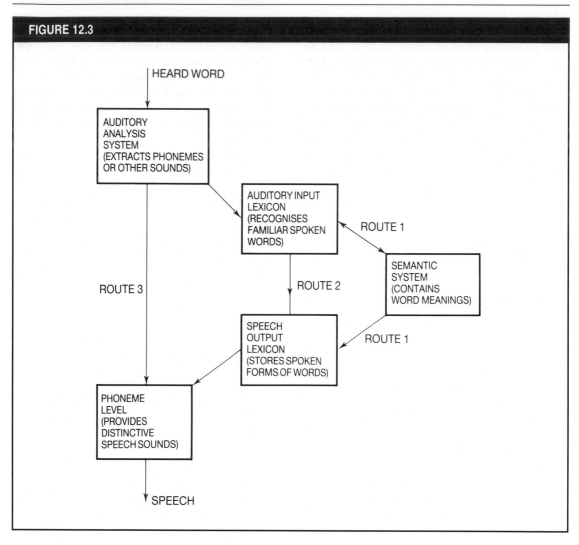

Processing and repetition of spoken words. Adapted from Ellis and Young (1988).

and even write them down to dictation. However, she found it very difficult to understand things that were said to her. When she was asked, "Do you like to come to Edinburgh?", she failed to understand the question. When she wrote the question down, however, it made sense to her.

Two additional cases of word-meaning deafness were reported by Kohn and Friedman (1986). Their symptoms resembled those of Bramwell's (1897) patient, but were rather less severe. Although the precise nature of the impairment producing this condition is not known for certain, Ellis and Young (1988, p.155) suggested it may represent "a complete or partial disconnection of the auditory input lexicon from the semantic system". This seems reasonable, because the ability of patients with word-meaning deafness to understand written words implies that the semantic system is relatively intact, and their ability to write to dictation implies that the auditory input lexicon is unimpaired. If there were problems of communication between the auditory input lexicon and the semantic system, the main consequence would be a difficulty in understanding spoken words, and that is precisely what is involved in word-meaning deafness.

Route 3

If a patient were to use only Route 3, then one would expect heard words and non-words to be repeated reasonably accurately, but with very poor comprehension. There do not appear to be any reported cases indicating precisely this pattern. However, McCarthy and Warrington (1984) reported on a patient, ART, who seemed to make use of Route 3. This patient had rather poor spontaneous speech, but he was consistently good at repeating spoken words regardless of whether they were common or rare. He was actually worse at repeating a word when it was preceded by an appropriate semantic context, suggesting that he could not take advantage of the semantic system to facilitate word recognition. However, the failure to investigate ART's ability to repeat non-words, which should theoretically have been good, means it is difficult to identify the precise nature of his impairment.

Deep dysphasia

Some brain-damaged patients have been found to make semantic errors when they are asked to repeat spoken words (i.e. they say words that are related in meaning to the words they are supposed to be saying). These patients have sometimes been termed "deep dysphasics". One of the most interesting cases was reported by Michel and Andreewsky (1983). Their patient made numerous semantic errors when repeating spoken words, but not when reading aloud. He was unable to repeat non-words, suggesting that he could not make use of Route 3. Presumably such a patient has a number of different impairments, so that none of the three routes between heard words and speech is intact. Route 1 is the route most commonly employed, but some impairment in or near the semantic system makes this route rather fallible.

Section summary

There has been relatively little research on auditory word recognition and comprehension in brain-damaged patients. As a result, it would be premature to draw any sweeping conclusions on the basis of the cognitive neuropsychological evidence. However, it has been established that there are different patterns of impairment in the ability to repeat and to understand spoken words. This encourages the belief that there are a number of separate components involved, and that there is more than one route between hearing a word and then saying it. Figure 12.3 represents a possible set of components and their interactions, but its validity will become clear only after considerable further research.

Cognitive neuropsychological research in this area has emphasised the differences between listening to speech and reading. For example, patients with word-meaning deafness can often understand written sentences reasonably well, but cannot make sense of the same sentences when spoken to them. This indicates strongly that rather different theories are needed to explain what happens when linguistic material is presented to our ears and to our eyes.

BASIC READING PROCESSES

Reading is an apparently straightforward and effortless activity for most adults. However, observation of young children struggling to make sense of simple stories provides some indication of its true complexity. Reading requires several different perceptual and other cognitive processes, as well as a good knowledge of language and of grammar. Indeed, almost all mental activities are related in some way to reading, and reading is sometimes referred to as "visually guided thinking".

Why is it important to investigate the skills involved in reading? Skilled reading has much value in contemporary society, and adults who fail to develop effective reading skills are at a great disadvantage. There are, thus, considerable practical benefits to be gained from discovering enough about the processes involved in reading to be able to sort out the problems of poor readers.

Some of the processes involved in reading are concerned with identifying and extracting meaning from individual words. Other processes operate at the level of the phrase or sentence, and still other processes deal with the overall organisation or thematic structure of an entire story or book.

However, research on reading is substantially biased in favour of some of these processes at the expense of others. As Ellis (1993, p.35) pointed out: "Scanning the literature on skilled reading, one could be forgiven for thinking that the goal of reading is to turn print into speech. Of course, it is not: the goal of reading is to understand (perhaps even to enjoy) a piece of text."

Research methods in reading research

There are several methods available for studying reading. Probably the most generally useful method is that of recording *eye movements* during reading (see Rayner & Sereno, 1994, for a review). This method has two particular strengths: (1) it provides a detailed on-line record of attention-related processes; and (2) it is unobtrusive, permitting the reader to read in a reasonably natural way. Indeed, the only major restriction on the reader whose eye movements are being recorded is that he or she should keep his or her head fairly still. The main disadvantage with eye-movement recordings is that it is generally difficult to be sure precisely what processing occurs during each fixation.

Another method that provides an on-line measure of reading involves making recordings of people *reading aloud*. This method permits analysis of the types of errors made in reading, and the ways in which readers react to deliberate inaccuracies in the text (e.g. misspellings) can be assessed. However, there are three main problems with this method. First, it is unnatural for most adults to read aloud. Second, the fact that reading aloud is about half as fast as silent reading suggests there are substantial differences between the two forms of reading. Third, the eye–voice span (the distance the eye is ahead of the voice) is approximately two words. Although this is not much, it nevertheless makes it possible that some of the errors made in reading aloud reflect memorial errors rather than genuine reading errors.

A third method for studying reading is known as *rapid serial visual presentation*. Words (generally one at a time) are presented rapidly in succession to the same part of a screen, so that a text can be read without the reader having to move his or her eyes. Comprehension of short passages is often reasonably good using this technique, even with presentation rates of up to approximately 1000 words a minute. The greatest advantage of the method of rapid serial visual presentation is that it gives the experimenter a considerable amount of control over what is presented and for how long. However, the method has the serious disadvantage that it differs from normal reading in at least two major ways: (1) it is not possible to re-read any of the text; and (2) the parafoveal processing (processing from outside the high-acuity foveal region) that plays an important role in normal reading is irrelevant when single words are presented at the fixation point.

A fourth method involves *subject-controlled presentation of text*. There are several variations on this method, but the basic notion is that the reader controls the rate of presentation of the text by pushing a button when she or he wants to see the next word or set of words. Just, Carpenter, and Woolley (1982) found a reasonable degree of similarity between the relative times taken to inspect words using this method and under normal reading conditions, but the overall reading rate was considerably slower with subject-controlled presentation. The method has the advantage over eye-movement recordings of being much easier to use, but it has various disadvantages. In particular, the imposition of an unnatural additional task (i.e. button pressing) probably changes the processes involved in reading. This is especially likely to be the case when words are presented singly, because parafoveal processing cannot be used.

A fifth method for studying reading involves a greater diversity of tasks than those that have been considered so far. Rayner and Pollatsek (1989) referred generally to these tasks as *word-identification techniques*, because they allegedly provide a good measure of the time taken for word identification. The tasks used include lexical decision (deciding whether or not a string of letters forms a word) and naming (saying the word out loud as rapidly as possible). For example, subjects might be asked to read sentences in which the final word was either highly or poorly predictable from the preceding context. On some trials, the reading task might be interrupted so that the subjects could perform a lexical decision or naming task on the final word, to see whether predictability affected word-identification time. The greatest advantage of word-identification techniques over eye movements is that they provide the assurance that certain processing has been performed on a given word in a given time, whereas identification may or may not occur during the time that a word is fixated. However, there are clear disadvantages. Normal reading processes are disrupted by the introduction of an additional task, and it is not clear precisely what processes are reflected in lexical decision or naming times.

Section summary
Five different methods for studying reading have been considered, all of which have their weaknesses. However, this is less problematic than it might appear. As Rayner and Pollatsek (1989, pp.186–187) pointed out:

> All methods are flawed, so the best strategy is to attack a question using a combination of methods. If these methods all appear to be converging on the same answer, then one can be reasonably sure that one has discovered something of importance ... if you want to study reading, then the primary data of interest are what happens when people are actually silently reading text. The only data, given the present technology, for studying people actually reading are eye move-ments.

Eye movements in reading
We have the impression that our eyes move smoothly across the page while reading, but this impression is quite mistaken. If you watch someone reading, you will see that their eyes actually move in rapid jerks (generally known as *saccades*). Saccades are ballistic in the sense that once initiated there is no way to change their direction. There are fairly frequent regressions in which the eyes move backwards in the text; these regressions account for 10–15% of all saccades. Saccades take only approximately 10–20 milliseconds to complete, and are separated by fixations lasting for about 200–250 milliseconds (see Rayner & Sereno, 1994).

The length of each saccade is influenced by a variety of factors (e.g. the complexity of the text), but is typically approximately eight letters or spaces. Information is extracted from the text only during each fixation, and not during the intervening saccades. Indeed, even a bright flash of light is generally not perceived if it is presented entirely within a saccade (Latour, 1962).

What determines where successive eye fixations fall? One extreme (and implausible) view is that the process is essentially random, that is, eye fixations are equally likely to occur at any point in the text. A more reasonable position known as cognitive guidance theory was proposed by O'Regan and Levy-Schoen (1987). According to them, fixations are guided by the visual system so that they tend to fall on words and parts of words that will be maximally informative. In line with this theory, they discussed evidence that relatively few fixations fall on punctuation marks, spaces, or very short words, with the word "the" receiving fewer fixations than other three-letter words. Fixations tend to fall on longer words (which are generally more informative than short words), and most fixations occur near the centre of such words. These findings may or may not provide strong support for cognitive guidance theory, but they certainly disprove the notion that eye fixations in reading are random.

An important issue in eye-movement research is that of establishing the amount of text from which useful information is obtained in each fixation. One would expect such information to be relatively limited in terms of the number of words of the text involved because of basic characteristics of the human visual system. There is a small area of high acuity in the centre of the retina known as the *fovea*, and visual perception is much less precise in the parafoveal area outside foveal vision (see Chapter 13). The limitations on intake of information from text have been established by using the "moving window" technique (see Rayner & Sereno, 1994). In essence, most of the text is mutilated except for an experimenter-defined area or window surrounding the reader's point of fixation. Every time the reader moves his or her eyes, different parts of the text are mutilated so as to permit normal reading within the window region. The effects of different-sized windows on reading performance can be compared.

An alternative method of assessing how much text can be processed in a single fixation is the boundary technique. With this technique, the entire text is displayed, but a critical letter or word is altered during a saccade. Evidence about the amount of text being processed can be obtained by varying the distance between the altered letter or word and the point of fixation.

The evidence suggests that the *perceptual span* (effective field of view) is affected to some extent by the difficulty of the text, the size of the print, and so on, but is relatively small under all conditions. It usually extends to no more than approximately three or four letters to the left of fixation and 15 letters to the right (see Fig. 12.4). This asymmetry presumably occurs because the most informative text lies to the right of the fixation point. The form of the asymmetry is clearly learned. Readers of Hebrew, which is read from right to left, show the opposite asymmetry (Pollatsek, Bolozky, Well, & Rayner, 1981). Finally, the perceptual span seems to be confined to the line of text currently being read, as no usable information is extracted from the line below (Pollatsek, Raney, LaGasse, & Rayner, 1993).

We have discussed the size of the perceptual span in terms of the number of letters it contains. However, there is evidence that matters are more complex than that. For example, the left boundary of the perceptual span is generally defined by the beginning of the fixated word (Rayner, Well, & Pollatsek, 1980), whereas the right boundary is defined mainly in terms of the number of letters (Rayner, Well, Pollatsek, & Bertera, 1982). On the basis of the available evidence, Rayner and Sereno (1994) came to the following conclusions:

- Three different spans can be distinguished:
  1. The first is *total perceptual span*, which consists of the total area from which useful information is extracted from a fixation;
  2. The second is *letter-identification span*, which is the area from which information about letters is obtained;
  3. The third is *word-identification span*, which is the area from which information relevant to word-identification processes is obtained.
- The total perceptual span is probably the longest of these three spans, and the word identification span is the shortest.

The size of the perceptual span means that parafoveal information outside the foveal region is used in reading. The relevance of parafoveal information is also shown by the fact that the length of the fixation on a word is shorter if that word was previously presented in the parafoveal part of the perceptual span than when it was not. What information is extracted at the parafoveal level? Rayner, Balota, and Pollatsek (1986) discovered that the fixation time on a word (e.g. tune) was reduced when a visually similar string of letters (e.g. turc) had just been presented to parafoveal vision. However, the processing of information at the parafoveal level does not appear to reach the semantic level (Rayner & Morris, 1992).

Meaning and fixations

It seems reasonable to assume that meaning would affect fixation times. One way in which meaning has an effect is via the context provided by the earlier part of the sentence. A word that is highly predictable on the basis of contextual information is fixated for less time than a relatively

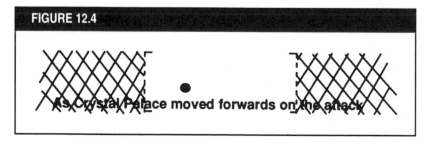

FIGURE 12.4

The perceptual span in reading.

unpredictable word (Balota, Pollatsek, & Rayner, 1985). It has proved surprisingly difficult to account for this finding. It is possible that the word is recognised more rapidly because it was expected. However, Fodor (1983) argued that context does not facilitate word recognition. According to him, word recognition is handled by a module that does not interact with other systems or modules, so that context merely reduces the time needed to integrate a word into the sentence meaning.

There are various arguments to support Fodor's (1983) position. Word recognition for isolated words generally occurs so rapidly and automatically in adult readers (see the next section) that there would probably be little benefit to be gained from attempting to make use of context. In any case, readers are not very successful at predicting the next word in most sentences, which suggests that the usefulness of context to word recognition is likely to be rather limited. Finally, using processing resources in the attempt to predict the forthcoming words in a sentence might well disrupt the other processes involved in reading.

Rayner and Sereno (1994) proposed a reasonable compromise. According to them, context has little or no effect on word recognition with a highly skilled and fluent process such as normal reading of text, but may have much more effect when word recognition is unusually difficult (e.g. trying to complete a clue in a crossword puzzle).

Word identification

If one considers children learning to read, then the main problem in reading may seem to be that of recognising individual words in the text. However, there are great doubts as to whether the same is true of normal adults. As college students typically read at approximately 300 words per minute, it is probable that they take no more than 200 milliseconds on average to identify each word. It has proved difficult to decide exactly how long word identification normally takes, in part because of imprecision about the meaning of "word identification": it can refer either to accessing the name of a word or to accessing its meaning. However, reading rate is slowed by only approximately 15% when a mask appears 50 milliseconds after the start of each eye fixation (Rayner et al., 1981); the implication is that word identication in both senses takes only a little more than 50 milliseconds.

Rayner and Sereno (1994), basing themselves in part on the evidence just outlined, argued that word identification is generally a relatively automatic process. This makes intuitive sense if you consider that the average college student has probably read somewhere between 20 and 70 million words in his or her lifetime. As we saw in Chapter 5, it has been argued that automatic processes are unavoidable and unavailable to consciousness. Some evidence that word identification may be unavoidable comes from the Stroop effect (Stroop, 1935): subjects have to name the colours in which words are printed as rapidly as possible, and naming speed is slowed when the words are conflicting colour names (e.g. the word RED printed in green). The Stroop effect suggests that word meaning is extracted even when subjects are attempting not to process it. Cheesman and Merikle (1984) replicated the Stroop effect, and discovered that the effect could be obtained even when the colour name was presented below the level of conscious awareness. This latter finding suggests that word identification does not depend on conscious awareness.

Another criterion for an automatic process is that it uses little or no processing capacity. The processing resources used in word identification have not been measured accurately. However, Rayner and Pollatsek (1989, p.75) argued that only modest processing resources are needed:

> the identification of a word ... appears to take at most about 60 to 70 msec. of mental activity. Since the average skilled reader reads even the simplest text at about 300 words a minute, or about 200 msec. per word, it thus appears that identifying the meaning of words takes at most something like one-third of the mental processing needed for reading.

In sum, there is reasonable evidence that word identification is often a relatively automatic process. However, it should be noted that this conclusion is based mainly on studies of very familiar words. It is entirely possible that automatic processes alone are insufficient to permit identification of relatively rare words.

Letter versus word identification

Common sense suggests that the recognition of a word on the printed page involves two successive stages: the first consists of identifying the individual letters in the word, and the second consists of the identification of the word. However, the notion that letter identification must be complete before word identification can begin appears to be wrong. For example, consider the "word superiority effect" (Reicher, 1969). A letter string is presented very briefly, and is followed by a pattern mask. The subject's task is to decide which of two letters was presented in a particular position (e.g. the third letter). The word superiority effect is defined by the fact that performance is better when the letter string forms a word than when it does not.

On the face of it, the word superiority effect indicates that information about the word presented can facilitate identification of the letters of that word. However, there is also a pseudo-word superiority effect, that is, letters are better recognised when presented in pronounceable non-words (e.g. "MAVE") than when presented in unpronounceable non-words or in isolation (e.g. Carr, Davidson, & Hawkins, 1978).

Interactive activation model

An influential account of word recognition and of the word superiority effect is the interactive activation model of McClelland and Rumelhart (1981), which is similar in a number of ways to the TRACE model of spoken word recognition proposed by McClelland and Elman (1986). McClelland and Rumelhart's (1981) interactive activation model is only designed to account for letter and word recognition in four-letter words written in capital letters, even though many of the principles incorporated into the model have more general applicability. Some of the major theoretical assumptions made by McClelland and Rumelhart (1981) are as follows (see Fig. 12.5):

- There are recognition units at three levels: the feature level at the bottom; the letter level in the middle; and the word level at the top.
- The features in individual letters are identified at the feature level; when a feature is detected (e.g. vertical line at the right-hand side of a letter), activation is sent to all of the letter units containing that feature (e.g. H, M, N) and inhibition is sent to all other letter units.
- Letters are identified at the letter level; when a letter in a particular position within a word is identified, activation is sent to the word level for all four-letter word units containing that letter in that position, and inhibition is sent to all other word units.
- Words are recognised at the word level; activated word units increase the level of activation in the letter-level units for the letters forming that word (e.g. activation of the word SEAT would increase activation for the four letters S, E, A, and T at the letter level) and inhibit activity of all other letter units.
- At each level in the system, activation of one particular unit leads to suppression or inhibition of competing units.

The interactive activation model may seem complicated, but the basic ideas contained in it are reasonably straightforward. McClelland and Rumelhart (1981) argued that bottom-up and top-down processes are both involved in letter identification and word recognition. The bottom-up processes stemming directly from the written word proceed from the feature level through the letter level to the word level by means of activation and inhibition. Top-down processing is involved in the activation and inhibition processes going from the word level to the letter level. The word superiority effect occurs because of the top-down influences of the word level on the letter level. Suppose the word SEAT is presented, and the subjects are asked whether the third letter is an A or an N. If the word unit for SEAT is activated at the word level, then this will increase the activation of the letter A at the letter level, and inhibit the activation of the letter N.

How can the pseudo-word superiority effect be explained within the interactive activation model?

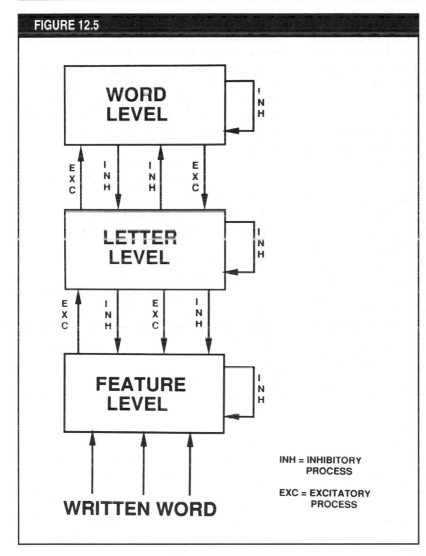

FIGURE 12.5

McClelland and Rumelhart's (1981) interactive activation model of visual word recognition. Adapted from Ellis (1984).

When letters are embedded in pronounceable non-words, there will generally be some overlap of spelling patterns between the pseudo-word and genuine words. This overlap can produce additional activation of the letters presented in the pseudo-word and thus lead to the pseudo-word superiority effect.

Evaluation

The interactive activation model has been extremely influential. It provides an interesting example of how a connnectionist processing system (see Chapter 1) can be applied to visual word recognition. The basic notion of an interactive system can be extended to cover other aspects of language processing, and that is exactly what McClelland (1987) proposed. He identified several different levels of language processing (e.g. semantic level; syntactic level; word-sense level; word level; letter level; phoneme level), and argued that these different levels all have interactive links with other components of the system. As we saw earlier in the chapter, many of the ideas incorporated in the interactive activation model were subsequently applied to spoken word recognition by McClelland and Elman (1986) in their TRACE model.

In spite of the general plausibility of the interactive approach, there are some limitations with the model put forward by McClelland and Rumelhart (1981). The most obvious one is that it was only designed to account for performance on four-letter words written in capital letters, and it is not clear how successfully it could be applied to longer words.

High-frequency or common words are more readily recognised than low-frequency or rare words, and this can be explained by assuming either that stronger connections are formed between the letter and word units of high-frequency words or that high-frequency words have a higher resting level of activation. However, it follows that there should be a larger word superiority effect for high-frequency words than for low-frequency words, because there should be more top-down activation from the word level to the letter level. In fact, the size of the word superiority effect is the same with high- and low-frequency words (Gunther, Gfoerer, & Weiss, 1984), and this is in apparent conflict with expectations from the interactive activation model.

The model proposed by McClelland and Rumelhart (1981) assumes that lexical access is determined by visual information. However, as we will see in the next section, this may be an over-simplification. In particular, there is evidence that the sound of a word sometimes plays a role in lexical access.

Visual versus phonological information
There is convincing evidence that phonological information (information about the sound of words) is often available to someone reading a text. For example, consider a study of reading by Baron (1973; discussed in more detail in Chapter 13). He gave subjects the task of deciding whether phrases were meaningful, and he was interested in finding out whether the sounds of the words influenced performance. He discovered that subjects had particular difficulties in rejecting phrases such as "tie the not", indicating that they were using phonological information.

Evidence such as that provided by Baron (1973) does not make it clear whether phonological information about words is generally available

before or only *after* they have been identified. One way of addressing this issue is to compare the identification times for regular words (whose pronunciation corresponds to their spelling) and for irregular words (whose pronunciation does not correspond to their spelling). If word identification is based only on visual information, then there should be no systematic differences in speed of identification between regular and irregular words. In contrast, if sound or phonology plays a role in word identification, then irregular words might well be more difficult to identify than regular ones. Unfortunately, there is a problem in testing these predictions, in that there is little agreement on how to classify words as regular or irregular. If it is argued that the rules of pronunciation are very simple, then up to 50% of words are irregular. If the rules of pronunciation are complex, then the number of irregular words is much lower.

The evidence is rather inconsistent, perhaps in part because of disagreements about classifying words as regular or irregular. However, there is reasonable evidence that whether or not there is a regularity effect depends on word frequency. For example, Seidenberg, Waters, Barnes, and Tanenhaus (1984) found no differences in naming times between common regular and irregular words, but rare irregular words took significantly longer to name than rare regular words.

Additional evidence that sound-based information can be used in accessing meaning has come from research by Van Orden (1987). He gave his subjects a categorical-decision task, in which they had to decide whether or not words belonged to certain categories (e.g. is BREAD a FOOD?). The crucial comparison was between non-members (e.g. MELT) and pseudomembers (homophones of members; e.g. MEET). Pseudomembers were falsely classified as category members approximately 30% of the time, whereas non-members were misclassified only 5% of the time. Javed and Seidenberg (1991) replicated these findings, and also found that the influence of phonology was greater for rare than for common words.

There are two possible problems with the studies of Van Orden (1987) and Javed and Seidenberg (1991). First, they used a somewhat artificial task that is far removed from normal reading. Second, it is possible that they were assessing the influence of phonological information at a stage of processing after word identification, and thus that their findings are not strictly relevant to the issue of whether phonology influences word identification.

A study by Daneman and Reingold (1993) appears to avoid these problems. Eye movements were recorded as subjects read a text containing homophonic errors ("He wore blew jeans") and non-homophonic errors ("He wore blow jeans"). If the sound or phonology of words is available before word identification, then presumably subjects should have experienced greater difficulties with homophonic errors than with non-homophonic errors. In fact, eye-fixation times on the crucial word (e.g. "blew"; "blow") were the same for homophonic and non-homophonic errors, and subsequent eye-movement regressions back to the area of the error were shorter in duration for homophonic than for non-homophonic errors. These findings do not indicate that phono-logical information is available prior to word identification.

Section summary

Some information about phonology or word sounds is available during reading. However, it remains controversial whether word identification is affected by the sound of a word as well as by its visual characteristics.

There is some evidence (e.g. Seidenberg et al., 1984) that phonology is more likely to be used when identifying rare words than common words. As a consequence of considerable experience with common words, they are typically identified rapidly, so that there is insufficient time for phonological information to be activated prior to identification. In contrast, rare words are identified more slowly and in a less automatic fashion, and this may permit phonological information to precede identification at least some of the time (Coltheart, 1978).

Routes from print to sound

Suppose you were asked to read out the following list of words and non-words:

CAT FOG COMB PINT MANTINESS FASS

You would probably find it a simple task, but it actually involves some hidden complexities. For example, how do you know that the "b" in "comb" is silent, and that "pint" does not rhyme with "hint"? Presumably you have specific information stored in long-term memory about how to pronounce these words. However, this cannot explain how you are able to pronounce non-words such as "mantiness" and "fass", because you do not have any stored information about their pronunciation. Accordingly, a rather different strategy must be used with these non-words. One possibility is that they are pronounced by analogy with real words (e.g. "fass" is pronounced to rhyme with "mass"). Another possibility is that the rules governing the translation of letter strings into sounds are used to generate a pronunciation for non-words. These alternative strategies are discussed in some detail by Patterson and Coltheart (1987).

The notion that there is more than one way in which readers can decide on the appropriate pronunciation of words and non-words was originally proposed a long time ago. Teachers and educationalists over the years have often drawn a distinction between two methods of reading:

- The look-and-say method, which is based on identifying words by their visual appearance.
- The phonic method, which involves sounding out the letters of a word (e.g. c-a-t) in order to work out its pronunciation.

Skilled adult readers can usually identify words correctly "by sight", and so only rarely need to resort to sounding them out in order to understand them. Young children, however, are familiar with the spoken versions of many words that they have rarely encountered in their written form. Therefore, saying words aloud or to themselves is the only way in which children can recognise many words.

The description of the reading of individual words that has been offered so far is an over-simplified one. The study of adult patients whose reading skills have been impaired as a result of brain damage suggests that there are several rather different reading disorders, depending on which part or parts of the cognitive system involved in reading are damaged. Some of the major findings from the cognitive neuropsychological approach are discussed in the following section.

Cognitive neuropsychology

Some of the processes and structures involved in reading are shown in Fig. 12.6. Ellis and Young (1988) identified these components on the basis of the study of acquired dyslexias (i.e. impairments of reading produced by brain damage in adults who were previously skilled readers). Only selected aspects of the cognitive neuropsychological account of reading will be presented here.

The most important message of Fig. 12.6 is the notion that there are three different routes between the printed word and speech. All three routes start with the visual analysis system, which has the functions of identifying and grouping letters in printed words. The simplest way of enabling the reader to make sense of Fig. 12.6 is by considering each of these routes in turn.

Route 1 (grapheme–phoneme conversion)
Route 1 differs from the other routes between the printed word and speech in making use of the process of grapheme–phoneme conversion. This process may well involve working out pronunciations for unfamiliar words and non-words in a piecemeal fashion by translating letters or letter groups into phonemes by the application of rules. However, not everyone agrees with this view. Kay and Marcel (1981) argued that unfamiliar words and non-words are actually pronounced by analogy with familiar words. In support of that argument, they discovered that the pronunciations of non-words by normal readers were sometimes altered to rhyme with real words that had just been presented. The similarities and differences between these two theoretical approaches are discussed by Patterson and Coltheart (1987).

If a brain-damaged patient could use only Route 1 when pronouncing words and non-words, what would one expect to find in their pronunciation performance? In essence, the use of

grapheme–phoneme conversion rules should permit accurate pronunciation of words having regular spelling– sound correspondences, but not of irregular words. If an irregular word such as "pint" has grapheme– phoneme conversion rules applied to it, it should be pronounced to rhyme with "hint". Finally, the grapheme–phoneme conversion rules can be used to provide pronunciations of non-words.

Patients who adhere most closely to exclusive use of Route 1 were labelled as surface dyslexics by Marshall and Newcombe (1973). The surface dyslexic JC was able to read 67 out of 130 regular words correctly, but he was successful with only 41 out of 130 irregular words. Similar, but more striking, findings were reported by Bub, Cancelliere, and Kertesz (1985). Their patient MP read non-words well, and had a reading accuracy of over 90% with common and rare regular words. In contrast, although common words were read with an accuracy of approximately 80%, only 40% of rare irregular words were read accurately.

The evidence from surface dyslexics such as JC and MP indicates that they have a strong, but not exclusive, reliance on Route 1. If all words were read by means of grapheme–phoneme conversion, then all irregular words would be mispronounced, and this simply does not happen. Presumably surface dyslexics can make some use of routes in reading other than Route 1, even though these other routes are severely impaired.

Finally, it should be noted that surface dyslexics vary considerably in the nature of the impairment that led them to adopt the strategy of grapheme–phoneme conversion. For example, JC had no problem with understanding words that he pronounced correctly, whereas MP frequently failed to understand words she could pronounce. The fact that the syndrome category of "surface dyslexia" camouflages important differences among patients suggests that it might usefully be abandoned.

Route 2 (lexicon plus semantic system)
Route 2 is the route generally used by adult readers. The basic idea is that representations of thousands of familiar words are stored in a visual input lexicon. Visual presentation of a word leads to activation in the visual input lexicon. This is

FIGURE 12.6

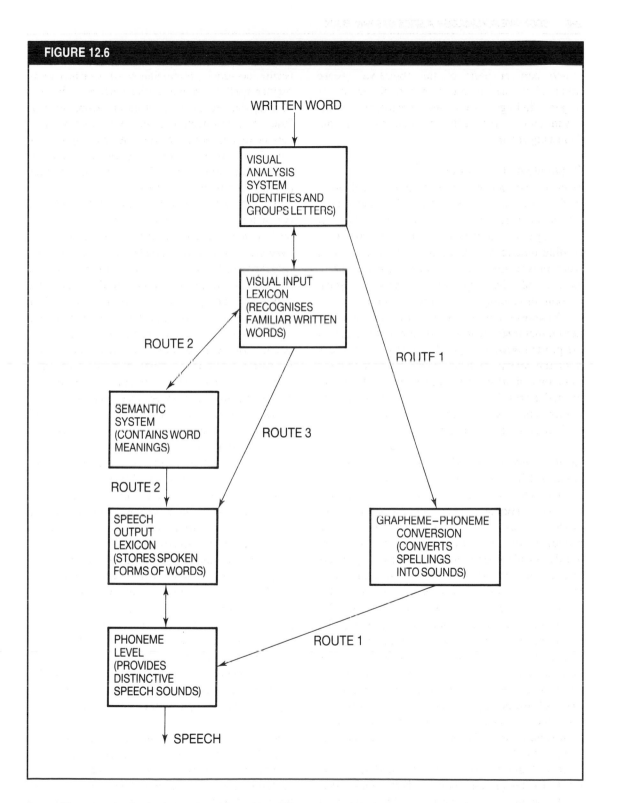

Some of the processes involved in reading. Adapted from Ellis and Young (1988).

followed by obtaining its meaning from the semantic system, after which the word can be spoken (see Fig. 12.6).

How could we identify patients who use Route 2 but not Route 1? Their intact visual input lexicon means that they should experience little or no difficulty in pronouncing familiar words. However, their inability to use grapheme–phoneme conversion should mean they find it very difficult to pronounce relatively unfamiliar words and non-words.

Phonological dyslexics fit this predicted pattern rather well. The first case of phonological dyslexia reported in a systematic fashion was the patient RG (Beauvois & Derousne, 1979). In one experiment with 40 words and 40 non-words, RG successfully read 100% of the real words but only 10% of the non-words. Similar findings with patient AM were reported by Patterson (1982). AM had problems in reading function words (e.g. with, if, yet), but was very successful in reading content words (nouns, verbs, and adjectives). In contrast, he managed to read correctly only 8% of a list of non-words.

Deep dyslexia is more severe and more mysterious than phonological dyslexia. Deep dyslexics resemble phonological dyslexics in finding it very difficult to read unfamiliar words and non-words, which indicates that they cannot use grapheme–phoneme conversion effectively. Deep dyslexics also make semantic errors, in which a word related in meaning to the printed word is read instead of the printed word itself. Examples are reading "costs" as "money" and "city" as "town". This pattern of impairments indicates that deep dyslexics mainly make use of Route 2, but damage within the semantic system itself or in the connections between the visual input lexicon and the semantic system makes this route error-prone.

Deep dyslexia poses theoretical problems, because the great majority of deep dyslexics exhibit a bewildering variety of symptoms. As well as the poor ability to read unfamiliar words and non-words, and their semantic errors, they make visual errors (e.g. reading "while" as "white"), they find low-imageability words harder to read than high-imageability words, and their writing (both spontaneous and to dictation) is impaired. One

theoretical approach is the right-hemisphere theory (Coltheart, 1983b), according to which many of the reading difficulties of deep dyslexics arise because they are relying heavily on the right hemisphere. This causes problems because in most normals the processes and structures best suited to reading are located in the left hemisphere.

There are certainly various similarities between reading performance in deep dyslexics and in patients with an isolated right hemisphere (Patterson, Vargha-Khadem, & Polky, 1989). However, there has been some controversy about exactly how similar reading performance is in those two groups (see Plaut & Shallice, 1993). In addition, a patient who exhibited many of the symptoms of deep dyslexia was completely unable to read after a second stroke in the left hemisphere (Roeltgen, 1987), which seems inconsistent with the right-hemisphere theory. Another problem with the right-hemisphere theory is that it focuses on the part of the brain involved in deep dyslexia, but is uninformative about the processes underlying the reading performance of deep dyslexics.

An ambitious theory of deep dyslexia was offered by Plaut and Shallice (1993). They proposed a type of connectionist network which was concerned with mapping orthography (word spellings) to meaning within the semantic system. This type of network possesses four key properties:

- Similar patterns of activation represent similar words in the orthographic and semantic domains.
- As a consequence of learning, the strengths of the connections between word spellings and meanings are altered.
- The initial pattern of semantic activity produced by a visually presented word moves towards (or is attracted by) the pattern of the nearest known meaning; this is known as the operation of attractors.
- The semantic representations of high-imageability words contain on average many more features than those of low-imageability words.

In order to simulate the symptoms of deep dyslexia with this connectionist network, Plaut and Shallice (1993) investigated the consequences of damage to the network. They discovered that virtually all of the main symptoms could either be simulated, or followed straightforwardly from their simulations. The only important symptom that did not emerge from damage to the connectionist network was impaired writing performance.

Plaut and Shallice's (1993) theory is widely regarded as the most successful account of the diverse symptoms of deep dyslexia. There are two main reasons for its success. First, it predicts about a dozen diverse symptoms of deep dyslexia on the basis of a rather small number of theoretical assumptions. Second, the theory is explicit, in that the processes involved were specified in detail before the simulations proceeded.

At a more general level, the Plaut-Shallice theory is an excellent example of what may be called "connectionist neuropsychology". The essence of connectionist neuropsychology is that the consequences of brain damage for cognitive performance are simulated by means of damage to a connectionist network. The work of Plaut and Shallice (1993) suggests that connectionist neuropsychology may soon become an important approach within cognitive psychology.

Route 3 (lexicon only)

Route 3 resembles Route 2 in that the visual input lexicon and the speech output lexicon are involved in the reading process. However, the semantic system is bypassed in Route 3, so that printed words that are pronounced are not understood. Otherwise, the expectations about reading performance for users of Route 3 are the same as those for users of Route 2: familiar regular and irregular words should be pronounced correctly, whereas most unfamiliar words and non-words should not (see Fig. 12.6).

Schwartz, Saffran, and Marin (1980) reported the case of WLP, a 62-year-old woman suffering from senile dementia. She showed a reasonable ability to read familiar words whether they were regular or irregular, but she often indicated that even words she pronounced correctly meant nothing to her. She was totally unable to relate the written names of animals to pictures of them, despite the fact that she was quite good at reading animal names aloud. Although these findings are consistent with the view that WLP was bypassing the semantic system when reading words, they are not definitive. It is possible that processing occurred in WLP's semantic system, but that she was unable to use such processing to facilitate performance on the tasks she was given.

Evaluation of the dual-route (or triple-route) model

The approach to reading that we have been discussing can be regarded as the triple-route model. However, as the fundamental distinction is between reading based on a lexical or dictionary look-up procedure on the one hand and reading based on a letter-to-sound procedure on the other hand, the approach is often referred to as the dual-route model. It is fairly generally accepted that the triple- or dual-route model provides a good account of normal reading and of abnormal reading in brain-damaged patients. However, there are some dissenters from this point of view. For example, Seidenberg and McClelland (1989, p.564) proposed a parallel-distributed processing model based on a single route from print to speech, arguing that "our model ... offers an alternative that dispenses with this two-route view in favour of a single system that also seems to do a better job of accounting for the behavioural data".

In essence, the Seidenberg-McClelland parallel-distributed processing network consists of 400 orthographic (letter) units, 460 phonological (sound) units, and 200 intervening hidden units (see Chapter 1 for a discussion of hidden units). Initially the network computes random pronunciations for letter strings presented to the orthographic units. However, learning via back-propagation (discussed in Chapter 1) alters the strengths of the links among units and produces steadily increasing accuracy in the reading of words and non-words. The crucial feature of this approach is that the processes underlying the pronunciation of words and non-words are essentially the same.

Seidenberg and McClelland (1989) used 2897 words in their training set. They claimed that their model could read regular words, irregular words, and non-words well, but this is not correct. Coltheart, Curtis, Atkins, and Haller (1993) discussed evidence indicating that the model could read correctly between 50% and 65% of non-words compared to normal human performance of 90% or better. Coltheart et al. (1993, p.597) concluded that the Seidenberg-McClelland model:

> reads exception words well; however, it cannot read non-words as well as people can, it cannot be used to explain acquired dyslexias (surface dyslexia and phonological dyslexia), and it cannot be used to explain developmental dyslexias (surface dyslexia and phonological dyslexia).

In spite of the limitations of the Seidenberg-McClelland model, Coltheart et al. (1993) admitted that it possesses two valuable features lacking in dual-route models: (1) it is explicitly computational; and (2) it learns from experience. They attempted to rectify these deficiencies by proposing a dual-route cascaded model of reading based loosely on the processes and structures shown in Fig. 12.6. Their focus was on non-lexical reading via Route 1, with the computational system learning the grapheme–phoneme rules embodied in an initial set of words. These rules were subsequently applied to previously unseen letter strings.

Coltheart et al. (1993) trained their computational model on the 2897 words used by Seidenberg and McClelland (1989). They then tested its performance when reading various non-words on which it had not been trained. It scored 90% correct, which is very close to the figure of 91.5% obtained by human subjects, and far higher than the 55% recorded by the Seidenberg-McClelland model. Thus, Coltheart et al.'s dual-route cascaded model appears to be clearly superior to the Seidenberg-McClelland model.

As yet, there is no implementation within the dual-route cascaded model of the lexical route in reading. However, Coltheart et al. (1993) suggested that a modified version of McClelland and Rumelhart's (1981) interactive-activation model (discussed earlier in this chapter) might account for visual word recognition, with Dell's (1986) spreading-activation model (see Chapter 14) being used to account for spoken word production.

Section summary

It has been argued (e.g. Seidenberg & McClelland, 1989) that the reading of individual words can be accounted for by a single processing system. However, the available evidence indicates that the dual-route (or triple-route) model offers the most adequate account of reading. In the words of Coltheart et al. (1993, p.606):

> Our ability to deal with linguistic stimuli we have not previously encountered (… to read a non-word aloud) can only be explained by postulating that we have learned systems of general linguistic rules, and our ability at the same time to deal correctly with exceptions to these rules (… to read an exception word aloud) can only be explained by postulating the existence of systems of word-specific lexical representations.

CHAPTER SUMMARY

Language processing usually appears to be relatively straightforward. In fact, however, there are numerous processes involved in the perception of speech and in reading. Many of these processes normally work rather rapidly and at the same time, in order to allow the efficient comprehension of speech and text.

The auditory signal in speech is usually unclear and somewhat ambiguous, and the listener has to contend with linearity, segmentation, and non-invariance problems As a consequence, identifying the words that are being spoken often involves reliance on the sentence context, and on the visual information conveyed by the speaker's lip movements. However, speech has the advantage over visual text that it contains prosodic cues (e.g. stress; rhythm) which provide useful information about grammar and meaning.

Spectrograms have proved very valuable in the investigation of speech perception; they provide a visible record of the component frequencies of sound over time. There is evidence that the perception of speech differs in significant ways from the perception of other auditory stimuli (e.g. speech perception exhibits a clear left-hemisphere bias). However, it is not clear that there is a separate module specialised for speech perception.

Research on spoken word recognition indicates that the presentation of the initial speech segment of a word leads to the activation of multiple candidate words, and that subsequent processes operate rapidly and in parallel. There is strong evidence that top-down processes (many of which are triggered by contextual information) combine in some fashion with bottom-up processes to achieve spoken word recognition, but the influence of top-down processes may have been exaggerated in some models (e.g. the TRACE model).

The investigation by cognitive neuro-psychologists of brain-damaged patients who experience difficulties in repeating spoken words has revealed some of the complexities involved in word recognition. More specifically, there is evidence suggesting that the task of saying a spoken word can be achieved in at least three different ways.

Analysis of eye movements has been used to reveal some of the processes involved in reading; this approach has the advantage that eye movements can be recorded in a relatively unobtrusive fashion that does not disrupt normal reading processes. We make a series of eye movements known as saccades during reading, but all of the information about the text is extracted during the fixation periods which generally last for about 200–250 milliseconds. Eye fixations tend to fall on those words or parts of words that are maximally informative for the reader.

Some of the processes involved in letter and word identification were identified by McClelland and Rumelhart (1981) in their interactive activation model. In this model, they assumed that bottom-up and top-down processes operate within a three-level system: feature, letter, and word levels. They focused on visual factors in word identification. However, there is evidence that phonological factors sometimes play a role, especially in the identification of rare words.

Research within cognitive neuropsychology has revealed that there are probably three routes between seeing a word on the page and saying it. The main evidence for this is that brain-damaged patients who cannot say printed words normally show considerable individual differences in the precise nature of their impairment. The triple-route (or dual-route) model has been challenged by Seidenberg and McClelland (1989), who proposed an alternative single system parallel-distributed processing model. However, the evidence is more in line with the triple-route or dual-route model than with the Seidenberg-McClelland model.

FURTHER READING

Ellis, A.W. (1993). *Reading, writing and dyslexia: A cognitive analysis* (2nd Edn.). Hove, UK: Lawrence Erlbaum Associates Ltd. This book provides an excellent introduction to reading research; it includes much information from the cognitive neuro-psychological perspective.

Lively, S.E., Pisoni, D.B., & Goldinger, S.D. (1994). Spoken word recognition: Research and theory. In M.A. Gernsbacher (Ed.), *Handbook of psycholinguistics*. New York: Academic Press. There is a particularly good account of theories of spoken word recognition in this chapter.

Rayner, K., & Sereno, S.C. (1994). Eye movements in reading: Psycholinguistic studies. In M.A. Gernsbacher (Ed.), *Handbook of psycholinguistics*. New York: Academic Press. An authoritative account of what has been learned about reading from the study of eye movements.

Yeni-Komshian, G.H. (1993). Speech perception. In J.B. Gleason & N.B. Ratner (Eds.), *Psycholinguistics*. Orlando, FL: Harcourt Brace. Most of the basic processes involved in speech perception are discussed in this review chapter.

13

Language Comprehension

INTRODUCTION

Many of the basic processes involved in the initial stages of reading and listening to speech were discussed in the previous chapter. At the end of that chapter, we had reached the point at which individual words were identified. The main objective of this chapter is to complete our account of reading and listening to speech, dealing with the ways in which phrases, sentences, and entire stories are processed and understood.

In crude terms, the previous chapter dealt with those aspects of language processing that differ between reading and listening to speech. In contrast, the higher-level processes involved in comprehension tend to be rather similar whether a story is being listened to or read. Because there has been far more research on comprehension processes in reading than on those in listening to speech, the emphasis will be on what is known about reading comprehension. However, it can usually be assumed that what is true of reading is also true of listening to speech. Any major discrepancies between reading and listening will be specifically dealt with as and when they occur.

SENTENCE PROCESSING

There are three main levels of analysis in the comprehension of sentences. First, there is an analysis of the syntactical (grammatical) structure of each sentence; this is known technically as *parsing*. Second, there is an analysis of the literal meaning of the sentence. Third, there is an interpretation of the sentence focusing on the intended meaning, which may not be the same as the literal meaning; the study of intended meaning is known as *pragmatics*. For example, suppose that a wife says to her husband, "Would you mind opening the window, dear?" He is asking for trouble if he only takes account of the literal meaning of the question, and responds "yes" or "no". Other cases in which the literal meaning is not the intended meaning include rhetorical devices such as irony, sarcasm, and understatement.

The relationship between syntactic and semantic analysis has been a matter of some controversy. One possibility is that syntactic analysis generally precedes (and influences) semantic analysis; another possibility is that semantic analysis usually occurs prior to syntactic analysis; and a further possibility is that syntactic and semantic analysis are carried out independently of each other. These issues will be addressed shortly.

Grammar or syntax

An infinite number of sentences is possible in any language, but these sentences are nevertheless systematic and organised in various ways. Linguists such as Chomsky (1957, 1965) have attempted to produce a set of rules that will take account of the productivity and the regularity of language. Such a set of rules is commonly referred to as a grammar. Ideally, a grammar should be able to generate all of the permissible sentences in a given language, while at the same time rejecting all of the unacceptable ones. For example, as Harris (1990) pointed out, our knowledge of grammar allows us to be confident that "Matthew is likely to leave" is grammatically correct, whereas the similar sentence "Matthew is probable to leave" is not.

Parsing

It might seem that parsing or assigning grammatical structure to sentences would be relatively straightforward. However, there are numerous sentences in the English language (e.g. "They are flying planes") that pose problems because their grammatical structure is ambiguous. As we will see, much of the research on parsing has focused on such ambiguous sentences. Why is that the case? Parsing operations generally occur very rapidly, and this makes it difficult to study the processes involved. In contrast, observing the problems encountered by readers struggling with ambiguous sentences can provide revealing information about parsing processes. It is conceivable that some of the processes used with ambiguous sentences differ from those used with unambiguous sentences, but there is no clear evidence of that.

As Mitchell (1994) pointed out in his review of research on parsing, there are several different ways in which readers might try to work out the grammatical structure of ambiguous sentences. For example, comprehension might proceed by the reader working out both or all of the possible

grammatical structures, and then using additional information (e.g. contextual knowledge) to eliminate all but one of them. An alternative approach would be to calculate only one grammatical structure, and to consider alternative structures only if that proves inadequate. Two different theories of parsing will now be considered.

Garden-path model

Frazier and Rayner (1982) proposed a *garden-path model*, which was so-called because readers or listeners can be misled or "led up the garden path" by ambiguous sentences. The model was based on the following notions:

- Only one syntactical structure is initially considered for any sentence.
- Meaning is not involved at all in the selection of the initial syntactical structure.
- The simplest syntactical structure is chosen, making use of two general principles: minimal attachment and late closure.
- According to the principle of minimal attachment, the grammatical structure producing the fewest nodes or units is preferred.
- The principle of late closure is that new words encountered in a sentence are attached to the current phrase or clause if this is grammatically permissible.

The principle of minimal attachment can be illustrated by the following example taken from Rayner and Pollatsek (1989). In the sentences, "The girl knew the answer by heart" and "The girl knew the answer was wrong", the minimal attachment principle leads to a grammatical structure in which "the answer" is regarded as the direct object of the verb "knew". This is appropriate for the first sentence, but inappropriate for the second sentence. So far as the principle of late closure is concerned, Rayner and Pollatsek (1989) gave an example of a sentence in which use of this principle would lead to an inaccurate syntactical structure: "Since Jay always jogs a mile seems like a short distance." In this sentence, the principle leads "a mile" to be placed in the preceding phrase rather than at the beginning of a new phrase. In contrast, the principle of late closure produces the correct grammatical structure in a sentence such as: "Since Jay always jogs a mile this seems like a short distance to him."

There are three main criticisms of this garden-path model. First, it seems inefficient that readers and listeners should frequently construct erroneous grammatical structures for sentences. Second, it seems rather strange that meaning plays no part at all in the initial assignment of grammatical structure to a sentence. Frazier and Rayner (1982) addressed the first criticism by claiming that the principles of minimal attachment and late closure are efficient because they help to minimise the pressure on short-term memory. They also provided experimental support for the view that only one grammatical structure is considered initially. They measured eye movements while subjects read sentences such as those given earlier. The crucial argument was as follows: if readers construct both possible syntactic structures, then there should be additional processing time at the point of disambiguation (e.g. "seems" in the first jogging sentence and "this" in the second jogging sentence). In contrast, according to the garden-path model, there should be increased processing time at the point of disambiguation only when the actual grammatical structure conflicts with the one produced by application of the principles of minimal attachment and late closure (e.g. the first jogging sentence). The eye-movement data consistently supported the predictions of the garden-path model.

The second criticism of the garden-path model (the implausibility of ignoring the role of meaning in determining assignment of grammatical structure) was considered by Rayner, Carlson, and Frazier (1983). They measured eye movements when readers were presented with sentences such as: "The florist sent the flowers was very pleased with herself" and "The performer sent the flowers was very pleased with herself." In both sentences, "sent" has to be interpreted within the grammatical structure as essentially "who was sent". If meaning played a part in determining choice of grammatical structure, then it would seem rather simpler to work out that the performer was the recipient of flowers than to decide that the florist received flowers. In fact, the pattern of eye movements was very similar with both sentences. Readers fixated for a long time at the point of disambiguation (the word "was"), but there was no difference as a function of the type of sentence.

The third criticism relates to the notion that the initial choice of grammatical structure depends only on the principles of minimal attachment and late closure. There is plentiful evidence that other factors are often involved (see Mitchell, 1994). For example, decisions about grammatical structure are influenced by punctuation when reading and by prosody (e.g. rhythm; stress) when listening to speech.

Context-guided processing theory

Taraban and McClelland (1988) disagreed with the theoretical position of Frazier and Rayner (1982). They proposed a *content-guided processing theory*, according to which meaning plays a role in determining the assignment of syntactical structure. More specifically, they claimed that readers' expectations of what is to come in the sentence are of importance. They analysed word-by-word reading times as readers were presented with sentences such as "The reporter exposed corruption in the article" (Type 1) and "The reporter exposed corruption in the government" (Type 2). The final word in these sentences served to resolve the syntactical ambiguity. According to Frazier and Rayner (1982), Type 1 sentences should be easier than Type 2 sentences, because they are in accord with the principle of minimal attachment. In contrast, Taraban and McClelland (1988) argued that the grammatical structure of Type 2 sentences is more in line with readers' expectations.

The key findings related to processing time on the final word in the sentence. Frazier and Rayner (1982) would predict that this processing time should be longer for Type 2 sentences than for Type 1 sentences, whereas Taraban and McClelland (1988) predicted exactly the opposite. The findings are shown in Fig. 13.1. They strongly support the predictions of the content-guided processing theory, indicating that meaning can override grammatical principles such as that of minimal attachment.

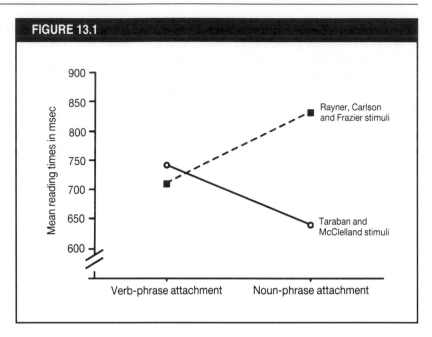

FIGURE 13.1

Mean reading time for noun-fillers with verb-phrase attachment and noun-phrase attachment for two sets of sentences. Adapted from Taraban and McClelland (1988).

Section summary

As Mitchell (1994, p.388) pointed out:

> the most viable models of ambiguity-handling strategies all presuppose that the parser has a tendency to make structural commitments somewhat prematurely ... there seems to be an unevenness of support for the various potential readings of any ambiguous structure, and this bias often appears to manifest itself well in advance of the appearance of any material that would licence a decision one way or the other.

The evidence reviewed in this section suggests that meaning can often influence such premature structural commitments, but that it may have little or no effect when a particular grammatical structure is strongly implied by a sentence. On balance, content-guided processing appears more generally applicable than the garden-path model.

INFERENCE DRAWING

Comprehension would be impossible without access to stored knowledge, and a simple illustration of the crucial role played by such knowledge is the process of inference or filling in of gaps. The importance of inference was emphasised by Schank (1976, p.168), who described it as "the core of the understanding process".

Some idea of how readily we make inferences can be formed if you try to understand what is going on in the following story taken from Rumelhart and Ortony (1977):

1. Mary heard the ice-cream van coming.
2. She remembered the pocket money.
3. She rushed into the house.

You probably made various assumptions or inferences while reading the story, perhaps including the following: Mary wanted to buy some ice-cream; buying ice-cream costs money; Mary had some pocket money in the house; and Mary had only a limited amount of time to get hold of some money before the ice-cream van arrived. The important point to note is that none of these assumptions is explicitly stated in the three sentences that were presented. It is so natural for us to draw inferences in order to facilitate understanding that we are often unaware that we are doing so.

A distinction is often drawn in the literature between *bridging inferences* and *elaborative inferences*. Bridging inferences need to be made in order to establish coherence between the current part of the text and the preceding text, whereas elaborative inferences serve to embellish the text. Most theorists accept that readers generally draw bridging inferences, which are essential for understanding; what is more controversial is the extent to which non-essential or elaborative inferences are drawn.

As we embark on a consideration of research on inference drawing, the reader should be warned that there is no entirely satisfactory way of deciding whether someone has drawn an inference. In addition, the findings obtained can vary considerably across different methods of investigating inferences.

Anaphora

Perhaps the simplest form of bridging inference is involved in *anaphora*, in which a pronoun or noun has to be identified with a previously mentioned noun or noun phrase (e.g. "Fred sold John his lawn mower, and then he sold him his garden hose"). It requires a bridging inference to realise that "he" refers to Fred rather than to John. How do people make the appropriate anaphoric inference? Sometimes gender makes the task very straightforward (e.g. "Juliet sold John her lawn mower, and then she sold him her garden hose"), and sometimes the number of the noun provides a useful cue (e.g. "Juliet and her friends sold John their lawn mower, and then they sold him their garden hose").

It seems reasonable that the ease of establishing the appropriate anaphoric inference should depend on the distance between the pronoun and the noun to which it refers: the *distance effect*. There is plenty of evidence for the distance effect, but Clifton and Ferreira (1987) demonstrated that distance is not always important. Their subjects presented themselves with passages one phrase at a time, and the reading time for the phrase containing the pronoun was measured. In essence, they found that the reading time was fast if the antecedent noun was still the topic of discourse, but it was slow otherwise; distance as such had no effect on reading time. Thus, the distance effect is found normally because greater distance reduces

the probability that the antecedent noun is still the topic of discourse when the pronoun is presented.

When are inferences drawn?

Consider the following passage from a study by O'Brien, Shank, Myers, and Rayner (1988):

> All the mugger wanted was to steal the woman's money. But when she screamed, he stabbed her with his weapon in an attempt to quiet her. He looked to see if anyone had seen him. He threw the knife into the bushes, took her money, and ran away.

O'Brien et al. (1988) were interested in seeing when readers drew the inference that the "weapon" referred to in the second sentence was in fact a knife. There are two major possibilities: (1) the inference was drawn immediately; (2) the inference was drawn only when the word "knife" was encountered in the final sentence. In order to distinguish between these alternatives, they compared reading time on the last sentence in the passage quoted here, and in an almost identical passage in which the word "weapon" was replaced by "knife". They found that there was no difference in the reading time, suggesting that the inference that the weapon was a knife had been drawn immediately by readers.

O'Brien et al. (1988) also considered reading time for the last sentence when the second sentence was altered so that the inference that the weapon was a knife was less clear ("But when she screamed, he assaulted her with his weapon in an attempt to quiet her"). This time, the last sentence took longer to read, presumably because the inference that the weapon was a knife was drawn only while the last sentence was being read.

One of the implications of the O'Brien et al. (1988) study is that it is only strong and obvious inferences that are drawn immediately. Findings obtained by Singer (1979) are consistent with that position. He asked subjects to read pairs of sentences. In some cases, the subject noun of the second sentence had been explicitly mentioned in the first sentence (e.g. "The boy cleared the snow with a shovel. The shovel was heavy."). In other cases, the subject noun had not been specifically referred to before (e.g. "The boy cleared the snow from the stairs. The shovel was heavy."). Singer (1979) found that the time taken to read the second sentence in the pair was greater when the subject noun of that sentence had not been explicitly mentioned before. This suggests that the inference that a shovel was used to clear the snow was not drawn while the first sentence was being read, but was drawn subsequently.

Which inferences are drawn?

Everyone agrees that various inferences are made while people are reading text or listening to speech. What is of interest theoretically is to understand *why* inferences are made, and to be able to predict which inferences are likely to be made. The constructionist approach originally proposed by Bransford (e.g. Bransford, Barclay, & Franks, 1972) and subsequently developed by others (e.g. Johnson-Laird, 1980; van Dijk & Kintsch, 1983) represents one very influential theoretical position. In essence, Bransford argued that comprehension typically requires our active involvement in order to supply information that is not explicitly contained in the text. Johnson-Laird (1980) argued that readers typically construct a relatively complete "mental model" of the situation and events referred to in a text (see Chapter 9). A key implication of the constructionist approach is that numerous elaborative inferences are typically drawn while reading a text.

Most of the early research supporting the constructionist position involved using memory tests to assess inference drawing. For example, Bransford et al. (1972) presented their subjects with sentences such as: "Three turtles rested on a floating log, and a fish swam beneath them." They argued that the inference would be drawn that the fish swam under the log. In order to test this, some subjects on a subsequent recognition memory test were given the sentence: "Three turtles rested on a floating log, and a fish swam beneath it." Most subjects were confident that this inference was the original sentence; indeed, the level of confidence was as high as it was when the original sentence was re-presented on the memory test! Bransford et al. (1972) concluded that inferences from text were

typically stored in memory in the same way as information directly presented in the text.

Memory tests provide a rather indirect measure of inferential processes, and there is the ever-present danger that any inferences that are found on a memory test were made at the time of test rather than during reading. This issue has been investigated in detail in a number of studies (e.g. Singer, 1980). The findings indicate that many (or most) inferences found on memory tests reflect reconstructive processes occurring during retrieval. As a consequence, there has been a marked reduction in the use of memory tasks in inference research.

The minimalist hypothesis

Problems of interpretation with the memory studies (e.g. Bransford et al., 1972) have suggested to some theorists that the evidence for the constructionist position is relatively weak. For example, McKoon and Ratcliff (1992, p.442) reached the following conclusion: "The widely accepted constructionist view of text processing has almost no unassailable empirical support … it is difficult to point to a single, unequivocal piece of evidence in favour of the automatic generation of constructionist inferences." McKoon and Ratcliff (1992, p.440) proposed an alternative view which they referred to as the *minimalist hypothesis*: "In the absence of specific, goal-directed strategic processes, inferences of only two kinds are constructed: those that establish locally coherent representations of the parts of a text that are processed concurrently and those that rely on information that is quickly and easily available."

In order to make sense of the minimalist hypothesis, it is necessary to clarify some of the notions contained in it. In summary form, here are the main assumptions made by McKoon and Ratcliff (1992):

* Inferences are either automatic or strategic (goal-directed).
* Some automatic inferences establish local coherence (two or three sentences making sense on their own or in combination with easily available general knowledge); these inferences involve parts of the text that are in working memory at the same

time (see Chapter 6 for a discussion of working memory).

• Other automatic inferences rely on information that is readily available either because it forms part of general knowledge or because it is explicitly stated in the text.

• Strategic inferences are formed in pursuit of the reader's goals; they sometimes serve to produce local coherence.

The greatest difference between the minimalist hypothesis and the constructionist position concerns the number of automatic inferences that are formed. Those who support the constructionist view claim that numerous automatic inferences are drawn in reading, whereas those who favour the minimalist hypothesis argue that there are very definite constraints on the number of inferences that are generated automatically.

McKoon and Ratcliff (1986) tested this discrepancy between the two theories. They argued that a sentence, such as "The actress fell from the fourteenth storey", would automatically lead to the inference that she died from the constructionist viewpoint but not from the minimalist hypothesis. Subjects read several short texts containing such sentences, followed by a recognition memory test on which they had to decide very rapidly whether or not certain words had been presented in any of the texts. There were critical test words which represented inferences from a presented sentence but which had not actually been presented (e.g. "dead" for the sentence about the actress). The correct response to these critical test words was "No". However, if subjects had formed the inference, then this would presumably lead to errors.

McKoon and Ratcliff (1986) found that the number of errors on critical test words was no higher than on control words when they were immediately preceded on the recognition memory test by the neutral word "ready". However, when they were preceded by a word from the relevant sentence (e.g. "actress"), there was an increase in the number of errors to the critical test words. The implication of these slightly complicated findings is that the inferences were not generated fully, which is in line with the minimalist hypothesis.

However, the fact that they were formed to a limited extent provides some support for the constructionists.

Evidence opposing the constructionist position and indicating the importance of the distinction between automatic and strategic inferences was obtained by Dosher and Corbett (1982). They studied instrumental inferences (e.g. a sentence such as "Mary stirred her coffee" has "spoon" as its instrumental inference). In order to decide whether subjects generated these instrumental inferences during reading, they made use of a somewhat unusual procedure. It is known from research on the Stroop effect that the time taken to name the colour in which a word is printed is affected if the word has recently been activated. Thus, if presentation of the sentence "Mary stirred her coffee" activates the word "spoon", then this should slow the time taken to name the colour in which the word "spoon" is printed on the Stroop task. In a control condition, the words presented on the Stroop task bore no relationship to the preceding sentences. There was no evidence that the instrumental inferences had been formed with normal reading instructions (see Fig. 13.2). However, when the subjects were instructed to guess the instrument in each sentence, then there were effects on the Stroop task.

What do these findings mean? First, they indicate clearly that whether an inference is drawn can depend on the reader's intentions or goals, which is one of the central assumptions made by McKoon and Ratcliff (1992). Second, the findings are very much at variance with the constructionist position. It is necessary to infer the instrument used in stirring coffee in order to attain full understanding, but the evidence indicates that such instrumental inferences are not normally drawn.

McKoon and Ratcliff (1992) assumed that automatic inferences are drawn to establish local coherence for information contained in working memory, but that global inferences (inferences connecting widely separated pieces of textual information) are not drawn automatically. They tested these assumptions with short texts containing a global goal (e.g. assassinating a president) and one or two local or subordinate goals

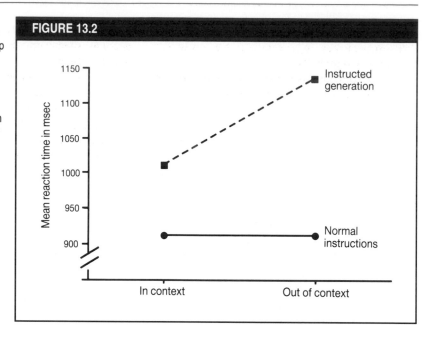

FIGURE 13.2

Colour-naming time in the Stroop task as a function of whether or not subjects had been asked to guess the instrument in preceding sentences, and as a function of whether the words on the Stroop task were in or out of context with the preceding sentences. Based on data in Dosher and Corbett (1982).

(e.g. using a rifle; using hand grenades). Active use of global and local inferences was tested by presenting a test word after each text, and instructing the subjects to decide rapidly whether the word had appeared in the text.

There was an important difference between local and global inferences, with the former being drawn automatically but the latter not. These findings are more consistent with the minimalist hypothesis than with the constructionist position, in which no distinction is drawn between local and global inferences.

Evaluation

One of the greatest strengths of the minimalist hypothesis is that it serves to clarify which inferences are and are not automatically drawn when someone is reading a text. In contrast, constructionist theorists often argue that those inferences that are needed to understand fully the situation described in a text are drawn automatically. This is rather vague, as there obviously could be considerable differences of opinion over exactly what information needs to be encoded for full understanding.

Another strength of the minimalist hypothesis is that it emphasises the distinction between auto-

matic and strategic inferences. The notion that many inferences will be drawn only if they are consistent with the reader's goal in reading is an important one.

On the negative side, it is not always possible to predict accurately from the hypothesis which inferences will be drawn. For example, automatic inferences are drawn if the necessary information is "readily available", but it can be problematic to establish the precise degree of availability of some piece of information.

Search-after-meaning theory

Since the appearance of McKoon and Ratcliff's (1992) minimalist hypothesis, there has been a counter-attack by constructionist theorists. Graesser, Singer, and Trabasso (1994) agreed with McKoon and Ratcliff (1992) that constructionist theories often fail to specify which inferences are drawn during comprehension. They attempted to eliminate this omission in their search-after-meaning theory, according to which readers engage in a search after meaning based on the following:

• The reader goal assumption: the reader constructs a meaning for the text that addresses his or her goals.

- The coherence assumption: the reader tries to construct a meaning for the text that is coherent locally and globally.
- The explanation assumption: the reader tries to explain the actions, events, and states referred to in the text.

Graesser et al. (1994) pointed out that the reader will not search after meaning if his or her goals do not necessitate the construction of a meaning representation of the text (e.g. in proofreading); if the text appears to lack coherence; or if the reader does not possess the necessary background knowledge to make sense of the text. Even if the reader does search after meaning, there are several kinds of inference that are not normally drawn according to the search-after-meaning theory. As can be seen in Fig. 13.3, these undrawn inferences include ones about future developments (causal

consequence); the precise way in which actions are accomplished (subordinate goal-actions); and the author's intent.

Nine different types of inference are described in Fig. 13.3. According to Graesser et al. (1994), it is assumed within search-after-meaning theory that six of these types of inference are generally drawn, whereas only three are drawn on the minimalist hypothesis. As can be seen in the last column of Fig. 13.3, the evidence seems to be more in line with the predictions of the search-after-meaning theory than those of the minimalist hypothesis.

Section summary

Inferences are generally drawn during the process of language comprehension. It used to be assumed by constructionist theorists that numerous inferences are made routinely during reading, but some of the studies apparently supporting that view

FIGURE 13.3

	Type of inference	Answers query	Predicted by constructionalists	Predicted by minimalists	Normally found
1.	Referential	To what previous word does this apply? (e.g. anaphora)	√	√	√
2.	Case structure role assignment	What is the role (e.g. agent, object) of this noun?	√	√	√
3.	Causal antecedent	What caused this?	√	√	√
4.	Supraordinate goal	What is the main goal?	√		√
5.	Thematic	What is the overall theme?	√		?
6.	Character emotional reaction	How does the character feel?	√		√
7.	Causal consequence	What happens next?			×
8.	Instrument	What was used to do this?			×
9.	Subordinate goal-action	How was the action achieved?			×

The types of inferences normally drawn, together with the predictions from the constructionist and minimalist perspectives. Adapted from Graesser et al. (1994).

are flawed because of a failure to discriminate between inferences formed during reading and those formed at the time of subsequent testing.

The main goal of recent theories is to identify more precisely which inferences are normally drawn. It may appear that there is a large gap between the minimalist hypothesis and the search-after-meaning theory, because the focus within the minimalist hypothesis is on a narrower set of inferences. However, it should be remembered that McKoon and Ratcliff (1992) accepted that many strategic inferences are formed in addition to the automatic inferences they discussed. All in all, there is a growing consensus on the types of inference that are generally made (e.g. inferential; causal antecedent), and on those that are rarely made (e.g. instrumental; causal consequence).

Some theorists (e.g. Johnson-Laird, 1983; Kintsch, 1994; van Dijk & Kintsch, 1983) have argued that readers often construct a mental model or representation of the situation described by the text (see Chapter 9). The information contained in mental models can go well beyond the information contained in a text, and such information is based on inferences. The notion of situational representations plays an important part in the theory of story processing proposed by van Dijk and Kintsch (1983), and so further discussion will be deferred until that theory is considered later in the chapter.

INNER SPEECH

An important issue of some controversy concerns the role of inner speech in reading comprehension. It has sometimes been argued that inner speech is of little or no value to adult readers. Children learn to read out loud before they can read silently, and inner speech while reading may simply be a habit that has persisted from childhood. A very different viewpoint was expressed by Huey (1908):

The carrying range of inner speech is considerably larger than that of vision … The inner subvocalisation seems to help hold the

word in consciousness until enough others are given to combine with it in touching off the unitary utterance of the sentence which they form … It is of the greatest service to the reader or listener that at each moment a considerable amount of what is being read should hang suspended in the primary memory of the inner speech.

From a common sense perspective, it seems implausible that most people would use inner speech throughout their adult lives if it served no useful purpose. However, that is a weak argument scientifically, and it is clearly important to consider the relevant experimental evidence. Before doing so, however, it is necessary to distinguish between two somewhat separate aspects of inner speech: (1) *subvocal articulation*, which involves movements in the speech tract; and (2) *phonological coding*, which gives rise to the experience of hearing your own voice as you read text. The precise relationship between subvocal articulation and phonological coding is not known, but it has been established that they are not simply different aspects of the same thing. As Rayner and Pollatsek (1989) pointed out, it is possible to have phonological coding without the appropriate subvocal articulation—if you read a text while saying "the the the" over and over again, it is still possible to hear your own voice.

Experimental evidence

One way to study the role of inner speech in reading comprehension is to take electromyographic (EMG) recordings of some of the muscles used in subvocal articulation. This is of interest because EMG activity in the speech tract typically increases considerably during reading. In one study, Hardyck and Petrinovich (1970) asked their subjects to read easy and difficult texts while EMG recordings were being made. In the key condition, a tone sounded every time the level of muscle activity in the speech tract was greater than that of a predetermined relaxation level. Subjects in this feedback condition were instructed to try to prevent the tone from being sounded. Reduction of EMG activity in the speech tract (and thus reduction of subvocal articulation) produced a significant impairment of comprehension for the difficult text, but had no efffect on comprehension of the easy text (see Fig. 13.4).

Another technique that has been used to study the role of subvocal articulation in reading is *articulatory suppression*. Readers are required to say something simple (e.g. "the the the"; "blah blah blah") over and over again while reading a text. This requirement prevents them from using the speech apparatus to produce subvocal articulation of the sentences in the text. If subvocal articulation of the text is important for comprehension, then an articulatory suppression task should severely impair comprehension.

Some of the early studies indicated that articulatory suppression can have surprisingly little effect on reading performance. For example, Baddeley (1979) discovered that articulatory suppression produced no increase in either processing time or errors on the task of deciding on the truth of simple sentences such as "Canaries have wings" and "Canaries have gills". However, Baddeley and Lewis (1981) obtained evidence that inner speech can affect comprehension. They presented sentences that were meaningful or anomalous because two words in a meaningful sentence were switched around (syntactic anomaly) or because a totally inappropriate word replaced one of the words in the sentence (semantic anomaly). Speed to decide whether each sentence was meaningful was unaffected by articulatory suppression, but suppression increased errors on the syntactic anomaly sentences from 15.9% to 35.6%, while also having a modest effect on the semantic anomaly sentences. The powerful effect of suppression on the syntactic anomaly sentences suggests that subvocal articulation is especially useful for retaining information about the order of words, because accurate retention of word order is crucial for successful performance.

Additional evidence that inner speech provides memory support during reading comprehension was obtained by Slowiaczek and Clifton (1980). They found that articulatory suppression did not affect memory for individual propositions of the form "The subject verbed the object", but it did reduce comprehension when information had to be integrated across sentences. Presumably this latter finding occurred because of the memory demands involved in such integration.

A third approach to inner speech involves what Rayner and Pollatsek (1989) referred to as the

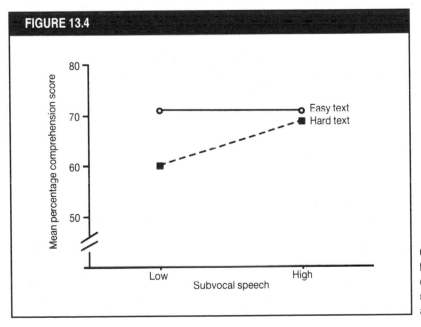

FIGURE 13.4

Mean percentage comprehension score

80
70
60
50

Low   High
Subvocal speech

○ Easy text
■ Hard text

Comprehension for text as a function of text difficulty and opportunity to use subvocal speech. Adapted from Hardyck and Petrinovich (1970).

homophonic reading paradigm. This paradigm makes use of homophones (different words which sound the same, such as "die" and "dye") or of words that are phonemically similar to each other. The underlying rationale is that the sounds of words should influence reading performance if phonological coding is important for comprehension.

In a study of homophonic reading, Baron (1973) asked subjects to decide on the meaningfulness of various phrases. The two crucial conditions were as follows: (1) visually and phonetically incorrect (e.g. "I am kill"); and (2) visually incorrect but phonetically correct (e.g. "Tie the not"). Subjects made substantially more errors with the latter phrases, presumably because information about the sounds of the words was taken into account when judging meaningfulness.

A rather similar conclusion was reached by Baddeley and Lewis (1981) using a different version of the homophonic reading paradigm. Subjects decided whether sentences were semantically acceptable. Some of the sentences were made up of phonemically similar words (e.g. "Crude rude Jude chewed stewed food"), whereas other sentences did not contain phonemically similar words. It took longer to make judgements of semantic acceptability with the phonemically similar sentences, indicating the relevance of the sounds of words to the comprehension process. They also discovered that articulatory suppression (i.e. continuous counting aloud) had no effect on the size of this phonemic similarity effect, although it led to a general increase in errors. This is an important finding. It suggests that the processes responsible for the phonemic similarity effect are rather different from those responsible for the effects of articulatory suppression. More specifically, phonological coding is probably involved in the phonemic similarity effect, whereas subvocal articulation is involved in articulatory suppression.

Speech comprehension and inner speech

So far we have considered the role of inner speech in reading. What about the situation with respect to listening to speech? According to the revised version of the working memory model (Baddeley,

1986; see Chapter 6), phonological or speech-based information about spoken words enters *directly* into a phonological store. In the case of reading, phonological information can be entered into the phonological store only *indirectly*: (1) through subvocal articulation; (2) through phonological information stored in long-term memory (called phonological coding earlier in the chapter). Readers typically have more control over their use of subvocal articulation than over their use of phonological information in long-term memory.

In essence, Baddeley (1986) proposed that much of the information contained in inner speech is directly and effortlessly available to someone listening to speech. In contrast, phonological information is available to readers only in relatively indirect ways.

Functions of inner speech

The evidence discussed earlier has consistently indicated that inner speech plays a useful role in reading comprehension unless the text is very easy. However, there are many complexities associated with understanding exactly how inner speech facilitates comprehension. One complexity is that there are important differences between overt speech and inner speech. Most adults read aloud at about 150–200 words per minute, whereas skilled readers typically have a silent reading rate of approximately 300 words per minute. Perfetti and McCutchen (1982) argued that normal reading rates are much faster than speech rates because the phonological specification of words in inner speech is incomplete. They speculated that consonant sounds are more likely than vowel sounds to be activated, that the beginings of words are favoured over the ends of words, and that content words have a greater probability than function words (e.g. prepositions; conjunctions) of being represented fully in inner speech.

The basic assumption of Perfetti and McCutchen (1982) is that the abbreviated phonological representation of inner speech is biased towards information that is of greatest use. Thus, for example, most words are specified more precisely by their consonants than by their vowels, and so consonant sounds are more likely to be included in the phonological representation.

However, we do not consciously experience inner speech as having the abbreviated nature proposed. It can also be argued that there is a simpler way of accounting for the high speed of silent reading. As Rayner and Pollatsek (1989, p.213) pointed out: "It is possible that the difference between oral and silent reading rates is because a motor response for actually pronouncing each word need not occur in silent reading."

What function or functions does inner speech play in reading comprehension? Probably the most obvious function is that of holding information about words and about word order in working memory so as to reduce the memory load involved in comprehension (e.g. Baddeley & Lewis, 1981; Slowiaczek & Clifton, 1980). Readers sometimes resort to regressions with their eyes in order to integrate the current part of a text with information presented previously, but a faster method of achieving such integration may involve relating current text to inner speech for earlier parts of the text. Inner speech preserves temporal order information, and thus may be of particular value when accurate comprehension depends on a precise recollection of word order (Baddeley & Lewis, 1981).

Some confirmatory evidence for these theoretical suggestions comes from a study by Bub, Black, Howell, and Kertesz (1987). They investigated a patient, MV, with very deficient inner speech. When written sentences were presented to her, she had problems with syntactically anomalous sentences in which the word order had been altered, but not with semantically anomalous sentences in which an inappropriate word replaced the correct one. This confirms the view that inner speech serves to preserve word order.

Another possible function of inner speech is that it may provide the prosodic structure (e.g. rhythm, intonation, stress) that is lacking in written text but present in spoken language. Slowiaczek and Clifton (1980) developed this notion. They argued that the prosodic structure of inner speech is in the form of "timing trees", which are hierarchically organised and based primarily on rhythm. According to this point of view, inner speech facilitates the task of identifying important information within a sentence. Although there is little or no direct supporting evidence, the fact that you can often "hear" someone's style of speaking when reading a letter they have written (Brown, 1970) is consistent with the general position adopted by Slowiaczek and Clifton (1980).

STORY PROCESSING

If someone asks us to tell them about a story or book that we have read recently, we discuss the major events and themes of the story and leave out virtually all the minor details. In other words, our description of the story is highly selective, and is determined by its meaning. Indeed, imagine the questioner's reaction if we simply recalled a random selection of sentences taken from the story!

Gomulicki (1956) provided a straightforward demonstration of the selective way in which stories are comprehended and remembered. One group of subjects wrote a précis (abstract or summary) of a story that was visible in front of them, and a second group of subjects recalled the story from memory. A third group of subjects who were given the précis and the recalls found it extremely difficult to tell which were which. Thus, story memory resembles a précis in that people focus on important information and ignore what is relatively unimportant.

Kintsch and van Dijk's Model

There have been several attempts to consider in some detail how readers discriminate between what is important in stories and what is unimportant. One of the most successful theories of story processing was proposed by Kintsch and van Dijk (1978) and modified by van Dijk and Kintsch (1983). The original version of the theory has been more influential than the modified version, because the modified version is less precise and so lends itself less well to experimental testing. Accordingly, our main focus will be on Kintsch and van Dijk (1978).

There are two basic units of analysis within their model: the *argument* (the representation of the meaning of a word) and the *proposition* (the smallest unit of meaning to which we can assign a truth value; generally a phrase or clause). The text of a story is processed so as to form structures at two main levels:

- The *micro-structure*: the level at which the propositions extracted from the text are formed into a connected structure.
- The *macro-structure*: the level at which an edited version of the micro-structure (resembling the gist of the story) is formed.

Kintsch and van Dijk (1978) argued that the propositions extracted from a story are entered into a short-term working buffer of limited capacity similar to the working memory system proposed by Baddeley and Hitch (1974; see Chapter 6). Additional propositions are formed from bridging inferences and added to those formed directly from the text itself. When the buffer contains a number of propositions, the reader attempts to link them together in a coherent fashion. More specifically, propositions that share an argument (i.e. two words having the same meaning) are linked. Linking of propositions occurs only within the buffer, and thus is limited by the capacity of short-term memory. There is a *processing cycle*: at regular intervals, the buffer is emptied of everything but a few key propositions. In general terms, propositions are retained in the buffer if they are high-level or central in the evolving structure of the story, or if they were presented recently.

The macro-structure of a story combines schematic information with an abbreviated version of the micro-structure. More specifically, various macro-rules are applied to the propositions of the micro-structure:

- *Deletion:* any proposition not required to interpret a subsequent proposition is deleted.
- *Generalisation:* a sequence of propositions may be replaced by a more general proposition.
- *Construction:* a sequence of propositions may be replaced by a single proposition that is a necessary consequence of the sequence.

Memory for the text depends on both the micro-structure and the macro-structure. Higher-level or more central propositions are remembered better than low-level propositions, because they are held longer in the working buffer and are more likely to be included in the macro-structure. This prediction has been confirmed several times (e.g. Kintsch et al., 1975).

Experimental evidence

One of the main assumptions of the theory is that stories can be regarded as consisting of a set of propositions. Some evidence for the importance of propositions was obtained by Kintsch and Keenan (1973). They manipulated the number of propositions in sentences and paragraphs, but equated the number of words. An example of a sentence with four propositions is: "Romulus, the legendary founder of Rome, took the women of the Sabine by force," whereas the following sentence contains eight propositions: "Cleopatra's downfall lay in her foolish trust of the fickle political figures of the Roman world." The reading time increased by approximately one second for each additional proposition.

Some of the most convincing evidence for the existence of propositions was reported by Ratcliff and McKoon (1978). Subjects were presented with sentences (e.g. "The mausoleum that enshrined the czar overlooked the square") followed by a recognition test in which they had to decide as rapidly as possible whether test words had been presented before. For the example given, the test word "square" was recognised more rapidly when the preceding test word was from the same proposition (e.g. "mausoleum") than when it was closer in the sentence but from a different proposition (e.g. "czar").

Propositions contain information about meaning rather than exact details of syntax or wording. It thus follows that memory for text should be better for meaning than for its wording. Dramatic evidence that it is generally the meaning that is remembered was provided by Johnson-Laird and Stevenson (1970). They presented short passages including a sentence such as: "John liked the painting and bought it from the duchess." On a recognition memory test shortly thereafter, subjects very often mistakenly claimed they had heard the following sentence: "The painting

pleased John and the duchess sold it to him."
Despite the substantial differences in wording and
syntax between the two sentences, the fact that they
are very similar in meaning confused the subjects.

One of the more convincing tests of the model
was carried out by McKoon and Ratcliff (1980).
Subjects were presented with a paragraph. This was
followed by tests of recognition memory, with
subjects deciding whether the ideas contained in
sentences had been presented in the paragraph. The
response times to perform this recognition
memory task were speeded up when a sentence was
preceded by another sentence from the paragraph,
and the crucial issue was whether this speeding-up
or priming effect was determined mainly by the
closeness of the two sentences in the text or by
closeness within the propositional structure of the
micro-structure. Priming was affected mainly by
propositional structure, thus providing evidence
for the reality of the micro-structure.

Kintsch (1974) distinguished between effects of
the micro-structure and of the macro-structure on
memory for text using a verification task. Subjects
decided whether explicit and implicit inferences
were consistent with a text which they had either
just read or had read approximately 15 minutes
earlier. Explicitly stated propositions were verified
faster than implicitly stated propositions on the
immediate test, but there was no difference in
verification time between the two kinds of
propositions after 15 minutes. According to the
theory, explicit propositions are better represented
than implicit propositions in the micro-structure,
but both are equally well represented in the
macro-structure. Information in the micro-
structure is much more available immediately than
after a delay, and this explains the different pattern
of results at the two time intervals.

Kintsch's construction–integration model

Kintsch (1988, 1992, 1994) proposed a
construction–integration model that developed and
extended his previous model in various ways. This
model provides more information about the ways
in which inferences are formed and how stored
knowledge interacts with textual information to
form the macro-structure.

The basic structure of the construction–
integration model is shown in Fig. 13.5. According
to the model, the following stages occur during the
comprehension process:

- Sentences in the text are turned into propositions representing the meaning of the text.
- These propositions are entered into a short-term
buffer and form a *propositional net*.
- Each proposition constructed from the text
retrieves a few associatively related propositions
(including inferences) from long-term memory.
- The propositions constructed from the text plus
those retrieved from *long-term memory* jointly
form the *elaborated propositional net*; this net will
usually contain many irrelevant propositions.
- A spreading activation process is then used to
select propositions for the text representation;
clusters of highly interconnected propositions
attract most of the activation and have the greatest
probability of inclusion in the text representation,
whereas irrelevant propositions are likely to be
discarded: "things that belong together
contextually become stronger, and things that do
not, die off" (Kintsch, 1994, p. 732); this is the
integration process.
- The *text representation* is an organised
structure which is stored in *episodic text memory*;
information about the relationship between any
two propositions is included if the two propositions
were processed together in the short-term buffer.
- As a consequence of these processes, three
levels of representation are constructed: surface
representation (the text itself); propositional
representation (propositions formed from the text);
and situational representation (a mental model
describing the situation referred to in the text).

The most distinctive feature of this model is the
assumption that the processes involved in the
construction of the elaborated propositional net are
relatively inefficient, with many irrelevant
propositions being included. This is basically a
bottom-up approach, in that the elaborated
propositional net is constructed without taking
account of the context provided by the overall
theme of the text. In contrast, as Kintsch, Welsch,
Schmalhofer, and Zimny (1990, p.136) pointed

FIGURE 13.5

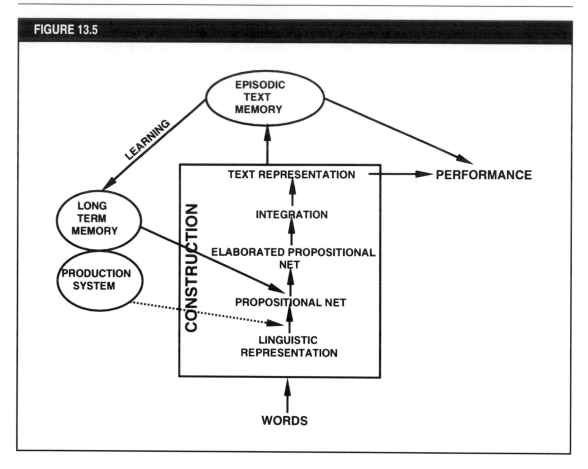

The construction–integration model. Adapted from Kintsch (1992).

out, "most other models of comprehension attempt to specify strong, 'smart' rules, which, guided by schemata, arrive at just the right interpretations, activate just the right knowledge, and generate just the right inferences". According to Kintsch et al. (1990), such strong rules would need to be very complex, and they might prove insufficiently flexible across different situations. In contrast, the weak rules incorporated into the construction–integration model are much more robust, and can be used in virtually all situations.

On the basis of a reasonably detailed specification of the model, Kintsch (1988) was able to produce some convincing computer simulations of parts of the model. Further testing of the model was carried out by Kintsch et al. (1990). They

investigated the assumption that text processing produces three levels of representation ranging from the surface level based directly on the text itself, through the propositional level, to the situational or mental model level (providing a representation that is similar to the one that would result from directly experiencing the situation described in the text). Subjects were presented with brief descriptions of very stereotyped situations (e.g. going to see a film), and then their recognition memory was tested immediately or at times ranging up to four days.

The main findings from the study by Kintsch et al. (1990) are shown in Fig. 13.6. The forgetting functions for the surface, propositional, and situational representations were distinctively

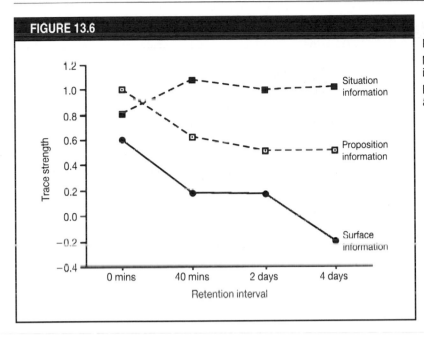

FIGURE 13.6

Forgetting functions for situation, proposition, and surface information over a four-day period. Adapted from Kintsch et al. (1990).

different. There was rapid and complete forgetting of the surface representation, whereas information from the situational representation showed no forgetting over four days. Propositional information differed from situational information in that there was forgetting over time, and it differed from surface information in that there was only partial forgetting. As Kintsch et al. (1990) had predicted, the most complete representation of the meaning of the text (i.e. the situational representation) was best remembered, and the least complete representation of textual meaning (i.e. the surface representation) was the worst remembered.

Evaluation

So far as the Kintsch and van Dijk (1978) model is concerned, there is reasonably strong evidence for the distinction between micro-structure and macro-structure, and it seems likely that proposition-like representations play a role in text comprehension and memory. The notion that propositions of central importance (e.g. those relating to the main theme) are especially well recalled because they spend a disproportionate amount of time in the working buffer is interesting and plausible.

Most of the major problems with the model proposed by Kintsch and van Dijk (1978) are concerned with what has been omitted from it. For example, the details of how propositions are formed are not spelled out, nor is it indicated exactly how bridging inferences are formed or how schematic knowledge interacts with textual information. As we have seen, the construction–integration model goes some way towards remedying these deficiencies.

Rayner and Pollatsek (1989, p.299) pointed out that "coherence and the understanding of discourse entails [*sic*] more than just tying propositions together with links, and hence ... other structures are going to be needed besides networks of propositions". For example, Kintsch and van Dijk (1978) were wrong to claim that the coherence of a text depends very largely on the same argument being repeated several times. On the one hand, a series of essentially unrelated statements about the same individual would not be coherent, but would be deemed to be so within the model. On the other hand, factors other than an overlap of arguments can promote coherence. For example, there is considerable evidence that sentences that are linked causally are read more rapidly and remembered better than those that are not (e.g. Trabasso & Sperry, 1985).

One of the greatest advantages of the construction–integration model and of van Dijk and Kintsch's (1983) theory over the original formulation of Kintsch and van Dijk (1978) is the assumption that there is a situational representation or mental model as well as a propositional representation. An interesting study suggesting the superiority of the mental model approach to the propositional approach was conducted by Glenberg, Meyer, and Lindem (1987). They presented their subjects with short passages such as the following:

> John was preparing for a marathon in August. After doing a few warm-up exercises, he (took off/put on) his sweatshirt and went jogging. He jogged halfway round the lake without too much difficulty. Further along the route, however, his muscles began to ache.

Subjects were then probed with the word "sweatshirt", and had to decide as rapidly as possible whether it had occurred in the passage. They responded significantly faster with the version of the story in which John put on his sweatshirt than when he took it off. This finding is rather mystifying from the perspective of a propositional theory, because the probe word is represented in only one proposition in both versions of the passage. In contrast, the finding is readily explicable from the mental model approach: if subjects construct mental models depicting the events described in the passage, then the sweatshirt has much greater prominence when John puts it on than when he takes it off.

Additional evidence for the importance of situational representations is discussed in a review by Fletcher (1994). However, it should be noted that situational representations or mental models are not always constructed. Zwaan and van Oostendop (1993) asked their subjects to read part of an edited mystery novel describing the details of a murder scene, including the locations of the body and various clues. Most subjects did not construct a situational or spatial representation when they read normally. However, such representations were constructed at the cost of a marked increase in reading time when the initial instructions emphasised the importance of constructing a spatial representation. These findings suggest that limited processing capacity may often restrict the formation of situational representations or mental models.

The construction–integration model has the advantage over its predecessors that the ways in which information in the text combines with related knowledge already possessed by the reader are spelled out in much more detail. In particular, the notion that propositions for the text representation are selected on the basis of a spreading activation process operating on propositions drawn from the text and from stored knowledge is an interesting one. This approach seems superior to the previous model's emphasis on integration based on linking together propositions sharing an argument.

There are two major problems with the construction–integration model. First, it is assumed within the model that numerous inferences are considered initially, with most of them being discarded before the reader becomes aware of them. This is a key theoretical assumption, but one that has not been tested systematically. Second, the model as a whole has not as yet been put to a searching test. Evidence supporting parts of the model has been obtained, but this evidence is insufficiently detailed to be convincing.

Schema approaches to story comprehension

Definitions

Several schema theories of story processing have been proposed, and it is worth considering the schema-based approach at this point. As we saw in Chapter 11, the term "schema" is used to refer to well-integrated chunks of knowledge about the world, about events, about people, and about actions. Scripts and frames are relatively specific kinds of schemas. Scripts deal with knowledge about events and consequences of events. Thus, for example, Schank and Abelson (1977) referred to a restaurant script, which contains information about the usual sequence of events involved in going to a restaurant to have a meal. In contrast, frames deal with knowledge about the properties of objects and locations.

The crucial function of all these kinds of schemas is that they allow us to form *expectations*. In a restaurant, for example, we expect to be shown to a table, to be given a menu by the waiter or waitress, to order the food and drink, and so on. If any of these expectations is violated, then we usually take appropriate action. For example, if no menu is forthcoming, we try to catch the eye of the waiter or waitress. As our expectations are generally confirmed, schemas help to make the world a more predictable place than it would be otherwise.

Rumelhart and Norman (1983) identified several characteristics of schemas. First, schemas vary enormously in the kinds of information they contain, ranging from the simple to the very complex. Second, schemas are often organised in a hierarchical fashion. For example, we have a restaurant schema or script, but also probably more specific schemas relating to the kinds of food and drink that one would expect to see on the menu of each type of restaurant (e.g. curry in an Indian restaurant). Third, schemas operate in a top-down or conceptually driven fashion to facilitate interpretation of the world about us.

Fourth, as we saw in Chapter 11, schemas have slots, some of which have fixed values and others of which have optional values. For example, the restaurant schema has sitting at a table and eating food as fixed values, but the people present at the meal, the number of courses, the type of food, and so on, all have optional values. Most importantly, slots often have *default values*, which means that plausible guesses or inferences are made if the relevant information is not explicitly supplied. Thus, we might well assume that people having a meal in a restaurant receive a bill and pay it even if we are not told so in unambiguous terms.

Story comprehension

Schema theories of story comprehension differ considerably from Kintsch's construction–integration theory (1988, 1992). Whereas construction–integration theory involves a largely bottom-up approach, schema theories focus on top-down processing. An extreme version of schema theory was proposed by Schank (1978, p.94): "We would claim that in natural language understanding, a simple rule is followed. Analysis proceeds in a top-down predictive manner. Understanding is expectation based. It is only when the expectations are useless or wrong that bottom-up processing begins."

Interesting evidence that schemas can influence the process of story comprehension was obtained by Bransford and Johnson (1972, p.722). They presented a passage in which it was very difficult to work out which schemas were relevant. This is the passage they used:

The procedure is quite simple. First, you arrange items into different groups. Of course one pile may be sufficient depending on how much there is to do. If you have to go somewhere else due to lack of facilities that is the next step; otherwise, you are pretty well set. It is important not to overdo things. That is, it is better to do too few things at once than too many. In the short run this may not seem important but complications can easily arise. A mistake can be expensive as well. At first, the whole procedure will seem complicated. Soon, however, it will become just another facet of life. It is difficult to foresee any end to the necessity for this task in the immediate future, but then, one never can tell. After the procedure is completed one arranges the materials into their appropriate places. Eventually, they will be used once more and the whole cycle will then have to be repeated. However, that is part of life.

Subjects who heard the above passage in the absence of a title rated it as incomprehensible and recalled an average of only 2.8 idea units, whereas those supplied beforehand with the title "Washing clothes" found it easy to understand and recalled 5.8 idea units on average. This effect of relevant schema knowledge occurred because it facilitated comprehension of the passage rather than because the title acted as a useful retrieval cue: subjects who received the title after hearing the passage but before attempting recall recalled only 2.6 idea units on average.

Bartlett (1932) was the first psychologist to argue persuasively that schemas play an important role in determining what we remember from stories (see also Chapter 11). According to him, memory is affected not only by the presented story itself but also by the subject's store of relevant prior knowledge or schemas. He had the ingenious idea of presenting his subjects with stories that produced a conflict between what was presented to them and their prior knowledge. If, for example, people read a story taken from a culture different from their own, then prior knowledge might produce distortions in the remembered version of the story, rendering it more conventional and acceptable from the standpoint of their own cultural background. Bartlett's (1932) findings supported his predictions. In particular, a substantial proportion of the recall errors were in the direction of making the story read more like a conventional English story. He used the term "rationalisation" to refer to this type of error.

There are various deficiencies with Bartlett's work. He did not give very specific instructions to his subjects (Bartlett, 1932, p.78): "I thought it best, for the purposes of these experiments, to try to influence the subjects' procedure as little as possible." As a consequence, it is possible that some of the distortions observed by Bartlett were due to conscious guessing rather than deficient memory. There is some force in this criticism, because instructions stressing the need for accurate recall eliminate almost half the errors usually obtained (Gauld & Stephenson, 1967).

Another problem is that Bartlett assumed that memorial distortions occur largely as a result of schema-driven reconstructive processes operating at the time of retrieval. As we have already seen in the study by Bransford and Johnson (1972), schemas often influence comprehension processes rather than retrieval processes. However, schemas do sometimes influence the retrieval of information from long-term memory. Anderson and Pichert (1978) asked subjects to read a story from the perspective of either a burglar or of someone interested in buying a home. After they had recalled the story, they were asked to shift to the alternative perspective and then to recall the story again. On the second recall, subjects recalled more information that was important only to the second perspective or schema than they had done on the first recall (see Fig. 13.7)

These findings of Anderson and Pichert (1978, p.10) confirm the notion of schema-driven retrieval. Further support comes from the subjects' introspective reports:

When he gave me the homebuyer perspective, I remembered the end of the story, you know, about the leak in the roof. The first time through I knew there was an ending, but I couldn't remember what it was. But it just popped into my mind when I thought about the story from the homebuyer perspective.

Some of the research on schemas and memory for text has focused on large-scale schemas. For example, Thorndyke (1977) proposed a *story grammar* (set of rules permitting the structure of any story to be generated). Stories possess a hierarchical structure within this story grammar, with the major categories of setting, theme, plot, and resolution at the top of the hierarchy. To test this theory, Thorndyke (1977) presented a story in which the theme was in its usual place at the beginning of the story, or it was placed at the end of the story, or it was omitted altogether. Memory for the story was best when the theme had been presented at the beginning of the story, and it was better when it had been presented at the end rather than not at all. This suggests that at least some of the story information could be organised after it had been read.

Other research based on similar notions has supported the view that stories are hierarchically organised. For example, Meyer and McConkie (1973) found that an event low down in the story hierarchy was much more likely to be recalled if the event immediately above it in the hierarchy had been recalled.

Evaluation
Our organised knowledge of the world is used in a systematic fashion to facilitate text comprehension and recall, but it has proved rather difficult to identify the characteristics of schemas with any

FIGURE 13.7

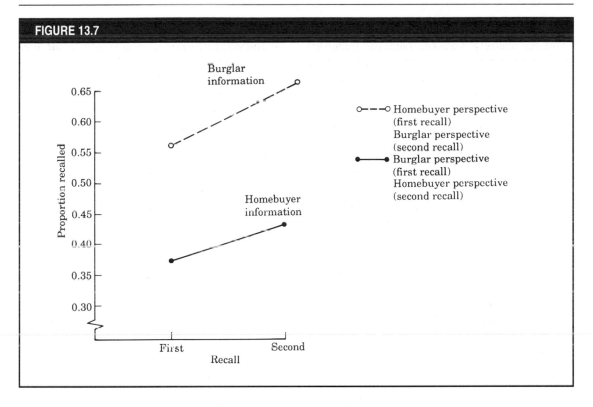

Recall as a function of perspective at the time of retrieval. Based on data in Anderson and Pichert (1978).

precision. More importantly, most versions of schema theory are sadly lacking in testability. If we are trying to explain text comprehension and memory in terms of the activation of certain schemas, then we really require independent evidence of the existence (and appropriate activation) of those schemas. However, such evidence is generally not available.

One of the major assumptions of schema theory is that top-down processes lead to the generation of numerous inferences during story comprehension. However, the evidence discussed earlier in the chapter (e.g. McKoon and Ratcliff, 1992) suggests that the number of inferences generated by the average reader is much less than is implied by schema theory.

Another problem with the schema-based approach is that many of its predictions are intuitively obvious, making one wonder whether such elaborate theorising is needed. For example, it is not clear that we require a complex story grammar in order to account for Thorndyke's

(1977) finding that memory for a story is best when the theme is presented early on.

Finally, the reader may have noticed that memory rather than comprehension was the primary focus of the research discussed in this section. Schema theory may be more useful in accounting for memory findings than it is in explaining the processes involved in comprehension. Real-world knowledge manifestly affects comprehension processes, but schema theory tells us rather little about how this happens.

THEORIES OF READING

Capacity theory

An important theory of language comprehension applicable to both reading and listening was proposed by Just and Carpenter (1992). Their capacity theory focuses on working memory, by which they mean "the part of the central executive in Baddeley's theory that deals with language comprehension" (p. 123; see Chapter 6). Within the theory, working memory is used for both storage and processing during comprehension. Storage and processing demands can be heavy, and it is assumed that working memory has a strictly limited capacity. As a consequence, one of the general characteristics of language processing is that storage demands are reduced to manageable proportions. For example, each word is often processed thoroughly when it is first encountered (this is known as the immediacy assumption— Beck and Carpenter, 1986), instead of storing it for future processing. Another way of reducing storage demands is to discard information that is no longer required. For example, syntactic information is often unavailable only a few seconds after a sentence has been processed (e.g. Johnson-Laird & Stevenson, 1970).

The central assumptions made by Just and Carpenter (1992) are that there are individual differences in the capacity of working memory, and that these individual differences have substantial effects on language comprehension. Working memory capacity is assessed by means of the reading-span task: subjects read a number of sentences, and then attempt to recall the final word of each sentence. The largest number of sentences for which a subject can recall all of the final words more than 50% of the time is defined as his or her reading span. It is assumed that the processes used in comprehending the sentences require a smaller proportion of the available working memory capacity of those with a large capacity, and thus they have more capacity for retaining the last words of the sentences.

There is good evidence that reading span is a useful measure. Just and Carpenter (1992) referred to studies indicating that reading span typically correlates about +0.8 with the ability to answer comprehension questions about a passage, and it correlates approximately +0.6 with verbal intelligence. In addition, those with high reading spans read difficult portions of a text considerably faster than those with low reading spans.

Capacity theory has been applied to some of the theoretical issues considered earlier in this chapter. For example, there has been controversy as to whether the initial syntactic parsing of a sentence is affected by meaning. In order to study this issue, Just and Carpenter (1992) examined reading times for sentences such as: "The evidence examined by the lawyer shocked the jury" and "The defendant examined by the lawyer shocked the jury." If meaning influences initial parsing, then sentences of the former type should be easier to understand than sentences of the latter type: "the evidence" (an inanimate noun) is unlikely to be doing the examining, whereas "the defendant" (an animate noun) might well be doing the examining. Accordingly, the actual syntactic structure of the sentence should come as more of a surprise to readers given sentence two than to those given sentence one. However, if meaning does not influence initial syntactic parsing, then the gaze duration on the critical phrase "by the lawyer" should be the same for both sentences.

What Just and Carpenter (1992) actually found was that the performance of subjects with high and low reading spans was quite different. As can be seen in Fig. 13.8, subjects with a low reading span did not appear to make any use of the valuable information provided by the inanimate subject noun when processing the crucial phrase, and so their syntactic parsing was unaffected by meaning. In contrast, subjects with a high reading span did make use of the cue of inanimacy, and so their initial parsing was affected by meaning. Presumably only those subjects with a high reading span had sufficient working memory capacity available to take the animacy/inanimacy of the subject noun into account when parsing the sentences. In other words, individual differences need to be considered when answering the question: "Does meaning affect initial syntactic parsing?"

Another area of controversy relates to the processing of sentences containing syntactic ambiguity. One possibility is that those encountering such an ambiguity attempt to retain both (or all) interpretations until disambiguating information is provided; alternatively, people might select a single interpretation, and retain it unless or until there is invalidating information. Just and Carpenter (1992) discussed a study in which sentences were presented in a self-paced, word-by-word, moving window paradigm. Some of the

FIGURE 13.8

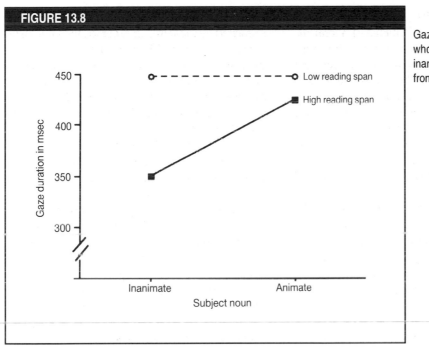

Gaze duration as a function of whether the subject noun was inanimate or animate. Adapted from Just and Carpenter (1992).

sentences were syntactically ambiguous until the end (e.g. "The experienced soldiers warned about the dangers before the midnight raid"), but were finally given the more predictable resolution; others were unambiguous (e.g. "The experienced soldiers spoke about the dangers before the midnight raid").

The key findings are shown in Fig. 13.9. Subjects with a high reading span processed the ambiguous sentences more slowly than the unambiguous ones, especially close to the part of the sentence in which the ambiguity was resolved. These subjects incurred a cost in terms of processing time for maintaining two different syntactic interpretations of the ambiguous sentences. In contrast, those with a low reading span did not differ in their processing times for ambiguous and unambiguous sentences, presumably because they did not attempt to maintain two interpretations of the ambiguous sentences (i.e. they treated such sentences as if they were unambiguous).

Evaluation

Probably the greatest strength of the capacity theory put forward by Just and Carpenter (1992) is the assumption that there are substantial individual differences in the processes used in language comprehension. It is not simply the case that some individuals comprehend text faster than others; rather, some individuals have more processing resources available than others, and so are able to carry out forms of processing that those with fewer processing resources are unable to do. This approach has shed important new light on some major controversies (e.g. the role of meaning in the initial parsing of sentences).

Capacity theory represents a refreshing change from much previous theorising on language comprehension in its emphasis on the importance of a very general capacity (i.e. working memory capacity). This can be contrasted with the cognitive neuropsychological approach, in which the focus is on numerous specific modules or mechanisms. General and specific processes both need to be considered in a complete theory of language comprehension, and Just and Carpenter (1992) have provided a timely reminder of that fact.

Individual differences in comprehension ability do not depend solely on working memory capacity. For example, Gernsbacher, Varner, and Faust (1990) argued that a major advantage of more

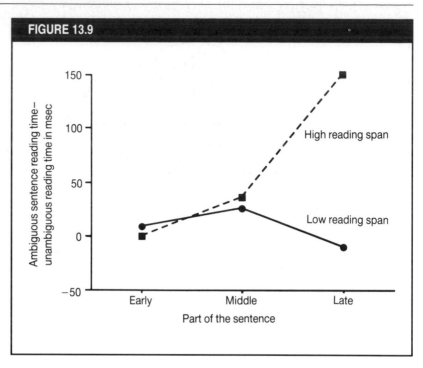

FIGURE 13.9

Differences in reading time per word between ambiguous and unambiguous sentences as a function of part of the sentence. Adapted from Just and Carpenter (1992).

skilled over less skilled comprehenders is that they are much better at rejecting inappropriate information because they have more efficient suppression mechanisms. In one of their experiments, subjects read a short sentence ("He dug with the spade") followed by a test word (e.g. "ACE"), and their task was to decide rapidly whether the test word matched the sentence. In the example given, there would be interference unless the inappropriate meaning of spade (related to playing cards) were quickly suppressed. More skilled comprehenders showed no interference when the test words were presented 850 milliseconds after the sentence had been read, whereas less skilled comprehenders showed substantial interference. The implication is that Just and Carpenter's (1992) theory needs to be extended to incorporate individual differences in suppression mechanisms.

Another limitation of capacity theory is that its emphasis on working memory capacity is to some extent at the expense of more specific processes involved in comprehension. In other words, Just and Carpenter (1992) do not provide us with a detailed account of comprehension processes. As a

consequence, capacity theory cannot be regarded as anything like a comprehensive account of language comprehension.

Interactive model of reading

One of the most detailed theories of reading was proposed by Rayner and Pollatsek (1989). They described it as an interactive model, in the sense that bottom-up and top-down processes are both involved in the reading process. However, the primary focus of the model is on bottom-up processes.

As can be seen in Fig. 13.10, two memory structures (working memory and long-term memory) are of central significance in the model. Working memory has various relevant modules or components:

- A module for the short-term retention of inner speech.
- A parser involved in syntactic processing.
- A thematic processor involved in selecting the most appropriate semantic interpretation of text.

FIGURE 13.10

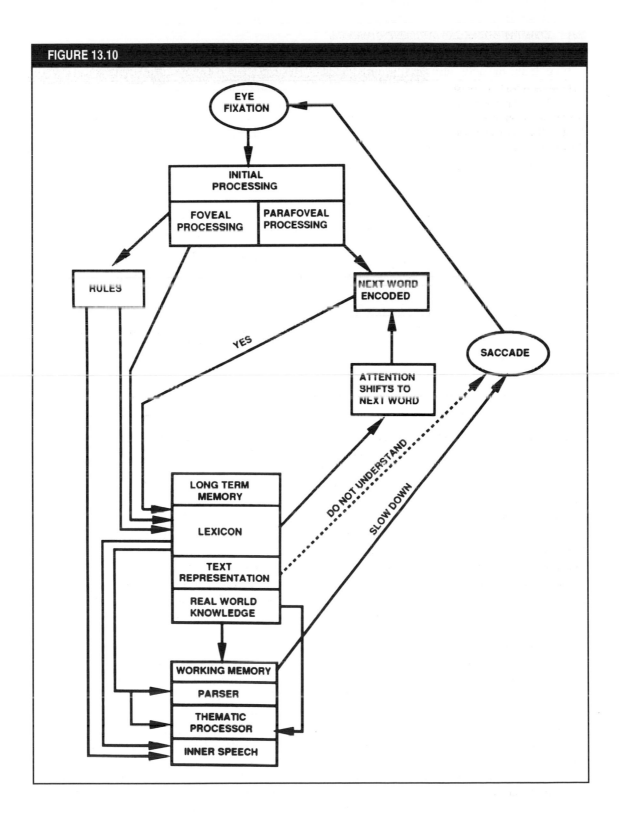

Rayner and Pollatsek's model of reading. Adapted from Rayner and Pollatsek (1989).

Long-term memory also has a number of components that are relevant to reading:

- The lexicon, which contains the meanings of all the words you know and which is highly organised.
- Real-world knowledge, which is often known as "semantic memory".
- The text representation, which is simply the text-related information that is stored in long-term memory.

The easiest way to understand the workings of the model is to consider the sequence of processes involved in reading. Foveal word processing is concerned with processing the currently fixated word; in contrast, parafoveal processing is directed to the right of the fixation point, and determines the location of the next eye fixation. Lexical access can occur directly as a consequence of foveal word processing, but it can also occur indirectly by means of the use of rules or analogies to create a phonological route to the lexicon. Inner speech (a transient holding system based on phonological coding and subvocal articulation) can be triggered by either the direct or the indirect route to lexical access. There can be complexities in terms of the programming of eye movements, but according to Rayner and Pollatsek (1989, p.474):

> most of the time the sequence of events is foveal word processing (with parafoveal processing occurring in parallel), lexical access, attention shift to the next word, saccade to the next word, and the cycle starts again (with the preview benefit useful in speeding the initial foveal processing).

After the meaning of a currently fixated word has been accessed in the lexicon, it is integrated into the developing text representation. If difficulties arise, there are various ways in which the reader may react: a second fixation on the word; a regression; or use of the information in the inner speech mechanism. During the process of text integration, the parser constructs a single syntactic representation of the current sentence. In doing this, the parser makes use of information from the lexicon about the syntactic or grammatical class of each word in the sentence. The initial syntactic representation is formed without taking account of word meanings. The thematic processor makes use of information from the parser, as well as information about the meanings of the words in the sentence, information from previous sentences, and real-world information. The task of the thematic processor is to select the most appropriate thematic interpretation of the text. If there is an inconsistency between the syntactic representation produced by the parser and other information available to the thematic processor, the parser computes a second syntactic representation.

Rayner and Pollatsek (1989, p.477) admitted that their model had little to say about the details of how the meaning of a text is constructed. In their own words: "The situation is pretty murky after we leave the lexicon."

Evaluation
The greatest strength of the model proposed by Rayner and Pollatsek (1989) is the way in which eye-movement findings are incorporated into the model. Eye movements provide valuable information about what is being attended to in a text, and so they are potentially very informative about the processes involved in reading. At the risk of over-simplification, the duration of eye fixations and the length of saccades are determined mainly by basic features of the text (e.g. length and familiarity of the word currently fixated; locations of the spaces between words; length of the next word to be fixated) and are relatively unaffected by top-down factors such as schematic knowledge. Thus, eye-movement data provide a solid basis for emphasising bottom-up processes in reading as was done by Rayner and Pollatsek (1989).

The greatest weakness of the model is the failure to deal convincingly with higher-level processes in reading. Little is said about how inferences are formed, how information from different sentences is integrated, whether textual information is represented in propositional or some other form, and so on. Thus, we are given an incomplete account of reading. Another weakness concerns the assumption that the parser constructs a syntactic representation of each sentence without taking into account the meanings of the words in the sentence. As we saw earlier in the chapter (Taraban & McClelland, 1988), this is probably an over-simplification.

CHAPTER SUMMARY

Comprehension of text or speech involves an analysis of the grammatical or syntactical structure of each sentence, followed by an analysis of its literal meaning, and by an interpretation of the sentence to ascertain its intended meaning. Frazier and Rayner (1982) argued that meaning plays no role in determining the initial syntactical or grammatical structure considered by the reader, but this was disputed by Taraban and McClelland (1988) in their content-guided processing theory. It is probable that meaning sometimes influences the initial selection of grammatical structure, but does not do so when a particular grammatical structure is strongly implied by a sentence.

There is general agreement that inferences are drawn during reading. The simplest form of inference is anaphora, in which a pronoun or noun in text has to be identified with some previously mentioned noun or noun phrase. According to the constructivist approach advocated by Bransford and others, numerous inferences are drawn. According to McKoon and Ratcliff's (1992) minimalist hypothesis, relatively few inferences are drawn automatically. Graesser et al. (1994), in their search-after-meaning theory, assumed that a relatively wide range of inferences is drawn, but they considered strategic as well as automatic inferences. What is important theoretically is to indicate precisely the conditions in which different kinds of inference will be drawn, and recent theorists are moving closer to that goal.

It has often been assumed that inner speech plays an important role in reading. There are two aspects to inner speech: (1) subvocal articulation; and (2) phonological coding, which allows readers to "hear" their own voices as they read. Inner speech facilitates comprehension during reading unless the text is very easy to understand. It is

useful because it permits the transient storage of information about words that have just been read; because it provides useful information about word order; and because it can provide some of the prosodic structure that is present in spoken but not in written language.

Kintsch and van Dijk (1978) put forward a very influential theory of story processing. They distinguished between the micro-structure, which consists of a set of propositions representing the meaning of the text, and the macro-structure, which is an edited version of the micro structure representing the gist of the text. The evidence indicates that the theory is on the right lines. However, many of the processes that are involved are not specified in detail, and it is doubtful whether a set of propositions provides the basis for understanding the meaning of a text as was assumed by Kintsch and van Dijk (1978).

Kintsch (1988, 1992, 1994) proposed construction–integration theory, which represents a modified version of his earlier model. According to this theory, propositions are constructed in a bottom-up fashion, and this is followed by an integration process involving a spreading activation process. This integration process serves as a kind of filter to eliminate irrelevant propositions from the final text representation. This theory emphasises the notion that there are three levels of representation (surface; propositional; and situational), and much of the available evidence provides support for this.

Schema theories emphasise the role of schemas or organised packets of knowledge in language comprehension and memory. In essence, it is assumed by schema theories that schemas operate in a top-down fashion to influence the processes involved in the initial comprehension and subsequent retrieval of written or spoken language. Language comprehension clearly depends extensively on stored knowledge, but it has not been established that top-down processes are as important as is assumed by schema theorists.

Just and Carpenter (1992) proposed a capacity theory of language comprehension. They assumed that there are individual differences in the capacity of working memory, and that these differences have important implications for language comprehension. More specifically, those with a small working memory capacity engage in fewer language-processing activities than those with a large capacity. The emphasis on the very general (i.e. working memory capacity) is justified, but the lack of consideration paid to suppression mechanisms and to more specific processes makes capacity theory of somewhat limited value.

Rayner and Pollatsek (1989) proposed a detailed theory of reading based on the working memory and long-term memory systems. It is largely a bottom-up theory, and it provides a very good account of the role of eye movements in reading. The theory is less explicit about high-level processes than about low-level ones, and has little to say about how inferences are drawn, whether propositions are formed, and so on.

FURTHER READING

Fletcher, C.R. (1994). Levels of representation in memory for discourse. In M.A. Gernsbacher (Ed.), *Handbook of psycholinguistics* (Chapter 17). London: Academic Press. The increasing influential view that there are three different levels of representation resulting from discourse processing is discussed in a comprehensive and informative fashion.

Kintsch, W. (1994). The psychology of discourse processing. In M.A. Gernsbacher (Ed.), *Handbook of psycholinguistics* (Chapter 22). London: Academic Press. This chapter provides an overview of research on reading and an up-to-date account of Kintsch's construction–integration model.

Mitchell, D. (1994). Sentence parsing. In M.A. Gernsbacher (Ed.), *Handbook of psycholinguistics* (Chapter 11). London: Academic Press. Most of the existing theory and research on the processes involved in assigning a grammatical structure to sentences is dealt with thoroughly in this chapter.

Rayner, K., & Pollatsek, T.A. (1989). *The psychology of reading.* London: Prentice-Hall. There is substantial coverage of comprehension in this book, especially in Chapters 7 and 8. In addition, there is an interesting discussion of theories of reading in Chapter 13.

14

Language Production: Speaking and Writing

We know more about language comprehension than we do about language production. Why should this be so? It is fairly easy to exercise experimental control over material to be comprehended, whereas it is much more difficult to constrain an individual's production of language. A further problem in accounting for language production (albeit one that is shared with language comprehension) is that more than a theory of language is needed. Language production is basically a goal-directed activity. People speak and write in order to influence other people, to impart information, to express concern, to be friendly, and so on. As a consequence, motivational and social factors need to be considered in addition to purely linguistic ones.

INTRODUCTION

The two major topics considered within this chapter are speech production and writing. More is known about speech production than about writing. Nearly everyone spends more time talking than

writing, and so it is of more practical use to understand the processes involved in talking than in writing. However, writing is clearly an important skill in contemporary Western society, and this justifies its inclusion in this chapter.

This chapter and the two previous ones are concerned with the processes involved in language. There are obviously links between language and thought, but there has been much controversy about their precise relationship. Some of the relevant issues are considered towards the end of this chapter, following our coverage of language production.

SPEECH PRODUCTION

Speech as communication

For most people (unless there is something seriously wrong with them), speech nearly always occurs as conversation in a social context: we speak because we want to communicate with other people. If that communication is to be successful, there has to be adherence to certain conventions.

Grice (1967) argued that the key to successful communication lies in the Co-operative Principle, according to which speakers and listeners must attempt to be co-operative.

In addition to the Co-operative Principle, Grice proposed a total of four maxims that the speaker should heed:

- *Maxim of quantity:* the speaker should be as informative as necessary, but not more so.
- *Maxim of quality:* the speaker should be truthful.
- *Maxim of relation:* the speaker should say things that are relevant to the situation.
- *Maxim of manner:* the speaker should make his or her contribution easy to understand.

Some evidence that speakers do heed the maxim of quantity was obtained by Olson (1970). He pointed out that what needs to be said depends on the context. For example, it is not possible to account for what someone says simply by focusing on what the speaker wishes to describe (often called the referent). It is also necessary to know the objects from which the referent must be differentiated. It is sufficient to say "The boy is good at football" if the other players in a football game are all men, but not if the other players are also boys. In the latter case, it is necessary to be more specific (e.g. "The boy with red hair is good at football").

In applying the maxim of quantity, the speaker also has to take account of what has been called the "common ground" (Clark & Carlson, 1981). The "common ground" between two people consists of their mutual suppositions, beliefs, and knowledge; it typically increases as two people interact more with each other. Clark (1994) proposed a distinction between communal common ground and personal common ground. Communal common ground refers to all the knowledge and beliefs universally held in the communities to which the two people belong, whereas personal common ground refers to the mutual knowledge and beliefs that two people have inferred from their dealings with each other.

The way in which personal common ground influences speakers can be seen if we consider a concrete example. If a speaker and his or her listener have several friends in common, then it may be reasonable for the speaker to say: "Willie bought Tom's old Beetle." However, if the listener does not know who Tom is, and only knows Willie as Dr. Smith, then the speaker will typically convey the information in a rather different fashion: "Dr. Smith bought the orange car parked outside your office." The key point is that the process of language production often involves deciding on the factual information to be expressed, and then deciding exactly how this information should be expressed in the light of factors such as the environmental context and the available knowledge of the listener.

The power of these influences can be observed if you overhear a conversation between two friends on a bus or train. Because you lack the personal common ground that they share, it can be amazingly difficult to make much sense of what they are saying to each other.

Conversational turns

Some of the factors determining who talks when were considered by Brennan (1990). One frequent way in which the conversation moves from one speaker to another is by means of an *adjacency pair*, in which what the first speaker says provides a strong invitation to the listener to take up the conversation; a question followed by an answer is a very common example of an adjacency pair. If the first speaker completes what he or she intended to say without producing the first part of an adjacency pair, then the next turn goes to the listener who speaks first. If none of the listeners speaks, then the first speaker is free to continue with another turn (known technically as a *turn-constructional unit*).

As Clark (1994) pointed out, spontaneous narratives in conversation (known as *intonation units*) tend to be approximately six words long, and are often preceded and followed by pauses. There tends to be a single point of highest pitch or loudness towards the end of the unit, and most units consist of a clause with a finite verb (Gee, 1986). Research on slips of the tongue (discussed later in the chapter) also suggests that speakers formulate their thoughts in units of about six words each.

Processes in speech production

We tend to take the skills involved in speech production for granted. Even young children are usually adept at talking in a reasonably sensible and grammatical way. However, speech is actually a complex activity involving a number of different skills. These include the ability to think of what one wants to say, to select the appropriate words to express it, to organise those words in a grammatical fashion, and to turn the sentences one wants to say into actual speech.

A consideration of hesitations and pauses in speech production suggests that speech tends to be planned in phrases or clauses. Pauses in spontaneous speech occur more often at grammatical junctures (such as the ends of phrases or clauses) than anywhere else. Boomer (1965) discovered that such pauses last longer on average than those at other locations (1.03 seconds vs. 0.75 seconds, respectively). Pauses that coincide with phrase boundaries tend to be filled with sounds such as "um", "er", or "ah", whereas those occurring within a phrase tend to be silent (Maclay & Osgood, 1959). A major reason for these longish pauses at the ends of phrases or clauses is probably to permit forward planning of the next utterance.

It is difficult to identify the processes involved in speech production, in part because they normally occur so rapidly (we produce two or three words per second on average). Many researchers have attempted to discover how people normally produce fluent speech by focusing on those occasions when errors creep into spoken language. As Dell (1986, p.284) pointed out: "The inner workings of a highly complex system are often revealed by the way in which the system breaks down."

Theories of speech production

Several theorists (e.g. Bock & Levelt, 1994; Dell, 1986; Dell & O'Seaghdha, 1991; Garrett, 1976, 1984) have used evidence from speech errors to construct theories of speech production. These theories have much in common. First it is assumed that there is a substantial amount of pre-production planning of speech; in other words, the speaker engages in fairly detailed planning of an utterance before speaking. Second, most theorists agree that there is a series of processing stages in speech production, and there is even agreement that there are four processing stages. Third, it is assumed that the processes involved in speech production proceed from the general (the intended meaning) to the specific (the units of sound to be uttered). In approximate terms, the processes in speech production resemble those involved in comprehension, except that the processes are in the opposite order. For example, the goal of comprehension is to understand the meaning of a message, whereas with speech production the meaning of the message is the starting point.

In view of the similarity among theories of speech production, only two theoretical approaches will be considered here. First, the spreading-activation theory of Dell (1986) and Dell and O'Seaghdha (1991) will be discussed for two main reasons: it has been a very influential theory, and it emphasises a psychological process (spreading activation) of general significance within language processing (see Chapter 12). Second, the theoretical approach of Levelt (1989) and of Bock and Levelt (1994) is discussed, because it is an important theory incorporating new insights and supported by a wide range of evidence.

Dell's theoretical approach

Dell (1986) and Dell and O'Seaghdha (1991) proposed a spreading-activation theory of speech production based on connectionist principles in which four separate levels were identified. The major assumptions of the theory (including descriptions of the four levels) are as follows:

- *Semantic level*: the meaning of what is to be said; this level is not considered in detail within the theory.
- *Syntactic level*: the grammatical structure of the words in the planned utterance.
- *Morphological level*: the morphemes or basic units of meaning in the planned sentence.
- *Phonological level*: the phonemes or basic units of sound within the sentence.
- A representation is formed at each level.
- Processing during speech planning occurs at the same time at all four levels, but is typically

more advanced at higher levels (e.g. semantic) than at lower levels (e.g. phonological).

According to spreading-activation theory, there are *categorical rules* at each level. These rules set constraints on the categories of items and on the combinations of categories that are acceptable. The rules at each level define categories that are appropriate to that level; for example, the categorical rules at the syntactic level specify the syntactic categories of items within the sentence.

In addition to the categorical rules, there is a *lexicon* (dictionary), which is in the form of a connectionist network. This lexicon contains nodes for concepts, words, morphemes, and phonemes. When a node is activated, it sends activation to all the nodes connected to it (see Chapter 1 for a discussion of activation in semantic networks). Finally, *insertion rules* select the items for inclusion in the representation at each level according to the following criterion: the most highly activated node belonging to the appropriate category is chosen. For example, if the categorical rules at the syntactic level dictate that a verb is required at a particular point within the syntactic representation, then that verb whose node is most activated will be selected. After an item has been selected, its activation level immediately reduces to zero; this prevents it from being selected repeatedly.

According to spreading-activation theory, speech errors occur because an incorrect item will sometimes have a higher level of activation than the correct item. The existence of spreading activation means that numerous nodes are all activated at the same time, and this increases the likelihood of errors being made in speech.

What kinds of errors are predicted by the theory? First, errors should belong to the appropriate category (e.g. an incorrect nouns replacing the correct noun), because of the operation of the categorical rules. As expected, most errors do belong to the appropriate category (Dell, 1986).

Second, many errors should be anticipation errors, in which a word is spoken earlier in the sentence than is appropriate (e.g. "The sky is in the sky"). This happens because all of the words in the sentence tend to become activated during the planning for speech.

Third, anticipation errors should often turn into exchange errors, in which two words within a sentence are swapped (e.g. "I must write a wife to my letter"). Remember that the activation level of a selected item immediately reduces to zero. Therefore, if "wife" has been selected too early, it is unlikely to compete successfully to be selected in its correct place in the sentence. This allows a previously unselected and highly activated item such as "letter" to appear in the wrong place. Many speech errors are of the exchange variety.

Fourth, anticipation and exchange errors generally involve words moving only a relatively short distance within the sentence. Those words relevant to the part of the sentence that is under current consideration will tend to be more activated than those words relevant to more distant parts of the sentence.

Fifth, it is predicted that speech errors should tend to consist of actual words or morphemes (this is known as the lexical bias effect). This effect was demonstrated by Baars, Motley, and MacKay (1975). Word pairs were presented briefly, and subjects had to say both words as rapidly as possible. The error rate was twice as great when the word pair could be re-formed to create two new words (e.g. "lewd rip" can be turned into "rude lip") than when it could not (e.g. "Luke risk" turns into "ruke lisk").

Sixth, the notion that the various levels of processing interact flexibly with each other means that speech errors can be multiply determined. Dell (1986) quoted the example of someone saying "Let's stop" instead of "Let's start". The error is certainly semantic, but it could also be regarded as phonological, because the substitute word shares a common sound with the appropriate word. Detailed investigation of such word-substitution errors reveals that the two words concerned (i.e. the spoken word and the intended word) tend to be more similar in sound than would be expected by chance alone (Dell & O'Seaghdha, 1991; Harley, 1984). However, Levelt et al. (1991a, b) have argued that phonological and semantic information do not combine in the way proposed by Dell (1986) and Dell and O'Seaghdha (1991). This issue is discussed later in the chapter.

According to spreading activation theory, most errors are caused by spreading activation. It might appear preferable if activation did not spread so widely through the lexicon, because then there would be fewer speech errors. Dell (1986) argued against this position. He claimed that widespread activation facilitates the production of novel sentences, and so prevents our utterances from becoming too stereotyped.

Evaluation
One of the strengths of spreading-activation theory is that it makes a series of reasonably precise and testable predictions about the kinds of errors that should occur most frequently in speech production. Another strength of the theory is that its emphasis on spreading activation provides links between speech production and other cognitive activities (e.g. word recognition: McClelland & Rumelhart, 1981). On the negative side, the focus of spreading activation theory is mainly on individual words or concepts. As a consequence, broader issues relating to the construction of a message with its intended meaning are de-emphasised.

Levelt's theoretical approach
The key features of the theoretical account of Levelt (1989) and Bock and Levelt (1994) can be seen in Fig. 14.1. There are four levels or stages involved in speech production, resembling those proposed by Dell (1986) and by Dell and O'Seaghdha (1991):

- *Message*: this consists of aspects of the speaker's intended meaning.
- *Functional processing*: it is at this stage that the outlines of the subsequent utterance are produced; these outlines possess grammatical structure or syntax. More specifically, there is *lexical selection* (word concepts of suitable meaning are selected) and there is *function assignment* (grammatical roles or syntactic functions such as subject and object are assigned). At this stage, the specific words to be spoken are not selected.
- *Positional processing*: at this stage structure is imposed on the sentence that is to be uttered.

Constituent assembly involves ordering the elements of the sentence in the appropriate sequence, and *inflection* involves adding the appropriate inflections (e.g. "-s", "-ing", "-ed") to those elements.
- *Phonological encoding*: the phonological or sound structure of the utterance is worked out, including its prosody (rhythm; stress).

One of the key features of Bock and Levelt's (1994) theory (and of the related theory put forward by Levelt, 1989) is the notion that information about meaning and syntax is generally available before information about sound. At the level of the individual word, Levelt (1989) and Bock and Levelt (1994) distinguished between a word's *lemma* (its meaning and syntactical role) and *lexeme* (its sound). Evidence that these two levels of representation are separate comes from the "tip-of-the-tongue" phenomenon, in which someone has a concept clearly in mind (a lemma), but searches in vain for the right word to describe it (a lexeme).

The tip-of-the-tongue phenomenon was first investigated systematically by Brown and McNeill (1966). They read out dictionary definitions of rare words, and asked their subjects to identify the words defined. Thus, for example, the correct answer to the definition "a navigational instrument used in measuring angular distances, especially the altitude of the sun, moon and stars at sea" is "sextant". If the subjects could not produce the right word, but felt the word was on the tip of their tongue, they tried to guess the initial letter and the number of syllables of the missing word. Those in the tip-of-the-tongue state often had access to some of the features of the word they were trying to recall. For example, subjects in that state were correct 57% of the time when guessing the word's initial letter.

Speech errors
Much of the support for theories, such as that of Bock and Levelt (1994), has come from collections of speech errors (e.g. Garrett, 1975; Stemberger, 1982). The errors in these collections consist of those that were personally heard by the researchers concerned. This procedure has some problems

Bock and Levelt's outline of the processes involved in speech production. Adapted from Bock and Levelt (1994).

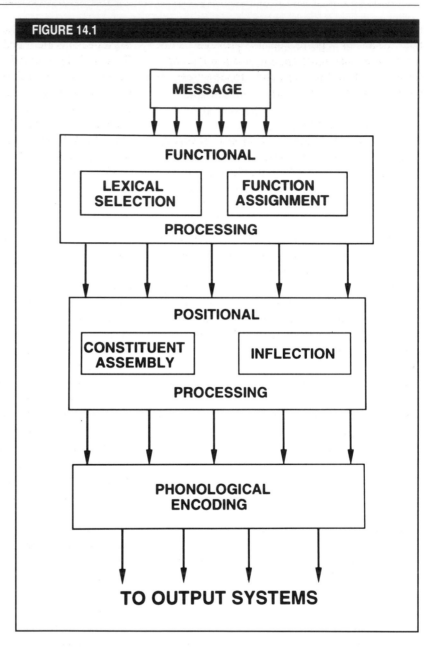

FIGURE 14.1

associated with it. For example, there may be systematic biases because some kinds of error are more readily detectable than others. Thus, we should be sceptical about percentage figures for the different kinds of speech errors. It is less clear that there are any major problems with the main categories of speech errors that have been identified. The existence of some types of speech errors has been confirmed by experimentation in which techniques have been used to create errors under laboratory conditions (see Dell, 1986).

Although care needs to be taken in interpreting the available information on speech errors, it is striking that some kinds of errors are considerably more common than others. For example, word-exchange errors (two words in a sentence switching places) nearly always involve two words belonging to the same part of speech (e.g. both nouns). The fact that there are strong constraints on the forms of speech errors provides some reassurance that most speech errors reflect in a fairly direct fashion specific imperfections in speech-production processes.

Functional processing

There are several forms of speech error involving functional processing, most of which involve lexical selection. A simple kind of lexical selection error involves *semantic substitution* (the correct word is replaced by another word of similar meaning, e.g. "Where is my tennis bat?" instead of "Where is my tennis racquet?" In 99% of cases, the substituted word is of the same form class as the correct word (e.g. nouns substitute for nouns, adjectives substitute for adjectives). Verbs are much less likely than nouns, adjectives, or adverbs to undergo semantic substitution (Hotopf, 1980), possibly because they are of central importance in function assignment.

Blending is another kind of lexical selection error (e.g. "The sky is shining" instead of "The sky is blue" or "The sun is shining"). A further kind of lexical selection error is the *word-exchange error* mentioned earlier (e.g. "I must let the house out of the cat" instead of "I must let the cat out of the house"). The two words involved in a word-exchange error are typically further apart in the sentence than the two words involved in sound-exchange errors (Garrett, 1980). This finding is consistent with Bock and Levelt's (1994) view that the order of the elements in spoken sentences has not been decided when lexical selection takes place.

Positional processing
and phonological encoding

Morpheme-exchange errors are of particular significance to the understanding of speech production processes. These errors involve inflections or suffixes remaining in place but attached to the wrong words (e.g. "He has already trunked two packs"). An implication from morpheme-exchange errors is that the positioning of inflections is dealt with by a rather separate process from the one responsible for positioning word stems (e.g. "trunk"; "pack"). There is some

evidence that the word stems are worked out before the inflections are added. Smyth, Morris, Levy, and Ellis (1987) pointed out that inflections are generally altered to fit in with the new word stems to which they are linked. For example, the "s" sound in the phrase "the forks of a prong" is pronounced in a way that is appropriate within the word "forks", but this is different to the "s" sound in the original word "prongs".

One of the best-known errors of spoken language is the spoonerism, in which the initial letter or letters of two or more words are switched. The Rev. William Archibald Spooner, after whom the spoonerism is named, is credited with several memorable examples, including "You have hissed all my mystery lectures" and "The Lord is a shoving leopard to his flock." Alas, there is a strong suspicion that many of the Rev. Spooner's gems were not produced spontaneously, but rather were the result of much painstaking effort.

The study of genuine spoonerisms reveals that consonants always exchange with consonants and vowels with vowels; it also reveals that the exchanging phonemes tend to be similar in sound (see Fromkin, 1993). Of particular importance, Garrett (1976) reported that 93% of the spoonerisms in his collection involved a switching of letters between two words within the same clause, suggesting that the clause is an important unit in speech production.

Experimental evidence

As we have seen, the focus of much research has been on speech errors and their theoretical significance. In spite of its popularity, there are limitations with this focus. Much of the information on speech errors was obtained in an informal fashion from studies lacking experimental control, and some of the main categories of speech errors have only a 1-in-10,000 incidence in normal speech (Hotopf, 1983). Such rare occurrences may well be of only partial relevance to an understanding of normal speech production. Another limitation of most research on speech errors is that information about prosodic structure (including features such as rhythm, intonation, and stress) is omitted. Such considerations led Levelt et al. (1991b, p.615) to argue that "an exclusively error-based approach to … speech production is as ill-conceived as an exclusively illusion-based approach in vision research".

Some key issues of speech production have been investigated under laboratory conditions. For example, Levelt (1989) and Bock and Levelt (1994) argued for a two-stage theory of lexical access, in which semantic but not phonological information is active during the first stage, whereas only phonological information is available during the second stage. This contrasts with the views of Dell (1986) and Dell and O'Seaghdha (1991), who argued that semantic and phonological information can be active at the same time.

The issue of whether lexical access always proceeds in the serial fashion assumed by the two-stage theory was investigated by Levelt et al. (1991a). Subjects named pictures as rapidly as possible. On some trials, an auditory probe was presented at a short, medium, or long delay after the onset of the picture; subjects had to make a lexical decision to the probe (is it a word?) before naming the picture. Some of the word probes were semantically related to the picture, whereas others were phonologically related to the picture, or were unrelated to it. Finally, some of the probes were mediated (e.g. if the picture were of a sheep, then "goal" would be a mediated probe because goat is semantically related to goat, and goal is phonologically related to goat).

There were two theoretically important findings. First, there were no effects of the semantically related probes at the long delay, suggesting that there is only phonological processing at that stage. Second, there was no effect of the mediated probes on picture-naming latencies. According to Levelt et al. (1991a, b), both of these findings are more consistent with the two-stage theory than with Dell's (1986) inter-active spreading-activation theory. For example, the absence of any effect of the mediated probes occurred because semantic and phonological information are not active at the same time. Counter-arguments were provided by Dell and O'Seaghdha (1991).

According to Levelt (1989) and Bock and Levelt (1994), sequential processes are involved in producing the prosodic representation of a sentence. Of particular importance, they assumed that key aspects of the prosodic structure (e.g. timing durations) are determined before the phonemic characteristics of the words to be spoken are known. For example, the most stressed word in a sentence is usually the last word. This is so even when the last word in the sentence is not the one intended (e.g. "I left the briefcase in my cigar", Garrett, 1980). The implication is that a sentence is assigned a prosodic pattern (including stress) before words are inserted into its structure.

Ferreira (1993) tested the views of Levelt (1989) and of Bock and Levelt (1994). Subjects were presented with sentences one at a time, and said each one from memory after it had been presented. The critical word in each sentence had a long duration (e.g. "drive") or a short duration (e.g. "stop"). This critical word came either at the end of a phrase (e.g. "Even though the chauffeur thought he could *stop*, the passengers were worried"; "Even though the chauffeur thought he could *drive*, the passengers were worried") or in the middle of a phrase (e.g. "The chauffeur thought he could *stop* the car"; "The chauffeur thought he could *drive* the car"). Information about the length of time taken to say the word plus the pause after it is shown in Fig. 14.2. The time devoted to word plus pause was greater at the end of the phrase than in the middle; of greater importance, the duration of the word had essentially no effect on that time. This suggests that the allocation of time within a phrase is decided before the exact words to be spoken have been worked out.

The findings of Ferreira (1993) provide impressive support for Levelt's views. However, when similar experiments were carried out in the Dutch language rather than in American English, the duration of the word did have an effect (Meyer, 1994). The most likely reason for the difference in findings is that some of the timing principles involved in speech production differ from one language to another.

Speech errors in patients

Bock and Levelt (1994) argued that there are various conceptually distinct processes involved in speech production. If that is indeed the case, then

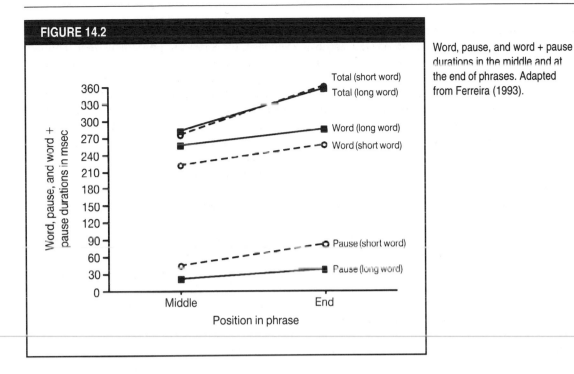

FIGURE 14.2

Word, pause, and word + pause durations in the middle and at the end of phrases. Adapted from Ferreira (1993).

presumably brain-damaged patients with impaired speech should vary in the specific process or processes that are disrupted. For example, it might be possible to identify some patients with particular problems at the message level, others with problems of functional processing, and so on. Many patients have widespread brain damage, so that most or all of the speech-production processes may be impaired. However, some patients have more circumscribed brain damage, and investigations of their speech impairments are of particular value.

Anomia

Many brain-damaged patients who cannot speak normally suffer from what is known as anomia. Such patients can construct sentence frames, but have great difficulties in accessing content words. The precise nature of the problem in anomic patients varies considerably. Anomia is sometimes associated with a semantic impairment, and sometimes not. In those cases where there is a semantic impairment, this would indicate the existence of a problem between the message and functional processing.

A case of anomia in which a semantic impairment appeared to be mainly responsible was reported by Howard and Orchard-Lisle (1984). The patient, JCU, had good object recognition and reasonable comprehension. However, she was very poor at naming the objects shown in pictures unless she was given the first phoneme or sound as a cue. If the cue was the first phoneme of a word closely related to the object shown in the picture, then JCU would often be misled into producing the wrong answer. This wrong answer she accepted as correct 76% of the time. In contrast, if she produced a name that was quite different in meaning to the object depicted, then she rejected it 86% of the time. The implication is that JCU had some access to semantic information, but the information was often insufficient to specify precisely what it was she was looking at.

A very different case of anomia was investigated by Kay and Ellis (1987). Their patient, EST, had very good comprehension. He did not have the semantic impairment shown by JCU on the tasks just described. Indeed, his performance on a range of tasks was so good that it appeared that he had no significant impairment to his semantic system. However, he had a very definite anomia, as can be seen from this attempt to describe a picture (Kay & Ellis, 1987):

> Er ... two children, one girl one male ... the ... the girl, they're in a ... and their, their mother was behind them in in, they're in the kitchen ... the boy is trying to get ... a ... er, a part of a cooking ... jar ... He's standing on ... the lad, the boy is standing on a ... standing on a ... standing on a ... I'm calling it a seat, I can't ... I forget what it's, what the name of it is ... It is er a higher, it's a seat, standing on that, 'e's standing on that ... this boy is standing on this, seat ... getting some of this er stuff to ... biscuit to eat.

Close inspection of EST's speech indicates that it is reasonably grammatical, and that his greatest problem lies in finding words other than those in very common usage. His problem may lie between functional and positional processing. More specfically, two major possibilities suggest themselves as to why most words cannot be found by EST:

- Information about them is no longer contained in the store that makes the spoken forms of words available.
- The information is still there, but for some reason is inaccessible.

The evidence tends to favour the second alternative. EST is better at repeating spoken words that he never uses in his spontaneous speech than he is at repeating spoken non-words, indicating that at least some residual information about most words is still present in his memory system.

What are we to make of EST's anomia? Kay and Ellis (1987) argued that his condition resembles in greatly magnified form that of the rest of us when in the "tip-of-the-tongue" state. The difference is that it is mostly relatively rare words that cause us problems with finding and saying the word corresponding to a concept that we have, whereas with EST the problem is present with all but the most common words.

Syntactic problems: Agrammatism

Suppose, for the sake of argument, that there are some patients who can formulate ideas clearly at the message level, but who have problems in speaking grammatically. According to the theory of Bock and Levelt (1994), such patients might well have problems with constituent assembly and inflections in positional processing, and possibly also problems with function assignment in functional processing. The speech of such patients would contain many meaningfully related words, but would lack the normal structure. The lack of appropriate grammatical structure seems to reveal itself mainly by the omission of inflections and function words from their speech. There is also inappropriate ordering of the words within a sentence. For example, the words in the following two phrases are the same, but the different ordering of the words makes a substantial difference to the meaning: "Dog bites man" and "Man bites dog." Patients who exhibit grammatical problems have been discovered, and are sometimes referred to by the rather vague term of "agrammatic aphasia".

Saffran, Schwartz, and Marin (1980a,b) investigated patients suffering from grammatical impairments. For example, one patient was asked to describe a picture of a woman kissing a man, and produced the following: "The kiss ... the lady kissed ... the lady is ... the lady and the man and the lady ... kissing." In addition, Saffran et al. found that agrammatic aphasics had great difficulty in putting the two nouns in the correct order when asked to describe pictures containing two living creatures in interaction.

The majority of patients who produce numerous grammatical errors in speaking also have problems in making use of grammatical information in comprehension. It is currently uncertain whether there are separate syntactic modules involved in comprehension and production, or whether there is a single syntactic module involved in both input and output.

Evaluation

The theoretical approach adopted by Levelt (1989) and by Bock and Levelt (1994) possesses a number of strengths. The notion that there are four different levels of stages of processing underlying speech production is in line with several previous theories (e.g. Garrett, 1976, 1984; Dell, 1986), and has received substantial support from studies of speech errors, from laboratory experimentation, and from studies on brain-damaged patients. The view that the processes involved in speech production should not only be studied by consideration of the relatively infrequent errors made in speech, but should also be investigated experimentally under error-free conditions, is undoubtedly correct. Furthermore, the emphasis on prosodic features of speech production remedies a deficiency in many previous approaches.

Probably the greatest problem facing theories of speech production is that speech errors can be interpreted in many different ways. As a consequence, we can have no real confidence that speech production proceeds in the fashion indicated by Bock and Levelt (1994). For example, Bock and Levelt (1994), in common with most theorists, assumed that speech production involves forming a grammatical structure, and then inserting specific words into that structure. In contrast, Dell, Juliano, and Goviadjie (1993) proposed a parallel distributed processing theory of speech production in which there is no explicit grammatical structure. In essence, they argued that many phonological speech errors are determined by two principles: (1) similarity (an incorrect sound typically resembles the correct sound); and (2) sequential bias (what is said is biased towards common sound sequences). As they concluded (1993, p.177), several phonological speech errors "can be produced by a mechanism that does not separate linguistic structure and content in an explicit a priori fashion".

Another limitation of the Levelt (1989) and Bock and Levelt (1994) approach is their relative neglect of cognitive processes and structures known to be of major importance in language processing. The working memory system (see Chapters 6 and 13) is presumably much involved in speech production, but its role is not discussed in detail. In similar fashion, spreading activation (at the heart of Dell's theoretical approach) is probably of more central importance in speech production than is acknowledged by Levelt.

WRITING

Writing involves several processes that are also used in other cognitive activities. For example, writing always involves memory retrieval, and it also involves goal setting, planning, problem solving, and evaluation. Thus, although writing is an important topic in its own right (no pun intended!), it should not be regarded as entirely separate from other language and non-language activities.

The processes involved in writing can be considered at several different levels. At the most specific level, we can focus on individual words (e.g. on systematic errors in spelling). At the most general level, we can focus on the overall structure of a piece of writing and on the major goal or goals being pursued by the writer. At an intermediate level, we can focus on the processes that mediate between goal-setting and writing sentences. It is of interest that the intermediate level has been a major focus of research on speech production, but has received less attention than the specific and general levels in writing research.

We will be considering all three levels, moving from the general to the specific. Because much of the most valuable information about the processes involved in spelling has emerged from cognitive neuropsychology, our discussion of spelling will largely revolve around research on brain-damaged patients.

Theoretical considerations

Probably the first systematic attempt to identify the major processes involved in writing was that of Hayes and Flower (1980). They argued that writing consists of the following main processes:

- *Planning:* generating information from long-term memory, organising, and goal-setting.
- *Translating:* producing language conforming in meaning to the information retrieved from the writer's long-term memory.
- *Reviewing:* reading and editing what has been written.

Hayes and Flower (1980) relied on *protocol analysis* to support their theoretical account. In protocol analysis, a writer verbalises his or her thoughts during writing, and a tape recording is made of these verbalisations. In addition, all the notes made by the writer are assessed. The writer they studied was particularly aware of the processes he used while writing. His protocol analysis suggested that he started by generating information, then proceeded to organising, and then to translating. Analysis of what he wrote confirmed this impression, because there was a definite progression over time from unorganised fragments to more structured items, and then to complete sentences. Finally, as expected, the flow of processing was often interrupted by the editing and generating processes.

Hayes and Flower (1986) developed some of their earlier theoretical views. They put more emphasis on the notion that writing is goal-directed. Evidence for this emerged clearly from protocol analysis. For example, someone who was asked to write about the role of women for a hostile audience focused very much on what he was trying to achieve: "I'm not really trying to persuade these people of anything. I'm simply being descriptive … I'm saying, 'This is the way the world is'."

The goals involved in writing tend to be hierarchically organised. Many writers prepare an outline before they start writing, including the major points they want to make and more minor points associated with the major ones. The writer who said that he was being descriptive analysed his writing goals as follows: "I think what I really want is to present maybe one [point] with a lot of illustrations."

Hayes and Flower (1986) identified planning, sentence generation, and revising as the key processes:

• The planning process involves producing ideas and organising them into a writing plan to satisfy the goals the writer is seeking to achieve.
• The sentence-generation process involves turning the writing plan into the actual writing of sentences.
• The revision process involves evaluating what has been written; this process can operate at a relatively specific level (i.e. individual words or phrases) or at a more general level (e.g. the structural coherence of the writing).
• The natural sequence is planning, sentence generation, and revision, but it is rarely the case that all of the planning is done before any of the sentence generation and revision.

Planning

Writing plans obviously depend heavily on the knowledge that the writer possesses about the topic in question, but the quality of a writing plan is not only influenced by the writer's topic knowledge. Experts are often notoriously poor at organising their ideas into a form that is comprehensible, in part because their expertise distances them from the problems in understanding experienced by the non-expert.

According to Hayes and Flower (1986), strategic knowledge plays a major role in the construction of a writing plan. Strategic knowledge concerns ways of organising the goals and sub-goals of writing so as to construct a coherent writing plan. Hayes and Flower (1986) found that good writers use strategic knowledge in a very flexible way. The structure of the writing plan often changes considerably during the writing period as new ideas occur to the writer, or dissatisfaction grows with the original plan. Hayes and Flower made the interesting suggestion that writers who are afflicted by writer's block tend to adhere rigidly to their original writing plan. If it becomes obvious that the plan is inadequate, then the writing process grinds to a halt.

Adults possessing either a lot of knowedge or relatively little on a topic were compared by Hayes and Flower (1986). The experts produced more goals and sub-goals, and so constructed a more complex overall writing plan. However, the greatest difference between the experts and the novices was in terms of plan integration: the various goals of the experts were much more interconnected.

Sentence generation

The gap between the writing plan and the actual writing of sentences is usually large. Kaufer, Hayes, and Flower (1986) compared the outlines that writers produced with the essays they wrote subsequently. Even for those writers who produced the longest outlines, the essay was approximately eight times longer than the outline. In some ways, the process going on here is the opposite of that involved in comprehension. Van Dijk and Kintsch (1983) argued that comprehension involves extracting the macro-structure from the micro-propositions (see Chapter 13), and sentence generation could be regarded as generating micro-propositions from the macro-structural plans.

The technique of asking writers to think aloud permitted Kaufer et al. (1986) to gain some insight into the process of sentence generation. Here is a typical verbal protocol of a writer engaged in writing, with dashes being inserted at those points where there was a pause of at least two seconds:

The best thing about it is (1) _____ what? (2) Something about using my mind (3)_____ it allows me the opportunity to (4) _____uh_____I want to write something about my ideas (5) _____ to put ideas into action (6) _____or _____to develop my ideas into (7) _____what? (8) _____ into a meaningful form? (9) Oh, Bleh! _____say it allows me (10) _____ to use (11) _____ Na _____allows me _____scratch that. The best thing about it is that it allows me to use (12) _____ my mind and ideas in a productive way (13).

In this protocol, fragments 12 and 13 formed the written sentence, and the earlier fragments 1, 4, 6, 7, 9, and 11 were attempts to produce parts of the sentence.

Kaufer et al. (1986) compared the sentence-generation styles of expert and average writers. Both groups accepted approximately 75% of the sentence parts they verbalised, and those sentence parts that were changed were nearly always those that had just been produced. The most interesting difference between the two groups was in terms of the length of the average sentence part that was proposed: it was 11.2 words for the expert writer compared with 7.3 words for the average writers. Thus, good writers make use of larger units or "building blocks" in writing than do others.

It is interesting to compare the size of the unit in writing with that in speech production. As we saw earlier in the chapter, there is evidence that the unit in speech production is approximately six words (Clark, 1994), which is comparable to the average writer's unit of approximately seven words. The size of these units is probably determined in part by the limited capacity of working memory (Chapter 6).

Revision

Expert writers differ from non-expert writers in terms of both the amount of time spent revising what they have written and how they approach the task of revision. Because increased expertise usually means that less time is needed to perform a task, it is perhaps surprising that expert writers typically spend longer than non-expert writers in revision. Matters become clearer, however, when one considers differences between the two groups in how they perceive the revision process. Expert writers tend to focus on the coherence and structure of the arguments expressed, whereas non-expert writers focus on individual words and phrases. It is much more complex and time-consuming to modify the hierarchical structure of a text than to change individual words.

Faigley and Witte (1983) compared the revisions made by writers at different levels of skill. They discovered that 34% of the revisions by experienced adult writers involved a change of meaning, against 25% of the revisions of experienced college writers, and only 12% of the revisions of inexperienced college writers. These differences probably occur because experienced writers are more concerned with the broad issues of coherence and meanings.

Further evidence on differences in revision processes between expert and non-expert writers was obtained by Hayes et al. (1985). They discovered that expert writers detected approximately 60% more problems in a text than did non-experts. Of the problems that were detected, the expert writers correctly identified the nature of the problem in 74% of the cases, against only 42% for the non-expert writers. Rather surprisingly, both groups often re-wrote sections of the text without working out what was deficient in the original.

One of the greatest problems in revision is to alter the text in such a way that it becomes more comprehensible to the intended reader or readers. This is a particularly acute problem in writing a textbook such as this, where the readers are likely to vary considerably in their previous knowledge of the topics being discussed. An interesting way of teaching writers to be more alert to the reader's needs was used by Schriver (1984). Students read an imperfect text, and tried to predict the comprehension problems that a reader would have with it. Then the students read a reader's verbal protocol, which was produced while he or she was struggling to understand that text. After the students had been given a number of texts and the accompanying reader's protocols, they became better at predicting the kinds of problems readers would have with new texts.

Writing expertise

It is a matter of considerable practical and theoretical interest to find out in detail why some writers are more skilful than others. We have already seen that more skilled writers differ from less skilled ones during all three stages of writing: planning, sentence generation, and revising. However, there is increasing evidence that individual differences in writing ability depend more on the processes involved in planning than on those involved in the other stages.

Bereiter and Scardamalia (1987) identified two major strategies that are used in the planning stage:

- a knowledge-telling strategy.
- a knowledge-transforming strategy.

The knowledge-telling strategy involves the writer simply writing down everything that he or she knows about a topic without any real planning or attempt to organise the information for the reader's benefit. The text that has already been generated is used to provide retrieval cues for generating the rest of the text. In the words of a 12-year-old child who used the knowledge-telling strategy (Bereiter & Scardamalia, 1987, p. 9), "I have a whole bunch of ideas and write them down until my supply of ideas is exhausted. Then I might try to think of more ideas up to the point when you can't get any more ideas that are worth putting down on paper and then I would end it".

The knowledge-transforming strategy is considerably more complex. It involves use of a *rhetorical problem space* and a *content problem space*. Rhetorical problems relate to the achievement of the goals of the writing task (e.g. "Can I strengthen the argument?"; "Can the main idea be expressed more simply?"), and content problems relate to the specific information to be written down (e.g. "The case of Smith vs. Jones strengthens the argument"). There should be movement of information in both directions between the content space and the rhetorical space. However, this is much more likely to happen with skilled writers using a knowledge-transforming strategy than with less skilled writers using the knowledge-telling strategy. In the words of Bereiter and Scardamalia (1987, p.303):

> The key requirement for reflective thought in writing ... is the translation of problems encountered in the rhetorical space back into subgoals to be achieved in the content spacee ... the novice possesses productions for transferring information from the content space to the rhetorical space, but lacks productions for the return trip.

Writers using a knowledge-transforming strategy should produce high-quality text that is more organised and more structured than the text produced by those using a knowledge-telling strategy. A major characteristic of well-organised or structured text is that it contains high-level main or central points capturing important themes. Accordingly, Bereiter, Burtis, and Scardamalia (1988) hypothesised that knowledge-transforming strategists would be more likely than knowledge-telling strategists to produce high-level main points. This hypothesis was tested by asking children and adults to write on the topic: "Should children be able to choose the subjects they study in school?" The subjects were told to think aloud while planning what to write, and what they said was later analysed for evidence of knowledge-transforming processes (e.g. organising the structure; focusing on a subset of ideas). Those subjects who produced a high-level main point used on average 4.75 different knowledge-transforming processes during planning, whereas those who produced a low-level main point used only 0.23 knowledge-transforming processes.

It has often been claimed that expert writers are helped by their use of either rough drafts (an initial version of the text) or outlines (focus on main themes). Kellogg (1988) assessed the value of rough drafts and outlines on a task in which subjects learned several facts about a controversy over bussing systems for the handicapped, and were then asked to write a business letter arguing for a particular system. Producing an outline increased the quality of the letter, whereas producing a rough draft did not.

The proportion of the time during writing devoted to different processes is shown in Fig. 14.3. Those who produced an outline devoted more of their time to translating or sentence generation than did the no-outline subjects, but less of their time to planning and reviewing or revising. Those who produced a rough draft focused on planning and translating or generating, whereas those who only did a polished draft attended to all three processes.

What do these results mean? Subjects who produced rough drafts or outlines had reduced processing load during the writing of the final text, in the sense that they did not have to focus on all three processes (i.e. planning, translating, and reviewing). However, the finding that outlines led to improved quality of final text, but rough drafts did not, means that reduced processing overload does not necessarily enhance quality. Planning is the most important and the most difficult process in writing, and producing an outline has the great advantage that the planning process can be virtually complete before starting to write the polished draft.

Evaluation

Hayes and Flower (1980, 1986) have greatly advanced our understanding of the processes involved in writing. However, protocol analysis (on which Hayes and Flower rely heavily) can provide information only about those processes of which there is conscious awareness. This criticism applies more to some aspects of their theorising than to others. Writers may generally have a clear idea of what they are trying to achieve during the revision process, but are unlikely to be aware of

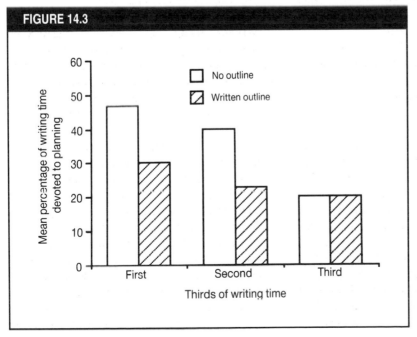

FIGURE 14.3

Percentage of writing time devoted to planning as a function of whether an outline had been prepared and its place in the writing period. Based on data in Kellogg (1988).

how they search long-term memory for ideas, how they think of inferences, and so on. There is probably little or no conscious awareness of many (or even most) of the processes involved in writing, and there is an urgent need to develop ways of investigating these processes.

One of the most valuable aspects of the approach taken by Hayes and Flower (1986) is their comparison of more- and less-skilled writers. This facilitates the identification of the specific strategies involved in skilled writing. It is also useful in terms of producing practical advice for those who find it dificult to develop adequate writing skills. The research of others (e.g. Bereiter et al., 1988; Kellogg, 1988) has confirmed that the planning process is of particular importance in determining writing quality.

On the negative side, there are some doubts as to whether the three processes of planning, sentence generation, and revision can be neatly separated from each other. In particular, planning and sentence generation are often almost inextricably bound up with each other. A further criticism was raised by Kellogg (1990), who argued that writing is more of a social act than was proposed by Hayes and Flower (1986). According to Kellogg (1990, p.376): "Instead of focusing on the cognitive processes of an individual, the social approach studies the writer as an agent in a literate community of discourse."

Writing problems:
Cognitive neuropsychology

Many brain-damaged patients who have particular problems with spelling and with writing have been studied (Ellis & Young, 1988). The focus here will be on two of the major issues in this area. First, there has been a certain amount of controversy about the role played by inner speech in the writing process. Second, there have been suggestions that the processes involved in spelling and writing can vary. The notion of different "routes" to the writing of words is considered in the light of the relevant cognitive neuropsychological evidence. It should be emphasised that cognitive neuropsychologists have focused only on certain limited aspects of writing, especially those concerned with the spelling of individual words. Some reasons for the

circumscribed nature of the cognitive neuropsychological approach are discussed in Chapter 19.

Inner speech and writing

It has often been assumed (e.g. Luria, 1970) that writing depends heavily on inner speech, and that one says words to oneself before writing them down. This makes intuitive sense, because we often have the impression that inner speech is accompanying the writing process. In addition, many of the spelling mistakes made in writing (e.g. "akshun" instead of "action") are consistent with the notion that spellings are sometimes based almost entirely on knowledge of word sounds.

These considerations suggest that inner speech is sometimes involved in writing. However, the key theoretical issue is whether inner speech is necessary for writing or whether it is an "optional extra". Perhaps the most direct way of tackling this issue is to consider brain-damaged patients who appear to have little or no inner speech, and see whether they are able to write in a reasonably normal fashion. Precisely this has now been done in a number of studies, and we now turn to the relevant evidence.

Levine, Calvanio, and Popovics (1982) reported on the case of EB, who was an engineer in his mid-fifties who had had a stroke. This stroke had virtually removed his ability to produce overt speech, but his comprehension of speech and of written text was very good. Of most immediate interest, his inner speech appeared to be practically non-existent. In one task, he was given a target picture and four further pictures. His task was to decide which of the four pictures had a name that rhymed with the name of the target picture. He was able to work out the names and spellings of most of the pictures, but could not use the sounds of the picture names to perform the task accurately. In another task, he could not match spoken and written non-words, presumably because he was unable to make use of inner speech.

In spite of his apparent lack of inner speech, EB's writing skills were largely intact. He sometimes experienced problems with grammatical structure in his writing, but the quality of his written language can be seen in this account

(Levine et al., 1982) of his first memories after his stroke:

> Gradually after what seemed days and days, got back enough strength to pull myself up and sit if I held on. I tilted off to the right and had a hard time maintaining my balance … The nurse and doctor and an orderly helped me up then … I got to another part of the hospital where there were two doctors asking me questions I couldn't answer.

The findings from EB are unusually clear. The great majority of aphasic patients are severely impaired in both writing and speaking, and so lack the marked discrepancy between writing and speaking skills shown by EB.

Further evidence that some brain-damaged patients do not rely on inner speech when engaged in writing comes from the study of patients suffering from what has been termed "neologistic jargonaphasia". Their speech is full of non-words which sound similar to the intended words (e.g. "skut" instead of "scout"; "orstrum" instead of "saucepan"). These errors do not seem to be due to problems of articulation, because patients with neologistic jargonaphasia can often pronounce common multi-syllabled words accurately.

If neologistic jargonaphasics relied on inner speech while writing, it would be expected that the kinds of errors present in their pronunciation of words would affect their spelling of the same words. The patient RD (Ellis, Miller, & Sin, 1983) was shown various pictures, and called an elephant an "enelust", a screwdriver a "kistro", and a penguin a "senstenz". Despite these substantial mispronunciations, his spellings of all of these words were completely accurate. However, the superiority of writing over speech that RD displayed may not be generally true of neologistic jargonaphasics.

Section summary

There are patients (e.g. EB) whose writing skills are reasonably intact, but who do not appear to use inner speech at all. Other patients (e.g. RD) can write many words accurately in spite of the fact that they cannot pronounce them correctly. It must be concluded that spelling and writing do not necessarily depend on inner speech. However, inner speech may often be used during writing by normal individuals.

Routes to spelling

In this section, we will consider the various ways in which we spell words that we hear. A sketch-map of what may be involved is shown in Fig. 14.4. The main points to be noted are as follows:

- There are several different routes between hearing a word and spelling it.
- The spelling of known or familiar words involves use of the *graphemic output lexicon* (a store containing information about the written forms of familiar words). Heard words can gain access to the graphemic output lexicon either through the *semantic system* (which stores word meanings), or through the *speech output lexicon* (which provides information about the spoken forms of words). Both routes are often used at the same time by normal individuals. This serves the function of minimising the number of errors in writing.
- The spelling of unknown words or non-words cannot involve use of the grapheme output lexicon, because no information about them is available in the lexicon. What happens is that spellings are constructed from the spoken or phonemic forms of words by means of *phoneme–grapheme conversion*, which capitalises on the regularities in the language. The irregularities of the English language mean that this route will often produce plausible but incorrect spellings of irregular words (e.g. "yacht" might be spelled as "yot").

This theoretical model makes several assumptions about the different components or modules that can be involved in spelling. In order to evaluate its adequacy, it will be useful to consider some of the evidence relating to each of the major assumptions incorporated in the model.

How do we know there are separate graphemic output and speech output lexicons? If information about the written forms (graphemic output lexicon) and the spoken forms (speech output lexicon) of words were stored in the same lexicon, then

FIGURE 14.4

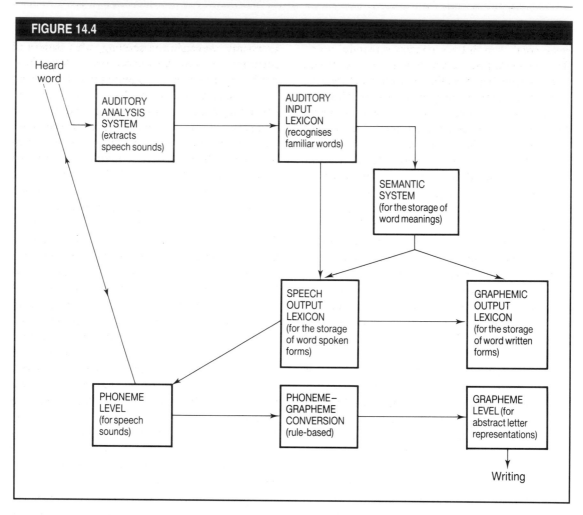

Components of a model for the spelling of heard words. Adapted from Ellis and Young (1988).

presumably patients who had problems with speaking would have problems with writing. We have seen already that this is not always the case. EB was able to write reasonably well despite apparently having no inner speech, and RD could write many words he could not say properly. Presumably patients such as EB and RD have a relatively intact graphemic output lexicon, but a severely impaired speech output lexicon (or connections to or from it). In contrast to EB and RD, the more common pattern among brain-damaged patients is to have a greater problem with writing than with speech. Such patients presumably have more severe impairment of the graphemic output lexicon than of the speech output lexicon.

How do we know that the semantic system is involved in the writing process? If, for some reason, only partial semantic information about a heard word was passed on from the semantic system to the graphemic output lexicon, then we would expect a word similar in meaning to be written down in place of the actual word. Precisely this has been observed in so-called "deep dysgraphics". Bub and Kertesz (1982) studied a young woman, JC, who made numerous semantic errors, writing "sun" when the word "sky" was spoken, writing "chair" when "desk" was said, and

to label the colours did worse than the non-labellers on a subsequent test of recognition memory, suggesting that colour memory was distorted by language in the form of labelling. In a study by Stefflre, Castillo Vales, and Morley (1966), memory for colour was compared in Spanish and Mayan speakers. There were significant differences, which were related to differences in linguistic codability (ease of verbal labelling) of the colours between the two languages.

We have seen that language can affect memory. There is also evidence that language sometimes affects perceptual processes. Miyawaki et al. (1975) compared English and Japanese speakers with respect to their perception of sounds varying between a pure /l/ and a pure /r/. English speakers make a sharp perceptual distinction between similar sounds on either side of the categorial boundary between "l" and "r". No such perceptual distinction is made by Japanese speakers, presumably because there is no distinction between /l/ and /r/ in the Japanese language.

A similar effect of language on perception was reported by Kay and Kempton (1984). Their subjects had to decide whether each of a set of test colour chips more closely resembled a blue or a green colour chip. English speakers were much influenced by which side of the English colour boundary each test chip lay, exaggerating the greenness or blueness of chips intermediate between blue and green. In contrast, speakers of the Mexican–Indian language Tarahumara (which does not have words for blue and green) did not show this exaggeration effect.

Recent interpretations of the Whorfian hypothesis

Hunt and Agnoli (1991) proposed a cognitive psychology account of the Whorfian hypothesis. The essence of their position is as follows (1991, p.379):

> Different languages lend themselves to the transmission of different types of messages. People consider the costs of computation when they reason about a topic. The language that they use will partly determine

those costs. In this sense, language does influence cognition.

In other words, any given language makes it easy to think in certain ways and difficult to think in other ways, and it is for this reason that thinking is influenced by language.

An especially interesting demonstration of how language can influence thinking was provided by Hoffman, Lau, and Johnson (1986). Bilingual English–Chinese speakers read descriptions of individuals, and were subsequently asked to provide free impressions of the individuals described. The descriptions were prepared in such a way as to conform to either Chinese or English stereotypes of personality. For example, there is a stereotype of the artistic type in English, consisting of a mixture of artistic skills, moody and intense temperament, and bohemian lifestyle, but this stereotype does not exist in Chinese. Bilinguals thinking in Chinese made use of Chinese stereotypes in their free impressions, whereas bilinguals thinking in English used English stereotypes. This suggests that the kinds of inferences we draw can be much influenced by the language in which we are thinking.

Hunt and Agnoli (1991) have provided a plausible cognitive account of the Whorfian hypothesis, and there is a fair amount of evidence that is consistent with their account. However, what is lacking is a systematic programme of research to establish clearly that language influences thought in the ways specified by Hunt and Agnoli.

CHAPTER SUMMARY

Speaking and writing are the two main forms of language production. Those who speak well generally also write well, whereas those who speak poorly tend to write poorly. This suggests that speaking and writing share common processes. However, cognitive neuropsychological evidence from brain-damaged patients has demonstrated that some of the processes involved in speaking and writing are quite different. There are some patients who can speak adequately but have immense problems with writing, and there are other patients who can write but not speak.

Speech production is best regarded as a form of communication. In order for that communication to be effective, there are certain rules that need to be heeded. For example, speakers should take account of the communal and personal common ground, consisting of the attitudes, knowledge, and so on shared by speakers and their listeners.

One of the key characteristics of speech is that there is typically a substantial amount of pre-production planning. In other words, a speaker's mind is generally on what will be said shortly rather than on what he or she is currently saying. Pre-production planning tends to move from the general (intended message) to the specific (sounds to be uttered), and from grammatical considerations to identification of the words to be said.

The speech of normal individuals is reasonably accurate, but various problems do occur from time to time. These include the tip-of-the-tongue state, word-exchange errors, morpheme-exchange errors, spoonerisms, and hesitations and pauses. It is probable that spreading activation is responsible for many of these speech errors (Dell, 1986; Dell & O'Seaghdha, 1991). The existence of so many different kinds of speech errors supports the view that there are several different stages of speech planning, each of which is fallible. The same view is supported by research on brain-damaged patients, who have impairments ranging from anomia (inability to find and say content words) to agrammatism (grammatically unstructured speech).

Writing resembles speaking in that there are various different stages involved. According to Hayes and Flower (1986), the major stages in writing are planning, sentence generation, and revising. Planning involves the generating of ideas that will satisfy the writing goals, and arranging them into a coherent structure. Sentence generation involves turning the results of the planning stage into actual sentences. Revising involves identifying deficiencies in what has been written. The stages generally proceed in the order planning, generation, and revising, but there are numerous exceptions to this order. Expert writers differ from non-expert writers at all stages, but the differences are particularly great at the planning stage.

Writers often feel that they say words and parts of sentences to themselves before writing them down. However, cognitive neuropsychologists have discovered that some patients who lack any inner speech can nevertheless write in a perfectly adequate fashion. This demonstrates that writing does not necessarily depend on inner speech. Cognitive neuropsychologists have also found that spelling and writing can occur in various ways, depending on such factors as whether it is a familiar or an unfamiliar word that must be written.

Research on the relationship between language and thought has provided support for the weak form of the Whorfian hypothesis, namely, that language influences thought. Most of this research has focused on memory and perception. Any language makes it easy to think in certain ways and difficult to think in other ways (Hunt & Agnoli, 1991), and it is for this reason that thought is often influenced by language.

FURTHER READING

Bock, K., & Levelt, W. (1994). Language production: Grammatical encoding. In M.A. Gernsbacher (Ed.), *Handbook of psycholinguistics*. London: Academic Press. Some of the main processes involved in speech production are discussed in detail.

Clark, H. H. (1994). Discourse in production. In M.A. Gernsbacher (Ed.), *Handbook of psycholinguistics*. London: Academic Press. The notion that speech production should be considered in its social context is explored in depth.

Fromkin, V.A. (1993). Speech production. In J.B. Gleason & N.B. Ratner (Eds.), *Psycholinguistics*. Orlando, FL: Harcourt Brace. This chapter deals with the processes involved in speech production in an accessible and comprehensive fashion.

Hunt, E., & Agnoli, F. (1991). The Whorfian hypothesis: A cognitive psychology perspective. *Psychological Review*, *98*, 377–389. The evidence relating to the weak form of the Whorfian hypothesis is discussed in the light of contemporary views on cognition.

Kellogg, R.T. (1990). Writing. In M.W. Eysenck (Ed.), *The Blackwell dictionary of cognitive psychology*. Oxford: Blackwell. This provides a succinct account of modern thinking about psychological factors affecting writing performance.

15

Solving Puzzles and Problems

OVERVIEW ON THINKING

Thinking is often considered one of the highest expressions of our mental development. Consider a sample of the sorts of things to which we apply the term "thinking".

First, consider a fragment of Molly Bloom's sleepy thoughts from James Joyce's *Ulysses* (1922/1960, pp.871–872), about Mrs. Riordan:

> ... God help the world if all the women in the world were her sort down on bathingsuits and lownecks of course nobody wanted her to wear I suppose she was pious because no man would look at her twice I hope I'll never be like her a wonder she didn't want us to cover our faces but she was a welleducated woman certainly and her gabby talk about Mr. Riordan here and Mr. Riordan there I suppose he was glad to get shut of her ...

Next, a person (S) answering an experimenter's (E) question about regulating the thermostat on a home-heating system (Kempton, 1986, p.83):

E: Let's say you're in the house and you're cold ... Let's say it's a cold day, you feel cold, you want to do something about it.

S: Oh, what I might do is, I might turn the thing up high to get out, to get a lot of air out fast, then after a little while turn it off or turn it down.

E: Uh-huh

S: So there are also, you know, these issues about, um, the rate at which the thing produces heat, the higher the setting is, the more heat that's produced per unit of time, so if you're cold, you want to get warm fast, um, so you turn it up high.

Finally, a protocol of one of the authors adding 457 and 638 aloud.

> Eight and seven is fifteen and then you carry one so, one and three is four and five is nine, and six and four is ten, so the final number is ... one, nought, nine, five; one thousand and ninety-five.

These three samples illustrate several general aspects of thinking. First, all the pieces involve individuals being *conscious* of their thoughts. Clearly, thinking must involve conscious awareness. However, we tend to be conscious of the products of thinking rather than the processes themselves. For example, we are conscious of taking eight and seven to add, to produce fifteen, but the thought processes responsible for the answer are unconscious and not open to introspection. Furthermore, even when we can introspect on our thoughts, our recollections of them are often inaccurate. Joyce does a good job of reconstructing the character of idle, associative thought in Molly Bloom's internal monologue, but if we interrupted her and asked her to tell us her thoughts from the previous five minutes, little of it would be recalled accurately. Similarly, in psychological experiments retrospective recollections of conscious thoughts are often unreliable. In fact, even introspective evidence taken as thoughts are being produced is only reliable under some conditions (see Ericsson & Simon, 1980, 1984; for more details see also Chapter 1).

Second, thinking can vary in the extent to which it is directed (Gilhooly, 1995). At one end of the scale it can be relatively undirected, and at the other extreme it can be sharply directed towards a specific goal. Molly Bloom's piece is more undirected relative to the other pieces. On the point of slipping into a dream, she is just letting one thought slide into another. If she has any goal it is a very general and ill-defined one (e.g. reflect on the day's happenings). In the other two pieces, the goal is much clearer and well-defined. In the addition example, a specific answer must be provided that is known to be either right or wrong (i.e. the goal is clearly defined and can be evaluated easily). As we shall see, most of the research on thinking has been concerned with relatively well-defined, goal-driven situations and, hence, these situations will be the main focus of the chapters in this part of the book (see Gilhooly, 1995, for an exploration of undirected thinking).

Third, the amount and nature of the knowledge used in different thinking tasks can vary enormously. For example, the knowledge required in the addition case is quite limited. It mainly hinges on knowing how to add any number between one and ten and the rule that you carry numbers above ten from one column to the next (see Anderson, 1993, for a production system model of this behaviour). On the other hand, Molly Bloom is using a vast amount of knowledge about the mores of old widows, expectations about what she herself will be like when old, general knowledge about the irony of those who criticise

that which they cannot do themselves, and much more besides. Technically, situations that require little knowledge are called *knowledge-lean*, whereas those requiring more knowledge are termed *knowledge-rich*. Knowledge-rich situations are much harder to characterise because of the amount of knowledge involved and the variety of ways it is used. For this very reason, much of the initial success in thinking research has come from examining knowledge-lean situations.

In considering the literature on problem solving, we will first concentrate in this chapter on research that examines puzzle problems, which tend to be knowledge-lean. In the next chapter, we will consider knowledge-rich types of problem solving: typically, this has been investigated by studying the problem-solving behaviour of experts. The puzzles of the present chapter differ considerably from everyday, real-world problems. However, as laboratory tasks they have allowed us to make initial inroads on human problem solving. Later, we will consider the "ecological-validity" of these problems and how they differ from real-world problems.

Overview of thinking chapters

In this part of the book, thinking research is divided up into three main categories: problem solving involving puzzles, expert problem solving, and reasoning. These divisions reflect the history and theoretical orientations of thinking research. They are unlikely to be reflected in everyday thought, which may involve a complex admixture of thinking styles. However, the subject matter is made more tractable by introducing these divisions. All these types of thinking share the property of being directed towards relatively definite goals.

These chapters are distinguished from many other chapters in the book by their silence on cognitive neuropsychology. In general, there is very little work on thinking from a cognitive neuropsychology perspective (see Shallice, 1988). Part of the reason for this must be the degree to which thinking depends on many diverse lower-level systems (e.g. attention, working memory, and language; see Fodor, 1983, for a deeper analysis of this situation).

This chapter and the next are broadly structured along historical lines. So, we begin with a review of early problem-solving research the Gestalt school—before turning to a treatment of the information-processing theories of problem solving that emerged in the 1950s and 1960s. We also consider how these information-processing theories have tried to account for the findings of early research. Then in Chapter 16 we follow the subsequent development of these theories in studies of expertise, mental models, analogy, and scientific discovery. Later in Chapter 17, we consider a very different research tradition on thinking devoted to understanding reasoning.

Section summary

The different forms of thinking behaviour vary along a number of dimensions. The degree to which we are conscious of our thought processes can vary considerably. We tend to be conscious of the products of thinking rather than the thinking processes themselves. Furthermore, even these conscious products may not be recalled accurately in retrospect by people. Thinking tasks can also be more or less directed. Some thinking tasks are directed towards specific, well-defined goals, whereas other forms are rambling and goal-less. Thinking episodes also differ in terms of the amount of knowledge that comes into play to achieve a goal; they may be knowledge-lean or knowledge-rich. Most of the early research on problem solving has examined directed thinking in knowledge-lean situations that have specific goals (i.e. puzzles). Later research considers more knowledge-rich situations (e.g. expert problem solving). Reasoning research can also be characterised along these dimensions, although it arises out of a different theoretical tradition.

EARLY RESEARCH: THE GESTALT SCHOOL

At the beginning of this century, adherents of the Gestalt school of psychology extended their theories of perception to problem-solving behaviour. These researchers were particularly creative in performing experimental tests of their theories, and produced a large corpus of evidence. During the behaviourist period much of this research was reinterpreted in behaviourist terms (see e.g. Maltzman, 1955), even though the basic experimental paradigms remained unchanged. During much of the 1950s and 1960s this type of problem-solving research became a background activity, although it has been researched actively again more recently, especially when it was reinterpreted in information-processing terms (see e.g. Ohlsson, 1984a, 1992; Raaheim, 1974; Weisberg & Suls, 1973).

Gestalt research on problem solving in animals

The work of the Gestalt school of psychology had its origins in problem-solving research on animals. Early associationist and behaviourist psychologists had characterised problem solving as the result of either trial-and-error or the reproduction of previously learned responses (e.g. Hull, 1930, 1931; Maltzman, 1955; Thorndike, 1911). Following Lloyd Morgan's (1894) observations of his dog, Thorndike's famous experiments on cats were taken as strong evidence for this view.

Thorndike had placed hungry cats in closed cages, within sight of a dish of food outside the cages. The cage doors could be opened when a pole inside the cage was hit. Initially, the animals thrashed about and clawed the sides of the cage. Inevitably, at some point, the cat hit the pole inside the cage and opened the door. On repeated trials, when the cat was placed in the cage again, similar energetic behaviour ensued but gradually the animal seemed to learn that hitting the pole opened the cage door. So, eventually, when placed in the cage it went to the pole, hit it and escaped. So, new problems were initially solved by trial-and-error behaviour and then accidental solutions were amalgamated into responses that were reproduced when the appropriate stimulus was presented.

One of the founders of the Gestalt school, Wolfgang Kohler, disagreed with this formulation and believed that there was more to animal problem solving than trial-and-error and reproductive responses. The Gestalt psychologists had been fairly successful in showing that perception was something more than mere associations (see

Chapter 3) and felt that the same ideas could be applied to problem solving. In the perception of illusions, like the Necker cube in Fig. 15.1, the corner marked "Y" sometimes appears to be to the front of the figure and other times to the back. In Gestalt terms, the figure is *restructured* to be perceived in one way or the other. In a similar fashion, Gestalt psychologists maintained that one could have "insight" into the problem's structure and "restructure" a problem in order to solve it.

Gestalt theory can be summarised by the following points (see e.g. Ohlsson, 1984a; Wertheimer, 1954):

- Problem-solving behaviour is both repro-ductive and productive.
- Reproductive problem solving involves the re-use of previous experience and can hinder successful problem solving (e.g. as in problem-solving set and functional-fixedness experiments).
- Productive problem solving is characterised by *insight* into the structure of the problem and by productive *restructurings* of the problem.
- Insight often occurs suddenly and is accompanied by an "ah-ha" experience.

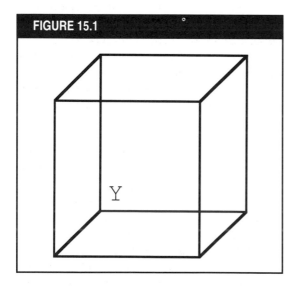

FIGURE 15.1

A Necker cube which illustrates the perceptual restructuring in which the corner marked by the "Y" alternates between being at the back and the front of the figure.

The classic example of Gestalt research was Kohler's (1927) study on problem solving in apes. In Kohler's experiments, apes had to reach bananas outside their cages, when sticks were the only objects available. On one occasion, he observed an ape take two sticks and join them together to reach the bananas, and heralded it as an example of insight. In contemporary terms, Kohler's point was that the animal had acted in a goal-directed way; it was trying to solve the problem using the sticks. He also pointed out that even though the ape had used the sticks initially in a trial-and-error manner, it was only after sitting quietly for a time that the animal produced the insightful solution. Kohler's evidence was not cast-iron because the previous experiences of this once-wild ape were not known. Later, Birch (1945) was to find little evidence of this sort of "insightful" problem solving in apes that were raised in captivity. However, such research set the agenda for later Gestalt psychologists to extend their analyses to human problem solving.

Restructuring and insight : The two-string problem

One of the better-known Gestalt problems (which is uncomfortably close to the ape studies), is Maier's (1931) "two-string" or "pendulum problem". In the original version of the problem, human subjects were brought into a room that had two strings hanging from the ceiling and a number of other objects (e.g. poles, pliers, extension cords). They were then asked to tie together the two strings that were hanging from the ceiling. However, they soon found out that when they took hold of one string and went to grab hold of the other, it was too far away for them to reach (see Fig. 15.2). Subjects produced several different types of solutions to this problem but the most "insightful" and infrequently produced solution was the pendulum solution. This involved taking the pliers, tying them to one of the strings and swinging them. So, while holding one string, it was possible to catch the other on its up-swing and tie the two together. Maier demonstrated a striking example of "problem restructuring" by first allowing subjects to get to a point where they were stuck and then (apparently accidentally) brushing against the string to set it

FIGURE 15.2

The two-string problem in which it is not possible to reach one string while holding the other.

swinging. Soon after this was done subjects tended to produce the pendulum solution, even though few reported noticing the experimenter brush against the string. According to Maier, this subtle hint resulted in a reorganisation or restructuring of the problem so that the solution emerged.

Functional fixedness: The candle problem and the nine-dot problem

At around the same time, another young researcher was also expanding Gestalt theory. During his twenties, Karl Duncker (1926, 1945) performed experiments on "functional fixedness" or "functional fixity", which continue to be replicated in various guises to this day. He demonstrated this phenomenon in an experiment where subjects were given a candle, a box of nails, and several other objects and asked to attach the candle to a wall by a table, so that it did not drip onto the table below (see Fig. 15.3). Duncker found that subjects tried to nail the candle directly to the wall or glue it to the wall by melting it, but few thought of using the inside of the nail-box as a candle holder and nailing it to the wall. In Duncker's terms, subjects were "fixated" on the box's normal function of holding nails and could not re-conceptualise it in a manner

that allowed them to solve the problem. Subjects' problem-solving success was hampered by reproductive behaviour (see Weisberg & Suls, 1973, for an information-processing account of the candle problem). Subjects' failure to produce the pendulum solution in the two-string problem can also be seen as a case of functional fixedness because subjects are unable to reconceive of the pliers as a pendulum weight (see Adamson & Taylor, 1954; Keane, 1985a, 1989).

Another famous problem from the Gestalt school is Scheerer's (1963) nine-dot problem. As can be seen in Fig. 15.4a, the problem involves nine dots organised in a three-by-three matrix. In order to solve the problem one must draw four continuous straight lines, connecting all the dots without lifting the pencil from the paper. The correct solution is shown in Fig. 15.4b (though see Adams, 1979, for several wild but valid alternatives). Most people cannot solve the problem because, Scheerer maintained, they assume that the lines must stay within the square formed by the dots. In Gestalt terms, subjects had "fixated" on the shape of the dots and could not solve the problem for this reason. We shall see that later research has shown that this is not the whole truth.

FIGURE 15.3

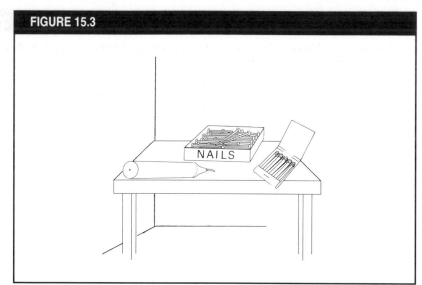

The objects presented to subjects in the candle problem. Adapted with the permission of Oxford University Press from R.W. Weisberg (1980), *Memory, thought, and behaviour*.

FIGURE 15.4

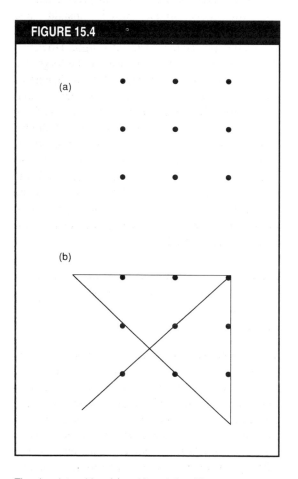

The nine-dot problem (a) and its solution (b).

Problem-solving set: The water-jug problems

A final set of experiments produced by the Gestalt school that deserve mention are the water-jug experiments of Luchins and Luchins (1959; Luchins, 1942). These experiments are another case of the general notion of fixation, where reproductive responses result in problem-solving failure rather than success. The Luchins termed the phenomenon *problem-solving set*. In a typical water-jug problem you have to imagine that you are given an eight-pint jug full of water, and a five-pint jug and three-pint jug that are empty (represented as 8–8, 5–0, 3–0, where the first figure indicates the size of the jug and the second the amount of water in that jug). Your task is to pour the water from one jug to another until you end up with four pints in the eight-pint jug and four pints in the five-pint jug (i.e. 8–4, 5–4, 3–0). Even though this problem appears straightforward it can take some time to solve (Table 15.1 shows one possible solution).

In order to demonstrate problem-solving set, Luchins and Luchins typically had two groups in their experiments: a set and a control condition. The set condition received a series of problems that could be solved using the same solution method, but the control group received problems that had to be solved using different methods. Then, both groups were given a test problem that could be

TABLE 15.1

Shortest Set of Moves to Solution in the Luchin's Water-jug Problem (8–8, 5–0, 3–0)

States	Jar 1	Jar 2	Jar 3
Initial	8–8	5–0	3–0
Intermediate	8–3	5–5	3–0
	8–3	5–2	3–3
	8–6	5–2	3–0
	8–6	5–0	3–2
	8–1	5–5	3–2
	8–1	5–4	3–3
Goal	8–4	5–4	3–0

solved using either a very simple method or the more complex method that the set condition subjects had been applying to all the previous problems. Not surprisingly, the control group tended to use the simple method, but the set group opted for the more complex method. In fact, they did not "see" the simpler method until it was pointed out to them. The set group had, in Gestalt terms, been fixated on the more complex method.

Evaluating Gestalt theory and its legacy

The Gestalt psychologists attacked associationist views from two sides. First, they tried to show that problem solving was something more than the "mere" reproduction of learned responses; that it involved the productive processes of insight and restructuring. Recall Maier's demonstration of the effects of the "swing" hint on the solution of the two-string problem. Second, they showed that problem solving that relied solely on past experience often led to failure; recall the demonstrations of problem-solving set (where a routine method is used) and functional fixedness (when the typical function of an object is assumed).

Gestalt theory was based on a perceptual metaphor carried over from their perceptual theories (and everyday life?). This metaphor makes the theory very attractive and comprehensible but it is also its main weakness. The concepts of "insight" and "restructuring" are attractive because they are easily understood and convey something of the mysterious dynamism of human creativity.

However, as theoretical constructs they are radically under-specified (see Chapters 1 and 2); the conditions under which insight and restructuring occur were unclear and the theory did not really specify the nature of insight. However, the Gestalt work is not a dinosaur to be forgotten. In many ways the spirit of Gestalt research, with its emphasis on the productive and non-associationistic nature of thinking, informed the information-processing approach that followed some decades later (see e.g. Holyoak, 1991; Newell, 1985; Ohlsson, 1984a). The school also left a large corpus of experimental materials (in the form of problems) and evidence that had to be reinterpreted by later information-processing theory (see later sections). The Gestalt legacy was, therefore, substantial.

NEWELL AND SIMON'S PROBLEM-SPACE THEORY

The problem-solving research of Allen Newell and Herb Simon, of Carnegie-Mellon University, is the bedrock of the information-processing framework. In the late 1950s, they produced the first computational models of psychological phenomena, and made milestone discoveries in cognitive psychology and artificial intelligence. Their problem-space theory of problem solving, recounted in their 1972 *magnum opus* entitled

Human problem solving, remains at the centre of current problem-solving research. In fact, many of the remaining areas reviewed in this chapter and the next are elaborations of Newell and Simon's basic views.

Problem-space theory

It is very natural to think of problems as being solved through the exploration of different paths to a solution. This is literally the case in finding your way through a labyrinth. You start from a point outside the maze and then progress through it to the centre. On your way, you reach junctions where you have to choose between going straight on, turning to the left or right, or turning back. Each of these alternative paths may branch again and again so that, in the maze as a whole, there are hundreds of alternative paths (only some of which will lead to the centre). Different strategies can be used to find one's way through a labyrinth (e.g. mark your past path, initially always take the left turn). Umberto Eco's (1984) novel *The name of the rose* gives a vivid description of using several strategies to pass through a deadly monastery labyrinth. These strategies provide you with a systematic method for searching the maze and help you to select one from among the many alternative paths.

Newell and Simon used parallels to these basic ideas to characterise human problem-solving behaviour. They suggested that the objective structure of a problem can be characterised as a set of states, beginning from an initial state (e.g. standing outside the maze), involving many intermediate states (e.g. moving through the maze), and ending with a goal state (e.g. being at the centre of the maze). Just as in the labyrinth, actions can be performed or "operators applied" (e.g. turn left, turn right). The application of these operators results in a move from one state to another. In any given state there may be several different operators that apply (e.g. turn left, turn right, go back) and each of these will generate numerous alternative states. Thus, there is a whole space of possible states and paths through this space (only some of which will lead to the goal state). *This problem space describes the abstract structure of a problem.*

Newell and Simon take the further step of proposing that when people solve problems they pass through similar "knowledge states" in their heads. They begin at an initial knowledge state and "search" through a space of alternative mental states until they reach a goal knowledge state. Moves from one knowledge state to the next are achieved by the application of "mental operators". As a given problem may have a large number of alternative paths, people use strategies (or heuristic methods) to move from the initial state to the goal state efficiently. Thus, subjects' conception of a problem (i.e. the nature of the initial state) and the knowledge they bring to it (the operators and strategies available to them) make important contributions to the observed problem-solving behaviour. Problem-space theory is summarised in Panel 15.1 (see Newell & Simon, 1972; Simon, 1978).

This theory pins down in explicit representational terms the various hypothetical knowledge states and processes that are used to solve many different problems. It also makes predictions about what makes problems difficult; for example, the size of the search space is clearly important to problem-solving success and the interaction between it and the method people use to search it. Newell and Simon's theory has been implemented in computer programs that usually take the form of production systems (see Chapter 1). In these models, the various knowledge states are held in a working memory, and long-term memory consists of a set of productions which encode the operators that modify these states in working memory. Their earliest and now-famous model was called the *General Problem Solver* (GPS; see Newell, Shaw, & Simon, 1958, 1960). Let us consider a typical problem to which the theory has been applied.

PROBLEM-SPACE THEORY AND THE TOWER OF HANOI

In the "Tower of Hanoi" problem, subjects are presented with three vertical pegs in a row, the first of which has a number of disks piled on it in order of size; that is, the largest disk is at the bottom, the

---

(Panel 15.1) Problem-space Theory

- For any given problem there are a large number of alternative paths from an initial state to a goal state; the total set of such states, as generated by the legal operators, is called the basic problem space.

- People's problem-solving behaviour can be viewed as the production of knowledge states by the application of mental operators, moving from an initial knowledge state to a goal, knowledge state.

- Mental operators encode legal moves that can be made and restrictions that explicitly disallow a move if certain conditions hold.

- People use their knowledge and various heuristic methods (like means–end analysis; see next section for details) to search through the problem space and to find a path from the initial state to the goal state.

- All of these processes occur within the limits of a particular cognitive system; that is, there may be working-memory limitations and limitations on the speed with which information can be stored and retrieved from long-term memory.

---

next largest on top of it, and so on to the smallest at the top (see Fig. 15.5). The goal of the problem is to have all the disks piled in the same order on the last peg. However, disks can only be moved in certain ways. Only one disk can be moved at a time and a larger disk cannot be placed on top of a smaller disk. The standard version of the problem uses three disks. Fig. 15.6 shows some of the legal states that make up the search space of the problem.

The state described in the problem statement, where all of the disks are stacked on the first peg, is the *initial knowledge state*, and the *goal knowledge state* consists of all the disks stacked on the last peg, in order of size. Subjects can use *mental operators* that move disks from one peg to another, with the restriction that no move places a larger disk on a smaller disk. This gives rise to varying numbers of alternative states after each possible move. From the initial state, if one applies the move operation, two alternative new states are possible; moving the small disk from the first peg to either the second or the third peg (i.e. states 2 and 3 in Fig. 15.6, respectively). Each of these intermediate states can, in turn, give rise to several alternatives (see Fig. 15.6). The number of these alternative states, between the initial and goal state, increases rapidly. In order to solve the problem people have to use a variety of strategies to reduce

the number of states they have to pass through to reach the goal. Newell and Simon described several such strategies, which they called *heuristic methods* or *heuristics*.

Heuristics are to be contrasted with algorithms. An *algorithm* is a method or procedure that will definitely solve a problem, if it is applied. For example, one could use a "check-every-state algorithm" to solve the Tower of Hanoi problem; by starting at the beginning and systematically checking every alternative state until the goal state is encountered. This method will take a long time and be inefficient but it is guaranteed to solve the problem. *Heuristics* are "rules-of-thumb" that do not guarantee a solution to the problem, but more often than not they will succeed and save a lot of time and effort in the process.

One of the most important heuristic methods proposed by Newell and Simon was means–ends analysis. *Means–ends analysis* consists of the following steps:

- note the difference between the current state and the goal state;
- create a subgoal to reduce this difference;
- select an operator that will solve this subgoal.

To illustrate means–ends analysis, let us assume that a problem solver is two steps off solving the

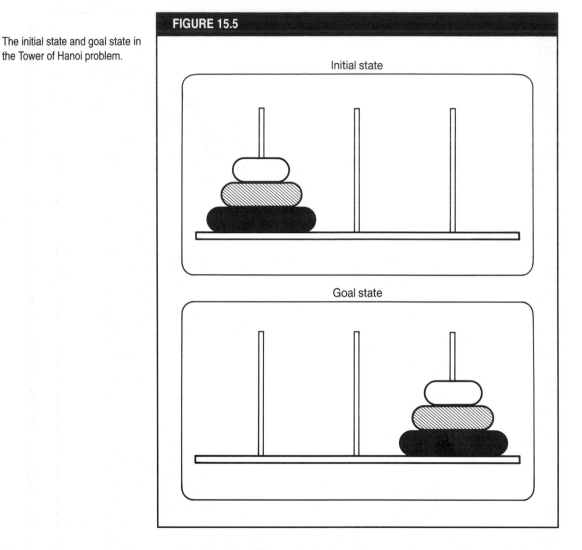

FIGURE 15.5

The initial state and goal state in the Tower of Hanoi problem.

Initial state

Goal state

Tower of Hanoi problem in state 15 in Fig. 15.6. At this point, three possible moves can be made (i.e. states 11, 14, 19), but only one of these moves will bring you closer to solving the problem (see state 19 in Fig. 15.6). Means–ends analysis proposes that you first note the difference between the current state and the goal state; here the important thing to notice is that the medium disk is on the second peg instead of the third peg. Second, establish the subgoal of reducing this difference; create the new subgoal of moving the medium disk to the third peg. Third, select an operator that solves this subgoal and apply it. So, the medium disk will be moved to the third peg and the problem will move closer to its solution. If you then apply this

method again, the goal state will be reached in the next step of the problem. Means–ends analysis can be applied from the initial state of the problem to select a set of operators that will construct a path from this state to the goal state. However, as with any heuristic method, it is not guaranteed to be successful in every case where is it applied.

Goal–subgoal structures in problem solving

The generation of appropriate subgoals on the way to solving the main goal is important to successful problem solving. So, if you can structure a problem into appropriate subgoals — subgoals like "attempt to get the largest disk onto the third peg" —then problem-solving performance should

FIGURE 15.6

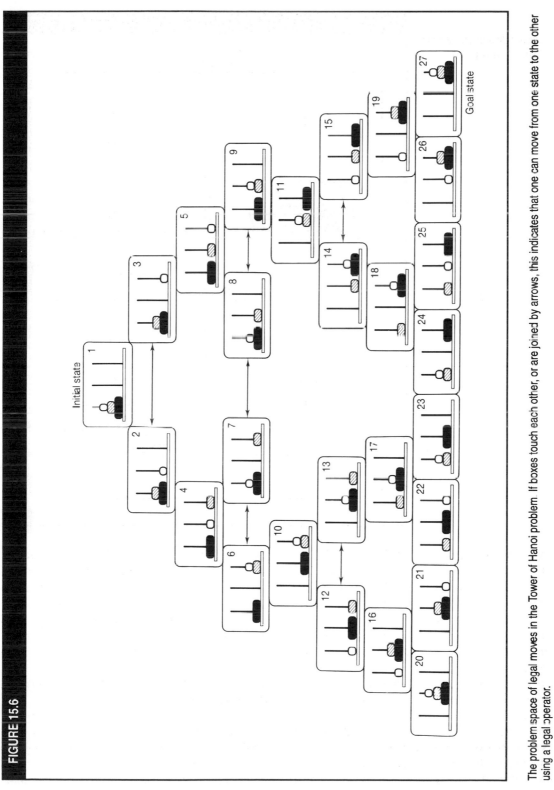

The problem space of legal moves in the Tower of Hanoi problem. If boxes touch each other, or are joined by arrows, this indicates that one can move from one state to the other using a legal operator.

improve. One possible source of such subgoal structures should be prior experience on related problems.

Several researchers have tested this prediction (Egan & Greeno, 1974; Luger, 1976). For instance, Egan and Greeno (1974) gave different groups of subjects complex five-disk and six-disk versions of the Tower of Hanoi. Experimental groups received prior experience on three-disk and four-disk problems, whereas controls did not. Egan and Greeno found that subjects with prior experience on the easier problems, which instilled an appropriate goal structure, showed some benefits. Furthermore, the error profiles (as measured by any deviation from the minimal solution path for each problem) indicated that subjects performed better as they neared important goals/subgoals and, conversely, tended to experience more difficulty when they were far from an important goal.

Learning different strategies

Egan and Greeno's work illustrates the effects that experience can have on subjects' ability to solve the problem. Egan and Greeno's subjects adopted the strategy of partitioning a complex problem into several simpler sub-problems and then solving each of these in turn. Anzai and Simon (1979) examined other strategies adopted by a single subject in four successive attempts to solve a five-disk version of the Tower of Hanoi (see Fig. 15.7).

On each of the four attempts the subject used a different strategy, becoming progressively more efficient at solving the problem. Initially, the subject seemed to explore the problem space without much planning of moves. Search at this stage seemed to be guided by avoidance of certain states rather than moves towards definite goal/subgoal states. Anzai and Simon argued that the subject was using general *domain-independent strategies*. These strategies included a *loop-avoidance strategy* to avoid returning to previously visited states, and a heuristic strategy that preferred shorter sequences of moves, to achieve a goal, to longer sequences. These general strategies allowed the subject to learn better sequences of moves, and these sequences were carried forward to be used in later attempts to solve the problem. Anzai and Simon developed an adaptive production system model that learned in the same manner. This model could create new production rules that were used to solve the problem on a later attempt. From Anzai and Simon's research, the general course of learning in these situations hinges on the initial use of general, domain-independent heuristics, which then allow one to learn domain-dependent or domain-specific heuristics (see also Anderson's, 1993, ACT-R theory).

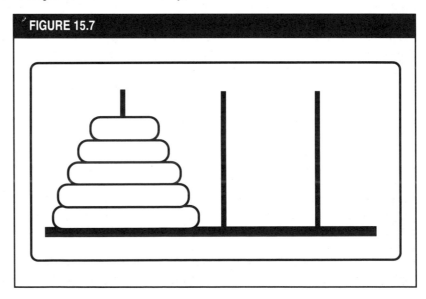

FIGURE 15.7

The initial state of the five-disk version of the Tower of Hanoi problem used by Anzai and Simon (1979).

Isomorphic problems: Understanding and problem representation

Clearly, the way you understand a problem should influence your ability to solve it. This intuition is specified in problem-space theory and has been borne out by a variety of findings on solving isomorphic problems. Two things are isomorphic if they have the same form or relational structure. So, in problem-space terms, two problems can be isomorphic if there is a one-to-one correspondence between the states and operators of the problems such that whenever two states are connected by an operator in one problem space, corresponding states are connected by the corresponding operator in the other problem space. Research has shown that slight differences in the way isomorphic problems are presented have significant effects on subjects' problem-solving success, presumably because the presentational differences affect their understanding of the problem. Furthermore, problem-space theory is specific enough to allow one to pin-point what it is about subjects' understanding of the problem that causes these effects.

Several studies of this type have been performed on variants of the Tower of Hanoi (see Hayes & Simon, 1974, 1977; Simon & Hayes, 1976). In one study, Simon and Hayes (1976) used problem isomorphs about a tea ceremony involving three different people (corresponding to the three pegs), carrying out three ritual tasks for one another (like the three disks), in differing orders of importance (like disks of different sizes). In other studies, Hayes and Simon used isomorphs to the Tower of Hanoi that involved monsters and globes. In the basic, monster–globe problem there are three monsters of different sizes (small, medium, and large), each holding different-sized globes (that are small, medium, and large). The small monster is holding the large globe, the medium-sized monster the small globe, and the large monster the medium-sized globe. The goal is to achieve a state in which each monster is holding a globe proportionate to its size (e.g. the small monster holding the smallest globe). However, monster etiquette demands that: (i) only one globe is transferred at a time, (ii) if a monster is holding two globes, only the larger of the two is transferred, and

(iii) a globe may not be transferred to a monster who is holding a larger globe. This monster–globe problem is, thus, a *move* problem with an isomorphic problem space to the Tower of Hanoi problem.

Simon and Hayes also had a *change* version of the monster–globe problem with the same monsters and globes, but subjects had to shrink and expand the globes held by the monsters rather than moving them; the rules were that: (i) only one globe may be changed (i.e. shrunk or expanded) at a time, (ii) if two globes have the same size, only the globe held by the largest monster may be changed, and (iii) a globe may not be changed to the same size as the globe of a larger monster.

Hayes and Simon's *rule-application hypothesis* predicted that the move version of the monster–globe problem should be easier than the change version, because the rules in the latter were more difficult to apply (i.e. they involved complex tests to determine legal operations). What they found was that the move problem was twice as easy as the change problem (see Hayes & Simon, 1977). However, apart from Hayes and Simon's rule-application hypothesis, Kotovsky, Hayes, and Simon (1985) proposed that a *rule-learning hypothesis* could also account for the data. That is, that some rules can be learned more easily than others and this contributes to the ease with which the problem is solved. In fact, Kotovsky et al. found evidence, from a task in which subjects simply learned the move and change rules, that they took longer to learn the change rules than the move rules. They also showed that the general ease of rule learning and rule application was likely to be influenced by: (i) the extent to which the rules are consistent with real-world knowledge, (ii) the memory load inherent in the problem; that is, how much of the problem solving could be performed in an external memory (e.g. on paper) rather than in working memory, and (iii) whether the rules could be easily organised in a spatial fashion or more easily imagined.

Recently, further work on the sources of difficulty in problems has emerged from tests of isomorphism of another problem: the Chinese ring puzzle (see Kotovsky & Simon, 1990). In the original version, this puzzle involves a complex arrangement of five interconnected metal rings on a bar, the task being to remove the rings from the bar (see Afriat, 1982). This puzzle has two important characteristics: (i) what constitutes a move is not immediately obvious, because the rings can be twisted and turned in a number of ways, and (ii) the problem space of moves, once found, is linear (i.e. a straight line of moves with no branching). The latter ensures that problem difficulty—which is considerable for this problem—cannot emerge from searching the problem space, but must be due to discovering how to make moves. Kotovsky and Simon developed a digitised version of this puzzle, involving the moving of five balls out of boxes. Their study showed that the major source of difficulty lay in discovering what a legal move was, rather than navigating through the problem space.

SOLVING THE MISSIONARIES AND CANNIBALS PUZZLE

Problem-space theory has also been applied, with some success, to the missionaries–cannibals puzzle. In this problem, subjects are given the task of transferring three missionaries and three cannibals across a river in a boat. Because the boat is fairly small, only two or fewer people can be taken across in it at a time, and someone must always accompany the boat back to the other side. Furthermore, at no point in the problem can there be more cannibals than missionaries left on one bank of the river or else the cannibals will have a religious feast. Figure 15.8 shows the legal search space for reaching the goal state. Researchers have argued that people use a variety of heuristics to solve different variants of this problem.

Thomas (1974) used a variant of this problem involving J.R.R. Tolkien's (1966) hobbits and orcs; in which orcs have a proclivity for gobbling hobbits. He showed that at some points in the problem — especially states 5 and 8 in Fig. 15.8 — subjects took considerably longer and produced more errors than at other points. Thomas maintained that the difficulties experienced at these

states had different cognitive sources. In the case of the state 5, the difficulty lies in the many alternative moves that are possible at this point (five in number). Only two of these moves are illegal and of the remaining three legal moves, only one is really helpful. In the case of state 8, subjects are misled because they need to move away from the goal state in order to get closer to it. As can be seen in Fig. 15.8, in going from state 8 to state 9, one enters a state that seems further away rather than closer to the goal. At this point, subjects typically think that they have reached a blind alley and start to backtrack. Figure 15.9 shows the distribution of incorrect responses by Thomas' subjects at each state in the problem.

Thomas also suggested that subjects made three or four major planning decisions in solving the problem, and, having made each of these decisions, carried out whole blocks of moves with increasing speed. Then, at the beginning of each planned sequence of moves, there would be a long pause before the next decision was made. Thomas' statistical analysis of the distributions of subjects' times-to-move supported this hypothesis.

Other researchers have looked at more complex versions of the problem and noted strategic changes in subjects' behaviour. Simon and Reed (1976) investigated a version of the missionaries–cannibals problem, involving five missionaries and five cannibals. This problem is more complex in that it has many more legal states even though it can be solved in just 11 moves. However, on average, subjects take 30 moves to solve the problem. Simon and Reed suggested that there were three main strategies used in solving the problem. Initially, subjects adopted a *balancing strategy* whereby they simply tried to ensure that equal numbers of missionaries and cannibals remained on either side of the river. This strategy avoids illegal moves, resulting in more cannibals than missionaries on either bank of the river. At a certain point, subjects become more oriented towards the goal state, and adopt a *means–ends strategy*. This strategy is manifested by a tendency to move more people to the goal side of the river. Finally, subjects use a simple *anti-looping heuristic* to avoid moves that reverse the immediately preceding move.

FIGURE 15.8

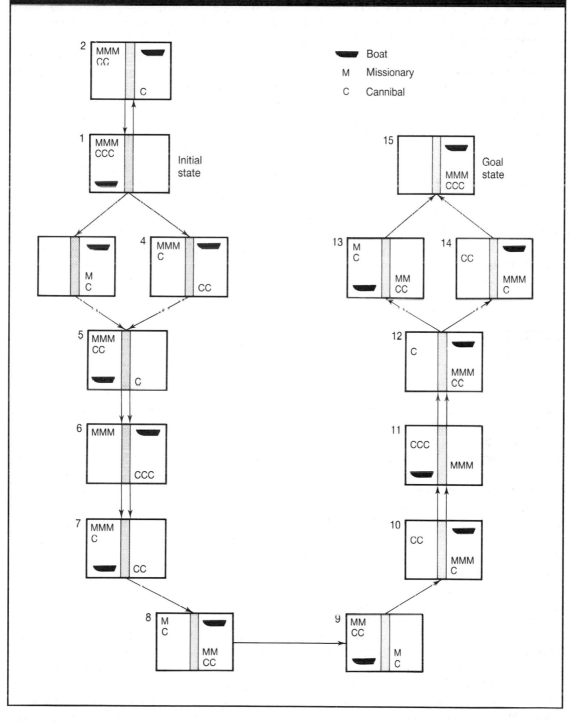

The search space intervening between the initial state and goal state of the missionaries–cannibals problem (M indicates a missionary and C a cannibal).

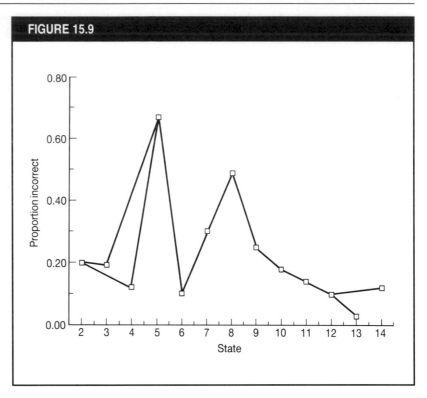

FIGURE 15.9

The proportion of incorrect responses in the various states of the hobbits–orcs problem (an isomorph of the missionaries–cannibals problem) from Thomas (1974). It shows the difficulties that subjects experience in states 5 and 8.

Simon and Reed maintained that the key to efficient solution of the problem rested on a *strategy shift* from the balancing strategy to the means–ends strategy. The trouble with the balancing strategy is that it leads one into blind-alley states in the problem. Thus, they predicted that any manipulation that increased the probability of a strategy shift would result in improved performance on solving the problem. In an experiment designed to test this prediction, a control group of subjects received the problem to solve with no hints, and an experimental group was given, as a hint, a subgoal to achieve on the way to solving the problem. This hint suggested that subjects should work to reach a state where three cannibals were on the goal side of the river on their own without a boat. Because this subgoal involves a state where there are unequal numbers of missionaries and cannibals on either side of the river, it was expected that this subgoal should discourage the use of the balancing strategy early on. This prediction was confirmed. Subjects in the experimental group tended to shift strategies after

about four moves, whereas those in the control group only shifted after about 15 moves. Figure 15.10 shows the much better performance of subjects in the subgoal condition versus controls who were not given the subgoal.

REINTERPRETING THE GESTALT FINDINGS

We began this chapter by considering the perceptual theories of problem solving proposed by the Gestalt school of psychology. Information-processing theory has inherited the burden of reinterpretation or explanation of the findings of Gestalt research in information-processing terms (see Chapter 1). This reconception of things past has been carried out since the 1970s (see e.g. Keane, 1985a, 1989; Metcalfe, 1986a; Newell, 1985; Ohlsson, 1984a, 1985, 1992; Simon, 1986; Sternberg & Davidson, 1982; Weisberg, 1980; Weisberg & Alba, 1981; Weisberg & Suls, 1973).

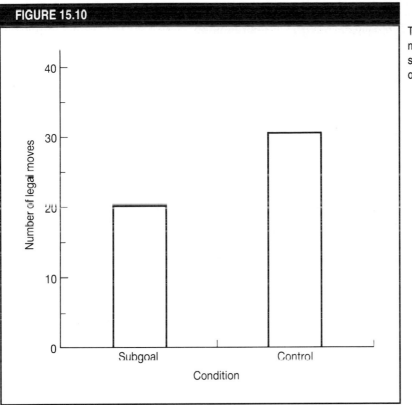

FIGURE 15.10

The mean number of legal moves made by subjects in the subgoal and control conditions of Simon and Reed (1976).

Problem-space models of water-jug problems

We saw earlier, that water-jug problems were intensively investigated by Gestalt researchers (see Luchins & Luchins, 1959). These problems are very amenable to a treatment in terms of problem-space theory. In the 8–8, 5–0 and 3–0 problem we encountered earlier (see Table 15.1), the initial state consists of the largest jug being full of water and the other two jugs empty, and the goal state has four pints of water in the largest and middle-sized jugs with nothing in the smallest. The operators consist of pouring various amounts of water from one jug to another, and the operator restrictions are that the water cannot be added to or flung away while solving the problem.

Atwood and Polson (1976) produced a state–space analysis of these problems in the context of a full process model for explaining subjects' behaviour on water-jug problems. They specified the various heuristic methods used by subjects and included assumptions about the limitations on human information processing (i.e. working memory limitations). Their model had the following main points:

- In planning moves, subjects only look ahead to a depth of one move.
- Moves are evaluated using a means–ends analysis method, where subjects look at the difference between the actual and goal quantities in the two largest jugs and see which of the next alternative states will bring them closer to the goal state.
- Subjects tend to avoid moves that return them to immediately preceding states (an anti-looping heuristic).
- There are limitations on the number of possible alternative moves that can be stored in working memory.
- This limitation can be somewhat alleviated by transferring information into long-term memory.

This model makes predictions about the difficulties that people should encounter in solving water-jug problems, which Atwood and Polson (1976) tested. They were particularly interested in two problems: one involving jugs of 8, 5, and 3 units and one involving jugs of 24, 21, and 3 units. In both cases, the largest jug is filled and the other jugs are empty, and the goal is to distribute the largest jug's contents evenly between the largest and middle jugs. Both problems are isomorphic in the number of moves one needs to consider to solve the problem. Their model predicted that the 8–8, 5–0, 3–0 problem should be harder than the 24–24, 21–0, 3–0, because the latter could be solved by simply applying the means–ends heuristic whereas the former required a violation of this heuristic. Their results showed that the mean number of moves to solve either problem confirmed this prediction.

Atwood, Masson, and Polson (1980) also tested the proposal that subjects only planned one move ahead to avoid overloading working memory. They assumed that any reduction of the memory load should have the effect of freeing up the problem solver for more long-term planning. To achieve this manipulation they provided subjects with information about all the different moves available from any state in the problem. One group of subjects received even more information in the form of a record of the previous states they had visited. However, although Atwood et al. (1980) discovered that the more information subjects received the fewer the number of moves they needed to consider in solving the problem, they did not find the big "planning improvement" they expected. It seems that when the information load is lifted subjects do not use the extra capacity to plan ahead, but rather become more efficient at avoiding states that lead them back to the initial state of the problem.

On the whole, this sort of model has been shown to be very useful. Jeffries, Polson, Razan, and Atwood (1977) and Polson and Jeffries (1982) have extended it to apply to versions of the missionaries–cannibals and Tower of Hanoi problems. So, the model combines predictive specificity with some generality in its applicability.

Problem-space accounts of insight and restructuring

Weisberg and Alba (1981) re-examined the nine-dot problem (see Fig. 15.4). In Scheerer's (1963) original paper on the nine-dot problem, he had argued that subjects failed to solve the problem because they assumed that the lines drawn had to stay within the square shape formed by the dots; they were "fixated" on the Gestalt of the nine dots. To test this, Weisberg and Alba gave subjects a hint that they could draw lines outside the square. However, with this hint, only 20% solved the problem. They therefore concluded that fixation on the square of dots was not the only factor responsible for subjects' failures. In further experiments, Weisberg and Alba used simpler versions of the problem (a four-dot task) and explored the use of specific hints (e.g. drawing some of the lines that led to the solution). From these experiments they concluded that in order to solve the problem subjects required highly problem-specific knowledge. In their eyes, this undercut the Gestalt concepts of "insight" and "fixation", which they argued were of dubious explanatory value (see also Weisberg, 1986).

However, several other researchers have argued and shown that the notion of "insight" is a key part of problem-solving theory (see Dominowski, 1981; Ellen, 1982; Lung & Dominowski, 1985; Metcalfe, 1986a; Ohlsson, 1992; Simon, 1986). For example, Metcalfe (1986a,b; Metcalfe & Weibe, 1987) asked subjects for their metacognitions—their assessment of their feeling-of-knowing a solution or feelings-of-closeness to a solution—on insight problems and trivia questions that they were unable to answer. She found that although people had reasonably accurate metacognitions for the memory/trivia questions, they had no predictive metacognitions for the insight problems. This indicates that the insight problems were not solved by an incremental accumulation of information from memory, but by a sudden illumination, which is best described as "insight".

Other theorists, like Ohlsson (1984a,b, 1985, 1992), have tried to reassess the Gestalt constructs of insight and restructuring in problem-space terms, rather than rejecting them (for related ideas see Keane, 1985b, 1989; Langley & Jones, 1988). Ohlsson's (1992, p.4) position is that "insight occurs in the context of an impasse, which is unmerited in the sense that the thinker is, in fact, competent to solve the problem". The impasse is unmerited because the thinker has the knowledge to solve the problem, but for some reason or another cannot use it. Given this definition, Ohlsson maintains that a theory of insight has to explain three things: (i) why the impasse is encountered, (ii) how the impasse is broken, and (iii) what happens after it is broken. Ohlsson's theory is summarised in Panel 15.2.

This account is consistent with the known evidence on insight problems and is supported by more recent research. For instance, Kaplan and Simon (1990) have shown how, when the representation of another insight problem—the "mutilated checker board problem"—is enriched or elaborated with other information, then its solution becomes easier. Furthermore, Yaniv and Meyer (1987) have demonstrated, in another feeling-of-knowing experiment, that unsuccessful attempts to retrieve inaccessible stored information can prime the recognition of later information by a process of spreading activation. Here initial retrieval attempts lead to a spread of activation from some concepts to other concepts in memory. This spread of activation then sensitises the problem solver to other, new information in the environment needed for an insightful solution (e.g. hints, or noticing that the swinging string in the two-string problem provides a solution; see Fig. 15.2). Bowers, Regehr, Balthazard, and Parker (1990) have also used spreading activation to account for intuitions and hunches in problem solving.

Is problem solving productive or reproductive?

Finally, what answer does information-processing psychology give to the core issue posed by the Gestalt school: is problem solving *productive*, as the Gestalt psychologists claimed, or *merely reproductive*, as the associationists claimed? Problem-space accounts of puzzle research can be read as support for the productive claim. This

---

(Panel 15.2) Ohlsson's (1992) Insight Theory

- The representation of insight problems is a matter of interpretation; so there may be many different mental representations of the same problem (i.e. the problems are ill-defined).

- People have many knowledge operators for solving problems, and therefore operators may have to be retrieved from memory; the retrieval mechanism is spreading activation (see Chapters 1 and 6).

- The current representation of the problem acts as a memory probe for relevant operators in memory.

- Impasses occur because the initial representation of the problem is a bad memory probe for retrieving the operators needed to solve the problem.

- Impasses are broken when the representation of the problem is changed (is reinterpreted, re-represented, or restructured) thus forming a new memory probe that allows the retrieval of the relevant operators.

- This re-representation can occur through (i) elaboration, adding new information about the problem from inference or the environment (e.g. hints), (ii) constraint relaxation, changing some of the constraints on the goal, (iii) re-encoding, changing aspects of the problem representation through re-categorisation or deleting some information (e.g. re-categorising the pliers in the two-string problem as a *building material* rather than a *tool*).

- After an impasse is broken a full or partial insight may occur; a full insight occurs if the retrieved operators bridge the gap between the impasse state and the goal state.

research shows us that people have general heuristics that they can apply to situations about which they have little prior knowledge. Hence, they are not merely recollecting solutions to problems, but are actively and dynamically constructing solutions by applying different heuristics.

However, in the next chapter, we will see that there is also a reproductive component to problem solving. People can recall partial solutions and use prior knowledge to classify and define problems. We think that a new sense of the term "reproductive" has emerged, which resists the "mere" prefix. Human problem solving seems to rely on a lot of specific knowledge about particular situations. Even though this is strictly speaking "reproduced knowledge", it is not "mere reproduced knowledge" because of the amazing variety of this knowledge, the complexity of the mechanisms used to acquire it, and the flexibility of the ways in which it is used. In the next chapter on expertise and creativity we explore the character of this form of thought.

EVALUATING RESEARCH ON PUZZLES

The research on solving puzzles in cognitive psychology has been one of the most successful areas in the discipline. Problem-space theory has remained undefeated since it was first proposed in the late 1950s, and has continued to expand steadily to encompass more and more problem-solving phenomena. In the next chapter, we will look at some further extensions of the theory. But before we do this it is perhaps a good idea to review the progress afforded by puzzle problems.

Benefits of problem-space research on puzzles

Newell and Simon's problem-space theory makes substantial and fundamental contributions to cognitive theory and to our understanding of people's problem-solving abilities. Theoretically, a fundamental contribution of problem-space theory that cannot be under-stressed, is that it contains a

normative theory of problem solving. It allows us to specify the structure of problems in an idealised way and to define the best solution to a problem. For most of the puzzles described here, we can elaborate the problem space and point to the *correct/best* solution to the problem by tracing the shortest sequence of moves from the initial state to the goal state. Thus, in a normative way, the theory tells us what an ideal thinker should do in this problem. From an empirical standpoint, such a normative theory allows us to look at how and why people's behaviour deviates from the ideal. We can also say what heuristic (or combination of heuristics) are the optimal ones to use to solve the problem successfully. The normative theory also allows us to determine when problems are structurally the same, even when they appear to be very different (i.e. problem isomorphs). Cognitive psychologists often borrow normative theories from other disciplines; for instance, in deductive reasoning, logic is used as the normative theory (see Chapter 17). One of the incredible things about Newell and Simon's work is that they created *both* the normative theory and psychological research that followed.

Problem-space theory advances our understanding of a very complex cognitive ability. Even though the research on puzzles is on a specific class of problems, which may be a long way from more everyday problems, it provides a solid foundation for other work. Research always has to start somewhere, and islands of understanding have to be built up. From these islands, our understanding can then extend to more complicated, real-world situations. Problem-space theory provides us with a specific account of the following:

- How people solve puzzles by applying very general rules (heuristics) to the reduce the complexity of alternative solutions that are possible.
- The type of learning that can occur in problem solving; namely, the acquisition and development of different strategies for solving problems (see Anzai & Simon, 1979).
- How the understanding of a problem can affect subsequent problem-solving performance (cf. the monster–globe problems).

- The theory is general enough to characterise different puzzle problems, showing the theoretical unity in many diverse instances of problem solving.
- The theory allows us to reinterpret previous research on other problems in an informative fashion (i.e. insight problems).
- The theory supports the standard model of memory with a limited-capacity working memory, which can retard problem-solving abilities (see the Atwood and Polson work).

As we shall see in later chapters, these benefits extend outwards to other areas of problem solving and thinking.

Limitations of problem-space research on puzzles

Having stated the benefits that have followed from puzzle research, it is also important to be clear about the limitations of this research. There is a question mark hanging over the ecological validity of these puzzle problems. They are a special class of problems that have different properties from other problems; indeed, extensions to problem-space theory are needed to extend the generality of the theory to other classes of problems.

Puzzle problems have several contrasting properties with more mundane problems. First, puzzle problems are unfamiliar problems about which we have little knowledge (this is less the case for some insight problems, like the two-string problem). Many of the problems encountered in everyday life require considerable amounts of knowledge. Second, the knowledge required to solve puzzle problems is present in the statement of the problem. In everyday life all the information required to solve problems is often not present. In fact, much of the difficulty in everyday problems may hinge on finding the relevant information in memory or the environment required to solve the problem. If you have to buy a house, you need to know all about mortgages and current houses on sale, and finding this information is a significant part of solving the problem. Third, the requirements in puzzle problems are relatively unambiguous; the start state and goal state are clearly specified, and what can and cannot be done

in the problems is known (i.e. the legal moves). In everyday problems, the real difficulty may amount to specifying the nature of the goal state. For instance, doing a masters or doctoral thesis is essentially a matter of specifying where you want to end up.

In short, problem-space theory on puzzles concentrates on *well-defined* as opposed to *ill-defined problems* (Reitman, 1965; Simon, 1973, 1978). In well-defined problems the operators, initial state, and goal state are well specified and subjects tend to have little specific knowledge about the problem. These problems tend to be solved by so-called *general-purpose* or *domain-independent heuristics*. That is, heuristics that can be applied to a wide range of situations and domains; they are rules that do not involve specific knowledge of the domain. In artificial intelligence, heuristics of this type are often called *universal, weak* methods. They are "universal" because they can be applied in many domains, and they are "weak" because they are often not very efficient. For instance, solving one of these puzzles takes time using means–ends analysis. However, if one had rules that were specific to the problem-solving domain, the solution could be found more quickly (as appears to be the case in the nine-dot problem).

In contrast, *ill-defined problems* can be under-specified in many ways and require the use of substantial amounts of *domain-specific knowledge*. First, the initial state of an ill-defined problem may be uncertain; what is and is not part of the initial state may be unclear from the situation. If someone locks their keys inside their car, it is clear that the car and the keys locked in it are part of the initial state, but coat hangers, brooms, the police, and owners of cars of a same make are also potentially part of the initial state too. Second, the operators and operator restrictions may have to be discovered and/or created. You may have to dredge your memory for suitable operators (e.g. using a coat hanger in a certain way, forcing a back window, finding a route into the car through the boot). Finally, the goal state may need definition. On the face of it, getting into the car is a reasonable goal state, but smashing a window to do this does not seem like a good solution; so you may want to define the goal further, to stipulate that you should get into the car without doing much damage. But what constitutes "much damage"? Ill-definition and knowledge go hand in hand because ill-defined problems are usually defined through the application of knowledge. In the next chapter we will see how people use domain-specific knowledge when they are experts in an area.

In conclusion, problem-space theory provides an adequate treatment of well-defined problems, but has to be extended in order to deal with more ill-defined problems. In the next chapter we will see some of these extensions.

CHAPTER SUMMARY

Thinking can differ along a number of dimensions; in terms how conscious we can be of it, how directed it is towards a specific goal and the amount of knowledge it involves. Early problem-solving research centred on the question, posed by the Gestalt school in opposition to associationist psychologists, of whether thinking was productive or reproductive. The Gestalt psychologists performed many experiments to demonstrate that problem solving could be productively successful and reproductively a failure; making use of concepts like insight, restructuring, and fixation.

One of the most successful theories of cognition that has emerged from the information-processing revolution is Newell and Simon's (1972) problem-space theory. At base, it characterises problem solving as a constrained and guided search through a space of alternative possibilities. This search is guided by various heuristic methods or rules of thumb that co-ordinate the application of various operators (moves) used for transforming one state into another. This theory has been used to predict problem-solving behaviour in puzzle problems,

like the Tower of Hanoi, the missionaries–cannibals problem, and water-jug problems. Computational models have been constructed for many of these problems that simulate subjects' behaviour. The strength of this approach has been its predictive success; its weakness is manifested in the narrow range of problem situations to which it has been applied. However, as we shall see in the next chapter, this is a "limitation in practice" rather than a "limitation in principle".

Problem-space theory has also been extended to reinterpret the findings of the Gestalt school. In one sense, this research is very consistent with the spirit of Gestalt research, because it supports the claim that problem solving has an important productive component. However, it also shows that problem solving must also have a measure of reproductiveness. Having said this, it should also be noted that our current conception of reproductive problem solving is a long way from associationist proposals.

FURTHER READING

Gilhooly, K.J. (1995). *Thinking: Directed, undirected and creative* (3rd Edn.). London: Academic Press. This provides more detail on some of the research covered here and explores other areas too.

Keane, M.T., & Gilhooly, K.J. (Eds.) (1992). *Advances in thinking research.* London: Harvester Wheatsheaf. This volume has reviews of several developing areas of thinking research.

Newell, A. (1990). *Unified theories of cognition.* Harvard, MA: Harvard University Press. This book proposes a unified theory of cognition, called SOAR, which is the most advanced expression of Newell and Simon's approach to problem solving.

Newell, A., & Simon, H.A. (1972). *Human problem solving.* Englewood Cliffs, NJ: Prentice-Hall. This is not an easy book to read but it is *the* presentation of problem-space theory.

16

Problem-solving Skill and Creativity

FROM PUZZLES TO CREATIVITY

In the previous chapter, we reviewed a variety of different types of puzzles and looked at theoretical explanations of them. Newell and Simon's problem-space theory emerged as the dominant theory from this review. Problem-space theory characterises problems as a space of states, starting with an initial state and ending with a goal state, where the application of problem-solving operators moves you from one knowledge state to the next. According to this view, problem solving is "a search through a problem space from an initial state to a goal state". Most of the puzzles we met were well defined, in the sense that the initial states, goal states, and operators were well specified. However, some of the puzzles were ill-defined problems; where the start states, end states, and operators were unspecified. Real-world problems tend to be ill-defined rather than well defined. In this chapter, we turn to these ill-defined problems. We consider how experts solve ill-defined problems in specific domains like chess, physics, and computer programming. We also look at how people use mental models to understand different

aspects of the world. Finally, we consider one of the highest expressions of human thought—creativity—by looking at how people make discoveries by using analogies and testing hypotheses.

The keynote of this chapter is the importance of knowledge to the solution of ill-defined problems. Problem-solving expertise hinges on having considerable knowledge of the problem domain; by definition, expertise means being good at specific problems in a specific domain. In the domain of physics, an undergraduate student has less knowledge than a lecturer. Even though both of them may have equivalent intellectual abilities, the differences in their knowledge makes one a *novice* and the other an *expert problem solver*. Many of the domains studied in expertise research have enormous practical significance, and represent a major move in cognitive psychology away from laboratory-based puzzles and towards everyday, ecologically valid problems. We review chess, physics, and computer programming because they manifest several important theoretical and practical aspects of expertise research.

Many puzzles are difficult because the problem solver has to search through a large problem space.

However, we also saw that people can encounter difficulties in encoding and representing problems; isomorphic problems with different cover stories can differ in difficulty because people represent them differently. In this chapter, we also see that a major source of difficulty is the representation/definition of problems. Expert problem solvers have the right sorts of knowledge to encode problems easily and represent them optimally, whereas novices often lack this knowledge.

THE SKILL OF CHESS MASTERS

Differences in problem-solving expertise were first studied in the domain of chess. One view is that chess masters are masters because they have much specific knowledge about the game. Chess fits nicely into problem-space theory. The initial state of a game consists of all the pieces on the board in their starting positions, and the goal state is some specific checkmate against an opponent. Many alternative moves are possible from any state; from the initial state one can move legally any of the pawns or either of the knights. For each possible turn, a player can make one of a large number of replies, and an opponent can counter each of these replies with many more moves and so on. In computational terms, one faces a "combinatorial explosion" of possibilities. The sheer number of possible paths is overwhelming; the problem space is truly vast. From the initial state after 2 ply (i.e. a turn each by both sides), given the 20 possible moves by both White and Black, there are 400 possible positions. At only 6 ply from the opening position there are more than 9 million distinct board positions.

Most chess-playing computer programs search through a considerable number of alternatives and evaluate each alternative. For example, Newell and Simon (1972) reported a program called MANIAC, developed at Los Alamos in the 1950s, that explored nearly 1,000,000 moves at each turn. Even so MANIAC only considered each alternative move to a depth of four turns (an initial move, an opponent's reply, a reply to this move,

and the opponent's counter move). Even with this brute-force computation, it did not play chess well and occasionally made serious mistakes. Current chess programs, which have reached Grand Master level, still do a lot at each search. The current state-of-the-art, Deep Blue, considers 90 billion moves at each turn, at a rate of 9 billion a second (Hsu, 1993). People do not appear to (want to) search this much, so *something else* seems to underlie the expertise of chess masters.

DeGroot's chess studies

DeGroot (1965, 1966) provided the first indication of what this "something else" might be. DeGroot compared the performance of five grand masters and five expert players on choosing a move from a particular board position. He asked his subjects to think aloud, and then determined the number and type of different moves they had considered. He found that grand masters did not consider more alternative moves than expert players, and did not search any deeper than expert players, although they took slightly less time to make a move. However, independent raters judged the final moves made by the masters to be better than those of expert players.

In contrast to chess programs, the human players manifested a paradoxical mix of laziness and efficiency. They tended to consider only around 30 alternative moves and about four alternative first moves. At most, they searched to a depth of six turns, although frequently they searched a lot less (see Charness, 1981a; Saariluoma, 1990). Wagner and Scurrah (1971) examined this behaviour in further detail and found that chess players used a *progressive deepening* strategy. Players only check a small number of alternative first moves. These moves are then returned to repeatedly and explored to a greater depth each time that they are re-examined.

So, where do the essential differences lie between grand masters and experts, and between human players and computer players? DeGroot proposed that experts and masters differed in their knowledge of different board positions. Chess players study previous games and can recall their own games in detail. Therefore, good chess players recognise previous board positions and remember good moves to make from these positions. This use of prior knowledge excludes the need to entertain irrelevant moves and a host of alternatives. DeGroot argued that if chess players had stored previous board positions in some schematic fashion (see Chapter 11), then this knowledge should be reflected in tasks that measure memory.

Therefore, he gave subjects brief presentations of board positions from actual games (i.e. ranging from 2 to 15 seconds) and, after taking the board away, he asked them to reconstruct the positions. The main finding was that chess masters could recall the positions very accurately (91% correct), whereas less expert players made many more errors (41% correct). Thus, chess masters were better at recognising and encoding the various configurations of pieces than expert players. Researchers working with DeGroot also found that when the pieces were randomly arranged on the board (i.e. were not arranged in a familiar configuration), both groups of players did equally badly. Neither group had the knowledge available to encode the unfamiliar configurations. This also showed that the group differences found did not depend on any general differences in memory ability.

Chunking in chess

Simon and his associates extended DeGroot's findings (see Fig. 16.1; Chase & Simon, 1973a,b; Simon & Barenfeld, 1969; Simon & Gilmartin, 1973; but see Vicente & Brewer, 1993, on mistakes surrounding the uptake of DeGroot's work). Chase and Simon proposed that players "chunked" the board (see Miller, 1956; and Chapter 6); that they memorised board positions by breaking them down into seven or so familiar units in short-term memory. The essential difference between chess masters and expert players lay in the size of the

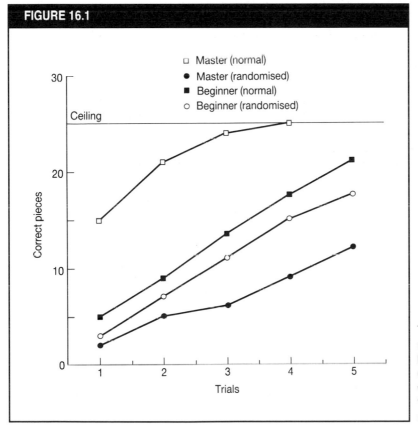

FIGURE 16.1

The number of pieces correctly recalled by masters and beginner chess players, from Chase and Simon (1973b), when they were presented with "normal" as opposed to randomised board positions.

chunk that they could encode. So, the seven chunks in a master's short-term memory contained more information than the seven chunks in a poorer player's memory.

Chase and Simon tested this hypothesis using a modified version of DeGroot's task. They asked subjects to reconstruct a board position on a second chess board with the first board still in view. They recorded the number and type of pieces subjects placed on the second board after a glance at the first board. The chunking hypothesis predicts that players should only place a few pieces after each glance, and that they should form some coherent whole. In each of the three players studied, Chase and Simon found that the average number of pieces taken in at a glance was small in number (i.e. about three) and similar in content. However, better players used significantly shorter glances to encode a chunk. Chase and Simon also discovered systematic differences in the number of pieces encoded in a chunk as a function of expertise. The strongest player encoded about 2.5 pieces per chunk, whereas the weakest player encoded only 1.9 pieces per chunk. So, their results showed that expert players can recognise chunks in a board position more quickly and can encode more information in these chunks than novice players.

Simon and Gilmartin (1973) modelled aspects of these results in a program called the Memory-Aided Pattern Perceiver (MAPP). The model contained a large number of different board patterns and encoded a "presented" board configuration into its short-term memory, by recognising various chunks of the total configuration. Simon and Gilmartin produced one version of the program with more patterns than another version (1114 patterns vs. 894 patterns) and ran both versions on board reconstruction tasks. They found that the version with fewer patterns performed the poorest. Thus, the model provided concrete support for the proposal that board-position knowledge was the key to understanding novice–expert differences in these tasks. Extrapolating from the model, Simon and Gilmartin estimated that master-level performance required a long-term memory of between 10,000 and 100,000 patterns.

Board-position knowledge and chess expertise?

However, chess expertise does not rely solely on knowledge of board positions. Performance differences between players reflect differences in the numbers of board patterns known by players (e.g. see MAPP), but players also have heuristic knowledge for evaluating moves that is quite independent of board-position knowledge (see Charness, 1981b, 1991; Holding, 1985, 1989). Holding and Reynolds (1982) presented players, rated as being of high or low ability, with random board positions for eight seconds, and asked them to recall them later. They found, like DeGroot, that irrespective of their ability, all subjects were poor at recalling the positions. However, when the players were asked to evaluate the strength of the board position and decide on the next best move to make, the high-ability players produced better-quality moves. So, even though the subjects had no specific schemata for these random board positions, they had other knowledge that allowed them to generate and evaluate potential moves from that position.

It is important that chess expertise relies on both board-position and evaluative knowledge because this shows that expertise is not just about memory for the routine problem solving (see Green & Gilhooly, 1992). Hatano and Inagaki (1986) have made a crucial distinction between different types of expertise, routine, and adaptive expertise (see also Holyoak, 1991; Lamberts & Pfeifer, 1992). *Routine expertise* manifests itself in the ability to solve familiar, standard problems in an efficient manner, and probably relies on schemata that encode the routine, like standard board-position knowledge. *Adaptive expertise* works best on non-standard, unfamiliar problems, and allows experts to develop *ad hoc* procedures and strategies for solving such problems. Evaluation knowledge seems to underlie adaptive expertise. It comes into play when a problem situation deviates from a known situation. In general, board-position knowledge allows the player to find out what parts of the board are relevant, whereas evaluation knowledge helps to develop moves from these positions and evaluate the consequences of these moves.

PHYSICS EXPERTISE

Anyone who has studied physics will recall (possibly with dread) problems like the following one:

A block of mass M is dropped from a height x onto a spring of force constant K. Neglecting friction, what is the maximum distance the spring will be compressed?

People solve physics problems by selecting appropriate principles from the physics domain and deriving a solution through the application of these principles. A problem solver must analyse the problem, build some cognitive representation of it that cues relevant principles, and then strategically apply these principles to solve it. Clearly, if someone represents the problem incorrectly they are less likely to solve it. If we follow the hypotheses from chess research, we should expect experts to have a larger repertoire of problem-solving knowledge than novices. In physics, this knowledge takes the form of schemata that link problem situations to principles (see Chapter 11). Without this knowledge both groups should fall back on more heuristic knowledge similar to that used in puzzle problems (e.g. means–ends analysis; see Chapter 15).

Evidence of novice–expert differences in physics

It has been proposed that expert physicists build better representations of the problem than novices, based on their schematic knowledge (Heller & Reif, 1984; Larkin, 1983, 1985). Chi, Feltovich, and Glaser (1981) asked novices and experts to sort problems into related groups, and found that the two groups classified problems differently. Novices tended to group together problems that had the same *surface features*; they grouped two problems together if they used pulleys or ramps. Novices were led by the keywords and the objects in the problem. However, experts classified problems in terms of their *deep structure*. That is, they grouped together problems that could be solved by the same principles, even though these

problems had different surface features (Chi, Glaser, & Rees, 1983; see Fig. 16.2).

Chi et al. (1981) also discovered that even though experts solved the problems four times faster than novices, they spent more time than novices analysing and understanding the problems. Unlike the novices who waded into the problem immediately applying equations, the experts elaborated the representation of the problem by selecting the appropriate principles that applied to it. Experts carried out a complex categorisation of the problem situation using their available knowledge.

Strategic differences have also been found between experts and novices. Experts tend to *work forwards* to a solution whereas novices tend to *work backwards* (Larkin, McDermott, Simon, & Simon, 1980). When they have analysed the problem, experts apply the principles they have selected to the given quantities in the problem. These principles generate the unknown quantities needed to solve the problem. This planned working-forward strategy is both efficient and powerful. Novices, in contrast, have an impoverished repertoire of available principles. Typically, they take the goal (e.g. what is the maximum distance the spring will be compressed?) and find a principle that contains the desired quantity and usually no more than one other unknown quantity. They then try to find this new unknown quantity and hence work backwards to the givens of the problem statement.

Symbolic and connectionist models of physics skills

Several computational models of physics problem solving have been produced to model physics experts and the shift in expertise from novices to experts (Elio & Sharf, 1990; Lamberts, 1990; Lamberts & Pfeifer, 1992; Larkin, 1979; Priest, 1986). Most of these models are conventional symbolic models, like production systems (see Chapter 1). However, recently Lamberts (1990) has produced an interesting *hybrid model* that mixes connectionist and production-system ideas. Lamberts noted that physics expertise seems to be a mix of knowledge of previous problems and strategic reasoning (e.g. forward reasoning). In his

FIGURE 16.2

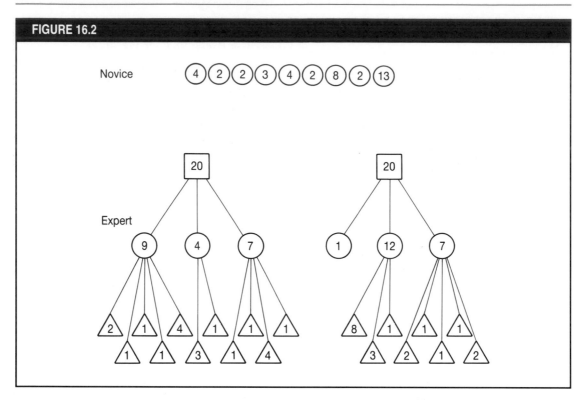

A schematic diagram of the sortings of physics problems by a novice and expert, from Chi, Glaser, and Rees (1983). The squares indicate higher-order categories which organise lower-order groupings (circles). The conceptual groups represented by circles can be further subdivided into smaller groupings (triangles). The numbers indicate the number of problems in the category. Note how the expert's categorisation reveals an hierarchical organisation that is missing from the novice's categorisation, which is completely flat.

model, a connectionist memory encodes previous problem-solving experience and a production system handles the strategic reasoning.

The model's long-term memory is a distributed memory that encodes previous problem situations (see Chapters 1 and 9). This memory has input units that are divided into three types: data units, final goal units, and subgoal units. The *data units* can encode different sorts of symbols in problem statements (e.g. the explicitly mentioned objects and variables), whereas the *final goal units* encode the required quantity to be found in the problem. Problems are encoded in memory using these two sets of units. From experience of solving previous problems, the memory learns an association between a particular set of problem statements (including their goals) and a set of useful subgoals (see Fig. 16.3).

The model goes through four main processing stages when solving a problem. First, the problem to be solved is encoded by both the distributed memory system and the production system. In the distributed memory, the problem statement is encoded as activations to the appropriate data and final goal units (it should be noted that no encoding of subgoals occurs). The production system encodes the problem as a structured representation in its working memory. Second, the encoded problem is processed by the distributed memory until it settles into a stable state, at which point one or more of the units in the subgoal set achieve a high activation. Third, the production system then comes into play and uses its sets of inference rules on the problem representation and the subgoals generated by the distributed memory. These inference rules are used to reach the goals of the

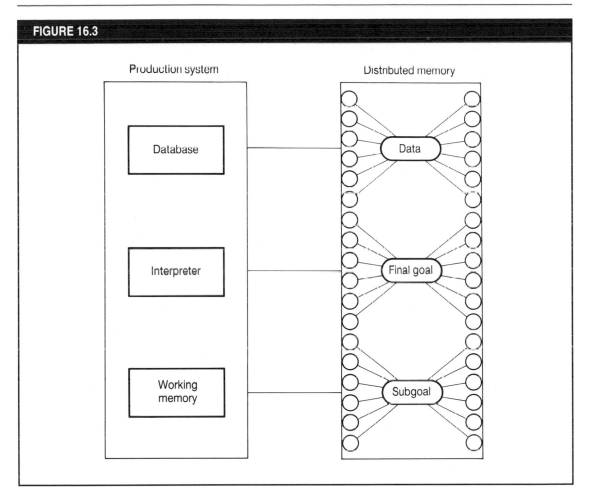

A schematic diagram of Lamberts' (1990) hybrid system for modelling physics expertise.

problem using forward inference. If forward inference fails then the system starts backward inference. Fourth, if a solution is learned in the third stage then the subgoals that were found to be useful are used, along with the problem statement and goal, to put the network through a learning cycle that encodes the association between these three entities. So, in the future, if the same or a similar problem is met the network will produce a certain set of suitable subgoals to be adopted. Lamberts has shown that the system, when trained, can produce solutions that closely correspond to those generated by human experts.

A number of theorists have suggested that connectionist models should form the basis of future accounts of expertise (see Holyoak, 1991;

Lamberts & Pfeifer, 1992). Their argument rests on the claim that connectionist models easily capture adaptive expertise, rather than just routine expertise (see Hatano & Inagaki, 1986). A case in point is the type of adaptive expertise manifested in solving problems by analogy, which we will encounter in a later section (see Holyoak & Thagard, 1989).

COMPUTER-PROGRAMMING SKILLS

With developments in information technology many people, other than computer scientists, have had to learn to program computers. Three unassailable facts have emerged from this experience. First, people do not find programming languages easy to learn. Second, even expert programmers frequently make mistakes. Third, all of this takes time and costs money. From a research perspective, the interest lies in fundamental questions about the cognitive demands of computer programming; about the features of programming languages that make them difficult to learn and use (see e.g. Anderson, Boyle, & Reiser, 1985; Eisenstadt, Keane, & Rajan, 1992; Kahney, 1989; Kahney, & Eisenstadt, 1982; Soloway & Spohrer, 1989).

Plans in programming

Like chess masters and expert physicists, the expert programmer appears to have developed elaborated schemata or abstract plans for programming tasks (see Chapter 11 on schemas). Soloway and his associates argue that expert programmers have script-like plans that are stereotypical chunks of code. For example, a programmer might have an "averaging plan", which contains the knowledge that an average is a sum divided by a count (see Rist, 1989; Spohrer, Soloway, & Pope, 1985). These plans are seen as being "natural" in the sense that programmers possess them before they learn to program. According to this view, programmers plan a program at an abstract level, by co-ordinating and sequencing these chunks to achieve the required task (see Erlich & Soloway, 1984).

Evidence for this theory has been found by Adelson (1981). She has shown, using a recall task, that expert programmers can recall more lines of code than novices and have a larger chunk size for encoding this information than novices (see also McKeithen, Reitman, Rueter, & Hirtle, 1981). Soloway and Erlich (1984) have supported the theory with evidence from a different fill-in-the-blanks task in which subjects have to add missing statements to a program. Expert programmers have less difficulty in filling in the blanks than novices. Skilled programmers appear to be able to select appropriate plans from memory and adapt them to the local requirements of a specific programming task. Soloway, Bonar, and Erlich (1983) have found direct evidence for the existence of such programming plans when the

requirements of the programming language conflict with programmers' "natural" plans from everyday life. Programmers order program statements according to the dictates of everyday knowledge, even when this ordering leads to bugs in their programs. For example, the process/read loop construct in PASCAL is a major source of bugs because it mismatches the normal course of events in the real world; in the real world we get an object (read it), and then do something with it (process it), but in the PASCAL loop world, items are processed first and then read.

However, Gilmore and Green (1988) have argued against the view that programming plans are necessarily natural and general. They asked skilled programmers in two languages—PASCAL and BASIC—to carry out plan-related and plan-unrelated tasks, when the plan structure of a program was highlighted. They reasoned that if plans were being used, then highlighting the structure of these plans should facilitate subjects in a plan-related task, but not in a plan-unrelated task. This prediction was only confirmed for PASCAL programs. They therefore proposed that the content of programming plans do not generalise across languages (even though they admitted that BASIC programmers may use other plans). In particular, they maintained that plans emerge from notational aspects of the programming language in question. So, the notation of PASCAL makes it easier to form plans than the notation of BASIC (see Davies, 1990a).

Davies (1990a,b) has produced a synthesis to heal the conflict between these findings and earlier work. His position is that natural plans exist but they may be harder to express in one language than in another. Furthermore, programmers may find it easier to express natural plans in a particular language after being trained in program design. Davies pointed out that Gilmore and Green's results could be due to the PASCAL programmers' previous training in design. He therefore performed a similar study looking at novice BASIC programmers with or without design experience. In contrast to Gilmore and Green's results, he found that BASIC programmers *could* benefit from the cues to plan structures in programs, but only when they had training in program design. So, to characterise the knowledge involved in programming expertise we need to consider three distinct factors: the structures in the problem domain (i.e. natural plans); the structures in the particular programming language domain (to do with the notation of the language); and the mapping between the former and the latter. Education in program design is seen as providing the basis for this mapping.

All these studies have concentrated on the comprehension and recall of programs, rather than on the coding or generation of programs. More recently, some studies have addressed code generation, showing that there are systematic changes in the strategies used by programmers as they move from being novices to experts (see Davies, 1991; Green, 1989, 1990; Rist, 1989). Theories of programming expertise now take into account the many ingredients that go into making up the skill: the programming language used, the background education of the programmer, the knowledge structures acquired, and the strategies employed to write the code.

LEARNING TO BE AN EXPERT

Thus far, we have seen some of the differences that exist between novices and experts in several different domains. We have not said how these differences come about; how novices become experts. Theoretically, we need an account of how people start as novices with little domain knowledge, using weak methods to solve problems, and end up as experts with elaborate, domain-specific knowledge structures and efficient problem-specific strategies. In this section, we review some explanations of how people become experts.

Practice makes perfect
Common sense suggests that one way to become an expert is to practice something. Chase and Simon (1973a) estimated that most grand masters had studied for at least 9–10 years to reach their level of expertise. The relationship between

practice and performance in perceptual-motor skills has been captured by one of the few "laws" in cognitive psychology: the Power Law of Practice. This law states that if the time per trial and number of trials are graphed on log–log co-ordinate axes, then a straight line results (Fitts & Posner, 1967). Some researchers have proposed that the power law also holds for purely cognitive skills, and have suggested a number of mechanisms to explain the effects of practice and the acquisition of expertise: chunking, proceduralisation, compression, induction (see Chapter 1; Anderson, 1982, 1987a, 1993; Newell, 1990; Rosenbloom & Newell, 1986). Most of these techniques have been developed in the context of production system models of cognition (Chapter 1).

Chunking
One proposal is that a form of *chunking* underlies practice effects (this is a very specific sense of the term, to be distinguished from Miller's, 1956, memory formulation; see Chapter 6). Rosenbloom and Newell (1986) have argued that, when a series of production rules is applied to solve a particular problem, a new rule can be created that does away with the chain of rules (moves) to get to the solution. For example, suppose an problem solver encounters a problem situation, state-a, and needs to reach a goal state, state-f. In solving the problem a chain of rules might be applied: rule1 changes state-a to state-b, rule 2 changes state-b to state-e, and rule 3 changes state-e to state-f. Put simply, chunking would create a new rule containing the relevant conditions that led to the goal state; a new rule that will change state-a to state-f in one step. An immediate implication of chunking is that the problem is solved in one step rather than a succession of steps, allowing the time taken to solve the problem to decrease significantly.

Knowledge compilation: Proceduralisation, composition, and tuning
Anderson (1982, 1983, 1987a, 1993) has proposed another mechanism called "knowledge compilation" in his theory of skill learning. His ACT models (*Adaptive Control of Thought*) have been applied to model the learning of geometry (Anderson, Greeno, Kline, & Neves, 1981),

computer programming (Anderson & Reiser, 1985; Pirolli & Anderson, 1985) and computer text-editing (Singley & Anderson, 1989). The ACT models tend to have three main components (see Fig. 16.4):

- a *declarative memory*; that is, a semantic network of interconnected concepts that have different activation strengths (see Chapters 1 and 10);
- a *procedural memory*, of production rules; and,
- a *working memory* that contains currently active information.

Declarative knowledge is knowledge that can be reported and is not tied to the situation in which it can be used (e.g. a memorised textbook procedure to apply a statistical test), whereas procedural knowledge often cannot be expressed, is applied automatically, and is specifically tuned to specific situations (e.g. the knowledge we use when adding numbers). Information can be *stored* and *retrieved* from declarative memory by a number of methods. Information in the production memory takes the form of production rules, which are *executed* when they *match* the contents of working memory. Production memory can also be applied to itself by *application processes*; new productions can be learned by examining existing productions. For the most part, Anderson explains skill acquisition as *knowledge compilation*; as a move from the use of declarative knowledge to procedural knowledge.

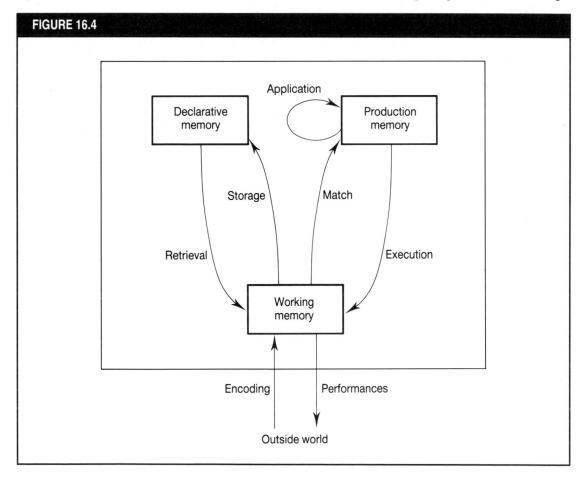

FIGURE 16.4

A schematic diagram of the major components and interlinking processes used in Anderson's (1983, 1993) ACT models.
Reprinted by permission of Harvard University Press. © 1983 President and Fellows of Harvard College. All rights reserved.

Knowledge compilation has two sub-processes: proceduralisation and composition.

Proceduralisation is the process that transforms declarative knowledge into production knowledge. Usually, problem solvers initially attempt to solve say a maths or programming problem from a textbook. In these solution attempts, the novice will generate a number of subgoals using a combination of weak methods (like hill climbing or means–ends analysis; see Chapter 15) and declarative knowledge from instruction. During repeated problem-solving episodes, a particular piece of declarative knowledge will occur repeatedly in the context of a particular subgoal. When this happens, a new production rule is created, which has the declarative knowledge as a pattern (its IF-part) and the executed action as its action (its THEN-part). This declarative–procedural change should result in a concurrent reduction in verbalisation by the problem solver. Correlatively, there is an increase in the automaticity of the problem-solving behaviour (see also Chapter 5). Reductions in verbalisation have been demonstrated repeatedly in the literature (Anderson, 1982; Sweller, Mawer, & Ward, 1983).

Composition is another method of knowledge compilation. It involves cutting out unnecessary productions from a sequence of productions. Problem solvers' initial attempts will involve many false paths and the use of incorrect strategies, but if they are subsequently asked to solve the same problem, they will generally have learned to ignore these false paths and produce the correct solution sequence. This type of learning is captured in the ACT models by a composition mechanism that prunes away the production rules used in false paths. Hence, a production is created that delivers the correct solution to the problem.

Anderson also maintained that production rules could be *tuned* by either strengthening, generalisation or discrimination. *Production tuning* is a method to account for speed-up as a result of practice on a problem, when little new knowledge is being acquired. Production rules are *strengthened* in their activation value every time they are used successfully, and the stronger a production is, the more likely it is to fire when it competes with other productions. Productions are *generalised* when part of their condition or "IF" patterns are replaced by variables. Finally, when a production cannot be executed for some reason, or an impasse is reached, *discrimination* occurs; that is, one production's activation is weakened relative to other more successful productions with similar conditions.

Rule induction

Anderson's account suggests that the novice–expert shift involves a gradual replacement of weak methods, like means–ends analysis, with domain-specific rules. However, in some mathematics problem solving, novices learn less if they adopt a means–ends heuristic. People use serial pattern learning if there is a salient pattern to the solution of a problem (see Kotovosky & Simon, 1973). For example, if a solution depends on applying one rule and then another repeatedly, then subjects notice this regular pattern and induce a rule that describes it (Sweller, 1983; Sweller, Mawer, & Ward, 1983). Furthermore, this form of rule induction is inhibited if subjects use means–ends analysis because it directs problem solvers' attention away from the important aspects of the problem's structure.

EVALUATION OF EXPERTISE RESEARCH

In this chapter, we have seen that problem-solving expertise relies on acquiring knowledge structures and strategies appropriate to a particular problem situation. Green and Gilhooly (1992) summarise the results of expertise research in five maxims, which we paraphrase as:

- Experts remember better.
- Experts employ different problem-solving strategies (e.g. they work forwards to solutions).
- Experts have better and more elaborated problem representations.
- Experts' superiority is based on knowledge not on some basic capacity.
- Experts become expert through extensive practice.

We have seen these maxims reflected in the three areas of expertise research that have been reviewed. The consensus on these maxims is some indication of the success of this research area.

Expertise research has been marked by success in several respects. First, it is an area where computational modelling has proved to be very informative. We now have very well-developed models of skill acquisition and expert problem solving. Indeed, both Anderson (1993) and Newell (1990) consider these production system models to be candidate cognitive architectures; that is, general theoretical frameworks for characterising all of cognition. Second, this research has considerable significance to everyday cognition; in particular, it is important in education where one view of the task of educators is to create experts.

Perhaps the biggest flaw in expertise research is that it has concentrated on routine expertise rather than on adaptive expertise (Hatano & Inagaki, 1986). However, this imbalance is likely to be redressed in the future.

MENTAL MODELS OF THE WORLD

The research on expertise brought thinking research face to face with real-world problem solving. However, expertise research focuses on specialist forms of thinking rather than commonplace, everyday thought. Happily, research on mental models has dealt with mundane thought;

dealing with the "naive theories" or "mental models" people use to understand the world (see Brewer, 1987; Gentner & Stevens, 1983; Norman, 1983; Rips, 1986; Vosniadou & Brewer, 1992). The theory of *mental models* is used to account for a variety of aspects of behaviour in novel, problem-solving situations. Although theorists use the term "mental model" to mean different things, Panel 16.1 shows several common properties that are shared by these different conceptions. However, it should be noted that this conception of mental models is quite different to that used in reasoning research (see Chapter 17; Johnson-Laird, 1983; Johnson-Laird & Byrne, 1991).

Mental models of home heating

Kempton's (1986) work is a prime example of the use of mental models. She proposed that when people regulated their thermostats to heat their houses they used one of two models of how a heating system works: a "feedback model" or a "valve model".

According to the *feedback model*, the thermostat turns the furnace on and off depending on the room temperature. So, when the room is too cold, the thermostat turns the furnace on, and when the room is warm enough, it turns the furnace off. The temperature at which the furnace is turned on, is determined by the setting on the thermostat's dial. This model posits that the furnace runs at a constant rate and so the only way that the thermostat can control the amount of heat in a room is by the length of time that the furnace is on. If the

---

(Panel 16.1) Mental Models

- Mental models constitute a person's causal understanding of a physical system, and are used to understand and make predictions about that system's behaviour.

- They are incomplete, unstable, and may be even partly *ad hoc*.

- These models can simulate the behaviour of a physical system and may be accompanied by visual imagery.

- They are unscientific; people maintain "superstitious" behaviour patterns even though they are known to be unnecessary, because they may cost little physical effort and save mental effort.

- They are usually characterised in propositional terms (see Chapter 9).

dial is adjusted upward only a little bit, the furnace will run a short time and turn off; if it is adjusted upward a large amount, the furnace must run for a longer period to heat the house sufficiently. Left at one setting, the thermostat will switch the furnace off and on as necessary to maintain the temperature on the dial setting.

In contrast, in the *valve model*, the thermostat controls the rate at which the furnace generates heat, rather than having a feedback function. So, the furnace runs at variable rates depending on the setting on the dial. To maintain a constant temperature in the house the setting is adjusted so that the amount of heat generated balances the amount being lost. In this model, the thermostat has no specific role as a regulator of heat; indeed, in one sense, it is the person adjusting the thermostat that acts as the regulator. Several other common physical devices operate in a similar manner and are used as analogies for the valve model. For example, when you turn a tap, more water comes out.

These models make different predictions about how heating systems work and about how energy can be saved in the home. However, even though they are elaborate and intriguing, neither of them is technically accurate. The valve model predicts that more fuel is consumed at higher settings than at lower settings. This prediction is correct but for the wrong reasons; the higher fuel consumption is not the result of the valve opening wider, but is due to higher internal temperatures in the house resulting in greater heat loss through walls, windows, and ceilings. Hence, people using the valve model tend to readjust their thermostats more frequently and be more efficient energy users. In contrast, the feedback model can, under certain circumstances, lead to fuel wastage. People using the feedback model tend to leave their thermostat settings at a set, often high, level for long periods of time; they assume that the thermostat will turn the heating off when the required temperature is reached. So, the heating is on more than is necessary. In an ecology-conscious world, the importance of these findings is enormous. Kempton estimates that if people had an appropriate and accurate model of home heating then the saving for all US households in a single year could be around $5 billion.

Home-heating models illustrate some of the main properties of mental models. First, mental models are predictive; they suggest different ways in which physical mechanisms operate. Second, they simulate physical mechanisms and phenomena, and are often accompanied by visual imagery. For example, someone using the valve model could easily imagine a signal going from the dial on the wall to the furnace causing the valve to open, stoking the flames of the boiler. Third, people can have multiple models to deal with different aspects of the same system; Kempton identified two different models but admitted that many people may have a mixture of both. Fourth, mental models are often inherently unscientific, in the sense that they are not tested carefully and vetted by their users. Fifth, mental models can be volatile; they can undergo sudden changes depending on the knowledge used to construct them and an individual's conception of the task situation. Finally, it is also possible that people's protocols, which appear to reflect model use, include *ad hoc* rationalisations to account for actions that have been taken. So, some of the information people report may not be part of the model at all.

Naive models of motion

Similar evidence for the use of mental models has been found in studies of people's naive theories of object motion (see Caramazza, McCloskey, & Green, 1981; McCloskey, 1983). These models are fairly consistent across individuals and can be applied in many different situations; however, they differ markedly from the fundamental principles of classical physics (interestingly enough, they parallel early pre-Newtonian physics). McCloskey and his colleagues examined these naive theories by looking at subjects' answers to problems like the following one (see Fig. 16.5):

In the diagram, a plane is flying along at a constant speed. The plane is also flying at a constant altitude, so that the flight path is parallel to the ground. The arrow shows the direction in which the plane is flying. When the plane is in the position shown in the diagram a large metal ball is dropped from

FIGURE 16.5

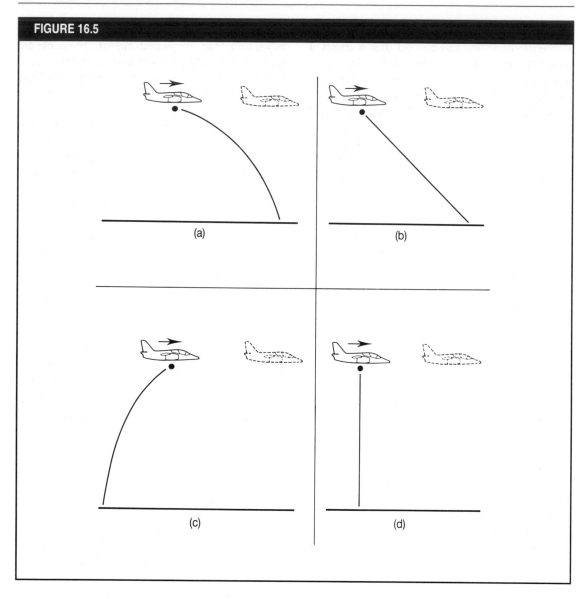

The correct response (a) and incorrect responses (b–d) for the airplane problem. Reproduced with the permission of Michael McCloskey from *Mental models* (edited by D. Gentner & A. Stevens) published by Lawrence Erlbaum Associates Inc., © 1983 Lawrence Erlbaum Associates Inc.

the plane. The plane continues flying at the same speed in the same direction and at the same altitude. Draw the path the ball will follow from the time it is dropped until it hits the ground. Ignore wind or air resistance. Also show as well as you can the position of the plane at the moment that the ball hits the ground.

Only one of the diagrams in Fig. 16.5 is correct (the first). When the ball is dropped it will ascribe a parabolic arc and the plane will be above the ball when it hits the ground. The total velocity of the ball is made up of two independent velocities; a horizontal and a vertical velocity. Before the ball is dropped, it has a horizontal velocity equal to that of the plane and a vertical velocity of zero. After the ball is released, it undergoes a constant vertical acceleration due to gravity, and thus acquires a constantly increasing vertical velocity. The ball's horizontal velocity, however, does not change; it continues to move horizontally at the same speed as the plane. It is the combination of the constant horizontal velocity and the continually increasing vertical velocity that produces a parabolic arc. Because the horizontal velocity of the ball equals that of the plane, it hits the ground directly beneath the plane.

However, few subjects appear to think about the problem in this way. Only 40% of subjects drew diagrams with parabolic arcs, and not all of these placed the plane above the ball as it hit the ground. The remaining 60% produced the other variants shown in Fig. 16.5. According to McCloskey (1983) these responses arise from a simple model of motion that he calls *impetus theory*. In deference to classical physics, impetus theory proposes that: (i) the act of setting an object in motion imparts to the object an internal force or "impetus" that serves to maintain the motion, and (ii) that a moving object's impetus gradually dissipates. McCloskey argued that this mental model was useful in predicting object motions in everyday life. However, the model is not true in general and leads to incorrect predictions in many contexts.

Many of these experiments were carried out on university-level subjects, and so illustrate surprising misconceptions in well-educated people. More recently, several investigators have questioned the generality of these findings and their explanation. It now seems that the results found are, in part, due to the use of paper-and-pencil tests. Kaiser, Jonides, and Alexander (1986) asked subjects to reason about similar problems in familiar contexts, and found that the majority of people produced correct predictions. Furthermore, if subjects are asked to make judgements about object motions as part of a dynamic simulation of ongoing events, then they rarely make errors (see Kaiser, Proffitt, & Anderson, 1985). It has also been shown that when people have made erroneous predictions on a picture-based task, they frequently view simulations of their predictions as being anomalous. So, people are not as poor at predicting particle motions as the McCloskey studies suggested. However, it does appear that people are quite poor at judgements of more complex events, like the dynamics of wheels, irrespective of the testing context used (see Proffitt, Kaiser, & Whelan, 1990).

Yates et al. (1988) have challenged the theoretical basis of McCloskey's work. They have argued that people do not have abstract theories about motion, but rather rely on imagery-based, prototypical motion events to construct specific "enactments" of the motions of objects. This theory predicts that the more "realistic" or familiar the testing scenario, the greater the likelihood that such prototypes would be cued and used to generate appropriate predictions. Ironically, the conception of mental models is wide enough to include both intuitive theories or prototypic motion events as instances of mental models. In conclusion, it should be noted that whatever mental model we *do* use, it may be entirely appropriate for making predictions about the motions of everyday objects, even though it may be at variance with the predictions of classical physics (see Springer, 1990, and Yates, 1990, for a discussion of this issue).

CREATIVITY, ANALOGY, AND DISCOVERY

The research reviewed so far in this chapter has been about relatively routine problem solving. It shows that we apply either schemata or mental models to solve familiar problems. However, people sometimes go beyond their knowledge to solve problems that are novel or unfamiliar. We can act creatively when we have no directly applicable knowledge to a problem situation. For example, Kekulé reported discovering the structure of the benzene ring after dreaming about a snake biting its tail.

In this section, we look at this type of behaviour. Initially, we consider some of the traditional research on creativity, before examining two recent research areas that shed light on the way discoveries are made, by using analogies and testing hypotheses.

Creativity

In the past, research on creativity has often been descriptive rather than explanatory. The classic example of this descriptive approach is Wallas's (1926) classification of the broad stages of the creative process into:

- Preparation, where the problem under consideration is formulated and preliminary attempts are made to solve it.
- Incubation, where the problem is left aside to work on other tasks.
- Illumination, where the solution comes to the problem solver as a sudden insight.
- Verification, in which the problem solver makes sure that the solution really works.

This classification appears to be supported by the reports of creative scientists. One such famous report is by French mathematician Henri Poincaré (1913). Poincaré reported working intensively on the development of Fuchsian functions for 15 days. At the end of this time he reported that:

> I wanted to represent these functions by the quotient of two series; this idea was perfectly conscious and deliberate; the analogy with elliptic functions guided me. I asked myself what properties these series must have if they existed, and succeeded without difficulty in forming the series I have called theta-Fuchsian.
>
> Just at that time I left Caen, where I was living, to go on a geologic excursion under the auspices of the school of mines. The changes in travel made me forget my mathematical work. Having reached Coutances, we entered an omnibus to go some place or other. At the moment when I put my foot on the step the idea came to me, without anything in my former thoughts seeming to have paved the way for it, that the transformations I had used to define Fuchsian functions were identical to those of non-Euclidean geometry. I did not verify the idea; I should not have had time, as, upon taking my seat in the omnibus, I went on with a conversation already commenced, but I felt a perfect certainty.

Poincaré's report fits Wallas's framework perfectly, with illumination following an incubation period after extensive preparation. However, even though Wallas's analysis provides us with a broad framework, it is really too general and descriptive. Fortunately, some attempts have been made to specify these stages; for example, incubation and illumination have been treated in Gestalt research on insight (see Chapter 15).

Incubation, illumination and creativity

Few studies have been carried out on incubation, although on balance they support the existence of the phenomenon (see Ohlsson, 1992; Kaplan & Simon, 1990). Incubation can be explained within problem-space theory as a special type of forgetting (see Simon, 1966). Simon (1966) makes the distinction between control information about a problem (e.g. a record of the subgoals tried in a problem) and factual information (e.g. some property of an object or substantive aspect of the problem). For example, in Maier's (1931) two-string problem, control knowledge might include the subgoal "try to reach something that is far away" and substantive information would be that "the string is a flexible object" (see Chapter 15 and Keane, 1989). Factual information discovered in the context of one subgoal will not be available to other goals. However, during incubation, control information decays faster than factual information. Therefore, after the problem has been set aside for a time, subgoal information will be lost but the factual information will be still present. This factual information will thus be available to newly generated subgoals of the problem, increasing the likelihood of the problem being solved.

Ohlsson (1992) maintains that there is very little empirical support for illumination; the literature on it seems to rely on two anecdotal reports by von Helmholtz and Poincaré (see Hadamard, 1945). If we are to relate the phenomenon to any literature, it is that on the use of hints in problem solving. Again, much of this work has been carried out within the Gestalt tradition (see Chapter 15). The current favoured account seems to be that any new information introduced into the problem or met in the environment may activate related concepts in memory, and result in the sudden emergence of a solution. For example, in the case of the two-string problem, Maier reported that when the experimenter brushed against the string, setting it swinging in the line of sight of subjects, many of them suddenly produced the solution of swinging the string and catching it on the up-swing, while holding the other string.

Recent accounts of creativity

Even though Wallas's stages of creativity have been very influential, his formulation is not the final word on creativity. More recently, several cognitive scientists have made a number of proposals about aspects of the phenomenon. None of these proposals is at variance with the theoretical proposals of these chapters, and many of the ideas have been modelled computationally already.

Johnson-Laird (1988) has contrasted two alternative accounts of creativity, based on an analogy to theories of evolution. The *Neo-Darwinian* model proposes that creativity involves the arbitrary combination of elements (ideas) to generate possible new ideas, followed by the application of constraints to rule out non-viable products. The *Neo-Lamarckian* alternative involves the initial use of constraints to generate viable possibilities and then the arbitrary choice among these possibilities.

Boden's (1991, in press) account of creativity makes the distinction between improbabilistic creativity and impossibilistic creativity. Improbabilistic discoveries involve novel combinations of familiar ideas; hence, they are discoveries that have a low probability of occurring. Boden sees this type of creativity as being the product of associationistic or analogical thinking (see next section). Impossibilistic discoveries are more radical in that ideas are generated that, in some sense, could not have been generated before. Boden argues that ideas are always generated within a conceptual space, like a problem space, which is generated by some set of rules or constraints. People explore these conceptual spaces using various conceptual maps, which characterise typical routes through the space. Some forms of creativity are linked to exploring new parts of the space, or in showing the limits of the space. Other forms of creativity

emerge when the fundamental rules of the space are violated or modified. When the space itself changes, ideas that could not have been generated before emerge. For example, James Joyce's *Ulysses* could be viewed as an exploration and extension of the space of literary styles used in the novel. This conceptual space is explored by writing different sections of *Ulysses* in widely differing styles (e.g. as a Middle-English, Chaucerian tale, or a threepenny-terrible, romantic novel). The space of styles used in the novel is extended by introducing the style of streaming consciousness, which is designed to mimic the flow of an individual's thoughts (see beginning of Chapter 15 for an example). Any computer program that changes its own rules and hence its conceptual space can be said to manifest impossibilistic creativity. Boden reviews some of the programs in artificial intelligence that have these abilities.

Analogical thinking

Analogical thinking has often been identified as a core method in creativity. Koestler (1964) gives accounts of creativity in disparate domains — including literature, the arts, and science — which result from the juxtaposition of two sets of very different ideas. Various creative individuals report solutions to unfamiliar problems based on deep analogies. For example, Rutherford used a solar system analogy to understand the structure of the atom; viewing the electrons as revolving around the nucleus in the same way that the planets revolve around the sun (see Gentner, 1980, 1983, and Fig. 16.6). Similarly, Einstein performed thought experiments based on analogies about riding on light beams and travelling in elevators. So, when people do not have knowledge that is directly relevant to a problem, they apply knowledge indirectly, by analogy to the problem. This use of analogy has been demonstrated in many domains: for example, in computer programming (Anderson & Reiser, 1985; Keane, Kahney, & Brayshaw, 1989), in the missionaries–cannibals problem (Reed, Ernst, & Banerji, 1974; Luger & Bauer, 1978) and in solving electric circuit problems (Gentner & Gentner, 1983).

Analogical thought involves a mapping of the conceptual structure of one set of ideas (called a

FIGURE 16.6

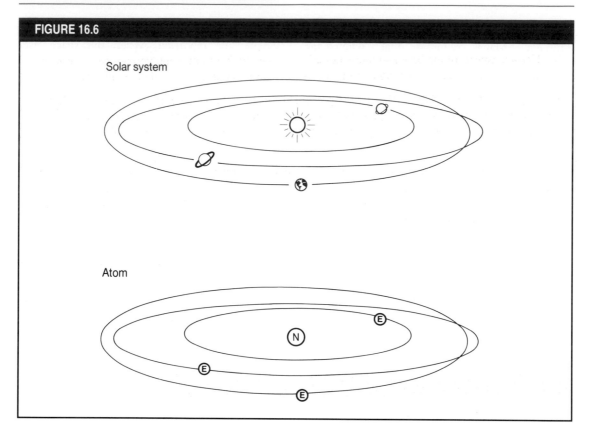

Solar system

Atom

A diagram of the solar system–atom analogy. The planets are attracted to the sun and revolve around it, just as the electrons (Es) are attracted to and revolve around the nucleus (N).

base domain) into another set of ideas (called a target domain); technically, this is called an *analogical mapping* from a base domain (like the solar system) to a target domain (like the atom; see Gentner, 1980, 1983; Holyoak, 1985; Keane, 1985b, 1988). Panel 16.2 provides a rough characterisation of analogical mapping.

Gick and Holyoak (1980, 1983) were the first to study this phenomenon of analogical mapping in problem-solving situations. They gave subjects analogous stories to Duncker's (1945) "radiation problem". The radiation problem involves a doctor's attempt to destroy a malignant tumour using rays. The doctor needs to use high-intensity rays to destroy the tumour, but these high-intensity rays will destroy the healthy tissue surrounding the tumour. If the doctor uses low-intensity rays then the healthy tissue will be saved but the tumour will remain unaffected too. This dilemma can be solved

by a "convergence solution" which proposes that the doctor send low-intensity rays from a number of different directions so that they converge on the tumour, summing to a high intensity to destroy it. However, only about 10% of subjects produce this solution if they are given the problem on its own.

Gick and Holyoak (1980) gave subjects a story about a general attacking a fortress. The general could not use his whole army to take the fortress because the roads leading to it were mined to explode if large groups of men passed over them. He therefore divided up his army into small groups of men and sent them along different roads to the fortress so that they converged on it. When subjects were given this analogous story to memorise and later asked if they could use it to solve the radiation problem the rates of convergence solutions rose to about 80% (see Fig. 16.7). So, people could use the analogous story to solve the

(Panel 16.2) Analogical Mapping

- Certain aspects of the base and target domains are *matched*; for example, you notice that objects in the solar system attract each other and objects in the atom attract each other (see Fig. 16.6).

- Aspects of the base domain that are not present in the target domain are transferred into the latter; for instance, relations about the planets "revolving around" the sun are *tranferred* into the atom domain to create some new conceptual structure there (i.e. that the electons revolve around the nucleus).

- When the knowledge is transferred from one domain to another, there is a tendency for coherent, integrated pieces of knowledge rather than fragmentary pieces to be transferred (see Gentner's 1983, *systematicity principle*); so, the integrated knowledge that attraction and weight difference *cause* the planets to revolve around the sun is transferred before non-integrated information about the earth having life on it.

- Sometimes knowledge is transferred because it is viewed as being pragmatically important or goal-relevant in some respect (see Holyoak, 1985; Keane, 1985b).

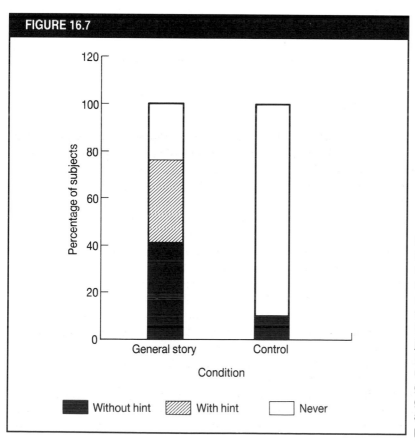

FIGURE 16.7

Some of the results from Gick and Holyoak (1980; Experiment 4) showing the percentage of subjects who solved the radiation problem when they were given an analogy (general-story condition) or were just asked to solve the problem (control condition). Note that just under half of the subjects in the general-story condition had to be given a hint to use the story analogue before they solved the problem.

problem. However, without a specific hint to use the analogy, subjects did not tend to notice it (see later section).

Several computational models of analogical mapping have been suggested: the Structure-Mapping Engine (SME; Falkenhainer, Forbus, & Gentner, 1986, 1989; Forbus, Ferguson, & Gentner, 1994), the Incremental Analogy Machine (IAM; see Keane & Brayshaw, 1988; Keane, Ledgeway, & Duff, 1994) and the Analogical Constraint Mapping Engine (ACME; Holyoak & Thagard, 1989). All of these models agree on the important processes in mapping; however, the IAM model predicts performance differences based on its incremental mode of operation. IAM predicts that the singleton-first problem should be easier to map than the singleton-last problem (see Table 16.1). This occurs because IAM is sensitive to the order of the sentences in the problem, and when the singletons are first in the lists the correct mapping follows more easily than when the order is different. Keane et al. (1994) confirmed this prediction with the finding that people were almost twice as fast at mapping singleton-first problems than singleton-last problems.

Noticing and retrieval in analogy

Gick and Holyoak (1980) also found interesting evidence about subjects' failure to notice the analogous story. If subjects were not directed explicitly to use the story, they often failed to notice that it was relevant to the problem. This suggested that people could not easily recall stories like the general story that lacked superficial similarities and were semantically remote. Keane (1987; see also Holyoak & Koh, 1987) tested this prediction by presenting subjects with either a semantically close story-analogue (about a surgeon using rays on a cancer) or a semantically remote analogue (namely, the general story). Subjects received the story during a weekly lecture and some days later were asked to take part in an experiment on problem solving. As expected it was found that many subjects spontaneously retrieved the close analogue (88%) but very few retrieved the remote analogue (12%). Keane also found that a story that was mid-way between these two extremes (about a general using rays to destroy a missile) produced intermediate rates of retrieval (see Fig. 16.8).

Apart from the difficulties involved in retrieving remote analogues, Gentner, Ratterman, and Forbus (1992; see also Gentner & Landers,

---

TABLE 16.1

Two Versions of the Attribute-mapping Problem (from Holyoak & Thagard, 1989)

Singleton-first		Singleton-last	
A	*B*	*A*	*B*
Steve is smart*	Fido is hungry*	Bill is smart	Fido is hungry*
Bill is tall	Blackie is friendly	Bill is tall	Blackie is friendly
Bill is smart	Blackie is frisky	Tom is timid	Blackie is frisky
Tom is tall	Rover is hungry	Tom is tall	Rover is hungry
Tom is timid	Rover is friendly	Steve is smart*	Rover is friendly

These were used by Keane et al. (1994) to test for the effects of order on analogical mapping. The IAM model predicts that the singleton-first problem should be easier than the singleton-last problem, because the mappings are constructed incrementally.

The correct mappings for both problems are Steve–Fido, Bill–Rover, Tom–Blackie, smart–hungry, tall–friendly, timid–frisky.

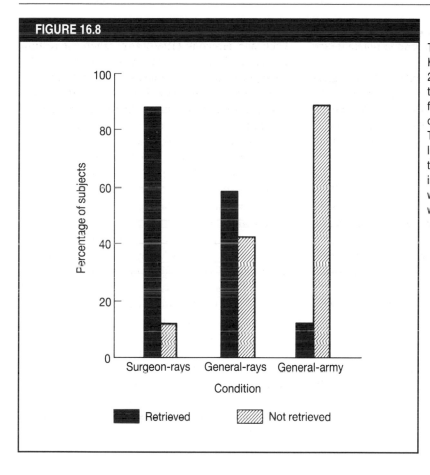

FIGURE 16.8

The percentage of subjects in Keane, 1987 (Experiments 1 & 2) who retrieved story analogues to the radiation problem, as a function of the semantic distance of the story from the problem. The surgeon-rays story was literally similar to the problem, the general-rays story was of intermediate semantic distance, whereas the general-army story was semantically remote.

1985) have shown that subjects tend to retrieve analogues that only share superficial features (so-called mere appearance matches). In other words, people are more likely to retrieve a story about doctors using rays, even if that story involves events that are irrelevant to the radiation problem. These results support the intuition that one reason why acts of creativity, involving remote analogies, are fairly rare is that most people have difficulties retrieving potentially relevant experiences from memory. However, Wharton et al. (1994) have shown that people may not be as poor at retrieval as they first seem. They found that subjects can retrieve deep analogues, once they are distinct from competing analogues stored in memory.

Several computational models have been produced to capture these retrieval results. All of these models use connectionist techniques and involve a two-stage retrieval process (see Keane,

1993, for a review). Thagard, Holyoak, Nelson, and Gochfeld's (1990) ARCS model uses parallel search to find a number of candidate analogues and then selects between these using analogical mapping processes. Gentner and Forbus's (1991) MAC/FAC model (many are called but few are chosen) uses a different form of parallel search to find a set of candidate memories, which are then distinguished by detailed mapping processes. At present, the MAC/FAC model provides the best model of the results found and is also very efficient in the way it computes retrievals (see Gentner & Forbus, 1991).

Scientific discovery and hypothesis testing

Analogical thinking is one technique for making discoveries in science; indeed, it may be used to generate novel hypotheses. However, analogy research will not provide a complete account of scientific discovery; there are other techniques for hypothesis formation. In the philosophy of science, Karl Popper (1968, 1969, 1972; see also Magee, 1973) argued that hypotheses could never be shown to be logically true by simply generalising from confirming instances (i.e. induction). As the philosopher Bertrand Russell pointed out, a scientist turkey might form the generalisation "Each day I am fed" because this hypothesis has been confirmed every day of his life. However, the generalisation provides no certainty that the turkey will be fed tomorrow, and if tomorrow is Christmas Eve then it is likely to be proved false. Popper concluded that the hallmark of science is not confirmation but falsification. Scientists attempt to form hypotheses that can be shown to be untrue by experimental tests. According to Popper, falsification separates scientific from unscientific activities, such as religion and pseudo-science (i.e. psychoanalysis and Marxism). Against Popper's dictates, most ordinary people, including scientists, often seek confirmatory rather than disconfirmatory evidence when testing their hypotheses (see Evans, 1989; Gorman, 1992; Mitroff, 1974; Mynatt, Doherty, & Tweney, 1977). For instance, Mitroff (1974) carried out a study of NASA scientists which revealed that they tended to seek confirmation of their hypotheses more often than disconfirmation.

Hypothesis testing in the 2-4-6 task

A number of key tasks have been used in the hypothesis testing literature, most notably the 2-4-6 task (see Wason, 1960, 1977, and Chapter 17 on the Wason selection task). In the 2-4-6 task, subjects have to discover a rule known to the experimenter, starting with the hint that the number triple 2-4-6 is an instance of it. The experimenter's rule is that the numbers are "an ascending sequence". Subjects have to write down additional triples along with their reason for suggesting them. So, a subject might write 6-8-10 giving "numbers ascending by twos" as the rationale, to which the experimenter would answer that "yes, this triple is also an instance of the rule". After the subject has generated a number of such triples (e.g. 20-22-24, 45-47-49) and has received the positive feedback that they are all instances of the rule, they can

declare what they think the rule to be (e.g. "numbers ascending by twos"). However, this is not the experimenter's rule and after they are informed of this, they must continue generating triples and proposing other rules until they guess correctly. The task allows subjects to generate an infinite variety of hypotheses and tests. Unfortunately, most of these alternatives are not the rule that is required. Wason (1960) found that subjects tended to gather evidence that confirmed their hypothesised rules, rather than generating examples that would falsify their hypotheses (like 33-31-32). He called this tendency a *confirmation bias*: Subjects sought confirmation for hypotheses rather than resorting to falsification. Mahony (1976) also found that scientists fared no better on the task than other groups (indeed, clergymen proved to be better at abandoning their hypotheses).

Confirmation bias appears to be quite prevalent. Mynatt, Doherty, and Tweney (1977) found similar results in a simulation world that is closer to real scientific testing. In this computer world, subjects fire particles at circles and triangles that are presented at two brightness levels (low and high). The world has other features but all of these are irrelevant to the task (see Fig. 16.9). Subjects were not told that the lower-brightness shapes had a 4.2cm invisible boundary around them that deflected particles. At the beginning of the experiment, they were shown arrangements of shapes which suggested the initial hypothesis that "triangles deflect particles". They were then presented with pairs of screens, where one screen contained similar features to those that deflected particles, and the other screen contained novel features. Subjects were divided into three groups that were instructed to adopt either a confirmatory strategy, a disconfirmatory strategy, or no particular strategy (i.e. a control). Again, as in the 2-4-6 task, subjects tended to confirm their hypotheses by picking the confirming screen 71% of the time. Furthermore, the strategy instructions did not deflect subjects from this confirmation bias. Mynatt, Doherty, and Tweney (1978) found similar results using an interactive version of this simulation world. They also found that subjects tended to ignore falsificatory evidence when it occurred.

FIGURE 16.9

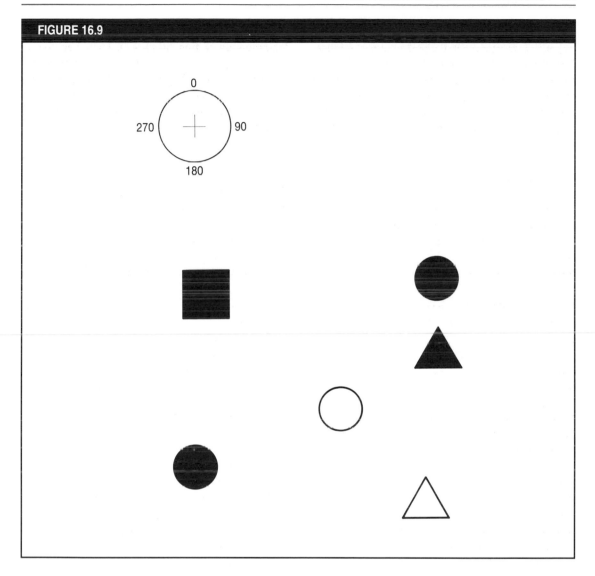

The type of display used by Mynatt et al. (1977) to study confirmation bias. Subjects had to direct a particle that was fired from the upper left part of the screen, by selecting the direction of its path. The relative shading of the objects indicates the two levels of brightness at which objects were presented.

The failure of instructions to undo people's confirmation bias led subsequent researchers to try a number of different manipulations to encourage disconfirmation. Tweney et al. (1980) used a manipulation that increased subjects' disconfirmatory responses by using either confirmatory instructions (it was pointed out that given an hypothetical triple 3-3-3 and the rule "three equal numbers", this rule could be tested with triples like 8-8-8 to confirm the hypothesis) or disconfirma- tory instructions (given an hypothetical triple 3-3-3 and the rule "three equal numbers", subjects were told that if triples like 5-7-9 were correct then the rule would be wrong). However, even though subjects changed their strategy, Tweney et al. did not find any improvement in their success on the problem. Gorman and Gorman (1984) observed greater success, along with an increase in the use of disconfirmation on the 2-4-6 task, when they instructed subjects to use a disconfirmatory strategy and did not give subjects feedback as to the correctness of their hypotheses (see Gorman, 1992, for other related studies).

All these studies indicate that confirmation bias is difficult to modify by instruction. However, some researchers have argued that the studies fail to prove that subjects *have the intention to confirm their hypotheses* (see Evans, 1983; Klayman & Ha, 1987; Wetherick, 1962). They point out that subjects are led to induce an hypothesis that is a specific version of the experimenter's rule (e.g. "numbers ascending by twos" is more specific than "any ascending sequence"). As the subject's rule is a restricted version of the experimenter's rule, any triple that fits the subject's hypothesis will also fit the experimenter's. Thus, they fail to produce triples that do not fit their rule, but do conform to the experimenter's rule. In other situations, an attempt to test an hypothesis with a triple could result in a falsification (which could be intended by subjects). However, the 2-4-6 problem is such that falsification can only be achieved by explicitly trying negative tests of the hypothesis.

However, there is one manipulation that has been surprisingly successful at improving subjects' performance on the 2-4-6 task; this involved indicating to subjects that there were two distinct rules to be considered. Tweney et al. (1980) told subjects that the experimenter had two rules in mind; one of these rules generated DAX triples and the other generated MED triples. They were also told that 2-4-6 was a DAX triple. The DAX rule was intended to be what has been called the experimenter's rule (i.e. "any ascending sequence"), whereas the MED rule characterised the rule that generated any other triple. Thus, instead of being told that their triples were right or wrong, subjects were told that they were DAX or MED. This manipulation led to the striking result that the majority of subjects generated the correct rule on their first attempt. Furthermore, this success occurred even though subjects continued to make "confirmatory" tests of their hypothesis. In this version of the task, subjects succeed because they do not have to disconfirm the DAX hypothesis; rather they can alternatively test the MED hypothesis (indicated by explicit labelling in the instructions). More generally, one of the things that

should be remembered about falsification and confirmation is that either may be appropriate at different times. Chalmers (1982) has pointed out that established theories should be falsifiable, but that it will often be more beneficial to a scientist to seek confirmatory evidence during the development of a new theory.

Problem-space accounts of scientific discovery

Traditionally, hypothesis testing and discovery have remained outside the problem-space tradition, although this is no longer the case. Kulkarni and Simon (1988, 1990) adopted a historical perspective by simulating Hans Kreb's discovery of the urea cycle in biochemistry in a system called Kekeda. One of the key phenomena modelled in this system is how surprising new results can lead to new hypotheses and theories.

Klahr and Dunbar (1988; Klahr, Fay, & Dunbar, 1993) have also looked at discovery in different task situations. In one task, they asked subjects to discover the function of a mystery button (labelled "RPT") for controlling a toy vehicle called Big Trak. Subjects tested the function of the button by including it in brief sets of instructions they had to write to make the toy move. Subjects, therefore, propose hypotheses about the function and then experimentally test them by seeing whether they work. Initially, subjects adopt a positive test strategy reasoning that "If Big Trak does X then my hypothesis is correct", although they are often forced to revise their theories by negative evidence.

Using problem-space theory, Klahr and Dunbar characterised scientific discovery as a *dual-space search*; one space contains the experimental possibilities in the situation and the other contains possible hypotheses. In searching the *hypothesis space*, the initial state is some knowledge of the domain and the goal state is an hypothesis that can account for that knowledge in a more concise, universal form. Hypothesis generation in this space may be the result of a variety of mechanisms (e.g. memory search, analogical mapping, or remindings). Search in the *experiment space* is directed towards experiments that will discriminate between rival hypotheses and yield interpretable outcomes. On the basis of protocol analysis, Klahr and Dunbar distinguished two groups of subjects, *theorists* who preferred to search the space of hypotheses, and *experimenters* who preferred to search the space of experiments. Gorman (1992) has suggested that much previous research has concentrated on the experiment space, ignoring the hypothesis space. The latter is important, as is illustrated in the DAX–MED study which shows how subjects' representation of hypotheses can be very important to their subsequent success on a task.

EVALUATING PROBLEM-SOLVING RESEARCH

Problem-solving research is important to cognitive psychology because it is a testbed for the methodology of cognitive science. Since the advent of information-processing psychology, problem-solving research has been marked by the development of computational models, hand in hand with empirical testing (cf. Newell & Simon, 1972). During this time, the area has made steady progress and is quite unified in embracing a common theoretical stance, based on problem-space theory. To conclude Chapters 15 and 16, we consider a number of core issues that are posed by this research. First, we consider what problem-space theory says about what makes problems difficult. Second, we broach the question of the ecological validity of problem-solving research. Finally, we consider whether thinking phenomena can be modelled using connectionist techniques.

Why are problems difficult?

Given 30 or so years of problem-solving research, we should be able to say something about what influences the ease of problem solving. First, problems are made more difficult if people have to search through a large problem space to find a solution. Stated more simply, problems get difficult when people have to "hold more in their heads" (for "heads" read "working memory"). Second, search difficulties can be alleviated by knowledge of the problem; whole parts of the problem can be

chunked and routine strategies used, all of which lightens the load on working memory. In everyday language, the more familiar a problem the easier it becomes. Third, problems can be difficult because they are ill-defined; again, the ability to define problems hinges on having the right sort of knowledge available. Problems may be difficult because it is not clear what they are about or how they can be solved.

The constant theme that emerges from this research is that problems are difficult because of two main limitations; resource limitations and limitations of knowledge. The major resource limitations lie in a working memory that can only process a certain quantity of information at a certain rate. Knowledge limitations can give rise to a wide range of difficulties. Furthermore, there is an interaction between these two limitations; the probability of being affected by resource limitations can decrease, the more knowledge one has of a problem (because of chunking). At the beginning of this chapter, we saw that the essential difference between expert problem solvers and novice problem solvers hinges on the amount and type of knowledge they have available about a domain; this knowledge may take the form of "facts" about the domain or "rules" about what to do in the domain. Knowledge is the key to unlocking difficult problems.

Indeed, many of the problem-solving methods we have encountered in these two chapters can be classified in terms of the amount and specificity of their domain knowledge (see Carbonell, 1986, and Fig. 16.10):

- In knowledge-poor, puzzle situations where we have little useful past experience, the only useful methods are universal, weak methods (e.g. means–ends analysis).
- A problem may be relatively familiar, but we may lack specific plans to solve it, in which case general plans may be applied; these plans will break the problem down into sub-problems, in a divide-and-conquer fashion, even though these sub-problems will not suggest immediate solutions.
- With more familiar problems we may have various specific plans or schemata about how to

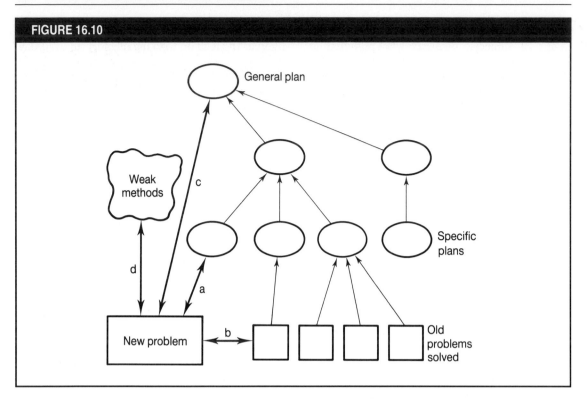

Problem solving may involve the following: (a) instantiating specific plans, (b) using analogical transformation to a known solution of a similar problem, (c) applying general plans to reduce the problem, (d) applying weak methods to search heuristically for a possible solution, or (e) using a combination of these approaches. Reproduced with the permission of the publishers from *Machine Learning: An Artificial Intelligence Approach*, Vol. 2, edited by R.S. Michalski, J.G. Carbonell, and T.M. Mitchell. © 1986 by Morgan Kaufmann, Inc.

solve them (e.g. the expert physicist); here, we can instantiate such schemata and solve any sub-problems that arise with other instantiated schemata.

• Finally, if problem solvers have no specific or general schemata, they may choose a specific past experience (e.g. a specific previously encountered problem) and apply it by analogy to solve the problem they face.

These four situations lay out the main ways in which researchers have proposed that different types of knowledge are used. Clearly, we would not want to maintain that the application of these approaches is mutually exclusive; people may use a combination of all four at different points in solving a particular problem. The key point, however, is that different methods of problem solving can be distinguished by the amount and types of knowledge they use.

Is problem-solving research ecologically valid?

Earlier, we encountered the criticism that problem-solving research was not ecologically valid because it only considered well-defined, puzzle-like problems. This criticism certainly held water in the early history of the area, but is less true today.

We have seen that studies on expertise and mental models have broadened research to consider problem solving in the classroom and other everyday, real-world situations. Investigations of physics expertise have important implications for the teaching of this discipline in schools. Research on programming expertise tackles a very important ability for technological development, and suggests better ways to design programming languages and the computers that use such languages. Some expert–novice research, which we have not reviewed, has been applied to everyday tasks in other domains. For example, Lesgold and his associates (Lesgold et al., 1988; see also Lesgold, 1988) have examined expertise in the reading of X-rays by radiologists. Patel and his associates (Patel & Groen, 1986, 1993; Patel, Groen, & Arocha, 1993) have examined the expertise underlying medical diagnosis. This work has taken cognitive psychology out into the world, and indeed has led some to argue that the everyday world is the most important context in which to test cognitive theories (see Anderson, 1987b).

Connectionism and thinking

The rise of the modelling techniques associated with connectionism appears to be at variance with the character of thinking and the classical, symbolic models that have tended to be used in this area. The argument that theorists often make is that thinking is inherently serial and therefore is not amenable to a parallel processing treatment. Intuitively, this looks like a reasonable proposal, but it does not stand up to much scrutiny. If one examines carefully the models of thinking in the literature, connectionist techniques are used repeatedly.

Consider Anderson's (1983, 1993) ACT models. Even though they use a production-rule system, the models also have a declarative memory, that is a network of concepts through which activation passes in parallel (indeed, it is a precursor of localist, connectionist nets; see Chapters 1 and 9). More recently, we have seen that connectionist models have been produced to model aspects of skill (see e.g. Lamberts, 1990). Indeed, Holyoak (1991) has suggested that the next generation of expertise models will all have a connectionist character. We have also seen that, in the area of analogical thinking, parallel constraint satisfaction has been used with some success; such methods seem central to analogue retrieval (see Thagard et al. 1990; Gentner & Forbus, 1991) and are an elegant solution to some aspects to analogical mapping (Holyoak & Thagard, 1989).

Holyoak and Spellman (1993) have argued that these techniques have a wider applicability in a range of problem-solving situations. Finally, Shastri and Ajjanagadde's (1993) work on dynamic binding suggests a general solution to modelling problems of seriality in many thinking phenomena.

CHAPTER SUMMARY

In this chapter, we have considered a broad range of thinking phenomena; from chess playing to scientific discovery. The emphasis in this chapter, as opposed to Chapter 15, has been on the role that various forms of knowledge play in problem solving. We have seen that expertise in chess, physics, and computer programming all hinge on having available specific knowledge about the domain in question. In chess, this knowledge has been characterised as board-position and evaluation knowledge. In physics, expertise depends on schemata that encode the important theorems in the discipline. In computer programming, we saw how various types of programming plans play a role. Experts and novices can also differ in the strategies they use to apply this knowledge.

All of this expertise research has been accompanied by extensive computational modelling; typically, using production system models. These models have been used to develop clear ideas of how knowledge can be acquired; several mechanisms for learning have been proposed including chunking, proceduralisation, compilation, and rule induction.

People can also have some expertise about various everyday phenomena. Again, here the knowledge that people bring to these everyday problems, in the form of mental models, is crucial to an understanding of how people manage in these situations.

In the domain of creativity, several broad frameworks have been replaced by more specific ideas about the nature of specific skills; like the use of analogy and hypothesis testing. A lot is now known about the key processes involved in analogy; including analogical mapping and retrieval. This understanding has been heavily supported by computational models. Similarly, the long research tradition on hypothesis testing is now coming into contact with computational models, which have arisen out of problem-space theory. It now remains to be seen whether this detailed work in laboratory situations scales up to acts of creation in everyday life.

FURTHER READING

Eisenstadt, M., Keane, M.T., & Rajan, T. (Eds.) (1992). *Novice programming environments*. Hove, UK: Lawrence Erlbaum Associates Ltd. This book deals with the development of computer systems to support novice and expert programmers.

Ericsson, A., & Smith, J. (Eds.) (1991). *Toward a general theory of expertise*. Cambridge: Cambridge University Press. This book provides a recent collection of research on expert–novice differences.

Gilhooly, K.J. (1995). *Thinking: Directed, undirected and creative* (3rd Edn.). London: Academic Press. This book provides more detail on some of the research covered here and explores other areas too.

Keane, M.T., & Gilhooly, K.J. (Eds.) (1992). *Advances in thinking research*. London: Harvester Wheatsheaf. This volume has recent reviews of several developing areas of thinking research.

Osherson, D.N., & Smith, E.E. (Eds.) (1990). *Thinking: An invitation to cognitive science*. Cambridge, MA: MIT Press. This book has a number of overview chapters on a variety of areas of thinking research.

17

Reasoning

INTRODUCTION

Deductive reasoning, as one of the oldest research areas in psychology, has concerned itself with a key question about human nature: "Are human beings rational?" Philosophers have tended to answer this question with a resounding "yes", with arguments that the laws of logic are the laws of thought (Boole, 1854; Mill, 1843). This basic idea has been used, albeit in more sophisticated forms, in the psychology of reasoning. The psychology of reasoning covers both deductive and inductive reasoning. When people carry out deductive reasoning they usually determine what conclusion, if any, *necessarily* follows when certain statements or premises are assumed to be true. In inductive reasoning, people make a generalised conclusion from premises that describe particular instances. Here, we concentrate on deductive reasoning rather than inductive reasoning (but see the 2-4-6 task in Chapter 16).

Johnson-Laird and Byrne (1991, p.3) point out that deductive reasoning is a central intellectual ability, which is necessary:

in order to formulate plans; to evaluate alternative actions; to determine the consequences of assumptions and hypotheses; to interpret and formulate instructions, rules and general principles; to pursue arguments and negotiations; to weigh evidence and to assess data; to decide between competing theories; and to solve problems. A world without deduction would be a world without science, technology, laws, social conventions and culture.

Deductive reasoning research makes central use of logical systems—especially the propositional calculus—to characterise the abstract structure of reasoning problems. So, we will review the logic of deduction in some detail before considering the psychological research. If you are not familiar with logic then you will find this section difficult because it *is* difficult. However, a little extra effort on it will improve your understanding of later sections.

The use of logic in reasoning research

Newell and Simon's problem-space theory uses the notion of an idealised problem space to characterise the abstract structure of a problem, quite independently of any psychological proposals (see Chapters 15 and 16). In reasoning research, some logics—usually, the propositional calculus—have been used in a similar manner. These logics are used to characterise the abstract structure of reasoning problems and to determine categories of responses (i.e. incorrect and correct answers). So, a clear understanding of this sub-section is essential to make sense of large portions of reasoning research.

In mathematical systems we use symbols to stand for things (e.g. let *h1* be the height of the Empire State building and *h2* be the height of the Eiffel Tower) and then apply mathematical operators to these symbols to manipulate them in various ways (the combined height of both buildings should be *h1 plus h2*, where *plus* is the operator used). In an analogous fashion, logical systems use symbols to stand for sentences and apply logical operators to them to reach conclusions. So, in the propositional calculus, we might use *P* to stand for the verbally expressible proposition "It is raining" and *Q* to stand for "Alicia gets wet", and then use the logical operator "*if … then*" to relate these two propositions: *if P then Q*. It is very important to remember that even though logical operators use common words (such as *or*, *and*, *if … then*), in logic these terms have very different meanings. The logical meaning of the conditional (i.e. *if … then*) is well specified and differs markedly from everyday conception of the words "If … then". In the next sub-section, we attempt to explain how logicians specify the meaning or semantics of these operators.

Truth tables and the "meaning" of logical operators

The propositional calculus has a small number of logical operators: *not, and, or, if … then, if and only if*. In this logical system, propositions can only have one of two truth-values; they are either true or false. For instance, if *P* stands for "it is raining" then *P* is either true (in which case it *is* raining) or *P* is false (it is not raining). The calculus does not admit any uncertainty about the truth of *P* (where it is not really raining but is so misty you could almost call it raining).

Logicians use a system of *truth tables* to lay out the possibilities for a proposition (i.e. whether it is true or false) and to explain how a logical operator acts on that proposition. For example, a single proposition *P* can be either true or false. In truth tables, this is notated by putting *P* as a heading and showing the two values of it, as follows:

P
T
F

If we want to indicate the effects of *not* on P, then we get the following truth table:

P	*not P*
T	F
F	T

This new column shows the effects of *not* on *P*, when *P* is true or false. So, when *P* is true the result of negating *P* will make that proposition false, and when *P* is false, negation will make *P* true. This truth table defines the "meaning" of *not*.

Consider the more complicated case of the conditional, which unlike negation involves two propositions (P, Q): *if P then Q*. On their own *P* and *Q* can each be true or false; when they are combined there are four possible states of affairs (see Table 17.1): both *P* and *Q* can be true, *P* can be true when *Q* is false and vice versa, and both can be false.

Now consider what happens when *if … then* is applied to these propositions. First, when *P* and *Q* are true, then clearly *if P then Q* is true. If we know that "it is raining" and that "Alicia is wet" then we can be confident that the assertion "If it is raining, Alicia gets wet" is true. However, if it is raining (*P* is true) and Alicia is not wet (*Q* is false) then clearly the assertion "If it is raining, Alicia gets wet" is false.

The next two cases are somewhat trickier. Imagine that it is not raining (*P* is false) and Alicia still gets wet (*Q* is true), then, psychologically, one may feel uncertain whether the statement *if P then Q* is true or false. You might want to say, "Well, the statement might be true" or "We don't know whether it's true or not". However, in the context of the logic, we are dealing with a world in which everything is either true or false. Hence, the logician's choice has been to maintain that the assertion is true, when *P* is false and *Q* is true; something else may have made Alicia wet— someone may have thrown a bucket of water over her—so we have no grounds for saying that "If it is raining, Alicia gets wet" is false; therefore, it is true. Again, when *P* and *Q* are false—when "it is

TABLE 17.1

The Truth Tables for the Conditional and the Biconditional

		Conditional	Biconditional
P	Q	if P then Q	if and only if P then Q
T	T	T	T
T	F	F	F
F	T	T	F
F	F	T	T

not raining" and "Alicia does not get wet"—the assertion is also considered to be true. This then is the logician's conception of the meaning of *if ... then* (see Table 17.1 for the truth table).

Furthermore, logicians distinguish this treatment of *if ... then* (called *material implication* in logic) from *if and only if*, the *biconditional* (or in logic *material equivalence*). The biconditional (notated as ↔) has a similar truth table to the conditional except for the *P* is false and *Q* is true case; it characterises this case as making the assertion false. The reason for this is that the biconditional rules out other states of affairs (like the bucket of water); that is, $P \leftrightarrow Q$ is read as "if and only if *P* is true, then *Q* is true".

As we shall see later, people often deviate from these logical interpretations in their reasoning. However, the logical analysis is critical because it allows us to characterise the abstract structure of reasoning problems, and gives us a criterion for determining whether a certain conclusion is valid or invalid, correct, or in error.

THEORETICAL APPROACHES TO REASONING

In this chapter, we focus on just three core research areas in deductive reasoning: conditional reasoning, reasoning in the selection task, and syllogistic reasoning (see Evans, Newstead, & Byrne, 1993, for a comprehensive coverage of these and other areas). Each of these three areas is

covered in the following structured fashion. First, we list the main empirical findings in the area. Second, we elaborate the different theories that have been proposed and some of the specific empirical results that support these theories. Finally, we evaluate these theoretical proposals.

Four main theoretical positions on deductive reasoning have emerged in the literature:

- Abstract rule theories, which view reasoning as the product of the application of abstract, content-free rules, in a manner that is similar to the derivation of proofs in logic.
- Domain-specific-rule theories, which see reasoning as being based on rules that are sensitive to the content of different situations; rules that are encoded in domain-specific schemas (see previous chapter).
- Model theories, which see reasoning as the construction, description, and validation of mental models that represent possible states-of-affairs in the world.
- Bias accounts, which see reasoning as being, in part, due to non-logical tendencies based on a response to superficial aspects of a task situation.

As we shall see, each of these approaches is represented in the three areas we review. Table 17.2 summarises the areas of deduction covered and the different theoretical approaches we consider in each.

Towards the end of the chapter, we deal with broader issues, like the nature of rationality and

TABLE 17.2	
The Main Theoretical Approaches to Reasoning and the Tasks they are Related to in the Present Chapter	
Theory	*Research Area*
abstract-rule	conditional reasonens
domain-specific-rule	Wason selection task
model theory	conditional reasoning, syllogistic reasoning
bias account	Wason selection task

comparative evaluation of the different theoretical approaches. However, before we move on to these matters, some of the logical backdrop to this research needs to be sketched.

HOW PEOPLE REASON WITH CONDITIONALS

The propositional calculus and reasoning based on it involve the use of a number of logical operators: *or*, *and*, *if … then*, *if and only if*. We deal just with conditionals; how people reason with statements using *if* (see Evans et al., 1993, for a full account of propositional reasoning). In research on conditional reasoning the question "Are people rational?" is re-cast as "Are they logical?" In other words, do people conform to the logical interpretation of *if … then*, make valid inferences, and reject the invalid inferences dictated by the propositional calculus (see section on logic). As we shall see, the simple answer is "No". However, before we consider the evidence, let us first define the valid and invalid inferences for the conditional.

Conditional inferences: Valid and invalid forms

Earlier, we saw how propositions, like P and Q, were acted on by logical operators. When a number of propositions are related together by a given logical operator we have a premise (e.g. *If P then Q*) . Logics define a variety of rules of inference that can be used to make logically valid conclusions from premises. Consider the inference rules used on premises involving the conditional. Two valid inferences that can be made using

conditionals are: *modus ponens* and *modus tollens*. An argument of the modus ponens form is as follows (it may help to keep the truth table in Table 17.1 close by, to understand the following discussion):

Valid: Modus Ponens

Premises

| If it is raining, then Alicia gets wet | *If P then Q,* |
| It is raining. | *P,* |

Conclusion

| Therefore, Alicia gets wet. | *Therefore, Q* |

So, if you are given the conditional about it raining and Alicia getting wet, and are then told that it is raining, you can validly conclude that "Alicia gets wet". To understand this conclusion, note that there is only one line in the truth table where P is true and *if P then Q* is true, and this is the one where Q is also true (see Table 17.1).

It is important to remember that logical validity is purely formal and is not affected by whether the propositions are really true (i.e. in the world). So, even premises and conclusions that we know to be patently ridiculous can be logically valid:

Valid: Modus Ponens

Premises

| If he is a cowboy, then he is a chair | *If P then Q,* |
| He is a cowboy. | *P,* |

Conclusion

| Therefore, he is a chair. | *Therefore, Q* |

The modus ponens form is obvious and most people readily make it when the content is sensible. However, the other valid inference made from the conditional — modus tollens — is not as intuitively obvious. This rule states that, if we are given the proposition *If P then Q* and that *Q* is false, then we can infer that *P* is false. Thus, the following argument is valid:

Valid: Modus Tollens

Premises

| If it is raining, then Alicia gets wet | *If P then Q,* |
| Alicia does not get wet. | *not Q* |

Conclusion

| Therefore, it is not raining. | *Therefore, not P* |

Again, this inference is consistent with the truth table (in Table 17.1). The line where *If P then Q* is true and *Q* is false, is that one in which *P* is false.

Modus ponens and modus tollens are the two valid inferences that can be drawn from simple conditional arguments. Two other inferences can be drawn but they are invalid (even though people often think them plausible). They are called the "affirmation of the consequent" and the "denial of the antecedent".

In the affirmation of the consequent, *if P then Q* is true and *Q* is true, for instance:

Invalid: Affirmation of the Consequent

Premises

| If it is raining, then Alicia gets wet | *If P then Q,* |
| Alicia is wet. | *Q,* |

Conclusion

| Therefore, it is raining. | *Therefore, P* |

One can see where this form gets its name, because the consequent of the conditional premise (i.e. *Q*) has been affirmed. But why is it considered invalid? If you examine the truth table for the lines where *If P then Q* is true and *Q* is true, you can see that there are two lines that meet this description. On one of these lines, *P* is true and on the other *P*

is false. This means that logically speaking the most we can conclude is that "no conclusion can be made". So, a conclusion that asserts that *P* is true is considered invalid.

A similar explanation can be made for the other invalid form, the denial of the antecedent; for example:

Invalid: Denial of the Antecedent

Premises

| If it is raining, then Alicia gets wet | *If P then Q,* |
| It is not raining. | *not P,* |

Conclusion

| Therefore, Alicia does not get wet. | *Therefore, not Q* |

Here one has denied the antecedent of the conditional (i.e. the *P*). There are two lines in the truth table where *If P then Q* is true and *P* is false. In one of these lines, *Q* is false and in the other *Q* is true. Therefore, again, no firm conclusion can be made. So, to conclude that *not-Q* is this case is invalid (these forms are summarised in Table 17.3). If you think that these two invalid forms yield plausible conclusions, you are not alone.

Evidence on conditional inference

The literature on conditional reasoning in cognitive science is vast, as is the range of findings on how people reason with conditionals (see Evans et al., 1993; Johnson-Laird & Byrne, 1991). We will consider just some of these findings; the patterns of valid and invalid inferences made by subjects and the effects of context. During our review of the various theories we will introduce further empirical tests that are based on the predictions made by different theories.

As we hinted earlier, it is not the case that people automatically make the valid modus ponens and modus tollens inferences and resist the invalid denial of the antecedent and affirmation of the consequence inferences. Sometimes people fail to make valid inferences, and consider invalid inferences to be acceptable. These results have been found in experiments where subjects are presented with a conditional statement (e.g. "if she

TABLE 17.3

Valid and Invalid Inferences for the Conditional

Valid		
	Modus Ponens	If P then Q, P, Therefore, Q
	Modus Tollens	If P then Q not Q Therefore, not P
Invalid		
	Affirmation of the Consequent	If P then Q Q, Therefore, P
	Denial of the Antecedent	If P then Q, not-P Therefore, not-Q

gets up early, she will go for a run") and a premise (e.g. "she gets up early") and are asked to evaluate a conclusion, draw a conclusion, or choose from a list of possible conclusions.

Figure 17.1 graphs the characteristic pattern of inferences for each of the four forms (from Experiment 2 by Marcus & Rips, 1979). Typically, nearly 100% of subjects make the valid modus ponens inference, but most people find the modus tollens inference much harder—about 50% or so of subjects do not make this inference. On the other hand, many subjects accept the invalid inferences; the rates for making the denial of the antecedent and affirmation of the consequent inferences can increase to around 70%. In the Marcus and Rips (1979) study, 21% of subjects make the denial of the antecedent inference and 33% make the affirmation of the consequent inference (although the difference is not always in this direction; see Evans, 1993a). As we will see, this pattern of inferences should be explained by any adequate theory of deductive reasoning.

However, in some circumstances people do *not* make these inferences. Context effects have also been demonstrated on subjects' inferences. The rates of invalid or fallacious inferences can be modified by contexts in which further information is given (Rumain, Connell, & Braine, 1983). For

example, if alternative antecedents to the conditional are provided then people avoid making the fallacious inferences (Markovits, 1984, 1985; Rumain et al., 1983). For example, the following argument explicitly indicates *alternative antecedents* to the consequent:

If it is raining then she will get wet,	*If P then Q,*
If it is snowing then she will get wet,	*If R then Q,*
She got wet,	*Q,*
Therefore,	*Therefore, ?*

The data show that people would be more likely to produce the correct answer (i.e. no conclusion can be made) than the fallacious *P* conclusion they usually make in the affirmation of the consequent. So, when people are told about an explicit alternative to the consequent, they can use this extra information to generate the logically appropriate inference. More generally, this suggests that extra information can help people to improve their logical reasoning.

However, this generalisation is unwarranted. Byrne (1989a; see also Cummins, Lubart, Alksnis, & Rist, 1991) has found, using a similar paradigm to Rumain et al., that the provision of extra information can suppress the *valid inferences* as well as the invalid inferences. Byrne replicated the

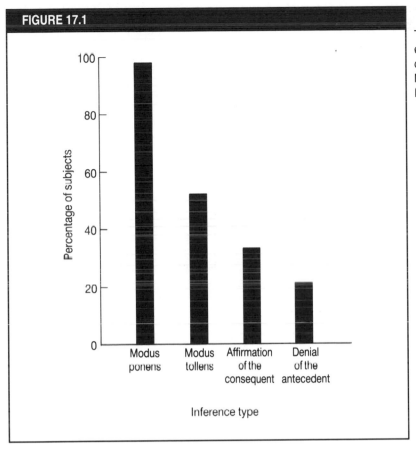

FIGURE 17.1

The percentage of subjects endorsing the various conditional inferences from Marcus and Rips (1979, Experiment 2).

alternative-antecedents effect, but also showed that *additional antecedents* reduced the frequency of valid modus ponens and modus tollens inferences (see Fig. 17.2).

So, when subjects were given:

If she has an essay to write then she will study late in the library,	*If P then Q,*
If the library stays open then she will study late in the library,	*If R then Q,*
She has an essay to write	*P*
Therefore	*Therefore, ?*

which contained the additional requirement of the "library staying open", people typically did not make the modus ponens inference to conclude that "she will study late in the library" (i.e. *Q*).

In the next two sections, we outline two theoretical accounts of the evidence reviewed here.

As we shall see, some of this evidence has played an important role in distinguishing between these two competing theories.

ABSTRACT-RULE THEORY OF CONDITIONAL REASONING

The evidence on conditional reasoning suggests that people are not wholly rational; they fail to make valid inferences and often make invalid inferences. Abstract-rule theories maintain that people are inherently rational; that they use a *mental logic*. According to this account, people only make invalid inferences because they misunderstand or misrepresent the reasoning task. After their initial misunderstanding, the reasoning itself is logical (Henle, 1962).

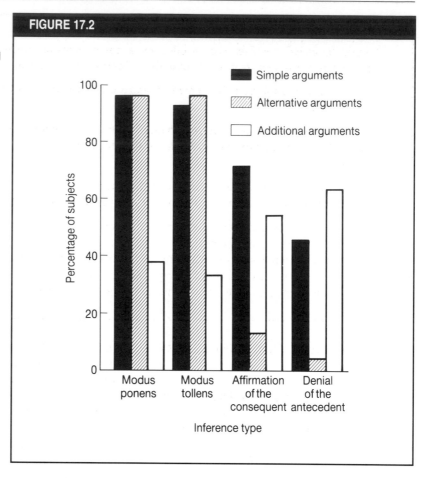

FIGURE 17.2

The percentage of subjects endorsing the various conditional inferences from Byrne (1989a) when they are given simple (standard conditional), alternative, and additional arguments.

Abstract-rule theories propose that humans reason using a set of very abstract, logic-like rules that can be applied to any domain of knowledge (e.g. rules like modus ponens). These abstract rules do not take the content of the premises into account (see e.g. Braine, 1978; Braine & O'Brien, 1991; Johnson-Laird, 1975; Osherson, 1975; Rips, 1983, 1990, 1994). From this theoretical perspective, people construct proofs to reach conclusions in a manner similar to logical proofs. For example, Rips (1983, p.40) says that "the sequence of applied rules forms a mental proof or derivation of the conclusion from the premises, where these implicit proofs are analogous to the explicit proofs of elementary logic". Although there are several variants of this theoretical position, we concentrate on a representative case: Braine's abstract-rule theory.

Braine's abstract-rule theory

Braine's (1978) theory maintains that deductive reasoning is mediated by basic, abstract rules or schemata (see Chapter 9). People comprehend the premises of an argument and encode them into abstract rules from which they make inferences. The theory is summarised in Panel 17.1 (see also Braine, 1978; Braine & O'Brien, 1991; Braine & Rumain, 1983; Braine, Reiser, & Rumain, 1984; O'Brien, Braine, & Yang, 1994; Rumain, Connell, & Braine, 1983).

Braine's theory uses abstract rules to account for reasoning behaviour. In Braine's view people are natural logicians who are slightly fallible at the edges. People would always reason validly except for extraneous influences from the comprehension of premises or the inherent limitations of working memory. In the following sections, we elaborate

---

(Panel 17.1) Braine's Abstract-rule Theory

- Natural language premises are encoded by a comprehension mechanism and the resulting representation is related to abstract, reasoning rules (uncovering the logical form of the sentence).

- These rules are considered to be elementary and are used to draw valid conclusions (e.g. a modus ponens rule).

- There are strategies that co-ordinate a chain of inferences, selecting the rule to be applied at each point in the reasoning process; this chain of inferences constitutes a mental proof or derivation to a conclusion.

- If this reasoning process does not deliver a straightforward conclusion then a set of non-logical rules determine the response (i.e. bias-type responses would arise).

- If a subject draws invalid conclusions or makes errors they may be of three types: comprehension errors, when the premises or conclusion are misconstrued in some fashion; heuristic inadequacy errors, when the conclusion to a reasoning problem fails to be reached because the strategies for co-ordinating numerous sets of reasoning rules are inadequate; processing errors resulting from lapses of attention or a failure to hold relevant information in working memory.

---

how the theory accounts for the different inferences made by people.

The abstract-rule account of valid inferences

Consider the abstract-rule account of how a conclusion is drawn for the following premises:

If I get hungry, then I will go for a walk,	*If P then Q*
If I go for a walk, I will feel much better,	*If Q then R*
I am hungry	*P*

Most abstract-rule theories have a reasoning rule that corresponds to modus ponens; theorists assume that because people find this inference so easy, there must be a mental rule to deal with it. A conclusion to the argument given here can be derived by the repeated application of this modus ponens rule. First, the rule is applied to the first premise (If I get hungry then I will go for a walk) and third premise (I am hungry) to produce the intermediate conclusion of "I will go for a walk"; then the rule is applied again to the second premise "If I go for a walk, I will feel much better" and the intermediate conclusion "I will go for a walk" to produce the final conclusion "I will feel much better" (see Byrne, 1989b, for explicit tests of these

chains of inferences). The rules are applied successively to the set of premises until a conclusion is derived.

The existence of a modus ponens rule accounts nicely for why people find this argument so easy, but why do they find the other valid form, modus tollens, so hard? In the abstract-rule theory, modus tollens is a harder inference to make because no single rule can be applied to it. Rather, a proof involving several different rules has to be formed to reach a conclusion. In general, the longer a derivation, the greater the likelihood that errors will occur or no conclusion will be reached.

The abstract-rule account of invalid inferences and context effects

In abstract-rule theories, people make the fallacious inferences, such as the invalid denial of the antecedent and affirmation of the consequent inferences, as a result of comprehension errors. One account maintains that people make the conversational assumptions used in everyday life, thus causing a reinterpretation of the premises. So, people still apply their logically valid rules but because the input to the rules is erroneous, the output is often erroneous too. Consider the detailed explanation for why people make the fallacious denial of the antecedent inference:

Invalid: Denial of the Antecedent

Premises

| If it is raining, then Alicia gets wet | *If P then Q,* |
| It is not raining. | *not P,* |

Conclusion

| Therefore, Alicia does not get wet. | *Therefore,* |
| | *not Q* |

Rumain et al. (1983) maintained that the conditional premise of this argument, *If P then Q,* was reinterpreted as *If not-P then not-Q.* As Geis and Zwicky (1971) have pointed out, the statement "if you mow the lawn I will give you five dollars" invites the inference "if you don't mow the lawn, I won't give you five dollars". If one starts with this as the conditional premise then by the application of the modus ponens rule one reaches the conclusion *not-Q.* For example:

Premises

If it is not raining,	*If not P*
then Alicia does not get wet	*then not Q,*
It is not raining.	*not P,*

Conclusion

| Therefore, Alicia does not get wet. | *Therefore,* |
| | *not Q* |

So, valid rules are still being applied, but to reinterpreted premises. A similar explanation can be made for the affirmation of the consequent fallacy.

This switch in the interpretation of the premise is said to occur because of Grice's (1975) *co-operative principle.* This principle maintains that a speaker tells a hearer exactly what they think the other needs to know. For example, if a speaker says "If it is raining, then Alicia will get wet" the hearer will assume, in the context of the conversation, that rain is the only likely event that will lead to Alicia getting wet. The hearer assumes that no other alternative *Ps* will play a role. So, during comprehension people make a reasonable assumption that modifies the premises. Having made this comprehension error, reasoning continues normally through the application of the

various reasoning rules (see Braine & O'Brien, 1991, for a recent elaboration of these proposals).

The abstract-rule account of context effects

The context effects reviewed earlier are also explained in terms of these conversational assumptions. Rumain et al. (1983) predicted that alternative antecedents undo these conversational assumptions resulting in the suppression of the invalid inferences. Rumain et al. (1983) took these results as evidence that there could not be rules for invalid inferences of the denial of the antecedent and the affirmation of the consequent. However, this conclusion is upset by the other half of the context effects; the suppression of the valid inferences by the provision of additional antecedents (see Byrne, 1989a). If the same argument is applied to Byrne's results, then abstract-rule theorists would also have to conclude that there are no mental inference rules for the valid inferences. Politzer and Braine (1991) have therefore challenged these results; they argued that Byrne's materials led subjects to doubt the truth of one of the premises because one premise was inconsistent with the other premises. If this was the case then Byrne's manipulation was radically different to Rumain et al's. However, in reply, Byrne (1991) has shown that the conclusions drawn by subjects in her experiments were not those predicted by Politzer and Braine's account (see Bach, 1993; Fillenbaum, 1993; Savion, 1993, Stevenson & Over, in press, for further work on these results).

Other evidence for abstract-rule theories

There is considerable evidence for the proposals of abstract-rule theory. For example, Braine et al. (1984) examined several predictions from the theory in a series of experiments. In one experiment, subjects were given a simple reasoning task about the presence or absence of letters on an imaginary blackboard (from Osherson, 1975). So, on being given a problem such as:

If there is a T, there is an L,
There is a T
? There is an L ?

subjects were asked to evaluate whether the provided conclusion was true. These problems were designed to be solved in a single step by one of the 16 rules proposed by the theory. The results showed that reasoning on these problems was essentially error-free. Difficulty measures were derived from subjects' performance on these problems, which were then used to predict behaviour on problems that involved short chains of reasoning (on the assumption that the difficulty measures for single rules would be additive in more complex tasks). A variety of measures were used to determine problem difficulty, including subjective ratings of difficulty, times taken to solve a problem, and the number of errors made. Braine et al. found high correlations between the difficulty measures of problems and the number of predicted inferences, from the repertoire of rules, required to solve the problems.

Evaluation of abstract-rule theories

The abstract-rule approach is very attractive in its promise to account for conditional reasoning with recourse to a limited set of reasoning rules. However, two main criticisms can be made of these theories.

First, abstract-rule theories achieve their elegance at the price of a considerable under-specification of the accompanying comprehension component. The core reasoning system is well-specified and makes predictions about what inferences people will and will not make. However, some predictions are grounded in a comprehension component that is considerably less specified (predictions on invalid inferences). As long as a comprehension component is under-specified the theory is incomplete. Rumain et al. (1983; Braine & O'Brien, 1991) have said more about the comprehension mechanisms responsible for the production of fallacious conclusions. However, as we have seen, the theoretical rationale for the results of their study causes problems for the theory when all the different context effects are considered.

The second main problem for abstract-rule theories is one of generality. Propositional reasoning is only one of many different sorts of reasoning that people engage in (although it may be implicated in other sorts of reasoning too; see Rips, 1989b, and Johnson-Laird & Byrne, 1990). There is no single abstract-rule theory that has been applied to all of these tasks. So, it remains to be proven whether these or similar ideas can account, in a complete manner, for the many different forms of reasoning. These issues will be returned to later when we evaluate the various theories of reasoning.

THE MODEL THEORY OF CONDITIONAL REASONING

We have seen how abstract-rule theories characterise people's reasoning as being rational, although this rationality may be derailed by various comprehension processes. The model theory also proposes that people are rational, but that their rationality can be hampered by processing limitations (e.g. limited working memory; Johnson-Laird & Byrne, 1993a). Furthermore, unlike abstract-rule theories, the model theory gives comprehension a central role in reasoning; people build models when they comprehend linguistic descriptions, and then their reasoning relies on these models. Indeed, the distinction between these two theories is paralleled by a distinction between different types of logical system. Logicians have also developed logical systems based on models or proofs. Logics based on models characterise the semantics or meaning of logical operators. The truth tables that we met earlier in this chapter are an instance of this type of system. Logics based on proofs consist of syntactic rules that are used to derive conclusions given certain axioms and premises. Abstract-rule theorists developed their ideas of rationality from logical syntactic systems, whereas model theorists have developed their ideas from logical, semantic systems. The proponents of this theory do not maintain that people use truth tables when they reason, but they see them as containing a kernel of psychological truth (see Johnson-Laird & Byrne, 1993b, p. 324).

The model theory

Stated simply, the model theory maintains that people reason by constructing a representation or model of the state of affairs described in the premises, based on the meanings of the premises and general knowledge. They then describe this model in a parsimonious manner to generate a conclusion, before validating the model. Validation is carried out by searching for alternative models that refute the conclusion drawn. If no such alternative models are found, then subjects view the inference as being valid (Johnson-Laird & Byrne, 1991, 1993a). The basic idea can be illustrated easily in simple spatial problems (see Byrne & Johnson-Laird, 1989; Erlich & Johnson-Laird, 1982; Mani & Johnson-Laird, 1982).

Consider the representation or model one might build from the following set of premises, given the instructions to imagine the state of affairs described in them:

The lamp is on the right of the pad
The book is on the left of the pad
The clock is in front of the book
The vase is in front of the lamp

Spatially, these objects can be viewed as being arranged in the following manner:

book   pad   lamp
clock   vase

So, one could make the novel inference from this model that "the clock is to the left of the vase". A novel inference or conclusion is any statement that follows from the premises and was not explicitly stated in them (so, many more could be made). If we try to refute this conclusion then we need to discover another layout or model of the objects that is consistent with the description in the premises, but is not consistent with the conclusion of "the clock is on the left of the vase". In fact, there is no such model.

But consider the following premises:

The lamp is on the right of the pad
The book is on the left of the lamp

The clock is in front of the book
The vase is in front of the pad

This is consistent with two distinct models (see Byrne & Johnson-Laird, 1989):

book   pad   lamp   pad   book   lamp
clock   vase   vase   clock

In this case, the conclusion that we might make from the first model, that "the clock is to the left of the vase", is inconsistent with an alternative model of the premises in which "the clock is to the right of the vase". Thus, in this case, one would have to admit that "there is no valid conclusion" to be made about the relationship of the vase and the clock on their own.

Several variants of the model theory have been proposed, that represent models in distinct ways; like Euler circles (Erickson, 1974; Guyote & Sternberg, 1981) or Venn diagrams (Newell, 1981). We will concentrate on a more general scheme initially proposed by Johnson-Laird (1983) and extended by Johnson-Laird and Byrne (1991, 1993a) which is summarised in Panel 17.2. We have already seen, in a rough fashion, how this theory is applied to spatial reasoning. Consider how it has been applied to conditional reasoning.

The model theory account of the valid inferences

Johnson-Laird and Byrne (1991; Byrne & Johnson-Laird, 1992; Johnson-Laird, Byrne, & Schaeken, 1992) have proposed a model theory of conditional reasoning. In this theory, a conditional premise like "If there is a circle then there is a triangle" is represented *explicitly* by the following three models:

O   Δ
¬O   Δ
¬O   ¬Δ

In this notation, each line represents a new model. These three models represent all those situations where the premise is true, but not the situation when the premise is false (compare it to the truth table in Table 17.1). The "¬" symbol is a

---

(Panel 17.2) The Model Theory

- Deductive reasoning involves three processes: the *comprehension* of premises to form a model, (or set of models); the *combining* and *description* of models to produce a conclusion; and the *validation* of this conclusion by eliminating alternative models of the premises that show the putative conclusion to be false.

- In *comprehending* the premises, various semantic procedures are used to construct models taking into account any background knowledge; the models are specific (i.e. they do not contain variables but specific mental tokens) and are structurally analogous (they parallel states of affairs in the world; see Chapter 9), where the mental tokens that make up models may be in visual images or they may be inaccessible to consciousness.

- The models of the premises have to be *combined* to form an integrated model (or set of models) and then this model is *described* in a parsimonious fashion to arrive at a conclusion.

- The *validation* of this conclusion involves a search for counterexamples or alternative models of the premises in which the putative conclusion is false; if there is no such model then the conclusion is valid; if a model is found that falsifies the conclusion then the ideal reasoner should attempt to discover whether there is any conclusion that is true in all the constructed models.

- Given the limited nature of working memory (see Chapter 6) several processing assumptions are made: (i) a task will increase in difficulty as a function of the number of explicit models the reasoner has to consider, (ii) a deduction made from initial models will be easier than one that is made from "fleshing-out" models with explicit information, (iii) it takes time to detect inconsistencies between elements in a model.

- Errors may therefore arise when conclusions are made from (i) initial models that have not been rigorously evaluated, or (ii) models that subjects have failed to flesh out.

---

propositional tag in the model, used to indicate "not". Intuitively, this means that when people understand the premise — "if there is a circle then there is a triangle" — they represent it by states of affairs described by this sentence; namely, a situation where there is a circle and a triangle, a situation where there is not a circle and there is a triangle, and a situation where there is neither a circle nor a triangle.

However, people attempt to represent as little information as possible because of their processing limitations and so they build representations that indicate the various alternative situations implicitly. So, Johnson-Laird and Byrne suggest that when people understand this premise they build the following initial models:

[O]   Δ
...

This representation contains just two models, one representing a situation where there is a circle and a triangle and one (indicated by the three dots or ellipsis) indicating that there are other alternative models (i.e. the two other explicit models shown earlier). These explicit models can be added or "fleshed out" later. The square brackets around the circle mean that the circle has been represented "exhaustively" in the model; that is, the alternative models will not contain a circle because in any other model where a circle occurs there has to be a triangle. When reasoners are given a second premise — "There is a circle" — they construct a model in which there is just a circle:

O

and when they combine this model and the original models, they get the following:

O   Δ

single model, with the implicit (ellipsis) model eliminated. The implicit model can be removed because all the other models it implicitly indicates are ones in which there is not a circle.

To form a conclusion this model is described in a parsimonious fashion with the sentence: "there is a triangle". This is how the model theory accounts for the valid, modus ponens inference. This inference can be made readily from the initial representation of the conditional, without any need to make the implicit information explicit. In the more difficult modus tollens inference, subjects are given the extra premise "There is not a triangle" represented by the model:

¬Δ

To combine this model with the initial models:

[O]   Δ
...

a lot more work must be carried out. First, the implicit aspects of the initial models must be fleshed out with the explicit models, for example:

O   Δ
¬O   Δ
¬O   ¬Δ

and then these models must be combined with the model of the second premise (i.e. ¬Δ), to get the following model:

¬O   ¬Δ

which can be described by the conclusion: "There is not a circle". Thus, modus tollens is more difficult than modus ponens because people have to flesh out the models and keep multiple alternatives in mind.

The model theory account of invalid inferences and context effects

Invalid inferences arise for two reasons: people can have different interpretations of the conditional premise, and they may fail to flesh out the explicit models for their interpretation. First, people can interpret the original premise — "If there is a circle,

there is a triangle" — as a biconditional; "if and only if there is a circle, there is a triangle".

In the minimal set of models adopted by subjects, this interpretation of the premise would be represented implicitly as:

[O]   [Δ]
...

where both components are exhaustively represented; indicating that any other models will not contain circles or triangles. Invalid inferences arise from these initial models. When subjects are given the extra information that: "There is a triangle" (Δ), the second model will be eliminated, leaving the affirmation of the consequent inference: "There is a circle."

When subjects are given the information: "There is not a circle" they can get the right answer for the wrong reason; that is, they may say that "nothing follows", simply because they cannot combine the model (¬O) with the initial set of models, regardless of whether those models are for the conditional or biconditional interpretation. However, if subjects flesh out the explicit models for the biconditional (see Table 17.1):

O   Δ
¬O   ¬Δ

then when they combine these models with the model of the second premise (¬O), the first model will be ruled out, and they will draw the denial of the antecedent inference: "There is not a triangle". In this way the theory explains why the denial of the antecedent inference is made less often than the affirmation of the consequent inference, as people can get the right answer for the wrong reason.

Regarding context effects, Byrne (1989a) has proposed that extra information leads to a different interpretation of the premises. Premises that contain alternatives as opposed to additionals result in different sets of models being constructed. The validation procedures that revise the models find that alternative antecedents act as counter-examples to the invalid inferences, whereas additional antecedents act as counterexamples to the valid inferences. So, the model theory can account for these effects.

Further evidence for the model theory

The model theory accounts for other evidence and novel predictions from it have been confirmed (see Evans et al., 1993, Chapter 2 for a review). Johnson-Laird, Byrne, and Schaeken (1992) have shown that the difficulty data, which abstract-rule theorists propose to be due to length of the mental derivation, can be explained in an alternative manner by the model theory. They showed that the simpler problems involved inferences that could be made from initial models, whereas the difficult problems required more models to be constructed. Furthermore, they also tested a novel prediction from the model theory, that modus tollens inferences should be easier from a biconditional than a conditional interpretation of the premises, whereas the rate of modus ponens inferences should remain constant (abstract rule theories predict no difference in either case). This result is

predicted because modus ponens can be made from just one explicit model from either interpretation, whereas modus tollens requires three explicit models to be considered for the conditional and just two explicit models for the biconditional. This prediction was confirmed (see Fig. 17.3).

Furthermore, Byrne and Johnson-Laird (1992) found evidence that people represent conditionals by an explicit model in which the events occur and an implicit model in which alternative events may occur. They gave subjects different versions of three assertions:

With Modal	*Without Modal*
John hires a gardener	John hires a gardener
John does some gardening	John does some gardening
John can get the grass cut	John gets the grass cut

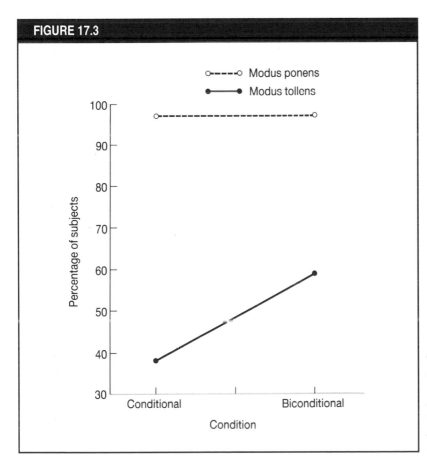

FIGURE 17.3

The percentage of subjects making modus ponens and modus tollens inferences when given two-premise conditional or biconditional problems from Johnson-Laird, Byrne, and Schaeken (1992, Experiment 2).

in which a modal (e.g. can) was present or absent, and asked subjects to paraphrase the assertions in a single sentence. As predicted by the model theory, they found that subjects tended to use a conditional-like paraphrase to combine the three assertions when the outcome contained a modal (e.g. John can get the grass cut; 36%) rather than when it does not (e.g. John gets the grass cut, 5%). The model cues people to think, at least implicitly, of alternative situations in which the events do not occur.

Evaluation of the model theory

Several objections have been made against the model theory account of conditional reasoning (see the final section for a wider evaluation). These objections can be divided into "in-principle" objections, theoretical objections, and empirical criticisms (for a wide variety of criticisms see Johnson-Laird & Byrne, 1993a).

Many commentators have argued that there is no difference *in principle* between abstract-rule theories and mental models (see Andrews, 1993; Bundy, 1993; Goldman, 1986; Rips, 1984, 1986). In logic, a distinction can be made between model-based systems and proof-based systems. However, in logic, this distinction is not clear cut. Hence, it has been argued that the parallel distinction made between model theories and abstract-rule theories is also unclear. How valid are these objections in a psychological context? The two theories propose different representations and cognitive processes and the fact that the two theories lead to different empirical predictions indicates that they are different. From a psychological perspective, they are clearly not the same theory.

A more subtle version of this type of objection has been to argue that the model theory implicitly assumes an abstract-rule system. Braine (1993) has argued the model theory implicitly assumes abstract inference rules. Johnson-Laird and Byrne agree that they use of rules to construct models; so, they do not reject rules *per se*, although they do reject the use of the abstract-inference rules of mental logics.

A number of theoretical criticisms have been made of the model theory. Perhaps the only one that

has stuck, and been admitted by model theorists, is that the theory is incomplete. First, the comprehension component of the theory is under-specified. Model theorists have maintained that background knowledge plays a role in constructing models of premises but they do not have a detailed account of this process. So, although they have computational models that simulate what happens in human reasoning with premises such as "if there is a circle, there is a triangle", they do not have similar models for context effects (see Byrne, 1989a). Second, they have no detailed account of how people validate models by searching for counterexamples because there is little available evidence on how people carry out this validation (see Polk, 1993; Rips, 1990).

From an empirical perspective, the coverage of the model theory is quite good. However, Evans (1993a,b) has questioned its applicability to conditionals using thematic content (see later sections on the selection task) and some of the predictions that the theory makes. Evans (1993a) has suggested some alternative formulations of the theory and shown that although some of them make inappropriate predictions, some deal with the findings in the literature.

REASONING IN WASON'S SELECTION TASK

Wason's selection task is a hypothetico-deductive reasoning task involving the use of conditionals that has been used in hundreds of experiments over the last 30 or so years (see Wason, 1966; Evans, 1982, 1989; Evans et al., 1993 for reviews). The original findings on the task were taken as evidence of people's tendency to confirm hypotheses in reasoning situations (see Chapter 16), although the task has now assumed a special place in reasoning research. In this section, we consider some of the basic empirical findings on the task, before reviewing some of the theories advanced to explain these findings. The main empirical findings deal with what happens in different versions of the basic task; for instance, abstract versus realistic versions of the task. Wason's selection task is living proof

Basic findings on the "abstract" selection task

The selection task, first proposed by Wason (1966), looks like an innocuous puzzle but it hides a multitude of difficulties. In the original version, subjects are shown four cards face down with letters or numbers on each of them (see Fig. 17.4). They are told that each of these cards has a letter on one side and a number on the other side, and they have to name the cards that *need* to be turned over to test the following rule:

If there is a vowel on one side of a card, then there is an even number on the other side of the card

Because you can turn over any of the four cards, there are four possible choices. However, subjects are asked to turn over only those cards that need to be turned over. The correct answer is to turn over just two cards, the E-card and the 7-card; but, few subjects spontaneously pick these cards on this abstract version of the task. To understand why this is the correct answer, first consider why the 4-card and K-card choices are wrong (and keep the truth table for *if ... then* in Table 17.1 handy).

In logic, the rule in the selection task is a conditional *if P then Q; P* here is the statement that "there is a vowel on one side of the card" and *Q* is "there is an even number on the other side of the card". So, each of the cards can be re-expressed as follows. the E-card is *P*, the K-card is *not-P*, the 4-card is *Q*, and the 7-card is *not-Q* (see Fig. 17.4). It is not a good idea to pick the *Q*-card (i.e. 4-card) because when *Q* is true and the rule *if P then Q* is true, *P* can be either true or false (see the truth table in Table 17.1); irrespective of what is on the other side of the 4-card (a vowel or a consonant), the rule

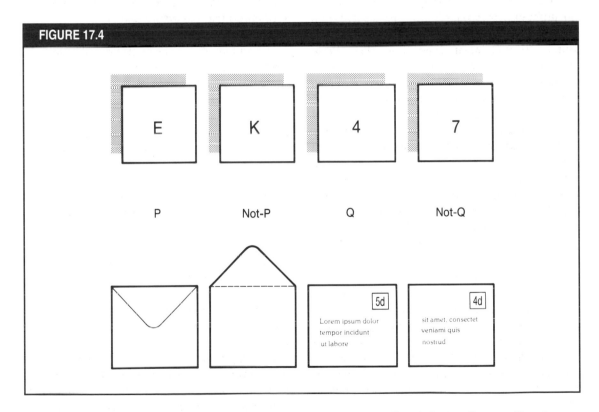

FIGURE 17.4

Examples of the abstract and concrete (postal) versions of Wason's selection task, with an indication of how the different cards/envelopes are labelled for the classification of subjects' choices in experiments.

will be true. Thus, turning over this card will tell you very little logically (cf. Oaksford & Chater, 1994). Of course, many subjects who turn over the *Q*-card may be making the fallacious affirmation of the consequent inference; they assume the rule *If P then Q* is true, they know *Q* to be true, and so they can conclude that *P* must be on the other side (see Table 17.3). So, if *not-P* is on the other side they feel they can conclude that the rule is not true. The same sort of reasoning may account for turning over the K-card, except here one is making an inference similar to the denial of the antecedent fallacy.

In contrast, the choices of the E-card (i.e. *P*) and the 7-card (i.e. *not-Q*) are correct because one is making logically valid inferences that may falsify the rule. When *P* is true and we turn over this card, then what we find on the other side will indicate whether the rule is true or false (see Table 17.1). If *Q* is on the other side then the rule is true, if *not-Q* then the rule is false (this is similar to a modus ponens inference). Similarly, if one turns over *not-Q* then a *P* on the other side will make the rule false, and a *not-P* on the other side will make the rule true (this is similar to a modus tollens inference; see Table 17.3).

The difficulty of reasoning in this problem should be apparent. What is typically found in abstract versions of the task (i.e. versions involving vowels and consonants) is that very few subjects make the correct choices. In Johnson-Laird and Wason's (1970) study only 5 subjects out of 128 chose the *P* cards and *not-Q* cards alone. The overwhelming majority of subjects chose either the *P* cards and *Q* cards (59 out of 128) or the *P* card alone (42 out of 128).

Originally, it was thought that subjects were trying to verify rather than falsify the rule (see e.g. Wason & Johnson-Laird, 1972; and Chapter 16); they turned over the *P* card to see if there is a *Q* (i.e. an even number) on the other side, and the *Q* card to see if there is a *P* (i.e. a vowel) on the other side. If they had wanted to falsify the rule they would have chosen the *P* card to see if there is *not-Q* on the other side (i.e. a consonant), and *not-Q* to see if there is *P* (i.e. a vowel) on the other side of it. However, as we shall see, variants of the task involving more realistic materials lead to very different behaviour.

The effects of negatives in the selection task

Evans has suggested that in abstract versions of the task subjects manifest a non-logical, matching bias (Evans 1984; Evans & Lynch, 1973; Wason & Evans, 1975). That is, subjects select those cards showing the symbols that are mentioned in the rule. So, when subjects are given another variant of the rule (i.e. "If there is a B on one side, there is not a 3 on the other side") they choose the B (*P*) and the 3 (*not-Q*) card because they are mentioned in the rule. In a separate conditional, truth-table task, Evans (1983) found that matching bias depended on the way the "negative cards" are presented; the negative cards, *not-P* and *not-Q*, can be presented as "explicit negatives" (e.g. *not-P* can presented as "not an A") or as "implicit negatives" (e.g. *not-P* presented as "K"). Evans found that the use of explicit negatives reduced matching bias and facilitated subjects' performance on the task.

Effects of realistic materials in the selection task

The most researched effect on performance in the selection task is the change in subjects' performance when they are given "concrete" or "realistic" or "thematic" content in the task (see Bracewell & Hidi, 1974; Gilhooly & Falconer, 1974; Wason & Shapiro, 1971). For example, Johnson-Laird, Legrenzi, and Sonino-Legrenzi (1972) used realistic materials; they asked subjects to imagine that they worked in a post office and had to discover whether the following rule had been violated given letters of different types (in the days when unsealed letters were cheaper to send):

If a letter is sealed, then it has a 5d. stamp on it

The envelopes provided were either sealed or unsealed and had a 4d. or a 5d. stamp on the side that was showing (see Fig. 17.4). Again, subjects had to make just those choices needed to determine if the rule was true. Johnson-Laird et al. also used an abstract version of the task involving an abstract rule (i.e. "If there is a D on one side, then there is a 5 on the other side"). They found that, of the 24 subjects who attempted the tasks, 92% (22) produced the correct choices on the realistic version and only 8% (2) were successful on the abstract version.

However, these results are not as straightforward as they first seem. Manktelow and Evans (1979) found no facilitation for other realistic materials (such as "If I eat haddock then I drink gin"). Later research suggested that people required specific prior experience of the situation to reason adequately about it; the so-called *memory-cueing hypothesis* (see e.g. Griggs, 1983; Griggs & Cox, 1982; Manktelow & Evans, 1979; Reich & Ruth, 1982). The availability of this prior experience was seen to provide counterexamples to the rule. That is, people must have encountered instances where the rule was not the case—for example, where there was "a sealed letter without a 5d. stamp on it"—and this specific knowledge helps them make the correct choice of the *P* cards and *not-Q* cards. This interpretation of the results was supported by Griggs and Cox's (1982) finding that when this postal rule lapsed, the facilitating effects of the realistic materials disappeared in young adults who had no experience with the old rule. However, Griggs and Cox still found the facilitating effect among Florida students for a drinking-age rule that was enforced in Florida (i.e. If a person is drinking beer then that person must be over 19 years of age). They also found that, in this realistic condition, the instruction to determine whether the rule had been violated (another variable quite separate from the content of the rule) improved performance over the standard instructions to see if the rule was true or false.

However, these accounts based on experience were upset by D'Andrade's finding that subjects could also solve tasks that involved realistic content, when they lacked direct experience (reported in Rumelhart, 1980; replicated by Griggs & Cox, 1983). He used a realistic version of the task in which subjects had to imagine they were Sears' store managers responsible for checking sales. Subjects had to test the rule: "If a purchase exceeds $30, then the receipt must be approved by the department manager." They were then shown four receipts: one for $15, one for $45, one signed and one not signed. Even without direct experience of this situation, subjects made the correct choices about 70% of the time.

The effects of realistic materials thus present us with a complicated picture. As we shall see, the impetus of domain-specific-rule theories has been to posit different forms of specific knowledge to deal with these results.

DOMAIN-SPECIFIC THEORIES OF THE SELECTION TASK

Any account of the selection task should explain why people do better on realistic versions than on abstract versions of the task. Abstract-rule theories predict no performance differences for these different versions, assuming extraneous factors are held constant (e.g. comprehension errors); both conditionals would be parsed into an *If P then Q* form. The model theory accounts for this finding by proposing that subjects consider only those cards that are explicitly represented in their models of the rule, and that they then select those cards for which the hidden value could have a bearing on the truth or falsity of the rule (see Johnson-Laird & Byrne, 1991). Recently, Oaksford and Chater (1994) have proposed an account based on probability theory. In this section, we will concentrate on those theories that have inspired recent research on the selection task; domain-specific-rule or schema theories.

Domain-specific-rule or schema theories of the selection task

Domain-specific-rule theories are a family of theories that have arisen to explain the various content effects on the selection task. These theories differ on the content of the domain-specific rules they posit. Some theories maintain that the content is very specific prior experience used by analogy (see Griggs, 1983; Chapter 16 on analogy), but most of these theories hinge on the use of schemas that are specific to classes of situations (e.g. permission situations or various contractual situations). Even though these schematic rules are relatively abstract, they are more specific than the content-free, abstract rules we met earlier. We consider two variants of domain-specific-rule theories before turning to specific tests of them.

Pragmatic reasoning schemata: Domain-specific rules for permissions and obligations

Cheng and Holyoak (1985; Cheng, Holyoak, Nisbett, & Oliver, 1986) have explained the effects of realistic contents by the application of rules that are sensitive to particular classes of situation. They call these rules pragmatic reasoning schemata because they are sensitive to the pragmatics of the situation (see Chapter 11 for more on schemata). Permission situations are one class of such situations that occur regularly in everyday life; for example, to gain permission to enter university you must satisfy the precondition of achieving a certain exam result. The schemata for such situations are abstract in that "they potentially apply to a wide range of content domains", but unlike abstract-rules "they are constrained by particular inferential goals and event relationships of certain broad types" (see Holland et al., 1986).

Pragmatic reasoning theory proposes that:

- People have specific rules that deal with particular types of situation; for instance, permission schemata and obligation schemata.
- Rules in the permission schemata take the form "If an action is to be taken, then a precondition must be satisfied"; if you are asked to test a rule that elicits a permission schema then the appropriate rule from this schema is applied (its logic is like that of the conditional in Table 17.1).
- Obligation schemata have also been elaborated for situations in which one is obliged to do something.

In this theory, errors occur when situations cannot be mapped easily into pragmatic schemata, or errors may arise directly from the inferences generated by schemata (because the rules in the schema may not conform to those sanctioned by propositional logic). Cheng and Holyoak have also suggested that in situations where the schemas do not apply (e.g. abstract content), abstract rules and other strategies may come into play.

Social contract theory: Domain-specific rules encoding contracts

Cosmides (1989) has an alternative domain-specific theory based on an evolutionary approach to cognition. She suggests that people have rules — called Darwinian algorithms — that maximise their ability to achieve their goals in social situations. She concentrates on situations involving social exchange, where two people must co-operate for mutual benefit. The social contract theory proposes that people have schemata pertaining to these sorts of social contracts, such as schemata that encode the following rules:

Standard Social contract: "If you take a benefit then you must pay the cost."

Switched Social contract: "If you pay the cost then you take the benefit."

Along with these schemata, for evolutionary reasons, people must have a mechanism for detecting people who might break a contract: a "look for cheaters" algorithm. If the standard contract schema is applied to the selection task, along with the cheater-detection algorithm, then people should make the correct selections (of P and not-Q), but when the switched-contract schema is applied they will make less optimal selections. Social contract situations are a subset of permission situations, so those permission situations that are social contracts will show facilitation, but permission situations that are not social contracts will not. The drinking-age and postal rules used in some realistic contents can be viewed as reified social contracts. Furthermore, instructions to find violators of the rule can be viewed as a means to facilitate the application of the cheater-detection algorithm (see also Gigerenzer & Hug, 1992, for a further elaboration of this theory).

Evidence for domain-specific-rule theories

Cheng and Holyoak have used a version of the selection task that manipulated the content and rationale for the task to test their theory. Subjects in Hong Kong and Michigan were given a version of the Johnson-Laird et al. postal problem and a variant about checking passengers' forms at an airport. The latter involved the testing of the following rule:

If the form says "ENTERING" on one side, then the other side includes cholera among the list of diseases.

Again, each problem had the appropriate *P*, *Q*, *not-P*, and *not-Q* cases. Neither group of subjects had direct experience of the airport problem, but the Hong Kong subjects were expected to be familiar with the postal rule. So, a memory-cueing hypothesis would predict that, on the airport problem, subjects in Hong Kong and Michigan should be equivalent. However, Hong Kong subjects should do better than Michigan subjects on the postal version because of their prior experience.

Cheng and Holyoak also provided a rationale for half the subjects on both the postal and airport tasks. The stated rationale for the postal task was that a sealed envelope indicated first-class mail, for which the post office received more revenue; the rationale for the airport task was that a cholera inoculation was required to protect the entering passengers from the disease. Cheng and Holyoak predicted that the rationale would cue the permission schema because it casts the problem as a situation in which some action/precondition Y must be carried out before another action is permitted. For example, the higher postage must be paid (precondition Y), before a letter can be mailed first class (action X). As the pattern of inferences suggested by the permission schema correspond closely to the logical treatment of *if ... then*, they predicted that the provision of the rationale would facilitate performance on the task. That is, all subjects should improve on both versions of the task (accepting that there may be a ceiling effect for the Hong Kong group on the postal task with the rationale).

Figure 17.5 shows the results of the experiment. They indicate that the memory-cueing hypothesis

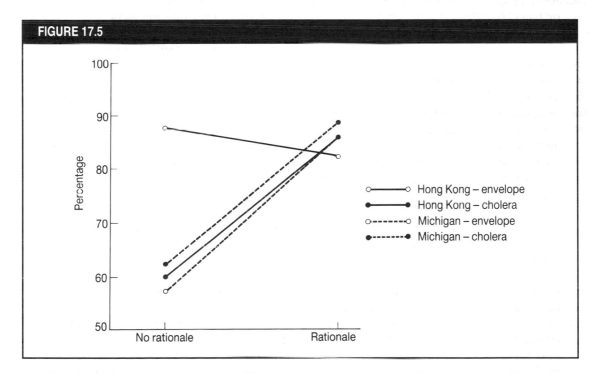

FIGURE 17.5

The percentage of subjects who solved Wason's selection task correctly in each condition as a function of provision of a rationale. Reproduced from Cheng and Holyoak (1985) with the permission of the authors and the publishers of *Cognitive psychology*, © 1985 by Academic Press, Inc.

has some validity but is clearly not the whole story. The Hong Kong subjects did do better on the postal task with no rationale relative to the comparable Michigan group. However, irrespective of prior experience, all subjects produced uniformly high rates of correct responses when the rationale was provided.

In a second experiment, Cheng and Holyoak found another interesting result. They demonstrated an improvement in performance for abstract materials, when the selection task was presented as an abstract description of a permission situation (i.e. If one is to take action A, then one must satisfy precondition P). Subjects in the abstract-permission version fared better (61% correct) than those in the usual version of the abstract task (19%). This finding is significant because "such facilitation had never been observed for any other abstract version of the standard selection task" (Jackson & Griggs, 1990). Cheng, Holyoak, Nisbett, and Oliver (1986) also pitted their theory against abstract rule theories in a series of training studies. These results indicated that if people are trained on standard logic they do not improve on the selection task, relative to training on rules that correspond to pragmatic schemata.

Some subsequent experiments have questioned Cheng and Holyoak's interpretation of the results. Evans (1983) had shown that subjects made fewer errors on a closely related task when they were given explicit negatives (the negation of A was indicated by "not-A") as opposed to implicit negatives (the negation of A was indicated by "B"). Jackson and Griggs (1990) pointed out that the condition in which subjects got the abstract-permission version of the selection task made use of explicit negatives. However, in the comparable condition, which used the standard abstract version of the task, subjects received the negative cards with both implicit and explicit negatives [e.g. the *not-P* card has "B (not A)" on it]. A consensus now seems to have emerged that supports Cheng and Holyoak's interpretation (see Girotto, Mazzacco, & Cherubini, 1992; Griggs & Cox, 1993; Kroger, Cheng, & Holyoak, 1993).

A second point arises from the argument that the effects do not hinge on the permission aspects of the situation but on its social-contractual aspects

(see Cosmides, 1989). When Cosmides examined cases of permission situations that were not social contracts she found less facilitation than in permission situations that were social contracts (see also Gigerenzer & Hug, 1992). However, the levels of correct responses in permission cases that were not social contracts were still higher than the usual levels on the abstract task. So, although social contract situations appear to be highly facilitating, there is also some facilitation for pure permission situations. Although many of Cosmides' results have been replicated and further clarified (see Platt & Griggs, 1993), some researchers contested her claims. For example, some have disputed her interpretation that some realistic content versions of the task are, in fact, social contracts; for example, the Sears' receipts version of the task seems to have no obvious contractual component to it (see Cheng & Holyoak, 1989; Gigerenzer & Hug, 1992).

Finally, is it really the permission or social contract nature of the content that results in the facilitation? Manktelow and Over (1991) have pointed to another possible source of the effects; all the realistic versions that facilitate reasoning (including permission and social contracts) use deontic forms rather than indicative forms of the conditional:

Indicative form: "If there is a p then there is a q"

Deontic form: "If you do p then you *must* do q"

The difficult abstract version of the task always has an indicative form of the rule whereas realistic versions have used deontic forms (but see Platt & Griggs, 1993, for further tests of this). Manktelow and Over maintain that the use of deontic conditionals turns the task into a decision-making rather than a reasoning task; a task in which people assess the utilities of actions (see also Evans, Manktelow, & Over, 1993).

Evaluation of domain-specific-rule theories
In general, domain-specific-rule or schema theories are an interesting addition to the theoretical corpus of research on the selection task.

They have been used to generate new predictions about the underlying basis of subjects' performance on the task and many of these predictions have been confirmed.

The major criticism of this view is that it is not a complete theory of reasoning; it can characterise some versions of the selection task, but does not go far beyond it. For example, it makes no predictions for other logical connectives (e.g. *and*; *or*) and it has no account of the pattern of selections on the abstract task. In other words, these theories are silent on what people are doing when they are *not* using domain-specific-rule schemata. Cheng and Holyoak suggest that some responses may be due to non-logical biases, but they do not elaborate this further. O'Brien (1993) has suggested a marriage between the abstract-rule account and their theories (see the later evaluation section for a discussion of this proposal).

Finally, the theories themselves have many under-specified components. Both pragmatic-rule and social-contract theory do not specify how natural language is parsed into the rules used for reasoning. So many aspects of their predictions could be open to *ad hoc* interpretations.

REASONING WITH SYLLOGISMS

Syllogistic reasoning comes from one of the first logics developed in the western world by Aristotle; so, it has a long tradition of study both in logic and as a reasoning task in psychology. A syllogism is any argument that consists of two premises and a conclusion. However, most experimental studies have looked at Aristotle's *categorical syllogisms*; for example:

All animals are mortal,	All B are A
All men are animals,	All C are B
Therefore, all men are mortal.	Therefore, all C are A

The conclusion drawn here is considered to be valid. Instead of just using the universal quantifier (i.e. all), syllogisms can also be constructed using the particular quantifier (i.e. some) and negatives

(i.e. not). This means that premises can occur in one of four "moods", which are conventionally designated by the mnemonics A, I, E, and O :

All A are B	(A; universal affirmative premise)
Some A are B	(I; particular affirmative premise)
No A are B	(E; universal negative premise)
Some A are not B	(O; particular negative premise)

The arrangements of terms in the premises, setting aside their moods, make up the four figures of the syllogism:

A-B	B-A	A-B	B-A
B-C	C-B	C-B	B-C

It should be appreciated immediately that the number of possible syllogisms is quite large. In fact, there are 64 possible logical forms for the premises of a syllogism (4 moods for each premise by 4 figures). Twenty-seven of these premise pairs yield valid conclusions interrelating the end terms, provided that one bears in mind that a conclusion may take the form A-C or C-A.

As in the case of conditional reasoning, early studies of syllogisms revealed that people often make errors or invalid conclusions, and their performance is affected by whether the content of the syllogism is abstract or concrete (see e.g. Wilkins, 1928; for a fuller treatment of the structure of the syllogism and evidence, see Evans et al., 1993).

One of the earliest explanations of performance on syllogistic tasks maintained that people were operating on the basis of a non-logical bias, called the "atmosphere effect" (Woodworth & Sells, 1935). The *atmosphere hypothesis* claimed that people failed to act in accordance with logical principles because their conclusions were affected by the atmosphere of the premises. Stated succinctly, it maintained:

- A negative premise creates a negative atmosphere, even when the other premise is affirmative, resulting in a negative conclusion being made.

- A particular premise creates a particular atmosphere, even when the other premise is universal, resulting in a particular conclusion being made.
- The effect appears to be stronger for valid than invalid conclusions, there also appears to be a contribution from some inferential mechanism.

However, as Johnson-Laird and Steedman (1978) pointed out, the most damning evidence against the hypothesis is that people often respond, with the wholly unpredicted conclusion, of "no valid conclusion follows". They even make this response when the atmosphere hypothesis predicts a valid conclusion, for example:

> Some B are A
> No C are B
> _____
> Some A are not C

Only 10% of subjects produce this valid conclusion, whereas 60% maintain that there is no valid conclusion.

Apart from negative findings, there are also alternative explanations of many of the atmosphere findings. Chapman and Chapman's (1959) *conversion hypothesis*, maintained that invalid conclusions are accepted because the premises are misinterpreted. Specifically, Chapman and Chapman argued that subjects commonly misinterpret universal affirmative propositions to mean that the converse is also true (e.g. "All As are Bs" is taken to mean "All Bs are As"). Similarly, particular negative premises are converted (e.g. "Some As are not Bs" is taken to mean "Some Bs are not As"). Some of the clearest support for the conversion hypothesis was obtained by Ceraso and Provitera (1971). They showed that when the premises were stated less ambiguously (e.g. "All As are Bs" was stated as "All As are Bs, but some Bs are not As"), there was a substantial improvement in performance.

The problem with accounts such as the atmosphere and conversion hypotheses is that they walk a very thin line between being "explanations"

and "descriptions of performance". If they *are* only descriptions of performance, then we are still left with the need to explain why subjects engage in this behaviour. For example, what is it that causes subjects to convert?

THE MODEL THEORY OF SYLLOGISTIC REASONING

We have already seen how the model theory proposes several processes of deductive reasoning: construct models of premises, combine models and describe them, and then validate these models (see Panel 17.2). Consider how this is applied to syllogistic reasoning (see Johnson-Laird, 1983; Johnson-Laird & Bara, 1984; Johnson-Laird & Byrne, 1989, 1991) .

Constructing models of the premises

During comprehension people try to build an integrated model of the premises. So given a premise like:

(1) Some of the artists   Some of the A are B
      are beekeepers

it is proposed that people construct initial models of the following type:

> artist   beekeeper
> artist   beekeeper
> …

Here the premise is characterised as two models in which there is an individual who is an artist and a beekeeper, and an implicit model which indicates that other models may be fleshed out. As in conditional reasoning, reasoners try to represent the least amount of information possible. Further models are possible that could contain individuals who are artists, but who are not beekeepers, as represented in the model:

> artist

These representations capture the logically correct interpretation of "some". In the logic of quantification, "some" means some and possibly all. So if a logician ever asks you for *some* of your crisps, be warned, he or she might eat the whole bag (without any logical qualms).

Of course, the other premises may have different moods:

(2) All of the beekeepers   All of the B are C
    are chemists

On its own this premise can be represented by the following set of models:

[beekeeper]	chemist
[beekeeper]	chemist
…	

These models represent individuals who are beekeepers and chemists, although there may be other chemists who are not beekeepers (as indicated by the implicit model, the " … "). The square-bracket notation is used to indicate "exhaustivity". In other words, there are no beekeepers in other models who are not chemists. The chemists, on the other hand, are not exhaustively represented, which means that there could be other chemists who are linked to other occupations.

Premises using negatives are captured in similar ways:

(7) None of the artists   None of the A are B
    are beekeepers

can be represented by the explicit models:

[artist]	
[artist]	
	[beekeeper]
	[beekeeper]
…	

Stated succinctly, this model shows that any given artist you might pick is not a beekeeper, and any given beekeeper you choose is not an artist. It should be noted that as in the treatment of

conditionals these models can also use propositional tags (i.e.$\neg$).

Combining and describing models

Comprehension must combine two premises in a single model by adding the information from subsequent premises to the model of earlier ones. So:

(1) Some of the artists   Some of the A are B
    are beekeepers
(2) All of the bee-   All of the B are C
    keepers are chemists

would be combined in the following model:

artist	[beekeeper]	chemist
artist	[beekeeper]	chemist
…		

Here, we have simply taken the model of the first premise and related the beekeepers in it to new tokens added for chemists, in accordance with the universal quantifier in the second premise. This set of models can then be described in a parsimonious fashion to form a conclusion. In syllogisms, the requirement is to relate the first and third terms, so we might state the conclusion as:

(3) Some of the artists   Some of the A are C
    are chemists

Note that this model is consistent with the possibility that there may be other artists who are not chemists.

Validating the conclusion by a search for counter-examples

There may be other sets of models that are also consistent with these premises. So, the conclusion must be validated by searching for other models that are consistent with the premises but are inconsistent with the conclusion; models in which the putative conclusion is untrue. In this problem, there is no alternative model to the one given earlier that refutes the conclusion.

However, in other problems, of course, there may be alternative models in which the initial conclusion is not true. Consider the premises:

(4) All of the artists are   All of the A are B
    beekeepers
(5) Some of the bee-   Some of the B are C
    keepers are chemists

These can be represented by the models:

[artist]	beekeeper	chemist
[artist]	beekeeper	chemist
…		

These initial models suggests the following conclusion:

(6) All of the artists are   All of the A are C
    chemists

But here there is another set of models that is consistent with the premises in which this conclusion is not the case, namely:

[artist]	beekeeper	
[artist]	beekeeper	
	beekeeper	chemist
	beekeeper	chemist
…		

In this representation, none of the artists are related to the chemists, because the subset of beekeepers who are artists are not chemists. Indeed, there is no conclusion that is true in both models, so the best we can say is that there is "no valid conclusion".

Evidence for the model theory

As before, errors can occur at any of the stages of reasoning; for instance, from failing to flesh out models. We will, however, concentrate on the predictions made about influences on the validation stage.

Different problems can require different numbers of models in order to determine a valid conclusion. The first problem we examined earlier [i.e. in sentences (1), (2), and (3)] admitted a valid conclusion from an initial single set of models. However, the second problem [i.e. (4), (5), and (6)], required two sets of models to be constructed before one could conclude that: "There is no valid conclusion relating the two terms." As people have a limited working memory, problems that require more models to be constructed will be more difficult because of information overload. This prediction has been confirmed in many experiments where subjects received different syllogisms that required one model or more than one model to be constructed (e.g. Johnson-Laird & Bara, 1984; Johnson-Laird & Byrne, 1991). Moreover, subjects' erroneous conclusions should be ones that followed if one or more of the possible models of the premises were neglected. This prediction has been supported; namely, that subjects' errors were the sorts of conclusions that one would expect subjects to make from initial models that had not been rigorously tested by searching for other alternative models.

More recently, Johnson-Laird and Byrne (1989) have investigated the use of "only" in syllogistic reasoning (e.g. Only criminals are psychopaths). *Only* is interesting because logically "All the psychopaths are criminals" is equivalent to "Only the criminals are psychopaths". However, they predicted that people's mental representation of *only* would be more complex than all because it makes negative relations between the sets of individuals salient. That is, with "Only criminals are psychopaths" one grasps immediately that some criminals are psychopaths and that anyone who is not a criminal is not a psychopath. However, in the case of "All psychopaths are criminals" one grasps that this is the case and that there may be criminals who are not psychopaths, but the latter is less obvious than in the "only" case. Assuming these representational differences between "all" and "only", Johnson-Laird and Byrne (1989) predicted that premises involving *only* would be harder than ones using *all*. This prediction was confirmed in their study and they also showed that inferences that required reasoners to consider explicit negatives were easier from *only* than from *all*.

Further research by Johnson-Laird, Byrne, and Tabossi (1989) has extended the theory to multiply quantified assertions. A singly quantified assertion is one like "All of the beekeepers are chemists", whereas a multiply quantified assertion is one like "None of the beekeepers is taller than any of the chemists". Inferences based on premises containing multiply quantified relations cannot be captured by model theories using Euler circles or Venn diagrams. Again, these experiments show that inferences requiring the construction of one model are considerably easier for subjects than those requiring more than one model. No abstract-rule theory exists that deals with these types of problems. Indeed, Johnson-Laird and Byrne (1991) argue convincingly that plausible extensions of current abstract-rule theories could not account for the results found.

Evaluation of the model theory of syllogistic reasoning

It seems to be generally recognised that the most complete and accurate account of syllogistic reasoning is provided by the model theory (see e.g. Evans et al., 1993; Newstead, 1990). In a recent set of commentaries on the theory several commentators raised the issue of how easy it was to determine the number of appropriate models for a given syllogism (see Garnham, 1993; Newstead, 1993; Polk, 1993). Johnson-Laird and Byrne (1993a) have, however, specified the procedure for model construction in a computer program.

Perhaps the critical empirical issue is to provide more detailed evidence on the sorts of models that people actually construct. The model theory goes some way towards doing this (see Byrne & Johnson-Laird, 1990; Johnson-Laird & Bara, 1984). For example, Byrne and Johnson-Laird (1990) have tested subjects' recognition memory for different conclusions to syllogisms. Their prediction was that subjects would falsely recognise conclusions they had generated from initial models predicted by the theory (but had rejected at a later stage), even if they had not finally produced these conclusions in their answers. The results confirmed their expectations.

EVALUATION OF REASONING RESEARCH

Throughout this chapter we have reviewed three main areas of research on reasoning. In the course of this review we have considered the theoretical accounts that have been posited to explain the behaviour of subjects on such tasks (see Table 17.2). In this section, we conclude with a consideration of wider issues. First, we evaluate all of the different theories of reasoning together. Then we consider the issue of rationality to tie up a thread that runs through much of the chapter.

Assessing competing theories

In this chapter, we have reviewed some of the key pieces of evidence in deductive reasoning. Along the way, we evaluated specific accounts with respect to the evidence found. In this section, we are left with the broader question: "What is the current best account of reasoning?" Usually, science seeks a single unified theory, rather than a cluster of alternative theories. So, we will assume that the answer to this question should be a single candidate theory.

On the whole, the biases view appears to be the least adequate. This approach is essentially a loose collection of task-specific heuristics, rather than a coherent theory. It can only gain coherence by combining with some theory of reasoning competence (an abstract-rule or model theory account). As such, it cannot serve as a stand-alone candidate theory of deductive reasoning on these tasks.

Domain-specific-rule theories can be criticised for similar reasons. They have not been rigorously applied to either conditional or syllogistic reasoning. Even on the selection task, they only account for realistic-materials effects, and they require additional biases or an abstract-rule theory to explain behaviour on the abstract task. So, this view is not close to being a complete theory of reasoning.

Abstract-rule theories have been applied to propositional reasoning. They can generate precise predictions about subjects' judgements of validity (Braine et al., 1984; Osherson, 1974, 1975; Rips, 1983), about the reaction times of subjects on tasks (Braine et al., 1984), and about inter-subject differences on problems (Rips & Conrad, 1983). They might also be applicable to classical syllogisms involving singly quantified assertions (Braine & Rumain, 1983; Osherson, 1976). The results of research on the selection task are more embarrassing. Realistic-materials effects can only be dealt with by adding assumptions on the effects of comprehension and other factors. Some abstract rule theorists have proposed that formal inference rules can be supplemented by domain-specific rules or by the addition of modal logics and non-logical operators (see Braine & O'Brien, 1991; Rips 1989a). However, the problem with this proposal is that it cannot provide a unique account of a variety of reasoning phenomena (see also Manktelow & Over's, 1991, criticisms of this proposition).

Finally, the model theory scores highly on generality. It has relatively complete accounts of conditional and syllogistic reasoning. Johnson-Laird and Byrne (1991) have proposed an account of all of the effects found on the selection task, although this proposal requires some fleshing out. At present, it looks like the most complete theory of human reasoning, although its opponents continue to challenge many of its foundations.

Are we rational?

The simple definition of rationality is that one acts in accordance with the laws of logic. However, modern logic consists of a huge number of logical systems, of which the propositional calculus is just one. So, it seems a little arbitrary to pick it and say it constitutes the laws of logic (e.g. see Cohen, 1981, for related arguments). It is, therefore, more reasonable to ask whether there is any sense in which people attempt to operate in accordance with a rational principle; whether they will try to deduce valid conclusions from the premises of an argument.

In fact, most theorists argue that people do operate in accordance with some rational principle. The most extreme anti-rationalist stance one can find is a biases approach to reasoning (see Evans, 1989). Recall, for example, the evidence from the selection task on the matching bias, in which subjects simply respond to superficial features of the task situation. However, even bias theorists do not postulate that people operate in this fashion all the time (see Evans, 1984). Could it be argued that a domain-specific-rule theorist, who does not admit the abstract rules of a abstract-rule theory, has a fundamentally anti-rationality view of human reasoning? From this perspective, people are always operating in accordance with their prior

experience and, as such, may perform in a reasonable but not a rational fashion. However, researchers like Cosmides might claim that to be able to detect cheaters is the hallmark of rationality (in some evolutionary sense of the term). Alternatively, as we saw in the sections on the selection task, one proposal is that a domain-specific-rule theory could act in concert with an abstract-rule theory, where the latter provides a grounding of logical competence (e.g. O'Brien, 1993).

The abstract-rule and model theories are committed to the view that people are rational. Abstract-rule theories assert this in their identification of people's mental logic with some rules of propositional logic. People are swayed from this rationality by reinterpreting information during comprehension and by the vagaries of their information-processing systems (e.g. working memory limitations). Johnson-Laird and Byrne (1993b) believe that people are rational in principle rather than in practice. Given sufficient time, the motivation, and a light working memory load, they can produce valid conclusions; that is, conclusions that arc true in all the possible models of the premises. People are able to make valid deductions. So, both of these theories suggest that people have the basic competence to be rational, but that they err in the execution or performance of this rationality. Thus, the burden of theoretical opinion seems to lie with the view that people can be rational.

CHAPTER SUMMARY

In this chapter, we have reviewed some of the major topics in deductive reasoning: conditional reasoning, reasoning on the selection task, and syllogistic reasoning. We have also seen how the phenomena in each of these areas are explained by the four main brands of reasoning theory; abstract-rule theories, the model theory, domain-specific-rule theories, and bias accounts.

In conditional reasoning, we saw that the patterns of inferences made by subjects do not correspond to those sanctioned by logic; people tend to avoid making some valid inferences and frequently make invalid inferences. The abstract-rule and model theories of reasoning both view people as being rational; people have a logical competence, albeit one that is not realised perfectly in their reasoning performance. However, the theories differ on how they conceptualise the reasoning process. Abstract-rule theories see reasoning as a proof-derivation process; in which successive abstract rules are applied to some representation of the premises. The model theory views reasoning as a matter of constructing, describing, and validating mental models. Both theories, therefore, realise logical competence in different ways, and also have different proposals about how logical performance is influenced. In recent, years several critical tests have been made that attempt to distinguish between these two approaches to conditional reasoning.

In the related Wason selection task, domain-specific-rule or schema theories have been applied extensively to explain the behaviour that arises when people solve different versions of the problem. In particular, pragmatic schema theory and social contract theory have been used to account for why subjects' performance improves on versions of the task involving realistic content. In recent, years this has been a heavily researched area, adding to an already large corpus of data on this task.

Finally, syllogistic reasoning has been characterised by the model theory; with a detailed account of the processes underlying subjects' patterns of inference. Again this account is based on the theory that people reason by constructing and validating mental models of these problems.

All the theories reviewed in this chapter have broad shortcomings; typically, they would have at least one unspecified processing component (e.g. a comprehension component) or fail to cover all the topic areas of deduction. With respect to the topics reviewed in this chapter, the model theory is currently the best candidate for a single unified theoretical account of deduction. None of the other theories has such a complete coverage. Indeed, to achieve a greater coverage, these other theories would have to combine with one or more of the other accounts. Of course, some would argue that the combined-theory rather than single-theory accounts are more plausible; it is possible to argue a priori that reasoning is not done by a single process, but rather involves some mixture of different processes (e.g. abstract-rules and biases or abstract- and domain-specific rules). However, if you think that the goal of a science is to seek a unity underlying a diversity of phenomena, then a preference for the model theory would seem to follow.

FURTHER READING

Evans, J. St.B. T., Newstead, S.E., & Byrne. R.M.J. (1993). *Human reasoning: The psychology of deduction*. Hove, UK: Lawrence Erlbaum Associates Ltd. This text provides a comprehensive review of recent reasoning research, covering some of the areas reviewed here, but in more detail.

Gilhooly, K.J. (1995). *Thinking: Directed, undirected and creative* (3rd Edn.). London: Academic Press. This book provides more detail on some of the research covered here and also other research not considered here.

Johnson-Laird, P.N., & Byrne, R.M.J. (1991). *Deduction*. Hove, UK: Lawrence Erlbaum Associates Ltd. This work provides the most up-to-date statement of recent developments and extensions of the model theory.

Keane, M.T., & Gilhooly, K.J. (1992). *Advances in the psychology of thinking*. London: Harvester Wheatsheaf. This collection of papers has a number of reviews of the current literature on reasoning.

Manktelow, K.I., & Over, D.E. (1993). *Rationality: Psychological and philosophical perspectives*. London: Routledge. This book is a collection of recent articles on the various proposals that have been made on the nature of rationality.

Rips, L.J. (1994). *The psychology of proof: Deductive reasoning in human thinking*. Cambridge, MA: MIT Press. This book provides a recent account of a major abstract-rule theory.

18

Cognition and Emotion

INTRODUCTION

As we have seen throughout this book, much of contemporary cognitive psychology is dominated by the computer analogy or metaphor. This has led to an emphasis on information-processing models, and these models have proved extremely fruitful. However, this approach does not lend itself readily to an examination of the relationship between cognition and emotion, in part because it is difficult to think of computers as possessing emotional states.

Most cognitive psychologists conducting research have chosen to ignore the issue of the effects of emotion on cognition by attempting to keep the emotional states of their subjects constant. Why do they take this evasive action? In the words of Gardner (1985, p.6), emotion is a factor "which may be important for cognitive functioning but whose inclusion at this point would un-necessarily complicate the cognitive-scientific enterprise".

In spite of this negative attitude, there is a growing volume of research on cognition and emotion. Some of that research, such as the role of emotional states in eyewitness testimony and autobiographical memory, was discussed earlier in the book (see Chapter 8). Probably the most common approach adopted by cognitive psychologists wishing to investigate the effects of emotion on cognition has involved manipulating subjects' emotional states in a systematic fashion. In contrast, some researchers (e.g. Smith & Lazarus, 1993) have studied the effects of cognition on emotion. As there are almost constant interactions between cognition and emotion in everyday life, any attempt to provide an adequate theory of cognition that ignores emotion is probably doomed to failure.

Before proceeding, it is worth considering some definitions. The term "affect" is very broad, and has been used to cover a wide variety of experiences such as emotions, moods, and preferences. In contrast, the term "emotion" tends to be used to refer to relatively brief but intense experiences, but is also used in a broader sense. Finally, "mood" or "state" are terms describing low-intensity but more prolonged experiences.

DOES AFFECT REQUIRE COGNITION?

Suppose that a stimulus (e.g. a spider) is presented to someone, as a consequence of which his or her affective response to that stimulus changes in a systematic way. Is it essential for the stimulus to be processed cognitively by that individual for the changed affective response to occur? This issue is of theoretical importance. If affective responses to all stimuli depend on cognitive processing, it follows that theories of emotion should have a distinctly cognitive flavour. In contrast, if cognitive processing is not necessary in the development of affective responses to stimuli, then a specifically cognitive approach to emotion may be less necessary.

There have been major disagreements about the answer to the question posed in the previous paragraph. Zajonc (1980, 1984) has consistently argued that the affective evaluation of stimuli is a basic process which can occur independently of cognitive processes. According to him (Zajonc, 1984, p.117), "affect and cognition are separate and partially independent systems and … although they ordinarily function conjointly, affect could be generated without a prior cognitive process". In contrast, Lazarus (1982, p.1021) claimed that some cognitive processing is an essential prerequisite for an affective reaction to a stimulus to occur: "Cognitive appraisal (of meaning or significance) underlies and is an integral feature of all emotional states."

Zajonc's theoretical position

As this controversy was started by Zajonc (1980), we will start with a consideration of his point of view. He claimed that we frequently make affective judgements about people and objects even though we have processed very little information about them. Zajonc (1980) discussed several studies which he believed provided support for his theoretical position. In these studies, stimuli such as melodies or pictures were presented either very briefly below the level of conscious awareness or while the subject was involved in a task. Even though these stimuli could not subsequently be recognised, subjects were still more likely to choose previously presented stimuli than equivalent new stimuli when asked to select the ones they preferred. Thus, there was a positive affective reaction to the previously presented stimuli (as assessed by the preference judgements), but there was no evidence of cognitive processing (as assessed by recognition-memory perform-

ance). This phenomenon is known as the "mere exposure" effect.

One limitation of studies on the "mere exposure" effect is that they they do not have much obvious relevance to ordinary emotional states. Subjects made superficial preference judgements about relatively meaningless stimuli of little relevance to their personal lives, and so no more than minimal affect was involved.

Another major problem with these studies is that the conclusion that the stimuli had not been processed cognitively was based on a failure of recognition memory. This conclusion may make sense if one equates cognition with consciousness, but very few cognitive psychologists would be willing to do so. The data do not rule out the possibility that there was extensive pre-conscious processing involving automatic and other processes.

Lazarus's theoretical position

Lazarus (1982) argued that *cognitive appraisal* plays a crucial role in emotional experience. Cognitive appraisal can be subdivided into three more specific forms of appraisal:

- *Primary appraisal:* an environmental situation is regarded as being positive, stressful, or irrelevant to well-being.
- *Secondary appraisal*: account is taken of the resources that the individual has available to cope with the situation.
- *Re-appraisal*: the stimulus situation and the coping strategies are monitored, with the primary and secondary appraisals being modified if necessary.

The importance of cognitive appraisal in determining emotional experience has been shown in several studies by Lazarus and his associates (e.g. Speisman, Lazarus, Mordkoff, & Davison, 1964). One approach involves presenting an anxiety-evoking film under various conditions. One film showed a Stone Age ritual in which adolescent boys had their penises deeply cut, and another film showed various workshop accidents. The most dramatic of these accidents involves a board caught in a circular saw which rams with tremendous force through the midsection of a worker, who dies writhing on the floor. Cognitive appraisal was manipulated by varying the accompanying soundtrack, and then comparing the stress experienced against a control condition in which there was no soundtrack. Denial was produced by indicating that the subincision film did not show a painful operation, or that those involved in the safety film were actors. Intellectualisation was produced in the subincision film by considering matters from the perspective of an anthropologist viewing strange native customs, and was produced in the workshop film by telling the viewer to consider the situation in an objective fashion. Various psychophysiological measures of arousal or stress (e.g. heart rate; galvanic skin response) were taken continuously during the viewing of the film.

The major finding of the various studies carried out by Lazarus and his associates was that denial and intellectualisation both produced substantial reductions in stress as indexed by the psychophysiological measures. Thus, manipulating an individual's cognitive appraisal when confronted by a stressful event can have a significant impact on physiological stress reactions. However, it should be noted that it has not always proved easy to replicate these findings (e.g. Steptoe & Vogele, 1986).

A somewhat different approach was used by Smith and Lazarus (1993). They proposed that there are six appraisal components, two of which involve primary appraisal and four of which involve secondary appraisal of situations:

- Primary: motivational relevance (related to personal commitments?).
- Primary: motivational congruence (consistent with the individual's goals?).
- Secondary: accountability (who deserves the credit or blame?).
- Secondary: problem-focused coping potential (can the situation be resolved?).
- Secondary: emotion-focused coping potential (can the situation be handled psychologically?).
- Secondary: future expectancy (how likely is it that the situation will change?).

Smith and Lazarus (1993) argued that different emotional states could be distinguished on the basis of which appraisal components are involved. Thus, for example, anger, guilt, anxiety, and sadness all possess the primary appraisal components of motivational relevance and motivational incongruence (these emotions only occur when goals are blocked), but they differ in terms of secondary appraisal components: anger involves other-accountability; guilt involves self-accountability; anxiety involves low or uncertain emotion-focused coping potential; and sadness involves low future expectancy for change.

Smith and Lazarus (1993) tested these theoretical ideas by using scenarios in which the subjects were told to identify with the central character. In one scenario, the central character has performed poorly in an important course, and he appraises the situation. Other-accountability was produced by having him put the blame on the unhelpful teaching assistants; self-accountability was produced by having him argue that he made a lot of mistakes (e.g. doing work at the last minute); low emotion-focused coping potential was produced by thinking that there was a great danger that he would finish with a poor academic record; and low future expectancy for change was produced by having him think that it was simply not possible to succeed with his chosen academic path. The appraisal manipulations generally had the predicted effects on the emotional states reported by the subjects, indicating that there are close links between appraisal on the one hand and experienced emotion on the other hand.

Lazarus (e.g. 1982) has argued consistently that cognitive appraisal always precedes any affective reaction, but that such appraisal may not be at the conscious level. However, the notion that pre-conscious cognitive processes determine affective reactions is often no more than an article of faith, because we generally have little direct evidence of either the existence or the nature of such cognitive processes. However, the literature on subliminal perception (see Chapter 4) suggests there are important pre-conscious cognitive processes.

Section summary

Zajonc (1980) and others have provided evidence that affective responses can occur in the absence of any conscious awareness of cognitive processing, and Lazarus (1982) does not dispute that this is possible. There is also agreement that cognition and emotion influence each other, and that these processes can be rather complex. Zajonc (1984, p.122) pin-pointed the controversial issue:

It is a critical question for cognitive theory and for theories of emotion to determine just what is the minimal information process that is required for emotion. Can untransformed, pure sensory input directly generate emotional reactions?

Until comparatively recently, it seemed that the answer to the question was "No." This was due in part to the fact that Lazarus made use of studies involving genuine emotional reactions to meaningful stimuli to support his argument that cognition always precedes affect, whereas Zajonc (1980) relied heavily on studies involving marginally emotional reactions to relatively meaningless stimuli to confirm his view that cognition does not necessarily precede affect. However, there is now reasonable evidence (see LeDoux, 1990, for a review) that physiological responses to emotional stimuli can be produced via a direct neural pathway that bypasses the cortex (i.e. affective responses can occur with little or no cognitive processing). Thus, although emotional experience is probably preceded by cognitive processes, Zajonc (1984) may be correct in assuming that this is not invariably the case.

FREUD'S CONTRIBUTION

Freud (1915, 1943) consistently emphasised the importance of emotional factors in memory. He argued that very threatening or anxiety-provoking material is often unable to gain access to conscious awareness, and he used the term *repression* to refer to this phenomenon. According to Freud (1915, p.86): "The essence of repression lies simply in the function of rejecting and keeping something out of consciousness." This is a very general definition, and Freud actually attached rather different meanings to the concept of "repression" at different times (Madison, 1956), sometimes using it to refer to the inhibition of the capacity for emotional experience. According to this definition, repression can occur even when there is conscious awareness of threatening ideas, provided that these ideas lack their normal emotional content.

Before discussing the experimental evidence on repression, we will consider the related phenomenon of perceptual defence, in which emotionally charged stimuli (e.g. taboo or obscene words) are perceived less readily than neutral stimuli. Freud's notion that the ego can be protected by refusing to acknowledge threatening environmental stimuli (sometimes termed *primary repression*) is consistent with the phenomenon of perceptual defence, and there is some link between perceptual defence and repression in memory. However, as Brewin (1988, p.28) pointed out, "the raising of a perceptual threshold is still a long way from the complete absence of a memory for a traumatic event".

Perceptual defence

The phenomenon of perceptual defence is generally demonstrated by presenting a word very briefly and then progressively increasing the presentation time until the subject identifies it. The minimal presentation time needed for identification tends to be greater for emotionally loaded words than for neutral words, even when the two types of stimuli are carefully matched for frequency, length, and so on.

It has been argued that the elevated recognition threshold for emotive stimuli such as taboo words is due to response bias rather than directly depending on perceptual processes. For example, subjects may sometimes recognise an embarrassing stimulus but be reluctant to report it. One way of attempting to reduce or eliminate this problem was used in a number of studies reviewed by Dixon (1981). Subjects initially learned paired associates. In the conditions of interest, an emotional word was paired with a neutral word (e.g. table-rape; whore-tree). Perceptual thresholds for the words were then assessed, with subjects being instructed not to say the word itself, but rather the word with which it had been paired. Thus, if the word "whore" were presented, subjects would respond "tree", and if the word "table" were presented, they would say "rape". This seems like a reasonably neat way of distinguishing between perceptual and response effects of emotional words, but studies using this method have produced inconsistent findings (see Dixon, 1981).

A superior way of reducing or eliminating the problem of response bias was used by Hardy and Legge (1968). In their first experiment, the visual recognition threshold for a neutral word or a rectangle was measured while at the same time an emotional or a neutral word was presented auditorily below the threshold of conscious awareness. The visual threshold was higher when emotional words were being presented, indicating that these words were having a general inhibitory effect on perceptual processing.

In a second experiment, Hardy and Legge asked their subjects to detect the presence of a faint auditory stimulus while watching a screen on which emotional or neutral words were presented subliminally (below the level of conscious awareness). The subjects did not notice the words, but the auditory threshold was higher when emotional words were being presented.

What is the relevance of Hardy and Legge's findings to the phenomenon of perceptual defence? Although they did not obtain direct evidence that emotionally loaded words are more difficult to perceive than neutral words, they did discover that the subliminal presentation of an emotionally loaded word has an inhibitory effect on perceptual processing. Presumably it is precisely such inhibitory effects that are responsible for producing the perceptual defence effect.

The fragmentation or partial cue hypothesis has often been used to explain perceptual defence. The basic idea is that conscious perception of part of a visually presented word (e.g. "sh*t") may inhibit further perceptual processing if it is suspected that the word may be rude or obscene. There is probably some truth in this hypothesis. However, it does not seem relevant to the study by Hardy and Legge (1968), because their subjects were not even aware

that any words had been presented. Furthermore, it is not altogether clear how inhibition of auditory perceptual processing would lead to elevation of the visual threshold, or how inhibition of visual processing would affect the auditory threshold.

Perceptual defence poses a problem for some theories of perception, largely because of the difficulty of deciding how it is that the perceiver can selectively defend himself or herself against an emotional stimulus unless he or she has already perceived the stimulus and identified it. In the words of Howie (1952, p.311):

To speak of perceptual defence is to use a mode of discourse which must make any precise or even intelligible meaning of perceptual defence impossible, for it is to speak of perceptual process as somehow being both a process of knowing and a process of avoiding knowing.

How can we resolve this paradox? The most straightforward answer (Dixon, 1981) is to reject the notion of perception as a unitary event, replacing it with a conceptualisation in which perception involves multiple processing stages or mechanisms, with consciousness perhaps representing the final level of processing. It is thus possible for a stimulus input to receive considerable perceptual processing without conscious awareness of the products of that processing, and this may well be the case with perceptual defence.

Repression

Freud's ideas on repression emerged from his clinical experiences, with the repression that he claimed to have observed mostly involving traumatic events that had happened to his patients. There are obvious ethical reasons why it is not possible to produce repression in the clinical sense under laboratory conditions, but there have been several attempts to study repression at an experimental level. Such attempts have generally involved creating anxiety in order to produce forgetting (repression), followed by removal of the anxiety in order to show that the repressed information is still stored ("return of the repressed"). In practical terms, anxiety has usually been produced by providing failure feedback to subjects performing a task, and anxiety has then been reduced either by reassuring the subjects that the failure feedback was not genuine or by providing success feedback on the task previously associated with failure.

Apparent evidence of repression and the return of the repressed has been obtained in several studies (see Holmes, 1990, for a review). However, the interpretation of the findings is controversial. It is possible that people show poor recall after a failure experience simply because they are thinking about their failure rather than devoting all of their attention to the recall test. D'Zurilla (1965) found that subjects exposed to failure feedback did indeed report more thoughts that were irrelevant to the subsequent task of recall than did subjects not exposed to failure feedback.

Holmes (1972) investigated this hypothesis further. Subjects were presented with a list of words. Subsequently, they received a personality test incorporating the same words, and were given ego-threatening, ego-enhancing, or neutral feedback. Holmes discovered that ego-enhancing feedback reduced recall to the same extent as ego-threatening feedback. As ego enhancement would not produce repression, it is likely that ego enhancement and ego threat were both associated with impaired memory, because they caused a relative lack of attention to the immediately following recall test.

In view of the limitations of the research, it is not surprising that Holmes (1990, p.97) concluded his review of experimental repression as follows: "Warning. The concept of repression has not been validated with experimental research and its use may be hazardous to the accurate interpretation of clinical behaviour."

Child sexual abuse

It is now time to consider repressed memories in the real world. Evidence is accumulating that large numbers of adults have repressed memories for sexual abuse which they suffered in childhood (see Loftus, 1993, for a review). For example, Herman and Schatzow (1987) found that 28% of a group of female incest victims reported severe memory

deficits from childhood, and such repressed memories were most frequent among women who had suffered violent abuse. In another study (Williams, 1992), 38% of a group of African–American women who were known to have been abused approximately 17 years previously reported repressed memories of that abuse.

The major problem with establishing the accuracy of repressed memories is that there is often no concrete evidence to provide corroboration or support. However, such evidence is sometimes discovered (e.g. pornographic photographs). In one case discussed by Loftus (1993), a 27-year-old man retrieved repressed memories of seeing his mother attempt suicide by hanging. The accuracy of these memories was confirmed by the man's father, who said that his son had witnessed such a suicide attempt when he was three years old.

There is evidence that people's memories of traumatic events can be wildly inaccurate. In one study (Pynoos & Nader, 1989), children's recollections of a sniper attack in a school playground were assessed. Here is one example of misreporting which they discovered (1989, p.238): "A boy who had been away on vacation said that he had been on his way to the school, had seen someone lying on the ground, had heard the shots, and then turned back."

Loftus (1993) discussed one of her studies in which an attempt was made to implant a false memory into a 14-year-old boy called Chris. Jim, who was Chris's older brother, was persuaded to tell Chris that he had been lost in a shopping mall when he was five years old. Chris was convinced that the story was true, and within two weeks his "memory" for the non-existent occurrence contained several details missing from his brother's brief account:

I was with you guys for a second and I think I went over to look at the toy store, the Kay-bee toy and uh, we got lost and I was looking around and I thought, 'Uh-oh. I'm in trouble now.' You know. And then I ... I thought I was never going to see my family again. I was really scared you know. And then this old man, I think he was wearing a blue flannel, came up to me ... he was kind of old. He was kind of bald on top ... he had like a ring of grey hair ... and he had glasses.

Even when Chris was told that his memory of getting lost was false, he found it hard to believe: "Really? I thought I remembered being lost ... and looking around for you guys. I do remember that. And then crying. And mom coming up and saying 'Where were you? Don't you ... don't you ever do that again'."

In the light of the evidence, Loftus (1993, p.534) came to the following conclusion:

We do not yet have the tools for reliably distinguishing the signal of true repressed memories from the noise of false ones ... Psychotherapists, counselors, social service agencies, and law enforcement personnel would be wise to be careful how they probe for horrors on the other side of some presumed amnesic barrier. They need to be circumspect regarding uncorroborated repressed memories that return.

Loftus' conclusion may be unduly pessimistic. Brewin, Andrews, and Gotlib (1993) argued that it is important to use structured interviews in which the focus is on eliciting *specific* personal memories rather than more general or global judgements about childhood experiences. This can be achieved in part by making use of explicit recognition cues relating to specific forms of behaviour that others (e.g. parents) may have engaged in when the individual was a child. When this is done, one can have some confidence in the memories that are reported (Brewin et al., 1993, p.94):

Social influences, childhood amnesia, and the simple fallibility of memory all impose limitations on the accuracy of recall, and fear of the consequences of disclosure may further disadvantage this process. However, provided that individuals are questioned about the occurrence of specific events or facts that they were sufficiently old and well placed to know about, the central features of their accounts are likely to be reasonably accurate.

MOOD AND MEMORY

Bower's network theory

Bower and his associates (e.g. Bower, 1981; Gilligan & Bower, 1984) proposed what they termed a very influential network theory of affect, aspects of which are shown in Fig. 18.1. The theory as expressed by Gilligan and Bower (1984) makes six assumptions:

• Emotions can be regarded as units or nodes in a semantic network, with numerous connections to related ideas, to physiological systems, to events, and to muscular and expressive patterns.
• Emotional material is stored in the semantic network in the form of propositions or assertions.
• Thought occurs via the activation of nodes within the semantic network.
• Nodes can be activated either by external or by internal stimuli.
• Activation from an activated node spreads in a selective fashion to related nodes; this assumption is crucial, because it means that activation of an emotion node (e.g. sadness) leads to activation of anxiety-related nodes or concepts (e.g. loss; despair; hopelessness) in the semantic network.
• "Consciousness" consists of a network of nodes which is activated above some threshold value.

These assumptions lead to the following hypotheses:

• *Mood-state-dependent recall:* recall is best when the mood at recall matches that at the time of learning.
• *Mood congruity:* emotionally toned information is learned best when there is correspondence between its affective value and the learner's current mood state.
• *Thought congruity:* an individual's free associations, interpretations, thoughts, and judgements tend to be thematically congruent with his or her mood state.
• *Mood intensity:* increases in intensity of mood cause increases in the activation of associated nodes in the associative network.

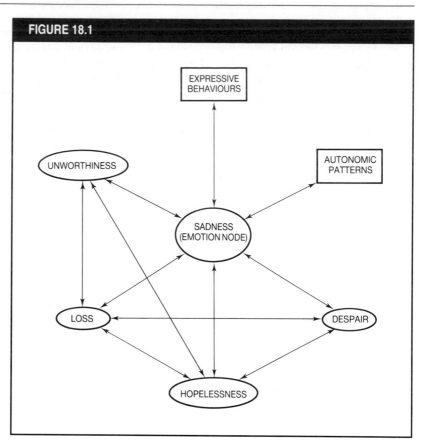

FIGURE 18.1

Bower's semantic network theory. The ovals represent nodes or units within the network. Adapted from Bower (1981).

How exactly do the four hypotheses relate to the six theoretical assumptions? So far as mood-state-dependent recall is concerned, associations are formed at the time of learning between the activated nodes representing the to-be-remembered items and the emotion node or nodes activated because of the subject's mood state. At the time of recall, the mood state at that time leads to activation of the appropriate emotion node. Activation then spreads from that emotion node to the various nodes associated with it. If there is a match between the mood state at learning and at recall, then this increases activation of the nodes of to-be-remembered items, and enhances recall. However, the associative links between the to-be-remembered stimulus material and the relevant emotion node are likely to be relatively weak. As a consequence, mood-state-dependent effects are likely to be much greater when the memory test is a difficult one offering few retrieval cues (e.g. free recall) than when the memory test

provides strong retrieval cues (e.g. recognition memory).

Mood-state-dependent effects are also predicted by other theories. According to Tulving's encoding specificity principle (discussed in Chapter 6), the success of recall or recognition depends on the extent to which the information available at the time of retrieval matches the information stored in memory. If information about the mood state at the time of learning is stored in memory, then being in the same mood state at the time of retrieval increases this information-matching. Theoretically, this should increase both recall and recognition.

Thought congruity occurs for two reasons. First, the current mood state leads to activation of the corresponding emotion node. Second, activation spreads from that emotion node to other, associately related nodes, which will tend to contain information emotionally congruent with the activated emotion node.

Mood congruity occurs when people in a good mood remember emotionally positive material better than those in a bad mood, whereas the opposite is true for emotionally negative material. According to Gilligan and Bower (1984), mood congruity depends on the fact that emotionally loaded information tends to be associated more strongly with its congruent emotion node than with any other emotion node. For example, those nodes containing information about sadness-provoking events and experiences are associatively linked to the emotion node for sadness (see Fig. 18.1). To-be-remembered material that is congruent with the current mood state links up with this associative network of similar information, and this leads to extensive or elaborative encoding of the to-be-remembered material. As we saw in Chapter 6, elaborate encoding is generally associated with superior long-term memory.

It seems reasonable to assume that the effects described here would become stronger as the intensity of the current mood increases, because the spread of activation from the activated emotion node to other related nodes would increase in line with the intensity with which emotion was experienced. However, a very sad mood may lead to a focus on internal information relating to failure, fatigue, and so on, and this may inhibit processing of all kinds of external stimuli whether or not they are congruent with the sad mood state.

Mood states

It is difficult to ensure that subjects are in the appropriate mood state. One method is to try to induce the required mood state under laboratory conditions, and another is to make use of naturally occurring mood states (e.g. in patients with mood disorders).

The most popular mood-induction approach is based on the procedure introduced by Velten (1968). Subjects read a set of sentences which are designed to induce increasingly intense feelings of elation or depression. Subjects typically report that their mood has altered in the expected direction, but they may simply be responding in the way they believe the experimenter wants. A further problem is that this mood-induction procedure usually

produces a blend of several different mood states rather than just the desired one (Polivy, 1981).

Bower (e.g. Bower, Gilligan, & Monteiro, 1981; Bower & Mayer, 1985) has used hypnosis combined with self-generated imagery. The subjects are hypnotised at the start of the experiment. When in the hypnotic state, they are asked to think of images of a past happy or sad emotional experience, using those images to produce the appropriate mood state. This approach produces strong and long-lasting moods, but it suffers from some disadvantages. It is necessary to use subjects who score highly on tests of hypnotic susceptibility, and it may be unwise to generalise from such subjects to people who are low in hypnotic susceptibility.

Some researchers have made use of naturally occurring mood states. For example, manic-depressive patients have very large mood swings between great excitement or mania and great sadness or depression. The strength of their mood states and the fact that their memory can be tested either in the same mood as at learning or in the opposite mood are two good reasons for studying such patients.

Experimental findings

As we will see, there is some experimental support for all four hypotheses proposed by Gilligan and Bower (1984). The strongest support has been for mood congruity (i.e. learning is best when the subject's mood matches the emotional tone of the to-be-learned material). However, there have been several failures to demonstrate mood-state-dependent recall, thought congruity, mood congruity, and effects of mood intensity.

Mood-state-dependent memory

Experimental studies testing for mood-state-dependent memory typically make use of either one or two learning lists of words. Learning occurs in one mood state (e.g. happy or sad), and recall occurs in the same mood state or in a different one (see Fig. 18.2). When two lists are presented (e.g. Bower, Monteiro, & Gilligan, 1978; Schare, Lisman, & Spear, 1984), one list is learned in one mood and the other list is learned in a different mood. Subsequently subjects are put back into one

FIGURE 18.2

Mood State at Learning	Mood State at Recall	Predicted Level of Recall
Happy	Happy	High
Happy	Sad	Low
Sad	Happy	Low
Sad	Sad	High

Design for a study of mood-state-dependent memory, together with the predicted results on Bower's (1981) theory.

of these two moods, and instructed to recall only the list learned first. It is predicted that recall should be higher when the mood state at the time of recall is the same as that at the time of learning.

Schare et al. (1984) and Bower et al. (1978) obtained mood-state-dependent recall with the two-list design but not with the one-list design. Perhaps subjects trying to recall the first list with the mood appropriate to the second list think of some of the words from the second list, and this interferes with the task of recalling first-list words.

Ucros (1989) reviewed 40 published studies of mood-state-dependent memory. According to her, the evidence indicates a moderate tendency for people to remember material better when there is a match between the mood at learning and the mood at retrieval. However, the magnitude of mood-state-dependent effects varies as a function of various factors. For example, the effects are generally stronger when subjects are in a positive mood than when they are in a negative mood. They are also greater when people try to remember personal events than when the learning material lacks personal relevance. Possible explanations for these effects are discussed later.

Until comparatively recently, only explicit memory involving conscious recollection of previous events was considered in studies of mood-state-dependent memory. However, there is now some evidence (e.g. Macaulay, Ryan, & Eich, 1993) that mood-state-dependent effects can also be obtained on tests of implicit memory (when conscious recollection is not required; see Chapter 6). Some potentially relevant evidence was reported by Nissen et al. (1988). They studied explicit and implicit memory in a 45-year-old woman suffering from multiple personality disorder, assuming that each of her separate personalities corresponded to a different mood state.

The woman studied by Nissen et al. (1988) has shown 22 different personalities ranging in age from 5 to 45, most of them female. One of her personalities is Alice, who is 39 years old, studying to be a ministerial counsellor, and who works as a nurses' assistant. Another of her personalities is Charles, who is 45 years old and is an aggressive heavy drinker, and a third personality is Bonnie, 36, who is very social and whose main interests lie in the theatre. On some tasks there were striking personality-dependent effects. The same story was read to five of the personalities in turn, with each personality providing almost immediate recall. As can be seen in Fig. 18.3, there was no systematic improvement in recall across personalities. On another task, memory for words was tested by means of an implicit memory test (word completion) and an explicit memory test (recall). Performance on both tests was considerably worse when the personality at the time of test was different from the personality at learning. In contrast, recognition memory for faces was almost as good when the personality changed between learning and test as when it remained the same (42% vs. 52%, respectively). Finally, there was an implicit task in which repeated and non-repeated words had to be identified from very brief presentations. Donna performed this task, then Charles, and then Donna again. Donna's performance on the repeated words was much

FIGURE 18.3

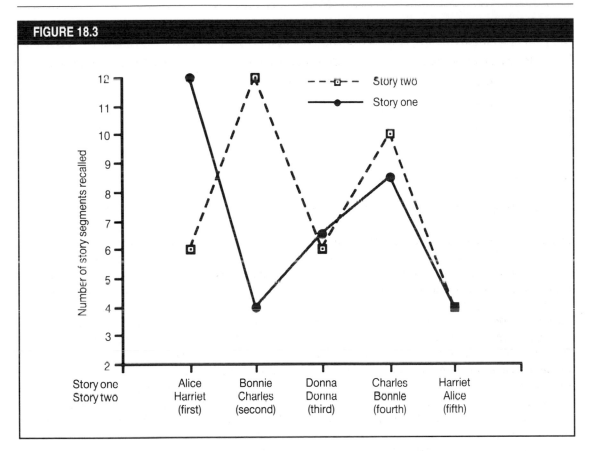

Memory performance in a woman suffering from multiple personality disorder. Based on data in Nissen et al. (1988).

better after Charles had performed the task than beforehand.

The findings from this woman with multiple personality disorder are rather varied. There was evidence of strong personality-dependent effects with some explicit and implicit memory tasks, but weak or non-existent personality-dependent effects with other explicit and implicit memory tasks. It is difficult to make sense of the pattern of findings, but Nissen et al. (1988, p.131) made the following attempt:

> Material that allows a variety of different interpretations or whose encoding is significantly guided by strategic processing, or whose interpretation might be expected to depend on one's mood and beliefs and biases is relatively inaccessible across personalities.

Mood congruity

There is more experimental support for mood congruity than for any of the other hypotheses put forward by Gilligan and Bower (1984). The usual procedure is that a mood is induced, followed by the learning of a list or the reading of a story containing emotionally toned material. There is then a memory test for the list or the story after the subject's mood has returned to normal. Mood congruity is demonstrated by recall being greatest when the affective value of the to-be-learned material matches the subject's mood state at the time of learning.

Bower et al. (1981) investigated mood congruity. Subjects who had been hypnotised to feel happy or sad read a story about two college men, Jack and André. Jack is very depressed and glum, because he is having problems with his academic work, with his girl-friend, and with his tennis. In contrast, André is very happy because things are going extremely well for him in all three areas. Bower et al. found that subjects reported identifying more with the story character whose mood resembled their own while they were reading the story. Subjects also recalled more information about the character whose emotional state was similar to their own when reading the story (see Fig. 18.4).

Although there are several experimental demonstrations of mood congruity, some doubts were raised by Perrig and Perrig (1988). They instructed their subjects to behave as if they were depressed or happy, but no attempt was made to induce any mood state. These instructions were followed by a word list containing positive, negative, and neutral words, which then had to be recalled. Those subjects indicating an awareness of mood-congruity effects produced results very similar to those obtained by Bower et al. (1981), whereas those subjects who did not showed no evidence of selective learning.

One interpretation of Perrig and Perrig's findings is that the subjects were simply behaving as they thought the experimenter wanted them to behave. It might even be that the mood-congruity effects obtained in mood-induction studies merely reflect a desire on the part of subjects to do what is expected of them. An alternative (and more plausible) interpretation was offered by Perrig and Perrig (1988, p.102): "Mood may be a sufficient but not a necessary condition to produce the mood-congruity effect of selective learning." In other words, mood-congruity effects can be produced either by means of genuine mood induction or by means of mood simulation, and researchers must attempt to distinguish between genuine mood effects and simulated mood effects.

Thought congruity

Thought congruity has been investigated in various ways. One method is to present subjects with a list of pleasant and unpleasant words prior to mood induction, and then to test for recall after mood

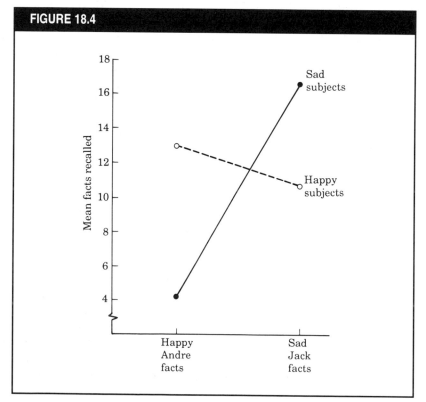

FIGURE 18.4

Recall of happy and sad facts by happy and sad subjects. Based on data in Bower et al. (1981).

induction. The prediction is that pleasant words will be recalled better after pleasant mood induction than after unpleasant mood induction, with the opposite being the case for unpleasant words. Another method is to ask subjects to recall autobiographical memories following mood induction. Pleasant moods should increase the number of pleasant memories recalled, and perhaps the speed with which they are recalled, and unpleasant moods should do the same for unpleasant memories.

Thought congruity has been shown in a number of studies using both of the methods just described (see Blaney, 1986, for a review). For example, Clark and Teasdale (1982) tested depressed patients on two occasions close in time, with the depth of the depression being more severe on one occasion than on the other. More depressing or unhappy memories and fewer happy memories were recalled on the more depressed occasion, with the opposite being the case on the less depressed occasion. As they pointed out, these findings are consistent with the notion of a vicious circle in depressed patients: depressed mood state leads to recall of depressing memories, and the recall of depressing memories exacerbates the depressed mood state.

Mood intensity

There has been relatively little work concerned with the mood intensity hypothesis. However, Rinck, Glowalla, and Schneider (1992) considered a related issue, namely, the emotional intensity of the stimulus material. Subjects who were put into a happy or sad mood rated words in terms of their pleasantness–unpleasantness. The following day they were given an unexpected recall test. As predicted, there was a mood-congruency effect for the intensely emotional words (i.e. strongly pleasant or unpleasant). Somewhat surprisingly, there was evidence for the opposite effect with weakly emotional words: recall was better for words that did not match the mood at learning.

Evaluation

Bower's network theory has provided an excellent focus for research on mood and memory. Indeed, his is the leading theory in the area, and it has

generated a considerable volume of research. Although the findings have been somewhat inconsistent, the effects of mood on learning and memory generally resemble those predicted. In spite of these successes, some problems with the theory will now be discussed.

First, negative moods have often failed to enhance the learning and recall of negative material. This was shown most strikingly by Williams and Broadbent (1986) in study of thought congruity. They investigated the retrieval of autobiographical memories to positive and negative cue words by people who had recently attempted suicide by overdose. The suicide attempters were slower than normal controls to retrieve personal memories to the positive cue words, but, however, they were no faster than normals in thinking of negative personal experiences. Presumably, it was so painful for the suicide attempters to retrieve unpleasant personal memories that they devoted some effort to inhibiting the retrieval of such memories.

Second, we have seen that mood-state effects are strongest when subjects learn and remember personal events (Ucros, 1989). This suggests that mood-state-dependent memory may be of more importance in everyday life than it generally is in the laboratory. It is not clear on Bower's (1981) original network theory why this should be so, but a possible reason for this difference is discussed shortly.

Third, the semantic network theory treats emotions as being rather similar to semantic concepts and ideas, in that emotions and semantic concepts are both represented as nodes within the same semantic network. This is an over-simplified view, because emotions and semantic concepts differ in various ways. For example, emotional states or moods can be experienced in several different intensities ranging from the very strong to the very weak, which is not the case with semantic concepts. Moods typically change relatively slowly over time, indicating that activated emotion nodes remain activated for some time, whereas semantic concepts are usually activated for only relatively short periods of time.

Other theoretical perspectives

In the years since Bower (1981) proposed his network theory, there have been various attempts to provide more adequate theoretical accounts of mood and memory. Bower (1992) offered an explanation of why mood-state effects are greatest when personal events are learned and remembered. He argued for a causal belongingness hypothesis, according to which mood state affects memory only when subjects attribute their emotional state at the time of learning as being caused by the to-be-learned stimuli. Causal attribution leads to an effective association between the stimulus and the emotional state. This is much more likely to occur with personal events (e.g. feeling delighted after succeeding in an important examination) than when an emotional state is induced before presenting the learning task.

An alternative position was advocated by Eich and Metcalfe (1989). They argued that mood state has more effect on *internal* events such as reasoning or imagination than it does on events that are more closely determined by *external* events. As a consequence, memory for internal events is more susceptible to mood effects than is memory for external events. They investigated this hypothesis in two different ways. First, subjects who had been put into a happy or sad mood were given either a read task or a generate task. The read task involved reading a category name followed by two exemplars (e.g. precious metals: silver–*gold*), whereas the generate task required the subject to complete the last word (e.g. precious metals: silver–g___?). It was assumed that internal events would be more important with the generate task than with the read task. Second, memory was tested with either free recall or recognition, and it was assumed that free recall would place more demands on internal events than would recognition memory. Thus, it was predicted that mood-state dependent effects would be greater with the generate condition than with the read condition and with free recall than with recognition memory.

Some of the main findings are shown in Fig. 18.5. They are in line with prediction. Mood-state-dependent effects were observable with free recall but not with recognition, and the effects on free recall were greater following the generate task than following the read task. Other similar studies provide additional support for the notion that

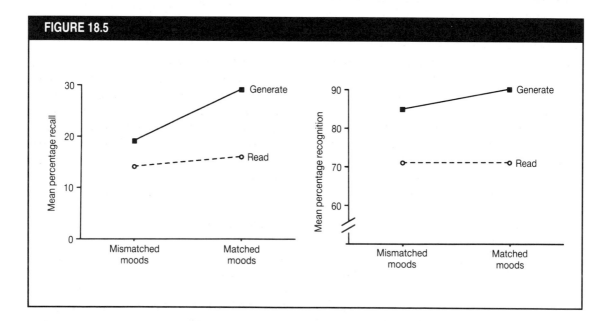

FIGURE 18.5

Memory performance (recall and recognition) as a function of learning conditions (generate vs. read) and match versus mismatch of moods at learning and test. Based on data in Eich and Metcalfe (1989).

mood-state effects are greater when internal events (rather than external events) are involved at learning and/or test (Macaulay, Ryan, & Eich, 1993).

ATTENTION AND PERCEPTION

Most of the research concerned with mood effects on attention and perception has focused on anxiety or depression. One reason is that they can be studied at both normal and clinical levels, because anxiety and depression are both common forms of emotional disorder. However, a problem with attempting to compare the effects of anxiety and depression on cognitive functioning is that individuals who are high in anxiety tend to be high in depression and vice versa. This is true of both normal and clinical populations.

Bower's (1981) network theory (discussed earlier in the chapter) is basically a theory of memory. However, it does have important implications for other aspects of cognitive functioning. According to the theory, whenever the node corresponding to an emotion is activated, activation spreads out to all of the related nodes. If someone is happy, then nodes relating to happy personal experiences, similar concepts to happiness (e.g. euphoria, joy, contentment, and so on) will be activated. This widespread activation should facilitate performance across a wide range of tasks involving processing of happiness-related information.

Before proceeding to discuss the effects of anxiety and depression on attention and perception, their effects on memory should be mentioned briefly. The main focus of the research has been on the *negative memory bias*, in which negative or threatening information is recalled relatively better than positive or neutral information. There is good evidence that depressed normals and depressed patients exhibit the negative memory bias, and the same is true of normals who are highly anxious (see Eysenck, 1992). However, it has not proved possible to obtain clear evidence of negative memory bias with generally anxious patients (Eysenck, 1992). Mogg, Mathews, and Weinman (1987) found, on tests of both recall and recognition, that generally anxious patients had poorer retention of threat-related words than did the control subjects, which is in exactly the opposite direction to a negative memory bias. It is not known why anxious patients do not show a negative memory bias, but it is possible that they find the negative material so threatening that they actively attempt to avoid processing it thoroughly.

Anxiety

Eysenck (1992) argued that the main functional value of anxiety is that it facilitates the detection of environmental threat. As a consequence, there are very important links between anxiety and attention. More specifically, he proposed that there are various ways in which anxiety may affect attentional processes:

• The *content* of the information to which attention is directed; anxious individuals are likely to attend selectively to threat-related stimuli, producing what is known as *selective attentional bias*.
• Attentional control or *distractibility*; the sensitivity to danger of anxious individuals may mean they cannot avoid attending to task-irrelevant stimuli, and are thus highly distractible.
• *Attentional breadth*; this refers to the extent to which attention is narrowly or broadly focused.

Eysenck (1992) also argued (on the basis of previous research) that anxious individuals might differ from non-anxious individuals in terms of perceptual processes. More specifically, he suggested that anxious individuals would exhibit an *interpretive bias* (the tendency to interpret ambiguous stimuli and situations in a threatening fashion).

This hypotheses can be investigated in normal and clinical populations. Among normal individuals, those high and low in anxiety can be identified by means of questionnaire assessment of trait anxiety (a personality dimension measuring susceptibility to anxiety). At the clinical level, there are various anxiety disorders. However, much of the research has focused on patients suffering from generalised anxiety disorder, a condition characterised by anxiety and worry about a very wide range of situations.

Attentional content

Common sense indicates that anxious individuals are more likely than non-anxious individuals to attend to threat-related stimuli (e.g. obscene words; words relating to social or physical threat such as "stupid" or "crippled"). However, it turns out that reality is more complicated than that. It has generally been found in studies of perceptual defence and other related phenomena that individuals high and low in trait anxiety do not differ in their processing of threatening stimuli (see Eysenck, MacLeod, & Mathews, 1987, for a review).

These non-significant findings may mean that individuals varying in anxiety level do not differ in their processing of threat-related stimuli. There is a more interesting possibility, namely that those high and low in anxiety differ in terms of a *selective attentional bias*. If a threat-related (social or physical threat) and a neutral stimulus are presented together, then individuals high in anxiety may selectively attend to the threat-related stimulus, whereas those low in anxiety selectively attend to the neutral stimulus. This hypothesis could account for the non-significant findings in most of the published research, in which only one stimulus was presented at a time. In such circumstances, selective allocation of processing resources was simply not possible.

This selective bias hypothesis was first tested in an experiment reported by Eysenck et al. (1987). They discovered that normals high in anxiety showed a selective attentional bias in favour of processing threatening words (e.g. grave, fail). The selective bias hypothesis has also been tested with generalised anxiety disorder patients. For example, MacLeod, Mathews, and Tata (1986) used a task in which two words were presented visually at the same time, and the upper word had to be read aloud. On some trials, a dot replaced one of the words, and the subjects responded as rapidly as possible to the dot. It was assumed that the faster the subjects responded to the dot, the more attention they were allocating to that part of the visual display. On some trials, a threatening and a neutral word were presented, and one of them was replaced by a dot.

The findings are shown in Fig. 18.6. The anxious patients showed attentional bias towards threatening words (e.g. humiliated, crippled), whereas the normal controls showed a slight bias away from threat. These findings indicate that anxious individuals selectively attend to threatening stimuli.

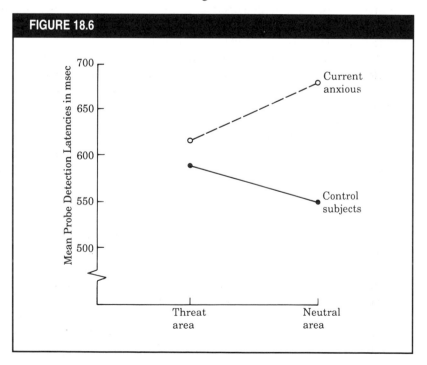

FIGURE 18.6

Mean detection times to probes as a function of the area of the screen where the probe was presented, and as a function of groups (anxious patients vs. normal controls). Data from MacLeod et al. (1986).

Distractibility

It has often been assumed that anxious individuals are more distractible than non-anxious ones. For example, Korchin (1964) concluded as follows on the basis of his clinical observations: "The anxious patient is unable to concentrate, hyper-responsive, and hyper-distractible." This distractibility may well extend to both external and internal stimuli, but it is difficult to assess the distracting power of internal stimuli (e.g. worries; self-concerns).

Most studies concerned with the effects of anxiety on distractibility have compared performance of a task in the presence or absence of task-irrelevant or distracting stimuli. Distractibility is assessed by the extent to which performance deteriorates in the presence of the task-irrelevant stimuli. There have been several such studies comparing normal individuals high and low in trait anxiety, and the typical finding is that those high in trait anxiety are significantly more distractible than those low in trait anxiety (see Eysenck, 1992, for a review).

Mathews, May, Mogg, and Eysenck (1990) investigated distractibility effects in generalised anxiety disorder patients and normal controls. Subjects had to detect target words, and the distractors consisted of threatening or non-threatening words. The anxious patients were more distracted than the normal controls by both kinds of distractor, but especially by the threatening distractors. These findings suggest that anxious patients have a rather general tendency to be distracted by task-irrelevant stimuli, but they also have a more specific tendency to have their attention captured by threat-related distractors.

Attentional breadth

Easterbrook (1959, p.193) argued that the range of environmental cues (i.e. the breadth of attention) reduces as anxiety or arousal increases, which "will reduce the proportion of irrelevant cues employed, and so improve performance. When all irrelevant cues have been excluded, however, ... further reduction in the number of cues employed can only affect relevant cues, and proficiency will fall".

Easterbrook's hypothesis has often been tested by requiring subjects to perform a main and a secondary task at the same time. The expectation is that the reduced range of cue utilisation in heightened anxiety should have a more adverse effect on performance of the secondary than of the main task. The reason for this is that the narrowing of attention produced by high anxiety will restrict the attention that can be directed to the secondary task. Eysenck (1982) reviewed 10 experiments with a main and secondary task in which there were normal groups high and low in trait anxiety. The two groups generally did not differ in performance of the main task, but the high-anxious group was significantly inferior to the low-anxious group on the secondary task. Such findings are consistent with Easterbrook's hypothesis.

Particularly impressive support for Easterbrook's hypothesis was reported by Koksal (1992). He presented his subjects with a visual display of 25 dots arranged over a small area or a large area. One dot moved to the left and then to the right for 80 milliseconds, and the subject's task was to identify which dot had moved. As can be seen in Fig. 18.7, there were no effects of anxiety with the small display. However, anxious individuals performed significantly worse than non-anxious ones with the large display, presumably because of attentional narrowing.

Interpretive bias

There is convincing evidence that anxious individuals possess an interpretive bias, meaning that they are more likely than non-anxious individuals to interpret ambiguous stimuli in a threatening way. For example, Eysenck et al. (1987) made use of a simple task in which subjects were asked to write down the spellings of auditorily presented words. Some of the words were homophones having both a threat-related and a neutral interpretation (e.g. die, dye; pain, pane). They reported a significant correlation of +0.60 between trait anxiety and the number of threatening homophone interpretations. These findings have been replicated (see Eysenck, 1992, for a review), and evidence of an interpretive bias has also been obtained in generalised anxiety disorder patients using ambiguous sentences such as "The two men watched as the chest was opened" (Eysenck et al., 1991).

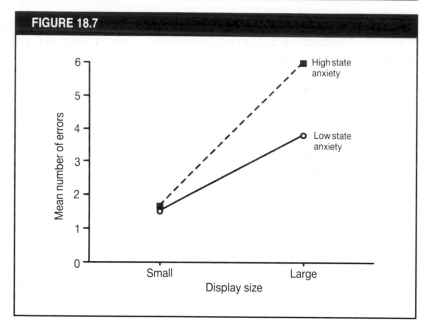

Mean errors in detecting a moving stimulus as a function of display size and state anxiety. Koksal (1992).

FIGURE 18.7

Section summary

We have seen that there is convincing evidence that anxiety is associated with mood-congruent effects on selective attention, interpretation of ambiguity, and memory (with the exception of anxious patients). Anxiety is also associated with enhanced distractibility and a narrowing of attention. Thus, anxiety has several effects on the cognitive system, with attention, perception and memory all affected.

Depression

So far as depression is concerned, we have already seen that it is associated with mood-congruent effects on memory. It follows from Bower's (1981) network theory that depressed individuals should also exhibit mood-congruent effects on selective attention and on interpretation of ambiguity, and these predictions are considered next.

So far as selective attentional bias is concerned, there is a lack of convincing evidence for its existence among depressed individuals. In a study discussed earlier in the chapter, MacLeod et al. (1986) found that anxious patients showed a selective attentional bias when a threatening and a neutral word were presented together. They also used a group of depressed patients who performed the same task. However, the depressed patients exhibited no selective attentional bias.

Other studies have produced similar findings. For example, Gotlib, McLachlan, and Katz (1988) used a modified version of the task employed by MacLeod et al. (1986), and they presented emotionally positive words as well as emotionally negative and neutral words. Depressed individuals did not show any tendency to attend selectively to the negative words or to avoid the positive words.

The effects of depression on interpretation of ambiguity have been assessed in several studies. The evidence consistently indicates that there is an interpretive bias in depressed individuals. A number of studies (discussed by MacLeod & Mathews, 1991) have made use of the Cognitive Bias Questionnaire. Events are described briefly, with subjects having to select one out of four possible interpretations of each event. Depressed patients consistently select more negative interpretations than control subjects, indicating the presence of an interpretive bias.

Theoretical analysis

The fact that anxiety is associated with a selective attentional bias but depression is not is inconsistent with Bower's (1981) network theory. According to that theory, individuals in a depressed mood should show facilitated processing of (and attention to) mood-congruent stimuli, and should thus exhibit a selective attentional bias. The findings indicate that Bower (1981) was wrong to assume that the effects of different mood states on cognition are comparable.

It is useful to consider the different functions of anxiety and depression if we are to understand why they have different effects on information processing. According to Eysenck (1992, p.4), "the key purpose or function of anxiety is probably to facilitate the detection of danger or threat in potentially threatening environments". It follows that anxiety should have a considerable impact on the attentional and other processes involved in threat detection, and the evidence on the selective attentional bias and the interpretive bias provides support for that prediction. It is also reasonable that anxious individuals who are concerned to detect threat should be more likely than non-anxious individuals to be distracted by, and to attend to, non-task stimuli in order to check their threat value. Finally, anxious individuals may exhibit a narrowing of attention because it is important to assess thoroughly the threat posed by any given stimulus in the environment.

It is more difficult to determine the major function of depression. However, it is likely that the passive disengagement or withdrawal from the external environment characteristic of depression permits the conservation of energy following loss or failure. If depressed individuals have withdrawn psychologically from the environment, it would be expected that their relative unresponsiveness to the changes in the environment would be reflected in their attentional processes. More specifically, as well as failing to allocate processing resources to mood-congruent stimuli, depressed individuals might show a lack of distractibility and attentional selectivity. Foulds (1952) found that a distracting task (repeating back digits spoken by the experimenter) actually enhanced depressed patients' performance speed on a maze task, although there was some increase in the number of errors. Campbell (1957) obtained very similar findings, and also found that the digit-repetition task did not speed up the performance of normal subjects.

So far as attentional selectivity is concerned, Hemsley and Zawada (1976) discovered that depressed patients exhibited less attentional selectivity than normals. Subjects were presented with a series of digits, some of which were spoken in a male voice and the others in a female voice. Normals had better digit recall when they were instructed which set of digits to recall before (rather than after) the digits were presented. In contrast, depressed patients were unaffected by the timing of the recall instructions, presumably because of their inability to focus attention selectively.

Section summary

In the early days of research on cognition and emotion it was assumed that the effects of different emotional states on cognition were broadly similar. However, this assumption no longer seems reasonable. Each emotion has its own function and significance, and it is thus not surprising that emotions should vary in their impact on the cognitive system. In order to understand the different effects of anxiety and depression on cognitive processes, it may be useful to consider a study by Finlay-Jones and Brown (1981). They found that depression tended to follow loss events (e.g. bereavement), whereas anxiety tended to follow danger events. If depressed individuals focus on the past, particularly on losses that have occurred, then it seems reasonable that they should show mood-congruent effects in memory rather than in attention. If anxious individuals focus on the present and the future, particularly on potential dangers, then it seems reasonable that they should show mood-congruent effects in attention.

In a nutshell, many of the differences between anxiety and depression seem to conform to the following generalisation: depressed individuals tend to focus on internal rather than external sources of threatening information, whereas anxious individuals do the opposite.

EMOTION AND PERFORMANCE

It is generally assumed that people in negative mood states, such as anxiety and depression, will perform most tasks less well than those in positive or neutral moods, and much of the evidence supports that assumption. However, although it is of interest to determine the effects of anxiety and depression on performance, it is also important to try to understand precisely *why* these effects occur. Accordingly, some of the relevant theories will now be discussed.

Anxiety

Much research on anxiety and performance has focused on state anxiety (the level of anxiety currently being experienced). Many definitions of state anxiety have been offered, of which the following one proposed by Spielberger (1972, p.29) is typical: "Unpleasant, consciously-perceived feelings of tension and apprehension, with associated activation or arousal of the autonomic nervous system." There has also been a focus on the personality dimension of trait anxiety and the related dimension of test anxiety, which is as the name implies is specifically concerned with the tendency to become anxious in test situations. Theorists such as Liebert and Morris (1967) argued that there are two major components of test anxiety: worry and emotionality. Worry is mainly cognitive concern about the consequences of failure, whereas emotionality relates to perceived changes in physiological functioning.

Performance on almost any task is affected adversely at extreme levels of state anxiety. For example, over 200 of the muzzle-loading rifles used in one of the battles during the American Civil War were loaded at least five times without being fired at all (Walker & Burkhardt, 1965). Under laboratory conditions, Patrick (1934a, b) used an apparently simple task, in which subjects had to discover which of four doors was locked. As the same door was never unlocked on two successive trials, the optimal strategy was to try each of the other doors in turn. When the conditions were non-stressful, approximately 60% of the solutions were optimal. This figure dropped to 20% when the subjects had cold water streams directed at them, or had their ears blasted by a car horn, or were given continuous electric shocks until they found the right door.

The finding that performance is impaired at high levels is consistent with what is known as the Yerkes-Dodson law (Yerkes & Dodson, 1908; see Fig. 18.8). According to this law, performance is best or optimal when the level of arousal (or anxiety) is intermediate, and it deteriorates as arousal or anxiety increases or decreases from that level. The Yerkes-Dodson law seems reasonable, in that neither low arousal stemming from boredom or uninvolvement nor high arousal stemming from terror would appear conducive to effective task performance. In order to provide good support for

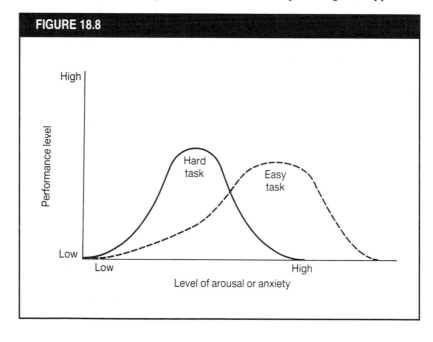

FIGURE 18.8

The Yerkes-Dodson law, proposed by Yerkes and Dodson (1908).

the Yerkes-Dodson law, however, it would be necessary to compare performance at several levels of arousal or anxiety, and this has very rarely been done. In addition, the Yerkes Dodson law suffers from the limitation that it is descriptive rather than explanatory. In other words, Yerkes and Dodson (1908) did not explain why low and high levels of arousal are associated with relatively poor performance.

Yerkes and Dodson (1908) also proposed that the optimal level of arousal is lower for difficult tasks than for easy ones. Thus, relatively high anxiety should have more detrimental effects on difficult or complex tasks than on easy ones. This has been found in several studies (see Eysenck, 1982, for a review). For example, Mayer (1977) considered the effects of trait anxiety on various simple problems, such as visual search and easy mathematical operations, as well as on much more complex cognitive tasks such as water-jar problems and anagrams. There was no effect of trait anxiety on performance of the simple problems, but high anxiety reduced the percentage of complex cognitive tasks solved correctly from approximately 80% to just over 40%.

Yerkes and Dodson (1908) unfortunately failed to explain why the effects of arousal or anxiety depend on task complexity. In order to do so, it is necessary to identify the major internal processes affected by anxiety. The theoretical attempts of Sarason (1988) and of Eysenck and Calvo (1992) to do this will be considered here; other theories of anxiety and performance are discussed by Eysenck (1992).

Cognitive interference theory
According to Sarason (1988, p.5): "Proneness to self-preoccupation and, most specifically, to worry over evaluation is a powerful component of what is referred to as test anxiety." He went on to argue that worry and self-evaluation over performance impair performance, a statement for which there is considerable evidence. For example, Spielberger et al. (1978) correlated the worry and emotionality components of test anxiety with a measure of academic achievement in students. For male students, worry correlated −0.47 with academic achievement, whereas emotionality correlated only

−0.13 with academic achievement; for female students, the correlations were −0.35 and 0.00, respectively.

Sarason (1988) also predicted that high test-anxious individuals are most likely to perform below the level of low test-anxious individuals when evaluative instructions are given, and when the task is relatively complex. Because worry allegedly interferes with attention to the task, it follows that the adverse effects of worry on task performance should be greatest on those tasks requiring the most attention, namely, relatively difficult tasks. As Sarason (1988) pointed out, these predictions have generally been supported.

In spite of the successes of Sarason's cognitive interference theory, he exaggerated the importance of self-preoccupation and worry. According to the theory, high-anxious individuals should perform most tasks less well than low-anxious individuals if they engage in significantly more self-preoccupations and worry. However, there are several studies in which that did not happen. For example, Blankstein, Flett, Boase, and Toner (1990) discovered that high test-anxious subjects had considerably more negative thoughts about themselves than did low test-anxious subjects, but the two groups did not differ in their anagram performance.

Another problem with Sarason's theoretical approach is its over-simplified account of the relationship between anxiety and task difficulty. Task difficulty is equated with the amount of attentional resources required by a task, whereas, in fact, there are other ways in which two tasks can differ in difficulty (e.g. reliance on short-term memory).

Processing efficiency theory
Eysenck and Calvo (1992) proposed processing efficiency theory. As with Sarason's (1988) theory, it is assumed that worry and self-concern have an important influence on performance. However, whereas Sarason argued that the effects of worry are negative, Eysenck and Calvo argued that worry has both negative and positive effects. The negative effects occur because worry pre-empts some of the resources of the working memory system (see Chapter 6), especially those of the attention-like

central executive, but also some of the resources of the articulatory loop. The positive effects occur because worry serves a motivational function. The presence of worry about task performance typically leads to the allocation of extra processing resources or effort to the task in an attempt to improve performance and thus to reduce or eliminate worry.

These theoretical assumptions lead to an important theoretical distinction between *performance effectiveness* and *processing efficiency*. Performance effectiveness refers to the quality of task performance; processing efficiency to the relationship between the effectiveness of performance and the effort or processing resources invested in performance. In approximate terms, processing efficiency can be defined as performance effectiveness divided by effort. According to processing efficiency theory, it is entirely possible for anxiety to have different effects on performance effectiveness and processing efficiency. More specifically, the worry associated with anxiety reduces processing efficiency because it uses up valuable resources of the working memory system, but the compensatory use of additional effort will often prevent anxiety from impairing performance effectiveness. Thus, the central prediction of processing efficiency theory is that anxiety will generally impair processing efficiency more than performance effectiveness.

Eysenck and Calvo (1992) discussed the findings from seven different types of studies, all of which supported processing efficiency theory. When those high and low in anxiety have comparable levels of task performance, most theorists would conclude that anxiety has failed to have any effect. In contrast, it is assumed on processing efficiency theory that comparable levels of performance may be camouflaging adverse effects of anxiety on processing efficiency. Several studies have supported that prediction, but for space reasons only two will be mentioned here.

Weinberg and Hunt (1976) discovered that there was no effect of trait anxiety on performance effectiveness on a throwing task. However, they also assessed efficiency by measuring muscle activity during the throwing task, which revealed clear evidence that high anxiety impaired efficiency (1976, p.223):

High-anxious individuals anticipated significantly longer with the agonists and shorter with the antagonists than did the low-anxious group. Therefore, they were preparing for the throw in all of the muscles while low-anxious subjects were preparing mostly with the antagonist muscles. This implies that high-anxious subjects were using more energy than necessary, and expending it over a greater period of time, than were low-anxious subjects.

Eysenck (1989) used a different approach. Subjects were instructed to perform a letter-transformation task as well as possible, and to devote any spare processing capacity to making a simple motor response to an occasional auditory signal. It was assumed that subjects who performed the letter-transformation task efficiently would have more spare processing capacity than those who performed it inefficiently, and that this greater spare capacity would be reflected in faster responding to the auditory signal. Subjects high and low in trait anxiety did not differ in their performance on the letter-transformation task, so there was no effect of anxiety on performance effectiveness. However, the high trait-anxious subjects took significantly longer than the low trait-anxious subjects to respond to the auditory signals, suggesting that they had lower processing efficiency.

As was mentioned earlier, one of the major assumptions of processing efficiency theory is that the worry associated with high anxiety pre-empts some of the available working memory capacity. As a consequence, anxious individuals have reduced working memory capacity available for task performance. If we make the further assumption that more complex tasks make more use of working memory capacity than do simple tasks, then processing efficiency theory can provide an explanation for the finding that anxiety has more detrimental effects on complex than on easy tasks.

MacLeod and Donnellan (1993) investigated the hypothesis that anxiety reduces the working memory capacity available for performance of a task in a rather direct fashion. Subjects were presented with a grammatical reasoning task (e.g. XY: X is preceded by Y) involving the use of working memory, and had to decide as rapidly as possible whether the sentence accurately described the spatial order of the accompanying letter pair. In order to vary the demands on working memory capacity, subjects had to maintain either a low or a high memory load in the form of digits while performing each trial on the reasoning task. The findings are shown in Fig. 18.9. Anxiety had only a small effect on speed of performance on the reasoning task when the memory load made few demands on working memory capacity, but it had a substantial adverse effect on performance speed when the memory load made large demands on working memory capacity. These findings clearly support the view that anxiety reduces available working memory capacity.

The theoretical assumption that anxious individuals respond to inefficient processing by increased effort and the allocation of additional processing resources requires more consideration in the future. What is needed is a more detailed understanding of how these additional resources are used. Some headway so far as reading performance is concerned has been made by Calvo. In one study (Calvo, Ramos, & Eysenck, 1993), subjects high and low in test anxiety were asked to

read a passage that was presented to them sentence by sentence. In one condition, subjects were presented with distracting speech during the reading task, whereas there was no distraction in a second condition. There were no effects of test anxiety on performance effectiveness as assessed by the comprehension test. However, the two anxiety groups differed, in that the high test-anxious group made more use than the low test-anxious group of overt articulation (i.e. lip movements and vocal utterances) during the reading task, especially when there was distracting speech. Thus, at least some of the additional resources used by the high test-anxious subjects were devoted to overt articulation, perhaps because this facilitated rehearsal of the information presented in the text.

Section summary

There is convincing evidence that anxious individuals worry more than non-anxious individuals, especially about being evaluated by other people. This worry often has detrimental effects on performance. However, there is evidence that worry can also have a beneficial effect on motivation, leading to increased effort and/or the use of additional processing resources. As a consequence of these effects, anxiety is more

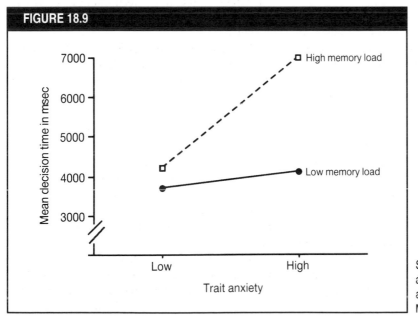

FIGURE 18.9

Speed of reasoning performance as a function of memory load and trait anxiety. Adapted from MacLeod and Donnellan (1993).

commonly associated with reduced processing efficiency than with reduced performance effectiveness. There is also evidence that anxiety reduces available working memory capacity, and this may explain why anxiety has more adverse effects on difficult than on easy tasks.

Depression

Much of the research on the effects of depression on performance has been carried out by Henry Ellis and his associates. They have investigated depression by means of mood manipulation rather than by studying depressed patients. The main reason for doing this is because it is easier to interpret the findings obtained (Leight & Ellis, 1981, p.251):

> Although it is important to understand memory processes of clinically diagnosed depressives, there is an inherent limitation in this endeavour; it does not involve the explicit manipulation of mood state. And without a direct manipulation of mood state, there is no clear way of separating these effects from any confounding related to the general syndrome associated with the clinical entity of depression.

Depressed individuals (whether clinically depressed or normals put into a depressed mood state) perform most tasks less well than non-depressed individuals (see Eysenck, 1992, for a review). Ellis and Ashbrook (1988) proposed a resource-allocation theory to account for the adverse effects of depression. According to this theory, depression reduces the processing capacity available as a consequence of task-irrelevant processing (e.g. negative thoughts about the self). The most obvious prediction from this theoretical position is that depressed patients should be at a greater disadvantage to normal controls on complex tasks with high processing demands than on simple tasks with much smaller demands.

Ellis, Thomas, and Rodriguez (1984) obtained evidence consistent with the predictions of this resource-allocation theory. Subjects were presented with incomplete sentences followed by two nouns, one of which fitted the sentence.

Selecting the appropriate noun was relatively straightforward in the low-effort condition (e.g. The girl was awakened by the frightening _____ [dream]), but was more difficult in the high-effort condition (e.g. The man was alarmed by the frightening _____ [dream]). There was a subsequent test of free recall for the words that completed the sentences. On the assumption that more processing resources were required in the high-effort than in the low-effort condition, it was predicted that any memory inferiority of sad or depressed subjects would be greater in the high-effort condition. As can be seen in Fig. 18.10, that is what was found.

The study by Ellis et al. (1984) indicated that sad or depressed mood can influence what happens at the time of learning. Ellis, Thomas, McFarland, and Lane (1985) demonstrated that depressed mood can also affect what happens at the time of retrieval. Subjects were initially presented with a mixture of base sentences (e.g. The hungry child opened the door) and elaborated sentences (e.g. The hungry child opened the door of the refrigerator). After that, subjects were placed in a depressed or neutral mood, and they were re-presented with the original sentences but with the adjectives missing (e.g. The _____ child opened the door). The task was to recall the missing adjectives. As can be seen in Fig. 18.11, the depressed subjects were much worse than those in neutral mood at taking advantage of the additional information provided by the elaborated sentences.

Processing resources versus effort

Ellis (e.g. Ellis & Ashbrook, 1988) argued in his resource-allocation theory that the poor memory performance of depressed individuals on demanding tasks could be explained by assuming that some of their available resources are depleted by task-irrelevant processing. Relevant evidence was reported by Ellis (1990), who asked subjects to verbalise their thoughts as they worked on a difficult learning task. Depressed subjects produced almost twice as many task-irrelevant thoughts as subjects in a neutral mood. Those subjects who produced the most task-irrelevant thoughts showed the poorest subsequent recall of the task.

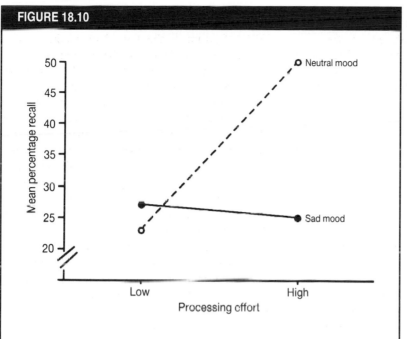

FIGURE 18.10

Recall performance as a function of mood (sad vs. neutral) and processing effort. Adapted from Ellis et al. (1984).

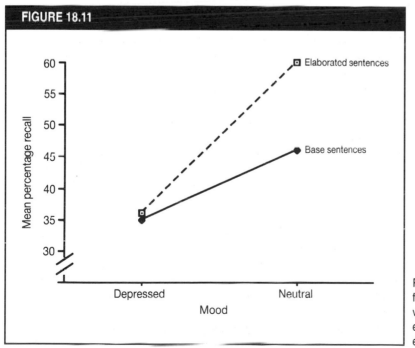

FIGURE 18.11

Recall performance as a function of mood (depressed vs. neutral) and sentence elaboration. Adapted from Ellis et al. (1985).

In spite of the successes of resource-allocation theory, there is a plausible alternative explanation for many of the findings. Depressed individuals report that they feel apathetic, lacking in energy, and generally poorly motivated. If these self-reports are genuine (and there is no reason to doubt their accuracy), then it may be that depressed individuals perform poorly on demanding tasks simply because they choose not to invest the processing resources necessary to perform well.

Some relevant evidence was obtained by Hertel and Hardin (1990), in a study involving homophones such as pear/pair or pain/pane. Subjects who were naturally depressed and subjects in a neutral mood were asked questions that included homophones (e.g. "What colour is a pear?"). Subsequently, they heard the homophones and were told to write down the spelling of each one. The tendency to write down the spellings that corresponded to those used in the questions provided a measure of implicit memory (memory not involving conscious recollection). Finally, the subjects were given a recognition memory test for the homophones presented in the questions. This test was either undirected, in the sense that no special instructions were given, or it was directed, with subjects being instructed to remember how they had spelled the word and to recollect the sentence in which the word had been presented initially.

The findings are shown in Fig. 18.12. Depression had no effect on the implicit memory test (homophone spelling), but it had an adverse effect on undirected recognition memory. There was no adverse effect of depression on directed recognition memory. What do these findings mean? They suggest that the reason for the depressed subjects' poor performance on the undirected recognition memory task was due to a lack of effort (or "cognitive initiative" as Hertel & Hardin, 1990, called it) rather than to inadequate processing resources. On the directed recognition memory test, the subjects were encouraged to use more effort, or cognitive initiative, and there was no evidence of any detrimental effects of depression on performance.

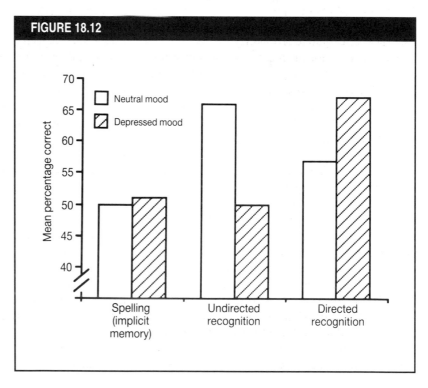

FIGURE 18.12

Memory performance as a function of mood (depressed vs. neutral) and type of memory test (spelling: undirected recognition; or directed recognition). Based on data in Hertel and Hardin (1990).

In sum, the available evidence (reviewed by Hartlage, Alloy, Vazquez, & Dykman, 1993) suggests that reduced processing capacity and poor motivation both contribute to the generally inferior cognitive performance of depressed individuals. It is a matter for future research to establish precisely the relative contributions of these two factors.

CHAPTER SUMMARY

Despite the importance of the relationship between cognition and emotion, most cognitive psychologists have not considered emotional factors in their research and theorising. However, there are signs of growing interest in this area, and some headway has been made.

Does affect require cognition? Affective responses can occur without any conscious awareness of cognitive processing, but that does not rule out the possibility of pre-conscious cognitive processing. It is difficult to investigate pre-conscious processing, but it is likely that such processing generally precedes any affective reaction in those cases where there is no conscious awareness of cognitive processing.

Freud argued for the importance of repression or motivated forgetting of anxiety-provoking events. He also proposed the notion of "primary repression", in which there is no conscious perception of threatening environmental stimuli. Perceptual defence (the tendency for the recognition threshold of emotionally charged words to be higher than that of neutral words) resembles primary repression. Much of the early work on perceptual defence was suspect, but more recent studies provide good support for its existence. Repression in memory has been studied under laboratory and clinical conditions (e.g. child sexual abuse), but the findings are somewhat inconclusive. There are ethical and methodological obstacles in the way of providing an adequate experimental test of repression theory in the laboratory, and it is difficult to check the accuracy of adults' repressed memories of childhood sexual abuse or other traumatic events.

Studies of mood and memory have mostly been based on Bower's semantic network theory. There is experimental support for mood congruity (material that is congruent with the learner's mood is remembered better than material that is incongruent) and mood-state-dependent recall (material is better remembered when the subject's mood at learning and at test is the same rather than different). However, various complications have emerged, and these have led to new theoretical formulations. Bower has proposed a causal belongingness theory, according to which memory is best when the learner perceives that his or her mood state has been caused by the learning material. Eich and Metcalfe argued that mood has stronger effects on memory for internal events than for external events.

Studies of attention and perception have revealed some differences between anxious and depressed individuals. Anxious individuals exhibit a range of attentional effects (e.g. selective attentional bias; distractibility; narrowing of attention) and they also exhibit an interpretive bias. Depressed individuals also show an interpretive bias, but they generally fail to show the attentional effects found in anxious individuals. To some extent, the cognitive effects of each emotion are unique and depend on the function it serves.

Depression generally has an adverse effect on cognitive performance, and anxiety often does as well. According to Eysenck and Calvo, anxiety is associated with worry, which has a negative effect on processing efficiency. However, worry also has motivational effects, and these motivational effects can compensate for the adverse effects of anxiety on efficiency. As a consequence, anxiety typically has more of a detrimental effect on processing efficiency than on performance effectiveness. Anxiety reduces the available capacity of working memory, and this has more serious consequences for the performance of hard than of easy tasks. Ellis has argued that depressed mood causes task-irrelevant processing and reduced processing capacity. In addition, however, the inferior cognitive performance of depressed individuals probably stems in part from their low level of motivation.

FURTHER READING

Bower, G.H. (1992). How might emotions affect learning? In S.-A. Christianson (Ed.), *The handbook of emotion and memory: Research and theory*. Hillsdale, NJ: Lawrence Erlbaum Associates Inc.

Eysenck, M.W. (1992). *Anxiety: The cognitive perspective*. Hove, UK: Lawrence Erlbaum Associates Ltd. Although this book focuses on the relationship between anxiety and cognition, there is also some coverage of the effects of depression.

Loftus, E. F. (1993). The reality of repressed memories. *American Psychologist, 48*, 518–537. Practical issues relating to the attitudes of therapists, judges, and jurors to claims about real-life repressed memories are discussed at length.

19

Cognitive Psychology: Present and Future

INTRODUCTION

The various facets of contemporary cognitive psychology have been discussed at some length in the previous chapters of this book. Cognitive psychologists have made considerable theoretical and empirical headway in making sense of human cognition, especially in recent years. Some of this progress is negative, in the sense that we now know that certain theoretical approaches that seemed promising at one time are actually dead ends. Of course, eliminating erroneous approaches is not the same as discovering the correct approach, but the history of science reveals that it is usually an important step along the way.

Most of the emphasis in this book has been on specific theories and bodies of research. In contrast, the primary aims of this chapter are to provide more global evaluations of the entire approach of cognitive psychology and of its three main perspectives (experimental cognitive psychology; cognitive neuropsychology; and cognitive science).

EXPERIMENTAL COGNITIVE PSYCHOLOGY

Strengths

The recent dramatic increase in the impact of cognitive neuropsychology and of cognitive science on cognitive psychology has led many people to de-emphasise the contribution made by the more traditional experimental cognitive approach. In fact, both cognitive neuropsychology and cognitive science owe much to experimental cognitive psychology. Cognitive neuropsychology became a significant discipline approximately 20 years after cognitive psychology. It was only when cognitive psychologists had developed reasonable accounts of normal human cognition that the performance of brain-damaged patients could be understood fully. Before that, it was very difficult to decide which patterns of cognitive impairment were of theoretical importance. In a similar fashion, the computational modelling activities of cognitive scientists are often informed to a major extent by pre-computational psychological theories.

One of the most striking successes of experimental cognitive psychology has been the way its approach has influenced several areas of psychology. For example, social, developmental, and clinical psychology have all become decidedly more "cognitive" in recent years. Many of the experimental paradigms used by researchers in those areas were initially developed in the research laboratories of experimental cognitive psychologists.

One of the greatest strengths of experimental cognitive psychology is its versatility: as we have seen throughout this book, experimental studies have provided valuable insights across the whole range of human cognition to a greater extent than has been the case with either cognitive neuropsychology or cognitive science. One of the reasons for this versatility is that experimental cognitive psychologists have an ever-increasing range of techniques at their disposal. Of particular significance for the future are likely to be the various techniques allowing relatively direct access to brain activity (see Chapter 1). These techniques have already demonstrated their great usefulness in areas such as perception (Chapter 2), attention (Chapter 5), and memory (Chapter 7).

Weaknesses

It has often been argued that cognitive psychology replaced behaviourism some time ago as the dominant paradigm or approach in psychology. However, Costall (1991) argued that the cognitive approach represents less of a departure from behaviourism than is generally believed. As he pointed out, both approaches rely heavily on detailed measures of behaviour, and both attempt to account for behaviour in terms of the processes occurring between stimulus and response. Miller, Galanter, and Pribram (1960) wrote one of the first books in cognitive psychology, claiming (p.12) that the aim of cognitive psychology is to put "a little wisdom between the stimulus and response". Later on in the same book they made the following revealing admission (p.211): "How does one characterise a position that seems to be such a mixture of elements usually considered incompatible? Deep in the middle of this dilemma it

suddenly occurred to us that we were subjective behaviourists."

Cognitive psychologists are generally much more interested than behaviourists in specifying the internal processes intervening between stimulus and response. However, most of the experiments carried out by cognitive psychologists involve a closer link between stimulus (e.g. presentation of a task) and response (e.g. task performance) than is usually recognised. An attempt is usually made to maximise the impact of the stimulus on internal cognitive processes by instructing subjects to process the task stimuli, by not presenting task-irrelevant stimuli, and so on. An attempt is also made to maximise the impact of internal task-relevant cognitive processes on responses by instructing subjects to respond as rapidly as possible. In other words, experiments are designed so that responses are closely determined by task stimuli in much the same way as was true of most behaviourist research. These limitations of cognitive research also apply to most of the computer simulations carried out in cognitive science.

Ecological validity

A recurring criticism of experimental cognitive psychology is that it lacks ecological validity (i.e. the findings cannot readily be extrapolated to real life). For example, so that the experimenter can produce a close link between stimulus and response, subjects in most cognitive experiments are well-motivated, undistracted, have no other goals competing with that of task completion, and know exactly what they are supposed to do with the task stimuli. The near-optimal conditions in which cognitive psychologists usually assess cognition can be contrasted with those prevailing in the workplace: many office workers have multiple work goals to satisfy, they have to devote time and effort to prioritising goals, they are distracted by phone calls and by people knocking on their door, and their behaviour is substantially affected by social pressures.

The $64,000 question is whether this really matters. That it may do so can be illustrated by means of an analogy. We could study the limits of people's mobility by having them run races of different distances on a fast running track wearing running spikes, singlet, and shorts. Measures of some of the processes involved could be obtained by recording heart rate, respiration rate, and so on. However, we would not expect that the information obtained would be of much value when predicting people's speeds when laden down with shopping or walking with their children, nor would we expect to be able to make accurate predictions of their heart rate or respiration rate under those conditions.

In the real world, people are constantly behaving in ways that will have an impact on the environment (e.g. turning on the television to watch a favourite programme). In other words, the responses that people make often change the stimulus situation. In contrast, most of the research of cognitive psychologists and cognitive scientists involves what Wachtel (1973) referred to as the "implacable [unyielding] experimenter". That is to say, the sequence of stimuli that the experimenter presents to the subject is not influenced by the behaviour of the subject, but is determined by the experimenter's predetermined plan.

As a consequence of the implacable experimenter, cognitive psychology is unduly limited in a number of respects. Consider what cognitive psychologists have discovered about attention (see Chapter 5). Many of the characteristics of divided and focused attention have been discovered, but it could be argued that fundamental aspects of attention have been de-emphasised. The focus of attention in most research is determined by the experimenter's instructions. As a consequence, relatively little is known of the factors that normally influence the focus of attention: relevance of stimuli to current goals; unexpectedness of stimuli; threateningness of stimuli; intensity of stimuli; and so on. This is an important limitation, because it would be impossible to predict someone's cognitive processes and behaviour in most situations in the absence of detailed knowledge of the factors determining attentional focus.

Another issue related to ecological validity is what has been called the "decoupling" problem. If a researcher wants to explore some aspect of, say, human memory, then an attempt is usually made to decouple the memory system from other cognitive

systems, and to minimise the impact of motivational and emotional factors on performance. Even if it is possible to study the memory system in isolation, it is clear that it usually operates in interaction with other functional systems. Accordingly, the more successful we are in examining part of the cognitive system in isolation, the less our data are likely to tell us about cognition in everyday life. For example, there are influences of emotional states on cognition, and of cognition on emotional states (see Chapter 18). As a consequence, the usual strategy of ignoring emotional factors cannot be recommended if we want to generalise from the circumscribed emotional states studied in the laboratory to the very different states often found in everyday life. In sum, we have seen that there are problems of ecological validity with much experimental cognitive psychology.

The key point can be expressed by referring to the distinction between internal validity (the validity of research within the confines of the context in which it is carried out) and external validity (the validity of research outside the research situation). In terms of that distinction, it could be argued that much of cognitive psychology is rather higher in internal than in external validity. However, it is only fair to point out that this criticism has lost some of its force in recent years. There are several examples in this book of the increased willingness of cognitive psychologists to move closer to "real life". For example, researchers have become more and more interested in perceptual processing of the human face (see Chapter 3), which is a highly significant stimulus in everyday life. In Chapter 5 there is a discussion of attentional and automatic processes in connection with the "real-world" phenomenon of absent-mindedness. Chapter 8 is devoted to everyday memory, Chapter 16 dealt with instances of skilled thinking in everyday life, and much of Chapters 12 and 13 is concerned with the important everyday activity of reading.

Although many experimental cognitive psychologists are aware that much of their research is somewhat lacking in ecological validity, they are rightly sceptical of a wholesale abandonment of experimental rigour and control in favour of a totally naturalistic approach. There are so many variables influencing behaviour in the real world, and it is so difficult to manipulate them systematically, that it can become almost impossible to assess the relative importance of each variable in determining behaviour. It is hard to achieve the desirable combination of experimental rigour and ecological validity, but some of the more successful endeavours in that direction have been discussed throughout this book.

Other issues

One of the most puzzling features of experimental cognitive psychology is the reluctance to take individual differences seriously. The typical research strategy is to use analysis of variance to assess statistically the effects of various experimental manipulations on cognitive performance, and to relegate individual differences to the error term. In effect, cognitive psychologists who adopt this strategy seem to be assuming implicitly that individual differences are unimportant and do not interact with any of the experimental manipulations.

The reality appears to be very different. Bowers (1973) considered 11 studies in which the percentages of the variance accounted for by individual differences, by situational factors, and by their interaction could be assessed. On average, individual differences accounted for 11.3% of the variance, the situation for 10.2%, and the interaction between individual differences and situation for 20.8%. In the light of such evidence, it seems perverse to ignore individual differences altogether!

A final problem with experimental cognitive psychology is that the emphasis has been on relatively specific theories which are applicable to only a narrow range of cognitive tasks. What has been lacking is an overarching theoretical architecture (see Chapter 1). Such an architecture would fulfil the function of clarifying the interrelationships among different components of the cognitive system. In recent years, several such candidate cognitive architectures have been proposed: most notably, Newell's (1990) SOAR architecture and Anderson's (1983, 1993) ACT models. Both of these cognitive architectures are based on production systems. These architectures have been applied to a wide range of tasks. However, their scope is still limited, in that their coverage is quite selective. Furthermore, in general, the research community has not abandoned specific theories in favour of using these architectures; researchers do not appear to be convinced that either of these is the "one true cognitive architecture". As long as there is not an overarching and accepted architecture, experimental cognitive psychology will always suffer from a certain lack of integration at the theoretical level.

COGNITIVE NEUROPSYCHOLOGY

Strengths

The cognitive neuropsychological approach has become much more influential within cognitive psychology over the past 20 years. One of the main reasons is that evidence about the cognitive performance of brain-damaged patients provides a good test-bed for evaluating theories originally based on the performance of normal individuals. For example, some of the most powerful evidence that there are at least two different routes involved in reading has come from studying brain-damaged patients largely lacking one route or the other (see Chapter 12). However, the contribution of cognitive neuropsychology does not consist only of testing pre-existing theories. Consider, for example, the study of amnesic patients (see Chapter 8). It became increasingly apparent that they could display good memory performance provided that conscious recollection of previous events was not required, and this finding was instrumental in establishing the key theoretical distinction between explicit and implicit memory. Thus, findings within cognitive neuropsychology have been used to generate new theories as well as to test existing ones.

The cognitive neuropsychological approach has been applied to several areas, including perception, attention, memory, and language. However, as was probably apparent from our treatment of these topics, cognitive neuropsychologists have carried out more research on language than on other topics, and rather little in areas such as reasoning or problem solving.

Why has language functioning received a disproportionate amount of research effort? In part, it reflects the increased interest in language by cognitive psychologists. In addition, however, it seems that language lends itself especially well to the cognitive neuropsychological approach. The comprehension and production of language involve a number of different skills (i.e. those of reading, listening, writing, and speaking), each of which has various modules or cognitive processes associated with it. In a nutshell, the investigation of brain-damaged patients by cognitive neuropsychologists has proved particularly successful in the identification of some of the modules involved in cognitive functioning, and the evidence so far suggests there may be more modules involved in language processing than in most other cognitive activities.

Weaknesses

There are various important cognitive activities (e.g. creative thought and organisational planning) that appear to be relatively resistant to a modular approach. For example, Fodor (1983, p.119) argued that nothing is known about the neuro-psychology of thought, adding "there is good reason why nothing is known about it—namely that there is nothing to know about it—in the case of central processes you get an approximation to universal connectivity, hence no stable neural architecture".

Although the study of language may be regarded as the "jewel in the crown" of cognitive neuropsychology, there are nevertheless signific-ant limitations apparent in the research that has been carried out. There has been a substantial amount of work on the reading and spelling of individual words by brain-damaged patients, but rather little on larger units of language. Many important language processes are involved in reading and spelling single words, but equally there are important additional factors (e.g. contextual influences; structural themes) which are only of relevance to larger units of language (see Chapter 12).

In more general terms, many of the weaknesses of experimental cognitive psychology apply equally to cognitive neuropsychology. Of particular importance is the tendency for studies in cognitive neuropsychology to lack ecological validity.

As well as the limitations of cognitive neuropsychology at the empirical level, there are further limitations at the theoretical level. The available neuropsychological evidence suggests that speaking and writing differ in that there are separate lexicons which contain information about the spoken and written forms of words, but which are similar in that they share the same semantic system. According to Ellis and Young (1988, p.223), "the semantic system is the (grossly underspecified) component in which word meanings are represented". The semantic system presumably plays some part (albeit rather modest) in planning the meaning of what is to be said (Garrett's, 1984, message level) and in the planning process in writing (Hayes & Flower, 1986). These planning activities are of fundamental importance to speaking and writing, but so far cognitive neuropsychology has not been able to provide anything approximating an adequate theoretical account of how they occur.

Why has cognitive neuropsychology been so uninformative about the planning processes involved in speaking and writing? Cognitive neuropsychology has been largely concerned with the identification of modules. Most of the modules identified by cognitive neuropsychologists are relatively peripheral (i.e. they are parts of the cognitive system that are close to either the input or the output of information), whereas planning processes occur at a relatively central level within the processing system. In other words, cognitive neuropsychology seems rather poorly equipped to provide detailed theoretical treatments of important cognitive functions that are central and non-modular.

In fairness to cognitive neuropsychologists, it should be pointed out that traditional cognitive psychology suffers from similar problems. There are good reasons for this. Central cognitive functions occur some time after the stimulus input has taken place, and can thus be difficult to manipulate effectively. They are also somewhat removed from response output, and so behavioural measures often provide a rather indirect reflection of their functioning. As a consequence, it will probably always be more difficult to pin-point central rather than peripheral processes.

COGNITIVE SCIENCE

For most of this book, we have concentrated on one dimension of the cognitive science perspective, namely the cross-disciplinary interaction between artificial intelligence and experimental cognitive psychology (for other interactions see Gardner, 1985). Many different opinions have been offered about the success (or otherwise) of the cognitive science approach. Some have merely sneered at practitioners in this area, dismissing them as an "artificial intelligentsia" whose activities have no tangible relationship to actual human behaviour. Others have been markedly more enthusiastic, none more so than Allport (1980, p.31): "The advent of Artificial Intelligence is the single most important development in the history of psychology."

The cognitive science approach will be evaluated shortly. Before doing so, however, we will consider the key issue of the degree to which computer processes are equivalent to the processes of the mind.

Computer programs and cognition
Many psychologists have argued that computer programs are no more than a metaphor, whereas others wish to go much further. According to Pylyshyn (1979, p.435):

> the notion of computation ... is not a metaphor but part of a literal description of cognitive activity ... it seems to me that computation, and all that it entails regarding rule-governed transformations on intentionally interpreted symbolic expressions, applies just as literally to mental activity as it does to the activity of digital computers.

Some cognitive scientists subscribe to the view that if a computer can be programmed to behave like a human, then it is intelligent in the same way as a human. So a program that enabled a computer to behave as if it understood Chinese would be able to understand Chinese in the same way as a person does. This position is often called the "Strong A.I. Position", and can be traced back to one of the founders of computational science, Alan Turing. The so-called "Turing Test" essentially proposed that if one could not distinguish the behaviour of a computer from that of a human on a given task, then the machine was intelligent like the human (see Turing, 1950).

Searle (1989) has countered this view clearly and forcefully. He admitted that cognitive scientists have been reasonably successful in using computer programs to simulate aspects of human cognitive performance, but claimed that they cannot duplicate human cognition; that is, crucial ingredients of human cognition are missing in the computer simulation. Searle supported this position by means of the so-called Chinese room thought experiment.

Imagine there is a person locked in a room containing several baskets full of Chinese symbols. This person does not understand Chinese at all, but is provided with a rule book in English which indicates how the Chinese symbols are to be manipulated. Thus, for example (Searle, 1989; p.32), one rule might be: "Take a squiggle-squiggle sign out of basket number one and put it next to a squoggle-squoggle sign from basket number two." The person armed with these rules might be able to answer questions in Chinese by passing the appropriate Chinese symbols out of the room. Indeed, the answers might be indistinguishable from those of a native Chinese person. However, this excellent level of performance would be achieved without the person involved having any understanding of Chinese. By analogy, even computers that have been programmed to respond in the same way as people are simulating human cognition rather than duplicating it: the computer has no understanding of what it is doing or why it is doing it. The computer program manipulates symbols in a purely syntactic manner; it does not know the meaning of these symbols. Searle argued that human brains differ crucially from computers precisely because they do manifest a high degree of understanding; they know the meaning of the symbols they manipulate. In essence, they are semantic rather than syntactic systems.

It should be pointed out that meaning plays more of a role in the Chinese room than was admitted by Searle (1989), in that the person in the room is able to extract meaning from the rule book written in English. However, it is probable that the key issue cannot be decided empirically, and that it is more a matter of what you accept as reasonable assumptions about the nature of artificial and human intelligence. At the very least, Searle's position signals an important point to keep in mind about computer models, namely that models of human cognitive functioning are only models. There is no guarantee that a given computational model of a specific behaviour actually captures the way in which humans produce that behaviour. The same specific behaviour can be modelled in many different ways. For example, the behaviour of drivers in the United Kingdom could be characterised by a model involving the following rule: "Drive in such a way that the steering wheel is nearest to the centre line of the road." A computer model incorporating that rule might simulate the driving behaviour of British people, but another model using a rule about driving on the left-hand side of the road would produce the same behaviour.

Strengths

There are a number of major items on the credit side of the balance sheet as far as cognitive science is concerned. The computational modelling of psychological theories enforces a strong test of their adequacy. Many theories from traditional cognitive psychology have been found to be inadequate because crucial aspects of the human information-processing system were (or could not be) spelled out computationally. For example, Marr (1982) discovered that previous theoretical assumptions about feature detectors in visual perception were over-simplified when he began to construct programs to specify precisely how feature extraction might occur (see Chapter 2). The intellectual discipline associated with the requirement to specify every process in detail often

gives the cognitive scientist a significant advantage over traditional cognitive psychologists.

A second advantage of the cognitive science approach is that, in theoretical terms, it tends to be very advanced. As a consequence, cognitive scientists have been more disposed than other cognitive psychologists to address fundamental or high-level theoretical issues concerning the forms of representation and the processes to be found in the human information-processing system. As we saw in Chapter 1, cognitive scientists have proposed computer models based on semantic networks, production systems, and connectionist networks. All of these modelling techniques can be applied to a wide range of topics within cognitive psychology. For example, connectionist networks have been used in theories of perception, learning, memory, and reading (see Chapters 6 and 12). Indeed, we have seen that some of these computational models have been proposed as general cognitive architectures that can be applied to the understanding of all cognitive functioning (see, for example, Newell, 1990; Rumelhart et al., 1986b). Such widely applicable theoretical notions have emerged less frequently from the work of traditional cognitive psychologists and cognitive neuropsychologists.

Many theorists have argued that connectionism and models based on parallel-distributed processing offer the prospect of providing better accounts of human cognition than previous approaches within cognitive science (see Chapters 2, 3, and 6). Some of the potential advantages of the newer approach can be seen with reference to the following quotation from Churchland (1989, p.100):

> The brain seems to be a computer with a radically different style. For example, the brain changes as it learns, it appears to store and process information in the same places ... Most obviously, the brain is a parallel machine, in which many interactions occur at the same time in many channels.

Connectionist models with their parallel-distributed processing resemble brain functioning more closely than do traditional computer models based on serial processing. Furthermore, their modifiable connections and their use of mechanisms such as the backward propagation of errors mean that such models can learn in the sense of progressively improving their performance (see Chapter 1).

In spite of the advantages of the connectionist approach, it appears to offer relatively low-level accounts of cognitive systems, and so may be unable to explain high-level systems such as the central executive component of the working memory system. In the words of Baddeley (1990, p.376):

> Models of a connectionist type may be appropriate for opaque processes, processes that operate relatively automatically, while models based on symbol processing will continue to provide a better account of those aspects of cognition that are transparent and open to conscious manipulation and control.

Weaknesses

Human cognition is influenced by several potentially conflicting motivational and emotional factors, many of which may be operative at the same time. This state of affairs can be contrasted (Boden, 1988, p.262) with the "single-minded nature of virtually all current computer programs". In future, the complexity of human purposes may be captured by more sophisticated computer programs, but the feasibility of devising such programs remains an article of faith.

Norman (1980) pointed out that human functioning involves an interplay between a cognitive system (which he called the Pure Cognitive System) and a biological system (which he called the Regulatory System). Much of the activity of the Pure Cognitive System is determined by the various needs of the Regulatory System, including the need for survival, for food and water, and for protection of oneself and one's family. Cognitive science, in common with most of the rest of cognitive psychology, focuses on the Pure Cognitive System and virtually ignores the key role played by the Regulatory System.

A final difference between humans and computers is that the behaviour of humans typically has

a social and moral dimension to it, whereas that of computers does not. The essence of that which computers lack and we possess in this area was expressed as follows by Shotter (1991, p.58):

> I want to argue that: (1) The computer model fails to characterise the way in which people's everyday actions are always "placed" within a social and moral, as well as a historically developed, political order, actual or imagined; (2) that the maintenance in good repair of that order is due to the social accountability of those "within" it; (3) that such accountability depends upon a first-person ability to distinguish eventualities for which one is oneself responsible, and those which lie outside one's own agency to control ... Computers, lacking any sense of being individually and personally "placed" in relation to those around them ... would lack the practical-moral social knowledge required to act in a socially responsible and responsive manner ... In short, they are unable to be accountable in their conduct to others.

However, the fact that the analogy between computer and human cognitive functioning breaks down in various ways may or may not pose serious problems. In spite of the fact that virtually all analogies or metaphors break down at some point, there are numerous examples in the history of science (e.g. Rutherford's planetary model of the atom) where analogies or metaphors have proved very useful in advancing theoretical understanding. The computer certainly provides a more plausible metaphor for brain functioning than most previous metaphors (e.g. the brain has been likened to a catapult, a telephone exchange, and a mill!). The computer metaphor has the advantage that the computer much more closely approximates the complexity of the human brain than does the catapult, the telephone exchange, or the mill. The computer metaphor has the additional advantage over previous metaphors that computers can be used in very flexible ways. As a consequence, the "fit" between brain and computer functioning has improved considerably in recent years, and can be relied on to improve still further in the future.

CHAPTER SUMMARY

Cognitive psychology has made considerable progress in the past 40 years or so, and it is now generally accepted as the dominant paradigm in psychology. It offers good accounts of the information processing triggered by external stimuli, but is less convincing in its attempts to explain the cognitive processes associated with active interactions with, or transformations of, the environment.

Experimental cognitive psychology has been successful in its own right and in its influence on the development of cognitive neuropsychology and cognitive science. One of its particular strengths is its versatility, as is illustrated by the way in which experimentation on normal individuals has proved of value across the whole area of cognitive psychology. Its limitations include some lack of ecological validity, the failure to develop overarching theoretical systems or architectures, and the relative neglect of individual differences. However, these limitations are increasingly being overcome.

Cognitive neuropsychology has become much more influential over the past 20 years Findings within cognitive neuropsychology have been used to test existing theories and to generate new ones that are applicable to normal cognitive functioning. Cognitive neuropsychology has been very successful in the task of identifying several of the modules or independent processors involved in cognition, especially in the field of language. However, it has failed to shed much light on some aspects of language such as the planning processes involved in speaking and writing. There is a suspicion that cognitive neuropsychology is better suited to an analysis of relatively peripheral modules than more central (and possibly non-modular) cognitive functions.

Cognitive science has been influential in the development of important new theoretical approaches and cognitive architectures. Connectionism and parallel-distributed processing models have been very important here, because they appear to offer more plausible accounts of learning and memory than were provided by previous models. Cognitive science has the strengths that it has required theorists to be very precise in their theoretical accounts of cognition, and it has provided the best available means for modelling cognitive processes. However, most computer models lack a social and moral dimension, and they do not take account of non-cognitive factors (e.g. biological influences). Although the computer analogy to human cognition breaks down at these points, it is still true that the computer analogy is rather adaptable, and that the "fit" between computer and brain functioning has improved progressively.

In view of the varied strengths and weaknesses of the three major perspectives in cognitive psychology, there are strong grounds for arguing that all three approaches are required. If all three approaches converge on an agreed theory in a particular area, then we can have some confidence that the theory is approximately correct. As the old saying has it, "Divided we fall, united we stand!"

FURTHER READING

Johnson-Laird, P.N. (1993). *The computer and the mind.* London: Fontana. Johnson-Laird is a leading authority on cognitive science, and in this book he provides an interesting account of that approach.

Still, A., & Costall, A. (Eds.) (1991). *Against cognitivism: Alternative foundations for cognitive psychology.* Hemel Hempstead, UK: Harvester Wheatsheaf. This book has proved controversial, with most cognitive psychologists disagreeing with its attacks on contemporary cognitive psychology. However, it contains several thought-provoking ideas.

Von Eckardt, B. (1993). *What is cognitive science?* Cambridge, MA: MIT Press. This is an extended attempt from a philosophy of science perspective to characterise cognitive science and where it is going.

References

Abbot, V., Black, J.B., & Smith, E.E. (1985). The representation of scripts in memory. *Journal of Memory and Language, 24,* 179–199.

Abelson, R.P. (1981). Psychological status of the script concept. *American Psychologist, 36,* 715–729.

Adams, D. (1979). *The hitch-hiker's guide to the galaxy.* London: Pan.

Adams, J.L. (1979). *Conceptual blockbusting: A guide to better ideas* (2nd Edn.). New York: W.W. Norton.

Adamson, R.E., & Taylor, D.W. (1954). Functional fixedness as related to elapsed time and set. *Journal of Experimental Psychology, 47,* 221–226.

Adelson, B. (1981). Problem solving and the development of abstract categories in programming languages. *Memory and Cognition, 9,* 422–433.

Afriat, S.N. (1982). *The ring of linked rings.* London: Duckworth.

Ahn, W.-K., Brewer, W., & Mooncy, R.J. (1992). Schema acquisition from a single example. *Journal of Experimental Psychology: Learning, Memory, and Cognition, 18,* 391–412.

Alba, J.W., & Hasher, L. (1983). Is memory schematic? *Psychological Bulletin, 93,* 203–231.

Allport, D.A. (1980). Attention and performance. In G. Claxton (Ed.), *Cognitive psychology: New directions.* London: Routledge & Kegan Paul.

Allport, D.A. (1989). Visual attention. In M.I. Posner (Ed.), *Foundations of cognitive science.* Cambridge, MA: MIT Press.

Allport, D.A. (1993). Attention and control: Have we been asking the wrong questions? A critical review of twenty-five years. In D.E. Meyer & S.M. Kornblum (Eds.), *Attention and performance* (Vol. XIV). London: MIT Press.

Allport, D.A., Antonis, B., & Reynolds, P. (1972). On the division of attention: A disproof of the single channel hypothesis. *Quarterly Journal of Experimental Psychology, 24,* 225–235.

Anderson, J.R. (1976). *Language, memory, and thought.* Hillsdale, NJ: Lawrence Erlbaum Associates Inc.

Anderson, J.R. (1978) Arguments concerning representations from mental imagery. *Psychological Review, 85,* 249–277.

Anderson, J.R. (1982). Acquisition of cognitive skill. *Psychological Review, 89,* 396–406.

Anderson, J.R. (1983). *The architecture of cognition.* Harvard: Harvard University Press.

Anderson, J.R. (1987a). Skill acquisition: Compilation of weak-method problem solutions. *Psychological Review, 94,* 192–210.

Anderson, J.R. (1987b). Methodologies for study ving human knowledge. *Behavioral and Brain Sciences, 10,* 467–505.

Anderson, J.R. (1989). A theory of the origins of human knowledge. *Artificial Intelligence, 40,* 313–351.

Anderson, J.R. (1993). *Rules of the mind.* Hillsdale, NJ: Lawrence Erlbaum Associates Inc.

Anderson, J.R., Boyle, C.F., & Reiser, B.J. (1985). Intelligent tutoring systems. *Science, 228,* 456–462.

Anderson, J.R., Greeno, J.G., Kline, P.J., & Neves, D.M. (1981). Acquisition of problem solving skill. In J.R. Anderson (Ed.), *Cognitive skills and their acquisition*. Hillsdale, NJ: Lawrence Erlbaum Associates Inc.

Anderson, J.R., & Reiser, B.J. (1985). The LISP tutor. *Byte, 10,* 159–175.

Anderson, R.C., & Ortony, A. (1975). On putting apples in bottles: A problem of polysemy. *Cognitive Psychology, 7,* 167–180.

Anderson, R.C., & Pichert, J.W. (1978). Recall of previously unrecallable information following a shift in perspective. *Journal of Verbal Learning and Verbal Behavior, 17,* 1–12.

Anderson, S.A., & Conway, M.A. (1993). Investigating the structure of autobiographical memories. *Journal of Experimental Psychology: Learning, Memory, and Cognition, 19,* 1178–1196.

Andrews, A.D. (1993). Review of "deduction". *Behavioral and Brain Sciences, 16,* 334.

Anzai, Y., & Simon, H.A. (1979). The theory of learning by doing. *Psychological Review, 86,* 124–180.

Arbib, M.A. (1987). Many levels: More than one is algorithmic. *Behavioral and Brain Sciences, 10,* 478–479.

Armstrong, S.L., Gleitman, L.R., & Gleitman, H. (1983). What some concepts might not be. *Cognition, 13,* 263–308.

Ashley, W.R., Harper, R.S., & Runyon, D.L. (1951). The perceived size of coins in normal and hypnotically induced economic states. *American Journal of Psychology, 64,* 564–572.

Atkinson, R.C., & Raugh, M.R. (1975). An application of the mnemonic keyword method to the acquisition of a Russian vocabulary. *Journal of Experimental Psychology: Human Learning and Memory, 104,* 126–133.

Atkinson, R.C., & Shiffrin, R.M. (1968). Human memory: A proposed system and its control processes. In K.W. Spence & J.T. Spence (Eds.), *The psychology of learning and motivation* (Vol. 2). London: Academic Press.

Atkinson, R.C., & Shiffrin, R.M. (1971). The control of short-term memory. *Scientific American, 225,* 82–90.

Atwood, M.E., Masson, M.E., & Polson, P.G. (1980). Further exploration with a process model for water jug problems. *Memory and Cognition, 8,* 182–192.

Atwood, M.E., & Polson, P.G. (1976). A process model for water jug problems. *Cognitive Psychology, 8,* 191–216.

Baars, B.J. (1988). *A cognitive theory of consciousness*. New York: Cambridge University Press.

Baars, B.J., Motley, M.T., & MacKay, D.G. (1975). Output editing for lexical status from artificially elicited slips of the tongue. *Journal of Verbal Learning and Verbal Behavior, 14,* 382–391.

Bach, K. (1993). Getting down to cases. *Behavioral and Brain Sciences, 16,* 334–335.

Baddeley, A.D. (1979). Working memory and reading. In P.A. Kolers, M.E. Wrolstad, & H. Bouma (Eds.), *Processing of visible language*. New York: Plenum .

Baddeley, A.D. (1982). Domains of recollection. *Psychological Review, 89,* 708–729.

Baddeley, A.D. (1984). Neuropsychological evidence and the semantic/episodic distinction. *Behavioral and Brain Sciences, 7,* 238–239.

Baddeley, A.D. (1986). *Working memory*. Oxford: Oxford University Press.

Baddeley, A.D. (1990). *Human memory: Theory and practice*. Hove, UK: Lawrence Erlbaum Associates Ltd.

Baddeley, A.D., Grant, S., Wight, E., & Thomson, N. (1975). Imagery and visual working memory. In P.M.A. Rabbitt & S. Dornic (Eds.), *Attention and performance* (Vol. V). London: Academic Press.

Baddeley, A.D., & Hitch, G.J. (1974). Working memory. In G.H. Bower (Ed.), *The psychology of learning and motivation* (Vol. 8). London: Academic Press.

Baddeley, A.D., & Lewis, V.J. (1981). Inner active processes in reading: The inner voice, the inner ear and the inner eye. In A.M. Lesgold & C.A. Perfetti (Eds.), *Interactive processes in reading*. Hillsdale, NJ: Lawrence Erlbaum Associates Inc.

Baddeley, A.D., & Lieberman, K. (1980). Spatial working memory. In R. Nickerson (Ed.), *Attention and performance* (Vol. VIII). Hillsdale, NJ: Lawrence Erlbaum Associates Inc.

Baddeley, A.D., Logie, R., Bressi, S., Della Sala, S., & Spinnler, H. (1986). Dementia and working memory. *Quarterly Journal of Experimental Psychology, 38A,* 603–618.

Baddeley, A.D., Thomson, N., & Buchanan, M. (1975). Word length and the structure of short-term memory. *Journal of Verbal Learning and Verbal Behavior, 14,* 575–589.

Baddeley, A.D., & Warrington, E.K. (1970). Amnesia and the distinction between long- and short-term memory. *Journal of Verbal Learning and Verbal Behavior, 9,* 176–189.

Baddeley, A.D., & Wilson, B. (1985). Phonological coding and short-term memory in patients without speech. *Journal of Memory and Language, 24,* 490–502.

Bahrick, H.P. (1970). Two-phase model for prompted recall. *Psychological Review, 77*, 215–222.

Ballard, D.H. (1986). Cortical connections and parallel processing. *Behavioral and Brain Sciences, 9*, 67–120.

Balota, D.A., Pollatsek, A., & Rayner, K. (1985). The interaction of contextual constraints and parafoveal visual information in reading. *Cognitive Psychology, 17*, 364–390.

Banaji, M.R., & Crowder, R.G. (1989). The bankruptcy of everyday memory. *American Psychologist, 44*, 1185–1193.

Banks, W.P., & Krajicek, D. (1991). Perception. In M.R. Rosenzweig & L.W. Porter (Eds.), *Annual Review of Psychology* (Vol. 42). Palo Alto, CA: Annual Reviews Inc.

Bannon, L.J. (1981). *An investigation of image scanning: Theoretical claims and empirical evidence.* Unpublished PhD Dissertation, University of Western Ontario, Canada.

Barclay, C.R. (1988). Truth and accuracy in auto-biographical memory. In M.M. Gruneberg, P.E. Morris, & R.N. Sykes (Eds.), *Practical aspects of memory: Current research and issues: Vol. 1. Memory in everyday life.* Chichester, UK: Wiley.

Bard, E.G., Shillcock, R.C., & Altmann, G.T. (1988). The recognition of words after their acoustic effects in spontaneous speech: Effects of subsequent context. *Perception and Psychophysics, 44*, 395–408.

Baron, J. (1973). Phonemic stage not necessary for reading. *Quarterly Journal of Experimental Psychology, 25*, 241–246.

Barsalou, L.W. (1982). Context-independent and context-dependent information in concepts. *Memory and Cognition, 10*, 82–93.

Barsalou, L.W. (1983). Ad hoc categories. *Memory and Cognition, 11*, 211–227.

Barsalou, L.W. (1985). Ideals, central tendency, and frequency of instantiation as determinants of graded structure in categories. *Journal of Experimental Psychology: Learning, Memory, and Cognition, 11*, 629–654.

Barsalou, L.W. (1987). The instability of graded structure: Implications for the nature of concepts. In U. Neisser (Ed.), *Concepts and conceptual development: Ecological and intellectual factors in categorisation.* Cambridge: Cambridge University Press.

Barsalou, L.W. (1988). The content and organization of autobiographical memories. In U. Neisser & E. Winograd (Eds.), *Remembering reconsidered: Ecological and traditional approaches to the study of memory.* New York: Cambridge University Press.

Barsalou, L.W. (1989). Intra-concept similarity and its implications for inter-concept similarity. In S. Vosniadou & A. Ortony (Eds.), *Similarity and analogical reasoning.* Cambridge: Cambridge University Press.

Barsalou, L.W., & Medin, D.L. (1986). Concepts: Fixed definitions or dynamic context-dependent representations. *Cahiers de Psychologie Cognitive, 6*, 187–202.

Bartlett, F.C. (1932). *Remembering: A study in experimental and social psychology.* Cambridge: Cambridge University Press.

Basso, A., Spinnler, H., Vallar, G., & Zanobio, E. (1982). Left hemisphere damage and selective impairment of auditory short-term memory: A case study. *Neuropsychologia, 20*, 263–274.

Battig, W.F., & Montague, W.E. (1969). Category norms for verbal items in 56 categories. *Journal of Experimental Psychology Monograph, 80*, 1–46.

Beach, C.M. (1990). The interpretation of prosodic patterns at points of syntactic structure ambiguity: Evidence for cue trading relations. *Journal of Memory and Language, 30*, 644–663.

Beasley, N.A. (1968). The extent of individual differences in the perception of causality. *Canadian Journal of Psychology, 22*, 399–407.

Beauvois, M.-F., & Derousne, J. (1979). Phonological alexia: Three dissociations. *Journal of Neurology, Neurosurgery and Psychiatry, 42*, 1115–1124.

Beck, I.L., & Carpenter, P.A. (1986). Cognitive approaches to understanding reading. *American Psychologist, 41*, 1088–1105.

Benson, D.F., & Greenberg, J.P. (1969). Visual form agnosia: A specific defect in visual discrimination. *Archives of Neurology, 20*, 82–89.

Bereiter, C., & Scardamalia, M. (1987). *The psychology of written composition.* Hillsdale, NJ: Lawrence Erlbaum Associates Inc.

Bereiter, C., Burtis, P.J., & Scardamalia, M. (1988). Cognitive operations in constructing main points in written composition. *Journal of Memory and Language, 27*, 261–278.

Berg, W.P., Wade, M.G., & Greer, N.L. (1994). Visual regulation of gait in bipedal locomotion: Revisiting Lee, Lishman, and Thomson (1982). *Journal of Experimental Psychology: Human Perception and Performance, 20*, 854–863.

Berlin, B. (1972). Speculations on the growth of ethnobiological nomenclature. *Language in Society, 1*, 51–86.

Berlin, B., Breedlove, D.E., & Raven, P.H. (1973). General principles of classification and nomenclature in folk biology. *American Anthropologist, 75,* 214–242.

Berlin, B., & Kay, P. (1969). *Basic colour terms: Their universality and evolution.* Berkeley, CA: University of California Press.

Berry, D.C., & Broadbent, D.E. (1984). On the relationship between task performance and associated verbalisable knowledge. *Quarterly Journal of Experimental Psychology, 36A,* 209–231.

Biederman, I. (1987). Recognition-by-components: A theory of human image understanding. *Psychological Review, 94,* 115–147.

Biederman, I., & Gerhardstein, P.C. (1993). Recognising depth-rotated objects: Evidence for 3-D viewpoint invariance. *Journal of Experimental Psychology: Human Perception and Performance, 19,* 1162–1182.

Biederman, I., Ju, G., & Clapper, J. (1985). *The perception of partial objects.* Unpublished manuscript, State University of New York at Buffalo.

Birch, H.G. (1945). The relationship of previous experience to insightful problem solving. *Journal of Comparative Psychology, 38,* 267–383.

Bisiach, E., & Luzzatti, C. (1978). Unilateral neglect of representational space. *Cortex, 14,* 129–133.

Blaney, P.H. (1986). Affect and memory: A review. *Psychological Bulletin, 99,* 229–246.

Blankstein, K.R., Flett, G.L., Boase, P., & Toner, B.B. (1990). Thought listing and endorsement measures of self-referential thinking in test anxiety. *Anxiety Research, 2,* 103–111.

Blasdel, G.G., & Salama, G. (1986). Voltage-sensitive dyes reveal a modular organisation in monkey striate cortex. *Nature, 321,* 579–585.

Blaxton, T.A. (1989). Investigating dissociations among memory measures: Support for a transfer-appropriate processing framework. *Journal of Experimental Psychology: Learning, Memory, and Cognition, 15,* 657–668.

Blaxton, T.A. (1992). Dissociations among memory measures in memory-impaired subjects: Evidence for a processing account of memory. *Memory and Cognition, 20,* 549–562.

Bobrow, D.G., & Norman, D.A. (1975). Some principles of memory schemata. In D.G. Bobrow & A. Collins (Eds.), *Representation and understanding: Essays in cognitive science.* New York: Academic Press.

Bock, K., & Levelt, W. (1994). Language production: Grammatical encoding. In M.A. Gernsbacher (Ed.), *Handbook of psycholinguistics.* London: Academic Press.

Boden, M. (1988). *Computer models of mind.* Cambridge: Cambridge University Press.

Boden, M. (1991). *The creative mind: Myths and mechanisms.* London: Abacus.

Boden, M. (in press). Precis of "The creative mind". *Behavioral and Brain Sciences.*

Bohannon, J.N. (1988). Flashbulb memories for the Space Shuttle disaster: A tale of two theories. *Cognition, 29,* 179–196.

Boles, D.B. (1983). Dissociated imagibility, concreteness, and familiarity in lateralized word recognition. *Memory and Cognition, 11,* 511–519.

Boole, G. (1854). *An investigation of the laws of thought on which are founded the mathematical theories of logic and probabilities.* London.

Boomer, D. (1965). Hesitation and grammatical encoding. *Language and Speech, 8,* 145–158.

Borges, J.-L. (1964). *Labyrinths.* London: Penguin.

Bower, G.H. (1970). Imagery as a relational organizer in associative learning. *Journal of Verbal Learning and Verbal Behavior, 9,* 529–533.

Bower, G.H. (1972). Mental imagery and associative learning. In L. Gregg (Ed.), *Cognition in learning and memory.* New York: John Wiley.

Bower, G.H. (1981). Mood and memory. *American Psychologist, 36,* 129–148.

Bower, G.H. (1992). How might emotions affect learning? In S.-A. Christianson (Ed.), *The handbook of emotion and memory: Research and theory.* Hillsdale, NJ: Lawrence Erlbaum Associates Inc.

Bower, G.H., Black, J.B., & Turner, T.J. (1979). Scripts in memory for text. *Cognitive Psychology, 11,* 177–220.

Bower, G.H., Gilligan, S.G., & Monteiro, K.P. (1981). Selectivity of learning caused by affective states. *Journal of Experimental Psychology: General, 110,* 451–473.

Bower, G.H., & Gilligan, S.G. (1979). Remembering information related to one's self. *Journal of Research in Personality, 13,* 420–432.

Bower, G.H., & Mayer, J.D. (1985). Failure to replicate mood dependent retrieval. *Bulletin of the Psychonomic Society, 23,* 39–42.

Bower, G.H., Monteiro, K.P., & Gilligan, S.G. (1978). Emotional mood as a context for learning and recall. *Journal of Verbal Learning and Verbal Behavior, 17,* 573–585.

Bower, G.H., & Winzenz, D. (1969). Group structure, coding and memory for digit series. *Journal of Experimental Psychology Monograph, 80* (No. 2, Pt. 2), 1–17.

Bowers, J., & Schacter, D.L. (1993). Priming of novel information in amnesic patients: Issues and data. In P. Graf & M.E.J. Masson (Eds.), *Implicit memory: New directions in cognition, development, and neuropsychology.* Hillsdale, NJ: Lawrence Erlbaum Associates Inc.

Bowers, K.S. (1973). Situationism in psychology: An analysis and a critique. *Psychological Review, 80,* 307–336.

Bowers, K.S., Regehr, G., Balthazard, C., & Parker, K. (1990). Intuition in the context of discovery. *Cognitive Psychology, 22,* 77–110.

Bracewell, R.J., & Hidi, S.E. (1974). The solution of an inferential problem as a function of stimulus materials. *Quarterly Journal of Experimental Psychology, 26,* 480–488.

Braddick, O.J. (1980). Low-level and high-level processes in apparent motion. *Philosophical Transactions of the Royal Society of London, Series B, 209,* 137–151.

Braine, M.D.S. (1978). On the relationship between the natural logic of reasoning and standard logic. *Psychological Review, 85,* 1–21.

Braine, M.D.S. (1993). Mental models cannot exclude mental logic and make little sense without it. *Behavioral and Brain Sciences, 16,* 338–339.

Braine, M.D.S., & O'Brien, D.P. (1991). A theory of If: A lexical entry, reasoning program and pragmatic principles. *Psychological Review, 98,* 182–203.

Braine, M.D.S., Reiser, B.J., & Rumain, B. (1984). Some empirical justification for a theory of natural propositional logic. In G.H. Bower (Ed.), *The psychology of learning, and motivation* (Vol. 18). New York: Academic Press.

Braine, M.D.S., & Rumain, B. (1983). Logical reasoning. In J.H. Flavell & E.M. Markman (Eds.), *Handbook of child psychology: Vol. 3. Cognitive development* (4th Edn.). New York: John Wiley.

Bramwell, B. (1897). Illustrative cases of aphasia. The Lancet, *1,* 1256–1259.

Brandimonte, M.A., & Gerbino, W. (1993). Mental image reversal and verbal recoding. *Memory and Cognition, 21,* 23–33.

Brandimonte, M.A., Hitch, G.J., & Bishop, D.V. (1992). Verbal recoding of visual stimuli impairs mental image transformations. *Memory and Cognition, 20,* 449–455.

Bransford, J.D., Barclay, J.R., & Franks, J.J. (1972). Sentence memory: A constructive versus interpretive approach. *Cognitive Psychology, 3,* 193–209.

Bransford, J.D., Franks, J.J., Morris, C.D., & Stein, B.S. (1979). Some general constraints on learning and memory research. In L.S. Cermak & F.I.M. Craik (Eds.), *Levels of processing in human memory.* Hillsdale, NJ: Lawrence Erlbaum Associates Inc.

Bransford, J.D., & Johnson, M.K. (1972). Contextual prerequisites for understanding: some investigations of comprehension and recall. *Journal of Verbal Learning and Verbal Behavior, 11,* 717–726.

Brennan, S.E. (1990). *Seeking and providing evidence for mutual understanding.* Unpublished PhD thesis, Stanford University, Stanford, CA.

Brewer, W.F. (1987) Schemas versus mental models in human memory. In P.E. Morris (Ed.), *Modelling cognition.* Chichester, UK: John Wiley.

Brewer, W.F. (1988). Memory for randomly sampled autobiographical events. In U. Neisser & E. Winograd (Eds.), *Remembering reconsidered: Ecological and traditional approaches to the study of memory.* New York: Cambridge University Press.

Brewer, W.F., & Dupree, D.A. (1983). Use of plan schemata in the recall and recognition of goal-directed actions. *Journal of Experimental Psychology: Learning, Memory, and Cognition, 9,* 117–129.

Brewin, C.R. (1988). *Cognitive foundations of clinical psychology.* Hove, UK: Lawrence Erlbaum Associates Ltd.

Brewin, C.R., Andrews, B., & Gotlib, I.H. (1993). Psychopathology and early experience: A reappraisal of retrospective reports. *Psychological Bulletin, 113,* 82–98.

Brindley, G.S., & Merton, P.A. (1960). The absence of position sense in the human eye. *Journal of Physiology, 153,* 127–130.

Broadbent, D.E. (1958). *Perception and communication.* Oxford: Pergamon.

Broadbent, D.E. (1982). Task combination and selective intake of information. *Acta Psychologica, 50,* 253–290.

Brooks, L. (1978). Non analytic concept formation and memory for instances. In E. Rosch & B.B. Lloyd (Eds.), *Cognition and categorisation.* Hillsdale, NJ: Lawrence Erlbaum Associates Inc.

Brown, C.H., Kolar, J., Torrey, B.J., Truong-Quang, T., & Volkman, P. (1976). Some general principles of biological and non-biological folk classification. *American Ethologist, 3,* 73–85.

Brown, N.R., Rips, L.J., & Shevell, S.K. (1985). The subjective dates of neural events in very-long-term memory. *Cognitive Psychology, 17,* 139–177.

Brown, N.R., Shevell, S.K., & Rips, L.J. (1986). Public memories and their personal context. In D.C. Rubin (Ed.), *Autobiographical memory.* Cambridge: Cambridge University Press.

Brown, R. (1970). Psychology and reading. In H. Levin & J.P. Williams (Eds.), *Basic studies on reading*. New York: Basic Books.

Brown, R., & Kulik, J. (1977). Flashbulb memories. *Cognition, 5*, 73–99.

Brown, R., & McNeill, D. (1966). The "tip of the tongue" phenomenon. *Journal of Verbal Learning and Verbal Behavior, 5*, 325–337.

Bruce, V. (1988). *Recognising faces*. Hove, UK: Lawrence Erlbaum Associates Ltd.

Bruce, V., & Green, P.R. (1990). *Visual perception: Physiology, psychology, and ecology* (2nd Edn.). Hove, UK: Lawrence Erlbaum Associates Ltd.

Bruce, V., & Valentine, T. (1988). When a nod's as good as a wink: The role of dynamic information in face recognition. In M. Gruneberg, P. Morris, & R. Sykes (Eds.), *Practical aspects of memory: Current research and issues* (Vol. 1.) Chichester, UK: John Wiley.

Bruce, V., & Young, A.W. (1986). Understanding face recognition. *British Journal of Psychology, 77*, 305–327.

Bruner, J.S. (1957). On perceptual readiness. *Psychological Review, 64*, 123–152.

Bruner, J.S., & Goodman, C.D. (1947). Value and need as organising factors in perception. *Journal of Abnormal and Social Psychology, 42*, 33–44.

Bruner, J.S., Goodnow, J.J., & Austin, G.A. (1956). *A study of thinking*. New York: John Wiley.

Bruner, J.S., Postman, L., & Rodrigues, J. (1951). Expectations and the perception of colour. *American Journal of Psychology, 64*, 216–227.

Bruno, N., & Cutting, J.E. (1988). Mini-modularity and the perception of layout. *Journal of Experimental Psychology: General, 117*, 161–170.

Bub, D., Black, S., Howell, J., & Kertesz, A. (1987). Speech output processes and reading. In M. Coltheart, G. Sartori, & R. Job (Eds.), *The cognitive neuropsychology of language*. Hove, UK: Lawrence Erlbaum Associates Ltd.

Bub, D., Cancelliere, A., & Kertesz, A. (1985). Whole-word and analytic translation of spelling to sound in a nonsemantic reader. In K.E. Patterson, J.C. Marshall, & M. Coltheart (Eds.), *Surface dyslexia: Neuropsychological and cognitive studies of phonological reading*. Hove, UK: Lawrence Erlbaum Associates Ltd.

Bub, D., & Kertesz, A. (1982). Deep agraphia. *Brain and Language, 17*, 146–165.

Bundy, A. (1993). "Semantic procedure" is an oxymoron. *Behavioral and Brain Sciences, 16*, 339–340.

Burton, A.M., & Bruce, V. (1992). I recognize your face but I can't remember your name: A simple explanation? *British Journal of Psychology, 83*, 45–60.

Burton, A.M., Bruce, V., & Johnston, R.A. (1990). Understanding face recognition with an interactive activation model. *British Journal of Psychology, 81*, 361–380.

Butters, N., & Cermak, L.S. (1980). *Alcoholic Korsakoff's syndrome: An information-processing approach*. London: Academic Press.

Butters, N., Heindel, W.C., & Salmon, D.P. (1990). Dissociation of implicit memory in dementia: Neurological implications. *Bulletin of the Psychonomic Society, 28*, 359–366.

Byrne, R.M.J. (1989a). Suppressing valid inferences with conditionals. *Cognition, 31*, 61–83.

Byrne, R.M.J. (1989b). Everyday reasoning with conditional sequences. *Quarterly Journal of Experimental Psychology, 41A*, 141–166.

Byrne, R.M.J. (1991). Can valid inferences be suppressed. *Cognition, 39*, 61–83.

Byrne, R.M.J., & Johnson-Laird, P.N. (1989). Spatial reasoning. *Journal of Memory and Language, 28*, 564–575.

Byrne, R.M.J., & Johnson-Laird, P.N. (1990). Models and deductive reasoning. In K.J. Gilhooly, M.T. Keane, R. Logie, & G. Erdos (Eds.), *Lines of thinking: Reflections on the psychology of thought* (Vol. 1). Chichester, UK: John Wiley.

Byrne, R.M.J., & Johnson-Laird, P.N. (1992). The spontaneous use of propositional connectives. *Quarterly Journal of Experimental Psychology, 44A*, 89–110.

Calvo, M.G., Ramos, P., & Eysenck, M.W. (1993). Estres, ansiedad y lectura: Eficiencia vs. eficacia. *Cognitiva, 5*, 77–93.

Campbell, D. (1957). *A study of some sensory-motor functions in psychiatric patients*. Unpublished PhD thesis, University of London.

Campion, J., & Latto, R. (1985). Apperceptive agnosia due to carbon poisoning: An interpretation based on critical band masking from disseminated lesions. *Behavioral Brain Research, 8*, 227–240.

Cantor, N., Smith, E.E., French, R.D., & Mezzich, J. (1980). Psychiatric diagnosis as prototype categorisation. *Journal of Abnormal Psychology, 89*, 181–193.

Caramazza, A., McCloskey, M., & Green, B. (1981). Naive beliefs in "sophisticated" subjects: Misconceptions about trajectories of objects. *Cognition, 9*, 117–123.

Carbonell, J.G. (1986). Derivational analogy: A theory of reconstructive problem solving and expertise acquisition. In R.S. Michalski, J.G. Carbonell, & T.M. Mitchell (Eds.), *Machine learning: Vol. II. An artificial intelligence approach.* Los Altos, CA: Morgan Kaufmann Publishers.

Carpenter, P.A., & Just, M.A. (1977). Reading comprehension as eyes see it. In M.A. Just & P.A. Carpenter (Eds.), *Cognitive processes in comprehension.* Hillsdale, NJ: Lawrence Erlbaum Associates Inc.

Carr, T.H., Davidson, B.J., & Hawkins, H.L. (1978). Perceptual flexibility in word recognition: Strategies affecting orthographic computations but not lexical access. *Journal of Experimental Psychology: Human Perception and Performance, 4,* 674–690.

Castiello, U., Paulignan, Y., & Jeannerod, M. (1991). Temporal dissociation of motor responses and subjective awareness. *Brain, 114,* 2639–2655.

Cavallo, V., & Laurent, M. (1988). Visual information and skill level in time-to-collision estimation. *Perception, 17,* 623–632.

Cave, C.B., & Kosslyn, S.M. (1993). The role of parts and spatial relations in object identification. *Perception, 22,* 229–248.

Ceci, S.J., Baker, J.E., & Bronfenbrenner, U. (1988). Prospective remembering, temporal calibration, and context. In M.M. Gruneberg, P.E. Morris, & R.N. Sykes (Eds.), *Practical aspects of memory: Current research and issues: Vol. 1. Memory in everyday life.* Chichester, UK: John Wiley.

Ceraso, J., & Provitera, A. (1971). Sources of error in syllogistic reasoning. *Cognitive Psychology, 2,* 400–410.

Cermak, L.S. (1979). Amnesic patients' level of processing. In L.S. Cermak & F.I.M. Craik (Eds.), *Levels of processing in human memory.* Hillsdale, NJ: Lawrence Erlbaum Associates Inc.

Cermak, L.S., Lewis, R., Butters, N., & Goodglass, H. (1973). Role of verbal mediation in performance of motor tasks by Korsakoff patients. *Perceptual and Motor Skills, 37,* 259–262.

Cermak, L.S., Talbot, N., Chandler, K., & Wolbarst, L.R. (1985). The perceptual priming phenomenon in amnesia. *Neuropsychologia, 23,* 615–622.

Challis, B.H., & Brodbeck, D.R. (1992). Level of processing affects priming in word fragment completion. *Journal of Experimental Psychology: Learning, Memory, and Cognition, 18,* 595–607.

Chalmers, A.F. (1982). *What is this thing called science?* Milton Keynes, UK: Open University Press.

Chambers, D., & Reisberg, D. (1985). Can mental images be ambiguous? *Journal of Experimental Psychology: Human Perception and Performance, 11,* 317–328.

Chambers, D., & Reisberg, D. (1992). What an image depicts depends on what an image means. *Cognitive Psychology, 24,* 145–174.

Chapman, J.L., & Chapman, J.P. (1959). Atmosphere re-examined. *Journal of Experimental Psychology, 58,* 220–226.

Charness, N. (1981a). Search in chess: Age and skill differences. *Journal of Experimental Psychology: Human Perception and Performance, 7,* 467–476.

Charness, N. (1981b). Aging and skilled problem solving. *Journal of Experimental Psychology: General, 110,* 21–38.

Charness, N. (1991). Expertise in chess: The balance between knowledge and search. In A. Ericsson & J. Smith (Eds.), *Toward a general theory of expertise.* Cambridge: Cambridge University Press.

Chase, W.G., & Simon, H.A. (1973a). Perception in chess. *Cognitive Psychology, 4,* 55–81.

Chase, W.G., & Simon, H.A. (1973b). The mind's eye in chess. In W.G. Chase (Ed.), *Visual information processing.* London: Academic Press.

Cheesman, J., & Merikle, P.M. (1984). Priming with and without awareness. *Perception and Psychophysics, 36,* 387–395.

Cheng, P.W. (1985). Restructuring versus automaticity: Alternative accounts of skills acquisition. *Psychological Review, 92,* 414–423.

Cheng, P.W., & Holyoak, K.J. (1985). Pragmatic reasoning schemas. *Cognitive Psychology, 17,* 391–416.

Cheng, P.W., & Holyoak, K.J. (1989). On the natural selection of reasoning theories. *Cognition, 33,* 285–314.

Cheng, P.W., Holyoak, K.J., Nisbett, R.E., & Oliver, L.M. (1986). Pragmatic versus syntactic approaches to training deductive reasoning. *Cognitive Psychology, 18,* 293–328.

Cherry, E.C. (1953). Some experiments on the recognition of speech with one and two ears. *Journal of the Acoustical Society of America, 25,* 975–979.

Chi, M.T.H., Feltovich, P.J., & Glaser, R. (1981). Categorization and representation of physics problems by experts and novices. *Cognitive Science, 5,* 121–152.

Chi, M.T.H., Glaser, R., & Rees, E. (1983). Expertise in problem solving. In R.J. Sternberg (Ed.), *Advances in the psychology of human intelligence* (Vol. 2). Hillsdale, NJ: Lawrence Erlbaum Associates Inc.

Chomsky, N. (1957). *Syntactic structures*. The Hague: Mouton.

Chomsky, N. (1959). Review of Skinner's "Verbal behaviour". *Language, 35*, 26–58.

Chomsky, N. (1965). *Aspects of the theory of syntax*. Cambridge, MA: MIT Press.

Churchland, P.M. (1981). Eliminative materialism and the propositional attitudes. *Journal of Philosophy, 78*, 67–90.

Churchland, P.S. (1989). From Descartes to neural networks. *Scientific American, July*, 100.

Churchland, P.S., & Sejnowski, T.J. (1991). Perspectives on cognitive neuroscience. In R.G. Lister & H.J. Weingartner (Eds.), *Perspectives on cognitive neuroscience*. Oxford: Oxford University Press.

Churchland, P.S., & Sejnowski, T.J. (1992). *The computational brain*. Cambridge, MA: MIT Press.

Claparede, E. (1911). Recognition et moité. *Archives de Psychologie, 11*, 75–90.

Clark, D.M., & Teasdale, J.D. (1982). Diurnal variation in clinical depression and accessibility of memories of positive and negative experiences. *Journal of Abnormal Psychology, 91*, 87–95.

Clark, H.H. (1994). Discourse in production. In M.A. Gernsbacher (Ed.), *Handbook of psycholinguistics*. London: Academic Press.

Clark, H.H., & Carlson, T.B. (1981). Context for comprehension. In J. Long & A. Baddeley (Eds.), *Attention and performance* (Vol. IX). Hillsdale, NJ: Lawrence Erlbaum Associates Inc.

Clifton, C., & Ferreira, F. (1987). Discourse structure and anaphora: Some experimental results. In M. Coltheart (Ed.), *Attention and performance* (Vol. XII). Hove, UK: Lawrence Erlbaum Associates Ltd.

Clocksin, W.F., & Mellish, C.S. (1984). *Programming in Prolog* (2nd Edn.). Berlin: Springer.

Cohen, B., & Murphy, G.L. (1984). Models of concepts. *Cognitive Science, 8*, 27–58.

Cohen, D., & Kubovy, M. (1993) Mental rotation, mental representation and flat slopes. *Cognitive Psychology, 25*, 351–382.

Cohen, G. (1983). *The psychology of cognition* (2nd Edn.). London: Academic Press.

Cohen, G. (1989). *Memory in the real world*. Hove, UK: Lawrence Erlbaum Associates Ltd.

Cohen, G. (1990). Why is it difficult to put names to faces? *British Journal of Psychology, 81*, 287–297.

Cohen, G., & Faulkner, D. (1988). Life span changes in autobiographical memory. In M.M. Gruneberg, P.E. Morris., & R.N. Sykes (Eds.), *Practical aspects of memory: Current research and issues* (Vol. 1). Chichester, UK: John Wiley.

Cohen, L.J. (1981). Can human irrationality be experimentally demonstrated? *Behavioral and Brain Sciences, 4*, 317–331.

Cohen, N. J. (1984). Preserved learning capacity in amnesia: Evidence for multiple memory systems. In L.R. Squire & N. Butters (Eds.), *Neuropsychology of memory*. New York: Guilford Press.

Cohen, N.J., & Squire, L.R. (1980). Preserved learning and retention of pattern-analyzing skill in amnesia using perceptual learning. *Cortex, 17*, 273–278.

Cole, R.A., Rudnisky, A.I., Zue, V.W., & Reddy, W. (1980). Speech as patterns on paper. In R.A. Cole (Ed.), *Perception and production of fluent speech*. Hillsdale, NJ: Lawrence Erlbaum Associates Inc.

Coleman, L., & Kay, P. (1981). Prototype semantics. *Language, 57*, 26–44.

Collins, A.M., & Loftus, E.F. (1975). A spreading-activation theory of semantic processing. *Psychological Review, 82*, 407–428.

Collins, A.M., & Quillian, M.R. (1969). Retrieval time from semantic memory. *Journal of Verbal Learning and Verbal Behavior, 8*, 240–248.

Collins, A.M., & Quillian, M.R. (1970). Does category size affect categorisation time. *Journal of Verbal Learning and Verbal Behavior, 9*, 432–438.

Coltheart, M. (1978). Lexical access in simple reading tasks. In G. Underwood (Ed.), *Strategies of information processing*. London: Academic Press.

Coltheart, M. (1983a). Ecological necessity of iconic memory. *Behavioral and Brain Sciences, 6*, 17–18.

Coltheart, M. (1983b). The right hemisphere and disorders of reading. In A.W. Young (Ed.), *Functions of the right cerebral hemisphere*. London: Academic Press.

Coltheart, M., Curtis, B., Atkins, P., & Haller, M. (1993). Models of reading aloud: Dual-route and parallel-distributed-processing approaches. *Psychological Review, 100*, 589–608.

Coltheart, M., Patterson, K.E., & Marshall, J.C. (Eds.). (1980). *Deep dyslexia*. London: Routledge & Kegan Paul.

Connine, C.M., Blasko, P.J., & Titone, D. (1993). Do the beginnings of spoken words have a special status in auditory word recognition? *Journal of Memory and Language, 32*, 193–210.

Conrad, C. (1972). Cognitive economy in semantic memory. *Journal of Experimental Psychology, 92*, 148–154.

Conway, M.A., Anderson, S.J., Larsen, S.F., Donnelly, C.M., McDaniel, M.A., McClelland, A.G.R., &

Rawles, R.E. (1994). The formation of flashbulb memories. *Memory and Cognition, 22,* 326–343.

Conway, M.A., & Bekerian, D.A. (1987). Organisation in autobiographical memory. *Memory and Cognition, 15,* 119–132.

Conway, M.A., & Rubin, D.C. (1993). The structure of autobiographical memory. In A.F. Collins, S.E. Gathercole, M.A. Conway, & P.E. Morris (Eds.), *Theories of memory.* Hove, UK: Lawrence Erlbaum Associates Ltd.

Cooper, L.A. (1975). Mental rotation of random two-dimensional shapes. *Cognitive Psychology, 7,* 20–43.

Cooper, L.A., & Podgory, P. (1976). Mental transformations and visual comparison processes. *Journal of Experimental Psychology: Human Perception and Perfomance, 2,* 503–514.

Cooper, L.A., & Shepard, R.N. (1973). Chronometric studies of the rotation of mental images. In W.G. Chase (Ed.), *Visual information processing.* New York: Academic Press.

Corballis, M.C. (1989). Laterality and human evolution, *Psychological Review, 96,* 492–505.

Corkin, S. (1968). Acquisition of motor skill after bilateral medial temporal-lobe excision. *Neuropsychologia, 6,* 255–265.

Corkin, S. (1982). Some relationships between global amnesias and the memory impairments in Alzheimer's disease. In S. Corkin, K.L. Davis, J.H. Growden, E. Usdin, & R.J. Wurtman (Eds.), *Alzheimer's disease: A report of research in progress.* New York: Raven Press.

Cornoldi, C., & Paivio, A. (1982). Imagery value and its effects on verbal memory: A review. *Archivio de Psicologia Neurologia e Psichiatria, 2,* 171–192.

Coslett, H.B., & Saffran, E.M. (1991). Simult-anagnosia: To see but not two see. *Brain, 114,* 1523–1545.

Cosmides, L. (1989). The logic of social exchange: Has natural selection shaped how humans reason? *Cognition, 31,* 187–276.

Costall, A. (1991). "Graceful degradation": Cognitivism and the metaphors of the computer. In A. Still & A. Costall (Eds.), *Against cognitivism: Alternative foundations for cognitive psychology.* Hemel Hempstead, UK: Harvester Wheatsheaf.

Costall, A., & Still, A. (1991). Introduction: Cognitivism as an approach to cognition. In A. Still & A. Costall (Eds.), *Against cognitivism: Alternative foundations for cognitive psychology.* Hemel Hempstead, UK: Harvester Wheatsheaf.

Costello, F., & Keane, M.T. (1992). Concept combination: A theoretical review. *Irish Journal of Psychology, 13,* 125–140.

Coughlan, A.K., & Warrington, E.K. (1978) Word-comprehension and word-retrieval in patients with localised cerebral lesions. *Brain, 101,* 163–185.

Craik, F.I.M. (1973). A "levels of analysis" view of memory. In P. Pliner, L. Krames, & T.M. Alloway (Eds.), *Communication and affect: Language and thought.* London: Academic Press.

Craik, F.I.M., & Lockhart, R.S. (1972). Levels of processing: A framework for memory research. *Journal of Verbal Learning and Verbal Behavior, 11,* 671–684.

Craik, F.I.M., & Tulving, E. (1975). Depth of processing and the retention of words in episodic memory. *Journal of Experimental Psychology: General, 104,* 268–294.

Crick, F. (1989). *What mad pursuit?* New York: Basic Books.

Crovitz, H.F., Harvey, M.T., & McClanahan, S. (1981). Hidden memory: A rapid method for the study of amnesia using perceptual learning. *Cortex, 17,* 273–278.

Cummins, D.D., Lubart, T., Alksnis, O., & Rist, R.S. (1991). Conditional reasoning and causation. *Memory and Cognition, 19,* 274–282.

Cutting, J.E. (1978). Generation of synthetic male and female walkers through manipulation of a biomechanical invariant. *Perception, 7,* 393–405.

Cutting, J.E. (1986). *Perception with an eye to motion.* Cambridge, MA: MIT Press.

Cutting, J.E., & Kozlowski, L.T. (1977). Recognising friends by their walk: Gait perception without familiarity cues. *Bulletin of the Psychonomic Society, 9,* 353–356.

Cutting, J.E., Proffitt, D.R., & Kozlowski, L.T. (1978). A biomechanical invariant for gait perception. *Journal of Experimental Psychology: Human Perception and Performance, 4,* 357–372.

Daneman, M., & Reingold, E. (1993). What eye fixations tell us about phonological recoding during reading. *Canadian Journal of Experimental Psychology, 47,* 153–178.

Danks, J.H., & Glucksberg, S. (1980). Experimental psycholinguistics. *Annual Review of Psychology, 31,* 391–417.

Darwin, C.J., Turvey, M.T., & Crowder, R.G. (1972). An auditory analogue of the Sperling partial report procedure: Evidence for brief auditory storage. *Cognitive Psychology, 3,* 255–267.

Davies, S.P. (1990a). The nature and development of programming plans. *International Journal of Man–Machine Studies, 32,* 461–481.

Davies, S.P. (1990b). Plans, goals and selection rules in the comprehension of computer programs. *Behaviour and Information Technology, 10,* 173–190.

Davies, S.P. (1991). The role of notation and knowledge representation in the determination of programming strategy. *Cognitive Science, 15,* 547–573.

Davison, G.C., & Neale, J.M. (1990). *Abnormal psychology* (5th Edn.). New York: John Wiley.

DeGroot, A.D. (1965). *Thought and choice in chess.* The Hague: Mouton.

DeGroot, A.D. (1966). Perception and memory versus thought. In B. Kleinmuntz (Ed.), *Problem solving.* New York: John Wiley.

De Haan, E.H.F., Young, A.W., & Newcombe, F. (1991). A dissociation between the sense of familiarity and access to semantic information concerning familiar people. *European Journal of Cognitive Psychology, 3,* 51–67.

Dell, G.S. (1986). A spreading-activation theory of retrieval in sentence production. *Psychological Review, 93,* 283–321.

Dell, G.S., Juliano, C., & Goviadjie (1993). Structure and content in language production: A theory of frame constraints in phonological speech errors. *Cognitive Science, 17,* 149–195.

Dell, G.S., & O'Seaghdha, P.G. (1991). Mediated and convergent lexical priming in language production: A comment on Levelt et al. (1991). *Psychological Review, 98,* 604–614.

Dennis, M. (1976). Dissociated naming and locating of body parts after left anterior lobe resection: An experimental case study. *Brain and Language, 3,* 147–163.

De Renzi, E. (1986). Current issues in prosopagnosia. In H.D. Ellis, M.A. Jeeves, F. Newcombe, & A. Young (Eds.), *Aspects of face processing.* Dordrecht: Martinus Nijhoff.

de Saussure, F. (1960). *Course in general linguistics.* London: Peter Owen.

Deutsch, J.A., & Deutsch, D. (1963). Attention: Some theoretical considerations. *Psychological Review, 70,* 80–90.

Deutsch, J.A., & Deutsch, D. (1967). Comments on "Selective attention: Perception or response?" *Quarterly Journal of Experimental Psychology, 19,* 362–363.

De Valois, R.L., & Jacobs, F.H. (1968). Primate colour vision. *Science, 162,* 533–540.

Dittrich, W.H., & Lea, S.E.G. (1994). Visual perception of intentional motion. *Perception, 23,* 253–268.

Dixon, N.F. (1981). *Preconscious processing.* Chichester, UK: John Wiley.

Dodd, B., & Campbell, R. (1986). *Hearing by eye: The psychology of lip reading.* Hove, UK: Lawrence Erlbaum Associates Ltd.

Dominowski, R.L. (1981). Comment on "an examination of the alleged role of 'fixation' in the solution of several insight problems" by Weisberg and Alba. *Journal of Experimental Psychology: General, 110,* 199–203.

Dorman, M.F., Raphael, L.J., & Liberman, A.M. (1979). Some experiments on the sound of silence in phonetic perception. *Journal of the Acoustical Society of America, 65,* 1518–1532.

Dosher, B.A., & Corbett, A.T. (1982). Instrument inferences and verb schemata. *Memory and Cognition, 10,* 531–539.

Douglas, M. (1966). *Purity and danger.* London: Routledge & Kegan Paul.

Driver, J., & Tipper, S.P. (1989). On the nonselectivity of "selective seeing": Contrast between interference and priming in selective attention. *Journal of Experimental Psychology: Human Perception and Performance, 15,* 304–314.

Driver, J., & Baylis, G.C. (1989). Movement and visual attention: The spotlight metaphor breaks down. *Journal of Experimental Psychology: Human Perception and Performance, 15,* 448–456.

Duhamel, J.-R., Colby, C.L., & Goldberg, M.E. (1992). The updating of the representation of visual space in parietal cortex by intended eye movements. *Science, 255,* 90–92.

Duncan, J. (1979). Divided attention: The whole is more than the sum of its parts. *Journal of Experimental Psychology: Human Perception, 5,* 216–228.

Duncan, J., & Humphreys, G.W. (1989). A resemblance theory of visual search. *Psychological Review, 96,* 433–458.

Duncan, J., & Humphreys, G.W. (1992). Beyond the search surface: Visual search and attentional engagement. *Journal of Experimental Psychology: Human Perception and Performance, 18,* 578–588.

Duncker, K. (1926). A qualitative (experimental and theoretical) study of productive thinking (solving of comprehensible problems). *Journal of Genetic Psychology, 68,* 97–116.

Duncker, K. (1945). On problem solving. *Psychological Monographs, 58* (Whole No. 270).

D'Zurilla, T. (1965). Recall efficiency and mediating cognitive events in "experimental repression". *Journal of Personality and Social Psychology, 3,* 253–256.

Dyer, M.G. (1983). *In-depth understanding: A model of integrated processing for narrative comprehension.* Cambridge, MA: MIT Press.

Easterbrook, J.A. (1959). The effect of emotion on cue utilization and the organisation of behaviour. *Psychological Review, 66,* 183–201.

Eco, U. (1984). *The name of the rose.* London: Picador.

Egan, D.W., & Greeno, J.G. (1974). Theories of rule induction: Knowledge acquired in concept learning, serial pattern learning and problem solving. In W.G. Gregg (Ed.), *Knowledge and cognition.* Hillsdale, NJ: Lawrence Erlbaum Associates Inc.

Ehrlichman, H., & Barrett, J. (1983). Right hemispheric specialisation for mental imagery: A review of the evidence. *Brain and Cognition, 2,* 55–76.

Eich, E., & Metcalfe, J. (1989). Mood dependent memory for internal versus external events. *Journal of Experimental Psychology: Learning, Memory, and Cognition, 15,* 443–455.

Eimas, P.D. (1985). The perception of speech in early infancy. *Scientific American, 252,* 46–52.

Eimas, P.D., Miller, J.L., & Juscyzk, P.W. (1987). On infant speech perception and the acquisition of language. In S. Harnad (Ed.), *Categorical perception: The groundwork of cognition.* New York: Cambridge University Press.

Eisenstadt, M., Keane, M.T., & Rajan T. (Eds.) (1992) *Novice programming environments.* Hove, UK: Lawrence Erlbaum Associates Ltd.

Elio, Y., & Sharf, P. (1990). Modeling novice-to-expert shifts in problem solving strategy and knowledge organization. *Cognitive Science, 14,* 579–639.

Ellen, P. (1982). Direction, past experience and hints in creative problem solving: A reply to Weisberg and Alba. *Journal of Experimental Psychology: General, 111,* 316–325.

Ellis, A.W. (1984). Introduction to Bramwell's (1897) case of word meaning deafness. *Cognitive Neuropsychology, 1,* 245–258.

Ellis, A.W. (1987). Intimations of modularity, or, the modularity of mind: Doing cognitive neuropsychology without syndromes. In M. Coltheart, G. Sartori, & R. Job (Eds.), *The cognitive neuropsychology of language.* Hove, UK: Lawrence Erlbaum Associates Ltd.

Ellis, A.W. (1993). *Reading, writing, and dyslexia: A cognitive analysis* (2nd Edn.). Hove, UK: Lawrence Erlbaum Associates Ltd.

Ellis, A.W., Miller, D., & Sin, G. (1983). Wernicke's aphasia and normal language processing: A case study in cognitive neuropsychology. *Cognition, 15,* 111–144.

Ellis, A.W., & Young, A.W. (1988). *Human cognitive neuropsychology.* Hove, UK: Lawrence Erlbaum Associates Ltd.

Ellis, H., Thomas, R.L., McFarland, A., & Lane, J. (1985). Emotional mood states and retrieval in episodic memory. *Journal of Experimental Psychology: Learning, Memory, and Cognition, 11,* 363–370.

Ellis, H., Thomas, R.L., & Rodriguez, I.A. (1984). Emotional mood states and memory: Elaborative encoding, semantic processing and cognitive effort. *Journal of Experimental Psychology: Learning, Memory and Cognition, 69,* 237–243.

Ellis, H.C. (1990). *The role of thoughts in influencing the effects of mood states on memory.* Speech at convention of the American Psychological Society, Dallas, TX.

Ellis, H.C., & Ashbrook, P.W. (1988). Resource allocation model of the effects of depressed mood states on memory. In K. Fiedler & J. Forgas (Eds.), *Affect, cognition, and social behaviour.* Toronto: Hogrefe.

Ellis, H.D., Shepherd, J.W., & Davies, G.M. (1979). Identification of familiar and unfamiliar faces from internal and external features: Some implications for theories of face recognition. *Perception, 8,* 431–439.

Ellis, J.A. (1988). Memory for future intentions: Investigating pulses and steps. In M.M. Gruneberg, P.E. Morris, & R.N. Sykes (Eds.), *Practical aspects of memory: Current research and issues: Vol. 1. Memory in everyday life.* Chichester, UK: John Wiley.

Elman, J., & McClelland, J. (1988). Cognitive penetration of the mechanisms of perception: Compensation for coarticulation of lexically restored phonemes. *Journal of Memory and Language, 27,* 143–165.

Enns, J.T., & Rensick, R.A. (1990). Sensitivity to three-dimensional orientation from line drawings. *Psychological Review, 98,* 335–351.

Erickson, J.R. (1974). A set analysis theory of behaviour in formal syllogistic reasoning tasks. In R. Solso (Ed.), *Loyola symposium* (Vol. 2). Hillsdale, NJ: Lawrence Erlbaum Associates Inc.

Ericsson A., & Smith, J. (Eds.) (1991). *Toward a general theory of expertise.* Cambridge: Cambridge University Press.

Ericsson, K.A. (1988). Analysis of memory performance in terms of memory skill. In R.J. Sternberg (Ed.), *Advances in the psychology of human intelligence* (Vol. 4). Hillsdale, NJ: Lawrence Erlbaum Associates Inc.

Ericsson, K.A., & Chase, W.G. (1982). Exceptional memory. *American Scientist, 70,* 607–615.

Ericsson, K.A., & Simon, H.A. (1980). Verbal reports as data. *Psychological Review, 87,* 215–251.

Ericsson, K.A., & Simon, H.A. (1984). *Protocol analysis.* Cambridge, MA: MIT Press.

Eriksen, C.W. (1990). Attentional search of the visual field. In D. Brogan (Ed.), *Visual search.* London: Taylor & Francis.

Erlich, K., & Johnson-Laird, P.N. (1982). Spatial descriptions and referential continuity. *Journal of Verbal Learning and Verbal Behavior, 21,* 296–306.

Erlich, K., & Soloway, E. (1984). An empirical investigation of tacit plan knowledge in programming. In J.C. Thomas & M.L. Schneider (Eds.), *Human factors in computing systems.* Norwood, NJ: Ablex.

Eslinger, P.J., & Damasio, A.R. (1985). Severe disturbance of higher cognition after bilateral frontal lobe ablation: Patient EVR. *Neurology, 35,* 1731–1741.

Estes, W.K. (1994). *Classification and cognition.* Oxford: Oxford University Press.

Evans, J. St. B.T. (1982). *The psychology of deductive reasoning.* London: Routledge & Kegan Paul.

Evans, J. St. B.T. (1983). Linguistic determinants of bias in conditional reasoning. *Quarterly Journal of Experimental Psychology, 35A,* 635–644.

Evans, J. St. B.T. (1984). Heuristic and analytic processes in reasoning. *British Journal of Psychology, 75,* 451–458.

Evans, J. St. B.T. (1989). *Bias in human reasoning.* Hove, UK: Lawrence Erlbaum Associates Ltd.

Evans, J. St. B.T. (1993a). The mental model theory of conditional reasoning: Critical appraisal and revision. *Cognition, 48,* 1–20.

Evans, J. St. B.T. (1993b). On rules, models and understanding. *Behavioral and Brain Sciences, 16,* 345–346.

Evans, J. St. B.T., & Lynch, L.S. (1973). Matching bias in the selection task. *British Journal of Psychology, 64,* 391–397.

Evans, J. St. B.T., Manktelow, K.I., & Over, D.E. (1993). Reasoning, decision making and rationality. *Cognition, 49,* 156–187.

Evans, J. St. B.T., Newstead, S.E., & Byrne, R.M.J. (1993). *Human reasoning: The psychology of deduction.* Hove, UK: Lawrence Erlbaum Associates Ltd.

Eysenck, M.W. (1978). Verbal remembering. In B.M. Foss (Ed.), *Psychology survey, No. 1.* London: Allen & Unwin.

Eysenck, M.W. (1979). Depth, elaboration, and distinctiveness. In L.S. Cermak & F.I.M. Craik (Eds.), *Levels of processing in human memory.* Hillsdale, NJ: Lawrence Erlbaum Associates Inc.

Eysenck, M.W. (1982). *Attention and arousal: Cognition and performance.* Berlin: Springer.

Eysenck, M.W. (1989). Stress, anxiety, and intelligent performance. In D. Vickers & P.L. Smith (Eds.), *Human information processing: Measures, mechanisms and models.* Amsterdam: Elsevier.

Eysenck, M.W. (1992). *Anxiety: The cognitive perspective.* Hove, UK: Lawrence Erlbaum Associates Ltd.

Eysenck, M.W., & Calvo, M.G. (1992). Anxiety and performance: The processing efficiency theory. *Cognition and Emotion, 6,* 409–434.

Eysenck, M.W., & Eysenck, M.C. (1980). Effects of processing depth, distinctiveness, and word frequency on retention. *British Journal of Psychology, 71,* 263–274.

Eysenck, M.W., MacLeod, C., & Mathews, A. (1987). Cognitive functioning and anxiety. *Psychological Research, 49,* 189–195.

Eysenck, M.W., Mogg, K., May, J., Richards, A., & Mathews, A. (1991). Bias in interpretation of ambiguous sentences related to threat in anxiety. *Journal of Abnormal Psychology, 100,* 144–150.

Faigley, L., & Witte, S. (1983). Analysing revision. *College Composition and Communication, 32,* 400–414.

Falkenhainer, B., Forbus, K.D., & Gentner, D. (1986). Structure-mapping engine. *Proceedings of the Annual Conference of the American Association for Artificial Intelligence.* Los Altos: Morgan Kaufmann.

Falkenhainer, B., Forbus, K.D., & Gentner, D. (1989). Structure-mapping engine. *Artificial Intelligence, 41,* 1–63.

Farah, M.J. (1984). The neurological basis of mental imagery: A componential analysis. *Cognition, 18,* 245–272.

Farah, M.J. (1988). Is visual imagery really visual? Overlooked evidence from neuropsychology. *Psychological Review, 95,* 307–317.

Farah, M.J., Gazzaniga, M.S., Holtzmann, J.D., & Kosslyn, S.M. (1985). A left-hemisphere basis for visual mental imagery? *Neuropsychologia, 23,* 115–118.

Farah, M.J., Hammond, K.M., Levine, D.N., & Calvanio, R. (1988). Visual and spatial mental imagery: Dissociable systems of representation. *Cognitive Psychology, 20,* 439–462.

Farah, M.J., Peronnet, F., Gonon, M.A., & Giard, M.H. (1988). Electrophysiological evidence for a shared representational medium for visual images and visual percepts. *Journal of Experimental Psychology: General, 117,* 248–257.

Farah, M.J., Weisberg, L.L., Monheit, M., & Peronnet, F. (1990). Brain activity underlying mental imagery: Event-related potentials during mental image generation. *Journal of Cognitive Neuroscience, 1,* 302–316.

Feldman, J.A., & Ballard, D.H. (1982). Connectionist models and their properties. *Cognitive Science, 6,* 205 254.

Ferreira, F. (1993). Creation of prosody during sentence production. *Psychological Review, 100,* 233–253.

Fillenbaum, S. (1993). Deductive reasoning: what are taken to be the premises and how are they interpreted? *Behavioral and Brain Sciences, 16,* 348–349.

Fillmore, C.J. (1968). The case for case. In E. Bach & R.T. Harms (Eds.), *Universals of linguistic theory.* New York: Holt, Rinehart, & Winston.

Fillmore, C.J. (1982). Frame semantics. In Linguistic Society of Korea (Eds.), *Linguistics in the morning calm.* Seoul: Hanshin.

Finlay-Jones, R.A., & Brown, G.W. (1981). Types of stressful life events and the onset of anxiety and depressive disorders. *Psychological Medicine, 11,* 803–815.

Fisher, R.P., Geiselman, R.E., & Amador, M. (1990). A field test of the cognitive interview: Enhancing the recollections of actual victims and witnesses of crime. *Journal of Applied Psychology, 74,* 722 727.

Fisher, R.P., Geiselman, R.E., Raymond, D.S., Jurkevich, L.M., & Warhaftig, M.L. (1987). Enhancing enhanced eyewitness memory: Refining the cognitive interview. *Journal of Police Science and Administration, 15,* 291–297.

Fitts, P.M., & Posner, M.I. (1967). *Human performance.* London: Prentice-Hall.

Fletcher, C.R. (1994). Levels of representation in memory for discourse. In M.A. Gernsbacher (Ed.), *Handbook of psycholinguistics.* London: Academic Press.

Flexser, A.J., & Tulving, E. (1978). Retrieval independence in recognition and recall. *Psychological Review, 85,* 153–171.

Flicker, C., Ferris, S.H., & Crook, T. (1987). Implications of memory and language dysfunction in naming deficit of senile dementia. *Brain and Language, 31,* 187 200.

Flude, B.M., Ellis, A.W., & Kay, J. (1989). Face processing and name retrieval in an anomic aphasia: Names are stored separately from semantic information about people. *Brain and Cognition, 11,* 60–72.

Fodor, J.A. (1983). *The modularity of mind.* Cambridge, MA: MIT Press.

Fodor, J.A., Garrett, M.F., Walker, E.C.T., & Parkes, C.H. (1980). Against definitions. *Cognition, 8,* 263–367

Fodor, J.A., & Pylyshyn, Z.W. (1981). How direct is visual perception? Some reflections on Gibson's "ecological approach". *Cognition, 9,* 139–196.

Fodor, J.D., Fodor, J.A., & Garrett, M.F. (1975). The psychological unreality of semantic representations. *Linguistic Inquiry, 4,* 515–531.

Forbus, K.D., Ferguson, R.W., & Gentner, D. (1994). Incremental structure mapping. In A. Ram & K. Eiselt (Eds.), *Sixteenth Annual Conference of the Cognitive Science Society.* Hillsdale, NJ: Lawrence Erlbaum Associates Inc.

Forster, K. (1979). Levels of processing and the structure of the language processor. In W.E. Cooper & E.C.T. Walker (Eds.), *Sentence processing: Psycholinguistic studies presented to Merrill Garrett.* Hillsdale, NJ: Lawrence Erlbaum Associates Inc.

Foulds, G.A. (1952). Temperamental differences in maze performance II: The effect of distraction and of electroconvulsive therapy on psychomotor retardation. *British Journal of Psychiatry, 43,* 33–41.

Fox, R., & McDaniel, C. (1982). The perception of biological motion by human infants. *Science, 218,* 486–487.

Francolini, C.N., & Egeth, H.E. (1980). On the non-automaticity of automatic activation: Evidence of selective seeing. *Perception and Psychophysics, 27,* 331–342.

Frauenfelder, U.H., Segui, J., & Dijkstra, T. (1990). Lexical effects in phonemic processing: Facilitatory or inhibitory? *Journal of Experimental Psychology: Human Perception and Performance, 16,* 77–91.

Frazier, L., & Rayner, K. (1982). Making and correcting errors during sentence comprehension: Eye movements in the analysis of structurally ambiguous sentences. *Cognitive Psychology, 14,* 178–210.

Frege, G. (1952). On sense and reference. In P. Geach & M. Black (Eds.), *Translations from the philosophical writings of Gottlob Frege.* Oxford: Basil Blackwell.

Freud, S. (1901). *The psychopathology of every-day life.* New York: W.W. Norton.

Freud, S. (1915). Repression. In *Freud's collected papers* (Vol. IV). London: Hogarth.

Freud, S. (1943). *A general introduction to psycho-analysis.* New York: Garden City.

Friedman, A. (1979). Framing pictures: The role of knowledge in automatised encoding and memory for gist. *Journal of Experimental Psychology: General, 108,* 316–355.

Frisby, J.P. (1986). The computational approach to vision. In I. Roth & J.P. Frisby (Eds.), *Perception and representation: A cognitive approach.* Milton Keynes, UK: Open University Press.

Frisby, J.P., & Mayhew, J.E.W. (1976). Rivalrous texture stereograms. *Nature, 264,* 53–56.

Fromkin, V. A. (1993). Speech production. In J.B. Gleason & N.B. Ratner (Eds.), *Psycholinguistics.* Orlando, FL: Harcourt Brace.

Fruzzetti, A.E., Toland, K., Teller, S.A., & Loftus, E.F. (1992). Memory and eyewitness testimony. In M. Gruneberg & P. Morris (Eds.), *Aspects of memory: The practical aspects.* London: Routledge.

Fry, G.A., Bridgman, C.S., & Ellerbrock, V.J. (1949). The effect of atmospheric scattering on binocular depth perception. *American Journal of Optometry, 26,* 9–15.

Funnell, E., & Sheridan, J. (1992). Categories of knowledge: Unfamiliar aspects of living and non-living things. *Cognitive Neuropsychology, 9,* 135–154.

Gabrieli, J.D.E., Cohen, N.J., & Corkin, S. (1988). The impaired learning of semantic knowledge following bilateral medial temporal-lobe resection. *Brain, 7,* 157–177.

Galambos, J.A., Abelson, R.P., & Black, J.B. (1986). *Knowledge structures.* Hillsdale, NJ: Lawrence Erlbaum Associates Inc.

Galambos, J.A., & Rips, L.J. (1982). Memory for routines. *Journal of Verbal Learning and Verbal Behavior, 21,* 260–281.

Galton, F. (1883). *Inquiries into human development and its development.* London: Macmillan.

Gardiner, J.M., & Java, R.I. (1993). Recognising and remembering, In A.F. Collins, S.E. Gathercole, M.A. Conway, & P.E. Morris (Eds.), *Theories of memory.* Hove, UK: Lawrence Erlbaum Associates Ltd.

Gardiner, J.M., & Parkin, A.J. (1990). Attention and recollective experience in recognition. *Memory and Cognition, 18,* 579–583.

Gardner, H. (1985). *The mind's new science.* New York: Basic Books.

Garnham, A. (1993). A number of questions about a question of number. *Behavioral and Brain Sciences, 16,* 350–351.

Garrett, M.F. (1975). The analysis of sentence production. In G.H. Bower (Ed.), *The psychology of learning and motivation* (Vol. 9). San Diego, CA: Academic Press.

Garrett, M.F. (1976). Syntactic processes in sentence production. In R.J. Wales & E. Walker (Eds.), *New approaches to language mechanisms.* Amsterdam: North-Holland.

Garrett, M.F. (1980). Levels of processing in sentence production. In B. Butterworth (Ed.), *Language production: Vol. 1. Speech and talk.* San Diego, CA: Academic Press.

Garrett, M.F. (1984). The organisation of processing structures for language production: Applications to aphasic speech. In D. Caplan, A.R. Lecours, & A. Smith (Eds.), *Biological perspectives on language.* Cambridge, MA: MIT Press.

Gauld, A., & Stephenson, G.M. (1967). Some experiments relating to Bartlett's theory of remembering. *British Journal of Psychology, 58,* 39–50.

Gee, J.P. (1986). Units in the production of narrative discourse. *Discourse Processes, 9,* 391–422.

Geis, M., & Zwicky, A.M. (1971). On invited inferences. *Linguistic Inquiry, 2,* 561–566.

Geiselman, R.E., Fisher, R.P., MacKinnon, D.P., & Holland, H.L. (1985). Eyewitness memory enhancement in police interview: Cognitive retrieval mnemonics versus hypnosis. *Journal of Applied Psychology, 70,* 401–412.

Gentner, D. (1975). Evidence for the psychological reality of semantic components: The verbs of possession. In D.A. Norman & D.E. Rumelhart (Eds.), *Explorations in cognition.* San Francisco: Freeman.

Gentner, D. (1980). The structure of analogical models in science. *BBN Technical Report No. 4454.*

Gentner, D. (1981). Verb structures in memory for sentences: Evidence for componential representation. *Cognitive Psychology, 13,* 56–83.

Gentner, D. (1983). Structure-mapping: A theoretical framework for analogy. *Cognitive Science, 7,* 155–170.

Gentner, D., & Forbus, K.D. (1991). MAC/FAC: A model of similarity-based retrieval. *Thirteenth Annual Conference of the Cognitive Science Society.* Hillsdale, NJ: Lawrence Erlbaum Associates Inc.

Gentner, D., & Gentner, D.R. (1983). Flowing waters and teeming crowds: Mental models of electricity. In D. Gentner & A.L. Stevens (Eds.), *Mental models*. Hillsdale, NJ: Lawrence Erlbaum Associates Inc.

Gentner, D., & Landers, R. (1985). Analogical reminding: A good match is hard to find. *Proceedings of the International Conference on Systems, Man and Cybernetics, IEEE*. Tucson, Arizona, November.

Gentner, D., Rattermann, M.J., & Forbus, K.D. (1992). The role of similarity in transfer. *Cognitive Psychology, 25,* 431–467.

Gentner, D., & Stevens, A.L. (1983). *Mental models*. Hillsdale, NJ: Lawrence Erlbaum Associates Inc.

Gernsbacher, M.A., Varner, K.R., & Faust, M. (1990). Investigating differences in general comprehension skill. *Journal of Experimental Psychology: Learning, Memory, and Cognition, 16,* 430–445.

Gibson, J.J. (1950). *The perception of the visual world*. Boston: Houghton Mifflin.

Gibson, J.J. (1966). *The senses considered as perceptual systems*. Boston: Houghton Mifflin.

Gibson, J.J. (1979). *The ecological approach to visual perception*. Boston: Houghton Mifflin.

Gick, M.L., & Holyoak, K.J. (1980). Analogical problem solving. *Cognitive Psychology, 12,* 306–355.

Gick, M.L., & Holyoak, K.J. (1983). Schema induction in analogical transfer. *Cognitive Psychology, 15,* 1–38.

Gigerenzer, G., & Hug, K. (1992). Domain specific reasoning: Social contracts, cheating and perspective change. *Cognition, 43,* 127–171.

Gilhooly, K.J. (1995). *Thinking: Directed, undirected and creative* (2nd Edn.). London: Academic Press.

Gilhooly, K.J., & Falconer, W. (1974). Concrete and abstract terms and relations in testing a rule. *Quarterly Journal of Experimental Psychology, 26,* 355–259.

Gilligan, S.G., & Bower, G.H. (1984). Cognitive consequences of emotional arousal. In C. Izard, J. Kagen, & R. Zajonc (Eds.), *Emotions, cognition, and behaviour*. New York: Cambridge University Press.

Gilmore, D.J., & Green, T.R.G. (1988). Programming plans and programming expertise. *Quarterly Journal of Experimental Psychology, 40A,* 423–442.

Girotto, V., Mazzacco, A., & Cherubini, P. (1992). Judgements of deontic relevance in reasoning: A reply to Jackson and Griggs. *Quarterly Journal of Experimental Psychology, 45A,* 547–574.

Glanzer, M., & Cunitz, A.R. (1966). Two storage mechanisms in free recall. *Journal of Verbal Learning and Verbal Behavior, 5,* 351–360.

Glass, A.L., & Holyoak, K.J. (1975). Alternative conceptions of semantic memory. *Cognition, 3,* 313–339.

Glenberg, A.M., Meyer, M., & Lindem, K. (1987). Mental models contribute to foregrounding during text comprehension. *Journal of Memory and Language, 26,* 69–83.

Godden, D.R., & Baddeley, A.D. (1975). Context-dependent memory in two natural environments: On land and under water. *British Journal of Psychology, 66,* 325–331.

Godden, D.R., & Baddeley, A.D. (1980). When does context influence recognition memory? *British Journal of Psychology, 71,* 99–104.

Goldberg, G. (1989). The ability of patients with brain damage to generate mental visual images. *Brain, 112,* 305–325.

Goldman, A.I. (1986). *Epistemology and cognition*. Cambridge, MA: Harvard University Press.

Goldstone, R.L., Medin, D.L., & Gentner, D. (1991). Relational similarity and the non-independence of features in similarity judgements. *Cognitive Psychology, 23,* 222–262.

Gomulicki, B.R. (1956). Recall as an abstractive process. *Acta Psychologica, 12,* 77–94.

Gordon, I.E. (1989). *Theories of visual perception*. Chichester, UK: John Wiley.

Gorman, M.E. (1992). Experimental simulations of falsification. In M.T. Keane & K.J. Gilhooly (Eds.), *Advances in the psychology of thinking*. London: Harvester Wheatsheaf.

Gorman, Michael E., & Gorman, Margaret E. (1984). A comparison of disconfirmation, confirmation and control strategy on Wason's 2–4–6 task. *Quarterly Journal of Experimental Psychology, 36A,* 629–648.

Gotlib, I.H., McLachlan, A.L., & Katz, A.N. (1988). Biases in visual attention in depressed and nondepressed individuals. *Cognition and Emotion, 2,* 185–200.

Gould, J.D. (1978). An experimental study of writing, dictating, and speaking. In J. Requin (Ed.), *Attention and performance* (Vol. VII). Hillsdale, NJ: Lawrence Erlbaum Associates Inc.

Gould, J.D. (1980). Experiments on composing letters: Some facts, some myths, and some observations. In L.W. Gregg & E.R. Sternberg (Eds.), *Cognitive processes in writing*. Hillsdale, NJ: Lawrence Erlbaum Associates Inc.

Graesser, A.C., Gordon, S.E., & Sawyer, J.D. (1979). Recognition memory for typical and atypical actions: Tests of a script pointer + tag hypothesis. *Journal of Verbal Learning and Verbal Behavior, 18,* 319–332.

Graesser, A.C., Singer, M., & Trabasso, T. (1994). Constructing inferences during narrative text comprehension. *Psychological Review, 101,* 371–395.

Graesser, A.C., Woll, S.B., Kowalski, D.J., & Smith, D.A. (1980). Memory for typical and atypical actions in scripted activities. *Journal of Experimental Psychology: Human Learning and Memory, 6,* 503–515.

Graf, P., & Masson, M.E.J. (1993). *Implicit memory: New directions in cognition, development, and neuropsychology.* Hillsdale, NJ: Lawrence Erlbaum Associates Inc.

Graf, P., & Schacter, D.L. (1985). Implicit and explicit memory for new associations in norma1 and amnesic subjects. *Journal of Experimental Psychology: Learning, Memory, and Cognition, 11,* 501–518.

Graf, P., Squire, L.R., & Mandler, G. (1984). The information that amnesic patients do not forget. *Journal of Experimental Psychology: Learning, Memory, and Cognition, 10,* 164–178.

Gray, J.A., & Wedderburn, A.A. (1960). Grouping strategies with simultaneous stimuli. *Quarterly Journal of Experimental Psychology, 12,* 180–184.

Green, A.J.K., & Gilhooly, K.J. (1992). Empirical advances in expertise research. In M.T. Keane & K.J. Gilhooly (Eds.), *Advances in the psychology of thinking.* London: Harvester Wheatsheaf.

Green, T.R.G. (1989). Cognitive dimensions of notation. In A. Sutcliffe & L. Macaulay (Eds.), *People and computers* (Vol. 5). Cambridge: Cambridge University Press.

Green, T.R.G. (1990). Programming languages as information structures. In J.-M. Hoc, T.R.G. Green, R. Samuray, & D.J. Gilmore (Eds.), *Psychology of programming.* London: Academic Press.

Greeno, J.G. (1994). Gibson's affordances. *Psychological Review, 101,* 336–342.

Gregory, R.L. (1970). *The intelligent eye.* New York: McGraw-Hill.

Gregory, R.L. (1972). Seeing as thinking. *Times Literary Supplement,* 23 June.

Gregory, R.L. (1973). The confounded eye. In R.L. Gregory & E.H. Gombrich (Eds.), *Illusion in nature and art.* London: Duckworth.

Gregory, R.L. (1980). Perceptions as hypotheses. *Philosophical Transactions of the Royal Society of London, Series B, 290,* 181–197.

Grice, H.P. (1967). Logic and conversation. In P. Cole & J.L. Morgan (Eds.), *Studies in syntax* (Vol. III). New York: Seminar Press.

Grice, H.P. (1975). Logic and conversation. In P. Cole & J.L. Morgan (Eds.), *Syntax and semantics: Vol. III. Speech acts.* New York: Seminar Press.

Griggs, R.A. (1983). The role of problem content in the selection task and THOG problem. In J. St. B.T. Evans (Ed.), *Thinking and reasoning: Psychological approaches.* London: Routledge & Kegan Paul.

Griggs, R.A., & Cox, J.R. (1982). The elusive thematic-material effect in Wason's selection task. *British Journal of Psychology, 73,* 407–420.

Griggs, R.A., & Cox, J.R. (1983). The effects of problem content and negation on Wason's selection task. *Quarterly Journal of Experimental Psychology, 35A,* 519–533.

Griggs, R.A., & Cox, J.R. (1993). Permission schemas and the selection task. *Quarterly Journal of Experimental Psychology, 46A,* 637–652.

Grudin, J.T. (1983). Error patterns in novice and skilled transcription typing. In W.E. Cooper (Ed.), *Cognitive aspects of skilled typewriting.* New York: Springer.

Gruneberg, M.M., & Morris, P.E. (Eds.) (1992a). *Aspects of memory: Vol. 1. The practical aspects.* London: Routledge.

Gruneberg, M.M., & Morris, P.E. (1992b). Applying memory research. In M. Gruneberg & P. Morris (Eds.), *Aspects of memory: Vol. 1. The practical aspects.* London: Routledge.

Gunther, H., Gfoerer, S., & Weiss, L. (1984). Inflection, frequency, and the word superiority effect. *Psychological Research, 46,* 261–281.

Guyote, M.J., & Sternberg, R.J. (1981). A transitive-chain theory of syllogistic reasoning. *Cognitive Psychology, 13,* 461–524.

Haber, R.N. (1983). The impending demise of the icon: A critique of the concept of iconic storage in visual information processing. *Behavioral and Brain Sciences, 6,* 1–11.

Hadamard, J. (1945). *A essay on the psychology of invention in the mathematical field.* New York: Dover.

Hampson, P.J. (1989). Aspects of attention and cognitive science. *The Irish Journal of Psychology, 10,* 261–275.

Hampton, J.A. (1979). Polymorphous concepts in semantic memory. *Journal of Verbal Learning and Verbal Behavior, 18,* 441–461.

Hampton, J.A. (1981). An investigation of the nature of abstract concepts. *Memory and Cognition, 9,* 149–156.

Hampton, J.A. (1982). A demonstration of intransitivity in natural categories. *Cognition, 12,* 151–164.

Hampton, J.A. (1983). *A composite prototype model of conceptual conjunction*. Unpublished manuscript, The City University, London.

Hampton, J.A. (1987). Inheritance of attributes in natural concept conjunctions. *Memory and Cognition, 15*, 55–71.

Hampton, J.A. (1988). Overextension of conjunctive concepts. *Journal of Experimental Psychology: Language, Memory, and Cognition, 14*, 12–32.

Hardy, G.R., & Legge, D. (1968). Cross-modal induction of changes in sensory thresholds. *Quarterly Journal of Experimental Psychology, 20*, 20–29.

Hardyck, C.D., & Petrinovich, L.F. (1970). Subvocal speech and comprehension level as a function of the difficulty level of reading material. *Journal of Verbal Learning and Verbal Behavior, 9*, 647–652.

Harley, T. (1984). A critique of top-down independent levels models of speech production: Evidence from non-plan-internal speech errors. *Cognitive Science, 8*, 191–219.

Harris, J.E., & Wilkins, A.J. (1982). Remembering to do things: A theoretical framework and an illustrative experiment. *Human Learning, 1*, 123–136.

Harris, M. (1990). Language and thought. In M.W. Eysenck (Ed.), *The Blackwell dictionary of cognitive psychology.* Oxford: Blackwell.

Harris, M.G., & Humphreys, G.W. (1994). Computational theories of vision. In A.M. Colman (Ed.), *Companion encyclopaedia of psychology* (Vol. 1). London: Routledge.

Hart, J., Berndt, R.S., & Caramazza, A. (1985). Category-specific naming deficit following cerebral infarction. *Nature, 316*, 439–440.

Hartlage, S., Alloy, L.B., Vazquez, C., & Dykman, B. (1993). Automatic and effortful processing in depression. *Psychological Bulletin, 113*, 247–278.

Harvey, L.O., Roberts, J.O., & Gervais, M.J. (1983). The spatial frequency basis of internal representations. In H.-G. Geissler, H.F.J.M. Buffart, E.L.J. Leeuwenberg, & V. Sarris (Eds.), *Modern issues in perception.* Rotterdam: North-Holland.

Hatano, G., & Inagaki, K. (1986). Two courses of expertise. In H. Stevenson, H. Azuma, & K. Hatuka (Eds.), *Child development in Japan.* San Francisco: Freeman.

Hatfield, F.M., & Patterson, K.E. (1983). Phonological spelling. *Quarterly Journal of Experimental Psychology, 35A*, 451–468.

Hayes, J.R., & Flower, L.S. (1980). Identifying the organisation of writing processes. In L.W. Gregg & E.R. Sternberg (Eds.), *Cognitive processes in writing.* Hillsdale, NJ: Lawrence Erlbaum Associates Inc.

Hayes, J.R., & Flower, L.S. (1986). Writing research and the writer. *American Psychologist, 41*, 1106–1113.

Hayes, J.R., Flower, L.S., Schriver, K., Stratman, J., & Carey, L. (1985). *Cognitive processes in revision* (Technical Report No. 12). Pittsburgh, PA: Carnegie Mellon University.

Hayes, J.R., & Simon, H.A. (1974). Understanding written problem instructions. In R.L. Gregg (Ed.), *Knowledge and cognition.* Hillsdale, NJ: Lawrence Erlbaum Associates Inc.

Hayes, J.R., & Simon, H.A. (1977). Psychological differences among problem isomorphs. In N.J. Castellan, D.B. Pisoni, & G.R. Potts (Eds.), *Cognitive theory* (Vol. 2). Hillsdale, NJ: Lawrence Erlbaum Associates Inc.

Hayes, P.J. (1985). Some problems and non-problems in representational theory. In R.J. Brachman & H.J. Levesque (Eds.), *Readings in knowledge representation.* Los Altos, CA: Morgan Kaufmann.

Hebb, D.O. (1949). *The organisation of behaviour.* New York: John Wiley.

Heider, E. (1972). Universals in colour naming and memory. *Journal of Experimental Psychology, 93*, 10–20.

Heider, F., & Simmel, M. (1944). An experimental study of apparent behavior. *American Journal of Psychology, 57*, 243–259.

Heindel, W.C., Butters, N., & Salmon, D.P. (1988). Impaired learning of a motor skill in patients with Huntingdon's disease. *Behavioural Neuroscience, 102*, 141–147.

Heller, J., & Reif, F. (1984). Prescribing effective human problem solving: Problem description in physics. *Cognition and Instruction, 2*, 191–203.

Helmholtz, H. von (1962). *Treatise on physiological optics* (Vol. III). New York: Dover (Original work published 1866.)

Hemsley, D.R., & Zawada, S.L. (1976). "Filtering" and the cognitive deficit in schizophrenia. *British Journal of Psychiatry, 128*, 456–461.

Henderson, J.M. (1992). Object identification in context: The visual processing of natural scenes. *Canadian Journal of Psychology, 46*, 319–341.

Henle, M. (1962). On the relation between logic and thinking. *Psychological Review, 69*, 366–378.

Herman, J.L., & Schatzow, E. (1987). Recovery and verification of memories of childhood sexual trauma. *Psychoanalytic Psychology, 4*, 1–14.

Hertel, P.T., & Hardin, T.S. (1990). Remembering with and without awareness in a depressed mood:

Evidence of deficits in initiative. *Journal of Experimental Psychology: General, 119*, 45–59.

Hinton, G.E. (1979). Some demonstrations of the effects of structural descriptions in mental imagery. *Cognitive Science, 3*, 231–251.

Hinton, G.E. (1989). Connectionist learning procedures. *Artificial Intelligence, 40*, 185–234.

Hinton, G.E., & Anderson, J.A. (1981). *Parallel models of associative memory*. Hillsdale, NJ: Lawrence Erlbaum Associates Inc.

Hinton, G.E., McClelland, J.L., & Rumelhart, D.E. (1986). Distributed representations. In D.E. Rumelhart, J.L. McClelland, & The PDP Research Group (Eds.), *Parallel distributed processing: Vol. 1. Foundations*. Cambridge, MA: MIT Press.

Hinton, G.E., & Shallice, T. (1991). Lesioning an attractor network: Investigations of acquired dyslexia. *Psychological Review, 98*, 74–95.

Hintzman, D.L. (1986). "Schema abstraction" in a multiple-trace memory model. *Psychological Review, 93*, 411–428.

Hintzman, D.L. (1990). Human learning and memory: Connections and dissociations. *Annual Review of Psychology, 41*, 109–139.

Hintzman, D.L., & Ludlam, G. (1980). Differential forgetting of prototypes and old instances: Simulation by an exemplar-based classification model. *Memory and Cognition, 8*, 378–382.

Hirst, W., Spelke, E.S., Reaves, C.C., Caharack, G., & Neisser, U. (1980). Dividing attention without alternation or automaticity. *Journal of Experimental Psychology: General, 109*, 98–117.

Hitch, G.J. (1978). The role of short-term working memory in mental arithmetic. *Cognitive Psychology, 10*, 302–323.

Hitch, G.J., & Baddeley, A.D. (1976). Verbal reasoning and working memory. *Quarterly Journal of Experimental Psychology, 28*, 603–621.

Hitch, G.J., & Ferguson, J. (1991). Prospective memory for future intentions: Such comparisons with memory for past events. *European Journal of Cognitive Psychology, 3*, 285–295.

Hockett, C. (1955). *Manual of phonology* (Publications in Anthropology and Linguistics, No. 11). Bloomington: Indiana University.

Hoffman, C., Lau, I., & Johnson, D.R. (1986). The linguistic relativity of person cognition. *Journal of Personality and Social Psychology, 51*, 1097–1105.

Hoffman, D.D., & Richards, W.A. (1984). Parts of recognition. *Cognition, 18*, 65–96.

Holding, D.H. (1985). *The psychology of chess*. Hillsdale, NJ: Lawrence Erlbaum Associates Inc.

Holding, D.H. (1989). *Human skills* (2nd Edn.). Chichester, UK: John Wiley.

Holding, D.H., & Reynolds, J.R. (1982). Recall or evaluation of chess positions as determinants of chess skill. *Memory and Cognition, 10*, 237–242.

Hollan, J.D. (1975). Features and semantic memory: Set-theoretic or network model. *Psychological Review, 82*, 154–155.

Holland, J.H., Holyoak, K.J., Nisbett, R.E., & Thagard, P. (1986). *Induction: Processes in inference, learning and discovery*. Cambridge, MA: MIT Press.

Holmes, D.S. (1972). Repression or interference? A further investigation. *Journal of Personality and Social Psychology, 22*, 163–170.

Holmes, D.S. (1990). The evidence for repression: An examination of sixty years of research. In J. Singer (Ed.), *Repression and dissociation: Implications for personality theory, psychopathology, and health*. Chicago: University of Chicago Press.

Holst, V.F., & Pezdek, K. (1992). Scripts for typical crimes and their effects on memory for eyewitness testimony. *Applied Cognitive Psychology, 6*, 573–587.

Holyoak, K.J. (1985). The pragmatics of analogical transfer. *The Psychology of Learning and Motivation, 19*, 59–87.

Holyoak, K.J. (1991). Symbolic connectionism: Toward third-generation theories of expertise. In A. Ericsson & J. Smith (Eds.), *Toward a general theory of expertise*. Cambridge: Cambridge University Press.

Holyoak, K.J., & Koh, K. (1987). Surface and structural similarity in analogical transfer. *Memory and Cognition, 15*, 332–340.

Holyoak, K.J., & Spellman, B.A. (1993). Thinking. *Annual Review of Psychology, 44*, 265–315.

Holyoak, K.J., & Thagard, P. (1989). Analogical mapping by constraint satisfaction. *Cognitive Science, 13*, 295–355.

Holyoak, K.J., & Thagard, P. (1990). A constraint satisfaction approach to analogical mapping and retrieval. In K.J. Gilhooly, M.T. Keane, R. Logie, & G. Erdos (Eds.), *Lines of thinking: Reflections on the psychology of thought* (Vol. 1). Chichester, UK: John Wiley.

Hotopf, W.H.N. (1980). Slips of the pen. In U. Frith (Ed.), *Cognitive processes in spelling*. London: Academic Press.

Howard, D., & Orchard-Lisle, V. (1984). On the origin of semantic errors in naming: Evidence from the case of a global aphasic. *Cognitive Neuropsychology, 1*, 163–190.

Howard, I.P., Bergstrom, S.S., & Masao, O. (1990). Shape from shading in different frames of reference. *Perception, 19,* 523–530.

Howie, D. (1952). Perceptual defence. *Psychological Review, 59,* 308–315.

Hsu, F.-H. (1993). IBM Deep Blue in Copenhagen. *International Computer Chess Association Journal, 16,* 53–56.

Huang, T., & Lee, C. (1989). Motion and structure from orthographic projections. *IEEE Transactions on Pattern Analysis and Machine Intelligence, 11,* 536–540.

Hubel, D.H., & Wiesel, T.N. (1962). Receptive fields, binocular interaction and functional architecture in the cat's visual cortex. *Journal of Physiology, 160,* 106–154.

Huey, E.B. (1908). *The psychology and pedagogy of reading.* New York: Macmillan.

Huggins, A.W.F. (1964). Distortion of the temporal pattern of speech: Interruption and alternation. *Journal of the Acoustical Society of America, 36,* 1055–1064.

Hull, C.L. (1930). Knowledge and purpose as habit mechanisms. *Psychological Review, 37,* 511–525.

Hull, C.L. (1931). Goal attraction and directing ideas conceived as habit phenomena *Psychological Review, 38,* 487–506.

Hummel, J.E., & Biederman, I. (1992). Dynamic binding in a neural network for shape recognition. *Psychological Review, 99,* 480–517.

Humphreys, G.W., & Bruce, V. (1989). *Visual cognition: Computational, experimental and neuropsychological perspectives.* Hove, UK: Lawrence Erlbaum Associates Ltd.

Humphreys, G.W., & Riddoch, M.J. (1984). Routes to object constancy: Implications from neurological impairments of object constancy. *Quarterly Journal of Experimental Psychology, 36A,* 385–415.

Humphreys, G.W., & Riddoch, M.J. (1985). Author corrections to "Routes to object constancy". *Quarterly Journal of Experimental Psychology, 37A,* 493–495.

Humphreys, G.W., & Riddoch, M.J. (1987). *To see but not to see: A case study of visual agnosia.* Hove, UK: Lawrence Erlbaum Associates Ltd.

Humphreys, G.W., & Riddoch, M.J. (1993). Interactions between object and space systems revealed through neuropsychology. In D.E. Meyer & S.M. Kornblum (Eds.), *Attention and performance* (Vol. XIV). London: MIT Press.

Humphreys, G.W., & Riddoch, M.J. (1994). Visual object processing in normality and pathology: Implications for rehabilitation. In M.J. Riddoch & G.W. Humphreys (Eds.), *Cognitive neuropsychology and cognitive rehabilitation.* Hove, UK: Lawrence Erlbaum Associates Ltd.

Humphreys, G.W., Riddoch, M.J., & Quinlan, P.T. (1985). Interactive processes in perceptual organization: Evidence from visual agnosia. In M.I. Posner & O.S.M. Marin (Eds.), *Attention and performance* (Vol. XI). Hillsdale, NJ: Lawrence Erlbaum Associates Inc.

Hunt, E., & Agnoli, F. (1991). The Whorfian hypothesis: A cognitive psychological perspective. *Psychological Review, 98,* 377–389.

Huppert, F.A., & Piercy, M. (1976). Recognition memory in amnesic patients: Effect of temporal context and familiarity of material. *Cortex, 4,* 3–20.

Huppert, F.A., & Piercy, M. (1978). The role of trace strength in recency and frequency judgements by amnesic and control subjects. *Quarterly Journal of Experimental Psychology, 30,* 346–354.

Hyde, T.S., & Jenkins, J.J. (1973). Recall for words as a function of semantic, graphic, and syntactic orienting tasks. *Journal of Verbal Learning and Verbal Behavior, 12,* 471–480.

Ittelson, W.H. (1951). Size as a cue to distance: Static localisation. *American Journal of Psychology, 64,* 54–67.

Ittelson, W.H. (1952). *The Ames demonstrations in perception.* New York: Hafner.

Jackson, S.L., & Griggs, R.A. (1990). The elusive pragmatic reasoning schemas effect. *Quarterly Journal of Experimental Psychology, 42A,* 353–374.

Jacoby, L.L. (1983). Remembering the data: Analysing interactive processing in reading. *Journal of Verbal Learning and Verbal Behavior, 22,* 485–508.

Jacoby, L.L., & Dallas, M. (1981). On the relationship between autobiographical memory and perceptual learning. *Journal of Experimental Psychology: General, 110,* 306–340.

Jacoby, L.L., Toth, J.P., & Yonelinas, A.P. (1993). Separating conscious and unconscious influences of memory: Measuring recollection. *Journal of Experimental Psychology: General, 122,* 139–154.

James, W. (1890). *Principles of psychology* New York: Holt.

Jansari, A., & Parkin, A.J. (submitted). Things that go bump in your life: explaining the reminiscence bump in autobiographical memory.

Javed, D., & Seidenberg, M.S. (1991). Does word identification proceed from spelling to sound to meaning? *Journal of Experimental Psychology: General, 120,* 358–394.

Jeannerod, M. (1994). The representing brain: Neural correlates of motor intention and imagery. *Behavioral and Brain Sciences, 17,* 187–202.

Jeffries, R., Polson, P., Razran, L., & Atwood, M.E. (1977). A process model for missionaries–cannibals and other river-crossing problems. *Cognitive Psychology, 9,* 412–440.

Johansson, G. (1973). Visual perception of biological motion and a model for its analysis. *Perception and Psychophysics, 14,* 201–211.

Johansson, G. (1975). Visual motion perception. *Scientific American, 232,* 76–89.

Johansson, G., von Hofsten, C., & Jansson, G. (1980). Event perception. *Annual Review of Psychology, 31,* 27–64.

Johnson-Laird, P.N. (1975). Models of deduction. In R.J. Falmagne (Ed.), *Reasoning: Representation and process in children and adults.* Hillsdale, NJ: Lawrence Erlbaum Associates Inc.

Johnson-Laird, P.N. (1977). Procedural semantics. *Cognition, 5,* 189–214.

Johnson-Laird, P.N. (1980). Mental models in cognitive science. *Cognitive Science, 4,* 71–115.

Johnson-Laird, P.N. (1983). *Mental models.* Cambridge: Cambridge University Press.

Johnson-Laird, P.N. (1988). Freedom and constraint in creativity. In R.J. Sternberg (Ed.), *The nature of creativity.* Cambridge: Cambridge University Press.

Johnson-Laird, P.N. (1989). Mental models. In M. Posner (Ed.), *Foundations of cognitive science.* Cambridge, MA: MIT Press.

Johnson-Laird, P.N. (1993). *The computer and the mind* (2nd Edn.). London: Fontana.

Johnson-Laird, P.N., & Bara, B.G. (1984). Syllogistic inference. *Cognition, 16,* 1–61.

Johnson-Laird, P.N., & Byrne, R.M.J. (1989). Only reasoning. *Journal of Memory and Language, 28,* 313–330.

Johnson-Laird, P.N., & Byrne, R.M.J. (1990). Metalogical reasoning: Knights, knaves and Rips. *Cognition, 36,* 69–84.

Johnson-Laird, P.N., & Byrne, R.M.J. (1991). *Deduction.* Hove, UK: Lawrence Erlbaum Associates Ltd.

Johnson-Laird, P.N., & Byrne, R.M.J. (1993a). Multiple book review of "Deduction". *Behavioral and Brain Sciences, 16,* 323–380.

Johnson-Laird, P.N., & Byrne, R.M.J. (1993b). Models and deductive rationality. In K.I. Manktelow & D.E. Over (Eds.), *Rationality: Psychological and philosophical perspectives.* London: Routledge.

Johnson-Laird, P.N., Byrne, R.M.J., & Schaeken, W. (1992). Propositional reasoning by model. *Psychological Review, 99,* 418–439.

Johnson-Laird, P.N., Byrne, R.M.J., & Tabossi, P. (1989). Reasoning by model: The case of multiple quantification. *Psychological Review, 96,* 658–673.

Johnson-Laird, P.N., Herrmann, D.J., & Chaffin, R. (1984). Only connections: A critique of semantic networks. *Psychological Bulletin, 96,* 292–315.

Johnson-Laird, P.N., Legrenzi, P., & Sonino-Legrenzi, M. (1972). Reasoning and a sense of reality. *British Journal of Psychology, 63,* 395–400.

Johnson-Laird, P.N., & Steedman, M.J. (1978). The psychology of syllogisms. *Cognitive Psychology, 10,* 64–99.

Johnson-Laird, P.N., & Stevenson, R. (1970). Memory for syntax. *Nature, 227,* 412.

Johnson-Laird, P.N., & Wason, P.C (1970). A theoretical analysis of insight into a reasoning task. *Cognitive Psychology, 1,* 134–148.

Johnston, W.A., & Dark, V.J. (1986). Selective attention. *Annual Review of Psychology, 37,* 43–75.

Johnston, W.A., & Heinz, S.P. (1978). Flexibility and capacity demands of attention. *Journal of Experimental Psychology: General, 107,* 420–435.

Johnston, W.A., & Wilson, J. (1980). Perceptual processing of non-targets in an attention task. *Memory and Cognition, 8,* 372–377.

Jones, G.V. (1982a). Tests of the dual-mechanism theory of recall. *Acta Psychologica, 50,* 61–72.

Jones, G.V. (1982b). Stacks not fuzzy sets: An ordinal basis for prototype theory of concepts. *Cognition, 12,* 281–290.

Joyce, J. (1960). *Ulysses.* London: Bodley Head. (Original work published 1922.)

Julesz, B. (1971). *Foundations of cyclopean perception.* Chicago: University of Chicago Press.

Julesz, B. (1975). Experiments in the visual perception of texture. *Scientific American, 212,* 38–48.

Julesz, B. (1981). Textons, the elements of texture perception, and their interactions. *Nature, 290,* 91–97.

Juola, J.F., Bowhuis, D.G., Cooper, E.E., & Warner, C.B. (1991). Control of attention around the fovea. *Journal of Experimental Psychology: Human Perception and Performance, 15,* 315–330.

Just, M.A., & Carpenter, P.A. (1992). A capacity theory of comprehension: Individual differences in working memory. *Psychological Review, 99,* 122–149.

Just, M.A., Carpenter, P.A., & Woolley, J.D. (1982). Paradigms and processes in reading comprehension. *Journal of Experimental Psychology: General, 111,* 228–238.

Kahneman, D., & Henik, A. (1979). Perceptual organisation and attention. In M. Kubovy & J.R. Pomerantz (Eds.), *Perceptual organisation.* Hillsdale, NJ: Lawrence Erlbaum Associates Inc.

Kahney, H. (1989). What do novice programmers know about recursion? In E. Soloway & J.C. Spohrer (Eds.), *Studying the novice programmer.* Hillsdale, NJ: Lawrence Erlbaum Associates Inc.

Kahney, H., & Eisenstadt, M. (1982). Programmers' mental models of their programming tasks. *Proceedings of the Fourth Annual Conference of the Cognitive Science Society.* Ann Arbor, Michigan.

Kaiser, M.K., Jonides, J., & Alexander, J. (1986). Intuitive reasoning about abstract and familiar physics problems. *Memory and Cognition, 14,* 308–312.

Kaiser, M.K., Proffitt, D.R., & Anderson, K. (1985). Judgements of natural and anomalous trajectories in the presence and absence of motion. *Journal of Experimental Psychology: Learning, Memory, and Cognition, 11,* 795–803.

Kanizsa, G. (1976). Subjective contours. *Scientific American, 234,* 48–52.

Kant, E. (1963). *Critique of pure reason* (2nd Edn.). London: Macmillan. (Original work published 1787.)

Kaplan, G.A., & Simon, H.A. (1990). In search of insight. *Cognitive Psychology, 22,* 374–419.

Kassin, S.M., Ellsworth, P.C., & Smith, U.L. (1989). The "general acceptance" of psychological research on eyewitness testimony. *American Psychologist, 44,* 1089–1098.

Katz, J.J., & Fodor, J.A. (1963). The structure of a semantic theory. *Language, 39,* 170–210.

Kaufer, D., Hayes, J.R., & Flower, L.S. (1986). Composing written sentences. *Research in the Teaching of English, 20,* 121–140.

Kay, J., & Ellis, A.W. (1987). A cognitive neuro psychological case study of anomia: Implications for psychological models of word retrieval. *Brain, 110,* 613–629.

Kay, J., & Marcel, T. (1981). One process not two in reading aloud: Lexical analogies do the work of nonlexical rules. *Quarterly Journal of Experimental Psychology, 39A,* 29–41.

Kay, P., & Kempton, W. (1984). What is the Sapir–Whorf hypothesis? *American Anthropologist, 86,* 65–79.

Keane, M. (1985a). Restructuring revised: A theoretical note on Ohlsson's mechanism of restructuring. *Scandinavian Journal of Psychology, 26,* 363–365.

Keane, M. (1985b). On drawing analogies when solving problems: A theory and test of solution generation in an analogical problem solving task. *British Journal of Psychology, 76,* 449–458

Keane, M. (1987). On retrieving analogues when solving problems. *Quarterly Journal of Experimental Psychology, 39A,* 29–41.

Keane, M.T. (1988). *Analogical problem solving.* Chichester, UK: Ellis Horwood (New York: John Wiley).

Keane, M.T. (1989). Modelling "insight" in practical construction problems. *Irish Journal of Psychology, 11,* 201–215.

Keane, M.T. (1993). The cognitive processes underlying complex analogies: Theoretical and empirical advances. *Ricerche di Psicologia, 17,* 9–36.

Keane, M.T., & Brayshaw, M. (1988). The incremental analogy machine: A computational model of analogy. In D. Sleeman (Ed.), *Third European working session on learning.* London: Pitman/San Mateo, CA: Morgan Kaufmann.

Keane, M.T., & Gilhooly, K.J. (Eds.) (1992). *Advances in thinking research.* London: Harvester Wheatsheaf.

Keane, M.T., Kahney, H., & Brayshaw, M. (1989). Simulating analogical mapping difficulties in recursion problems. *Proceedings of the Annual Conference of the Society for the Study of Artificial Intelligence and Simulation of Behaviour.* London: Pitman.

Keane, M.T, Ledgeway, T., & Duff, S. (1994). Constraints on analogical mapping: A comparison of three models. *Cognitive Science, 18,* 287–334.

Keil, F.C. (1989). *Concepts, kinds and conceptual development.* Cambridge, MA: MIT Press.

Kellogg, R.T. (1988). Attentional overload and writing performance: Effects of rough draft and outline strategies. *Journal of Experimental Psychology: Learning, Memory, and Cognition, 14,* 355–365.

Kellogg, R.T. (1990). Writing. In M.W. Eysenck (Ed.), *The Blackwell dictionary of cognitive psychology.* Oxford: Blackwell.

Kempton, W. (1986). Two theories used of home heat control. *Cognitive Science, 10,* 75–91.

Kimchi, R. (1992). Primacy of wholistic processing and global/local paradigm: A critical review. *Psychological Bulletin, 112,* 24–38.

Kinchla, R.A. (1992). Attention. In M.R. Rosenzweig & L.W. Porter (Eds.), *Annual Review of Psychology* (Vol. 43). Palo Alto, CA: Annual Reviews Inc.

Kinchla, R.A., & Wolfe, J.M. (1979). The order of visual processing: "Top-down", "bottom up", or "middle-out". *Perception and Psychophysics, 25,* 225–231.

Kintsch, W. (1974). *The representation of meaning in memory.* Hillsdale, NJ: Lawrence Erlbaum Associates Inc.

Kintsch, W. (1980). Semantic memory: A tutorial. In R.S. Nickerson (Ed.), *Attention and performance* (Vol. VIII). Hillsdale, NJ: Lawrence Erlbaum Associates Inc.

Kintsch, W. (1988). The role of knowledge in discourse comprehension: A construction– integration model. *Psychological Review, 95,* 163–182.

Kintsch, W. (1992). A cognitive architecture for comprehension. In H.L. Pick, P. van den Broek, & D.C. Knill (Eds.), *Cognition: Conceptual and methodological issues.* Washington, DC: American Psychological Association.

Kintsch, W. (1994). The psychology of discourse processing. In M.A. Gernsbacher (Ed.), *Handbook of psycholinguistics.* London: Academic Press.

Kintsch, W., & Keenan, J.M. (1973). Reading rate and retention as a function of the numer of propositions in the base structure of sentences. *Cognitive Psychology, 5,* 257–274.

Kintsch, W., Kozminsky, E., Streby, W.J., McKorn, G., & Keenan, J.M. (1975). Comprehension and recall of text as a function of content variables. *Journal of Verbal Learning and Verbal Behavior, 14,* 196–214.

Kintsch W., & van Dijk, T.A. (1978). Toward a model of text comprehension and production. *Psychological Review, 85,* 363–394.

Kintsch, W., Welsch, D., Schmalhofer, F., & Zimny, S. (1990). Sentence memory: A theoretical analysis. *Journal of Memory and Language, 29,* 133–159.

Klahr, D., & Dunbar, K. (1988). Dual space search during scientific reasoning. *Cognitive Science, 12,* 1–55.

Klahr, D., Fay, A.L., & Dunbar, K. (1993). Heuristics for scientific experimentation: A developmental study. *Cognitive Psychology, 25,* 111–146.

Klayman, J., & Ha, Y.-W. (1987). Confirmation, disconfirmation, and information in hypothesis testing. *Psychological Review, 94,* 211–228.

Klein, F.B., & Kihlstrom, J.F. (1986). Elaboration organisation and the self-reference effect in memory. *Journal of Experimental Psychology: General, 115,* 26–38.

Koestler, A. (1964). *The act of creation.* London: Picador.

Koffka, K. (1935). *Principles of Gestalt psychology.* New York: Harcourt Brace.

Kohler, W. (1927). *The mentality of apes* (2nd Edn.). New York: Harcourt Brace.

Kohn, S.E., & Friedman, R.B. (1986). Word-meaning deafness: A phonological-semantic dissociation. *Cognitive Neuropsychology, 3,* 291–308.

Koksal, F. (1992). *Anxiety and narrowing of visual attention.* Unpublished manuscript, Bogazici University, Istanbul, Turkey.

Kolodner, J.L. (1984). *Retrieval and organizational strategies in conceptual memory.* Hillsdale, NJ: Lawrence Erlbaum Associates Inc.

Kolodner, J.L., & Simpson, R. (1986). Using experience as a guide for problem solving. In T.M. Mitchell, J.G. Carbonell, & R.S. Michalski (Eds.), *Machine learning: A guide to current research.* Lancaster, UK: Kluwer Academic Publishers.

Komatsu, L.K. (1992). Recent views of conceptual structure. *Psychological Bulletin, 112,* 500–526.

Korchin, S. (1964). Anxiety and cognition. In C. Scheeser (Ed.), *Cognition: Theory, research, promise.* New York: Harper & Row.

Korsakoff, S.S. (1889). Über eine besondere Form psychischer Störung, kombiniert mit multiplen Neuritis. *Archiv für Psychiatrie und Nervenkrankheiten, 21,* 669–704.

Kosslyn, S.M. (1975). Information representation in visual images. *Cognitive Psychology, 7,* 341–370.

Kosslyn, S.M. (1976). Can imagery be distinguished from other forms of internal representation? Evidence from studies of information retrieval time. *Memory and Cognition, 4,* 291–297.

Kosslyn, S.M. (1978). Measuring the visual angle of the mind's eye. *Cognitive Psychology, 10,* 356–389.

Kosslyn, S.M. (1980). *Image and mind.* Cambridge, MA: Harvard University Press.

Kosslyn, S.M. (1981). The medium and the message in mental imagery: A theory. *Psychological Review, 88,* 44–66.

Kosslyn, S.M. (1983). *Ghosts in the mind's machine: Creating and using images in the brain.* New York: Norton.

Kosslyn, S.M. (1987). Seeing and imagining in the cerebral hemispheres: A computational approach. *Psychological Review, 94,* 148–175.

Kosslyn, S.M. (1994). *Image and brain: The resolution of the imagery debate.* Cambridge, MA: MIT Press.

Kosslyn, S.M., Alpert, N.M., Thompson, W.L., & Maljkovic, V. (1993). Visual mental imagery activates topographically organized visual cortex: PET investigations. *Journal of Cognitive Neuroscience, 5,* 263–287.

Kosslyn, S.M., Ball, T.M., & Reiser, B.J.(1978). Visual images preserve metric spatial information: Evidence from studies of image scanning. *Journal of Experimental Psychology: Human Perception and Performance, 4,* 47–60.

Kosslyn, S.M., Flynn, R.A., Amsterdam, J.B., & Wang, G. (1990). Components of high-level vision: A cognitive neuroscience analysis and accounts of neurological syndromes. *Cognition, 34,* 203–277.

Kosslyn, S.M., Holtzmann, J.D., Farah, F., & Gazzaniga, M.S. (1985). A computational analysis of mental image generation: Evidence from functional dissociations in split-brain patients. *Journal of Experimental Psychology: General, 114,* 311–341.

Kosslyn, S.M., & Koenig, O. (1992). *Wet mind: The new cognitive neuroscience.* New York: Free Press.

Kosslyn, S.M., & Shwartz, S.P. (1977). A simulation of visual imagery. *Cognitive Science, 1,* 265–295.

Kotovsky, K., Hayes, J.R., & Simon, H.A. (1985). Why are some problems hard? Evidence from the Tower of Hanoi. *Cognitive Psychology, 17,* 248–294.

Kotovosky, K., & Simon, H.A. (1973). Empirical tests of a human theory of acquisition of concepts for sequential patterns. *Cognitive Psychology, 4,* 399–424.

Kotovsky, K., & Simon, H.A. (1990). What makes some problems really hard. *Cognitive Psychology, 22,* 143–183.

Kozlowski, L.T., & Cutting, J.E. (1978). Recognising the gender of walkers from point-lights mounted on ankles: Some second thoughts. *Perception and Psychophysics, 23,* 459.

Kroger, J.K., Cheng, P.W., & Holyoak, K.J. (1993). Evoking the permission schema: The impact of explicit negation and a violation-checking context. *Quarterly Journal of Experimental Psychology, 46A,* 615–636.

Kruk, R., & Regan, D. (1983). Visual test results compared with flying performance in telemetry-tracked aircraft. *Aviation, Space, and Environmental Medicine, 54,* 906–911.

Kruschke, J.K. (1992). ALCOVE: An exemplar-based connectionist model of category learning. *Psychological Review, 99,* 22–44.

Kuhn, T.S. (1970). *The structure of scientific revolutions.* Chicago: Chicago University Press.

Kuhn, T.S. (1977). *The essential tension: Selected studies in scientific tradition and change.* Chicago: Chicago University Press.

Kulkarni, D., & Simon, H.A. (1988). The processes of scientific discovery: The strategy of experimentation. *Cognitive Science, 12,* 139–175.

Kulkarni, D., & Simon, H.A. (1990). Experimentation in machine discovery. In J. Shrager & P. Langley (Eds.), *Computational models of scientific discovery and theory formation.* San Mateo, CA: Morgan Kaufmann.

Kunnapas, T.M. (1968). Distance perception as a function of available visual cues. *Journal of Experimental Psychology, 77,* 523–529.

Kutas, M., & Van Petten, C.K. (1994). Psycholinguistics electrified. In M.A. Gernsbacher (Ed.), *Handbook of psycholinguistics.* New York: Academic Press.

Kvavilashvili, L. (1987). Remembering intention as a distinct form of memory. *British Journal of Psychology, 78,* 507–518.

LaBerge, D. (1983). Spatial extent of attention to letters and words. *Journal of Experimental Psychology: Human Perception and Performance, 9,* 371–379.

LaBerge, D., & Buchsbaum, M.S. (1990). Positron emission tomography measurements of pulvinar activity during an attention task. *Journal of Neuroscience, 10,* 613–619.

Lachman, R., Lachman, J.L., & Butterfield, E.C. (1979). *Cognitive psychology and information processing.* Hillsdale, NJ: Lawrence Erlbaum Associates Inc.

Laird, J.E., Newell, A., & Rosenbloom, P. (1987). SOAR: An architecture for general intelligence. *Artificial Intelligence, 33,* 1–64.

Lakoff, G. (1973). Hedges: A study of meaning criteria and the logic of fuzzy concepts. *Journal of Philosophical Logic, 2,* 458–508.

Lakoff, G. (1982). Categories and cognitive models. *Berkeley Cognitive Science Report No.2,* November.

Lakoff, G. (1987). *Women, fire, and dangerous things.* Chicago: Chicago University Press.

Lamberts, K. (1990). A hybrid model of learning to solve physics problems. *European Journal of Cognitive Psychology, 2,* 151–170.

Lamberts, K., & Pfeifer, R. (1992). Computational models of expertise. In M.T. Keane & K.J. Gilhooly (Eds.), *Advances in the psychology of thinking.* London: Harvester Wheatsheaf.

Langley, P., & Jones. R. (1988). A computational model of scientific insight. In R.J. Sternberg (Ed.), *The nature of creativity: Contemporary psychological approaches.* Cambridge, MA: Cambridge University Press.

Larkin, J.H. (1979). Information processing models and science instructions. In J. Lochhead & J. Clement

(Eds.), *Cognitive process instructions*. Philadelphia, PA: Franklin Institute Press.

Larkin, J.H. (1983). The role of problem representation in physics. In D. Gentner & A.L. Stevens (Eds.), *Mental models*. Hillsdale, NJ: Lawrence Erlbaum Associates Inc.

Larkin, J.H. (1985). Understanding problem representations and skill in physics. In S.F. Chipman, J.W. Segal, & R. Glaser (Eds.), *Thinking and learning skills: Vol. 2. Research and open questions*. Hillsdale, NJ: Lawrence Erlbaum Associates Inc.

Larkin, J.H., McDermott, J., Simon, D., & Simon, H.A. (1980). Expert and novice performance in solving physics problems. *Science, 208,* 1335–1342.

Lashley, K.S., Chow, K.L., & Semmes, J. (1951). An examination of the electrical field theory of cerebral integration. *Psychological Review, 58,* 123–136.

Latour, P.L. (1962). Visual threshold during eye movements. *Vision Research, 2,* 261–262.

Lawson, R., Humphreys, G.W., & Watson, D.G. (1994). Object recognition under sequential viewing conditions: Evidence for viewpoint-specific recognition procedures. *Perception, 23,* 595–614.

Lazarus, R.S. (1982). Thoughts on the relations between emotion and cognition. *American Psychologist, 37,* 1019–1024.

LeDoux, J.E. (1990). Fear pathways in the brain: Implications for a theory of the emotional brain. In P.F. Brain, S. Parmigiani, R.J. Blanchard, & D. Mainardi (Eds.), *Fear and defence*. London: Harwood.

Lee, D.N. (1976). A theory of visual control of braking based on information about time-to-collision. *Perception, 5,* 437–459.

Lee, D.N., Lishman, J.R., & Thomson, J.A. (1982). Regulation of gait in long-jumping. *Journal of Experimental Psychology: Human Perception and Performance, 8,* 448–459.

Lee, D.N., Young, D.S., Reddish, P.E., Lough, S., & Clayton, T.M.H. (1983). Visual timing in hitting an accelerating ball. *Quarterly Journal of Experimental Psychology, 35A,* 333–346.

Leech, G. (1974). *Semantics*. Harmondsworth, UK: Penguin.

Lehnert, W.G., Dyer, M.G., Johnson, P.N., Yang, C.J., & Harley, S. (1983). BORIS: An experiment in in-depth understanding of narratives. *Artificial Intelligence, 20,* 15–62.

Leight, K.A., & Ellis, H.C. (1981). Emotional mood states, strategies, and state-dependency in memory. *Journal of Verbal Learning and Verbal Behavior, 20,* 251–266.

Lekhy, S.R., & Sejnowski, T.J. (1988). Network model of shape-from-shading: Neural function arises from both receptive and projective fields. *Nature, 333,* 452–454.

Lenneberg, E.H., & Roberts, J.M. (1956). *The language of experience, memoir 13*. Indiana: University of Indiana, Publications in Anthropology and Linguistics.

Lesgold, A.M (1988). Problem solving. In R.J. Sternberg & E.E. Smith (Eds.), *The psychology of human thought*. Cambridge: Cambridge University Press.

Lesgold, A.M., Rubinson, H., Feltovich, P., Glaser, R., Klopfer, D., & Wang, Y. (1988). Expertise in a complex skill: Diagnosing X-ray pictures. In M.T.H. Chi, R. Glaser, & M. Farr (Eds.), *The nature of expertise*. Hillsdale, NJ: Lawrence Erlbaum Associates Inc.

Levelt, W.J.M. (1989). *Speaking: From intention to articulation*. Cambridge, MA: MIT Press.

Levelt, W.J.M., Schriefers, H., Vorberg, D., Meyer, A.S., Pechmann, T., & Havinga, J. (1991a). The time course of lexical access in speech production: A study of picture naming. *Psychological Review, 98,* 122–142.

Levelt, W.J.M., Schriefers, H., Vorberg, D., Meyer, A.S., Pechmann, T., & Havinga, J. (1991b). Normal and deviant lexical processing: Reply to Dell and O'Seaghdha (1991). *Psychological Review, 98,* 615–618.

Levine, D.N., Calvanio, R., & Popovics, A. (1982). Language in the absence of inner speech. *Word, 15,* 19–44.

Liberman, A.M., Cooper, F.S., Shankweiler, D.S., & Studdert-Kennedy, M. (1967). Perception of the speech code. *Psychological Review, 74,* 431–461.

Liberman, A.M., Delattre, P.C., & Cooper, F.S. (1952). The role of selected stimulus variables in the perception of the unvoiced stop consonants. *American Journal of Psychology, 65,* 497–516.

Lieberman, P. (1963). Some effects of semantic and grammatical context on the production and perception of speech. *Language and Speech, 6,* 172–187.

Liebert, R.M., & Morris, L.W. (1967). Cognitive and emotional components of test anxiety: A distinction and some initial data. *Psychological Reports, 20,* 975–978.

Lindsay, D.S. (1990). Misleading suggestions can impair eyewitnesses' ability to remember event details. *Journal of Experimental Psychology: Learning, Memory, and Cognition, 16,* 1077–1083.

Lindsay, R.C.L., Lea, J.A., Nosworthy, G.J., Fulford, J.A., Hector, J., LeVan, V., & Seabrook, C. (1991). Biased lineups: Sequential presentation reduces the problem. *Journal of Applied Psychology, 76,* 741–745.

Lindsay, R.C.L., & Wells, G.L. (1980). What price justice? Exploring the relationship of lineup fairness to identification accuracy. *Law and Human Behavior, 4,* 303–314.

Linton, M. (1975). Memory for real-world events. In D.A. Norman & D.E. Rumelhart (Eds.), *Explorations in cognition* (Chapter 14). San Francisco: Freeman.

Lively, S.E., Pisoni, D.B., & Goldinger, S.D. (1994). Spoken word recognition: Research and theory. In M.A. Gernsbacher (Ed.), *Handbook of psycholinguistics.* New York: Academic Press.

Locke, J. (1924). *Essay on human understanding.* Oxford: Clarendon Press. (Original work published 1690.)

Loftus, E.F. (1973). Category, dominance, instance dominance, and categorisation time. *Journal of Experimental Psychology, 97,* 70–74.

Loftus, E.F. (1979). *Eyewitness testimony.* Cambridge, MA: Harvard University Press.

Loftus, E.F. (1993). The reality of repressed memories. *American Psychologist, 48,* 518–537.

Loftus, E.F., & Burns, H.J. (1982). Mental shock can produce retrograde amnesia. *Memory and Cognition, 10,* 318–323.

Loftus, E.F., & Palmer, J.C. (1974). Reconstruction of automobile destruction: An example of the interaction between language and memory. *Journal of Verbal Learning and Verbal Behavior, 13,* 585–589.

Loftus, E.F., & Zanni, G. (1975). Eyewitness testimony: The influence of the wording of a question. *Bulletin of the Psychonomic Society, 5,* 86–88.

Logan, G.D. (1988). Toward an instance theory of automatisation. *Psychological Review, 95,* 492–527.

Logie, R., & Baddeley, A.D. (1989). Imagery and working memory. In P.J. Hampson, D.F. Marks, & J.T.E. Richardson (Eds.), *Imagery: Current developments.* London: Routledge.

Logie, R.H. (1986). Visuo-spatial processes in working memory. *Quarterly Journal of Experimental Psychology, 38A,* 229–247.

Logvinenko, A.D., & Belopolskii, V.I. (1994). Convergence as a cue for distance. *Perception, 23,* 207–217.

Loveless, N.E. (1983). Event-related brain potentials and human performance. In A. Gale & J.A. Edwards (Eds.), *Physiological correlates of human behaviour: Vol. II. Attention and performance.* London: Academic Press.

Luchins, A.S. (1942). Mechanisation in problem solving. The effect of Einstellung. *Psychological Monographs, 54,* (248).

Luchins, A.S., & Luchins, E.H. (1959). *Rigidity of behaviour.* Eugene, OR: University of Oregon Press.

Lucy, J., & Schweder, R. (1979). Whorf and his critics: Linguistic and non-linguistic influences on colour memory. *American Anthropologist, 81,* 581–615.

Luger, G.F. (1976). The use of the state space to record the behavioural effects of sub-problems and symmetries in the Tower of Hanoi problem. *International Journal of Man–Machine Studies, 8,* 411–421.

Luger, G.F., & Bauer, M.A. (1978). Transfer effects in isomorphic problem situations. *Acta Psychologica, 34,* 121–131.

Lung, C.T., & Dominowski, R.L. (1985). Effects of strategy instructions and practice on nine-dot problem solving. *Journal of Experimental Psychology: Learning, Memory, and Cognition, 11,* 804–811.

Luria, A.R. (1970). *Traumatic aphasia.* The Hague: Mouton.

Luria, A.R. (1975). *The mind of a mnemonist.* New York: Basic Books.

Lyman, R.S., Kwan, S.T., & Chao, W.H. (1938). Left occipito-parietal brain tumor with observations on alexia and agraphia in Chinese and English. *Chinese Medical Journal, 54,* 491–516.

Macaulay, D., Ryan, L., & Eich, E. (1993). Mood dependence in implicit and explicit memory. In P. Graf & M.E.J. Masson (Eds.), *Implicit memory: New directions in cognition, development, and neuropsychology.* Hillsdale, NJ: Lawrence Erlbaum Associates Inc.

Maclay, H., & Osgood, C.E. (1959). Hesitation phenomena in spontaneous English speech. *Word, 15,* 19–44.

MacLeod, C., & Donnellan, A.M. (1993). Individual differences in anxiety and the restriction of working memory capacity. *Personality and Individual Differences, 15,* 163–173.

MacLeod, C., & Mathews, A. (1991). Cognitive-experimental approaches to the emotional disorders. In P.R. Martin (Ed.), *Handbook of behaviour therapy and psychological science: An integrative approach.* Oxford: Pergamon.

MacLeod, C., Mathews, A., & Tata, P. (1986). Attentional bias in emotional disorders. *Journal of Abnormal Psychology, 95,* 15–20.

MacNeilage, P.F. (1972). Speech physiology. In J.H. Gilbert (Ed.), *Speech and cortical functioning.* New York: Academic Press.

Madison, P. (1956). Freud's repression concept: A survey and attempted clarification. *International Journal of Psychoanalysis, 37,* 75–81.

Magee, B. (1973). *Popper.* London: Fontana.

Mahony, M.J. (1976). *Scientist as subject: The psychological imperative.* Cambridge, MA: Ballinger.

Maier, N.R.F. (1931). Reasoning in humans II: The solution of a problem and its appearance in consciousness. *Journal of Comparative Psychology, 12,* 181–194.

Malone, D.R., Morris, H.H., Kay, M.C., & Levin, H.S. (1982). Prosopagnosia: A double dissociation between the recognition of familiar and unfamiliar faces. *Journal of Neurology, Neurosurgery and Psychiatry, 45,* 820–822.

Malt, B.C. (1994). When water is not H_2O. *Cognitive Psychology, 27,* 41–70.

Malt, B.C., & Smith, E.E. (1983). Correlated properties in natural categories. *Journal of Verbal Learning and Verbal Behavior, 23,* 250–269.

Maltzman, I. (1955). Thinking: From a behaviouristic point of view. *Psychological Review, 62,* 275–286.

Mandler, J.M., & Mandler, G. (1964). *Thinking: From association to gestalt.* New York: John Wiley.

Mani, K., & Johnson-Laird, P.N. (1982). The mental representation of spatial descriptions. *Memory and Cognition, 10,* 181–187.

Manktelow, K.I., & Evans, J. St. B.T. (1979). Facilitation of reasoning by realism: Effect or non-effect? *British Journal of Psychology, 70,* 477–488.

Manktelow, K.I., & Over, D.E. (1991). Social role and utilities in reasoning with deontic conditionals. *Cognition, 43,* 183–186.

Manktelow, K.I., & Over, D.E. (1993). *Rationality: Psychological and philosophical perspectives.* London: Routledge.

Mäntylä, T., & Bäckman, L. (1992). Aging and memory for expected and unexpected objects in real world settings. *Journal of Experimental Psychology: Learning, Memory, and Cognition, 18 ,* 1298–1309.

Marcus, S.L., & Rips, L.J. (1979). Conditional reasoning. *Journal of Verbal Learning and Verbal Behavior, 18,* 199–233.

Marin, O.S.M. (1987). Dementia and visual agnosia. In G.W. Humphreys & M.J. Riddoch (Eds.), *Visual object processing: A cognitive neuropsychological approach.* Hove, UK: Lawrence Erlbaum Associates Ltd.

Markman, A.B., & Gentner, D. (1993a). Splitting the differences: A structural alignment view of similarity. *Journal of Memory and Language, 32,* 517–535.

Markman, A.B., & Gentner, D. (1993b). Structural alignment during similarity comparisons. *Cognitive Psychology, 26,* 356–397.

Markovits, H. (1984). Awareness of the "possible" as a mediator of formal thinking in conditional reasoning problems. *British Journal of Psychology, 75,* 367–376.

Markovits, H. (1985). Incorrect conditional reasoning among adults: Competence or performance? *British Journal of Psychology, 76,* 241–247.

Marr, D. (1976). Early processing of visual information. *Philosophical Transactions of the Royal Society (London), B275,* 483–524.

Marr, D. (1982). *Vision: A computational investigation into the human representation and processing of visual information.* San Francisco: W.H. Freeman.

Marr, D., & Hildreth, E. (1980). Theory of edge detection. *Proceedings of the Royal Society of London, B207,* 187–217.

Marr, D., & Nishihara, K. (1978). Representation and recognition of the spatial organisation of three-dimensional shapes. *Philosophical Transactions of the Royal Society (London), B200,* 269–294.

Marr, D., & Poggio, T. (1976). Cooperation computation of stereo disparity. *Science, 194,* 283–287.

Marschark, M., & Cornoldi, C. (1990). Imagery and verbal memory. In C. Cornoldi, & M McDaniel (Eds.), *Imagery and cognition.* New York: Springer.

Marschark, M., & Hunt, L. (1989). A reexamination of the role of imagery in learning and memory. *Journal of Experimental Psychology: Learning, Memory, and Cognition, 15,* 710–720.

Marschark, M., Richman, C.L., Yuille, J.C., & Hunt, R.R. (1987). The role of imagery in memory: On shared and distinctive information. *Psychological Bulletin, 102,* 28–41.

Marschark, M., & Surian, L. (1992). Context effects in free recall: The role of imaginal and relational processing. *Memory and Cognition, 20,* 612–620.

Marshall, J.C., & Newcombe, F. (1973). Patterns of paralexia: A psycholinguistic approach. *Journal of Psycholinguistic Research, 2,* 175–199.

Marslen-Wilson, W.D. (1990). Activation, competition, and frequency in lexical access. In G.T.M. Altmann (Ed.), *Cognitive models of speech processing: Psycholinguistics and computational perspectives*. Cambridge, MA: MIT Press.

Marslen-Wilson, W.D., & Tyler, L.K. (1980). The temporal structure of spoken language understanding. *Cognition, 8*, 1-71.

Marsolek, C.J., Kosslyn, S.M., & Squire, L.R. (1992). Form specific visual priming in the right cerebral hemisphere. *Journal of Experimental Psychology: Learning, Memory, and Cognition, 18*, 492–508.

Martin, A., & Fedio, P. (1983). Word production and comprehension in Alzheimer's disease: The breakdown of semantic knowledge. *Brain and Language, 19*, 121–141.

Martone, M., Butters, N., Payne, M., Becker, J.T., & Sax, D.S. (1984). Dissociations between skill learning and verbal recognition in amnesia and dementia. *Archives of Neurology, 41*, 965–970.

Masson, M.E.J., & Graf, P. (1993). Introduction: Looking back and into the future. In P. Graf & M.E.J. Masson (Eds.), *Implicit memory: New directions in cognition, development, and neuropsychology*. Hillsdale, NJ: Lawrence Erlbaum Associates Inc.

Mathews, A., May, J., Mogg, K., & Eysenck, M.W. (1990). Attentional bias in anxiety: Selective search or defective filtering? *Journal of Abnormal Psychology, 99*, 166–173.

Mattingly, I.G., & Liberman, A.M. (1990). Speech and other auditory modules. In G.M. Edelman, W.E. Gall, & W.M. Cowan (Eds.), *Signal and sense: Local and global order in perceptual maps*. New York: Wiley.

Mayer, R.E. (1977). Problem-solving performance with task overload: Effects of self-pacing and trait anxiety. *Bulletin of the Psychonomic Society, 9*, 283–286.

Mayes, A.R. (1988). *Human organic memory disorders*. Cambridge: Cambridge University Press.

Mayes, A.R., Meudell, P.R., & Pickering, A. (1985). Is organic amnesia caused by a selective deficit in remembering contextual information? *Cortex, 21*, 167–202.

Mayhew, J.E.W., & Frisby, J.P. (1981). Psychophysical and computational studies towards a theory of human stereopsis. *Artificial Intelligence, 17*, 349–385.

McCarthy, R., & Warrington, E.K. (1984). A two-route model of speech production. *Brain, 107*, 463–485.

McClelland, J.L. (1981). Retrieving general and specific information from stored knowledge of specifics. *Proceedings of the Third Annual Meeting of the Cognitive Science Society*, 170–172.

McClelland, J.L. (1987). The case for interactionism in language processing. In M. Coltheart (Ed.), *Attention and performance* (Vol. XII). Hove, UK: Lawrence Erlbaum Associates Ltd.

McClelland, J.L. (1991). Stochastic interactive processes and the effect of context on perception. *Cognitive Psychology, 23*, 1–44.

McClelland, J.L., & Elman, J.L. (1986). The TRACE model of speech perception. *Cognitive Psychology, 18*, 1–86.

McClelland, J.L., & Rumelhart, D.E. (1981). An interactive activation model of context effects in letter perception. Part 1. An account of basic findings. *Psychological Review, 88*, 375–407.

McClelland, J.L., & Rumelhart, D.E. (1985). Distributed memory and the representation of general and specific information. *Journal of Experimental Psychology: General, 114*, 159–188.

McClelland, J.L., & Rumelhart, D.E. (1986a). A distributed model of human learning and memory. In D.E. Rumelhart, J.L. McClelland, & The PDP Research Group (Eds.), *Parallel distributed processing: Vol. 2. Psychological and biological models*. Cambridge, MA: MIT Press.

McClelland, J.L., & Rumelhart, D.E. (1986b). Amnesia and distributed memory. In D.E. Rumelhart, J.L. McClelland, & The PDP Research Group (Eds.), *Parallel distributed processing: Vol. 2. Psychological and biological models*. Cambridge, MA: MIT Press.

McClelland, J.L., Rumelhart, D.E., & Hinton, G.E. (1986). The appeal of parallel distributed processing. In D.E. Rumelhart, J.L. McClelland, & The PDP Research Group (Eds.), *Parallel distributed processing: Vol. 1. Foundations*. Cambridge, MA: MIT Press.

McClelland, J.L., Rumelhart, D.E., & The PDP Research Group (Eds.), (1986). *Parallel distributed processing: Vol. 2, Psychological & biological models*. Cambridge, MA: MIT Press.

McCloskey, M. (1980). The stimulus familiarity problem in semantic memory research. *Journal of Verbal Learning and Verbal Behavior, 19*, 485–504.

McCloskey, M. (1983). Intuitive physics. *Scientific American, 24*, 122–130.

McCloskey, M., & Egeth, H. (1983). Eyewitness identification: What can a psychologist tell a jury? *American Psychologist, 38*, 550–563.

McCloskey, M.E., & Glucksberg, S. (1977). Natural categories: Well-defined or fuzzy sets. *Memory and Cognition, 6*, 462–472.

McCloskey, M., Wible, C.G., & Cohen, N.J. (1988). Is there a special flashbulb-memory mechanism? *Journal of Experimental Psychology: General, 117,* 171–181.

McCloskey, M., & Zaragoza, M.S. (1985). Misleading postevent information and memory for events: Arguments and evidence against memory impairment hypotheses. *Journal of Experimental Psychology: General, 114,* 1–16.

McCulloch, W.S., & Pitts, W. (1943). A logical calculus of the idea imminent in nervous activity. *Bulletin of the Mathematical Biophysics, 5,* 115–133.

McGurk, H., & MacDonald, J. (1976). Hearing lips and seeing voices. *Nature, 264,* 746–748.

McKee, R., & Squire, L.R. (1992). Equivalent forgetting rates in long-term memory for diencephalon and medial temporal lobe amnesia. *Journal of Neuroscience, 12,* 3765–3772.

McKeithen, K.B., Reitman, J.S., Rueter, H.H., & Hirtle, C. (1981). Knowledge organization and skill differences in computer programmers. *Cognitive Psychology, 13,* 307–325.

McKoon, G., & Ratcliff, R. (1980). Priming in item recognition: The organization of propositions in memory for text. *Journal of Verbal Learning and Verbal Behavior, 19,* 369–386.

McKoon, G., & Ratcliff, R. (1986). Inferences about predictable events. *Journal of Experimental Psychology: Learning, Memory, and Cognition, 12,* 82–91,

McKoon, G., & Ratcliff, R. (1992). Inference during reading. *Psychological Review, 99,* 440–466.

McLeod, P. (1977). A dual-task response modality effect: Support for multiprocessor models of attention. *Quarterly Journal of Experimental Psychology, 29,* 651–667.

McNamara, T.P., & Sternberg, R.J. (1983). Mental models of word meaning. *Journal of Verbal Learning and Verbal Behavior, 22,* 449–474.

Meacham, J.A. (1988). Interpersonal relations and prospective remembering. In M.M. Gruneberg, P.E. Morris, & R.N. Sykes (Eds.), *Practical aspects of memory: Current research and issues: Vol. 1. Memory in everyday life.* Chichester, UK: John Wiley.

Meacham, J.A., & Singer, J. (1977). Incentive in prospective remembering. *Journal of Psychology, 97,* 191–197.

Medin, D.L., Goldstone, R.L., & Gentner, D. (1990). Similarity involving attributes and relations: Judgements of similarity and difference are not inverses. *Psychological Science, 1,* 64–69.

Medin, D.L., Goldstone, R.L., & Gentner, D. (1993). Respects for similarity. *Psychological Review, 100,* 254–278.

Medin, D.L., & Ortony, A. (1989). Psychological essentialism. In S. Vosniadou & A. Ortony (Eds.), *Similarity and analogical reasoning.* Cambridge: Cambridge University Press.

Medin, D.L., & Shaffer, M.M. (1978). Context theory of classification learning. *Psychological Review, 85,* 207–238.

Medin, D.L., & Shoben, E.J. (1988). Context and structure in conceptual combination. *Cognitive Psychology, 20,* 158–190.

Medin, D.L., & Smith, E.E. (1984). Concepts and concept formation. *Annual Review of Psychology, 35,* 113–138.

Medin, D.L., Wattenmaker, W.D., & Hampson, S.E. (1987). Family resemblance, conceptual cohesiveness and category construction. *Cognitive Psychology, 19,* 242–279.

Menzel, E.W. (1978). Cognitive mapping in chimpanzees. In S.H. Hulse, F. Fowler, & W.K. Honig (Eds.), *Cognitive processes in animal behaviour.* Hillsdale, NJ: Lawrence Erlbaum Associates Inc.

Mervis, C.B., Catlin, J., & Rosch, E. (1976). Relationships among goodness-of-example, category norms, and word frequency. *Bulletin of the Psychonomic Society, 7,* 283–284.

Metcalfe, J. (1986a). Feeling of knowing in memory and problem solving. *Journal of Experimental Psychology: Learning, Memory, and Cognition, 12,* 288–284.

Metcalfe, J. (1986b). Premonitions of error predict impending insight. *Journal of Experimental Psychology: Learning, Memory, and Cognition, 12,* 623–634.

Metcalfe, J., & Weibe, D. (1987). Intuition in insight and noninsight problem solving. *Memory and Cognition, 15,* 238–246.

Meudell, P.R., & Mayes, A.R. (1981). The Claparede phenomenon: A further example in amnesics, a demonstration of a similar effect in normal people with attenuated memory, and a reinterpretation. *Current Psychological Research, 1,* 75–88.

Meyer, A.S. (1994). Timing in sentence production. *Journal of Memory and Language, 33,* 471–492.

Meyer, B.J.F., & McConkie, G.W. (1973). What is recalled after hearing a passage? *Journal of Educational Psychology, 65,* 109–117.

Meyer, D.E., & Schvaneveldt, R.W. (1971). Facilitation in recognising pairs of words: Evidence of a dependence between retrieval operations. *Journal of Experimental Psychology, 90,* 227–234.

Michel, F., & Andreewsky, E. (1983). Deep dysphasia: An analogue of deep dyslexia in the auditory modality. *Brain and Language, 18,* 212–223.

Michotte, A. (1963). *The perception of causality.* New York: Basic Books.

Mill, J.S. (1843). *A system of logic.* London: Longman.

Miller, G.A. (1956). The magic number seven, plus or minus two: Some limits on our capacity for processing information. *Psychological Review, 63,* 81–93.

Miller, G.A., Galanter, E., & Pribram, K.H. (1960). *Plans and the structure of behaviour.* New York: Holt, Rinehart & Winston.

Miller, G.A., & Johnson-Laird, P.N. (1976). *Language and perception.* Cambridge: Cambridge University Press.

Miller, G.A., & Nicely, P. (1955). An analysis of perceptual confusions among some English consonants. *Journal of the Acoustical Society of America, 27,* 338–352.

Milner, A.D., Carey, D.P., & Harvey, M. (1994). Visually guided action and the "need to know". *Behavioral and Brain Sciences, 17,* 213–214.

Milner, A.D., Perrett, D.I., Johnston, R.S., Benson, P.J., Jordan, T.R., Heeley, D.W., Bettuci, D., Mortora, F., Mutani, R., Terazzi, E., & Davidson, D.L.W. (1991). Perception and action in visual form agnosia. *Brain, 114,* 405–428.

Minsky, M. (1975). A framework for representing knowledge. In P.H. Winston (Ed.), *The psychology of computer vision.* New York: McGraw-Hill.

Minsky, M., & Papert, S. (1969). *Perceptrons.* Cambridge, MA: MIT Press.

Minsky, M., & Papert, S. (1988). *Perceptrons* (2nd Edn.). Cambridge, MA: MIT Press.

Mishkin, M., & Ungerleider, L. G. (1982). Contribution of striate inputs to the visuospatial functions of parieto-preoccipital cortex in monkeys. *Behavioural Brain Research, 6,* 57–77.

Mitchell, D. (1994). Sentence parsing. In M.A. Gernsbacher (Ed.), *Handbook of psycholinguistics.* London: Academic Press.

Mitroff, I. (1974). *The subjective side of science.* Amsterdam: Elsevier.

Miyawaki, K., Strange, W., Verbrugge, R., Liberman, A.M., Jenkins, J.J., & Fujimura, O. (1975). An effect of linguistic experience. The discrimination of [r] and [l] by native speakers of Japanese and English *Perception and Psychophysics, 18,* 331–340.

Mogg, K., Mathews, A., & Weinman, J. (1987). Memory bias in clinical anxiety. *Journal of Abnormal Psychology, 96,* 94–98.

Moray, N. (1959). Attention in dichotic listening: Affective cues and the influence of instructions. *Quarterly Journal of Experimental Psychology, 11,* 56–60.

Moray, N. (1969). *Attention: Selective processes in vision and hearing.* London: Hutchinson.

Morgan, L. (1894). *An introduction to comparative psychology.* London: Scott.

Morris, C.D., Bransford, J.D., & Franks, J.J. (1977). Levels of processing versus transfer appropriate processing. *Journal of Verbal Learning and Verbal Behavior, 16,* 519–533.

Morris, P.E. (1992). Prospective memory: Remembering to do things. In M. Gruneberg & P. Morris (Eds.), *Aspects of memory: Vol. 1, The practical aspects.* London: Routledge.

Morris, P.E., & Reid, R.L. (1970). The repeated use of mnemonic imagery. *Psychonomic Science, 20,* 337–338.

Morris, R.G. (1987). The effect of concurrent articulation on memory span in Alzheimer-type dementia. *British Journal of Clinical Psychology, 26,* 233–234.

Morris, R.G. (1991). The nature of memory impairment in Alzheimer-type dementia. In J. Weinman & J. Hunter (Eds.), *Memory: Neurochemical and abnormal perspectives.* London: Harwood.

Morton, J. (1969). Interaction of information in word recognition. *Psychological Review, 76,* 165–178.

Morton, J. (1979). Facilitation in word recognition: Experiments causing change in the logogen model. In P.A. Kolers, M. Wrolstead, & H. Bouma (Eds.), *Processing of visible language* (Vol. 1). New York: Plenum Press.

Moscovitch, M. (1984). The sufficient conditions for demonstrating preserved memory in amnesia: A task analysis approach. In L.R. Squire & N. Butters (Eds.), *Neuropsychology of memory.* New York: Guilford.

Muller, H.J., & Rabbitt, P.M. (1989). Reflexive and voluntary orienting of visual attention. *Journal of Experimental Psychology: Human Perception and Performance, 17,* 125–141.

Murphy, G.L., & Medin, D.L. (1985). The role of theories in conceptual coherence. *Psychological Review, 92,* 289–316.

Muter, P. (1978). Recognition failure of recallable words in semantic memory. *Memory and Cognition, 6,* 9–12.

Mynatt, C.R., Doherty, M.E., & Tweney, R.D. (1977). Confirmation bias in a simulated research environment. *Quarterly Journal of Experimental Psychology, 29,* 85–95.

Mynatt, C.R., Doherty, M.E., & Tweney, R.D. (1978). Consequences of confirmation and disconfirmation in a simulated research environment. *Quarterly Journal of Experimental Psychology, 30,* 395–406.

Navon, D. (1977). Forest before trees: The precedence of global features in visual perception. *Cognitive Psychology, 9,* 353–383.

Nebes, R.D. (1989). Semantic memory in Alzheimer's disease. *Psychological Bulletin, 106,* 380–408.

Nebes, R.D., Brady, C.B., & Huff, F.J. (1989). Automatic and attentional mechanisms of semantic priming in Alzheimer's disease. *Journal of Clinical and Experimental Neuropsychology, 2,* 219–230.

Neisser, U. (1964). Visual search. *Scientific American, 210,* 94–102.

Neisser, U. (1967). *Cognitive psychology.* New York: Appleton-Century-Crofts.

Neisser, U. (1976). *Cognition and reality.* San Francisco: W.H. Freeman.

Neisser, U. (1978). Memory: What are the important questions? In M.M. Gruneberg, P.E. Morris, & R.N. Sykes (Eds.), *Practical aspects of memory.* London: Academic Press.

Neisser, U. (1981). John Dean's memory: A case study. *Cognition, 9,* 1–22.

Neisser, U. (1982). *Memory observed.* San Francisco: Freeman.

Neisser, U., & Becklen, P. (1975). Selective looking: Attending to visually superimposed events. *Cognitive Psychology, 7,* 480–494.

Nelson, K. (1993). Explaining the emergence of autobiographical memory in early childhood. In A.F. Collins, S.E. Gathercole, M.A. Conway, & P.E. Morris (Eds.), *Theories of memory.* Hove, UK: Lawrence Erlbaum Associates Ltd.

Newell, A. (1981). Reasoning, problem solving and decision processes. In R.S. Nickerson (Ed.), *Attention and performance* (Vol. VIII). Hillsdale, NJ: Lawrence Erlbaum Associates Inc.

Newell, A. (1985). Duncker on thinking: An inquiry into progress in cognition. In S. Koch & D. Leary (Eds.), *A century of psychology as science: Retrospections and assessments.* New York: McGraw-Hill.

Newell, A. (1990). *Unified theories of cognition.* Cambridge, MA: Harvard University Press.

Newell, A., Shaw, J.C., & Simon, H.A. (1958). Elements of a theory of human problem solving. *Psychological Review, 65,* 151–166.

Newell, A., Shaw, J.C., & Simon, H.A. (1960). Report on a general problem solving program for a computer. In *Information processing: Proceedings of the International Conference on Information Processing.* Paris: UNESCO.

Newell, A., & Simon, H.A. (1972). *Human problem solving.* Englewood Cliffs, NJ: Prentice Hall.

Newstead, S.E. (1990). Conversion in syllogistic reasoning. In K.J. Gilhooly, M.T. Keane, R. Logie, & G. Erdos (Eds.), *Lines of thinking: Reflections on the psychology of thought* (Vol. 1). Chichester, UK: John Wiley.

Newstead, S.E. (1993). Do mental models provide an adequate account of syllogistic reasoning performance? *Behavioral and Brain Sciences, 16,* 358–359.

Nielsen, J.M. (1946). *Agnosia, apraxia, aphasia: Their value in cerebral localization.* New York: Paul B. Hoeber.

Nisbett, R.E., & Wilson, T.D. (1977). Telling more than we can know: Verbal reports on mental processes. *Psychological Review, 84,* 231–259.

Nissen, M., Ross, J., Willingham, D., Mackenzie, T., & Schachter, D. (1988). Memory and amnesia in a patient with multiple personality disorder. *Brain and Cognition, 8,* 117–134.

Norman, D.A. (1980). Twelve issues for cognitive science. *Cognitive Science, 4,* 1–32.

Norman, D.A. (1981). Categorisation of action slips. *Psychological Review, 88,* 1–15.

Norman, D.A. (1983). Some observations on mental models. In D. Gentner & A.L. Stevens (Eds.), *Mental models.* Hillsdale, NJ: Lawrence Erlbaum Associates Inc.

Norman, D.A., & Rumelhart, D.E. (1975). *Explorations in cognition.* San Francisco: Freeman.

Norman, D.A., & Shallice, T. (1980). *Attention to action: Willed and automatic control of behaviour.* CHIP Document No. 99, Centre for Human Information Processing, University of California, San Diego, La Jolla.

Norman, D.A., & Shallice, T. (1986). Attention to action: Willed and automatic control of behaviour. In R.J. Davidson, G.E. Schwartz, & D. Shapiro (Eds.), *The design of everyday things.* New York: Doubleday.

Norris, D. (1994). Shortlist: A connectionist model of continuous speech recognition. *Cognition, 52,* 189–234.

Norvig, R. (1992). *Paradigms for artificial intelligence programming*. Los Altos: Morgan Kaufmann.

Nosofsky, R.M. (1988). Exemplar-based accounts of relations between classification, recognition and typicality. *Journal of Experimental Psychology: Learning, Memory, and Cognition, 14*, 700–708.

Nosofsky, R.M. (1991). Tests of an exemplar model for relating perceptual classification and recognition memory. *Journal of Experimental Psychology: Learning, Memory, and Cognition, 17*, 3–27.

Oaksford, M., & Chater, N. (1994). A rational analysis of the selection task as optimal data selection. *Psychological Review, 101*, 608–631.

O'Brien, D.P. (1993). Mental logic and irrationality. In K.I. Manktelow & D.E. Over (Eds.), *Rationality: Psychological and philosophical perspectives*. London: Routledge.

O'Brien, D.P., Braine, M.D.S., & Yang, Y. (1994). Propositional reasoning by mental models? Simple to refute in principle and in practice. *Psychological Review, 101*, 701–724.

O'Brien, E.J., Shank, D.M., Myers, J.L., & Rayner, K. (1988). Elaborative inferences during reading: Do they occur on-line? *Journal of Experimental Psychology: Learning, Memory, and Cognition, 14*, 410–420.

Ohlsson, S. (1984a). Restructuring revisited I: Summary and critique of Gestalt theory of problem solving. *Scandinavian Journal of Psychology, 25*, 65–76.

Ohlsson, S. (1984b). Restructuring revisited II: An information processing theory of restructuring and insight. *Scandinavian Journal of Psychology, 25*, 117–129.

Ohlsson, S. (1985). Retrieval processes in restructuring: Answer to Keane. *Scandinavian Journal of Psychology, 26*, 366–368.

Ohlsson, S. (1992). Information processing explanations of insight and related phenomena. In M.T. Keane & K.J. Gilhooly (Eds.), *Advances in the psychology of thinking*. London: Harvester Wheatsheaf.

Olson, D.R. (1970). Language and thought: Aspects of a cognitive theory of semantics. *Psychological Review, 77*, 257–273.

O'Regan, K., & Levy-Schoen, A. (1987). Eye-movement strategy and tactics in word recognition and reading. In M. Coltheart (Ed.), *Attention and performance* (Vol. XII). Hove, UK: Lawrence Erlbaum Associates Ltd.

Osherson, D.N. (1974). *Logical abilities in children* (Vol. 2). Hillsdale, NJ: Lawrence Erlbaum Associates Inc.

Osherson, D.N. (1975). *Logical abilities in children* (Vol. 3). Hillsdale, NJ: Lawrence Erlbaum Associates Inc.

Osherson, D.N. (1976). *Logical abilities in children* (Vol. 4). Hillsdale, NJ: Lawrence Erlbaum Associates Inc.

Osherson, D.N., & Smith E.E. (Eds.) (1990). *Thinking: An invitation to cognitive science*. Cambridge, MA: MIT Press.

Osherson, D.N., & Smith, E.E. (1981). On the adequacy of prototype theory as a theory of concepts. *Cognition, 9*, 35–58.

Osherson, D.N., & Smith, E.E. (1982). Gradedness and conceptual conjunction. *Cognition, 12*, 299–318.

Paivio, A. (1971). *Imagery and verbal processes*. New York: Holt, Rinehart, & Winston. (Reprinted by Lawrence Erlbaum Associates Inc. in 1979.)

Paivio, A. (1975). Coding distinctions and repetition effects in memory. In G.H. Bower (Ed.), *The psychology of learning and motivation* (Vol. 9). New York: Academic Press.

Paivio, A. (1979). Psychological processes in the comprehension of metaphor. In A. Ortony (Ed.), *Metaphor and thought*. New York: Cambridge University Press.

Paivio, A. (1983). The empirical case for dual coding. In J.C. Yuille (Ed.), *Imagery, memory, and cognition: Essays in honor of Allan Paivio*. Hillsdale, NJ: Lawrence Erlbaum Associates Inc.

Paivio, A. (1986). *Mental representations: A dual coding approach*. Oxford: Oxford University Press.

Paivio, A. (1991). Dual coding theory: Retrospect and current status. *Canadian Journal of Psychology, 45*, 255–287.

Paivio, A., & Csapo, K. (1973). Picture superiority in free recall: Imagery or dual coding? *Cognitive Psychology, 5*, 176–206.

Paivio, A., & te Linde, J. (1982). Imagery, memory and brain. *Canadian Journal of Psychology, 36*, 243–272.

Paivio, A., Yuille, J.C., & Madigan, S.A. (1968). Concreteness, imagery and meaningfulness values for 925 nouns. *Journal of Experimental Psychology Monographs, 78* (1, Pt. 2).

Palmer, S.E. (1975). The effects of contextual scenes on the identification of objects. *Memory and Cognition, 3*, 519–526.

Palmer, S.E. (1989). Levels of description in information processing theories of analogy. In S. Vosniadou & A. Ortony (Eds.), *Similarity and analogical reasoning*. Cambridge: Cambridge University Press.

Palmer, S. E., & Kimchi, R. (1986). The information processing approach to cognition. In T. Knapp & L.C. Robertson (Eds.), *Approaches to cognition: Contrasts and controversies.* Hillsdale, NJ: Lawrence Erlbaum Associates Inc.

Parkin, A.J. (1979). Specifying levels of processing. *Quarterly Journal of Experimental Psychology, 31,* 175–195.

Parkin, A.J. (1990). Recent advances in the neuropsychology of memory. In J. Hunter & J. Weinman (Eds.), *Mechanisms of memory: Clinical and neurochemical contributions.* London: Harwood.

Parkin, A.J. (1993). *Memory: Phenomena, experiment and theory.* Oxford: Blackwell.

Parkin, A.J., & Leng, N.R.C. (1993). *Neuropsychology of the amnesic syndrome.* Hove, UK: Lawrence Erlbaum Associates Ltd.

Parkin, A.J., & Steward, F. (1993). Category-specific impairments? Yes. *Quarterly Journal of Experimental Psychology, 46A,* 505–510.

Pashler, H. (1990). Do response modality effects support multiprocessor models of divided attention? *Journal of Experimental Psychology: Human Perception and Performance, 16,* 826–842.

Pashler, H. (1993). Dual-task interference and elementary mental mechanisms. In D.E. Meyer & S. Kornblum (Eds.), *Attention and performance* (Vol. XIV). London: MIT Press.

Patel, V.L., & Groen, G.J. (1986). Knowledge-based solution strategies in medical reasoning. *Cognitive Science, 10,* 91–116.

Patel, V.L., & Groen, G.J. (1993). Confusing apples and oranges: Some dangers in confusing frameworks with theories. *Cognitive Science, 17,* 135–141.

Patel, V.L., Groen, G.J., & Arocha, J. (1993). Medical expertise as a function of task difficulty. *Memory and Cognition, 18,* 394–406.

Patrick, J.R. (1934a). Studies in rational behaviour and emotional excitement: I. Rational behaviour in human subjects. *Journal of Comparative Psychology, 18,* 1–22.

Patrick, J.R. (1934b). Studies in rational behaviour and emotional excitement: II. The effect of emotional excitement on rational behaviour in human subjects. *Journal of Comparative Psychology, 18,* 153–195.

Patterson, K.E. (1982). The relation between reading and phonological coding: Further neuropsychological observations. In A.W. Ellis (Ed.), *Normality and pathology in cognitive functions.* London: Academic Press.

Patterson, K.E., & Coltheart, V. (1987). Phonological processes in reading: A tutorial review. In M. Coltheart (Ed.), *Attention and performance* (Vol. XII). Hove, UK: Lawrence Erlbaum Associates Ltd.

Patterson, K.E., Vargha-Khadem, F., & Polky, C.E. (1989). Reading with one hemisphere. *Brain, 112,* 39–63.

Pazzani, M.J. (1990). *Creating a memory of causal relationships.* Hillsdale, NJ: Lawrence Erlbaum Associates Ltd.

Pazzani, M.J. (1991a). Influence of prior knowledge on concept acquisition: Experimental and computational results. *Journal of Experimental Psychology: Learning, Memory, and Cognition, 15,* 416–432.

Pazzani, M.J. (1991b) A computational theory of learning causal relationships. *Cognitive Science, 15,* 401–424.

Pazzani, M.J. (1993). Learning causal patterns. *Machine Learning, 11,* 173–194.

Perfetti, C.A., & McCutchen, D. (1982). Speech processes in reading. In N. Lass (Ed.), *Speech and language: Advances in basic research and practice* (Vol. 7). New York: Academic Press.

Perret, D.I., Oram, M.W., Hietanen, J.K., & Benson, P.J. (1994). Issues of representation in object vision. In M.J. Farah & G. Ratcliff (Eds.), *The neuropsychology of higher vision: Collated tutorial essays.* Hillsdale, NJ: Lawrence Erlbaum Associates Inc.

Perrig, W.J., & Perrig, P. (1988). Mood and memory: Mood-congruity effects in absence of mood. *Memory and Cognition, 16,* 102–109.

Petersen, S.E., Corbetta, M., Miezin, F.M., & Shulman, G.L. (1994). PET studies of parietal involvement in spatial attention: Comparison of different task types. *Canadian Journal of Experimental Psychology, 48,* 319–338.

Petersen, S.E., Fox, P.T., Posner, M.I., Mintun, M., & Raichle, M.E. (1988). Positron emission tomographic studies of the cortical anatomy of single-word processing. *Nature, 331,* 585–589.

Peterson, M.A., Kihlstrom, J.F., Rose, P.M., & Glinsky, M.L. (1992). Mental images can be ambiguous: Reconstruals and reference frame reversals. *Memory and Cognition, 20,* 107–123.

Piaget, J. (1967). *The child's conception of the world.* Totowa, NJ: Littlefield, Adams.

Piaget, J. (1970). Piaget's theory. In J. Mussen (Ed.), *Carmichael's manual of child psychology* (Vol. 1). New York: Basic Books.

Pillemer, D.B., Goldsmith, L.R., Panter, A.T., & White, S.H. (1988). Very long-term memories of the first year in college. *Journal of Experimental Psychology: Learning, Memory, and Cognition, 14,* 709–715.

Pirolli, P.L., & Anderson, J.R. (1985). The role of learning from examples in the acquisition of recursive programming skill. *Canadian Journal of Psychology, 39,* 240–272.

Platt, R.D., & Griggs, R.A. (1993). Darwinian algorithms and the Wason selection task: A factorial analysis of social contract selection task problems. *Cognition, 48,* 163–192.

Plaut, D.C., & Shallice, T. (1993). Deep dyslexia: A case study of connectionist neuropsychology. *Cognitive Neuropsychology, 10,* 377–500.

Poincaré, H. (1913). Mathematical creation. In H. Poincaré, *The foundations of science.* New York: Science Press.

Politzer, G., & Braine, M.D.S. (1991). Responses to inconsistent premises cannot count as suppression of valid inferences. *Cognition, 38,* 103–108.

Polivy, J. (1981). On the induction of emotion in the laboratory: Discrete moods or multiple affect states? *Journal of Personality and Social Psychology, 41,* 803–817.

Polk, T. (1993). Mental models, more or less. *Behavioral and Brain Sciences, 16,* 362–363.

Pollatsek, A., Bolozky, S., Well, A.D., & Rayner, K. (1981). Asymmetries in the perceptual span for Israeli readers. *Brain and Language, 14,* 174–180.

Pollatsek, A., Raney, G.E., LaGasse, L., & Rayner, K. (1993). The use of information below fixation in reading and in visual search. *Canadian Journal of Experimental Psychology, 47,* 179–200.

Polson, P., & Jeffries, R. (1982). Problem solving as search and understanding. In R.J. Sternberg (Ed.), *Advances in the psychology of human intelligence* (Vol. 1). Hillsdale, NJ: Lawrence Erlbaum Associates Inc.

Popper, K.R. (1968). *The logic of scientific discovery.* London: Hutchinson.

Popper, K.R. (1969). *Conjectures and refutations.* London: Routledge & Kegan Paul.

Popper, K.R. (1972). *Objective knowledge.* Oxford: Oxford University Press.

Posner, M.I., & Keele, S.W. (1968). On the genesis of abstract ideas. *Journal of Experimental Psychology, 77,* 353–363.

Posner, M.I., & Petersen, S.E. (1990). The attention system of the human brain. *Annual Review of Neuroscience, 13,* 25–42.

Posner, M.I., Rafal, R.D., Choate, L.S., & Vaughan, J. (1985). Inhibition of return: Neural basis and function. *Cognitive Neuropsychology, 2,* 211–228.

Posner, M.I., Walker, J.A., Friedrich, F.J., & Rafal, R.D. (1984). Effects of parietal lobe injury on covert orienting of visual attention. *Journal of Neuroscience, 4,* 1863–1874.

Pressley, M., & McDaniel, M.A. (1988). Doing mnemonics research well: Some general guidelines and a study. In M.M. Gruneberg, P.E. Morris, & R.N. Sykes (Eds.), *Practical aspects of memory: Current research and issues: Vol. 2. Clinical and educational implications.* Chichester, UK: John Wiley.

Priest, A.G. (1986). Inference strategies in physics problem-solving. In A.G. Cohn & J.R. Thomas (Eds.), *Artificial intelligence and its applications.* Chichester, UK: John Wiley.

Proffitt, D.R., Kaiser, M.K., & Whelan, S.M. (1990). Understanding wheel dynamics. *Cognitive Psychology, 22,* 342–373.

Putnam, H. (1975a). Is semantics possible? In H. Putnam (Ed.), *Philosophical papers* (Vol. 2). Cambridge: Cambridge University Press.

Putnam, H. (1975b). The meaning of "meaning". In H. Putnam (Ed.), *Philosophical papers* (Vol. 2). Cambridge: Cambridge University Press.

Pylyshyn, Z.W. (1973). What the mind's eye tells the mind's brain. *Psychological Bulletin, 80,* 1–24.

Pylyshyn, Z.W. (1979). Metaphorical imprecision and the "top-down" research strategy. In A. Ortony (Ed.), *Metaphor and thought.* Cambridge: Cambridge University Press.

Pylyshyn, Z.W. (1981). The imagery debate: Analogue media versus tacit knowledge. *Psychological Review, 88,* 16–45.

Pylyshyn, Z.W. (1984). *Computation and cognition.* Cambridge, MA: MIT Press.

Pynoos, R.S., & Nader, K. (1989). Children's memory and proximity to violence. *Journal of the American Academy of Child and Adolescent Psychiatry, 28,* 236–241.

Quillian, M.R. (1966). *Semantic memory.* Unpublished PhD Dissertation, Carnegie Institute of Technology, Pittsburgh, PA.

Raaheim, K.J. (1974). *Problem solving and intelligence.* Bergen: Universitetforlaget.

Rabinowitz, J.C., Mandler, G., & Patterson, K.E. (1977). Determinants of recognition and recall: Accessibility and generation. *Journal of Experimental Psychology: General, 106,* 302–329.

Rafal, R.D., & Posner, M.I. (1987). Deficits in human visual spatial attention following thalamic lesions. *Proceedings of the National Academy of Science, 84,* 7349–7353.

Rajaram, S. (1993). Remembering and knowing: Two means of access to the personal past. *Memory and Cognition, 21,* 89–102.

Ramachandran, V.S. (1988). Perception of shape from shading. *Nature, 331,* 163–166.

Ramachandran, V.S., & Anstis, S.M. (1986). The perception of apparent motion. *Scientific American, 254,* 80–87.

Rapp, B.C., & Caramazza, A. (1989). General to specific access in word meaning: A claim re-examined. *Cognitive Neuropsychology, 6,* 251–272.

Ratcliff, R., & McKoon, G. (1978). Priming in item recognition: Evidence for the propositional structure of sentences. *Journal of Verbal Learning and Verbal Behavior, 20,* 204–215.

Rayner, K., Balota, D.A., & Pollatsek, A. (1986). Against parafoveal semantic preprocessing during eye fixations in reading. *Canadian Journal of Psychology, 40,* 473–483.

Rayner, K., Carlson, M., & Frazier, L. (1983). The interaction of syntax and semantics during sentence processing: Eye movements in the analysis of semantically biased sentences. *Journal of Verbal Learning and Verbal Behavior, 22,* 358–374.

Rayner, K., Inhoff, A.W., Morrison, R.E., Slowiaczek, M.L., & Bertera, J.H. (1981). Masking of foveal and parafoveal vision during eye fixations in reading. *Journal of Experimental Psychology: Human Perception and Performance, 7,* 167–179.

Rayner, K., & Morris, R.K. (1992). Eye movement control in reading: Evidence against semantic preprocessing. *Journal of Experimental Psychology: Human Perception and Performance, 18,* 163–172.

Rayner, K., & Pollatsek, A. (1989). *The psychology of reading.* London: Prentice-Hall.

Rayner, K., & Sereno, S.C. (1994). Eye movements in reading: Psycholinguistic studies. In M.A. Gernsbacher (Ed.), *Handbook of psycholinguistics.* New York: Academic Press.

Rayner, K., Well, A.D., & Pollatsek, A. (1980). Asymmetry of the effective visual field in reading. *Perception and Psychophysics, 27,* 537–544.

Rayner, K., Well, A.D., Pollatsek, A., & Bertera, J.H. (1982). The availability of useful information to the right of fixation in reading. *Perception and Psychophysics, 31,* 537–550.

Reason, J.T. (1979). Actions not as planned: The price of automatisation. In G. Underwood & R. Stevens (Eds.), *Aspects of consciousness: Vol. 1. Psychological issues.* London: Academic Press.

Reason, J.T. (1992). Cognitive underspecification: Its variety and consequences. In B.J. Baars (Ed.), *Experimental slips and human error: Exploring the architecture of volition.* New York: Plenum Press.

Reber, A.S. (1989). Implicit learning and tacit knowledge. *Journal of Experimental Psychology: General, 118,* 219–235.

Reed, S.K., Ernst, G.W., & Banerji, R. (1974). The role of analogy in transfer between similar problem states. *Cognitive Psychology, 6,* 436–450.

Regan, D., Beverley, K.I., & Cynader, M. (1979). The visual perception of motion in depth. *Scientific American, 241,* 136–151.

Reich, S.S., & Ruth, P. (1982). Wason's selection task: Verification, falsification and matching. *British Journal of Psychology, 73,* 395–405.

Reicher, G.M. (1969). Perceptual recognition as a function of meaningfulness of stimulus material. *Journal of Experimental Psychology, 81,* 274–280.

Reitman, J.S. (1974). Without surreptitious rehearsal, information in short-term memory decays. *Journal of Verbal Learning and Verbal Behavior, 13,* 365–377.

Reitman, W. (1965). *Cognition and thought.* New York: John Wiley.

Remez, R.E., Rubin, P.E., Pisoni, D.B., & Carrell, T.D. (1981). Speech perception without traditional speech cues. *Science, 212,* 947–950.

Repp, B.H. (1984). Categorical perception: Issues, methods and findings. In N.J. Lass (Ed.), *Speech and language: Advances in basic research and practice* (Vol. 10). New York: Academic Press.

Restle, F. (1979). Coding theory of the perception of motion configuration. *Psychological Review, 86,* 1–24.

Rhodes, G., Brennan, S., & Carey, S. (1987). Identification and ratings of caricatures: Implications for mental representations of faces. *Cognitive Psychology, 19,* 473–497.

Richardson, J.T.E. (1980). *Mental imagery and human memory.* London: Macmillian.

Riddoch, M.J., & Humphreys, G.W. (1987). Visual object processing in optic aphasia: A case of semantic access agnosia. *Cognitive Neuropsychology, 4,* 131–185.

Rinck, M., Glowalla, U., & Schneider, K. (1992). Mood-congruent and mood-incongruent learning. *Memory and Cognition, 20,* 29-39.

Rips, L.J. (1983). Cognitive processes in propositional reasoning. *Psychological Review, 90,* 38–71.

Rips, L.J. (1984). Reasoning as a central intellective ability. In R.J. Sternberg (Ed.), *Advances in the study of intelligence.* Hillsdale, NJ: Lawrence Erlbaum Associates Inc.

Rips, L.J. (1986). Mental muddles. In M. Brand & R.M. Harnish (Eds.), *Problems in the representation of knowledge and belief.* Tucson, AZ: University of Arizona Press.

Rips, L.J. (1989a). Similarity, typicality and categorisation. In A. Ortony & S. Vosniadou (Eds.), *Similarity and analogical reasoning* Cambridge: Cambridge University Press.

Rips, L.J. (1989b). The psychology of knights and knaves. *Cognition, 31,* 85–116.

Rips, L.J. (1990). Reasoning. *Annual Review of Psychology, 41,* 321–353.

Rips, L.J. (1994). *The psychology of proof: Deductive reasoning in human thinking.* Cambridge, MA: MIT.

Rips, L.J., & Collins, A. (1993). Categories and resemblance. *Journal of Experimental Psychology: General, 122,* 468–486.

Rips, L.J., & Conrad, F.J. (1983). Individual differences in deduction. *Cognition and Brain Theory, 6,* 259–285.

Rips, L.J., Shoben, E.J., & Smith, E.E. (1973). Semantic distance and the verification of semantic relations. *Journal of Verbal Learning and Verbal Behavior, 12,* 1–20.

Rist, R.S. (1989). Schema creation in programming. *Cognitive Science, 13,* 389–414

Roberts, A., & Bruce, V. (1988). Feature saliency in judging the sex and familiarity of faces. *Perception, 17,* 475–481.

Rock, I. (1973). *Orientation and form.* New York: Academic Press.

Roediger, H.L. (1980). Memory metaphors in cognitive psychology. *Memory and Cognition, 8,* 231–246.

Roediger, H.L. (1990). Implicit memory: Retention without remembering. *American Psychologist, 45,* 1043–1056.

Roediger, H.L., & Blaxton, T.A. (1987). Effects of varying modality, surface features, and retention interval on priming in word-fragment completion. *Memory and Cognition, 15,* 379–388.

Roeltgen, D.P. (1987). Loss of deep dyslexic reading ability from a second left hemisphere lesion. *Archives of Neurology, 44,* 346–348.

Rogers, B.J., & Collett, T.S. (1989). The appearance of surfaces specified by motion parallax and binocular disparity. *Quarterly Journal of Experimental Psychology, 41A,* 697–717.

Rogers, B.J., & Graham, M.E. (1979). Motion parallax as an independent cue for depth perception. *Perception, 8,* 125–134.

Rogers, T.B., Kuiper, N.A., & Kirker, W.S. (1977). Self-reference and the encoding of personal information. *Journal of Personality and Social Psychology, 35,* 677–688.

Rosch, E. (1973). Natural categories. *Cognitive Psychology, 4,* 328–350.

Rosch, E. (1975a). The nature of mental codes for colour categories. *Journal of Experimental Psychology: General, 104,* 192–233.

Rosch, E. (1975b). Cognitive reference points. *Cognitive Psychology, 7,* 532–547.

Rosch, E. (1978). Principles of categorisation. In E. Rosch & B.B. Lloyd (Eds.), *Cognition and categorisation.* Hillsdale, NJ: Lawrence Erlbaum Associates Inc.

Rosch, E., & Mervis, C.B. (1975). Family resemblances: Studies in the internal structure of categories *Cognitive Psychology, 7,* 573–605.

Rosch, E., Mervis, C.B., Gray, W.D., Johnson, D.M., & Boyes-Braem, P. (1976). Basic objects in natural categories. *Cognitive Psychology, 8,* 382–439.

Rosch, E., Simpson, C., & Miller, R.S. (1976). Structural bases of typicality effects. *Journal of Experimental Psychology: Human Perception and Performance, 2,* 491–502.

Rosenblatt, F. (1959). Two theorems of statistical separability in the perceptron. In *Mechanisations of thought processes: Proceedings of a symposium held at the National Physical Laboratory, November 1958* (Vol. 1). London: HM Stationery Office.

Rosenbloom, P., & Newell, A. (1986). The chunking of goal hierarchies: A generalised model of practice. In R.S. Michalski, J.G. Carbonell, & J.M. Mitchell (Eds.), *Machine learning II: An artificial intelligence approach.* Los Altos, CA: Morgan Kaufmann.

Rosenbloom, P., & Newell, A. (1987). Learning by chunking: A production system model of practice. In D. Klahr, P. Langley, & R. Neches (Eds.), *Production system model of learning and development.* Cambridge, MA: MIT Press.

Roth, I. (1986). An introduction to object perception. In I. Roth & J.P. Frisby (Eds.), *Perception and representation: A cognitive approach.* Milton Keynes, UK: Open University Press.

Roy, D.F. (1991). Improving recall by eye-witnesses through the cognitive interview: Practical applications and implications for the police service. *The Psychologist: Bulletin of the British Psychological Society, 4,* 398–400.

Rubin, D.C., Wetzler, S.E., & Nebes, R.D. (1986). Autobiographical memory across the life span. In

D.C. Rubin (Ed.), *Autobiographical memory.* Cambridge: Cambridge University Press.

Rumain, B., Connell, J., & Braine, M.D.S. (1983). Conversational comprehension processes are responsible for reasoning fallacies in children as well as adults: IF is not the Biconditional. *Developmental Psychology, 19,* 471–481.

Rumelhart, D.E. (1975). Notes on a schema for stories. In D.G. Bobrow & A. Collins (Eds.), *Representation and understanding: Studies in cognitive science.* New York: Academic Press.

Rumelhart, D.E. (1980). Schemata: The basic building blocks of cognition. In R. Spiro, B. Bruce, & W. Brewer (Eds.), *Theoretical issues in reading comprehension.* Hillsdale, NJ: Lawrence Erlbaum Associates Inc.

Rumelhart, D.E. Hinton, G.E., & McClelland, J.L. (1986c). A general framework for parallel distributed processing. In D.E. Rumelhart, J.L. McClelland, & The PDP Research Group (Eds.), *Parallel distributed processing: Vol. 1. Foundations.* Cambridge, MA: MIT Press.

Rumelhart, D.E., Hinton, G.E., & Williams, R.J. (1986b). Learning representations by back-propagating errors. *Nature, 323,* 533–536.

Rumelhart, D.E., McClelland, J.L., & The PDP Research Group (Eds.) (1986a). *Parallel distributed processing: Vol. 1. Foundations.* Cambridge, MA: MIT Press.

Rumelhart, D.E., & Norman, D.A. (1981). Analogical processes in learning. In J.R. Anderson (Ed.), *Cognitive skills and their acquisition.* Hillsdale, NJ: Lawrence Erlbaum Associates Inc.

Rumelhart, D.E., & Norman, D.A. (1983). Representation in memory. In R.C. Atkinson, R.J. Herrnstein, B. Lindzey, & R.D. Luce (Eds.), *Handbook of experimental psychology.* Chichester, UK: John Wiley.

Rumelhart, D.E., & Ortony, A. (1977). The representation of knowledge in memory. In R.C. Anderson, R.J. Spiro, & W.E. Montague (Eds.), *Schooling and the acquisition of knowledge.* Hillsdale, NJ: Lawrence Erlbaum Associates Inc.

Rumelhart, D.E., Smolensky, P., McClelland, J.L., & Hinton, G.E. (1986d). Schemata and sequential thought processes in PDP models. In J.L. McClelland, D.E. Rumelhart, & The PDP Research Group (Eds.), *Parallel distributed processing: Vol. 2. Psychological and biological models.* Cambridge, MA: MIT Press.

Runeson, S., & Frykholm, G. (1983). Kinematic specifications of dynamics as an informational basis for person-and-action perception: Expectation, gender recognition, and deceptive intention. *Journal of Experimental Psychology: General, 112,* 585–615.

Rylander, G. (1939). Personality changes after operations on the frontal lobes. *Acta Psychiatrica Neurologica* (Supplement No. 30).

Ryle, G. (1949). *The concept of mind.* London: Hutchinson.

Saariluoma, P. (1990). Apperception and restructuring in chess players' problem solving. In K.J. Gilhooly, M.T.G. Keane, R. Logie, & G. Erdos (Eds.), *Lines of thinking: Reflections on the psychology of thought* (Vol. 2). Chichester, UK: John Wiley.

Saffran, E.M., Schwartz, M.F., & Marin, O.S.M. (1980a). Evidence from aphasia: Isolating the components of a production model. In B. Butterworth (Ed.), *Language production* (Vol. 1). London: Academic Press.

Saffran, E.M., Schwartz, M.F., & Marin, O.S.M. (1980b). The word order problem in agrammatism: II. Production. *Brain and Language, 10,* 249–262.

Saint-Cyr, J.A., Taylor, A.E., & Lang, A.E. (1988). Procedural learning and neostriatal dysfunction in man. *Brain, 111,* 941–959.

Salzman, C.D., Murasugi, C.M., Britten, K.H., & Newsome, W.T. (1992). Microstimulation in visual area MT: Effects on direction discrimination performance. *Journal of Neuroscience, 12,* 2331–2355.

Samuel, A.G. (1981). Phonemic restoration: Insights from a new methodology. *Journal of Experimental Psychology: General, 110,* 474–494.

Sanford, A.J., & Garrod, S.C. (1981). *Understanding written language.* New York: John Wiley.

Sarason, I.G. (1988). Anxiety, self-preoccupation and attention. *Anxiety Research, 1,* 3–7.

Sargent, J. (1990). The neuropsychology of visual image generation. *Brain and Cognition, 13,* 98–129.

Savelsberg, G.J.P., Whiting, H.T.A., & Bootsma, R.J. (1991). Grasping tau. *Journal of Experimental Psychology: Human Perception and Performance, 17,* 315–322.

Savion, L. (1993). Review of "Deduction". *Behavioral and Brain Sciences, 16,* 364–365.

Schacter, D.L. (1983). Amnesia observed: Remembering and forgetting in a natural environment. *Journal of Abnormal Psychology, 92,* 236–242.

Schacter, D.L. (1987). Implicit memory: History and current status. *Journal of Experimental Psychology: Learning, Memory, and Cognition, 13,* 501–518.

Schacter,   D.L. (1992). Understanding   implicit memory: A cognitive neuroscience approach. *American Psychologist, 47*, 559–569.

Schafer, R., & Murphy, G. (1943). The role of autism in visual figure-ground relationship. *Journal of Experimental Psychology, 32*, 335–343.

Schank, R.C. (1972). Conceptual dependency: A theory of natural language understanding. *Cognitive Psychology, 3*, 552–631.

Schank, R.C. (1976). *Conceptual information processing*. Amsterdam: North-Holland.

Schank, R.C. (1978). Predictive understanding. In R.N. Campbell & P.T. Smith (Eds.), *Recent advances in the psychology of language: Formal and experimental approaches*. New York: Plenum Press.

Schank, R.C. (1982). *Dynamic memory*. Cambridge: Cambridge University Press.

Schank, R.C. (1986). *Explanation patterns*. Hillsdale, NJ: Lawrence Erlbaum Associates Inc.

Schank, R.C., & Abelson, R.P. (1977). *Scripts, plans, goals and understanding*. Hillsdale, NJ: Lawrence Erlbaum Associates Inc.

Schare, M.L., Lisman, S.A., & Spear, N.E. (1984). The effects of mood variation on state-dependent retention. *Cognitive Therapy and Research, 8*, 387–408.

Scheerer, M. (1963). Problem-solving. *Scientific American, 208*, 118–128.

Schiff, W., & Detwiler, M.L. (1979). Information used in judging impending collision. *Perception, 8*, 647–658.

Schneider, W., & Shiffrin, R.M. (1977). Controlled and automatic human information processing: 1. Detection, search, and attention. *Psychological Review, 84*, 1–66.

Schneider, W., & Shiffrin, R.M. (1985). Categorisation (restructuring) and automatisation: Two separable factors. *Psychology Review, 92*, 424–428.

Schooler, J.W., & Engstler-Schooler, T.Y. (1990). Verbal overshadowing of visual memories: Some things are better left unsaid. *Cognitive Psychology, 22*, 36–71.

Schriver, K. (1984). *Revised computer documentation for comprehension: Ten lessons in protocol-aided revision* (Tech. Rep. No. 14). Pittsburgh, PA: Carnegie Mellon University.

Schuman, H., & Rieger, C. (1992). Collective memory and collective memories. In M.A. Conway, D.C. Rubin, H. Spinnler, & W. Wagenaar (Eds.), *Theoretical perspectives on autobiographical memory*. Dordrecht: Kluwer Academic Publishers.

Schwartz, M.F., Marin, O.S.M., & Saffran, E.M. (1979). Dissociation of language function in dementia: A case study. *Brain and Language, 7*, 277–306.

Schwartz, M.F., Saffran, E.M., & Marin, O.S.M. (1980). Fractionating the reading process in dementia: Evidence for word-specific print-to-sound associations. In M. Coltheart, K.E. Patterson, & J.C. Marshall (Eds.), *Deep dyslexia*. London: Routledge & Kegan Paul.

Scoville, W.B., & Milner, B. (1957). Loss of recent memory after bilateral hippocampal lesions. *Journal of Neurology, Neurosurgery, and Psychiatry, 20*, 11–21.

Searle, J. (1989). *Minds, brains, and science*. Harmondsworth, UK: Penguin.

Sedgwick, H.A. (1973). *The visible horizon*. PhD thesis, Cornell University.

Segal, S.J., & Fusella, V. (1970). Influence of imaged pictures and sounds on detection of visual and auditory signals. *Journal of Experimental Psychology, 83*, 458–464.

Seger, C.A. (1994). Implicit learning. *Psychological Bulletin, 115*, 163–196.

Seidenberg, M.S., & McClelland, J.L. (1989). A distributed, developmental model of word recognition and naming. *Psychological Review, 96*, 523–568.

Seidenberg, M.S., Waters, G.S., Barnes, M.A., & Tanenhaus, M. (1984). When does irregular spelling or pronunciation influence word recognition? *Journal of Verbal Learning and Verbal Behavior, 23*, 383–404.

Seifert, C.M., & Black, J.B. (1983). Thematic connections between episodes. *Proceedings of the Fifth Annual Conference of the Cognitive Science Society*, Hillsdale, NJ: Lawrence Erlbaum Associates Inc.

Seifert, C.M., McKoon, G., Abelson, R.P., & Ratcliff, R. (1986). Memory connections between thematically-similar episodes. *Journal of Experimental Psychology: Learning, Memory, and Cognition, 12*, 220–231.

Sejnowski, T.J., & Rosenberg, C.R. (1987). Parallel networks that learn to pronounce English text. *Complex Systems, 1*, 145–168.

Sekuler, R., & Blake, R. (1994). *Perception* (3rd Edn.). New York: McGraw-Hill.

Sellen, A.J., & Norman, D.A. (1992). The psychology of slips. In B.J. Baars (Ed.), *Experimental slips and human error: Exploring the architecture of volition*. New York: Plenum Press

Sergent, J., Ohta, S., & MacDonald, B. (1992). Functional neuroanatomy of face and object processing. *Brain, 115,* 15–36.

Shaffer, L.H. (1975). Multiple attention in continuous verbal tasks. In P.M.A. Rabbitt & S. Dornic (Eds.), *Attention and performance* (Vol. V). London: Academic Press.

Shallice, T. (1981). Phonological agraphia and the lexical route in writing. *Brain, 104,* 413–429.

Shallice, T. (1982). Specific impairments of planning. *Philosophical Transactions of the Royal Society of London, B 298,* 199–209.

Shallice, T. (1988). *From neuropsychology to mental structure.* Cambridge: Cambridge University Press.

Shallice, T. (1991). From neuropsychology to mental structure. *Behavioral and Brain Sciences, 14,* 429–439.

Shallice, T., & Warrington, E.K. (1970). Independent functioning of verbal memory stores: A neuropsychological study. *Quarterly Journal of Experimental Psychology, 22,* 261–273.

Shallice, T., & Warrington, E.K. (1974). The dissociation between long-term retention of meaningful sounds and verbal material. *Neuropsychologia, 12,* 553–555.

Shapiro, P.N., & Penrod, S. (1986). Meta-analysis of facial identification studies. *Psychological Bulletin, 100,* 139–156.

Shastri, L., & Ajjanagadde, V. (1993). From simple associations to systematic reasoning: A connectionist representation of rules, variables and dynamic bindings. *Behavioral and Brain Sciences, 16,* 417–194.

Shepard, R.N. (1978). The mental image. *The American Psychologist, 33,* 125–137.

Shepard, R.N., & Metzler, J. (1971). Mental rotation of three-dimensional objects. *Science, 191,* 701–703.

Shiffrar, M., & Freyd, J.J. (1990). Apparent motion of the human body. *Psychological Science, 1,* 257–264.

Shiffrin, R.M., & Schneider, W. (1977). Controlled and automatic human information processing: II. Perceptual learning, automatic attending, and a general theory. *Psychological Review, 84,* 127–190.

Shimamura, A.P., Janowsky, J., & Squire, L.R. (1990). Memory for temporal order of events in patients with frontal lobe lesions and amnesic patients. *Neuropsychologia, 28,* 803–813.

Shoham, Y. (1993). *Prolog programming.* Cambridge, MA: MIT Press.

Shotter, J. (1991). The rhetorical-responsive nature of mind: A social constructionist account. In A. Still & A. Costall (Eds.), *Against cognitivism: Alternative foundations for cognitive psychology.* Hemel Hempstead: Harvester Wheatsheaf.

Silveri, M.C., & Gainotti, G. (1988). Interaction between vision and language in category specific semantic impairment for living things. *Cognitive Neuropsychology, 5,* 677–710.

Simon, H.A. (1966). Scientific discovery and the psychology of problem solving. In *Mind and cosmos: Essays in contemporary science and philosophy.* Pittsburgh, PA: University of Pittsburgh Press.

Simon, H.A. (1973). The structure of ill-structured problems. *Artificial Intelligence, 4,* 181–201.

Simon, H.A. (1974). How big is a chunk? *Science, 183,* 482–488.

Simon, H.A. (1978). Information-processing theory of human problem solving. In W.K. Estes (Ed.), *Handbook of learning and cognitive processes* (Vol. 5). Hillsdale, NJ: Lawrence Erlbaum Associates Inc.

Simon, H.A. (1980). Cognitive science: The newest science of the artificial. *Cognitive Science, 4,* 33–46.

Simon, H.A. (1986). The information processing explanation of Gestalt phenomena. *Computers in Human Behaviour, 2,* 241–255.

Simon, H.A., & Barenfeld, M. (1969). Information processing analysis of perceptual processes in problem solving. *Psychological Review, 76,* 473–483.

Simon, H.A., & Gilmartin, K. (1973). A simulation of memory for chess positions. *Cognitive Psychology, 5,* 29–46.

Simon, H.A., & Hayes, J.R. (1976). The understanding process: Problem isomorphs. *Cognitive Psychology, 8,* 165–190.

Simon, H.A., & Kaplan, C.A. (1989). Foundations of cognitive science. In M.I. Posner (Ed.), *Foundations of cognitive science.* Cambridge, MA: MIT Press.

Simon, H.A., & Reed, S.K. (1976). Modelling strategy shifts on a problem solving task. *Cognitive Psychology, 8,* 86–97.

Singer, M. (1979). Processes of inference during sentence encoding. *Memory and Cognition, 7,* 192–200.

Singer, M. (1980). The role of case filling inferences in coherence of brief passages. *Discourse Processes, 3,* 185–201.

Singley, M.K., & Anderson, J.R. (1989). *The transfer of cognitive skill.* Cambridge, MA: Cambridge University Press.

Slowiaczek, M.L., & Clifton, C. (1980). Subvocalisation and reading for meaning. *Journal of Verbal Learning and Verbal Behavior, 19,* 573–582.

Smith, C.A., & Lazarus, R.S. (1993) Appraisal components, core relational themes, and the emotions. *Cognition and Emotion, 7,* 233–269.

Smith, D.E., & Hochberg, J.E. (1954). The effect of "punishment" (electric shock) on figure– ground perception. *Journal of Psychology, 38,* 83–87.

Smith, E.E. (1978). Theories of semantic memory. In W.K. Estes (Ed.), *Handbook of learning and cognitive processes* (Vol. 6). Hillsdale, NJ: Lawrence Erlbaum Associates Inc.

Smith, E.E. (1988). Concepts and thought. In R.J. Sternberg & E.E. Smith (Eds.), *The psychology of human thought.* Cambridge: Cambridge University Press.

Smith, E.E., & Medin, D.L. (1981). *Categories and concepts.* Harvard. Harvard University Press.

Smith, E.E., & Osherson, D.N. (1984). Conceptual combination with prototype concepts. *Cognitive Science, 8,* 337–361.

Smith, E.E., Osherson, D.N., Rips, L.J., & Keane, M. (1988). Combining prototypes: A modification model. *Cognitive Science, 12,* 485–528.

Smith, E.E., Shoben, E.J., & Rips, L.J. (1974). Structure and process in semantic memory: A featural model for semantic decisions. *Psychological Review, 81,* 214–241.

Smolensky, P. (1988). On the proper treatment of connectionism. *Behavioral and Brain Sciences, 11,* 1–74.

Smyth, M.M., Morris, P.E., Levy, P., & Ellis, A.W. (1987). *Cognition in action.* Hove, UK: Lawrence Erlbaum Associates Ltd.

Smyth, M.M., & Scholey, K.A. (1994). Characteristics of spatial memory span: Is there an analogy to the word length effect, based on movement time? *Quarterly Journal of Experimental Psychology, 47A,* 91–117.

Soloway, E., Bonar, J., & Erlich, K. (1983). Cognitive strategies and looping constructs: An empirical study. *Communications of the ACM, 26,* 853–860.

Soloway, E., & Erlich, K. (1984). Empirical studies of programming knowledge. *IEEE Transactions of Software Engineering, 5,* 595–609.

Soloway, E., & Spohrer, J.C. (1989). *Studying the novice programmer.* Hillsdale, NJ: Lawrence Erlbaum Associates Inc.

Speisman, J.C., Lazarus, R.S., Mordkoff, A.M., & Davison, L.A. (1964). Experimental reduction of stress based on ego-defence theory. *Journal of Abnormal Psychology, 68,* 367–380.

Spelke, E.S., Hirst, W.C., & Neisser, U. (1976). Skills of divided attention. *Cognition, 4,* 215–230.

Sperling, G. (1960). The information available in brief visual presentations. *Psychological Monographs, 74* (Whole No. 498), 1–29.

Spielberger, C.D. (1972). Anxiety as an emotional state. In C.D. Spielberger (Ed.), *Anxiety: Current trends in theory and research* (Vol. 1). London: Academic Press.

Spielberger, C.D., Gonzalez, H.P., Taylor, C.J., Algaze, B., & Anton, W.D. (1978). Examination stress and test anxiety. In C.D. Spielberger & I.G. Sarason (Eds.), *Stress and anxiety* (Vol. 5). London: Halsted.

Spohrer, J.C., Soloway, E., & Pope, E. (1985). A goal–plan analysis of buggy Pascal programs. *Human–Computer Interaction, 1,* 163–207.

Springer, K. (1990) In defence of theories. *Cognition, 35,* 293–298.

Squire, L.R. (1987). *Memory and brain.* Oxford: Oxford University Press.

Squire, L.R., Knowlton, B., & Musen, G. (1993). The structure and organisation of memory. *Annual Review of Psychology, 44,* 453–495.

Squire, L.R., Ojemann, J.G., Miezin, F.M., Petersen, S.E., Videen, T.O., & Raichle, M.E. (1992). Activation of the hippocampus in normal humans: A functional anatomical study of memory. *Proceedings of the National Academy of Science, USA, 89,* 1837–1841.

Srinivas, K., & Roediger, H.L. (1990). Classifying implicit memory tests: Category association and anagram solution. *Journal of Memory and Language, 29,* 389–412.

Steele, G.L. (1990). *Common LISP: The language* (2nd Edn.). Bedford, MA: Digital Press.

Stefflre, V., Castillo Vales, V., & Morley, L. (1966). Language and cognition in Yucatan: A cross cultural replication. *Journal of Personality and Social Psychology, 4,* 112–115.

Stein, N.L., & Glenn, C.G. (1979). An analysis of story comprehension in elementary school children. In R. Freedle (Ed.), *Multidisciplinary perspectives in discourse comprehension.* Norwood, NJ: Ablex.

Stemberger, J.P. (1982). The nature of segments in the lexicon: Evidence from speech errors. *Lingua, 56,* 235–259.

Steptoe, A., & Vogele, C. (1986). Are stress responses influenced by cognitive appraisal? An experimental comparison on coping strategies. *British Journal of Psychology, 77,* 243–255.

Sternberg, R.J., & Davidson, J.E. (1982). Componential analysis and componential theory. *Behavioral and Brain Sciences, 53,* 352–353.

Stevens, J.K., Emerson, R.C., Gerstein, G.L., Kallos, T., Neufield, G.R., Nichols, C.W., & Rosenquist, A.C. (1976). Paralysis of the awake human: Visual perceptions. *Vision Research, 16,* 93–98.

Stevenson, R., & Over, D.E. (in press). Deduction from uncertain premises. *Quarterly Journal of Experimental Psychology.*

Steward, F., Parkin, A.J., & Hunkin, N.M. (1992). Naming impairments following recovery from herpes simplex encephalitis: Category-specific? *Quarterly Journal of Experimental Psychology, 44A,* 261–284.

Stewart, D., Cudworth, C.J., & Lishman, J.R. (1993). Misperception of time-to-collision by drivers in pedestrian accidents. *Perception, 22,* 1227–1244.

Still, A., & Costall, A. (Eds.) (1991). *Against cognitivism: Alternative foundations for cognitive psychology.* Hemel Hempstead: Harvester Wheatsheaf.

Stonham, J. (1986). Practical face recognition and verification with WISARD. In H.D. Ellis, M.A. Jeeves, F. Newcombe, & A.W. Young (Eds.), *Aspects of face processing.* Dordrecht: Martinus Nijhoff.

Stroop, J.R. (1935). Studies of interference in serial verbal reactions. *Journal of Experimental Psychology, 18,* 643–662.

Sullivan, L. (1976). Selective attention and secondary message analysis: A reconsideration of Broadbent's filter model of selective attention. *Quarterly Journal of Experimental Psychology, 28,* 167–178.

Sweller, J. (1983). Control mechanisms in problem solving. *Memory and Cognition, 11,* 32–40.

Sweller, J., Mawer, R.F., & Ward, M.R. (1983). Development of expertise in mathematical problem solving. *Journal of Experimental Psychology: General, 112,* 639–661.

Takano, Y. (1989). Perception of rotated forms. *Cognitive Psychology, 21,* 1–59.

Taraban, R., & McClelland, J.L. (1988). Constituent attachment and thematic role assignment in sentence processing: Influences of content-based expectations. *Journal of Memory and Language, 27,* 597–632.

Tarr, M.J., & Pinker, S. (1989). Mental rotation and orientation-dependence in shape recognition. *Cognitive Psychology, 21,* 233–282.

Tartter, V.C. (1986). *Language processes.* New York: Holt, Rinehart and Winston.

Teuber, H.-L., Milner, B., & Vaughan, H.G. (1968). Persistent anterograde amnesia after stab wound of the basal brain. *Neuropsychologia, 6,* 267–282.

Thagard, P. (1984). Conceptual combination and scientific discovery. In P. Asquith & P. Kitcher (Eds.), *PSA* (Vol.1). East Lansing, MI: Philosophy of Science Association.

Thagard, P., Holyoak, K.J., Nelson, G., & Gochfeld, D. (1990). Analogue retrieval by constraint satisfaction. *Artificial Intelligence, 46,* 259–310.

Thomas, J.C. (1974). An analysis of behaviour in the hobbits–orcs problem. *Cognitive Psychology, 6,* 257–269.

Thomson, D.M., & Tulving, E. (1970). Associative encoding and retrieval: Weak and strong cues. *Journal of Experimental Psychology, 86,* 5–262.

Thorndike, E.L. (1911). *Animal intelligence.* New York: Macmillan.

Thorndyke, P.W. (1977). Cognitive structures in comprehension and memory of narrative discourse. *Cognitive Psychology, 9,* 77–110.

Thorndyke, P.W., & Yekovich, F.R. (1980). A critique of schema-based theories of human memory. *Poetics, 9,* 23–49.

Tipper, S.P., & Driver, J. (1988). Negative priming between pictures and words: Evidence for semantic analysis of ignored stimuli. *Memory and Cognition, 16,* 64–70.

Tipper, S.P., Lortie, C., & Baylis, G.C. (1992). Selective reaching: Evidence for action-centred attention. *Journal of Experimental Psychology: Human Perception and Performance, 18,* 891–905.

Tippett, L.J. (1992). The generation of visual images: A review of neuropsychological research and theory. *Psychological Bulletin, 112,* 415–432.

Todd, J.T., & Akerstrom, R.A. (1987). Perception of three-dimensional form from patterns of optical texture. *Journal of Experimental Psychology: Human Perception and Performance, 13,* 242–255.

Todd, J.T., & Norman, J.F. (1991). The visual perception of smoothly curved surfaces from minimal apparent motion sequences. *Perception and Psychophysics, 50,* 509–523.

Tolkien, J.R.R. (1966). *The hobbit* (3rd Edn.). London: Allen & Unwin.

Trabasso, T., & Sperry, L.L. (1985). Causal relatedness and importance of story events. *Journal of Memory and Language, 24,* 595–611.

Treisman, A.M. (1964). Verbal cues, language, and meaning in selective attention. *American Journal of Psychology, 77,* 206–219.

Treisman, A.M. (1988). Features and objects: The fourteenth Bartlett memorial lecture. *Quarterly Journal of Experimental Psychology, 40A,* 201–237.

Treisman, A.M. (1991). Search, similarity, and integration of features between and within dimensions. *Journal of Experimental Psychology: Human Perception and Performance, 17,* 652–676.

Treisman, A.M. (1992). Spreading suppression or feature integration? A reply to Duncan and Humphreys (1992). *Journal of Experimental Psychology: Human Perception and Performance, 18,* 589–593.

Treisman, A.M., & Davies, A. (1973). Divided attention to ear and eye. In S. Kornblum (Ed.), *Attention and performance* (Vol. IV). London: Academic Press.

Treisman, A.M., & Geffen, G. (1967). Selective attention: Perception or response? *Quarterly Journal of Experimental Psychology, 19,* 1–18.

Treisman, A.M., & Gelade, G. (1980). A feature integration theory of attention. *Cognitive Psychology, 12,* 97–136.

Treisman, A.M., & Riley, J.G.A. (1969). Is selective attention selective perception or selective response: A further test. *Journal of Experimental Psychology, 79,* 27–34.

Treisman, A.M., & Sato, S. (1990). Conjunction search revisited. *Journal of Experimental Psychology: Human Perception and Performance, 16,* 459–478.

Treisman, A.M., & Schmidt, H. (1982). Illusory conjunctions in the perception of objects. *Cognitive Psychology, 14,* 107–141.

Tresilian, J.R. (1994). Two straw men stay silent when asked about the "direct" versus "inferential" controversy. *Behavioral and Brain Sciences, 17,* 335–336.

Tulving, E. (1972). Episodic and semantic memory. In E. Tulving & W. Donaldson (Eds.), *Organisation of memory.* London: Academic Press.

Tulving, E. (1974). Cue-dependent forgetting. *American Scientist, 62,* 74–82.

Tulving, E. (1979). Relation between encoding specificity and levels of processing. In L.S. Cermak & F.I.M. Craik (Eds.), *Levels of processing in human memory.* Hillsdale, NJ: Lawrence Erlbaum Associates Inc.

Tulving, E. (1982). Synergistic ecphory in recall and recognition. *Canadian Journal of Psychology, 36,* 130–147.

Tulving, E. (1983). *Elements of episodic memory.* Oxford: Oxford University Press.

Tulving, E. (1989). Memory: Performance, knowledge, and experience. *The European Journal of Cognitive Psychology, 1,* 3–26.

Tulving, E., & Flexser, A.J. (1992). On the nature of the Tulving–Wiseman function. *Psychological Review, 99,* 543–546.

Tulving, E., Mandler, G., & Baumal, R. (1964). Interaction of two sources of information in tachistoscopic word recognition. *Canadian Journal of Psychology, 18,* 62–71.

Tulving, E., & Schacter, D.L. (1990). Priming and human memory. *Science, 247,* 301–306.

Tulving, E., Schacter, D.L., & Stark, H.A. (1982). Priming effects in word-fragment completion are independent of recognition memory. *Journal of Experimental Psychology: Learning, Memory, and Cognition, 17,* 595–617.

Tulving, E., & Thomson, D.M. (1973). Encoding specificity and retrieval processes in episodic memory. *Psychological Review, 80,* 352–373.

Turing, A. (1950). Computing machinery and intelligence. *Mind, 59,* 433–460.

Tversky, A. (1977). Features of similarity. *Psychological Review, 84,* 327–352.

Tversky, A., & Gati, I. (1978). Studies of similarity. In E. Rosch & B.B. Lloyd (Eds.), *Cognition and categorisation.* Hillsdale, NJ: Lawrence Erlbaum Associates Inc.

Tweney, R.D., Doherty, M.E., Worner, W.J., Pliske, D.B., Mynatt, C.R., Gross, K.A., & Arkkelin, D.L. (1980). Strategies for rule discovery in an inference task. *Quarterly Journal of Experimental Psychology, 32,* 109–123.

Tzeng, O.J.L. (1973). Positive recency effects in delayed free recall. *Journal of Verbal Learning and Verbal Behavior, 12,* 436–439.

Ucros, C.G. (1989). Mood state-dependent memory: A meta-analysis. *Cognition and Emotion, 3,* 139–167.

Underwood, B.J., & Postman, L. (1960). Extra-experimental sources of interference in forgetting. *Psychological Review, 67,* 73–95.

Underwood, G. (1974). Moray vs. the rest: The effects of extended shadowing practice. *Quarterly Journal of Experimental Psychology, 26,* 368–372.

Valentine, T. (1988). Upside-down faces: A review of the effect of inversion upon face recognition. *British Journal of Psychology, 79,* 471–491.

van Dijk, T.A., & Kintsch, W. (1983). *Strategies of discourse comprehension.* New York: Academic Press.

Van Kleeck, M.H., & Kosslyn, S.M. (1993). Visual information processing: A perspective. In D.E. Meyer & S. Kornblum (Eds.), *Attention and performance* (Vol. XIV). London: MIT Press.

Van Mechelen, I., Hampton, J.A., Michalski, R.S., & Theuns, P. (1993). *Concepts and categories.* London: Academic Press.

Van Orden, G.C. (1987). A ROWS is a ROSE: Spelling, sound, and reading. *Memory and Cognition, 15,* 181–198.

Vaughan, J. (1985). *Hoping and commanding: Prototype semantics demonstrated.* Unpublished BA Thesis, Dept. of Psychology, Trinity College, Dublin, Ireland.

Velten, E. (1968). A laboratory task for induction of mood states. *Behaviour Research and Therapy, 6,* 473–482.

Vera, A., & Simon, H.A. (1994). Reply to Touretsky and Pomerleau: Reconstructing physical symbol systems. *Cognitive Science, 18,* 355–360.

Vincente, K.J., & Brewer, W.F. (1993). Reconstructive remembering of the scientific literature. *Cognition, 46,* 101–128.

Von Eckardt, B. (1993). *What is cognitive science?* Cambridge, MA: MIT Press.

Von Wright, J.M., Anderson, K., & Stenman, U. (1975). Generalisation of conditioned G.S.R.s in dichotic listening. In P.M.A. Rabbitt & S. Dornic (Eds.), *Attention and performance* (Vol. V). London: Academic Press.

Vosniadou, S., & Brewer, W. (1992) Mental models of the earth: A study of conceptual change in childhood. *Cognitive Psychology, 24,* 535–585.

Wachtel, P. (1973). Psychodynamics, behaviour therapy and the implacable experimenter: An inquiry into the consistency of personality. *Journal of Abnormal Psychology, 82,* 324–334.

Wagenaar, W.A. (1986). My memory: A study of autobiographical memory over six years. *Cognitive Psychology, 18,* 225–252.

Wagner, D.A., & Scurrah, M.J. (1971). Some characteristics of human problem solving in chess. *Cognitive Psychology, 2,* 451–478.

Walker, C.H., & Yekovich, F.R. (1984). Script-based inferences: Effects of text and knowledge variables on recognition memory. *Journal of Verbal Learning and Verbal Behavior, 23,* 357–370.

Walker, J.H. (1975). Real-world variability, reason-ableness judgements, and memory representations for concepts. *Journal of Verbal Learning and Verbal Behavior, 14,* 241–252.

Walker, N.K., & Burkhardt, J.F. (1965). The combat effectiveness of various human operator controlled systems. *Proceedings of the 17th military operations research symposium.* New York: Plenum.

Wallas, G. (1926). *The art of thought.* London: Cape.

Walsh, V., & O'Mara, S.M. (1994). A selection on attention: Special issue on attention. *Cognitive Neuropsychology, 11,* 97–98.

Warren, R. (1976). The perception of egomotion. *Journal of Experimental Psychology: Human Perception and Performance, 2,* 448–456.

Warren, R.M., & Warren, R.P. (1970). Auditory illusions and confusions. *Scientific American, 223,* 30–36.

Warren, W.H., Morris, M.W., & Kalish, M.L. (1988). Perception of translational heading from optical flow. *Journal of Experimental Psychology: Human Perception and Performance, 14,* 646–660.

Warrington, E.K. (1975). The selective impairment of semantic memory. *Quarterly Journal of Experimental Psychology, 27,* 635–657.

Warrington, E.K., & Shallice, T. (1972). Neuropsychological evidence of visual storage in short-term memory tasks. *Quarterly Journal of Experimental Psychology, 24,* 30–40.

Warrington, E.K., & Shallice, T. (1984). Category-specific semantic impairments. *Brain, 107,* 829–853.

Warrington, E.K., & Taylor, A.M. (1978). Two categorical stages of object recognition. *Perception, 7,* 695–705.

Wason, P.C. (1960). On the failure to eliminate hypotheses in a conceptual task. *Quarterly Journal of Experimental Psychology, 12,* 129–140.

Wason, P.C. (1966). Reasoning. In B.M. Foss (Ed.), *New horizons in psychology.* Harmondsworth, UK: Penguin.

Wason, P.C. (1977). On the failure to eliminate hypotheses … A second look. In P.N. Johnson-Laird & P.C. Wason (Eds.), *Thinking: Readings in cognitive science.* Cambridge: Cambridge University Press.

Wason, P.C., & Evans, J. St. B.T. (1975). Dual processes in reasoning? *Cognition, 3,* 141–154.

Wason, P.C., & Johnson-Laird, P.N. (1972). *The psychology of reasoning: Structure and content.* Cambridge, MA: Harvard University Press.

Wason, P.C., & Shapiro, D. (1971). Natural and contrived experience in a reasoning problem. *Quarterly Journal of Experimental Psychology, 23,* 63–71.

Watkins, M.J., & Gardiner, J.M. (1979). An appreciation of generate–recognise theory of recall. *Journal of Verbal Learning and Verbal Behavior, 18,* 687–704.

Watson, J.D. (1968). *The double helix: A personal account of the discovery of the structure of DNA.* London: Hutchinson.

Watt, R.J. (1988). *Visual processing: Computational, psychophysical, and cognitive research.* Hove, UK: Lawrence Erlbaum Associates Ltd.

Watt, R.J., & Morgan, M.J. (1984). Spatial filters and the localisation of luminance changes in human vision. *Vision Research, 24,* 1387–1397.

Weinberg, R.S., & Hunt, V. (1976). The inter-relationships between anxiety, motor performance, and electromyography. *Journal of Motor Behavior, 8,* 219–224.

Weisberg, R.W. (1980). *Memory, thought, and behaviour.* Oxford: Oxford University Press.

Weisberg, R.W. (1986). *Creativity, genius and other myths.* New York: W.H. Freeman.

Weisberg, R.W., & Alba, J.W. (1981). An examination of the alleged role of "fixation" in the solution of several insight problems. *Journal of Experimental Psychology: General, 110,* 169–192.

Weisberg, R.W., & Suls, J. (1973). An information-processing model of Duncker's candle problem. *Cognitive Psychology, 4,* 255–276.

Weiskrantz, L. (1986). *Blindsight: A case study and its implications.* Oxford: Oxford University Press.

Weiskrantz, L. (1990). Blindsight. In M.W. Eysenck (Ed.), *The Blackwell dictionary of cognitive psychology.* Oxford: Blackwell.

Weisstein, N., & Harris, C.S. (1974). Visual detection of line segments: An object-superiority effect. *Science, 186,* 752–755.

Welford, A.T. (1952). The psychological refractory period and the timing of high speed performance. *British Journal of Psychology, 43,* 2–19.

Wells, G.L. (1993). What do we know about eye-witness identification? *American Psychologist, 48,* 553–571.

Wertheim, A.H. (1994). Motion perception during self-motion: The direct versus inferential controversy revisited. *Behavioral and Brain Sciences, 17,* 293–311.

Wertheimer, M. (1912). Experimentelle Studien über das Sehen von Bewegung. *Zeitschrift für Psychologie, 61,* 161–265.

Wertheimer, M. (1954). *Productive thinking.* New York: Harper Row.

Wetherick, N.E. (1962). Eliminative and enumerative behaviour in a conceptual task. *Quarterly Journal of Experimental Psychology, 14,* 246–249.

Wharton, C.M., Holyoak, K.J., Downing, P.E., Lange, T.E., Wickens, T.D., & Melz, E.R. (1994). Below the surface: Analogical similarity and retrieval competition in reminding. *Cognitive Psychology, 26,* 64–101.

Wheatstone, C. (1838). Contributions to the physiology of vision. Part 1: On some remarkable and hitherto unobserved phenomena of binocular vision. *Philosophical Transactions of the Royal Society of London, 128,* 371–394.

Whorf, B.L. (1956). *Language, thought, and reality: Selected writings of Benjamin Lee Whorf.* New York: John Wiley.

Wickelgren, W.A. (1968). Sparing of short-term memory in an amnesic patient: Implications for strength theory of memory. *Neuropsychologia, 6,* 235–244.

Wickens, C.D. (1984). Processing resources in attention. In R. Parasuraman & D.R. Davies (Eds.), *Varieties of attention.* London: Academic Press.

Wilding, J., & Valentine, E. (1991). Superior memory ability. In J. Weinman & J. Hunter (Eds.), *Memory: Neurochemical and abnormal perspectives.* London: Harwood.

Wilding, J., & Valentine, E. (1994). Memory champions. *British Journal of Psychology, 85,* 231–244.

Wilensky, R. (1983). *Planning and understanding: A computational approach to human reasoning.* Massachusetts: Addison-Wesley.

Wilkins, M.C. (1928). The effect of changed material on the ability to do formal syllogistic reasoning. *Archives of Psychology, 16,* no. 102.

Wilkinson, D.A., & Carlen, P.L. (1982). Chronic organic brain syndromes associated with alcoholism: Neuropsychological and other aspects. In Y. Israel, S. Jones, & N.J. Cohen (Eds.), *Research advances in alcohol and drug problems* (Vol. 6). New York: Plenum Press.

Williams, J.M.G., & Broadbent, K. (1986). Auto-biographical memory in suicide attempters. *Journal of Abnormal Psychology, 95,* 144–149.

Williams, L.M. (1992). Adult memories of childhood abuse: Preliminary findings from a longitudinal study. *The Advisor, 5,* 19–20.

Wiseman, S., & Tulving, E. (1976). Encoding specificity: Relations between recall superiority and recognition failure. *Journal of Experimental Psychology: Human Learning and Memory, 2,* 349–361.

Wisniewski, E.J., & Medin, D.L. (1994). On the interaction of theory and data in concept learning. *Cognitive Science, 18,* 221–281.

Witherspoon, D., & Moscovitch, M. (1989). Stochastic independence between two implicit memory tasks. *Journal of Experimental Psychology: Learning, Memory, and Cognition, 15,* 22–30.

Wittgenstein, L. (1958). *Philosophical investigations.* (2nd Edn.). Oxford: Blackwell.

Woodworth, R.S., & Schlosberg, H. (1954). *Experimental psychology* (2nd Edn.). New York: Holt, Rinehart, & Winston.

Woodworth, R.S., & Sells, S.B. (1935). An atmosphere effect in formal syllogistic reasoning. *Journal of Experimental Psychology, 18,* 451–460.

Yaniv, I., & Meyer, D.E. (1987). Activation and metacognition of inaccessible information: Potential bases for incubation effects in problem solving. *Journal of Experimental Psychology: Learning, Memory, and Cognition, 13,* 187–205.

Yates, F.A. (1966). *The art of memory.* London: Routledge & Kegan Paul.

Yates, J. (1990). What is a theory? A response to Springer. *Cognition, 36,* 91–96.

Yates, J., Bessman, M., Dunne, M., Jertson, D., Sly, K., & Wendelboe, B. (1988). Are conceptions of motion based on a naive theory or on prototypes? *Cognition, 29,* 251–275.

Yeni-Komshian, G.H. (1993). Speech perception. In J.B. Gleason & N.B. Ratner (Eds.), *Psycholinguistics.* Orlando, FL: Harcourt Brace.

Yerkes, R.M., & Dodson, J.D. (1908). The relation of strength of stimulus to rapidity of habit-formation. *Journal of Comparative and Neurological Psychology, 18,* 459–482.

Young, A.W., Hay, D.C., & Ellis, A.W. (1985). The faces that launched a thousand slips: Everyday difficulties and errors in recognising people. *British Journal of Psychology, 76,* 495–523.

Young, A.W., Hellawell, D., & Hay, D.C. (1987). Configurational information in face perception. *Perception, 16,* 747–759.

Young, A.W., McWeeny, K.H., Hay, D.C., & Ellis, A.W. (1986a). Naming and categorisation latencies for faces and written names. *Quarterly Journal of Experimental Psychology, 38A,* 297–318.

Young, A.W., McWeeny, K.H., Hay, D.C., & Ellis, A.W. (1986b). Matching familiar and unfamiliar faces on identity and expression. *Psychological Research, 48,* 63–68.

Zadeh, L. (1982). A note on prototype theory and fuzzy sets. *Cognition, 12,* 291–297.

Zaidel, E. (1976). Auditory vocabulary of the right hemisphere following brain bisection or hemidecortication. *Cortex, 12,* 191–211.

Zajonc, R.B. (1980). Feeling and thinking: Preferences need no inferences. *American Psychologist, 35,* 151–175.

Zajonc, R.B. (1984). On the primacy of affect. *American Psychologist, 39,* 117–123.

Zaragoza, M.S., & McCloskey, M. (1989). Misleading postevent information and the memory impairment hypothesis: Comment on Belli and reply to Tversky and Tuchin. *Journal of Experimental Psychology: General, 118,* 92–99.

Zeki, S. (1992). The visual image in mind and brain. *Scientific American, 267,* 43–50.

Zeki, S. (1993). *A vision of the brain.* Oxford: Blackwell.

Zhang, G., & Simon, H.A. (1985). STM capacity for Chinese words and idioms: Chunking and acoustical loop hypotheses. *Memory and Cognition, 13,* 193–201.

Zihl, J., von Cramon, D., & Mai, N. (1983). Selective disturbance of movement vision after bilateral posterior brain damage, further evidence and follow-up observations. *Brain, 114,* 2235–2252.

Zwaan, R.A., & van Oostendop, U. (1993). Do readers construct spatial representations in naturalistic story comprehension? *Discourse Processes, 16,* 125–143.

Author Index

Subject Index